THE PAPERS
OF
JOHN MARSHALL

Sponsored by
The College of William and Mary
and
The Institute of Early American History and Culture
under the auspices of
The National Historical Publications and Records
Commission

JOHN MARSHALL
Engraving by Francis Kearny based on portrait by Joseph Wood, 1817.
Courtesy of The New-York Historical Society

THE PAPERS

OF

JOHN MARSHALL

Volume VIII

Correspondence, Papers, and Selected Judicial Opinions
March 1814–December 1819

CHARLES F. HOBSON, *Editor*

LAURA S. GWILLIAM, *Editorial Associate*

The University of North Carolina Press, Chapel Hill
in association with the
Institute of Early American History and Culture
Williamsburg, Virginia

*The Institute of Early American History and Culture
is sponsored jointly by
The College of William and Mary in Virginia
and The Colonial Williamsburg Foundation.*

© *1995 The University of North Carolina Press
All rights reserved
Manufactured in the United States of America
Set in Linotron Baskerville by
Keystone Typesetting, Inc.
ISBN 0-8078-2221-3*

The ornament on the title page is based upon John Marshall's personal seal, as it appears on a gold watch fob that also bears the seal of his wife, Mary Willis Marshall. It was drawn by Richard J. Stinely of Williamsburg, Virginia, from the original, now owned by the Association for the Preservation of Virginia Antiquities, Richmond, Virginia, and is published with the owner's permission.

Library of Congress Cataloging-in-Publication Data
(Revised for volume 8)

Marshall, John, 1755–1835.
  The papers of John Marshall.
  Vol. 5–   : Charles F. Hobson, editor.
  "Sponsored by the College of William and Mary and the Institute of Early American History and Culture under the auspices of the National Historical Publications Commission."
  Includes bibliographical references and indexes.
  CONTENTS: v. 1. Correspondence and papers, November 10, 1775–June 23, 1788. Account book, September 1783–June 1788. [etc.] v. 7. Correspondence, papers, and selected judicial opinions, April 1807–December 1813. v. 8. Correspondence, papers, and selected judicial opinions, March 1814–December 1819.
  1. Marshall, John, 1755–1835—Manuscripts. 2. United States—Politics and government—1775–1783—Sources. 3. United States—Politics and government—1783–1865—Sources. 4. Statesmen—United States—Manuscripts. 5. Judges—United States—Manuscripts. 6. Manuscripts, American. 7. Judicial opinions. I. Johnson, Herbert Alan, ed. II. Cullen, Charles T., 1940–   , ed. III. Hobson, Charles F., 1943–   , ed. IV. Title.
  E302.M365   347.73'2634   347.3073534   74-9575
                ISBN 0-8078-1233-1 (v. 1)
                ISBN 0-8078-1302-8 (v. 2)
                ISBN 0-8078-1337-0 (v. 3)
                ISBN 0-8078-1586-1 (v. 4)
                ISBN 0-8078-1746-5 (v. 5)
                ISBN 0-8078-1903-4 (v. 6)
                ISBN 0-8078-2074-1 (v. 7)
                ISBN 0-8078-2221-3 (v. 8)

Publication of this volume has been assisted by grants from the National Endowment for the Humanities, the National Historical Publications and Records Commission, the Robert G. III & Maude Morgan Cabell Foundation, and the William Nelson Cromwell Foundation.

CONTENTS

MARCH 1814–DECEMBER 1819

1814

1815

1818

1819

ILLUSTRATIONS

Preface

Volume VIII of *The Papers of John Marshall* chronicles Marshall's life and career from 1814 through 1819. During these six years the United States successfully concluded a war with Great Britain, enjoyed an interval of commercial prosperity and political harmony, and then endured a financial panic, the beginning of an economic depression, and a breakdown of the nationalist consensus. These broad historical currents are but partly and imperfectly reflected in the documentary record of Marshall's life and career for this period. Like its two predecessors, Volume VIII brings together Marshall's correspondence, assorted miscellaneous papers, and a selection of his judicial opinions. Although this volume contains more letters than were presented in Volume VII, the surviving correspondence for these years remains sparse and occupies a distinctly smaller proportion of the volume than do the judicial papers. More than a third of the documents (exceeding 50 percent of the bulk of the volume) fall within a single year, 1819, when Marshall penned three notable opinions and a series of newspaper essays.

For the Supreme Court these were years of internal stability and unity, in which the Court consolidated its institutional strength and enhanced its reputation as an authoritative expositor of national law. Along with the chief justice and Bushrod Washington, whose judicial tenure had begun during the Adams administration, the Court consisted of William Johnson, Brockholst Livingston, Thomas Todd, Joseph Story, and Gabriel Duvall, appointees of Presidents Jefferson and Madison. The most recent appointment had occurred in 1811, and there would be no further changes in personnel until 1823. On the first Monday in February these justices convened in Washington for six or seven weeks to hear arguments, confer about cases, and deliver judgments. Daily sessions in the courtroom (in the Capitol basement) usually lasted from eleven to four, after which the justices adjourned to the informal setting of their Capitol Hill lodgings and resumed deliberations over dinner and wine. Sharing living quarters and taking meals together encouraged a frank yet cordial exchange of views, fostered collegiality, and served a style of leadership that aspired to reach a true "opinion of the court" through persuasion and consensus building. No one understood better than the chief justice the importance of communal living arrangements. When the British invasion of August 1814 left much of the capital city in ruins, Marshall anxiously inquired about accommodations for the approaching term: "If it be practicable to keep us together you know how desirable this will be. It that be impracticable we must be as near each other as possible. Perhaps we may dine together should we even be compelled to lodge in different houses" (to Bushrod Washington, 29 December 1814).

Only by adhering to a strict regime of work both in and outside the courtroom could the justices hope to get through an increasingly crowded docket. The War of 1812 presented the Court with new and difficult cases involving prize law, violations of nonintercourse laws, and the rights of neutrals. Many of these cases attracted a numerous audience that crowded into the gallery to hear the great legal gladiators of the day—William Pinkney, Samuel Dexter, Robert G. Harper, Thomas A. Emmet, among others. Their forensic duels were a favorite entertainment of Washington society, whose season coincided with the opening of the Supreme Court. In addition to cases, the justices regularly received cards of invitation from the president, cabinet officials, members of Congress, and foreign ministers, which tested the limits of their self-discipline. "Since being in this place I have been more in company than I wish & more than is consistent with the mass of business we have to go through," wrote Marshall early in the 1817 term (to Mary W. Marshall, 14 February 1817). The chief justice once declined an invitation from John Randolph for a Wednesday evening, explaining that the justices had mutually pledged "to continue at home for the purpose of conferring on the causes under consideration." This rule did not apply to Sundays, however, when several of the judges visited with their families and "our conferences are of course broken up" (to John Randolph, 4 March 1816).

Among the significant prize cases decided by the Supreme Court during these years were *The Venus* (1814) and *The Nereide* (1815), both of which brought forth masterly expositions of the law of nations from Marshall (see Opinions, 12 March 1814, 11 March 1815). In the area of constitutional law the 1819 term of the Supreme Court stands preeminent in Marshall's chief justiceship as the occasion of three major constitutional pronouncements: *Dartmouth College* v. *Woodward*, *Sturgis* v. *Crowninshield*, and *McCulloch* v. *Maryland*. The first two opinions further extended the application of the contract clause to state legislation; the last affirmed the powers of the national government on the basis of implied powers and national supremacy (see Opinions, 2 February, 17 February, 1 March 1819). In another leading case, *Martin* v. *Hunter's Lessee* (1816), the Supreme Court (speaking through Justice Story) sustained its appellate jurisdiction over decisions of the state courts. Although Marshall did not sit in *Martin* because of his personal interest in the Fairfax lands litigation, two documents in his hand pertaining to the case have been found in the appellate case files (see Petition for Writ of Error, [ca. 16 December 1815]; Fragment of Argument, [ca. December 1815–March 1816]).

In the wake of the *McCulloch* decision the Supreme Court during the spring of 1819 was subjected to a torrent of public criticism, originating largely in Virginia and from the pens of two eminent state judges, William Brockenbrough and the redoubtable Spencer Roane. Writing to Washington and Story, Marshall expressed growing alarm at the intensity of these attacks, which he regarded as striking at the vitals of the Constitution and Union. He concluded the situation was too critical to let these censures go unanswered and resolved to take up the cause himself, concealing his identity under the pseudonyms "A Friend to the Union" and "A Friend of the Constitution." Marshall's defense ultimately produced eleven separate installments (see Essays Defending McCulloch v. Maryland, editorial note).

Chief Justice Marshall's life followed a settled pattern of presiding over the Supreme Court during the winter, attending his Raleigh, North Carolina, and Richmond, Virginia, circuits in the spring and fall, spending summers in the "upper country" (Fauquier and Frederick counties), and enjoying his close circle of family and friends at home in Richmond. Until *McCulloch* thrust the Court into the midst of controversy, the chief justice remained largely detached from the leading public issues of the day. In keeping with his disengagement "from the busy active world," Marshall's surviving letters exhibit little political commentary, instead focusing on legal questions and personal concerns (to Louis Marshall, 23 December 1816). Those to Washington and Story, his closest correspondents, discuss such topics as bankruptcy, patents, piracy, and admiralty law.

Marshall was not only chief justice of the United States but also head of a large extended family with branches in various parts of Virginia and Kentucky. He gave as close and devoted attention to this responsibility as he did to his official duties. In 1815, the year he turned sixty, Marshall still had three sons of minor age (the youngest was born in 1805) who needed to be educated and established in professions. He had sent the two older of these boys, John and James Keith, to Harvard College, in what proved to be an ill-advised venture. In the spring of 1815 both sons abruptly withdrew from the college under circumstances that caused their father no little mortification and parental distress. Although James's misconduct consisted of petty violations of college rules, Marshall decided to remove him from Harvard and consign him to a Philadelphia countinghouse, whose proprietor was to "exercise the authority of a Father, a Guardian & a master" (to Bushrod Washington, 16 March 1815; to Willing & Francis, 2 May 1815). Son John had no choice but to leave, having been dismissed by the faculty for unspecified "immoral & dissolute conduct." Blaming himself in part for placing "unlimited confidence" in John, Marshall brought him home in the hope that his then-unrepentant son would undergo a thorough reformation (to [Joseph G. Cogswell?], 9 April 1815).

A rebellious streak, a disposition toward unruly behavior, also manifested itself in other young men of the family. On receiving reports of the indiscretions of a nephew attending the military academy at West Point, Marshall advised his immediate withdrawal. Not only were the prospects unfavorable for "a young man in the military line in this country," but there was "danger of his acquiring very pernicious habits. He is at a time of life when it is extremely dangerous to trust him to such a place without a prudent & experienced person who will in some measure superintend his education" (to Lucy Marshall, 26 August 1817). Another nephew, who had been sent to be educated by Marshall's brother Louis in Kentucky, also had difficulty adjusting to a regime of study and self-discipline far from home. "Tom is unfortunately unused to discipline, & submits to it, no doubt, very unwillingly," Marshall explained, adding: "Early indulgence has very probably given him ideas of self importance which render him less tractable than boys ought to be. You my dear brother are the best judge of what the occasion may require, & will I doubt not mingle as much mildness with authority as the state of things will justify" (to Louis Marshall, 7 Dec. 1817).

Illness and death were frequent visitors to the Marshall family during these years. The chief justice himself continued to enjoy robust health, but his wife's increasingly invalid state was a source of constant worry. Polly Marshall's "wretched health" and extreme nervous condition made unbearable the mere act of sitting in a room "while a person walks across the floor." Marshall was "entirely excluded from society by her situation," and three times he stayed home with her rather than attend his Raleigh circuit (to Louis Marshall, 23 Dec. 1816, 7 Dec. 1817). When apart from her during his winter sojourn in Washington, the chief justice expressed anxious concern about the cold weather: "Indeed my dearest Polly as we grow older we suffer more from the cold & ough[t] to use more precautions against it. Your fears of being too warm push you into the other extreme & you expose yourself to more cold than is consistent with your health or safety. Let me entreat you to be more careful in this particular" (to Mary W. Marshall, 16 February 1818). While Polly still had more than a dozen years to live, death claimed two of Marshall's brothers and one sister in the brief space of less than a year (to St. George Tucker, [25 May 1816]; to Martin Marshall, 24 May 1817).

Judicial duties and family preoccupations kept Marshall busily employed as he entered advanced age. Other projects also engaged his attention. He did preliminary work on an edition of George Washington's correspondence, though he and Bushrod Washington eventually turned this enterprise over to Jared Sparks (to Bushrod Washington, 3 April 1815). He contemplated a new edition of *The Life of George Washington*, hoping to make amends for having written that work too hastily and allowing it to be rushed into print without sufficient time for revision. His plan was to revise and abridge the *Life of Washington* at leisure, withholding publication until there was an indication of public demand for the work. "I do not think a new edition ought to be hurried," he advised Bushrod. "It cannot be pressed on the public. We must wait till it is required" (to Bushrod Washington, 10 September 1816). Jurist, family chieftain, and author, Marshall was also a serious farmer, regularly escaping the bustle of town life for his farm on the Chickahominy River a few miles outside Richmond. Although complaining lightheartedly to Richard Peters (a fellow jurist-farmer) that his plantation was "productive only of expence & vexation," Marshall spent many pleasant hours there in *"laborious relaxation"* (to Richard Peters, 12 October 1815; to James Monroe, 25 June 1812, *The Papers of John Marshall,* VII, 333). Even in the midst of his Supreme Court term in Washington, the chief justice directed his thoughts to the Chickahominy farm, anxious to know whether the overseer was carrying out his "explicit instructions" about preparing plaster and drawing "in the stalks & hay" and also how "the grubbing & cutting" was progressing (to Jaquelin A. Marshall, [16 February 1818]).

Acknowledgments

The editors are pleased to recognize the following persons and institutions who assisted in the preparation of this volume: the staffs of the Earl Gregg Swem Library and the Marshall-Wythe Law Library, College of William and Mary; Margaret Cook and Ellen Strong of Special Collections, Swem Library; Conley Edwards and Minor Weisiger of the Virginia State Library, Richmond; Beth-Carroll Horrocks of the American Philosophical Society, Philadelphia; Dr. Robert Plowman of the National Archives, Mid-Atlantic Region, Philadelphia; Charles Reeves of the National Archives, Southeast Region, East Point, Georgia; and Patrice Donoghue of the Harvard University Archives, Pusey Library, Cambridge.

Timothy Connelly, research archivist at the National Historical Publications and Records Commission, deserves special thanks for his patient and painstaking searches for documents in various record groups in the National Archives.

Wade L. Shaffer, now assistant professor of history at West Texas A & M University, served as research assistant on the editorial staff from August 1993 to August 1994. Besides providing reliable research, Mr. Shaffer made a valuable contribution to this volume by diligently performing various editorial tasks such as proofreading, verifying citations, and collecting illustrations. The volume also owes much to the formidable research and editorial skills of Suzanne E. Coffman, who resigned as assistant editor in August 1992 to join the Colonial Williamsburg Publications Department as associate editor. For six months in 1993 the project had the benefit of the services of Suzanne D. Cooper, a graduate student in the history department at William and Mary.

This editorial enterprise has the good fortune to be sponsored by the College of William and Mary and the Institute of Early American History and Culture. The college provides generous monetary and in-kind support; the Institute provides the resources and editorial skills of a distinguished book publishing program. The editors are grateful to Fredrika J. Teute and Gilbert Kelly of the Institute publications staff for helpful advice. The National Endowment for the Humanities has contributed major financial support to the editing of this volume. Additional support has been supplied by grants from the National Historical Publications and Records Commission, the Robert G. III & Maude Morgan Cabell Foundation, and the William Nelson Cromwell Foundation.

The Plan of the Volume
and
Editorial Policy

Volume VIII is composed of 114 documents published in full and another 130 that are either calendared or listed. Most of the documents fall into two broad categories, correspondence and judicial papers, which together record Marshall's public and private activities through December 1819. The greater part of the volume consists of judicial opinions given in the Supreme Court and the U.S. Circuit Court for Virginia and a series of essays Marshall wrote in 1819 to answer attacks on the opinion in *McCulloch* v. *Maryland*.

CORRESPONDENCE

Large portions of Marshall's correspondence have been lost or destroyed. What survives does not form a continuous record and consists overwhelmingly of letters Marshall wrote to others. Of a total of seventy-nine letters published in full in Volume VIII, sixty-nine are from Marshall to various recipients. Fourteen of these are to Bushrod Washington, including five previously unknown letters purchased by the College of William and Mary in 1985. They are published here for the first time. The next most frequent correspondent is Joseph Story (making his first appearance in this edition), with whom Marshall exchanged seven letters. Aside from judicial business, correspondence in this volume yields information about Marshall's private pursuits and family concerns. Thirteen letters are addressed to family members, including half a dozen to his Kentucky relations—all of which portray Marshall in the role of patriarch of an extended clan.

JUDICIAL PAPERS

Over the course of his long judicial tenure, Marshall delivered nearly seven hundred reported opinions in the Supreme Court and in the U.S. Circuit Courts for Virginia and North Carolina. From 1801 on, judicial opinions constitute an ever-increasing proportion of the documentary record of his career. The editors have adopted the following policy with respect to this voluminous material.

This edition is not a documentary history of the Supreme Court from 1801 to 1835. Nor does its scope entail reproducing all 550 opinions Marshall delivered on the Supreme Court, the full texts of which are accessible in the official *United States Reports*. The original drafts of the great majority of his opinions have not survived, and their loss precludes rendering more accurately the texts that we now have. Only 88 of Marshall's manuscript opinions (16 percent of the total) are extant, most of them dating from his last years in office. (For a fuller description of the sources documenting Marshall's Supreme Court career, see *The Papers of John Marshall*, VI, 69–73.) Yet an edition of Marshall's papers cannot omit altogether such a large and important group of documents. As a workable compromise between total inclusion and total exclusion, this edition is publishing in full most of the constitutional opinions (about thirty) and a small but representative selection of nonconstitutional opinions. It also presents calendar entries for all the opinions given by the chief justice during the years covered by a volume. (See Appendix I for a list of the opinions from 1814 through 1819.)

Selecting from the huge mass of nonconstitutional opinions presents an editorial problem that admits of no fully satisfactory solution. Even eliminating many relatively insignificant cases that were disposed of in a brief opinion still leaves a sizable body of judicial literature. From this corpus the editors have attempted to provide a sampling of Marshall's jurisprudence in the several fields that occupied the major share of the Court's attention, including procedure, real property, contracts and commercial law, admiralty, and international law. With this general purpose in mind, they have flexibly applied several other criteria to shorten the list of potential choices. Priority is given to opinions that illuminate Marshall's broader views on politics, society, and economy; that reflect an important public issue or policy of the time; and that can be amply documented from the official case file and other sources, especially if the supplementary materials provide new information about the case not found in the printed report. Another important consideration is the availability of the original manuscript opinion, though this criterion will not often come into play until the later years of Marshall's chief justiceship. There is, to be sure, an unavoidable element of arbitrariness in the selection process. For every opinion chosen for inclusion, many others could equally suffice as examples of the chief justice's style, mode of reasoning, and learning in a particular field of law.

Although publishing in full only a small fraction of the Supreme Court opinions, this edition presents complete texts of all extant opinions given in the U.S. Circuit Courts for Virginia and North Carolina. Marshall spent much the greater part of his judicial life on circuit, yet this side of his career is relatively unknown, and the documents are less accessible. His circuit court papers include more than sixty autograph opinions delivered in the Virginia court. The one previous edition of Marshall's circuit opinions, prepared by John W. Brockenbrough in 1837, is extremely rare. While Brockenbrough's reports have been reprinted in *Federal Cases*, the alphabetical arrangement of that work scatters Marshall's opinions over many volumes. The editors believe that bringing the opinions together in the present edition serves a sound documentary purpose. By comparison with the Virginia materials, judicial papers from the North Carolina court are scanty—no manuscript opinions and only a handful of published reports of cases. (Marshall's circuit court papers are described at greater length in *The Papers of John Marshall*, VI, 126–29, 142–44.)

Eight Supreme Court opinions are published in the main body of Volume VIII. They deal with questions of constitutional law, prize law, and the law of nations. The volume presents fourteen circuit opinions, all but one issuing from the U.S. Circuit Court for Virginia. Half of these are prize and admiralty cases and cases arising from the embargo and revenue laws. Other opinions concern aspects of equity law such as decedents' estates, trusts, and mercantile accounts. Attention should be called to one other judicial opinion, *The Brig Caroline* v. *United States*, which appears in Appendix III. Marshall's manuscript of this opinion is in a collection of his circuit court opinions, and Brockenbrough published it as such under date of November 1819. The opinion in fact belongs to a case decided by the Supreme Court in 1813 and reported by William Cranch, though his report did not include the opinion.

OMITTED PAPERS

As a general editorial policy, dinner invitations and routine documents arising from Marshall's financial transactions—bills of exchange, promissory notes, bank drafts, and the like—are omitted entirely, though they may be referred to in the annotation. The same holds true for land deeds, even though in previous volumes these have been calendared and sometimes printed in full.

Editorial Apparatus

Editorial Method

The editors have applied modern historical editing standards in rendering the texts of documents. Transcriptions are as accurate as possible and reflect format and usage as nearly as is feasible, with the following exceptions. The first letter of a sentence is capitalized, and redundant or confusing punctuation has been eliminated. Superscript letters have been brought down to the line, and thorns ("ye," "yt," "yn") have been expanded. Words abbreviated by a tilde (~) have not been expanded, but the tilde has been omitted and a period added. Layout and typography attempt to replicate the appearance of the originals. The location of the dateline in letters, however, has been standardized, placed on the first line of the letter, flush to the right margin. The salutation has been set flush to the left margin. The complimentary closing has been run into the last paragraph of letters. Signatures, regardless of whether they are autograph, have been set in large and small capital letters and indented one space from the right margin. Other names at the foot of a document (for example, those of witnesses, sureties, and pledges) are rendered in the same distinctive type as signatures and are placed approximately where they appear in the originals.

Obvious slips of the pen, usually repeated words, have been silently corrected, as have typographical errors in printed sources. Words or parts of words illegible or missing because of mutilation are enclosed in angle brackets; letters or punctuation added by the editors for clarity's sake are set off by square brackets. If the editors are uncertain about their rendition, the words are enclosed within brackets followed by a question mark. If a portion of the manuscript is missing, the lacuna is shown by ellipsis points within angle brackets. Undecipherable words or phrases are indicated by the word "illegible" set in italics within angle brackets. Official and corporate seals are designated by the word "seal" set in capital letters and enclosed within square brackets. Wafer, or signature, seals are denoted by the initials "L.S." (*Locus Sigilli* [place of the seal]) within square brackets.

This volume follows the format first adopted in Volume V. Footnotes follow immediately at the end of the document, and identification of the source occurs in an unnumbered provenance note (referred to as "n." in cross-references) preceding the first numbered footnote. This note also supplies information on other copies, endorsements, dating, description, or peculiarities of the original. The provenance contains a full citation for the source of each document, except that National Union Catalog Symbols for depositories are used throughout. Elsewhere the editors have employed abbreviated titles for the most frequently cited public collections of manuscripts and secondary sources. These appear below in the lists of symbols and short titles. For other publications, a full citation is given the first time a source is cited in a document.

For books, periodicals, and articles, the editors follow the style of citation used in standard academic history. Reports of cases, however, are given in legal citation form. The name of the case is followed by the volume number and abbreviated title (usually the reporter's last name); the page number on which the case begins; and, if needed, the court and year within parentheses. For the old English cases, the volume number and page of the reprint of the case in *The English Reports* (abbreviated "Eng. Rep.") are also given. Full titles of all reports cited in this volume are provided in the short-title list. References to statutes also follow the historical style. In citing English statutes, the editors use the standard abbreviated form giving the regnal year, chapter and section (if appropriate), and year of enactment (if not otherwise indicated), e.g., 13 Edw. I, c. 31 (1285); 4 and 5 Anne, c. 3, sec. 12 (1705).

Annotation consists of footnotes to documents, occasional editorial notes preceding a document or group of documents, and short contextual notes preceding Marshall's court opinions. The guiding principle is to supply enough information and explanation to make the document intelligible to the general reader. The editors prefer to let the documents speak for themselves as much as possible. This laissez-faire policy is more easily followed in the case of personal correspondence. Legal materials by nature require denser annotation. Without presuming any knowledge of law on the reader's part, the editors attempt to strike a balance between too little and too much commentary.

The provenance note is followed, if needed, by one or more numbered footnotes that address matters arising immediately from the document: identifications of persons, places, technical words and phrases, statutes, authorities, cases, pamphlets, newspaper articles, and the like. If the information is available in a standard reference or secondary work, the note is brief, often no more than a citation to that source. Three standard reference works are not cited: *Dictionary of American Biography*, *Dictionary of National Biography*, and *Biographical Directory of Congress*. If the source is a manuscript collection or archival record group that is relatively inaccessible, the information derived from it is reported in greater detail. Cross-references to other documents or notes in the same volume are kept to a minimum, relying on the index to bring them all together. Editorial notes provide more extensive information or interpretation than can be conveniently included in footnotes. They serve to introduce documents of unusual significance or important subjects or episodes that are reflected in a number of documents. In Volume VII the editors adopted the practice of supplying brief contextual notes to introduce court opinions. Unlike editorial notes, these notes are concerned only with setting the immediate context of the opinion to follow. They typically provide the full names of the parties, the essential facts of the dispute (including, in the case of Supreme Court appellate opinions, the history of the case in the lower federal court or in the state court), and the particular point or motion addressed by the opinion.

Textual Notes

Marshall's manuscript drafts of judicial opinions receive special editorial treatment. With these documents, Marshall's intent as author takes on additional importance, for he meant them to be officially promulgated. In his opinions, Marshall made many deletions and insertions, which reveal his thought process at work; his choice of words and redrafting of phrases show a careful consideration of meaning. The final result was what he intended the public to hear, and, in keeping with that object, the editors have followed their standard rules of transcription and editorial method in presenting nearly clear texts of these documents as the main entries. In order to provide an inclusive list of Marshall's alterations in the manuscript, however, they have appended a set of textual notes, following the annotation, to each of these autograph opinions and drafts. By this means, a genetic text can be reconstructed, and a complete record of Marshall's revisions is preserved.

Marshall made changes in his text in a variety of ways: he struck through words, erased them, wrote over them, added words above the line, or indicated by means of a superscript symbol an addition to be inserted from the margin or a separate sheet. In recording Marshall's alterations, the editors have not distinguished among his various modes of deleting words, or between words inserted above the line as opposed to altered on the line. Marshall made many of his changes on the line, indicating that he amended as he was writing. The editors believe that the alterations were part of his process of refining his opinions and that he incorporated them into his final statement from the bench. He apparently did not go back later and revise his opinion as delivered orally in court.

Deletions are indicated by canceled type (~~ease~~), and insertions are surrounded by up and down arrows (↑court↓). Deleted punctuation will appear below the strike-through rule (~~, appeal~~). Illegible erasures or deletions are denoted by *"erasure"* within square brackets. Uncertain renderings are followed by a question mark within square brackets. Insertions within insertions are not indicated, but deletions within insertions are. Insertions within a deletion appear in canceled type and are set off by arrows.

Characteristically, in changing a preposition, article, indefinite pronoun, or verb ending, Marshall wrote over the end of the existing word to alter it to a new form. For instance, he transformed "that" to "this" by writing "is" over "at" and "on" to "in" by writing "i" over "o." Rather than placing internal marks within words to replicate Marshall's process of altering them, the editors have represented the change in substance by entering complete words. Canceled type shows his first version; up and down arrows indicate his substitution. Thus, a change from "that" to "this" will appear in the text notes as ~~that~~ ↑this↓, rather than ~~that~~ ↑is↓. Although this method sacrifices the exact recording of how Marshall entered a change, it does make clear the alteration of the content of what he wished to say. Marshall's intentions are not always self-evident; irregularities in pen, ink, and manuscript preclude certainty in some instances. Sometimes it is not possible to know whether he added or erased a word, or whether he had crowded words on a line or blotted a drop of ink. Where Marshall inadvertently repeated a word or words, the repetition is left out in the main text but is recorded verbatim in the textual notes.

All deletions and insertions, as the editors have been best able to determine from appearance and context of the manuscript, are listed by paragraph and line numbers of the printed document. (Paragraph numbers appear in the margin of the main text to facilitate use.) A word or two before and after the alteration is included to aid the reader in finding the phrase and following the change. The succeeding designations indicate alterations made in places other than in the middle of the text: "Title," in the title of an opinion; "mar.," in a marginal note; "footnote," in a note at the bottom of the manuscript page; "beg.," at the beginning of a paragraph before the first word of the main text. To avoid confusion, footnote numbers in the document have been dropped from words appearing in the textual notes.

Descriptive Symbols

AD	Autograph Document
ADf	Autograph Draft
ADS	Autograph Document Signed
ALS	Autograph Letter Signed
Df	Draft
JM	John Marshall
MS	Manuscript
Tr	Transcript

All documents in an author's hand are designated as autograph items (e.g., ALS). If the attribution of autograph is conjectural, a question mark within parentheses follows the designation. Documents can be in the hand of someone else but signed by persons under whose names they are written (e.g., DS). If the signature has been cropped or obliterated, the "S" appears within square brackets (e.g., AL[S]). Copies are contemporary replications of documents; if they are made by the author, the type of document will be indicated by one of the above symbols followed by "copy" or "letterbook copy" within parentheses. For instance, an unsigned copy of a letter retained by the writer will be described as AL (copy). Thomas Jefferson's letterpress copies are designated as ALS (press copy). Transcripts are transcribed versions of documents made at a later time by someone other than the author.

Location Symbols

CtY	Yale University, New Haven, Conn.
DLC	Library of Congress, Washington, D.C.
DNA	National Archives, Washington, D.C.
InU-Li	Lilly Library, Indiana University, Bloomington, Ind.
KU	University of Kansas, Lawrence, Kans.
KyLoF	Filson Club, Louisville, Ky.
MdHi	Maryland Historical Society, Baltimore, Md.
MH-H	Houghton Library, Harvard University, Cambridge, Mass.
MHi	Massachusetts Historical Society, Boston, Mass.
MWA	American Antiquarian Society, Worcester, Mass.
NcD	Duke University, Durham, N.C.
NcU	University of North Carolina, Chapel Hill, N.C.
NhD	Dartmouth College, Hanover, N.H.
NhHi	New Hampshire Historical Society, Concord, N.H.
NHi	New-York Historical Society, New York, N.Y.
NN	New York Public Library, New York, N.Y.
NNC	Columbia University, New York, N.Y.
NNPM	Pierpont Morgan Library, New York, N.Y.
PHi	Historical Society of Pennsylvania, Philadelphia, Pa.
PP	Free Library of Philadelphia, Philadelphia, Pa.
PPAmP	American Philosophical Society, Philadelphia, Pa.
PU	University of Pennsylvania, Philadelphia, Pa.
Vi	Virginia State Library, Richmond, Va.
ViHi	Virginia Historical Society, Richmond, Va.
ViU	University of Virginia, Charlottesville, Va.
ViW	College of William and Mary, Williamsburg, Va.

Record Groups in the National Archives

RG 15	Records of the Veterans Administration
RG 21	Records of the District Courts of the United States

RG 24	Records of the Bureau of Naval Personnel
RG 45	Naval Records Collection of the Office of Naval Records and Library
RG 46	Records of the United States Senate
RG 49	Records of the Bureau of Land Management
RG 59	General Records of the Department of State
RG 60	General Records of the Department of Justice
RG 94	Records of the Adjutant General's Office, 1780s–1917
RG 107	Records of the Office of the Secretary of War
RG 267	Records of the Supreme Court of the United States

Abbreviations for Court and Other Records

App. Cas.
Appellate Case
RG 267, National Archives

U.S. Cir. Ct., N.C.
  Min. Bk.
U.S. Circuit Court, N.C.
  Minute Book
RG 21, National Archives

U.S. Cir. Ct., Va.
  Ord. Bk.
  Rec. Bk.
U.S. Circuit Court, Va.
  Order Book
  Record Book
Virginia State Library

U.S. Dist. Ct., Va.
  Ord. Bk.
U.S. District Court, Virginia
  Order Book
Virginia State Library

U.S. Sup. Ct.
  Minutes
  Dockets
U.S. Supreme Court
  Minutes
  Dockets
RG 267, National Archives

After the first citation of legal papers in a case, the court reference is omitted, and the suit record is designated simply by the names of plaintiff v. defendant. The exception is the provenance note, where complete depository information will be given for the document printed.

Abbreviations for English Courts

Adm.	Admiralty
Ch.	Chancery
K.B.	King's Bench
N.P.	Nisi Prius

Short Titles

The expanded titles for the English reports are taken chiefly from W. Harold Maxwell and Leslie F. Maxwell, *A Legal Bibliography of the British Commonwealth of Nations,* Volume I: *English Law to 1800* (2d ed.; London, 1955).

Annals of Congress
> *Debates and Proceedings in the Congress of the United States* (1789–1824) (42 vols.; Washington, D.C., 1834–56).

ASP
> *American State Papers. Documents, Legislative and Executive, of the Congress of the United States . . .* (38 vols.; Washington, D.C., 1832–61).

Blackstone, *Commentaries*
> William Blackstone, *Commentaries on the Laws of England* (4 vols.; 13th ed.; Dublin, 1796).

Brock.
> John W. Brockenbrough, *Reports of Cases Decided by the Honorable John Marshall . . . in the Circuit Court of the United States for the District of Virginia and North Carolina, from 1802 to 1833 [1836] Inclusive* (2 vols.; Philadelphia, 1837).

Call
> Daniel Call, *Reports of Cases Argued and Adjudged in the Court of Appeals of Virginia* (6 vols.; Richmond, Va., 1801–33). Beginning with vol. IV, the title reads: *Reports of Cases Argued and Decided. . . .*

Carth.
> Thomas Carthew, *Reports of Cases Adjudged in the Court of King's Bench, from the Third Year of King James the Second, to the Twelfth Year of King William the Third* (London, 1728).

Cranch
> William Cranch, *Reports of Cases Argued and Adjudged in the Supreme Court of the United States* (1801–15) (9 vols.; New York and Washington, D.C., 1804–17).

C. Rob.
> Chr. Robinson, *Reports of Cases Argued and Determined in the High Court of Admiralty; Commencing with the Judgments of the Right Hon. Sir Wm. Scott from 1798–1808, with the Orders of the Court* (6 vols.; London, 1799– 1808).

Dall.
> Alexander J. Dallas, *Reports of Cases Ruled and Adjudged in the Several Courts of the United States, and of Pennsylvania . . .* (4 vols.; Philadelphia, 1790–1807).

Dy.
> James Dyer, *Ascuns Nouel Cases. Les Reports des divers select Matters and Resolutions* (London, 1585).

Eng. Rep.
> The English Reports (176 vols.; reprint of all the early English reporters).

Eq. Cas. Abr.
> General Abridgment of Cases in Equity Argued and Adjudged in the High Court of Chancery . . . (2 vols.; London, 1732–56).

Fed. Cas.
> Federal Cases (1789–1880) (30 vols.; St. Paul, Minn., 1894–97).

Gunther, Marshall's Defense
> Gerald Gunther, ed., John Marshall's Defense of McCulloch v. Maryland (Stanford, Calif. 1969).

Hening, Statutes
> William Waller Hening, ed., The Statutes at Large; Being a Collection of All the Laws of Virginia, from the First Session of the Legislature . . . (13 vols.; 1819–23; Charlottesville, Va., 1969 reprint: vols. I–IV from 2d ed.; vols. V–XIII from 1st ed.).

Hob.
> Henry Hobart, The Reports of That Reverend and Learned Judge, the Right Honourable Sr. Henry Hobart . . . (5th ed.; London, 1724).

Munf.
> William Munford, Reports of Cases Argued and Determined in the Supreme Court of Appeals of Virginia (6 vols.; New York, Philadelphia, Fredericksburg, Richmond, 1812–21).

Paxton, Marshall Family
> W. M. Paxton, The Marshall Family . . . (1885; Baltimore, 1970 reprint).

PJM
> Herbert A. Johnson et al., eds., The Papers of John Marshall (7 vols. to date; Chapel Hill, N.C., 1974–).

P. Wms.
> William Peere Williams, Reports of Cases Argued and Determined in the High Court of Chancery, and of Some Special Cases Adjudged in the Court of King's Bench (3 vols.; London, 1740–49).

Raym. Ld.
> Robert, Lord Raymond, Reports of Cases Argued and Adjudged in the Courts of King's Bench and Common Pleas . . . (2 vols.; London, 1743).

Rossiter, Federalist Papers
> Clinton Rossiter, ed., The Federalist Papers (New York, 1961).

S
> Ralph R. Shaw and Richard H. Shoemaker, eds., American Bibliography . . . 1801–1819 (22 vols.; New York, 1958–66).

S & R
> Thomas Sargeant & William Rawle, Jr., Reports of Cases Adjudged in the Supreme Court of Pennsylvania (Philadelphia, 1871).

Shepherd, *Statutes*
Samuel Shepherd, ed., *The Statutes at Large of Virginia, from October Session 1792, to December Session 1806, Inclusive* (3 vols.; 1835; New York, 1970 reprint).
Story, *Life and Letters*
William W. Story, ed., *Life and Letters of Joseph Story* . . . (2 vols.; Boston, 1851).
U.S. Statutes at Large
The Public Statutes at Large of the United States of America, 1789– 1873 (17 vols.; Boston, 1845–73).
Vattel, *Law of Nations* (1805 ed.)
[Emmerich de] Vattel, *The Law of Nations; or Principles of the Law of Nature; Applied to the Conduct and Affairs of Nations and Sovereigns* (Northampton, Mass., 1805; S# 9650).
Ves. jun. or Ves. (after vol. II)
Francis Vesey, Jr., *Reports of Cases Argued and Determined in the High Court of Chancery* . . . (20 vols.; London, 1795–1822).
Ves. & Bea.
Francis Vesey, Jr., and John Beames, *Reports of Cases Argued and Determined in the High Court of Chancery, in the Time of Lord Chancellor Eldon* . . . (2d ed.; London, 1818).
VMHB
Virginia Magazine of History and Biography.
Wash.
Bushrod Washington, *Reports of Cases Argued and Determined in the Court of Appeals of Virginia* (2 vols.; Richmond, Va., 1798–99).
Wheat.
Henry Wheaton, *Reports of Cases Argued and Adjudged in the Supreme Court* (1816–27) (12 vols.; Philadelphia, 1816–27).

MARSHALL CHRONOLOGY
7 February 1814–31 December 1819

1814

7 February–12 March	At Washington, attends Supreme Court.
5 May	At Richmond, attends convention of Protestant Episcopal Church, Virginia, as lay deputy of the Monumental Church.
12–14 May	At Raleigh, attends U.S. circuit court.
23 May–7 June	At Richmond, attends U.S. circuit court.
12 November	Misses term of U.S. circuit court, Raleigh.
22 November–3 December	At Richmond, attends U.S. circuit court.

1815

January	Awarded LL.D. by University of Pennsylvania.
6 February–11 March	At Washington, attends Supreme Court.
12–17 May	At Raleigh, attends U.S. circuit court.
22 May–3 June	At Richmond, attends U.S. circuit court.
13 November	Misses term of U.S. circuit court, Raleigh, because of wife's illness.
22 November–3 December	At Richmond, attends U.S. circuit court.

1816

5 February–22 March	At Washington, attends Supreme Court.
13–16 May	At Raleigh, attends U.S. circuit court.
22 May–6 June	At Richmond, attends U.S. circuit court (absent 28–29 May).
ca. 10 September	Returns to Richmond from upper country.
12–15 November	At Raleigh, attends U.S. circuit court.
ca. 22 November–mid-December	At Richmond, attends U.S. circuit court.

1817

3 February–15 March	At Washington, attends Supreme Court.
4 March	Administers oath of office to James Monroe.
12–14 May	At Raleigh, attends U.S. circuit court.
ca. 22 May–early June	At Richmond, attends U.S. circuit court.
Late August	Returns to Richmond from upper country.
12–14 November	At Raleigh, attends U.S. circuit court.
ca. 22 November–mid-December	At Richmond, attends U.S. circuit court.

1818

2 February–14 March	At Washington, attends Supreme Court.
12–13 May	At Raleigh, attends U.S. circuit court.
ca. 22 May–early June	At Richmond, attends U.S. circuit court.
12–13 November	At Raleigh, attends U.S. circuit court.
ca. 22 November–mid-December	At Richmond, attends U.S. circuit court.

1819

1 February–12 March	At Washington, attends Supreme Court.
2 February	Delivers opinion in *Dartmouth College* v. *Woodward*.
17 February	Delivers opinion in *Sturgis* v. *Crowninshield*.
6 March	Delivers opinion in *McCulloch* v. *Maryland*.
Before 24 March	Returns to Richmond.
Early April	Writes "A Friend to the Union" essays in defense of McCulloch opinion.
ca. 15 April	Visits upper country.
28 April	Returns to Richmond.
12–14 May	Misses term of U.S. circuit court, Raleigh, because of family illness.
ca. 22 May–early June	At Richmond, attends U.S. circuit court.

ca. 15 June–1 July	Writes "A Friend of the Constitution" essays in defense of McCulloch opinion.
12–13 November	At Raleigh, attends U.S. circuit court.
ca. 22 November–mid-December	At Richmond, attends U.S. circuit court.

CORRESPONDENCE, PAPERS,

AND

SELECTED JUDICIAL OPINIONS

March 1814–December 1819

Brown v. United States
Opinion
U.S. Supreme Court, 2 March 1814

This was an appeal from a decree rendered in the U.S. Circuit Court, Massachusetts, October 1813 term, reversing a district court sentence. Judge Joseph Story's circuit court decree condemned as enemy property the cargo of the *Emulous*, which included a quantity of timber owned by a British merchant firm. The timber was subsequently (after the declaration of war between the United States and Great Britain) sold to Armitz Brown, a Philadelphia merchant and claimant in the present case. The appeal to the Supreme Court was conducted without oral argument. Daniel Davis submitted a written brief on behalf of Brown, while Attorney General Richard Rush relied on Story's circuit opinion embodied in the appellate record. In reversing the circuit court decree, Marshall presented a major statement of the principle that the sovereign right of confiscation cannot be exercised without express authority from the legislature (8 Cranch 110, 121; Brown v. U.S., record on appeal, 1, 35–49, App. Cas. No. 650; U.S. Sup. Ct. Minutes, 2 Mar. 1814).

The material facts in this case are these:

The *Emulous* owned by John Delano and others citizens of the United States, was chartered to a company carrying on trade in Great Britain, one of whom was an American citizen, for the purpose of carrying a cargo from Savannah to Plymouth. After the cargo was put on board, the vessel was stopped in port by the embargo of the 4th of April, 1812.[1] On the 25th of the same month, it was agreed between the master of the ship and the agent of the shippers, that she should proceed with her cargo to New Bedford, where her owners resided, and remain there without prejudice to the charter party. In pursuance of this agreement, the Emulous proceeded to New Bedford, where she continued until after the declaration of war. In October or November, the ship was unloaded and the cargo, except the pine timber, was landed. The pine timber was floated up a salt water creek, where, at low tide, the ends of the timber rested on the mud, where it was secured from floating out with the tide, by impediments fastened in the entrance of the creek. On the 7th of November, 1812, the cargo was sold by the agent of the owners, who is an American citizen, to the Claimant, who is also an American citizen.[2] On the 19th of April, a libel was filed by the attorney for the United States, in the district Court of Massachusetts, against the said cargo, as well on behalf of the United States of America as for and in behalf of John Delano and of all other persons concerned. It does not appear that this seizure was made under any instructions from the president of the United States; nor is there any evidence of its having his sanction, unless the libels being filed and prosecuted by the law officer who represents the government, must imply that sanction.

On the contrary, it is admitted that the seizure was made by an individual, and the libel filed at his instance, by the district attorney who acted from his own impressions of what appertained to his duty. The property was claimed by Armitz Brown under the purchase made in the preceding November.

The district Court dismissed the libel. The Circuit Court reversed this sentence, and condemned the pine timber as enemy property forfeited to the United States. From the sentence of the Circuit Court, the Claimant appealed to this Court.

The material question made at bar is this. Can the pine timber, even admitting the property not to be changed by the sale in November, be condemned as prize of war?

The cargo of the Emulous having been legally acquired and put on board the vessel, having been detained by an embargo not intended to act on foreign property, the vessel having sailed before the war, from Savannah, under a stipulation to re-land the cargo in some port of the United States, the re-landing having been made with respect to the residue of the cargo, and the pine timber having been floated into shallow water, where it was secured and in the custody of the owner of the ship, an American citizen, the Court cannot perceive any solid distinction, so far as respects confiscation, between this property and other British property found on land at the commencement of hostilities. It will therefore be considered as a question relating to such property generally, and to be governed by the same rule. Respecting the power of government no doubt is entertained. That war gives to the sovereign full right to take the persons and confiscate the property of the enemy wherever found, is conceded. The mitigations of this rigid rule, which the humane and wise policy of modern times has introduced into practice, will more or less affect the exercise of this right, but cannot impair the right itself. That remains undiminished, and when the sovereign authority shall chuse to bring it into operation, the judicial department must give effect to its will. But until that will shall be expressed, no power of condemnation can exist in the Court.

The questions to be decided by the Court are:

1st. May enemy's property, found on land at the commencement of hostilities, be seized and condemned as a necessary consequence of the declaration of war?

2d. Is there any legislative act which authorizes such seizure and condemnation?

Since, in this country, from the structure of our government, proceedings to condemn the property of an enemy found within our territory at the declaration of war, can be sustained only upon the principle that they are instituted in execution of some existing law, we are led to ask,

Is the declaration of war such a law? Does that declaration, by its own operation, so vest the property of the enemy in the government, as to support proceedings for its seizure and confiscation, or does it vest only a right, the assertion of which depends on the will of the sovereign power?

The universal practice of forbearing to seize and confiscate debts and credits, the principle universally received, that the right to them revives on the restoration of peace, would seem to prove that war is not an absolute confiscation of this property, but simply confers the right of confiscation.[3]

Between debts contracted under the faith of laws, and property acquired in the course of trade, on the faith of the same laws, reason draws no distinction; and, although, in practice, vessels with their cargoes, found in port at the declaration of war, may have been seized, it is not believed that modern usage would sanction the seizure of the goods of an enemy on land, which were acquired in peace in the course of trade. Such a proceeding is rare, and would be deemed a harsh exercise of the rights of war. But although the practice in this respect may not be uniform, that circumstance does not essentially affect the question. The enquiry is, whether such property vests in the sovereign by the mere declaration of war, or remains subject to a right of confiscation, the exercise of which depends on the national will: and the rule which applies to one case, so far as respects the operation of a declaration of war on the thing itself, must apply to all others over which war gives an equal right. The right of the sovereign to confiscate debts being precisely the same with the right to confiscate other property found in the country, the operation of a declaration of war on debts and on other property found within the country must be the same. What then is this operation?

Even *Bynkershoek*, who maintains the broad principle, that in war every thing done against an enemy is lawful; that he may be destroyed, though unarmed and defenceless; that fraud, or even poison, may be employed against him; that a most unlimited right is acquired to his person and property; admits that war does not transfer to the sovereign a debt due to his enemy; and, therefore, if payment of such debt be not exacted, peace revives the former right of the creditor; "because," he says, "the occupation which is had by war consists more in fact than in law." He adds to his observations on this subject, "let it not, however, be supposed that it is only true of actions, that they are not condemned *ipso jure*, for other things also belonging to the enemy may be concealed and escape condemnation."[4]

Vattel says, that "the sovereign can neither detain the persons nor the property of those subjects of the enemy who are within his dominions at the time of the declaration."[5]

It is true that this rule is, in terms, applied by *Vattel* to the property of those only who are personally within the territory at the commencement of hostilities; but it applies equally to things in action and to things in possession; and if war did, of itself, without any further exercise of the sovereign will, vest the property of the enemy in the sovereign, his presence could not exempt it from this operation of war. Nor can a reason be perceived for maintaining that the public faith is more entirely pledged for the security of property trusted in the territory of the nation in time of peace, if it be accompanied by its owner, than if it be confided to the care of others.

Chitty, after stating the general right of seizure, says, "But, in strict justice, that right can take effect only on those possessions of a belligerent which have come to the hands of his adversary after the declaration of hostilities."[6]

The modern rule then would seem to be, that tangible property belonging to an enemy and found in the country at the commencement of war, ought not to be immediately confiscated; and in almost every commercial treaty an article is inserted stipulating for the right to withdraw such property.

This rule appears to be totally incompatible with the idea, that war does of itself vest the property in the belligerent government. It may be considered as the opinion of all who have written on the *jus belli*, that war gives the right to confiscate, but does not itself confiscate the property of the enemy; and their rules go to the exercise of this right.

The constitution of the United States was framed at a time when this rule, introduced by commerce in favor of moderation and humanity, was received throughout the civilized world. In expounding that constitution, a construction ought not lightly to be admitted which would give to a declaration of war an effect in this country it does not possess elsewhere, and which would fetter that exercise of entire discretion respecting enemy property, which may enable the government to apply to the enemy the rule that he applies to us.

If we look to the constitution itself, we find this general reasoning much strengthened by the words of that instrument.

That the declaration of war has only the effect of placing the two nations in a state of hostility, of producing a state of war, of giving those rights which war confers; but not of operating, by its own force, any of those results, such as a transfer of property, which are usually produced by ulterior measures of government, is fairly deducible from the enumeration of powers which accompanies that of declaring war. "Congress shall have power"—"to declare war, grant letters of marque and reprisal, and make rules concerning captures on land and water."

It would be restraining this clause within narrower limits than the words themselves import, to say that the power to make rules concerning captures on land and water, is to be confined to captures which are exterritorial. If it extends to rules respecting enemy property found within the territory, then we perceive an express grant to congress of the power in question as an independent substantive power, not included in that of declaring war.

The acts of congress furnish many instances of an opinion that the declaration of war does not, of itself, authorize proceedings against the persons or property of the enemy found, at the time, within the territory.

War gives an equal right over persons and property: and if its declaration is not considered as prescribing a law respecting the person of an enemy found in our country, neither does it prescribe a law for his property. The act concerning alien enemies, which confers on the president very great discretionary powers respecting their persons, affords a strong implication that he did not possess those powers by virtue of the declaration of war.[7]

The "act for the safe keeping and accommodation of prisoners of war," is of the same character.[8]

The act prohibiting trade with the enemy, contains this clause:

"And be it further enacted, That the president of the United States be, and he is hereby authorized to give, at any time within six months after the passage of this act, passports for the safe transportation of any ship or other property belonging to British subjects, and which is now within the limits of the United States."[9]

The phraseology of this law shows that the property of a British subject was not considered by the legislature as being vested in the United States by the declaration of war; and the authority which the act confers on the president, is manifestly considered as one which he did not previously possess.

The proposition that a declaration of war does not, in itself, enact a confiscation of the property of the enemy within the territory of the belligerent, is believed to be entirely free from doubt. Is there in the act of congress, by which war is declared against Great Britain, any expression which would indicate such an intention?

That act, after placing the two nations in a state of war, authorizes the president of the United States to use the whole land and naval force of the United States to carry the war into effect, and "to issue to private armed vessels of the United States, commissions or letters of marque and general reprisal against the vessels, goods and effects of the government of the united kingdom of Great Britain and Ireland, and the subjects thereof."[10]

That reprisals may be made on enemy property found within the United States at the declaration of war, if such be the will of the nation, has been admitted; but it is not admitted that, in the declaration of war, the nation has expressed its will to that effect.

It cannot be necessary to employ argument in showing that when the attorney for the United States institutes proceedings at law for the confiscation of enemy property found on land, or floating in one of our creeks, in the care and custody of one of our citizens, he is not acting under the authority of letters of marque and reprisal, still less under the authority of such letters issued to a private armed vessel.

The "act concerning letters of marque, prizes and prize goods," certainly contains nothing to authorize this seizure.[11]

There being no other act of congress which bears upon the subject, it is considered as proved that the legislature has not confiscated enemy property which was within the United States at the declaration of war, and that this sentence of condemnation cannot be sustained.

One view, however, has been taken of this subject which deserves to be further considered.

It is urged that, in executing the laws of war, the executive may seize and the Courts condemn all property which, according to the modern law of nations, is subject to confiscation, although it might require an act of the legislature to justify the condemnation of that property which, according to modern usage, ought not to be confiscated.[12]

This argument must assume for its basis the position that modern usage constitutes a rule which acts directly upon the thing itself by its own force, and not through the sovereign power. This position is not allowed. This usage is a guide which the sovereign follows or abandons at his will. The rule, like other precepts of morality, of humanity, and even of wisdom, is addressed to the judgment of the sovereign; and although it cannot be disregarded by him without obloquy, yet it may be disregarded.

The rule is, in its nature, flexible. It is subject to infinite modification. It is not an immutable rule of law, but depends on political considerations which may continually vary.

Commercial nations, in the situation of the United States, have always a considerable quantity of property in the possession of their neighbors. When war breaks out, the question, what shall be done with enemy property in our country, is a question rather of policy than of law. The rule which we apply to the property of our enemy, will be applied by him to the property of our citizens. Like all other questions of policy, it is proper for the consideration of a department which can modify it at will; not for the consideration of a department which can pursue only the law as it is written. It is proper for the consideration of the legislature, not of the executive or judiciary.

It appears to the Court, that the power of confiscating enemy property is in the legislature, and that the legislature has not yet declared its will to confiscate property which was within our territory at the declaration of war. The Court is therefore of opinion that there is error in the sentence of condemnation pronounced in the Circuit Court in this case, and doth direct that the same be reversed and annulled, and that the sentence of the District Court be affirmed.[13]

Printed, William Cranch, *Reports of Cases Argued and Adjudged in the Supreme Court of the United States* . . . , VIII (Washington, D.C., 1816), 121–29.

1. *U.S. Statutes at Large*, II, 700–1.

2. The agent of the British company was Elijah Brown of Philadelphia. His brother, James Brown, then residing in London, was a partner in the British firm. Armitz Brown, the claimant, was apparently a brother of Elijah and James. Story was inclined to believe that the sale to Armitz Brown was "colorable," not bona fide (8 Cranch 130, 136).

3. Counsel for the claimant cited Ware v. Hylton, the celebrated "British debts" case, which Marshall had argued as an attorney in 1796 (8 Cranch 117–18). See *PJM*, V, 295–329.

4. Cornelius van Bynkershoek, *A Treatise on the Law of War* (Philadelphia, 1810), 56, 57.

5. Vattel, *Law of Nations* (1805 ed.), Bk. III, chap. iv, sec. 63, p. 386.

6. Joseph Chitty, *A Practical Treatise on the Law of Nations* . . . (Boston, 1812; S #25063), 67.

7. Act of 6 July 1798 (*U.S. Statutes at Large*, I, 577–78).

8. Act of 6 July 1812 (ibid., II, 777).

9. Act of 6 July 1812, sec. 6 (ibid., 780).

10. Act of 18 June 1812 (ibid., 755).

11. Act of 26 June 1812 (ibid., 759–64).

12. In his circuit court opinion, Story contended that "the executive may authorize all captures which, by the modern law of nations, are permitted and approved," adding "that in this doctrine I do not mean to include the right to confiscate debts due to enemy subjects. This, though a strictly national right, is so justly deemed odious in modern times, and is so generally discountenanced, that nothing but an express act of congress would satisfy my mind that it ought to be included among the fair objects of warfare" (8 Cranch 145–46).

13. After JM delivered the opinion of the majority, Story read his circuit court opinion and made some additional remarks, in which he had "the concurrence" of one other justice. The Massachusetts jurist argued for a broad executive discretion to prosecute the war: "My argument proceeds upon the ground, that when the legislative authority, to whom the right to declare war is confided, has declared war in its most unlimited manner, the executive authority, to whom the execution of the war is confided, is bound to carry it into effect. He has a discretion vested in him, as to the manner and extent. . . . The sovereignty, as to declaring war and limiting its effects, rests with the legislature. The sovereignty, as to its execution, rests with the president" (8 Cranch 153–54).

The Venus
Opinion
U.S. Supreme Court, 12 March 1814

The Venus was one of many prize cases arising from the War of 1812 that involved application of the legal rule adopted by prize courts that residence or domicile determines the national character of a merchant. The ship *Venus*, owned by the New York merchant firm of Lenox & Maitland, sailed from Liverpool in July 1812 and was captured by the American privateer *Dolphin* in August. The vessel and cargo were subsequently libeled in the U.S. District Court of Massachusetts. The libelants sought condemnation on the ground that the claimants, naturalized American citizens residing in Great Britain when war was declared and at the time the *Venus* was captured, must be considered British subjects. The claimants contended that their property was shipped before they knew of the declaration of war and that, once war broke out, they should have reasonable time to leave Great Britain before forfeiting their American national character. The district court decreed restitution of the ship and a portion of the cargo; the circuit court affirmed this decree pro forma, and both parties appealed to the Supreme Court. The case was argued in the Supreme Court on 23, 24, and 26 February 1814 by John Pitman and Samuel Dexter for the captors and Richard Stockton and Robert G. Harper for the various claimants. The Court, speaking through Justice Bushrod Washington on 12 March, reversed so much of the circuit court sentence as restored the *Venus* and cargo to the claimants, holding that the entire cargo and vessel should be condemned as lawful prize. Marshall dissented from the majority opinion (The Venus, App. Cas. Nos. 633, 634; U.S. Sup. Ct. Minutes, 23–24, 26 Feb., 12 Mar. 1814; 8 Cranch 253–87).

I entirely concur in so much of the opinion delivered in this case, as attaches a hostile character to the property of an American citizen continuing, after the declaration of war, to reside and trade in the country of the enemy; and I subscribe implicitly to the reasoning urged in its support. But from so much of that opinion as subjects to confiscation the property of a citizen shipped before a knowledge of the war, and which disallows the defence founded on an intention to change his domicil and to return to the United States, manifested in a sufficient manner, and within a reasonable time after knowledge of the war, although it be subsequent to the capture, I feel myself compelled to dissent.[1]

The question is undoubtedly complex and intricate. It is difficult to draw a line of discrimination which shall be at the same time precise and equitable. But the difficulty does not appear to me to be sufficient to deter Courts from making the attempt.

A merchant residing abroad for commercial purposes may certainly intend to continue in the foreign country so long as peace shall exist, provided his commercial objects shall detain him so long, but to leave it the instant war shall break out between that country and his own. This intention, it is not necessary to manifest during peace; and when war shall commence, the belligerent cruizer may find his property on the ocean, and may capture it, before he knows that war exists. The question whether this be enemy property or not, depends, in my judgment, not exclusively on the residence of the owner at the time, but on his residence taken in connexion with his national character as a citizen, and with his intention to continue or to discontinue his commercial domicil in the event of war.

The evidence of this intention will rarely, if ever, be given during peace. It must, therefore, be furnished, if at all, after the war shall be known to him; and that knowledge may be preceded by the capture of his goods. It appears to me, then, to be a case in which, as in many others, justice requires that subsequent testimony shall be received to prove a pre-existing fact. Measures taken for removal immediately after a war, may prove a previous intention to remove in the event of war, and may prove that the captured property, although, *prima facie*, belonging to an enemy, does, in fact, belong to a friend. In such case, the citizen, in my opinion, has a right, in the nature of the *jus postlimi-nii*,[2] to claim restitution.

As this question is not only decisive of many claims now depending before this Court, but is also of vast importance to our merchants generally, I may be excused for stating, at some length, the reasons on which my opinion is founded.

The whole system of decisions applicable to this subject, rests on the law of nations as its base. It is, therefore, of some importance to enquire how far the writers on that law consider the subjects of one power residing within the territory of another, as retaining their original character, or partaking of the character of the nation in which they reside.

Vattel, who, though not very full to this point, is more explicit and more satisfactory on it than any other whose work has fallen into my hands, says, "the citizens are the members of the civil society; bound to this society by certain duties, and subject to its authority, they equally participate in its advantages. The *natives*, or *indigenes*, are those born in the country, of parents who are citizens. Society not being able to subsist and to perpetuate itself but by the children of the citizens, those children naturally follow the condition of their fathers, and succeed to all their rights."[3]

"The inhabitants, as distinguished from citizens, are strangers who are permitted to settle and stay in the country. Bound by their residence to the society, they are subject to the laws of the state, while they reside there, and they are obliged to defend it, because it grants them protection, though they do not participate in all the rights of citizens. They enjoy only the advantages which the laws, or custom gives them. The *perpetual inhabitants* are those who have received the right of perpetual residence. These are a kind of citizens of an inferior order, and are united and subject to the society, without participating in all its advantages."[4]

"The domicil is the habitation fixed in any place, with an intention of always staying there. A man does not, then, establish his domicil in any place, unless he makes sufficiently known his intention of fixing there, either tacitly or by an express declaration. However, this declaration is no reason why, if he afterwards changes his mind, he may not remove his domicil elsewhere. In this sense, he who stops, even for a long time, in a place, for the management of his affairs, has only a simple habitation there, but has no domicil."[5]

A domicil, then, in the sense in which this term is used by *Vattel*, requires not only actual residence in a foreign country, but "an intention of always staying there." Actual residence without this intention, amounts to no more than "simple habitation."

Although this intention may be implied without being expressed, it ought not, I think, to be implied, to the injury of the individual, from acts entirely equivocal. If the stranger has not the power of making his residence perpetual, if circumstances, after his arrival in a country, so change, as to make his continuance there disadvantageous to himself, and his power to continue, doubtful; "an intention always to stay there" ought not, I think, to be fixed upon him, in consequence of an unexplained residence previous to that change of circumstances. Mere residence, under particular circumstances, would seem to me, at most, to prove only an intention to remain so long as those circumstances continue the same, or equally advantageous. This does not give a domicil. The intention which gives a domicil is an unconditional intention "to stay always."

The right of the citizens or subjects of one country to remain in another, depends on the will of the sovereign of that other; and if that will be not expressed otherwise than by that general hospitality which receives and affords security to strangers, it is supposed to terminate with the relations of peace between the two countries. When war breaks out, the subjects of one belligerent in the country of the other are considered as enemies, and have no right to remain there. *Vattel* says, "enemies continue such wherever they happen to be. The place of abode is of no account here. It is the political ties which determine the quality. While a man remains a citizen of his own country, he remains the enemy of all those with whom his nation is at war."[6]

It would seem to me, to require very strong evidence of an intention to become the permanent inhabitant of a foreign country, to justify a court in presuming such intention to continue, when that residence must expose the person to the inconvenience of being considered and treated as an enemy. The intention to be inferred solely from the fact of residence during peace, for commercial purposes, is, in my judgment, necessarily conditional, and dependent on the continuance of the relations of peace between the two countries.

So far is the law of nations from considering residence in a foreign country in time of peace, as evidence of an intention "always to stay there," even in time of war, that the very contrary is expressed. *Vattel* says, "the sovereign declaring war can neither detain those subjects of the enemy who are within his dominions at the time of the declaration, nor their effects. They came into his country on the public faith. By permitting them to enter his territory and to continue there, he tacitly promised them liberty and security for their return. He is therefore to allow them a reasonable time for withdrawing with their effects; and if they stay beyond the time prescribed, he has a right to treat them as enemies, though as enemies disarmed."[7]

The stranger merely residing in a country during peace, however long his stay, and whatever his employment, provided it be such as strangers may engage in, cannot, on the principles of national law, be considered as incorporated into that society, so as, immediately on a declaration of war, to become the enemy of his own. "His property," says *Vattel*, "is still a part of the totality of the wealth of his nation."[8] "The citizen or subject of a state, who absents himself for a time, without any intention to abandon the society of which he is a member, does not lose his privilege by his absence; he preserves his rights, and remains bound by the same obligations. Being received in a foreign country, in virtue of the natural society, the communication and commerce, which nations are obliged to cultivate with each other, he ought to be considered there as a member of his own nation, and treated as such."[9]

The subject of one power inhabiting the country of another, ought not to be considered as a member of the nation in which he resides, even by foreigners; nor ought he, on the first commencement of hostilities, to be treated as an enemy by the enemies of that nation.

Burlamaqui says, "as to strangers, those who settle in the enemy's country after a war is begun, of which they had previous notice, may justly be looked upon as enemies and treated as such. But in regard to such as went thither before the war, justice and humanity require that we should give them a reasonable time to retire; and if they neglect that opportunity, they are accounted enemies."[10]

If this rule be obligatory on foreign nations, much more ought it to bind that of which the individual is a member.

I think I cannot be mistaken when I say that, in all the views taken of this subject by the most approved writers on the law of nations, the citizen of one country residing in another, is not considered as incorporated in that other, but is still considered as belonging to that society of which he was originally a member. And if war break out between the two nations, he is to be permitted, and is expected, to return to his own. I do not perceive in those writers any exception with regard to merchants.

It must, however, be acknowledged that the great extension of commerce has had considerable influence on national law. Rules have been adopted, perhaps by general consent, principles have been engrafted on the original stalk of public law, by which merchants, while belonging politically to one society, are considered commercially as the members of another. For commercial purposes the merchant is considered as a member of that society in which he has his domicil; and less conclusive evidence than would seem to be required in general cases, by the law of nations, has been allowed to fix the domicil for commercial purposes.

But I cannot admit that the original meaning of the term is to be entirely disregarded, or the true nature of this domicil to be overlooked. The effects of the rule ought to be regulated by the motives which are presumed to have induced its establishment, and by the convenience it was intended to promote.

The policy of commercial nations receives foreign merchants into their bosom; and permits their own citizens to reside abroad for the purposes of trade without injury to their rights or character as citizens. This free intercommunication must certainly be believed, by the nations who allow it, to be promotive of their interests. Nor is this opinion ill founded. Nothing can be more obvious than that the affairs of a commercial company will be transacted to most advantage by being conducted, as it respects both purchase and sale, under the eye of a person interested in the result. The nation which takes an interest in the prosperity of its commerce, can feel no inclination to restrain its citizens from residence abroad for the purposes of commerce; nor will it hastily construe such residence into a change of national character, to the injury of the individual. It is not the policy of such a nation, nor can it be its wish, to restrain its citizens from pursuing abroad a business which tends to enrich itself. It ought not, then, to consider them as enemies in consequence of their having engaged in such pursuit in the country of a friend, who, before their removal, becomes an enemy.

If, indeed, it be the real intention of the citizen permanently to change his national character, if it be his choice to remain in the country of the enemy during war, there can be no harshness—no injustice in treating him as an enemy. But if, while prosecuting his business in a foreign country, he contemplates a return to his own; if, in the prosecution of that business, he is promoting rather than counteracting the interests and policy of the country of which he is a member, it would seem to me to be pressing the principle too far, and to be drawing conclusions which the premises will not warrant, to infer, conclusively, an intention to continue in a country which has become hostile, from a residence and trading in that country while it was friendly; and to punish him by the confiscation of his goods, as if he was fully convicted of that intention.

It is admitted to be a general rule, that, while the state of things remains unaltered, while the motives which carried the citizen abroad continue, while he still prosecutes a business of uncertain duration, his capacity to prosecute which is not impaired, his mercantile character is confounded with that of the country in which he resides, and his trade is considered as the trade of that country.

It will require but a slight examination of the subject to perceive the reason of this rule; and that, to a certain extent, it is convenient without being unjust.

In times of universal peace, the question of national character can arise only when some privilege or some disability is attached to it, or in cases of insurance. A particular trade may be allowed or be prohibited to the merchants of a particular nation, or property may be warranted to be of a particular nation. If, in such cases, the residence of the individual be received as evidence of his national mercantile character, the subjects of enquiry are simplified, the questions are reduced to a plain one, and the various complex enquiries, which might otherwise arise, are avoided. There is, therefore, much convenience in adopting this principle in such a state of things; and it is not perceived that any injustice can grow out of it; since the individual to whom the rule is applied is not surprised by any new or unlooked for event.

So if war exists between two nations. Each belligerent having a right to capture the property of the other found on the ocean, each being intent on destroying the commerce of the other, and on depriving it of every cover under which it may seek to shelter itself, will certainly not allow the advantages of neutrality to a merchant residing in the country of his enemy. Were this permitted, the whole trade of the enemy could assume, and would assume, a neutral garb.

There is, in general, no reason for supposing that a merchant residing in a foreign country, and carrying on trade, means to withdraw from it, on its engaging in war with any other country to which he is bound by no obligation. By continuing, during war, the domicil acquired in peace, he violates no duty, offends against no generally acknowledged principle, and retains all his rights of residence and commerce. The war, then, furnishes no motive for presuming that he is about to change his situation, and to resume his original national character.

These reasons appear to me to require the rule as a general one, and to justify its application to general cases. But they do not, in my opinion, justify its application to the case of a merchant whom war finds engaged in trade in a country which becomes the enemy of his own. His country ought not, I think, to bind him by his residence during peace; nor to consider him as precluded by it from showing an intention that it should terminate with the relations of peace.

When it is considered that his right to remain and prosecute that trade in which he had been engaged during peace, is forfeited; that his duty, and most probably his inclinations, call him home; that he has become the enemy of the country in which he resides; that his continuance in it exposes him to many and serious inconveniences; that his person and property are in danger; it is not, I think, going too far to say that this change in his situation may be considered as changing his intention on the subject of residence, and as affording a presumption of intending to return.

Let it be remembered that, according to the law of nations, domicil depends on the intention to reside permanently in the country to which the individual has removed; and that a change of this intention is, at any time, allowable. If, upon grounds of general policy and general convenience, while the circumstances under which the residence commenced, continue the same, residence and employment in permanent trade be considered as evidence of an intention to continue permanently in the country, and as giving a commercial national character, may not a total change in circumstances—a loss of the capacity to carry on the trade, be received, in the absence of all conflicting proof, as presumptive evidence of an intention to leave the country, and as extricating the trade, carried on in the time of supposed peace, from the national character, so far as to protect it from the perils of war? At any rate, do not reason and justice require that this change of circumstances should leave the question open to be decided on such other evidence as the war must produce?

The great object for which an American merchant fixes himself in a foreign country, is, most generally, to carry on trade between that country and his own. In almost every case of this description before the Court, the Claimant is a member of a house established in the United States; and his business abroad is subservient to the business at home. This trade is annihilated by the war.

If, while peace subsists between the United States and Great Britain, while the American merchant possesses there all the commercial rights allowed to the citizens of a friendly nation, and may carry on uninterruptedly his trade to his own country, he is presumed, his intentions being unexplained, to intend remaining there always, and may, for general convenience, be clothed with the commercial character of the nation in which he resides, ought this presumption to be extended, by his own government, beyond the facts out of which it grows, if the interest of the individual be materially affected by that extension? Do not reason and justice require that we should consider his original intention as being only co-extensive with the causes which carried him to and detained him in the country, as being, in its nature, conditional, and dependent on the continuance of those causes?

If such a person were required, on his arrival in a foreign country, to declare his real intentions on the subject of residence, he would, most probably, say, if he spoke honestly, "I come for the purpose of trade: I shall remain while the situation of the two countries permits me to carry on my trade lawfully, securely, and advantageously: when that situation so changes as to deprive me of these rights, I shall return." His intention, then, to reside in the country, his domicil in it, and, consequently, his commercial character, unless he continued his trade after war, would be clearly limited by the duration of peace. It would not, I think, be unreasonable to say that the intention, to be implied from his conduct, ought to have the same limitation.

To me it seems that a mere commercial domicil acquired in time of peace, necessarily expires at the commencement of hostilities. Domicil supposes rights incompatible with a state of war. If the foreign merchant be not compelled to abandon the country, it is not because his commercial character confers on him a legal right to stay, but because he is specially permitted to stay. If in this I am correct, it would seem to follow, that, if all the legal consequences of a residence in time of peace do not absolutely terminate with the peace, yet the national commercial character which that residence has attached to the individual, is not so conclusively fixed upon him as to disqualify him from showing that, within a reasonable time after the commencement of hostilities, he made arrangements for returning to his own country. If a residence and trading after the war be not indispensably necessary to give the citizen merchant or his property a hostile character, yet removal, or measures showing a determination to remove, within a reasonable time after the war, may retroact upon property shipped before a knowledge of the war, and rescue that property from the hostile character attached to the property of the nation in which the individual resided.

The law of nations is a law founded on the great and immutable principles of equity and natural justice. To draw an inference against all probability, whereby a citizen, for the purpose of confiscating his goods, is clothed, against his inclination, with the character of an enemy, in consequence of an act which, when committed, was innocent in itself, was entirely compatible with his political character as a citizen, and with the political views of his government, would seem to me to subvert those principles. The rule which, for obvious reasons, applies to the merchant in time of peace or in time of war, the national commercial character of the country in which he resides, cannot, in my opinion, without subverting those principles, apply a hostile character to his trade carried on during peace, so conclusively as to prevent his protecting it by changing that character within a reasonable time after a knowledge of the war.

My opinion, then, is, that a mere commercial domicil acquired by an American citizen in time of peace, especially if he be a member of an American house, and is carrying on trade auxiliary to his trade with his own country, ought not to be considered positively as continuing longer than the state of peace. The declaration of war is a fact which removes the causes that induced his residence in the foreign country. They no longer operate upon him. When they cease, their effects ought to cease. An intention which they produced, ought not to be supposed to continue. The character of his property shipped before a knowledge of the war, ought not to be decided absolutely by his residence at the time of shipment or capture, but ought to depend on his continuing to reside and trade in the enemy country, or on his taking prompt measures for returning to his own.

This is the conclusion to which my mind would certainly be conducted, might I permit it to be guided by the lights of reason and the principles of natural justice. But it is said that a course of adjudications has settled the law to be otherwise—that we cannot, without overturning a magnificent system bottomed on the broad base of national law, and of which the facts[11] are admirably adjusted to each other, yield to the dictates of humanity on this particular question. *Sir William Scott*, it is argued at the bar, has, by a series of decisions, developed the principles of national law on this subject, with a perspicuity and precision which mark plainly the path we ought to tread.

I respect *sir William Scott*, as I do every truely great man; and I respect his decisions; nor should I depart from them on light grounds: but it is impossible to consider them attentively, without perceiving that his mind leans strongly in favor of the captors. Residence, for example, in a belligerent country, will condemn the share of a neutral in a house, trading in a neutral country; but residence in a neutral country will not protect the share of a belligerent or neutral in a commercial house established in a belligerent country. In a great maritime country, depending on its navy for its glory and its safety, the national bias is perhaps so entirely in this direction, that the judge, without being conscious of the fact, must feel its influence. However this may be, it is a fact of which I am fully convinced; and, on this account, it appears to me to be the more proper to investigate rigidly the principles on which his decisions have been made, and not to extend them where such extension may produce injustice.

While I make this observation, it would betray a want of candor not to accompany it with the acknowledgement that I perceive in the opinions of this eminent judge, no disposition to press this principle with peculiar severity against neutrals. He has certainly not mitigated it when applying it to British subjects.

With this impression respecting the general character of British admiralty decisions, I proceed to examine them so far as they bear on the question of domicil.

The case of the *Vigilantia*[12] does not itself involve the point. But in delivering his opinion, the judge cited two cases of capture which have been quoted and relied on at bar. In each of these, the share of the partner residing in the neutral country, was restored, and that of the partner residing in the belligerent country was condemned. But these decisions applied to a trade continued to be carried on during war.

In a subsequent case, the share of the partner residing in the neutral country also was condemned; and the lords commissioners said that the principle on which restitution was decreed in each of the first mentioned cases, was, "that they were merely at the commencement of a war." They said that "a person carrying on trade habitually in the country of the enemy, though not resident there, should have time to withdraw himself from that commerce; that it would press too heavily on neutrals to say that, immediately, on the first breaking out of a war, their goods would become subject to confiscation."[13] On these cases it is to be observed, that, although the two first happened at the commencement of the war, yet they happened during a war; and the partners whose interest was condemned, do not appear to have discontinued their residence and trading in the country of the enemy, after war had taken place. The declaration "that it would press too heavily on neutrals to say that, immediately on the first breaking out of a war, their goods would become subject to confiscation," though applied to a neutral not residing in the belligerent country, clearly discriminates, in a case of capture, between the rights of parties at the commencement of a war, and at a subsequent period. But it is sufficient to say that neither the case itself, nor the cases and opinions cited in it, apply directly to the question before this Court.

In the case of the *Harmony*,[14] the property of Mr. Murray, an American citizen residing in France, was condemned on account of that residence. But Mr. Murray had removed to France, during the war, and had continued there for four years.

The scope of the argument of *sir William Scott* goes to show that the single circumstance of residence in the enemy country, if not intended to be permanent, will not give the enemy character to the property of such resident captured in a trade between his own country and that of the enemy. It is material that the conduct of Mr. Murray, subsequent to the capture, had great influence in determining the fate of his property. Had he returned to the United States immediately after that event, I do not hazard much in saying that restitution would have been decreed.

In the case of the *Indian Chief*,[15] Mr. Johnson, an American citizen domiciliated in England, had engaged in a merchantile enterprize to the British East Indies—a trade allowed to an American citizen, but prohibited to a British subject. On its return, the vessel came into Cowes, and was seized for being concerned in illicit trade. Mr. Johnson had then left England for the United States. He was considered as not being a British subject at the time of capture, and restitution was decreed.

In delivering his opinion in this case, *sir William Scott* said, "Taking it to be clear that the national character of Mr. Johnson, as a British merchant, was founded in residence only, that it was acquired by residence, and rested on that circumstance alone, it must be held, that, from the moment he turns his back on the country where he has resided, on his way to his own country, he was in the act of resuming his original character, and is to be considered as an American. The character that is gained by residence, ceases by nonresidence. It is an adventitious character that no longer adheres to him from the moment that he puts himself in motion, *bona fide*, to quit the country *sine animo revertendi*."[16]

This case undoubtedly proves, affirmatively, that the national character gained by residence ceases with that residence; but I cannot admit it to prove, negatively, that this national character can be laid down by no other means. I cannot, for instance, admit that an American citizen, who had gained a domicil in England during peace, and was desirous of returning home on the breaking out of war, but was detained by force, could, under the authority of this opinion, be treated as a British trader, with respect to his property embarked before a knowledge of the war.

In the case of *La Virginie*,[17] the property of a Mr. Lapierre, who was probably naturalized in the United States, but who had returned to St. Domingo, and had shipped the produce of that island to France, was condemned. But he was considered as a Frenchman, was residing at the time in a French colony, and was engaged in a trade between that colony and the mother country. The case, the judge observed, might have been otherwise decided, had the shipment been made to the U. States.

In the case of the *Jonge Clarissa*,[18] Mr. Ravie had a license to make certain importations as a British subject. He had a house in Amsterdam, went there in person during the war, and made the shipment under his own inspection and control. It was determined that, in this transaction, he acted in his character as a Dutch merchant, and was not protected by his license. This was a trading during war.

In the case of the *Citto*,[19] the property of Mr. Bowden, a British subject residing in Holland, was condemned. It appeared that he had settled in Amsterdam, where he had resided, carrying on trade, for six years. In 1795, when the French troops took possession of that country, he left it and settled in Guernsey. The *Citto* was a Danish vessel captured in April, 1796, on a voyage from a Spanish port to Guernsey, where Mr. Bowden then resided. In June, 1796, after the capture of the *Citto*, he returned to Holland. In argument, it was contended, that it appeared that British subjects might reside in Holland, without forfeiting their British character, from the proclamation of the 3d of September, 1796, which directs the landing of goods, imported under that order into the united provinces, to be certified by *British merchants resident there*.

The judge was desirous of knowing the nature of Mr. Bowden's residence in Holland—whether he had confined himself to the object of withdrawing his property, or had been engaged in the general traffic of the place. If the former, "he may," said the judge, "be entitled to restitution; more especially adverting to the order in council, which is certainly so worded as not to be very easy to be applied."

The cause stood for further proof.

It is plain that, in this opinion, the residence of the Claimant at the time of capture was not considered as conclusive. Had it been so, restitution must have been decreed, because Mr. Bowden was a British subject, and, at that time, resided in Guernsey. It is equally apparent, that, had his subsequent residence in the enemy country been for the sole purpose of withdrawing his property, the law was not understood to forbid restitution. The language of *sir William Scott* certainly ascribes considerable influence to the proclamation, but does not rest the right of the Claimant altogether on that fact.

On the 17th of March, 1800, an affidavit of Mr. Bowden, made the 6th of August, 1799, was produced, in which he stated his residence in Holland previous to the invasion by the French. That he quitted Holland and landed in England, the 20th of January, 1795, whence he proceeded to Guernsey, where he resided with his family. That, in the month of June, 1796, he was under the absolute necessity of returning to Holland, for the purpose of recovering debts due and effects belonging to the partnership, his partner remaining in Guernsey.

The affidavit then proceeded to state many instances of his attachment to his own government, and concluded with averring that he was still under the necessity of remaining in Holland, for the purpose of recovering part of the said debts and effects, which would be impossible were he to leave the country; but that it was his intention to return to his native country, so soon as his affairs would permit where his mother and his relations reside.

The Court observed that it appeared, from the affidavit, that Mr. Bowden was, at that time, in Holland; and added, "it would be a strange act of injustice, if while we are condemning the goods of persons of all nations resident in Holland, we were to restore the goods of native British subjects resident there. An Englishman residing and trading in Holland, is just as much a Dutch merchant as a Swede or a Dane would be."[20]

This case was decided in 1800. Mr. Bowden had returned to Holland in 1796, during the war, and had continued in the country of the enemy. It is not denied that he continued his trade, and the fact that he did continue it is fairly to be inferred, not only from his omitting to aver the contrary, but from the language of *sir William Scott.* "An Englishman residing and *trading* in Holland," says that judge, "is just as much a Dutch merchant as a Swede or a Dane would be." The case of Mr. Bowden, then, is the case of a British subject who continued to reside and trade in the enemy country four years after the commencement of hostilities. His property must have been condemned on one of two principles. Either the judge must have considered his residence in Guernsey, from January, 1795 to June, 1796, as a temporary interruption of his permanent residence in Holland, and not as a change of domicil, since he returned to that country, and continued in it, as a trader, to the rendition of the final sentence; or he must have decided that, although Mr. Bowden remained and intended to remain in fact a British subject, yet the permanent national commercial character which he acquired after this capture, retroacted on a trade which, at the time of capture was entirely British, and subjected the property to confiscation. On whichsoever of these principles the case was decided, it is clear that the hostile character attached to the property of Mr. Bowden in consequence of his residing and trading in the country of the enemy during the war. This case is, I think, materially variant from one in which the residence and trading took place during peace, and the capture was made before a change of residence could be conveniently effected.

The *Diana*[21] is also a case, of considerable interest, which contains doctrines entitled to attentive consideration.

During the war between Great Britain and Holland, which commenced in 1795, the island of Demarara, surrendered to the British arms. By the treaty of Amiens, it was restored to the Dutch. That treaty contained an article allowing the inhabitants, of whatever country they might be, a term of three years, to be computed from the notification of the treaty, for the purpose of disposing of their property acquired and possessed before or during the war, in which term they may have the full exercise of their religion and enjoyment of their property.

Previous to the declaration of war against Holland, in 1803, the *Diana* and several other vessels, loaded with colonial produce, were captured on a voyage from Demarara to Holland. Immediately after the declaration of war, and before the expiration of three years from the notification of the treaty of Amiens, Demarara again surrendered to Great Britain. Claims to the captured property were filed by original British subjects, inhabitants of Demarara, some of whom had settled in the colony while it was in possession of Great Britain, others before that event. The trial came on after the island had again become a British colony.

Sir William Scott decreed restitution to these British subjects who had settled in the colony while in British possession, but condemned the property of those who had settled there before that time. He held, that their settling in Demarara while belonging to Great Britain, afforded a presumption of their intending to return, if the island should be transferred to a foreign power; which presumption, recognized in the treaty, relieved those Claimants from the necessity of proving such intention. He thought it highly reasonable that they should be admitted to their *jus postliminii*, and be held entitled to the protection of British subjects.

But the property of those Claimants who had settled before it came to the possession of Great Britain, was condemned. "Having settled without any faith in British possession, it cannot be supposed," he said, "that they would have relinquished their residence, because that possession had ceased. They had passed from one sovereignty to another with indifference; and if they may be supposed to have looked again to a connexion with this country, they must have viewed it as a circumstance that was in no degree likely to affect their intention of continuing there." "On the situation of persons settled there previous to the time of British possession, I feel myself," said the judge, "obliged to pronounce that they must be considered in the same light as persons resident in Amsterdam. It must be understood, however, that if there were among these, any who have been actually removing, and that fact is properly ascertained, their goods may be capable of restitution. All that I mean to express is, that there must be evidence of an intention to remove, on the part of those who settled prior to British possession, the presumption not being in their favor."[22]

This having been a hostile seizure, though made before the declaration of war, the property is held equally liable to condemnation as if captured the instant of that declaration.

So much of the case as relates to those Claimants who had settled during British possession, proves that other circumstances than an actual getting into motion for the purpose of returning to his own country, may create a presumption of intending to return; and may put off that hostile commercial character which a British subject residing and trading in the country of an enemy, is admitted to acquire. The settlement having been made in a country which, at the time, was in possession of Great Britain, though held only by the right of conquest— a tenure known to be extremely precarious, and rarely to continue longer than the war in which the acquisition is made, is sufficient to create this presumption; but the case does not declare negatively that no other circumstances would be sufficient.

I am aware that the part of the case which applies to Claimants who had settled previous to British possession, will, at first view, appear to have a strong bearing on the question before the Court. The shipment was in time of peace, and the seizure was made before the declaration of war. The trade was one in which a British subject, in time of peace, might lawfully engage. However strong his intention might be to return to his native country in the event of war, he could not be expected to manifest that intention before the actual existence of war. The reconquest of the island followed the declaration of war so speedily, as scarcely to leave time for putting in execution the resolution to return, had one been formed. Taking these circumstances into view, the condemnation would seem to be one of extreme severity. Yet even this case, admitting the decision to be perfectly correct, does not, I think, when accurately examined, go so far as to justify a condemnation under such circumstances as belong to some of the cases at bar.

The island having surrendered during war, such of its inhabitants as were originally British subjects were not allowed to derive, from this reannexation to the dominions of Great Britain, the advantages to which a voluntary return to their own country, of the same date, would have entitled them. They were considered as if they had been "residents of Amsterdam."

But *sir William Scott* observes, that "if there are among these any who have been actually removing, and that fact is properly ascertained, their goods may be capable of restitution." "Actually removing"— when? Not, surely, before the seizure; for that was made in time of peace. Not before the declaration of war, when the original seizure was converted into a belligerent capture; for until that declaration was known, a person whose intention to remain or return was dependant on peace or war, would not be "actually removing." On every principle of equity, then, the time to which these expressions refer, must be the surrender of Demarara, or a reasonable time after the declaration of war was known there. The one period or the other would be subsequent to that event which was deemed equivalent to capture.

It is not unworthy of remark, that *sir William Scott* adds explanatory words which qualify and control the words "actually removing," and show the sense in which he used them. "All," says the judge, "that I mean to express is, that there must be evidence of an *intention* to remove, on the part of those who settled prior to British possession, the presumption not being in their favor."

It would, then, I think, be rejecting a part, and a material part, of the opinion, to say that an intention to remove clearly proved, though not accompanied by the fact of removal, would have been deemed insufficient to support the claim for restitution.

Were there no other circumstances of real importance in this case— did it rest solely on the sentiments expressed by the judge, unconnected with those circumstances, I should certainly consider it as leaving open to the Claimants before this Court, the right of proving an intention to return within a reasonable time after the declaration of war, by other overt-acts than an actual removal.

But there are other circumstances which I cannot deem immaterial; and, as the opinions of a judge are always to be taken with reference to the particular case in which they are delivered, I must consider these expressions in connexion with the whole case.

The probability is, that the Claimants were not merely British merchants. Though the fact is not expressly stated, there is some reason to believe that they had become proprietors of the soil, and were completely incorporated with the Dutch colonists. They are not denominated merchants. They are spoken of, through the case, not as residents, but as settlers. "They had passed," said sir William Scott, "from one sovereignty to another with indifference." This mode of expression appears to me to indicate a more permanent interest in the country—a more intimate connexion with it than is acquired by a merchant removing to a foreign country, and residing there in time of peace, for the sole purpose of trade. And in another of the same class of cases, it is said that, previous to the last war, the principal plantations of the island were in possession of British planters from the other British islands.

The voyage, too, in making which the *Diana* was captured, was a direct voyage between the colony and the mother country. The trade was completely Dutch; and the property of any neutral, wherever residing, if captured in such a voyage, during war, would be condemned.

But it is still more material that those who settled in Demarara before British possession, must have settled during the war which was terminated by the treaty of Amiens; or, if they settled in time of peace, must have continued there while the colony was Dutch, and while Holland was at war with Great Britain. Which ever the fact might be, whether they had settled in an enemy country during war, or had continued, through the war, a settlement made in time of peace, they had demonstrated that war made no change in their residence. In their case, then, it might be correctly said, "that war created no presumption of an intention to return"—"that they passed from one sovereignty to another with indifference."

I cannot consider claims under these circumstances, as being in the same equity with claims made by persons who had removed into a foreign country, in time of peace, for the sole purpose of trade, and whose trade would be annihilated by war.

The case of the *Boedes Lust*[23] differs from the *Diana* only in this: the Claimants are not alleged to have been originally British subjects. Restitution was asked, because the property did not belong to an enemy at the time of shipment, nor at the time of seizure, nor at the time of adjudication. These grounds were all declared to be insufficient. The original seizure was provisionally hostile; and the declaration of war consummated the right to condemn, and vested the property in the crown, as enemy property. The subsequent change in the character of the Claimants, who became British subjects by the surrender of Demarara, could not divest it. "Where property is taken in a state of hostility," said *sir William Scott*, "the universal practice has ever been to hold it subject to condemnation, although the Claimants may have become friends and subjects prior to adjudication." "With as little effect," he added, "can it be contended that a *postliminium* can be attributed to these parties. Here is no return to the original character, on which only a *jus postliminii* can be raised. The original character at the time of seizure, and immediately prior to the hostility which has intervened, was Dutch. The present character, which the events of war have produced, is that of British subjects; and, although the British subject might, under circumstances, acquire the *jus postliminii*, upon the resumption of native character, it never can be considered that the same privilege accrues upon the acquisition of a character totally new and foreign."[24]

This opinion is certainly not decisive; but it appears to me rather to favor than oppose the idea, that a merchant residing abroad, and taking measures to return on the breaking out of war, may entitle himself to the *jus postliminii*, with respect to property shipped before a knowledge of the war.

The *President*[25] was captured on a voyage from the Cape of Good Hope to Europe. Mr. Elmslie,[26] the Claimant, was born a British subject, but claimed as a citizen of the United States. He had removed to the Cape of Good Hope, during the preceding war, and still resided there. The property was condemned. In delivering his opinion, *sir William Scott* observed, "It is said the Claimant is intitled to the benefit of an intention of removing to Philadelphia, in a few months. A mere intention to remove, has never been held sufficient without some overt-act, being merely an intention residing secretly and undistinguishable in the breast of the party, and liable to be revoked every hour. The expressions of the letter in which this intention is said to be found, are, I observe, very weak and general, of an intention merely *in futuro*. Were they even much stronger than they are, they would not be sufficient. Something more than mere verbal declaration, some solid fact showing that the party is in the act of withdrawing, has always been held necessary in such cases."[27]

It is to be held in mind, that this opinion is delivered in the case of a person who had fixed his residence in an enemy country, during war, and that he claimed to be the subject of a neutral state. For both these reasons, the war afforded no presumption of his intending to return either to his native or adopted country. To the vague expression of an intention to return at some future indefinite time, no influence can be ascribed. When the judge says that "something more than mere verbal declaration, some solid fact showing that the party is in the act of withdrawing, has always been held necessary in such cases," I do not understand him to say that the person must have put himself in personal motion to return, must have commenced his voyage homeward, in order to be considered as in "the act of withdrawing." Many other overt-acts, as selling a commercial establishment, stopping business, making preparations to return, accompanied by declarations of the intent, and not opposed by other circumstances, may, in my opinion, be considered as acts of withdrawing.

In the case of the *Ocean*,[28] *sir William Scott* said, "This claim relates to the situation of British subjects settled in a foreign state, in time of amity, and taking early measures to withdraw themselves, on the breaking out of war. The affidavit of claim states that this gentleman had been settled as a partner in a house of trade in Holland, but that he had made arrangements for the dissolution of the partnership, and was only prevented from removing personally, by the violent detention of all British subjects who happened to be within the territories of the enemy, at the breaking out of the war. It would, I think, under these circumstances, be going further than the principle of law requires, to conclude this person by his former occupation, and by his present constrained residence in France, so as not to admit him to have taken himself out of the effect of supervening hostilities, by the means which he had used for his removal."

If other means for removal were taken, than arrangements for the dissolution of the partnership, they are not stated; and it is fairly to be presumed, that these arrangements were the most permanent[29] of them, since that fact is alone selected and particularly relied upon. In his statement of the case, the reporter says that the Claimant had actually made his escape and returned to England, in July, 1803; (the trial was in January, 1804) but this must be a mistake, or is a fact not adverted to by the judge, since he says, in his opinion, that the Claimant is, at the time, "a constrained resident of France."

I shall notice two other cases which are frequently cited, though I have seen no full report of either of them.

The first is the case of Mr. *Curtissos*.[30] This gentleman, who was a British subject, had gone to Surinam in 1766, and from thence to St. Eustatius, where he remained till 1776. He then went to Holland to settle his accounts, and with an intention, "*as was said*," of returning afterwards to England to take up his final residence. In December, 1780, orders of reprisal were issued by England against Holland. On the first of January, 1781, the *Snelle Zeylder* was captured, and, on the 5th of March and 10th of April, 1781, the vessel and cargo were condemned as Dutch property. On the 27th of April, 1781, Mr. *Curtissos* returned to England: and, on an appeal, the sentence of condemnation was reversed by the lords of appeals, and restitution decreed.

Other claims of Mr. *Curtissos* were brought before the Court of admiralty; and, on a full disclosure of these circumstances, restitution was decreed, before the decree of the lords in the case of the *Snelle Zeylder* was pronounced.

The principle of this decree is said to be, that Mr. *Curtissos* was *in itinere*, and had put himself in motion, and was in pursuit of his original British character.

I do not mean to find fault with this decision; but certainly it presents some strong points more unfavorable to the Claimant than will be found in some of the cases now before this Court. Mr. *Curtissos* had obtained a commercial domicil in the country of the enemy. At the time of the sailing, capture and condemnation of the *Snelle Zeylder*, he still resided in the country of the enemy. But it is said he was *in itinere*; he was in motion in pursuit of his original British character. What was this journey he is said to have been performing in pursuit of his original character? He had passed from one part of the dominions of the united provinces to another. He had moved his residence from St. Eustatius to

Holland, where he remained from the year 1776 till 1781—a time of sufficient duration for the acquisition of a domicil, had he not previously acquired it. This change of residence, to make the most of it, is an act too equivocal in itself to afford a strong presumption that it was made for the purpose of returning to England. Had his stay in Holland even been short, a colonial merchant trading to the mother country, may so frequently be carried there on the business of his trade, that the fact can afford but weak evidence of an intention to discontinue that trade: but an interval of between four and five years elapsed between his arrival in Holland and his departure from that country, during which time he is not stated to have suspended his commercial pursuits, or to have made any arrangements, such as transferring his property to England, or making an establishment there, which might indicate, by overt-acts, the intention of returning to his native country. This journey to Holland, connected with this long residence, would seem to me to be made as a Dutch merchant for the purpose of establishing himself there, rather than as preparatory to his return to England. But it was said that he intended to return to England. How was this intention shown? If not by his journey to Holland and his long residence there, it was only shown by his being employed in the settlement of his accounts while a merchant at St. Eustatius, a business in which he would of course engage, whatever his future objects might be. This equivocal act does not appear to have been explained, otherwise than by his own declarations; nor does it appear that these declarations were made previous to the capture. But could I even admit that the journey from St. Eustatius to Holland was made with a view of passing ultimately from Holland to England, yet the intention was not to be immediately executed. The time of carrying it into effect, was remote and uncertain; subject to so many casualties that, had not the war supervened, it might never have been carried into effect.

But laying aside these circumstances, the case proves only that being *in itinere*, in pursuit of the native character, divests the enemy character acquired by residence and trading; it is not insinuated that this character can be divested by no other means.

Mr. *Whitehills*[31] case, though one of great severity, does not, I think, overturn the principle I am endeavoring to sustain. He went to St. Eustatius but a few days before admiral Rodney and the British forces made their appearance before that place. But it was proved that he went for the purpose of making a permanent settlement there. No intention to return appears to have been alleged. The recency of his establishment seems to have been the point on which his claim rested.

This case, in principle, bears on that before the Court, so far only as it proves that war does not, under all circumstances, necessarily furnish a presumption, that the foreigner residing in the enemy country, intends to return to his own. The circumstances of this case, so far as we understand them, were opposed to the presumption that war could affect Mr. *Whitehills* residence. War actually existed at the time of his removal; and had that fact been known to him, there would have been no hardship in his case. He would have voluntarily taken upon himself the enemy character at the same time that he took upon himself the Dutch character. There is reason to believe that the Court considered him in equal fault with a person removing to a country known to be hostile. St. Eustatius was deeply engaged in the American trade, which, from the character of the contest, was, at that time, considered by England as cause of war, and was the fact which drew on that island the vengeance of Britain. Mr. *Whitehill* could have fixed himself there only for the purpose of prosecuting that trade. "He went," says *sir William Scott*, "to a place which had rendered itself particularly obnoxious by its conduct in that war."[32] This was certainly a circumstance which could not be disregarded, in deciding on the probability of his intending to remain in the country in the event of war.

These are the cases which appear to me to apply most strongly to the question before this Court. No one of them decides, in terms, that the property of a British subject residing abroad in time of amity, which was shipped before a knowledge of war, and captured by a British cruizer, shall depend, conclusively, on the residence of the Claimant at the time of capture, or on his having, at that time, put himself in motion to change his residence. In no case which I have had an opportunity of inspecting, have I seen a *dictum* to this effect. The cases certainly require an intention, on the part of the subject residing and trading abroad, to return to his own country, and that this intention should be manifested by overt-acts; but they do not, according to my understanding of them, prescribe any particular overt act, as being exclusively admissible; nor do they render it indispensable that the overt act should, in all cases, precede the capture. If a British subject residing abroad for commercial purposes, takes decided measures, on the breaking out of war, for returning to his native country, and especially if he should actually return, his claim for the restitution of property shipped before his knowledge of the war, would, I think, be favorably received in a British Court of admiralty, although his actual return, or the measures proving his intention to return, were subsequent to the capture. Thus understanding the English authorities, I do not consider them as opposing the principle I have laid down.

An American citizen having merely a commercial domicil in a foreign country, is not, I think, under the British authorities, concluded, by his residence and trading in time of peace, from averring and proving an intention to change his domicil on the breaking out of war, or from availing himself of that proof in a Court of admiralty. The intrinsic evidence arising from the change in his situation, produced by war, renders it extremely probable that in this new state of things he must intend to return home, and will aid in the construction of any overt-act by which such intention is manifested. Dissolution of partnership, discontinuance of trade in the enemy country, a settlement of accounts, and other arrangements obviously preparatory to a change of residence, are, in my opinion, such overt-acts as may, under circumstances showing them to be made in good faith, entitle the Claimant to restitution.

I do not perceive the mischief or inconvenience that can result from the establishment of this principle. Its operation is confined to property shipped before a knowledge of the war. For if shipped afterwards, it is clearly liable to condemnation, unless it be protected by the principle that it is merely a withdrawing of funds. Being confined to shipments made before a knowledge of the war, the evidence of an intention to change or continue a residence in the country of the enemy, must be speedily given. A continuance of trade after the war, unless, perhaps, under very special circumstances, and for the mere purpose of closing transactions already commenced, would fix the national character and the domicil previously acquired. An immediate discontinuance of trade, and arrangements for removing, followed by actual removal within a reasonable time, unless detained by causes which might sufficiently account for not removing, would fix the intention to change the domicil, and show that the intention to return had never been abandoned; that the intention to remain always had never been formed. It is a case in which, if in any that can be imagined, justice requires that the citizen, having entirely recovered his national character by his own act, and by an act which shows that he never intended to part with it finally, should, by a species of the *jus postliminii*, be allowed to aver the existence of that character at the instant of capture. In the establishment of such a principle, I repeat, I can perceive no danger. In its rejection, I think I perceive much injustice. An individual whose residence abroad is certainly innocent and lawful, perhaps advantageous to his country, who never intended that residence to be permanent, or to continue in time of war, finds himself, against his will, clothed with the character of an enemy, so conclusively that not even a return to his native country can rescue from that character and from confiscation, property shipped in the time of real or supposed peace. My sense of justice revolts from such a principle.

In applying this opinion to the Claimants before the Court, I should be regulated by their conduct after a knowledge of the war. If they continued their residence and trade after that knowledge, at any rate after knowing that the repeal of the orders in council was not immediately followed by peace, their claim to restitution would be clearly unsustainable. If they took immediate measures for returning to this country, and have since actually returned, or have assigned sufficient reasons for not returning, their property I think may be capable of restitution. Some of the Claimants would come within one description, some within the other. It would, under the opinion given by the Court, be equally tedious and useless to go through their cases.

My reasoning has been applied entirely to the case of native Americans. This course has been pursued for two reasons. It presents the argument in what I think its true light; and the sentence of condemnation makes no discrimination between native and other citizens.

The Claimants are natives of that country with which we are at war, who have been naturalized in the United States. It is impossible to deny that many of the strongest arguments urged to prove the probability that war must determine the native American citizen to abandon the country of the enemy and return home, are inapplicable, or apply but feebly, to citizens of this description. Yet I think it is not for the United States, in such a case as this, to discriminate between them.

I will not pretend to say what distinctions may or may not exist between these two classes of citizens, in a contest of a different description. But in a contest between the United States and the naturalized citizen, in a claim set up by the United States to confiscate his property, he may, I think, protect himself by any defence which would protect a native American. In the prosecution of such a claim, the United States are, I think, if I may be excused for borrowing from the common law a term peculiarly appropriate, *estopped* from saying that they have not placed this adopted son on a level with those born in their family.

Printed, William Cranch, *Reports of Cases Argued and Adjudged in the Supreme Court of the United States . . .* , VIII (Washington, D.C., 1816), 288–317.

1. Justice Washington conceded that a merchant's national character acquired by residence could "be thrown off at pleasure" by returning to the country of citizenship, but that a mere declaration of an intention to return "ought never to be relied upon, when contradicted, or at least rendered doubtful, by a continuance of that residence which impressed the character." To guard against frauds, courts in such cases required evidence of a clear intention to remove before notice of the capture. In this particular case one of the claimants had returned to the U.S.; the other two were still in Great Britain. Washington founded his opinion on the judgments of Sir William Scott (1745–1836), judge of the British High Court of Admiralty from 1798 to 1828 (8 Cranch 273–87 [quotations at 280, 281]).

2. *Jus postliminii*—a term of international law. The right of postliminy is the restoration to the former state of persons and things taken in war when they come again into the power of the nation to which they belonged.

3. Vattel, *Law of Nations* (1805 ed.), Bk. I, chap. xix, sec. 212, p. 162.

4. Ibid., Bk. I, chap. xix, sec. 213, p. 162.

5. Ibid., Bk. I, chap. xix, sec. 218, pp. 163–64.

6. Ibid., Bk. III, chap. v, sec. 71, p. 390.

7. Ibid., Bk. III, chap. iv, sec. 63, p. 386.

8. Ibid., Bk. II, chap. viii, sec. 109, p. 238.

9. Ibid., Bk. II, chap. viii, sec. 107, pp. 237–38.

10. J. J. Burlamaqui, *The Principles of Natural and Politic Law* (5th ed.; 2 vols.; Cambridge, Mass., 1807), II, pt. IV, chap. vi, sec. vi, p. 195.

11. This should be "parts," as JM indicated in his letter to Henry Wheaton, 27 Oct. 1816, upon reading the proof sheets of the eighth volume of Cranch. Wheaton (1785–1848), who was appointed court reporter in 1816, oversaw the publication of the last three volumes of Cranch's reports. This particular correction was not included in the "Errata" list at the beginning of the volume.

12. The "Vigilantia," 1 C. Rob. 1, 165 Eng. Rep. 74 (Adm., 1798).

13. 1 C. Rob. 14–15, 165 Eng. Rep. 78–79.

14. The "Harmony," 2 C. Rob. 322, 165 Eng. Rep. 331 (Adm., 1800).

15. The "Indian Chief," 3 C. Rob. 12, 165 Eng. Rep. 367 (Adm., 1801).

16. 3 C. Rob. 20–21, 165 Eng. Rep. 371. *Sine animo revertendi* (without the intention of returning).

17. "La Virginie," 5 C. Rob. 98, 165 Eng. Rep. 711 (Adm., 1804).

18. The "Jonge Klassina," 5 C. Rob. 297, 165 Eng. Rep. 782 (Adm., 1804).

19. The "Citto," 3 C. Rob. 38, 165 Eng. Rep. 377 (Adm., 1800).

20. 3 C. Rob. 39–41, 165 Eng. Rep. 377–78.

21. The "Diana," 5 C. Rob. 59, 165 Eng. Rep. 697 (Adm., 1803).

22. 5 C. Rob. 64–66, 165 Eng. Rep. 699–700.

23. "Boedes Lust," 5 C. Rob. 233, 165 Eng. Rep. 759 (Adm., 1804).

24. 5 C. Rob. 247–48, 250, 165 Eng. Rep. 764, 765.

25. The "President," 5 C. Rob. 277, 165 Eng. Rep. 775 (Adm., 1804).

26. John Elmslie, Jr., had been U.S. consul at the Cape of Good Hope while JM was secretary of state (*PJM*, VI, 521).

27. 5 C. Rob. 280, 165 Eng. Rep. 776.

28. The "Ocean," 5 C. Rob. 90, 165 Eng. Rep. 708 (Adm., 1804).

29. This should be "prominent," as JM noted in his letter to Wheaton, 27 Oct. 1816. This correction was not included in the "Errata" for the eighth volume of Cranch.

30. JM's discussion of the unreported Curtisso's Case was taken from Scott's judgment in The "Indian Chief," 3 C. Rob. 21 and n., 165 Eng. Rep. 371 and n.

31. Scott mentioned the unreported Whitehill's Case in The "Diana," 5 C. Rob. 60, 165 Eng. Rep. 697.

32. 5 C. Rob. 65, 165 Eng. Rep. 699.

To Samuel M. Burnside

Sir   Washington March 13th. 1814

I received in the city of Richmond in Virginia your letter of the 10th. of January informing me that the American Antiquarian society holden at Boston had done me the honor to elect me as a member.[1] I inclose you a note for five dollars which you will please to consider as my contribution in advance, so far as it exceeds that which is required for the present year.[2] I am Sir, respectfully, Your Obedt Servt

J MARSHALL

ALS, MWA. Addressed to Burnside in Worcester, Mass., and marked "Hond by/Judge Story." Endorsed.

1. Letter not found. JM was elected a member at the 22 Dec. 1813 meeting. Burnside was then the society's recording secretary (American Antiquarian Society, *Proceedings, 1812–1849* [Worcester, Mass., 1912], 7, 41).

2. The treasurer reported receiving JM's five dollars at the society's 24 Oct. 1814 meeting (ibid., 49).

To Jonathan Williams

Sir   Washington March 13th. 1814
    I received a letter some time past from the Treasurer of the United States Military philosophical society informing me that twenty five dollars would be received from those members who chose to pay a sum in gross in lieu of their annual contribution.[1] I now take the liberty to inclose that sum to you. Very respectfully I am Sir, Your Obedt
                                                    J MARSHALL

ALS, INu-Li.

1. Letter not found. On Williams, see *PJM*, VI, 429, 430 n. 1.

To Timothy Pickering

My Dear Sir,   Richmond April 11. 1814.
    I had yesterday the pleasure of receiving your letter of the 8th accompanying Mr. Lowell's very masterly review of the treatise on expatriation.[1] I have read it with great pleasure, & thank you very sincerely for this mark of your recollection.
    Could I have ever entertained doubts on the subject, this review would certainly have removed them. Mingled with much pungent raillery is a solidity of argument and an array of authority which in my judgement is entirely conclusive. But in truth it is a question upon which I never entertained a *scintilla* of doubt; and have never yet heard an argument which ought to excite a doubt in any sound & reflecting mind. It will be to every thinking American a most afflicting circumstance, should our government on a principle so completely rejected by the world proceed to the execution of unfortunate, of honorable, & of innocent men.[2] With great & sincere respect & esteem, I am dear sir your obedt. servt.
                                                    J. MARSHALL

Tr, Pickering Papers, MHi.

1. Letter not found. John Lowell (1769–1840), a Massachusetts lawyer and Federalist political writer, had recently published his *Review of a Treatise on Expatriation . . .* (Boston, 1814; S #31967), a reply to George Hay's *A Treatise on Expatriation* (Washington, D.C., 1814; S #31670). Hay's pamphlet refuted the British doctrine of perpetual allegiance,

which maintained that a person born in Great Britain remained a British subject even after immigration to or naturalization by another country. The British government used this principle to justify impressment of sailors on American ships.

2. Lowell characterized Hay's tract as administration-inspired propaganda, one purpose of which was to prepare the public mind for the "murder" of twenty-three British officers then being held hostage to guarantee the safety of twenty-three American soldiers imprisoned in England. The latter prisoners were British-born, mostly Irishmen, some of them naturalized American citizens and others having resided many years in America. They had been captured in Oct. 1812 at the Battle of Queenston, Upper Canada, and transported to England for trial on treason charges. The U.S. responded to this action by making hostages of the twenty-three British officers. In turn, the governor-general of Canada placed forty-six additional American prisoners of war in close confinement and threatened to execute two American soldiers for every British soldier killed in retaliation for the execution of the Americans in England. Eventually all officers held by either side as prisoners of war in North America were kept as hostages under threat of execution. No retaliatory executions were carried out, however, and both sides released their hostages after peace was restored (Lowell, *Review of a Treatise on Expatriation*, 4; Donald R. Hickey, *The War of 1812: A Forgotten Conflict* [Urbana, Ill., 1989], 177–80).

To Bushrod Washington

My dear Sir   Richmond April 19th. 1814

Your letter of the 13th. reached me this morning.[1] The question you propose had never before attracted my attention. Without examining the subject, I had taken it for granted that the power of passing bankrupt laws resided in the states.[2] It now appears to me more doubtful than I had supposed it to be. Congress has power "to establis[h] an uniform rule of naturalization & uniform laws on the subject of bankruptcies throughout the United States." This would seem to empower Congress to regulate the whole bankrupt system, & to require in all the states a conformity to the laws of the national legislature. But unless Congress shall act on the subject, I should feel much difficulty in saying that the legislative power of the states respecting it is suspended by this part of the constitution.[3]

That part of the constitution which inhibits the passage of any "law impairing the obligation of contracts" was probably intended to prevent a mischief very different from any which grows out of a bankrupt law. Those laws exist in commercial countries where credit is in its most flourishing state, & were I believe common in the commercial states of the Union at the adoption of the constitution. I do not recollect that they excited any complaints or were considered as impairing credit in the states in which they were in operation. The fears & apprehensions which produced that limitation on the legislative power of the states were of a different description. Paper money, the tender of useless property, & other laws acting directly on the engagements of individuals were then objects of general alarm & were probably in the mind of the convention. Yet the words may go further; if they do on a fair & necessary construction, they must have their full effect.

The words of the Constitution are prospective. "No state shall" &c. They do not then act on the existing bankrupt system of any state. I should not willingly admit a construction which tolerated bankrupt laws in some states in which they already existed, but forbade their enactment in other states.

It may also be doubted whether a bankrupt law applying to contracts made subsequent to its passage may fairly be termed a law impairing the obligation of contracts. Such contract is made with a knowlege that it may be acted on by the law. But this would not apply to contracts made out of the state. I should feel no hesitation in saying that a particular act of the state legislature discharging a particular individual who had surrendered his property was invalid. But a general prospective act presents a question of considerable difficulty. I have not thought of the question long enough, nor viewed it in a sufficient variety of lights to have a decided opinion on it, but the biass of my mind at the moment is rather in favor of the validity of the law though I acknowlege I feel very great doubts whether I shall retain that opinion.[4] Your own judgement, you having heard the argument, is much more to be relied on than mine. I am my dear Sir very sincerely, Your affectionate

J MARSHA⟨LL⟩

ALS, Marshall Papers, ViW. Addressed to Washington in Philadelphia; postmarked [Richmond?] 19 Apr. Endorsed by Washington. MS torn where seal was broken.

1. Letter not found.

2. Washington was then preparing his opinion in the case of Golden v. Prince, which was heard at the April term of the U.S. Circuit Court for Pennsylvania (10 Fed. Cas. 542).

3. In Golden v. Prince, Washington held a Pennsylvania insolvency statute of 1812 to be unconstitutional on two grounds: (1) that it impaired the obligation of contracts and (2) that it was incompatible with Congress's power to enact uniform laws on the subject of bankruptcies. In striking down the state law, Washington placed greater emphasis on the second point, a position that the Supreme Court later rejected in Sturgis v. Crowninshield (10 Fed. Cas. 542–47). See Sturgis v. Crowninshield, Opinion, 17 Feb. 1819.

4. Because the Pennsylvania insolvency statute operated retrospectively, Washington voided the law as impairing the obligation of contracts. At the same time, however, he declared that "a law prospective in its operation, under which a contract afterwards made, may be avoided in a way different from that provided by the parties, would be clearly constitutional." On this point, Washington's view ultimately prevailed in the Supreme Court in the 1827 case of Ogden v. Saunders. Although the "biass" of JM's mind in 1814 was in favor of a prospective bankruptcy law, when the question finally came before him judicially in Ogden v. Saunders, he concluded (in dissent) that such a law unconstitutionally impaired the obligation of contracts (10 Fed. Cas. 544; 12 Wheat. 213, 332).

United States v. Jones
Opinion
U.S. Circuit Court, Virginia, 30 May 1814

At the May 1813 term the circuit court affirmed a district court judgment against George Pegram, Jr., on an embargo bond. In satisfaction of this judgment, Robert Colquhoun, Pegram's administrator, paid into court the sum of $46,300. Various claims were then exhibited against all or portions of this amount. U.S. Attorney Hay moved that the entire sum be deposited to the credit of the United States; Joseph Jones, the collector at Petersburg, requested payment to him, half of which he would pay to the United States, the other half to himself and John H. Peterson, surveyor at City Point; Thomas Shore, executor of John Shore, late collector at Petersburg, claimed half the money, to be distributed equally between himself and Reuben Gilliam, administrator of Andrew Forborne, late surveyor at City Point. Peterson and Gilliam also filed separate petitions on their behalf. Marshall's opinion below was addressed to Hay's motion (*PJM*, VII, 398–404; U.S. v. Jones and others; Shore's Executor v. Jones and others, U.S. Cir. Ct., Va., Rec. Bk. X, 146–66).

The U.S.

v

Money deposited in the Bank.[1]

¶1   A judgement having been rendered in this court in favor of the United States against _____ admr. of Pegram for $46300 the penalty of an embargo bond, the defendant paid into court the amount thereof & the money has been deposited in bank subject to the order of the court. This motion is made for the purpose of deciding to whom it is now to be delivered.

¶2   The United States claim the whole sum. Thomas Shore exr. of John Shore decd. who was collector of the port when the bond was executed & also when it was put in suit, & Joseph Jones who was collector when the final judgement was rendered & is still collector, contend that the United States are entitled only to a moity of the judgement; & that the other moity is subject to distribution. Should the court be of this opinion, each claims for himself that part of the money which is by law bestowed on the collecter.

¶3   This question depends on the 12th. Sec. of the act of Jany. 1809 commonly called ["]The Enforcing act." That sec. is in these words "And be it further enacted That all penalties & forfeitures" &c.[2]

¶4   It is admitted on the part of the United States that this judgement was rendered for a penalty, but not for such a penalty as is by law rendered distributable.

The importance of the question and the decision of the Treasury ¶5
department upon it, furnish peculiar motives for a rigid examination
of the principles on which the opinion of the court must depend.[3]

The words of the section could not be more comprehensive than ¶6
they are. "All penalties & forfeitures incurred by force of the act laying
an embargo &c shall be distributed &c." This being a penalty, & being a
penalty imposed by the act laying an embargo, is of course comprehended within the distributive clause, unless the U.S. can show that it is
excepted by the general spirit & true meaning of the act.

In the attempt to prove such exception the first & material proposi- ¶7
tion is, that this penalty is not included in the words "all penalties
incurred by force of the act laying an embargo &c." Penalties are of two
descriptions. The one nominal, as that in a bond conditioned to be void
on the payment of a smaller sum, or on the performance of some act
contracted to be performed. Against these penalties relief was originally granted in a court of chancery; & at length it was provided by
Statute that they should stand meerly as security for the sum equitably
due. Congress has adopted this principle, & has provided that, in all
covenants with a penalty, judgement shall be rendered for such sum
only as shall be assessed by a jury.

The other class of penalties is something more than form. The pen- ¶8
alty is intended as a punishment for some violation of law. Judgement
is rendered for the whole sum, & payment of the whole is enforced.

Now can it be doubted to which class the penalty imposed by the act ¶9
laying an embargo belongs? Can it be doubted that the words laying an
embargo on vessels bound to any foreign port or place, import a prohibition to sail to any foreign port or place? Would any gentleman
seriously contend that a vessel sailing after knowlege of this act, from a
port of the U.S. to a foreign port, had not violated the law? If, as is
truely urged on the part of the United States, this act was passed with
precipitation, that circumstance furnishes an additional motive for a
construction conforming to the obvious intent of the legislature. Now
can any gentleman read this act & resist the conviction that the legislature in imposing the embargo intended to prevent vessels in port from
sailing to a foreign country? If it be true that no punishment could be
inflicted upon this section for this violation of law; that is a consequence of the structure of our government & of our system of jurisprudence: but this failure to provide a punishment for the performance of
a prohibited act can never prove that the act is not prohibited.

Having thus laid an embargo on vessels bound to foreign ports, ¶10
which *ex vi termini* prohibits their sailing to such ports, the legislature
was aware that this prohibition might be eluded by clearing for a port
in the U.S. & sailing to a foreign port. To prevent this, & to punish the
fact if committed, it is enacted that no vessel shall depart from one port

of the United States to any other, unless the Master &c shall give bond with one or more sureties in a sum of double the value of the vessel & cargo conditioned that the goods shall be relanded in some port of the United States. This is substantially a penalty on the master or owner of a vessel which shall be cleared out for a port of the United States & shall sail to a foreign port. In its operation & its consequences it is not the less a penalty for being secured by a bond. Had this precaution been omitted, the person on whom the penalty was imposed might have placed himself beyond the reach of the United States. To prevent this the penalty is to be secured. But it remains a penalty. It is still a punishment for a violation of law, & is a punishment of precisely the same character as if the bond had not been exacted.

¶11 The distinction then taken by the attorney for the United States between those penalties which are to secure the performance of a contract, as in the case he has put of duty bonds; and those which are intended as a punishment for offences, altho it be a correct distinction, has no tendency to support the claim of the U.S. since this penalty is in the nature of a punishment for an offence.

¶12 This part of the case was decided in rendering the judgement in satisfaction of which the money now claimed was paid into court. By the express provision of law the court is inhibited from rendering judgement in case of a penalty for the performance of contract, for any larger sum than is due in equity, or shall be assessed by a jury. It would be very strange if in the same cause, the same court should, for the purpose of charging the obligors with the whole penalty, declare it to be inflicted as a punishment for an offence; &, then, for the sake of ousting those who claimed distribution, declare it to be, not a punishment for an offence, but a penalty in the nature of contract.

¶13 The next argument on the part of the United States in support of this proposition is that the words "all penalties" are qualified & restrained by the subsequent words "incurred by force of the act entitled an act laying an embargo &c." & that this penalty is not incurred *exclusively* by force of that act, but also by force of the bond on which the judgement has been rendered.

¶14 That these words constitute a material part of the description is admitted. Certainly no penalties are distributable under this clause, other than those which are incurred by force of the act. But on what tenable ground can it be contended that a penalty imposed by the act is not incurred by force of the act? To the argument which contends that this penalty is not incurred *exclusively* by force of the act, it would perhaps be sufficient to answer that the word "*exclusively*" is not in the law. It is first found in the argument, & is there used as if it had been introduced into the act.

¶15 But to the court it appears that this penalty is incurred as entirely by force of the act as if it had not been secured by a bond. The act creates the penalty & directs the bond. The bond then is the creature of the act. It is the mode by which the will of the law is carried into effect. It is the meer instrument by which the law acts, the road by which it travels to its object. The penalty is secured by the bond directed by law, but is incurred by force of the law creating the penalty, & the act of the party violating that law.

The act of sailing to a foreign port is indifferent in itself, but is made ¶16 an offence against the United States by the statute which prohibits it. The prohibitory statute annexes a penalty to the offence & directs this penalty to be secured by bond. To the court it seems perfectly clear that if the penalty be incurred it is incurred by force of the act.

The law directing the distribution refers to the act of 1799.[4] It has ¶17 been contended that as that act distributes no penalties secured by bond, the act of 1809 ought not to be construed to distribute such penalties. In illustration of this argument it has been contended that the penalties accruing on exportation bonds are not distributed under the 91st. Sec. of the act of 1799.

This fact is not certain—but it is not deemed material; because As ¶18 the act of 1809 refers to the act of 1799 not for the purpose of ascertaining what description of penalty shall be distributed, but solely for the mode of distribution, it may very well be that penalties are distributable under the one act which are not distributable under the other.

This observation applies equally to the arguments founded on the ¶19 provisos to the 91st. Sec. of the act of 1799. Those arguments as understood by the court were urged for the sole purpose of showing that the act of 1799 did not contemplate the distribution of penalties secured by bond. But it is immaterial what penalties were in contemplation of the legislature at the passage of that act, if only its mode of distribution, not its penalties are adopted by the act of 1809.

If the question depended solely on those parts of the act of 1809 ¶20 which have been already noticed, the court could not hesitate respecting its true construction; but one argument has been urged by the counsel for the Collectors which is really so conclusive, that, had not this been a case in which the decision of a great department of government in the line of its duty is resisted, the court would have rested its opinion on that single point. It is that the act of 1809 declares that all penalties & forfeitures incurred by force of the original embargo act shall be distributed as directed by the act of 99; & there is no penalty to which this provision can apply other than those secured by bond.

The words certainly evince the legislative opinion that there were ¶21 penalties or forfeitures or both incurred by force of the original embargo act; & direct positively that those penalties & forfeitures, if both are incurred by force of the act, shall be distributed. If penalties alone are created by that act, then the act of 1809 can admit of no other construction than that those penalties, if they be of one description only, must be all distributable. That these laws are to be construed as if the original act created no forfeiture is apparent from the supplemental act passed on the 9th. of Jany. 1808, the 3d. Sec. of which expressly confiscates any vessel which shall violate the original act by sailing to a foreign port.[5] The act of 1809 therefore must be construed on the idea that the forfeiture was created by the supplemental & not by the original, act. If so the words "all penalties & forfeitures incurred by force of the act laying an embargo shall be distributed" &c are totally inoperative & mean nothing unless they distribute the penalties secured by bond. Now if there are penalties imposed by that act, & no forfeitures, what court can dare to say that those penalties are not distributable, either because they were secured by bond, or because the officers entitled to distribution under the act have not rendered services equivalent to the rewards they will receive?

¶22   It has been said that these acts were drawn with precipitation. But the enforcing act passed more than 12 months after the original act & is obviously drawn with great care & attention. It was designed to remedy all the omissions & imperfections in the preceding acts, & it is apparent that in preparing it those preceding acts were revised & considered. Upon this revisal it was discovered that no distribution had been made of the penalties incurred by force of the original law & to cure that defect the provision was made which has been discussed in this case. Why else did the legislature look back & declare that all penalties incurred by force of the original act should be distributed?

¶23   Suppose this provision had been introduced into the original act. The word forfeitures would be omitted as inapplicable. It seems scarcely necessary to add that other parts of the act support this construction. For example—After directing that all penalties & forfeitures shall be distributed according to the rules prescribed by the act of 99 the legislature adds "And may be mitigated or remitted in the manner prescribed by the act entitled an act &c." Now it is clear that those penalties only come within the latter clause which were embraced by the foregoing. Has it ever been doubted that the penalties imposed by the original embargo act might be mitigated or remitted?

¶24   The court, let it be repeated, has felt it necessary to subject the opinion which was quickly formed in this case to a very rigorous examination, & is incapable of discerning any principle of sound construction which would sustain the claim made on the part of the U.S. to the whole money paid into court in satisfaction of this judgement. One moity of it must be distributed according to the rules prescribed in the act of 1799.

AD, Tucker-Coleman Papers, ViW. Endorsed by Tucker, "Court's Opinion/May 30. 1814." For JM's deletions and interlineations, see Textual Notes below.

1. St. George Tucker summarized this opinion in his casebook under date of 30 May 1814. There is no mention of the case under this date in the court order book ("Cases in the Courts of the United States, 25 February 1813–November 1834," No. 1, p. 37, Tucker-Coleman Papers, ViW).

2. *U.S. Statutes at Large*, II, 510.

3. In making his motion, Hay referred to a letter from the comptroller of the treasury, 27 Sept. 1813, directing him to pay the $46,300 into the Bank of Virginia, to the credit of the U.S. (U.S. Cir. Ct., Va., Rec. Bk. X, 146).

4. The 1809 act prescribed distribution of penalties according to the 1799 act to regulate collection of import and tonnage duties (*U.S. Statutes at Large*, II, 510; I, 697).

5. Ibid., II, 453–54.

Textual Notes

¶		
¶ 1 l. 2		for $~~43300~~ ↑$46300↓ the
	l. 3	defendent [*erasure*] ~~brought~~ paid
	ll. 3–4	amount ~~of the p~~ ↑thereof & the money↓ has
¶ 2 l. 4		is ~~now~~ ↑still↓ collector,
	ll. 6–7	distribution. ~~Each~~ ↑Should the court be of this opinion, each↓ claims
¶ 3 l. 2		called ["] ~~the~~ ↑The↓ Enforcing
¶ 6 l. 2		by ↑force of↓ the
	l. 4	imposed [*erasure*] ↑by↓ the
¶ 7 ll. 1–2		prove [*erasure*] ↑such↓ exception the first ~~argument is~~ ↑& material proposition↓ is,
	l. 3	an ~~embag~~ ↑embargo↓ &c."
	l. 5	or ~~in~~ ↑on↓ the
	l. 8	Statute [*erasure*] ↑that↓ they
	ll. 9–10	in ~~every such case~~ ↑all covenants with a penalty↓ , judgement
¶ 8 l. 1		penalties ~~consists~~ is
¶ 9 l. 2		words [*erasure*] ↑laying↓ an
	l. 5	that ~~th~~ ↑a↓ vessel
	ll. 5–6	a ~~foreign~~ port
	ll. 6–7	is ↑truely↓ urged
	l. 7	this ~~law~~ ↑act↓ was
	l. 11	embargo ~~did not~~ intended to prevent vessels ↑in port↓ from
	ll. 12–13	no ~~proceedings~~ ↑punishment↓ could be ~~sustained against a vessel or~~ ↑inflicted upon this section for↓ this
	l. 16	act ~~does not~~ ↑can never↓ prove
¶10 l. 1		vessels ~~vo~~ ↑bound to↓ foreign
	l. 3	this ~~embargo~~ ↑prohibition↓ might
	l. 5	committed, ~~the~~ ↑it↓ is
	l. 6	States ↑to any other,↓ unless
	l. 9	penalty ~~of~~ ↑on↓ the
	l. 10	the [*erasure*] United
¶11 l. 3		case ↑he has put↓ of
¶12 ll. 3–4		judgement ~~for~~ ↑in case of↓ a

¶13 l. 1   next ~~proposition~~ ↑argument↓ on

    ll. 1–2   States ↑in support of this proposition↓ is

    l. 3   the ~~subsq~~ ↑subsequent↓ words

    l. 6   judgement ~~was~~ ↑has been↓ rendered.

¶14 l. 5   which ~~says~~ ↑contends↓ that

¶15 l. 1   is ~~an~~ ↑incurred↓ as

    l. 3   bond ↑then↓ is

    l. 5   acts, ~~in effecting~~ ↑the road by which it travels to↓ its

¶16 l. 1 beg.   ~~To the court it seems extremely~~ The

    l. 2   by ↑the↓ statute

    ll. 3–4   offence ~~which~~ ↑&directs this↓ penalty ~~is~~ ↑to be↓ secured

¶17 l. 1 beg.   ~~As the~~ ↑The↓ law

    l. 1   of [erasure] ↑1799.↓ It

    l. 3   1809 [erasure] ↑ought↓ not

    l. 6   of [erasure] ↑1799.↓

¶18 l. 1   ↑This fact is not certain [erasure] but it is not deemed material; because↓ As

    l. 2   of [erasure] ↑1799↓ not

¶19 ll. 2–3   of [erasure] ↑1799.↓ Those arguments ↑as understood by the court↓ were

    l. 4   of [erasure] ↑1799↓ did

¶20 ll. 2–3   respecting ~~the~~ ↑its true↓ construction;

    l. 3   urged ~~a~~ ↑by↓ the

    ll. 5–6   department ↑of government↓ in

    l. 8   forfeitures ~~inflicted under the act of~~ ↑incurred by force of the original↓ embargo

    l. 9   as ~~the~~ ↑directed↓ by

    l. 9   no ~~other~~ penalty

¶21 l. 14   embargo " [erasure] ↑shall↓ be

    ll. 15–16   nothing ↑unless they distribute the penalties secured by bond.↓ Now

    l. 17   that ~~they~~ ↑those penalties↓ are

    l. 20   they ↑will↓ receive?

¶22 l. 1 beg.   ~~S~~ It

    l. 2   12 ~~mont~~ months

    ll. 4–5   is ~~obvious~~ ↑apparent↓ that

    l. 7   incurred [erasure] ↑by↓ force

    ll. 7–8   law ~~,t~~ ↑&↓ to cure that defect ↑the↓ provision

¶23 ll. 1–2   ↑Suppose this provision had been introduced into the original act. The word forfeitures would be omitted as inapplicable.↓ It

    l. 4   After ~~saying~~ ↑directing↓ that

    ll. 7–8   only ~~com are embraced by~~ ↑come within↓ the

    ll. 8–9   foregoing. ~~Those penal~~ Has

    l. 9   penalties ~~as~~ imposed

¶24 l. 1   to ~~examine this~~ subject

    l. 4   would ~~justif~~ sustain

    l. 5   money ~~recovered by this judge~~ ↑paid in↓ paid

Shore's Executor v. Jones
Opinion
U.S. Circuit Court, Virginia, 6 June 1814

After ruling that the United States was entitled to only half the judgment against Pegram (see U.S. v. Jones, Opinion, 30 May 1814), the court had to consider the further question of who was entitled to the other half. Should it be paid to Joseph Jones, the collector at Petersburg, to be distributed between himself and John H. Peterson, the surveyor at City Point? Or were the proper recipients the representatives of the late collector John Shore and late surveyor Andrew Forborne, who held those offices at the time the original action against Pegram commenced? Thomas Shore, John Shore's executor, and Reuben Gilliam, Forborne's administrator, filed their bill on the chancery side of the court, claiming $23,150 (half the judgment sum) as justly due them. On this question, Marshall and District Court Judge St. George Tucker were either opposed or else agreed to divide in order to have the case certified to the Supreme Court for decision. Marshall's opinion below, then, is his personal view of the question, not the official holding of the circuit court (U.S. Cir. Ct., Va., Rec. Bk. X, 146–47, 153–58).

OPINION

There are some incidental points in this case, which, though, not relied upon, it may be proper to dispose of, in the first instance, for the purpose of simplifying the question.

The deputy of John Shore, having continued to act as his deputy, until the judgment was rendered in the district court, the rights of John Shore are considered as preserving the same validity, as if he had been at that time in life, retaining his office and performing its duties.[1] The rights of Joseph Jones, could not commence, until he became the officer.

The judgment of the district court, having been brought into the circuit court, not by appeal, but by writ of error, and having been affirmed, the rights of all the parties under it, remain the same is if the writ of error had never been sued out. The contest, then, in this case is, between the representatives of the person who was collector when the penalty was incurred, and who remained the collector, until the judgment was rendered;[2] and the person who is collector, when the distribution of the penalty is to be made.

This question depends in a great degree, on the true construction of the act, "to regulate the collection of duties on imports and tonnage," passed the 2d day of March, 1799, since this penalty is to be distributed according to the rules prescribed in that act. In construing it, the attention of the Court has been directed to the phraseology of the 89th section,[3] and it has been contended, very truly, that the word "collector," throughout that section, applies to the collector for the time being, only. Yet, this construction must be sustained, rather by the necessary meaning, than by the grammatical arrangement of the sentence; rather by the life, than by the dead letter of the law. "The collector, within whose district the seizure shall be made," &c. It would seem, if we examine this sentence, without considering the nature of the duty intended to be performed, that the person who commenced the duty, must end it. "The said collector," &c., that is, the collector who instituted the suit, &c. But when we look to this duty, the contrary construction is at once adopted. The duty is entirely official, not in any degree personal, and must be performed by the tenant of the office.

But suppose the collector who receives the money, dies before payment and distribution. This duty must necessarily be performed by his executors, not by the collector for the time being.

The 91st sec. distributes the fines, forfeitures, and penalties, imposed by the act. It declares that "one moiety shall be for the use of the United States, and be paid into the treasury thereof, by the collector receiving the same: the other moiety shall be divided between, and paid in equal proportions to, the collector, and naval officer of the district, and surveyor of the port, wherein the same shall have been incurred, or to such of the said officers as there may be in the said district."[4]

Were this clause to be construed, without reference to the object of the Legislature, it will readily be admitted, that the officer for the time being, and the officer at the moment of distribution, is the person designated by the law. But no legislative act, no instrument of any description, is construed without regard to the object and intent of its framers, as manifested by itself. Language is too imperfect to admit of such a rule. The same words, in different connexion have a different import. The intention, therefore, must be regarded; and to find that intention, whatever relates to the subject must be inspected.

If the moiety of this penalty be a gratuity to the officer of the district, or a donation to the office, then there is nothing to control that construction, which the words most naturally import. If it be not a gratuity, but a compensation for service, or a stimulus to those who are to perform the service, and on whom the stimulus is to operate, and if such officers will come within the description of the law, they are the persons designated by the law.

The attempt to prove that this is not a mere donation to the officers, would be a waste of words and of time. If it be a compensation for services, or a stimulus for the performance of services, it must be bestowed on those who have performed, or who are expected to perform, the services which the law intends to remunerate.

Penalties are imposed for the purpose, not of[5] enriching the treasury, but of enforcing the execution of laws, and the legislature, is, therefore, uniformly liberal in its compensation out of penalties, to those who have contributed to the punishment of offenders, and, through that medium, to the enforcement of the law. Any thing like a rateable portion, therefore, of reward to service, is not to be expected; but the kind of service for which the reward is intended, must be looked for and discovered when the reward is claimed by different persons. The same inquiry must be made, if we consider the reward as a stimulus to the officer.

On the part of Mr. Jones, it is contended that, in the view of the legislature, the whole transaction, from its commencement, to its final termination; from the commission of the act, on which the penalty is to accrue, to the receipt of the money, is to be considered as one entire thing, consisting of different parts, deemed equal by the legislature; and that the compensation is bestowed on the person who happens to perform the concluding part of the service, that is, to receive the money, or who is then in office. This construction, which is admitted to be rather favoured by the words of the distributing clause of the section, is said to be equally consistent with the intent and spirit of the law; since the service is equally meritorious with any other that is performed, and since this construction will, equally with any other, stimulate the officer to exertion.

On the part of Mr. Shore, it is contended, that the duties intended to be stimulated and rewarded, terminate with the judgment, if not before, and that the receipt of the money has no connexion with the right to a distributive share of it.

In arguing the merits of the claimants, it has been contended, that no service is to be performed, previous to the judgment, of such importance as to give the officers of that period a superior claim to their successors, or to justify an opinion, that the legislature intended the reward to stimulate those services, which were to be performed anterior to that period, rather than such as might afterwards become necessary for the collection of the money.

In support of this proposition, the argument has been confined to the very case before the Court; to an embargo bond. But it is to be recollected, that this is only one of many cases, to which the same principle of distribution applies. The act of 1799, which gives the principle, creates a great number of penalties and forfeitures, and adapts their distribution to the nature of those penalties and forfeitures, and to the services which are to be rendered for their detection and punishment. The act of 1809 then, adopts the rule of distribution prescribed in the act of 1799. Perhaps the persons favoured by that rule, may be most certainly discerned by looking something further into the nature of the service to be performed by those who, under that act, might claim reward.

These penalties are imposed, some for acts of omission, others for acts of commission. In cases of omission, the labour of the officer is not considerable, but is perhaps essential to the security of the revenue. In all of them this attention must be kept alive, in order to observe the conduct of those who are transacting business in the office, and he must be on the alert to take care that all the formalities prescribed by law are observed. If, in any instance, they are neglected, he must take care that measures are pursued which shall enable the United States to convict the offender.

Those of commission are very numerous. It would be tedious to recapitulate them, but it may not be improper to mention one or two as examples.

If any part of the cargo of a ship bound to the United States, shall be unladen within the limits thereof, without authority, the goods are forfeited, and the master and the mate shall respectively pay $1000. So, if any person shall assist in such unlading, he forfeits treble the value of the goods and the vessel which shall receive them, if they be put on board a vessel.[6]

If a part of these penalties and forfeitures be given to the revenue officers, what are the services it is given to remunerate, and what are the services the reward is intended to stimulate? To discover these frauds, the officers of the revenue must be watchful, they must be on the alert. If they are not, the frauds will be committed, and they will escape punishment. It is detection which saves the law from infraction, and secures the punishment.

So, there is a penalty for sailing from a district before entry, or for not making a full entry within a limited time. These penalties are inflicted for the security of the revenue, and they require the attention of the officers to vessels arriving within the district, in order to secure the observance of the law.

So, penalties and forfeitures are incurred, if a vessel, sailing from one port to another, does not obtain at the port of departure, certain certificates required by law, and exhibit those certificates at the port of delivery within a limited time after her arrival. It is obvious, that the enforcement of this provision depends entirely on the officers at the time of incurring the penalty, and of its detection.

Thus too, baggage is exempted from duty, and certain forms are to be observed by the persons claiming it, but the officer may examine the baggage, and if upon examination any article be found subject to duty, not mentioned by the owner, the article is forfeited, and a penalty of treble the value imposed on the person committing the offence. Again we find the law enforced by the watchfulness and attention of the officer.

It is unnecessary to continue this examination of particular cases. Go through the law, and it will be perceived that the government rests for the security of its revenue on the fidelity and vigilance of those officers who act at the time of the offence, at the time of its detection, and during its prosecution.

If we turn from these to the embargo laws, in order to ascertain the motives which induced the legislature to adopt the principle of distribution, prescribed in the act of 1799, we shall derive some aid from looking into other penalties than that incurred by the breach of the bond.

Any vessel which sails from a port of the United States without a permit, or which sails to a foreign port, is liable to forfeiture.

Any foreign vessel, taking on board any specie or cargo, is liable, with the specie or cargo, to forfeiture, and every person concerned in such unlawful shipment, is liable to a penalty, not less than $1000, nor more than $20,000.[7]

In these, and in many other cases, the most entire reliance is placed on the officers of the revenue, to secure the law from violation by their vigilance; and, certainly, it is reasonable to suppose, that it was the object of the legislature to stimulate this vigilance by rewarding it.

If, in the particular case of an embargo bond, there was really no merit in the revenue officers who took and prosecuted the bond, this might be a reason with the legislature for not classing it with cases in which such merit exists, but can furnish no reason to the Court for withdrawing it from the influence of those cases. There is not, however, this total destitution of merit which has been insisted on. A degree of skill and attention is requisite in taking the bonds, to avoid the object being defeated, (as has happened in this Court in several cases,) by the officers' mistaking the proper form in which they should be taken. The vessel and cargo must be valued, the bond must conform to that valuation, and evidence of value must be furnished on the trial. The taking of the bond is preceded by that vigilance, which is requisite to prevent the vessel from sailing without giving the bond. These considerations might be sufficient to induce the legislature to leave this penalty on the footing of all others, incurred under the different acts of congress, on this subject, and under the duty law.

The Court will now pass from the services which it is reasonable to suppose the legislature intended to reward, in order to examine the provisions and phraseology of the law, for further lights on this question, whether services up to the judgment, or subsequent to the judgment, were the objects of this legislative bounty.

It is first observable, that the bounty is payable in equal proportions to the collector, naval officer, and surveyor.[8] If the receipt of the money is the fact for which compensation is made, why this distribution? Why are the naval officer and the surveyor put on an equal footing with the collector? They incur no portion of the risk or trouble incurred in receiving and paying away the money, nor do they participate in the commission allowed for collecting duties.

If, however, this compensation is intended, not as a reward for collecting the money recovered, but for the vigilance required for the execution of the law, the motives to this distribution are obvious. They are equally sentinels on the port, equally on the conduct of those who are to be watched; and having, on this account, equal claims, are thus prevented from entertaining those reciprocal jealousies which might seduce them to thwart the operations of each other, and, perhaps, impede detection, if the particular informer engrossed the prize. The reward is given, "to such of the said officers as there may be in the said district." As there may be when? Certainly, when the reward is earned. Suppose, after judgment, and before the receipt of the money, one of these officers should be discontinued by law. Would he lose any share of the penalty? Suppose another officer, a naval officer in the district of Petersburg, should be added. Would he be entitled to a share of the penalty? It is admitted, that this is merely stating the question in controversy, but it is stating in a form which leads, in some measure, to an opinion on it.

If the revenue officers, who are the legal sentinels, and whose duty it is to watch, do not detect the offences, the reward is divided between the informer, and the unsuccessful sentinels. Yet the informer has nothing to do with collecting the money. In the case of the officers of the revenue cutter, who are entitled to a moiety of the penalty, if it be recovered on any information given by them, it seems to be admitted, that the officers at the time of discovery, are entitled to claim the reward. This is admitted, because they claim solely in the character of informers. But the words applicable to them, are the same as those applied to the revenue officers, and not more susceptible of an interpretation, according to the nature of the case. The clause respecting the witness, would, unquestionably, be equally proper, whether the interest of the person called on, be certain or contingent: but there is something in its language, which deserves some, though not much attention. The share, says the law, to which the witness would otherwise be entitled, shall *revert* to the United States.

The right of the United States, is inchoate on the commission of the offence, and is consummated by the judgment. The term revert, which is here used, indicates, that in the mind of the legislature, something was done, in consequence of which, a portion of this right had passed out of the United States, which returned on the fact of calling the person to whom it had passed, as a witness. And the same words are applied to an officer of the revenue, an officer of the revenue cutter, and a common informer. In such case, the share to which the witness would otherwise have been entitled, reverts to the United States.

It is more worthy of remark, that the appropriate compensation for receiving money, is a commission on the money received, to be retained by the receiver. The appropriate and usual reward for those who detect offences against the laws, and prosecute them to punishment, is a part of the penalty, and the language and provisions of this section, seem to proceed on that idea. It directs, that "one moiety shall be paid to the United States, by the collector receiving the same; the other shall be divided in equal proportions between the collector and naval officer of the district, and surveyor of the port wherein the same shall have been incurred." If the part of the collector had belonged to him who received the money, he would not be directed to *pay* it to the collector of the district, but to *retain* it himself. The language of payment and retainer, are too distinct to be confounded with each other.

It is perfectly understood, that this phraseology is to be accounted for, by the fact, that the suit may be prosecuted, and money may be received by the collector of the district, in which the seizure was made, while the beneficial interest is in the revenue officers of the district in which the penalty was incurred. But this does not impair the argument. If the receipt of the money induced the reward, why is it not bestowed on the officer who collects it? Why on the officer who does not, and who has, in law, no right to collect it?

It would seem, as if the language and provisions of the law, excluded the idea, that any part of the penalty was intended as a compensation for its collection.

The idea that this is a gift bestowed on the office for the purpose of enhancing its emoluments, is not sustained by the general course of legislation on the subject. If the acts respecting the emoluments of the office of collector be examined, it will be found that the legislature has required the collector to show regularly the amount of the commissions, has reduced the per centage by several successive acts, and has finally directed that the emoluments of office shall not exceed a specific sum. This regulation does not comprehend penalties, but it shows that the share of penalties is not given to the office for the purpose of annexing value to it, but is given to the individual to stimulate and to reward his services in enforcing the execution of the laws.

The counsel for Mr. Jones have, with great force of argument, called on their opponents to say at what time a right to a share of the penalty vests in the individual, and have urged the difficulty of doing this, as a reason for fixing on the moment of distribution as that at which the right vests. This difficulty is not imaginary, but is felt as a real one. In this case, however, the only contest is between those who claim at the time of the judgment, and those who claim after it. There are some reasons, in addition to those which have already been urged, for supposing the judgment to fix ultimately the rights of the parties. The judgment changes entirely the nature of the right. From a claim to a penalty or forfeiture depending on evidence, the right to which is contested, it becomes a positive debt, and the right is vested absolutely in the United States. It would seem reasonable that all rights which were, pending the action, contingent and uncertain, should then, likewise vest in the persons entitled to them. No further proof is requisite, no further vigilance necessary, no further controversy exists, a claim to a penalty is converted into a debt. If collection may be delayed by fraudulent covers of property, it is equally the case in every other debt, and furnishes in no other instance a motive for giving more than a commission.

Neither can the idea, that because this is a perpetual office, the officer can be considered as always in being under contemplation of law, as in the case of the king or other sole corporation, avail the plaintiff. The office is not hereditary. It is filled by individuals appointed by the executive, and between the removal of one officer, and the appointment of another, a long interval may elapse. Though the office never dies, the individuals who fill it do, and as their emoluments are considered in the light of compensation for services, the rewards of services rendered by one, ought not to be bestowed on another.

The result of the best consideration which the Court has been able to bestow on the subject, is, that the acts, taken altogether, show the intention of the legislature, in giving to its revenue officers a portion of the penalties and forfeitures, inflicted for a violation of the embargo laws, to have been to stimulate those officers to vigilant exertion of duty in detecting offences and prosecuting the offenders to conviction, and that those alone are entitled to those rewards who have performed the service. This intention is sufficiently apparent to give to those words of the distributive section a construction different from that which they most naturally bear, if separated from every other part of the act, and to apply them to those who were officers when the service was performed, not to those who are officers when the distribution is to be made.[9]

Printed, John W. Brockenbrough, *Reports of Cases Decided by the Honourable John Marshall* . . . , I (Philadelphia, 1837), 287–97.

1. John Shore was collector at Petersburg until his death on 30 Oct. 1811. Thomas Shore continued to act as deputy collector until 14 Dec. 1811 (U.S. Cir. Ct., Va., Rec. Bk. X, 151–52).

2. Judgment in the district court in U.S. v. Pegram was rendered on 30 Nov. 1811 (proceedings in U.S. District Court [copy], 30 Nov. 1811, Pegram's Administrator v. U.S., U.S. Cir. Ct., Va., Ended Cases [Unrestored], 1813, Vi).

3. *U.S. Statutes at Large*, I, 695–96.

4. Ibid., 697.

5. Brockenbrough's text has "if," probably a printer's error.

6. *U.S. Statutes at Large*, I, 648. Here and below JM's references are to various sections of the 1799 act regulating the collection of duties (ibid., 627–704).

7. The supplementary embargo act of January 1808 (ibid., II, 453–54).

8. Here and below JM refers to sec. 91 of the 1799 collection law (ibid., I, 697).

9. The Supreme Court, speaking through Justice Story, sustained JM's opinion (Jones v. Shore's Executor; U.S. v. Jones, 1 Wheat. 468–76 [1816]).

From John Jay

Sir   Bedford[1] 7 June 1814

The Revd. Doctr Richd Channing Moore has been consecrated Bishop of the episcopal church in virginia, and appointed Rector of a church at Richmond, of the Vestry of which you are a member.[2] He has requested from me a Line of Introduction to you. Altho in an ordinary case, I should doubt the Propriety of my taking this Liberty, yet considering the Relation in which you stand to the church of which he is to be the Rector, I presume that a Compliance with his Request will be agreable to you as well as to him.

Doctr. Moore is a Native of New York, and of a Family which from their first Settlement in it, have enjoyed Consideration and Respect. I have known and esteemed him for many Years; and I concur in the general Belief and opinion that few of his Profession have, under similar Circumstances, done more good or deserved more Commendation.

The Impressions made on my mind by many things which I have read and heard, prompt me to embrace this opportunity to assure you of the great Respect and Esteem with which I have the Honor to be, Sir, Your obt. Servt.[3]

ADf, Jay Papers, NNC.

1. Jay's estate in Westchester County, N.Y.

2. Moore (1762–1841) was consecrated bishop in Philadelphia on 18 May 1814. He headed the Virginia episcopate until his death, serving also as rector of Monumental Church. JM was one of the original members of Monumental Church, which was built on the site of the theater fire that killed many prominent Richmonders in Dec. 1811 (Geo[rge] D. Fisher, *History and Reminiscences of the Monumental Church, Richmond, Va., from 1814 to 1878* [Richmond, Va., 1880], 35, 65).

3. In his draft of a letter to Moore the same day, Jay described JM as someone "whom I greatly esteem, but with whom I have had but little personal acquaintance" (Jay to Moore, 7 June 1814, Jay Papers, NNC).

Mutter's Executors v. Munford
Opinion
U.S. Circuit Court, Virginia, 7 June 1814

This complicated suit began in December 1803 with the filing of a bill in chancery by George Alston and others of North Carolina, executors of Thomas Mutter, against William Munford and others, heirs and devisees of Robert Munford of Mecklenburg County. William Munford (1775–1825), the principal defendant, was a lawyer and legislator who achieved prominence in his lifetime as a court reporter, poet and author, and translator of the classics. He was the only son of Robert Munford (d. 1784), the Revolutionary patriot who was also a poet and playwright. Besides Mutter's executors, who sought to recover a judgment obtained by Mutter in North Carolina against Munford's executors, other creditors joining this suit as plaintiffs included the British merchant firms William Cunningham & Company and Buchanan, Hastie & Company. After various pleas and answers were filed, the commissioner in chancery made a report in November 1806. To this report the defendant William Munford entered various exceptions, and Marshall issued an interlocutory decree on 14 December 1807 ordering the commissioner to make certain alterations. The commissioner then prepared a second report, dated 8 May 1808, which gave rise to the following opinion (Pamela I. Gordon, "William Munford," in W. Hamilton Bryson, ed., *The Virginia Law Reporters Before 1880* [Charlottesville, Va., 1977], 25–32; U.S. Cir. Ct., Va., Ord. Bk. IV, 497; VI, 324–26; IX, 303–4; bill in chancery [Dec. 1803]; commissioner's report, 20 Nov. 1806; William Munford's exceptions to commissioner's report, 27 Nov. 1806; decree, 14 Dec. 1807, Mutter's Executors v. Munford, U.S. Cir. Ct., Va., Ended Cases [Unrestored], 1824, Vi).

Alston &c
    v   }
Munford &c

¶1   So far as these suits[1] affect the heir it becomes material to distinguish those claims which may at this time be asserted against the real estate, & then to enquire what claims may be supported upon the principle of Marshalling assets.

¶2   The first claim which has been discussed is that of the exrs. of Samuel Beall decd. This was a judgement obtained by Samuel Beall in his life time against Robert Munford in his life time which was revived after the death of Munford to wi⟨t⟩ in 1784 or 1785 against his exrs.[2]

¶3   The great objection to this debt is that the judgement as against the real assets is barred by the act of limitations.

¶4   By an act passed in the year 1792 it is declared that Judgements in any court of record within this commonwealth may be revived within ten years next after the date of such judgement & not after.[3]

¶5   The words of this act taken in their strict literal sense certainly extend to this case; but it is contended that this strict construction must yield to one more favorable to the creditor, & Eppes & Randolph has been cited in support of this position.[4]

¶6   In Eppes v Randolph the obligation of a judgement of much older date was unquestionably admitted without controversy, but in that case the point was not made at the bar nor decided by the bench & in that case the claim was asserted within less than ten years after the passage of the act.

¶7   In the construction of this act some difficulty is producd by the circumstance that the draftsman has omitted to change the phraseology when a new provision was introduced so as to adapt the language of the act to the subject. Actions had been previously limited & this act does in general only reenact what was law before & therefore it would have been improper in most of its provisions to give time for the institution of a suit subsequent to the passage of the act. For example   The first section gives a right to sue forth a writ of formedon within twenty years after the cause of action accrued & not after.[5] If the whole twenty years had elapsed before the passage of the act, the action would be barred, or if nineteen years had elapsed the action must be brought within one year or the action would be barred. This is very proper & was undoubtedly within the intention of the legislature. Previous acts of limitation which were repealed by this had created the same bar to this action, & if a time for bringing it had been given after the passage of this act, it would have exempted from the operation of former acts claims which had been already barred by them, or might have given to the claimants a much longer time to assert those claims than they would otherwise have been entitled to. It was the intention of the legislature meerly to bring all former acts into one & not to change the rights or situation of parties so far as former statutes had provided for the case. But no former act of limitations had extended to judgements. Had the legislature adverted to this circumstance it is probable that a certain time would have been given after the passage of the act for the revival of judgements previously rendered. Not adverting to this circumstance they have employed terms which strictly interpreted must bar immediately any action on judgements of more than ten years standing unless they be so construed as to exclude those judgements entirely from their operation.

There is a peculiar degree of carelessness in the phraseology of the ¶8 two sections on this subject. The first, which is the 5th., sec. of the act, uses the appropriate terms for those judgements only which had been actually rendered when the act passed, & would therefore justify the idea that the act speaks as at the point of time when the scire facias issues; but the succeeding section applies itself expressly both to judgements which had been rendered before the passage of the act & to those which might thereafter be rendered.[6] This produces the necessity of applying the preceding section to the same judgements.

Whether the state courts would in the construction of this law supply ¶9 words which would give those entitled to judgements before its passage time to revive those judgements by scire facias is rendered by the length of time which has already elapsed a question of not much conse-qu⟨ence.⟩ The same principle may however arise in the case of a judgement on which an execution has issued or which has been enjoined, where, after the lapse of ten years from its rendition one of the parties dies. I shall not enquire what would be the law in such a case but think that in general where after the passage of the act ten years have passed away without a scire facias it is too late to sue out that writ. If then in this case there had been no scire facias against the exr. nor injunction on that judgement I should think it too late to proceed against the heir.[7] But those circumstances change the nature of the case as will hereafter be more particularly noticed.

¶10   The next claim to be considered is that of Buchanan Hastie & Co.[8]

¶11   In this case judgement was rendered in this court on a bond carrying interest for a specific sum altho the verdict on which that judgement was rendered found the penalty of the bond to be discharged by a less sum with interest.[9]

¶12   It is apparent that the entry of the judgement which appears to have been the meer act of the clerk deriving no sanction from any act of the court is a clerical misprision, & such a judgement must have been reversed on writ of error. But without enquiring whether it is not amendable & whether in making out a record of the cause it ought or ought not to be considered as the real judgement I think it perfectly clear that the heir cannot take advantage of it. A verdict can never be given in evidence in favor of a party if it might not be given in evidence against him. The heir therefore cannot avail himself of this judgement.

¶13   The claim of John MCrea is on a bond dated in April 1776.[10] The objection to this is the length of time which has elapsed since its date. If it is the wish of the heir I shall direct an issue to be tried at this bar to ascertain whether the bond has been paid or not.

———

¶14   The claim of William Cuninghame & Co being on a bill of exchange does not bind the heir.[11]

¶15   The claim of Conway Whittle is for a legacy given to his wife by Theoderick Munford one of whose exrs. Robert Mumford was.[12]

¶16   The principle objection to this claim is that Robert Mumford as exr. of Theoderic Mumford paid this money to himself as the Guardian of his ward & that as testamentary guardian he gave no bond, & consequently his heirs are not bound.

¶17   The legacy is a specific legacy to Frances Munford the wife of Conway Whittle of a bond of John Banister amounting to £1809. This bond was delivered to Robert Munford on the 2d. of Jany. 1777 by Archibald Carlos.

¶18   On the same day Robert Munford in his account with the estate of Theoderic Munford charges himself with this bond. On the credit side of that account is the following entry.

¶19   To John Banisters bond to be paid to Frances Munford. £1809.

¶20   This last entry is under date of the 12th. of July 1778.

¶21   A letter appears to have been written by Robert Munford to John Banister on the 13th of June 1780 in which he speaks of having received from Mr. Banister a payment of £1000 in paper money intrinsically worth only £200 &, after expressing his confidence that Mr. Banister would not avail himself of that payment adds "Agreeable to your request I shall make myself debtor to my niece for the amount of her pecuniary legacy from her Father & consider you as debtor to me for the bond & interest inclosed in your letter."

I do not know what other construction to put upon this entry than to ¶22 consider it as the consent of the exr. to the legacy & a payment of that legacy to the guardian. The terms of the entry show that the bond was no longer to be considered as a subject on which the exr. was to act. It was to be paid to Frances Munford, & in his executors account he takes credit for it. This credit is entered among his payments & bears date more than 12 months after the exr. debits himself with the bond.

It has been contended that this transaction, were it even unequivo- ¶23 cal, could not discharge the exr. because there were four testamentary guardians & they must act jointly.

Whatever force might be allowed to this argument as applicable to ¶24 the commutation of the bond which seems to be alluded to in the letter of the 13th. of June 1780 I cannot admit its validity when applied to the payment made by the exr. to the Guardian. When there is more than one testamentary guardian it may be necessary that they should unite in any act which disposes of the property of the ward but I cannot concieve that the absence of one disables the other from collecting a debt due to the ward. I cannot conceive that a joint receipt is necessary to the discharge of the debtor. This would be extremely inconvenient & I should require an express authority to the point before I could admit the principle. Whether the principle laid down in 3d. Ba. 407 that "from the nature of the thing the authority of guardians must be joint & several" be true in all cases or not, I think it must be true in the case of receiving the money of the ward.[13]

To me then it appears that Robert Munford was chargeable with this ¶25 bond in his character of Guardian, & as he gave no bond in that charac- ter, his heir is not bound. The debt remains a debt of the first dignity as against the personal estate.[14]

The extent to which the heir is directly liable being stated, with the ¶26 exception of Bealls judgement, it remains to inquire how far he is to be made liable on the principle of Marshaling assets.

The principle on which the court proceeds in marshaling assets is ¶27 discussed very much at large in a case reported in 8th. Vesey jr. 382.[15] The principle is that a creditor having his choice of two funds ought to exercise his right of election in such manner as not to injure other creditors who can resort to only one of these funds. But if, contrary to equity, he should so exercise his legal rights as to exhaust the fund to which alone other creditors can resort, then those other creditors will be placed by a court of equity in his situation so far as he has applied their fund to the satisfaction of his claim.

In the application of this principle no doubt can exist so far as re- ¶28 spects creditors by specialty in which the heir is bound. Such a case is precisely within the principle, & is the case to which the principle has been most frequently applied.[16]

¶29   It has been contended by the heir that monies applied by the exr. in payment for lands purchased by the ancester & not conveyed to him are not to be considered as being now chargeable on the real estate. But in such case the creditor had his election to proceed by way of eject-ment, & if the heir should enjoin & call on the exr. to satisfy the debt out of the personal estate, a court of equity would certainly not decree such satisfaction to the injury of simple contract creditors. Such a case therefore seems to come precisely within the general principle, for the creditor had his election of two funds at law. But this question came on to be considered in Trimmer v Bayne reported in 9th. Vesey 209 where the decision was against the heir.[17]

¶30   The question about which I have felt most difficulty is that which relates to the claims of simple contract creditors founded on payments made on judgements obtained against the testator in his life time.

¶31   On this subject I have searched every book of chancery reports to which I have access, & can find nothing completely satisfactory respect-ing it. In the case of Finch v The Earl of Winchelsea reported in a note in 3 P. W. 399.[18] it was contended by counsel at the bar that simple contract creditors were entitled to take the place of judgement credi-tors so far as the latter had exhausted the personal fund, & the court did not negative the doctrine; but the case was decided on another point, & the reporter adds a quere.

¶32   In 4th. Vesey jr.   (copied)   it is stated in the index & in the marginal note to have been expressly determined that assets could not be marshaled in consequence of payments made out of the per-sonal fund to judgement creditors;[19] but on examining the case itself, the decision of the Chancellor is not found to be so express as it is stated to be in the index & marginal note.[20] The implication however is in favor of the opinion that simple contract creditors are not permitted to take the place of judgement creditors as against the real fund.

¶33   It has considerable weight with me that there is not a case in the books, nor a dictum from the bench, in which it is said that simple contract creditors may stand in the place of judgement creditors who have exhausted the personal fund altho the principle of marshaling assets has been discussed perhaps as frequently as any other on which a court of equity acts. That principle is continually stated as applicable to payments made out of the personal fund to specialty creditors & mort-gagees, but never to judgement creditors.

¶34   There being no express authority which is satisfactory, the question was to be considered on principle. In taking this view of the subject it became necessary to enquire whether the creditor possessed at law his election of two funds or was under the necessity of pursuing the per-sonal fund in the first instance.

The oldest case I have seen on this point is that in Dyer 208[21] which ¶35
was cited by the counsel for the plf. In that case an elegit appears to
have been awarded agt. the terre tenents & it is to be presumed that no
previous scire facias issued against the exr.[22] But the question was not
made and the reporter adds a quere whether there ought not to be first
a scire facias against the exr., & on nihil[23] returned, then a scire facias
against the terre tenent, as was decided in Henry 4th. But as such a
scire facias on a recognizance is given in the judicial register he doubts
if the law be not the same as to judgements. In a note to the same report
it is said to have been afterwards stated in another case to have been the
course of the exchequer not to charge the land in the hands of the heir
for the debt of the King until the personal estate be exhausted.

In Carthew 107 it is stated expressly by counsel to be the admitted ¶36
law that a scire facias cannot issue against the heir until the personal
estate shall have been exhausted.[24] In support of this position many
decisions from the year books are cited, & it is not contradicted by the
court or by counsel. This position is introduced into Bacon, & stands in
the new edition as law, nor is any opposing principle laid down, or any
contrary authority cited.[25]

In 14th. Viner. title. Heir, letter R. sec. 2.[26] It is stated that an applica- ¶37
tion was made to the Kings bench for a scire facias agains⟨t⟩ the Heir
before process against the exr. which was refused.

The weight of authority therefore appears to be decidedly in favor of ¶38
the opinion that the judgement creditor cannot proceed against the
heir until he has exhausted the personal estate.

I am the more satisfied with these authorities because they appear to ¶39
me to lay down the positive rule in strict conformity with principle.

The writ of elegit in virtue of which the land is charged by a judge- ¶40
ment against the ancester, does not issue singly against the land but
orders the sheriff to deliver all the chattels, oxen & beasts of the plough
excepted, & a moity of the lands to the creditor. In his commentary on
this statute 2 inst. 395 Lord Coke says that if the chattels be sufficient to
satisfy the debt then the land ought not to be extended.[27] Upon view-
ing the writ of elegit given by our act of Assembly[28] I have no doubt but
that the same rule would regulate the conduct of the sheriff.

Since then upon an elegit issued on the judgement against the ances- ¶41
ter the personal estate is first liable, it would seem to be reasonable that
the same judgement would after his decease affect his estate in the
same order & that the personal fund should be applied first to its
discharge.

If this be the law, then the judgement creditor has no election. He is ¶42
under the necessity of proceeding in the first instance against the personal estate & the principle on which assets are marshaled would not
apply to the case.

If there be two mortgagees **A** the prior mortgagee upon two tracts & ¶43

B the subsequent mortgagee on one only of those tracts: if A should appropriate to his debt the land mortgaged to B then B would be permitted to take the place of A with respect to the other tract; but if by the terms of A's mortgage he was bound first to apply the tract mortgaged to B then B would not be allowed to take the place of A. The reason on which he could in the case first put be permitted so to do would cease.

¶44   I am therefore of opinion that in Marshaling assets simple contract creditors cannot charge the lands for so much of the personal fund as has been applied to the payment of debts due by judgements obtained against the ancester.

¶45   It is very possible that this decision may in this case be extremely unfavorable to the heir.

¶46   If the personal estate must be exhausted before the judgement creditor can proceed against the real estate, so that the proceeding against the heir is dependent on the proceeding against the exr. it would seem to follow that the act respecting the renewal of judgements ought not to be so construed as to bar a scire facias against the heir provided the creditor has been employed in pursuing the personal estate; & especially if a court of equity has prevented him from exhausting the personal estate.

¶47   It is with regret I give gentlemen of the bar additional trouble. But I was at the argument of this case so satisfied that this judgement could not be revived against the heir, as ten years had elapsed since its rendition & since the passage of the act, that I did not sufficiently advert to those other arguments which respected the claim of Bealls representatives. This opinion was not shaken until I considered that question in connection with the right of the creditor to proceed immediately against the heir. It was then out of my power to recall the other points on which the liability of the heir for the balance of Bealls judgement depends.

¶48   The arguments which have been urged at bar to show that the heir is not liable on account of the payments made to the creditors of Theoderic Mumford are in my opinion conclusive. I do not think the devastavit[29] fixed; nor do I think him bound by the report in chancey as by an exhibit produced & relied on by him. That report is to be considered as an exhibit admitted by both parties to be substituted in the place of a report made to this court by one of its commissioners. It is consequently open to all the exceptions which might have been made to it if returned directly to this court.

¶49   The objections made to the jurisdiction of this court are not deemed sufficient to prevent a decree on the interests of all the parties. In addition to other considerations urged in favor of a decision on the whole subject the argument founded on the bill for marshaling assets is conclusive. The creditors who have a direct charge on the lands must come in on that fund before it can be touched by the simple contract creditors. Consequently the court must direct them to be satisfied before it can apply the surplus to creditors by simple contract. The case then is like that of a subsequent mortgagee wishing to foreclose. All prior incumbrancers must be brought before the court & satisfied before he can obtain a decree.[30]

This cause came on afterward to be argued on the question whether ¶50 the heir was liable for profits received before the filing of the bill: and the court determined that he was not; but that opinion is lost.[31]

AD, Marshall Judicial Opinions, PPAmP; printed, John W. Brockenbrough, *Reports of Cases Decided by the Honourable John Marshall . . .* , I (Philadelphia, 1837), 272–85. For JM's deletions and interlineations, see Textual Notes below.

1. The points to be decided arose from that part of the report of 8 May 1808 dealing with Otway Byrd's administration of Robert Munford's estate. This report is missing from the case papers (U.S. Cir. Ct., Va., Ord. Bk. IX, 303–4).

2. John Pierce, Beall's surviving executor and trustee, was made a plaintiff at the May 1808 term and filed his bill to recover a debt founded on a judgment rendered in the General Court in 1783. To this bill (not found but summarized in 1 Brock. 271), William Munford filed his plea and answer on 11 June 1808 (U.S. Cir. Ct., Va., Ord Bk. VII, 93; plea and answer of William Munford, 11 June 1808, Mutter's Executors v. Munford).

3. Sec. 5 of the 1792 act reads: "Judgments in any court of record within this commonwealth where execution hath not issued may be revived by *scire facias* or an action of debt brought thereon within ten years next after the date of such judgment, and not after; or where execution hath issued and no return is made thereon, the party in whose favor the same was issued shall and may obtain other executions, or move against any sheriff or other officer . . . for not returning the same for the term of ten years from the date of such judgment, and not after" (Shepherd, *Statutes*, I, 27–28).

4. Wayles's Executors v. Randolph, 2 Call 125 (1799). JM argued this case in the Virginia Court of Appeals. See *PJM*, V, 117–60.

5. Shepherd, *Statutes*, I, 27.

6. Sec. 6 of the 1792 act was a proviso in favor of infants, married women, incompetents, prisoners, and those out of the state at the time judgment was rendered. This section begins, "*Provided*, That if any person or person entitled to such judgment, where execution hath not issued, or where execution hath issued, and no return made (in either case) shall be or were under the age of twenty-one years, *feme covert, non compos mentis*, imprisoned, or not within this commonwealth at the time of such judgment being awarded . . . " (ibid., 28).

7. Beall revived his judgment in Charles City County Court. He and other creditors were subsequently enjoined from proceeding on their judgments by a decree of the High Court of Chancery (plea and answer of William Munford, 11 June 1808, Mutter's Executors v. Munford).

8. This judgment was founded on a bond executed in 1772 by Robert Munford to the British firm (bill not found but summarized in 1 Brock. 269).

9. Judgment in the case of Buchanan, Hastie & Co. v. Otway Byrd, executor of Robert Munford, was rendered at the Dec. 1798 term for the penal sum of the bond—£1,167.7, or $3,890—to be discharged by payment of $1,221 in damages. The clerk in recording the jury verdict of $1,221 damages omitted that part of the verdict awarding interest from 1780 (U.S. Cir. Ct., Va., Ord. Bk. III, 180–81).

10. The surviving case papers contain nothing relating to this claim.

11. This claim was founded on a bill of exchange drawn by Robert Munford in Feb. 1776 on William Cunningham of Glasgow, payable to William Cunningham & Co. It was protested for nonacceptance, and judgment for $5,530 (plus interest from April 1785) was rendered at the Dec. 1798 term of the federal court against Otway Byrd, Munford's executor (U.S. Cir. Ct., Va., Ord. Bk. III, 183). The bill in chancery on behalf of Cunningham & Co. has not been found but is summarized in 1 Brock. 269.

12. The surviving case papers contain nothing relating to this claim.

13. Matthew Bacon, *A New Abridgment of the Law* (1st Am. ed., from the 6th London ed.; 7 vols.; Philadelphia, 1811), III, 407 (s.v., "Guardian").

14. Debts due from guardians to wards were to be paid before any other debts (Hening, *Statutes*, XII, 152, 197).

15. Aldrich v. Cooper, 8 Ves. 382, 32 Eng. Rep. 402 (Ch., 1803).

16. A creditor by bond ("specialty") could satisfy his debt out of the personal or real estate. If he exhausted the personal estate, however, a simple contract creditor was allowed in equity to stand in the place of the bond creditor and recover from the real estate. JM had discussed the principle of marshaling assets as counsel in Wayles's Executors v. Randolph (*PJM*, V, 148–49).

17. Trimmer v. Bayne, 9 Ves. 209, 32 Eng. Rep. 582 (Ch., 1803).

18. The report of Finch v. Earl of Winchelsea is in a note to the report of Robinson v. Tonge, 3 P. Wms. 399, 401, 24 Eng. Rep. 1118, 1119 (Ch., 1735). It is also reported (from the note in Peere Williams) in 2 Eq. Cas. Abr. 257–58, 460–61, 22 Eng. Rep. 218, 392 (Ch., 1719).

19. Sharpe v. Earl of Scarborough, 4 Ves. 538, 31 Eng. Rep. 276 (Ch., 1799). The marginal note reads: "An equity of redemption of a mortgage in fee is not equitable assets, at least, as against judgment creditors; who have a right to redeem. Assets are not marshalled against judgment creditors."

20. Lord Chancellor Loughborough: "Where there is a mortgage, then a judgment, and then a second mortgage, the judgment creditor may redeem the first mortgage. . . . The directions must be given upon the principle, that the judgment creditors are to be paid in the first instance" (4 Ves. 542, 31 Eng. Rep. 278).

21. Bricknold v. Owen, 2 Dy. 208a, 73 Eng. Rep. 458 (K.B., 1560).

22. The writ of elegit gave the creditor a right of execution against half the debtor's lands. A terre-tenant was the actual possessor of the land. See *PJM*, V, l, 150–51.

23. *Nihil habet* (He has nothing), the return made by a sheriff to a scire facias that he has been unable to serve on the defendant.

24. Panton v. Hall, Carth. 105, 107, 90 Eng. Rep. 665, 666 (K.B., 1689): "and where a judgment is had against one who dies before execution, a sci. fa. will not lie against his heir and tertenants until a nichil is returned against his executor."

25. Bacon, *Abridgment*, VI, 114.

26. Charles Viner, *A General Abridgment of Law and Equity* . . . (22 vols.; n.p., 1742–53), XIV, 276.

27. Edward Coke, *The Second Part of the Institutes of the Laws of England* . . . (2 vols.; London, 1797), II, 395.

28. Shepherd, *Statutes*, I, 209.

29. A devastavit was a charge against an executor or administrator for his waste or mismanagement of a decedent's estate (*PJM*, V, 46 n. 8).

30. In the formal decree accompanying the opinion, the court recommitted the report to the commissioner and ordered a supplemental report to show the sums actually received by the executor in his lifetime on behalf of Munford's estate and sums paid by him to creditors of the estate (U.S. Cir. Ct., Va., Ord. Bk. IX, 303–4).

31. JM added this note at a later time. In an 1821 case, he also noted that his opinion on the heir's liability for profits had "been mislaid." The decree which this "lost" opinion accompanied has not been found in the surviving records. It may have occurred sometime between 1816 and 1820, the years covered by a missing order book. By an order of

31 May 1824 the suit was dismissed as to one of the creditors. It was subsequently revived by Mutter's executors in Dec. 1826, but there are no further entries after that date (Backhouse v. Jett, 1 Brock. 515; U.S. Cir. Ct., Va., Ord. Bk. XI, 451, 486; XII, 146).

Textual Notes

¶ 1 l. 1		these ~~case~~ suits
	l. 1	to ~~enquire to~~ distinguish
¶ 3 ll. 1–2		the ~~heir is bound~~ ↑real assets↓ is
¶ 5 l. 1		taken ↑in their strict &↓ literal sense ~~would~~ certainly
¶ 6 l. 1		Randolph ~~a~~ the
	l. 2	was ~~certainly~~ unquestionably
	l. 3	made ↑at the bar↓ nor
¶ 7 l. 11		if ~~only~~ nineteen
	l. 14	limitation ↑which were repealed by this↓ had
	l. 15	bringing ~~them~~ ↑it↓ had
	l. 17	claims ~~by~~ ↑which↓ ~~they~~ had ↑been↓ already
	ll. 26–27	must ~~be constru~~ bar
¶ 8 l. 1		in ↑the phraseology of↓ the
	ll. 2–3	5th., ~~sec. of the act~~ ↑sec. of the act,↓ uses
	ll. 3–4	which ~~w~~ ↑had↓ been ↑actually↓ rendered
	l. 4	passed, ~~but the succeeding~~ & would ↑therefore↓ justify
¶ 9 ll. 1–2		supply ~~the~~ words "after th which
	l. 9	in ~~this case~~ ↑general↓ where
	l. 10	without ~~reviving t~~ a scire facias ~~against the heir~~ it
	ll. 10–14	writ. ↑If then in this case there had been no scire facias against the exr. nor injunction on that judgement I should think it too late to proceed against the heir. Bu⟨t⟩ those circumstances change the nature of the case as will hereafter be more particularly noticed. ↓
¶11 ll. 1–2		this ~~case~~ ↑court on a bond carrying interest↓ for
	l. 3	the ~~judgement~~ ↑verdict↓ on which that ~~sum~~ judgement
¶13 l. 1		The ~~clam~~ ↑claim↓ of
¶15 l. 2		Mumford ↑one of↓ whose
¶17 l. 2		of ~~the~~ ↑a↓ bond
¶18 l. 1		Munford ~~charges himself~~ in his account with the ~~the~~ estate
¶21 ll. 3–4		money ~~& after expressing~~ intrinsically
¶22 l. 2		consent ~~to~~ ↑of↓ the
	l. 4	as ~~an~~ ↑a↓ subject
	l. 7	months [erasure] after
¶24 l. 1 beg.		~~However~~ Whatever
	l. 5	may ~~p~~ ↑be↓ necessary
	ll. 11–14	principle. ↑Whether the principle laid down in 3d. Ba. 407 that "from the nature of the thing the authority of guardians must be joint & several" be true in all cases or not, I think it must be true in the case of receiving the money of the ward. ↓
¶26 l. 1		The ~~next subject~~ extent to which ~~is~~ the
¶27 l. 2		case ~~which was freque~~ reported
	l. 7	then ↑those↓ other

¶29 ll. 2–3   payment ~~of~~ ↑for↓ lands purchased by the ancester ↑& not conveyed to him↓ are

l. 6   estate, ~~the~~ ↑a↓ court

¶30 ll. 1–2   difficulty ↑is that which↓ relates to ~~pay~~ the

l. 3   obtained ~~by~~ ↑against↓ the

¶31 l. 1 beg.   ~~To satisf~~ To satisfy my mind on ↑On↓ this

l. 1   every ↑book of↓ chancery ~~report~~ ↑reports↓ to

ll. 2–3   satisfactory ~~on the subject.~~ ↑respecting it.↓ In

¶33 l. 2   bench, ~~in which~~ in

l. 5   assets ~~is stated~~ ↑has been discussed↓ perhaps

¶35 l. 2   the ~~deft.~~ ↑plf.↓ In

l. 3   awarded ↑agt. the terre tenents↓ &

¶36 l. 1   107 ~~this principle~~ ↑it↓ is

l. 5   ~~In 14th. Viner~~ [erasure] ↑This position is introduced↓ into

¶38 l. 2   the ~~heir~~ ↑judgement creditor↓ cannot

¶40 ll. 1–2   elegit ↑in virtue of which the land is charged by a judgement against the ancester,↓ does

¶41 l. 1 beg.   ~~It follows that~~ ↑Since then↓ upon an elegit issued ↑on the judgement↓ against

¶43 ll. 1–2   mortgagees ~~one~~ ↑A the prior mortgagee↓ upon two tracts & ~~the other~~ ↑B the subsequent mortgagee↓ on ~~onl~~ ↑one↓ only

l. 7   could ↑in the case first put↓ be

¶44 l. 2   lands ~~on account of~~ for

¶46 ll. 6–8   estate~~.~~ ↑; & especially if a court of equity has prevented him from exhausting the personal estate.↓

¶47 l. 2   that ~~the~~ ↑this↓ judgement

l. 5   those ↑other↓ arguments

¶48 l. 5   on ↑by↓ him.

¶49 l. 3   decision ~~of~~ ↑on↓ the

¶50 l. 2   the ~~institution~~ ↑filing of the↓ bill:

To [John Lauris] Blake

Sir   Richmond Decr. 27th. 1814

I have given your book of elements a reading which, though rapid, was as attentive as the time it remained in my possession would permit.[1]

Without pretending to that professional skill which would enable me to speak decidedly on the relative value of books to be used in schools for the tuition of youth, I may be permitted to say that yours appears to me to be well calculated for that purpose. In the department of geography especially (which I have read with most care) I think it has great merit & may be employed to much advantage. With great respect I am Sir, Your Obedt. Servt

J MARSHALL

ALS, MH-H. Addressed to "The Reverend/Mr Blake." Endorsed.

1. The recipient was probably John Lauris Blake (1788–1857), a clergyman, schoolmaster, and prolific author. Born in New Hampshire, Blake graduated from Brown University in 1812. After serving briefly as a Congregational minister, he turned to the Episcopal Church. He taught for many years in various New England locations and in New York. Blake wrote or compiled almost fifty works, primarily school textbooks. JM evidently referred to Blake's *A Text-Book, in Geography and Chronology, with Historical Sketches. For Schools and Academies* (Providence, R.I., 1814; S #30942).

To Bushrod Washington

My dear Sir   Richmond Decr. 29th. [1814]

As the time for our session approaches I become anxious to know what our situation will be. Can you inform me what provision is made for us? Where and in what kind of a room are we to sit?[1]

We must also rely on you to make enquiries, &, if in your power to make arrangements for our accomodation. If it be practicable to keep us together you know how desirable this will be. If that be impracticable we must be as near each other as possible. Perhaps we may dine together should we even be compelled to lodge in different houses. Do me the favor to give me all the inteligence in your power on this interesting subject.

Are we to have peace; or is the war to be continued till we are dismembered? Your affectionate

J MARSHALL

ALS, Marshall Papers, ViW. Addressed to Washington at Mount Vernon; postmarked Richmond, 30 Dec. Endorsed by Washington.

1. The Supreme Court, which since 1810 had met in the basement of the north wing of the Capitol, lost its meeting place when the British burned the Capitol on 24 Aug. 1814. During the 1815 term the Court met at the home of Elias B. Caldwell, clerk of the Supreme Court, on Pennsylvania Avenue. The Court moved back to the Capitol in 1817, meeting first in temporary quarters and then, by the 1819 term, in its permanent basement location (Charles Warren, *The Supreme Court in United States History* [rev. ed.; 2 vols.; Boston, 1922], I, 457–60).

From William Wirt

Dear Sir.   Richmond. January 7. 1815.

In making a new arrangement of my books, I discover one of yours among them which ought long since to have been sent home—Prior Documents.[1] The only atonement which I can offer for the omission, is to enable you to correct an error in the next edition of your life of

U.S. CAPITOL, AFTER FIRE OF 1814
Aquatint by William Strickland after George Munger, ca. 1814. *Courtesy of Prints and Photographs Division, Library of Congress*

Washington into which this Book has led you—it is in the Resolutions which you report as having been adopted in 1765 on the motion of Patrick Henry.[2] I send you the journals of that year by which you will see that you have not stated the resolutions which were adopted, correctly. The passage in the journal is marked with a paper on which is a copy of a writing left sealed by Patrick Henry, and professing to contain a copy of the Resolutions as adopted, differing both from the journal and Prior Documents. Mr. Jefferson who was present at the Debate states that a fifth resolution was passed, which he thinks was, *in substance at least*, the 5th. in Prior Documents, but which was expunged from the Journals the next day.[3] Yrs. with great respect

WM. WIRT

As the journal is borrowed & the manuscript copy of the resolutions, the only one I have, I wd. thank you to return them, as soon as convenient.[4]

ALS, Sparks Papers, MH-H.

1. The reference is to [John Almon], comp., *A Collection of Interesting, Authentic Papers, relative to the Dispute between Great Britain and America; Shewing the Causes and Progress of That Misunderstanding, from 1764 to 1775* (London, 1777). The volume was published as a companion to [John Almon and Thomas Pownall], *The Remembrancer, or Impartial Repository of Public Events* (17 vols.; London, 1775–84). The collection was called "Prior Documents" because it examined events that occurred before those covered in the "Remembrancer"; the first page of text is headed "PRIOR DOCUMENTS." Wirt was working on his biography of Patrick Henry, *Sketches of the Life and Character of Patrick Henry* (Philadelphia, 1817).

2. JM published Virginia's resolutions against the Stamp Act in the appendix to the second volume of *The Life of George Washington . . .* (5 vols.; Philadelphia, 1804–7), II, app., 25–27. In 1824 the first volume (and that part of the second introducing the War of Independence) was republished as *A History of the Colonies Planted by the English on the Continent of North America . . .* (Philadelphia, 1824). The appendix to that volume reprints the Stamp Act resolves with the following note subjoined: "These resolutions are in a small degree different from those published in the Introduction to the Life of Washington. They are copied from Mr. Wirt's Life of Patrick Henry. That gentleman having been fortunate enough to obtain a copy of the journals of the house of Burgesses for that session, the resolutions extracted from them by him are supposed to be accurate" (*History of the Colonies*, 469–70 and n.).

3. For a discussion of the variant texts of the resolves, see Edmund S. Morgan and Helen M. Morgan, *The Stamp Act Crisis: Prologue to Revolution* (rev. ed., New York, 1963), 123–32; Edmund S. Morgan, *Prologue to Revolution: Sources and Documents on the Stamp Act Crisis, 1764–1766* (Chapel Hill, N.C., 1959), 46–50.

4. For a photograph of the manuscript copy of the resolves, see John P. Kennedy, ed., *Journals of the House of Burgesses of Virginia, 1761–1765* (Richmond, Va., 1907). The manuscript copy is now in the collections of the Colonial Williamsburg Foundation.

From Noah Zane

D Sir[1]   Wheeling 14th Feby. 1815
I take the liberty of introducing to you My friend Col. Woods one of our most distinguished Citizens.[2]

Col. Woods Commands the detachment for this place that goes for the defence of your eastern frontier, he is highly deserving of any attentions that may be paid him by the Citizens of Richmond, and any civilities you may shew him will confer additional obligations on, Dear Sir, your obt. Servt.

NOAH ZANE

ALS, Archibald Woods Papers, ViW. Addressed to JM in Richmond and marked "Col. Woods."

1. Noah Zane of Ohio County (now West Va.) served in the Virginia Senate from 1812 to 1816 (Earl G. Swem and John W. Williams, *A Register of the General Assembly of Virginia, 1776–1918, and of the Constitutional Conventions* [Richmond, Va., 1918], 450).

2. Archibald Woods (1764–1846) served in the Virginia Convention of 1788 and represented Ohio County in the House of Delegates during the 1790s (*VMHB*, IV [1896–97], 459–61; Swem and Williams, *Register*, 448).

To [James Monroe?]

Dear Sir[1]   Washington March 10th. 1815
Charles Marshall a son of my deceased brother a youth of about 14 or 15 years of age wishes to be admitted as a student in the Military academy & his mother has requested me to mention the subject to you.[2] With very much respect & esteem, I am Sir your obedt. servt

J MARSHALL

ALS, RG 94, DNA. Endorsed by clerk.

1. The recipient was probably James Monroe, who had been commissioned secretary of state on 28 Feb. 1815 but continued to act as secretary of war until 14 Mar. (Robert Brent Mosher, comp., *Executive Register of the United States, 1789–1902* [Washington, D.C., 1905], 84).

2. Charles C. Marshall (1799–1849), son of the late Charles Marshall (1767–1805) and Lucy Pickett Marshall (1767–1825), was appointed to the academy but resigned two years later (Paxton, *Marshall Family*, 53, 147; Charles C. Marshall to Alexander J. Dallas, 28 May 1815, RG 94, DNA; *List of Cadets Admitted into the United States Military Academy . . .* [West Point, N.Y., 1912], 52; JM to Lucy Marshall, 26 Aug. 1817 and n. 2).

The Nereide
Opinion
U.S. Supreme Court, 11 March 1815

This prize case raised important questions of international law concerning the rights of neutrals. Manuel Pinto, a Spanish subject and resident of Buenos Aires, claimed restoration of his property shipped on the British armed merchant ship *Nereide*. In August 1813 Pinto, then in London, chartered the *Nereide* to carry his valuable cargo (estimated at £10,000 sterling) of iron, steel, coal, tools, and dry goods. Sailing under convoy, the *Nereide* cleared Portsmouth in late November bound for Buenos Aires. A month later, after becoming separated from her escort, the vessel was captured near Madeira by the American privateer *Governor Tompkins*. Brought into New York port in February 1814, the *Nereide* and her cargo were condemned as prize of war by the U.S. District Court in August. Soon thereafter the U.S. Circuit Court affirmed this decree pro forma so that an appeal could be brought in time for hearing at the 1816 term of the Supreme Court. The case required four days of argument, from 6 to 9 March, with Josiah Ogden Hoffman and Thomas Addis Emmet representing Pinto and Alexander J. Dallas and William Pinkney appearing on behalf of the captors. Pinto claimed restitution on the ground that his part of the *Nereide*'s cargo was neutral property. Although international law held that neutral goods were exempt from condemnation even if found on belligerent vessels, an unsettled question was whether such exemption applied to cases in which the belligerent vessel was armed and resisted capture. Speaking for a divided Court on 11 March, Marshall reversed the lower court's decree and upheld Pinto's claim (The Nereide, App. Cas. No. 707; U.S. Sup. Ct. Minutes, 6–9 Mar. 1815; 9 Cranch 388–412; *New-York Evening Post*, 15 Mar. 1815).

In support of the sentence of condemnation in this case, the captors contend,

1. That the Claimant, Manuel Pinto, has neither made sufficient proof of his neutral character nor of his property in the goods he claims.

2. That by the treaty between Spain and the United States the property of a Spanish subject in an enemy's vessel is prize of war.

3. That on the principles of reciprocity this property should be condemned.

4. That the conduct of Manuel Pinto and of the vessel has impressed a hostile character on his property and on that of other Spaniards laden on board of the Nereide.

1. Manuel Pinto is admitted to be a native of Buenos Ayres, and to carry on trade at that place in connexion with his father and sister, who are his partners, and who also reside at Buenos Ayres; but it is contended that he has acquired a domicil in England, and with that domicil the English commercial character.

Is the evidence in any degree doubtful on this point? Baltaza Ximenes, Antonio Lynch, and Felix Lynch, three Spaniards, returning with Pinto in the Nereide, all depose that Buenos Ayres is the place of his nativity and of his permanent residence, and that he carries on trade at that place.[1]

In his test affidavit Manuel Pinto swears in the most explicit terms to the fact that Buenos Ayres is, and always has been the place of his permanent residence; that he carries on business there on account of himself, his father, and sister, and that he has been absent for temporary purposes only. His voyage to London, where he arrived in June, 1813, was for the purpose of purchasing a cargo for his trade at Buenos Ayres, and of establishing connexions in London for the purposes of his future trade at Buenos Ayres.[2]

This plain and direct testimony is opposed,

1. By his examination *in preparatorio*.[3]

In his answer to the first interrogatory he says that he was born at Buenos Ayres, that for seven years last past, he has lived and resided in England and Buenos Ayres, that he now lives at Buenos Ayres, that he has generally lived there for thirty-five years last past, and has been admitted a freeman of the new government.

Whatever facility may be given to the acquisition of a commercial domicil, it has never heretofore been contended that a merchant having a fixed residence, and carrying on business at the place of his birth, acquires a foreign commercial character by occasional visits to a foreign country. Had the introduction of the words *"seven years last past"* even not been fully accounted for by reference to the interrogatory, those words could not have implied such a residence as would give a domicil. But they are fully accounted for.

In his answer to the 12th interrogatory he repeats that he is a Spanish American; now lives and carries on trade at Buenos Ayres, and has generally resided there.

2. The second piece of testimony relied on by the counsel for the captors is the charter party.[4] That instrument states Manuel Pinto to be of Buenos Ayres now residing in London.

The charter party does not state him to have been formerly of Buenos Ayres, but to be, at its date, of Buenos Ayres. Nothing can be more obvious than that the expression, *now residing in London*, could be intended to convey no other idea than that he was then personally in London.

As little importance is attached to the covenant to receive the return cargo at the wharf in London. The performance of this duty by the consignee of the cargo as the agent of Pinto, would be a complete execution of it.

Had the English character been friendly and the Spanish hostile, it would have been a hardy attempt indeed in Mr. Pinto to found, on these circumstances, a claim to a domicil in England.

The question respecting ownership of the goods is not so perfectly clear.

The evidence of actual ownership, so far as the claim asserts property existing, at the time, in himself and partners, is involved in no uncertainty. The test affidavit annexed to the claim is full, explicit, and direct. It goes as far as a test affidavit can go in establishing the right which the claim asserts. All the documentary evidence, relating to this subject, corroborates this affidavit. The charter party shows an expectation that, of a freight of 700*l.* the goods of Mr. Pinto would pay 400*l.* The very circumstance that he chartered the whole vessel furnishes strong inducement to the opinion that a great part of her cargo would be his own.

The witnesses examined *in preparatorio*, so far as they know any thing on the subject, all depose to his interest. William Puzey was clerk to Pinto, and he deposes to the interest of his employer, on the knowledge acquired in making out invoices and other papers belonging to the cargo.[5] His belief too is, in some degree, founded on the character of Pinto in London, where he was spoken of as a man of great respectability and property; and from the anxiety he discovered for the safety of the property after the Nereide was separated from her convoy.

The bills of lading for that part of the cargo which is claimed by Pinto, are filled up, many of them with his name, some to order, and the marginal letters in the manifest would also denote the property to be his. Where he claims a part of a parcel of goods the invoice is sometimes to order, and the marginal letters would indicate the goods to be the property of Pinto and some other person.

This testimony proves, very satisfactorily, the interest of Pinto's house in the property he claims. There is no counter testimony in the cause, except the belief expressed by Mr. Puzey, that for a part of the goods Pinto was agent for the government of Buenos Ayres. This belief of Mr. Puzey is supposed to derive much weight from his character as the clerk of Mr. Pinto. The importance of that circumstance, however, is much diminished by the fact that he had seen Pinto only a week before the sailing of the Nereide, and that he does not declare his belief to be founded on any papers he had copied or seen; or on any communication made to him by his employer. There are other and obvious grounds for his suspicion. A part of the cargo consisted of arms and military accoutrements; and it was not very surprising that Puzey should conjecture that they were purchased for a government about to sustain itself by the sword. But this suspicion is opposed by considerations of decisive influence, which have been stated at the bar. The demand for these articles in Buenos Ayres by the government would furnish sufficient motives to a merchant for making them a part of his cargo. In a considerable part of this warlike apparatus, British subjects were jointly concerned. It is extremely improbable, that, if acting for his government, he would have associated its interests with those of British merchants. Nor can a motive be assigned for claiming those goods for himself instead of claiming them for his government. They would not by such claim become his if restored. He would still remain accountable to his government, and the truth would have protected the property as effectually as a falshood, should it remain undetected. By claiming these goods for himself, instead of his government, he would commit a perjury from which he could derive no possible advantage, and which would expose to imminent hazard, not only those goods but his whole interest in the cargo. The Court, therefore, must consider this belief of Mr. Puzey as a suspicion, which a full knowledge of the facts ought entirely to dissipate. If there was nothing in the cause but this suspicion, or this belief of Mr. Puzey, the court would not attach any importance to it. But Mr. Pinto himself has, in his examination *in preparatorio*, been at least indiscreet in asserting claims not to be sustained; and in terms which do not exhibit the real fact in its true shape. In his answer to the 12th interrogatory he says "And this deponent also has one-fourth interest as owner of the following goods, &c. viz. 15 bales of merchandize," &c. In his claim he thus states the transaction under which his title to the one-fourth of these goods accrued. He had agreed with certain persons in England to select for them a parcel of goods for the market of Buenos Ayres, of which he was to be the consignee, and which he would sell on a commission of 10 per cent. on the amount of sales at Buenos Ayres. These goods were selected, purchased, and consigned to Manuel Pinto. The bills of lading were in his possession, and he considered his interest under this contract as equal to one-fourth of the value of the goods, "wherefore," he says, "he did suppose that he was interested in the said goods and merchandize for himself, his father, and sister, and well entitled, as the owner thereof, or otherwise, to an equal fourth part of the said goods, inasmuch as his commissions as aforesaid, would have been equal to such fourth."[6]

It is impossible to justify this representation of the fact. The reasoning might convince the witness, but the language he used was undoubtedly calculated to mislead the Court, and to extricate property to which the captors were clearly entitled, although the witness might think otherwise. Such misrepresentations must be frowned on in a prize Court, and must involve a claim, otherwise unexceptionable, in doubt and danger. A witness ought never to swear to inferences without stating the train of reasoning by which his mind has been conducted to them. Prize Courts are necessarily watchful over subjects of this kind, and demand the utmost fairness in the conduct of Claimants. Yet prize Courts must distinguish between misrepresentations which may be ascribed to error of judgement, and which are, as soon as possible, corrected by the party who has made them, and wilful falsehoods which are detected by the testimony of others, or confessed by the party when detection becomes inevitable. In the first case there may be cause for a critical and perhaps suspicious examination of the claim and of the testimony by which it is supported; but it would be harsh indeed to condemn neutral property, in a case in which it was clearly proved to be neutral, for one false step, in some degree equivocal in its character, which was so soon corrected by the party making it.

The case of Mr. Paul's printing press is still less dubious in its appearance. It would require a very critical investigation of the evidence to decide whether this press is stated in his answer to the 12th interrogatory to be his property or not. Four presses are said in that answer to belong to him; but he also says in his answer to another interrogatory, perhaps the 26th, that Mr. Paul had one printing press on board.[7] Whether there were five presses in the cargo, or only four, has not been decided, because the declaration made in his examination in *preparatorio* that one of the presses belonged to Mr. Paul proves unequivocally that the mistake, if he made one, was not fraudulent.

That he should state as his, the property which belonged to a house in Buenos Ayres, whose members all resided at the same place, and of which he was the acting and managing partner, was a circumstance which could not appear important to himself, and which was of no importance in the cause. These trivial and accidental inaccuracies are corrected in his claim and in his test affidavit. The Court does not think them of sufficient importance to work a confiscation of goods, of the real neutrality of which no serious doubt is entertained.

2. Does the treaty between Spain and the United States subject the goods of either party, being neutral, to condemnation as enemy property, if found by the other in the vessel of an enemy? That treaty stipulates that neutral bottoms shall make neutral goods, but contains no stipulation that enemy bottoms shall communicate the hostile character to the cargo.[8] It is contended by the captors that the two principles are so completely identified that the stipulation of the one necessarily includes the other.

Let this proposition be examined.

The rule that the goods of an enemy found in the vessel of a friend are prize of war, and that the goods of a friend found in the vessel of an enemy are to be restored, is believed to be a part of the original law of nations, as generally, perhaps universally, acknowledged. Certainly it has been fully and unequivocally recognized by the United States. This rule is founded on the simple and intelligible principle that war gives a full right to capture the goods of an enemy, but gives no right to capture the goods of a friend. In the practical application of this principle, so as to form the rule, the propositions that the neutral flag constitutes no protection to enemy property, and that the belligerent flag communicates no hostile character to neutral property, are necessarily admitted. The character of the property, taken distinctly and separately from all other considerations, depends in no degree upon the character of the vehicle in which it is found.

Many nations have believed it to be their interest to vary this simple and natural principle of public law. They have changed it by convention between themselves as far as they have believed it to be for their advantage to change it. But unless there be something in the nature of the rule which renders its parts unsusceptible of division, nations must be capable of dividing it by express compact, and if they stipulate either that the neutral flag shall cover enemy goods, or that the enemy flag shall infect friendly goods, there would, in reason, seem to be no necessity for implying a distinct stipulation not expressed by the parties. Treaties are formed upon deliberate reflection. Diplomatic men read the public treaties made by other nations and cannot be supposed either to omit or insert an article, common in public treaties, without being aware of the effect of such omission or insertion. Neither the one nor the other is to be ascribed to inattention. And if an omitted article be not necessarily implied in one which is inserted, the subject to which that article would apply remains under the ancient rule. That the stipulation of immunity to enemy goods in the bottoms of one of the parties being neutral does not imply a surrender of the goods of that party being neutral, if found in the vessel of an enemy, is the proposition of the counsel for the Claimant, and he powerfully sustains that proposition by arguments arising from the nature of the two stipulations. The agreement that neutral bottoms shall make neutral goods is, he very justly remarks, a concession made by the belligerent to the neutral. It enlarges the sphere of neutral commerce, and gives to the neutral flag a capacity not given to it by the law of nations.

The stipulation which subjects neutral property, found in the bottom of an enemy, to condemnation as prize of war, is a concession made by the neutral to the belligerent. It narrows the sphere of neutral commerce, and takes from the neutral a privilege he possessed under the law of nations. The one may be, and often is, exchanged for the other. But it may be the interest and the will of both parties to stipulate the one without the other; and if it be their interest, or their will, what shall prevent its accomplishment? A neutral may give some other compensation for the privilege of transporting enemy goods in safety, or both parties may find an interest in stipulating for this privilege, and neither may be disposed to make to, or require from, the other the surrender of any right as its consideration. What shall restrain independent nations from making such a compact? And how is their intention to be communicated to each other or to the world so properly as by the compact itself?

If reason can furnish no evidence of the indissolubility of the two maxims, the supporters of that proposition will certainly derive no aid from the history of their progress from the first attempts at their introduction to the present moment.

For a considerable length of time they were the companions of each other—not as one maxim consisting of a single indivisible principle, but as two stipulations, the one, in the view of the parties, forming a natural and obvious consideration for the other. The celebrated compact termed the armed neutrality, attempted to effect by force a great revolution in the law of nations. The attempt failed, but it made a deep and lasting impression on public sentiment. The character of this effort has been accurately stated by the counsel for the Claimants.[9] Its object was to enlarge, and not in any thing to diminish the rights of neutrals. The great powers, parties to this agreement, contended for the principle, that free ships should make free goods; but not for the converse maxim; so far were they from supposing the one to follow as a corollary from the other, that the contrary opinion was openly and distinctly avowed. The king of Prussia declared his expectation that in future neutral bottoms would protect the goods of an enemy, and that neutral goods would be safe in an enemy bottom. There is no reason to believe that this opinion was not common to those powers who acceded to the principles of the armed neutrality.

From that epoch to the present, in the various treaties which have been formed, some contain no article on the subject and consequently leave the ancient rule in full force. Some stipulate that the character of the cargo shall depend upon the flag, some that the neutral flag shall protect the goods of an enemy, some that the goods of a neutral in the vessel of a friend shall be prize of war, and some that the goods of an enemy in a neutral bottom shall be safe, and that friendly goods in the bottom of an enemy shall also be safe.

This review which was taken with minute accuracy at the bar, certainly demonstrates that in public opinion no two principles are more distinct and independent of each other than the two which have been contended to be inseparable.

Do the United States understand this subject differently from other nations? It is certainly not from our treaties that this opinion can be sustained. The United States have in some treaties stipulated for both principles, in some for one of them only, in some that neutral bottoms shall make neutral goods and that friendly goods shall be safe in the bottom of an enemy. It is therefore clearly understood in the United States, so far as an opinion can be formed on their treaties, that the one principle is totally independent of the other. They have stipulated expressly for their separation, and they have sometimes stipulated for the one without the other.

But in a correspondence between the secretary of state of the United States and the minister of the French republic in 1793, Prussia is enumerated among those nations with whom the United States had made a treaty adopting the entire principle that the character of the cargo should be determined by the character of the flag.[10]

Not being in possession of this correspondence the Court is unable to examine the construction it has received. It has not deferred this opinion on that account, because the point in controversy at that time was the obligation imposed on the United States to protect belligerent property in their vessels, not the liability of their property to capture if found in the vessel of a belligerent. To this point the whole attention of the writer was directed, and it is not wonderful that in mentioning incidentally the treaty with Prussia which contains the principle that free bottoms make free goods, it should have escaped his recollection that it did not contain the converse of the maxim. On the talents and virtues which adorned the cabinet of that day, on the patient fortitude with which it resisted the intemperate violence with which it was assailed, on the firmness with which it maintained those principles which its sense of duty prescribed, on the wisdom of the rules it adopted, no panegyric has been pronounced at the bar in which the best judgment of this Court does not concur. But this respectful defference may well comport with the opinion, that an argument incidentally brought forward by way of illustration, is not such full authority as a decision directly on the point might have been.

3. The third point made by the captors is, that whatever construction might be put on our treaty with Spain, considered as an independent measure, the ordinances of that government would subject American property, under similar circumstances, to confiscation, and therefore the property, claimed by Spanish subjects in this case, ought to be condemned as prize of war.

The ordinances themselves have not been produced, nor has the Court received such information respecting them as would enable it to decide certainly either on their permanent existence, or on their application to the United States. But be this as it may, the Court is decidedly of opinion that reciprocating to the subjects of a nation, or retaliating on them, its unjust proceedings towards our citizens, is a political not a legal measure. It is for the consideration of the government not of its Courts. The degree and the kind of retaliation depend entirely on considerations foreign to this tribunal. It may be the policy of the nation to avenge its wrongs in a manner having no affinity to the injury sustained, or it may be its policy to recede from its full rights and not to avenge them at all. It is not for its Courts to interfere with the proceedings of the nation and to thwart its views. It is not for us to depart from the beaten track prescribed for us, and to tread the devious and intricate path of politics. Even in the case of salvage, a case peculiarly within the discretion of Courts, because no fixed rule is prescribed by the law of nations, congress has not left it to this department to say whether the rule of foreign nations shall be applied to them, but has by law applied that rule. If it be the will of the government to apply to Spain any rule respecting captures which Spain is supposed to apply to us, the government will manifest that will by passing an act for the purpose. Till such an act be passed, the Court is bound by the law of nations which is a part of the law of the land.

Thus far the opinion of the Court has been formed without much difficulty. Although the principles, asserted by the counsel, have been sustained on both sides with great strength of argument, they have been found on examination to be simple and clear in themselves. Stripped of the imposing garb in which they have been presented to the Court, they have no intrinsic intricacy which should perplex the understanding.

The remaining point is of a different character. Belligerent rights and neutral privileges are set in array against each other. Their respective pretensions, if not actually intermixed, come into close contact, and the line of partition is not so distinctly marked as to be clearly discernible. It is impossible to declare in favor of either, without hearing, from the other, objections which it is difficult to answer and arguments, which it is not easy to refute. The Court has given to this subject a patient investigation, and has endeavored to avail itself of all the aid which has been furnished by the bar. The result, if not completely satisfactory even to ourselves, is one from which it is believed we should not depart were further time allowed for deliberation.

4. Has the conduct of Manuel Pinto and of the Nereide been such as to impress the hostile character on that part of the cargo which was in fact neutral?

In considering this question the Court has examined separately the parts which compose it.

The vessel was armed, was the property of an enemy, and made resistence. How do these facts affect the claim?

Had the vessel been armed by Pinto, that fact would certainly have constituted an important feature in the case. But the Court can perceive no reason for believing she was armed by him. He chartered, it is true, the whole vessel, and that he might as rightfully do as contract for her partially; but there is no reason to believe that he was instrumental in arming her. The owner stipulates that the Nereide "well manned, victualled, equipped, provided and furnished with all things needful for such a vessel," shall be ready to take on board a cargo to be provided for her.[11] The Nereide, then, was to be put, by the owner, in the condition in which she was to sail. In equipping her, whether with or without arms, Mr. Pinto was not concerned. It appears to have been entirely and exclusively the act of the belligerent owner.

Whether the resistance, which was actually made, is in any degree imputable to Mr. Pinto, is a question of still more importance.

It has been argued that he had the whole ship, and that, therefore, the resistance was his resistance.

The whole evidence upon this point is to be found in the charter party, in the letter of instructions to the master, and in the answer of Pinto to one of the interrogatories *in preparatorio.*

The charter party evinces throughout that the ship remained under the entire direction of the owner, and that Pinto in no degree participated in the command of her. The owner appoints the master and stipulates for every act to be performed by the ship, from the date of the charter party to the termination of the voyage. In no one respect, except in lading the vessel, was Pinto to have any direction of her.

The letter of instructions to the master contains full directions for the regulation of his conduct, without any other reference to Mr. Pinto than has been already stated.[12] That reference shows a positive limitation of his power by the terms of the charter party. Consequently he had no share in the government of the ship.

But Pinto says in his answer to the 6th interrogatory that "he had control of the said ship and cargo."[13]

Nothing can be more obvious than that Pinto could understand himself as saying no more than that he had the control of the ship and cargo so far as respected her lading. A part of the cargo did not belong to him, and was not consigned to him. His control over the ship began and ended with putting the cargo on board. He does not appear ever to have exercised any authority in the management of the ship. So far from exercising any during the battle, he went into the cabin where he remained till the conflict was over. It is, then, most apparent that when Pinto said he had the control of the ship and cargo, he used those terms in a limited sense. He used them in reference to the power of lading her, given him by the charter party.

If, in this, the Court be correct, this cause is to be governed by the principles which would apply to it had the Nereide been a general ship.

The next point to be considered is the right of a neutral to place his goods on board an armed belligerent merchantman.

That a neutral may lawfully put his goods on board a belligerent ship for conveyance on the ocean, is universally recognized as the original rule of the law of nations. It is, as has already been stated, founded on the plain and simple principle that the property of a friend remains his property wherever it may be found. "Since it is not," says Vattel, "the place where a thing is which determines the nature of that thing, but the character of the person to whom it belongs, things belonging to neutral persons which happen to be in an enemy's country, or on board an enemy's ships, are to be distinguished from those which belong to the enemy."[14]

Bynkershoek lays down the same principles in terms equally explicit; and in terms entitled to the more consideration, because he enters into the enquiry whether a knowledge of the hostile character of the vessel can effect the owner of the goods.[15]

The same principle is laid down by other writers on the same subject, and is believed to be contradicted by none. It is true there were some old ordinances of France declaring that a hostile vessel or cargo should expose both to condemnation. But these ordinances have never constituted a rule of public law.

It is deemed of much importance that the rule is universally laid down in terms which comprehend an armed as well as an unarmed vessel; and that armed vessels have never been excepted from it. Bynkershoek, in discussing a question suggesting an exception, with his mind directed to hostilities, does not hint that this privilege is confined to unarmed merchantmen.

In point of fact, it is believed that a belligerent merchant vessel rarely sails unarmed, so that this exception from the rule would be greater than the rule itself. At all events, the number of those who are armed and who sail under convoy, is too great not to have attracted the attention of writers on public law; and this exception to their broad general rule, if it existed, would certainly be found in some of their works. It would be strange if a rule laid down, with a view to war, in such broad terms as to have universal application, should be so construed as to exclude from its operation almost every case for which it purports to provide, and yet that not a *dictum* should be found in the books pointing to such construction.

The antiquity of the rule is certainly not unworthy of consideration. It is to be traced back to the time when almost every merchantman was in a condition for self-defence, and the implements of war were so light and so cheap that scarcely any would sail without them.

A belligerent has a perfect right to arm in his own defence; and a neutral has a perfect right to transport his goods in a belligerent vessel. These rights do not interfere with each other. The neutral has no control over the belligerent right to arm—ought he to be accountable for the exercise of it?

By placing neutral property in a belligerent ship, that property, according to the positive rules of law, does not cease to be neutral. Why should it be changed by the exercise of a belligerent right, universally acknowledged and in common use when the rule was laid down, and over which the neutral had no control?

The belligerent answers, that by arming his rights are impaired. By placing his goods under the guns of an enemy, the neutral has taken part with the enemy and assumed the hostile character.

Previous to that examination which the Court has been able to make of the reasoning by which this proposition is sustained, one remark will be made which applies to a great part of it. The argument which, taken in its fair sense, would prove that it is unlawful to deposit goods for transportation in the vessel of an enemy generally, however imposing its form, must be unsound, because it is in contradiction to acknowledged law.

It is said that by depositing goods on board an armed belligerent the right of search may be impaired, perhaps defeated.

What is this right of search? Is it a substantive and independent right wantonly, and in the pride of power, to vex and harrass neutral commerce, because there is a capacity to do so? or to indulge the idle and mischievous curiosity of looking into neutral trade? or the assumption of a right to control it? If it be such a substantive and independent right, it would be better that cargoes should be inspected in port before the sailing of the vessel, or that belligerent licenses should be procured. But this is not its character.

Belligerents have a full and perfect right to capture enemy goods and articles going to their enemy which are contraband of war. To the exercise of that right the right of search is essential. It is a mean justified by the end. It has been truely denominated a right growing out of, and ancillary to the greater right of capture. Where this greater right may be legally exercised without search, the right of search can never arise or come into question.

But it is said that the exercise of this right may be prevented by the inability of the party claiming it to capture the belligerent carrier of neutral property.

And what injury results from this circumstance? If the property be neutral, what mischief is done by its escaping a search. In so doing there is no sin even as against the belligerent, if it can be effected by lawful means. The neutral cannot justify the use of force or fraud, but if by means, lawful in themselves, he can escape this vexatious procedure, he may certainly employ them.

To the argument that by placing his goods in the vessel of an armed enemy, he connects himself with that enemy and assumes the hostile character; it is answered that no such connexion exists.

The object of the neutral is the transportation of his goods. His connexion with the vessel which transports them is the same, whether that vessel be armed or unarmed. The act of arming is not his—it is the act of a party who has a right so to do. He meddles not with the armament nor with the war. Whether his goods were on board or not, the vessel would be armed and would sail. His goods do not contribute to the armament further than the freight he pays, and freight he would pay were the vessel unarmed.

It is difficult to perceive in this argument any thing which does not also apply to an unarmed vessel. In both instances it is the right and the duty of the carrier to avoid capture and to prevent a search. There is no difference except in the degree of capacity to carry this duty into effect. The argument would operate against the rule which permits the neutral merchant to employ a belligerent vessel without imparting to his goods the belligerent character.

The argument respecting resistance stands on the same ground with that which respects arming. Both are lawful. Neither of them is chargeable to the goods or their owner, where he has taken no part in it. They are incidents to the character of the vessel; and may always occur where the carrier is belligerent.

It is remarkable that no express authority on either side of this question can be found in the books. A few scanty materials, made up of inferences from cases depending on other principles, have been gleaned from the books and employed by both parties. They are certainly not decisive for or against either.

The celebrated case of the Swedish convoy has been pressed into the service.[16] But that case decided no more than this, that a neutral may arm, but cannot by force resist a search. The reasoning of the judge on that occasion would seem to indicate that the resistance condemned the cargo, because it was unlawful. It has been inferred on the one side that the goods would be infected by the resistance of the ship, and on the other that a resistance which is lawful, and is not produced by the goods, will not change their character.

The case of the Catharine Elizabeth approaches more nearly to that of the Nereide, because in that case as in this there were neutral goods and a belligerent vessel.[17] It was certainly a case, not of resistance, but of an attempt by a part of the crew to seize the capturing vessel. Between such an attempt and an attempt to take the same vessel previous to capture, there does not seem to be a total dissimilitude. But it is the reasoning of the judge and not his decision, of which the Claimants would avail themselves. He distinguishes between the effect which the employment of force by a belligerent owner or by a neutral owner would have on neutral goods. The first is lawful, the last unlawful. The belligerent owner violates no duty. He is held by force and may escape if he can. From the marginal note it appears that the reporter understood this case to decide in principle that resistance by a belligerent vessel would not confiscate the cargo.[18] It is only in a case without express authority that such materials can be relied on.

If the neutral character of the goods is forfeited by the resistance of the belligerent vessel, why is not the neutral character of the passengers forfeited by the same cause? The master and crew are prisoners of war, why are not those passengers who did not engage in the conflict also prisoners? That they are not would seem to the Court to afford a strong argument in favor of the goods. The law would operate in the same manner on both.

It cannot escape observation, that in argument the neutral freighter has been continually represented as arming the Nereide and impelling her to hostility. He is represented as drawing forth and guiding her warlike energies. The Court does not so understand the case. The Nereide was armed, governed, and conducted by belligerents. With her force, or her conduct the neutral shippers had no concern. They deposited their goods on board the vessel, and stipulated for their direct transportation to Buenos Ayres. It is true that on her passage she had a right to defend herself, did defend herself, and might have captured an assailing vessel; but to search for the enemy would have been a violation of the charter party and of her duty.

With a pencil dipped in the most vivid colours, and guided by the hand of a master, a splendid portrait has been drawn exhibiting this vessel and her freighter as forming a single figure, composed of the most discordant materials, of peace and war. So exquisite was the skill of the artist, so dazzling the garb in which the figure was presented, that it required the exercise of that cold investigating faculty which ought always to belong to those who sit on this bench, to discover its only imperfection; its want of resemblance.[19]

The Nereide has not that centaur-like appearance which has been ascribed to her. She does not rove over the ocean hurling the thunders of war while sheltered by the olive branch of peace. She is not composed in part of the neutral character of Mr. Pinto, and in part of the hostile character of her owner. She is an open and declared belligerent; claiming all the rights, and subject to all the dangers of the belligerent character. She conveys neutral property which does not engage in her warlike equipments, or in any employment she may make of them; which is put on board solely for the purpose of transportation, and which encounters the hazard incident to its situation; the hazard of being taken into port, and obliged to seek another conveyance should its carrier be captured.

In this it is the opinion of the majority of the Court there is nothing unlawful.[20] The characters of the vessel and cargo remain as distinct in this as in any other case. The sentence, therefore, of the Circuit Court must be reversed, and the property claimed by Manuel Pinto for himself and his partners, and for those other Spaniards for whom he has claimed, be restored, and the libel as to that property, be dismissed.[21]

Printed, William Cranch, *Reports of Cases Argued and Adjudged in the Supreme Court of the United States* . . . , IX (Washington, D.C., 1817), 412–31.

1. Depositions of Balthazer Ximenes, 21 Feb. 1814; Antonio Linch, 25 Feb. 1814; Felix Linch, 25 Feb. 1814 (The Nereide, record on appeal, 13–34, 133–46, 147–64, App. Cas. No. 707).

2. Pinto's affidavit, sworn in open court, 15 Mar. 1814 (The Nereide, record on appeal, 363–72).

3. In prize proceedings, the examinations *in preparatorio* of all captured persons were taken soon after the captured vessel was brought into port. These depositions consisted of answers to standing interrogatories and were filed with the libel (Henry Wheaton, *A Digest of the Law of Maritime Captures and Prizes* [New York, 1815], 280–81). In the U.S. District Court of New York, witnesses were required to answer forty standing interrogatories. For Pinto's examination *in preparatorio*, 17 Feb. 1814, see The Nereide, record on appeal, 63–94. Dallas pointed out discrepancies between Pinto's examination *in preparatorio* and his subsequent claim and answer (9 Cranch 397–99).

4. A charter-party is a contract between a shipper and the owner of a vessel. The charter-party between John Drinkald, owner of the *Nereide*, and Manuel Pinto was executed in London on 26 Aug. 1813 (The Nereide, record on appeal, 177–82).

5. Puzey's deposition, 13 Feb. 1814 (The Nereide, record on appeal, 35–62).

6. JM quoted from Pinto's examination *in preparatorio* and claim (The Nereide, record on appeal, 75–77, 359–61).

7. The statement about the printing presses appeared in Pinto's answer to the sixth interrogatory. John Paul, a London printer, was going to Buenos Aires to establish a business (ibid., 68, 86, 369).

8. Article XV of the 1795 treaty between the U.S. and Spain (Hunter Miller, ed., *Treaties and Other International Acts of the United States of America*, II [Washington, D.C., 1931], 329).

9. In response to British and French searches and seizures of neutral vessels, Russia, Denmark, and Sweden formed the League of Armed Neutrality in 1780 to protect their ocean commerce. Other European powers joined the league during the next several years (Samuel Flagg Bemis, *A Diplomatic History of the United States* [New York, 1936], 38–41). See Emmet's argument, 9 Cranch 408.

10. In argument Dallas cited Jefferson's letter to Genet, 24 July 1793 (9 Cranch 399). For this correspondence, see *ASP, Foreign Relations*, I, 166–67.

11. The Nereide, record on appeal, 177.

12. Letter from John Drinkald to William Bennett, 24 Nov. 1813 (ibid., 201–4).

13. Ibid., 70.

14. [Emmerich de] Vattel, *The Law of Nations, or Principles of the Law of Nature, Applied to the Conduct and Affairs of Nations and Sovereigns*, Bk. III, chap. v, sec. 75 (Philadelphia, 1817), 322.

15. Cornelius van Bynkershoek, *A Treatise on the Law of War* (Philadelphia, 1810), 102.

16. The "Maria," 1 C. Rob. 340, 165 Eng. Rep. 199 (Adm., 1799). This case and The "Catherina Elizabeth" (see n. 17) were cited by counsel from the American edition of Robinson's reports, which has a different pagination from the English edition.

17. The "Catherina Elizabeth," 5 C. Rob. 232, 165 Eng. Rep. 759 (Adm., 1804).

18. The marginal note reads: "Resistance by an enemy master will not affect the cargo, being the property of a neutral merchant."

19. JM alluded to Pinkney's speech (9 Cranch 406).

20. The majority consisted of four justices, including Johnson, who delivered a concurring opinion. Story dissented and was joined by one other (unnamed) justice. Todd did not sit.

21. After the case was remanded to the circuit court in Apr. 1815, a question arose as to the rate of the duties to be paid on Pinto's restored property. On a division of opinion, the case was certified to the Supreme Court, which ruled at the Feb. 1816 term that duties were to be charged at the same rate as duties on goods imported in foreign vessels (The Nereid, 1 Wheat. 171–78; judgment, [8 Mar. 1816], The Nereide, App. Cas. No. 707; U.S. Sup. Ct. Dockets, App. Cas. No. 798).

To Bushrod Washington

My dear Sir   Richmond March 16th. 1815

As peace will I hope restore commerce to the United States I have again turned my attention to the profession for which I originally intended my son James. He is now at Cambridge, but I should remove him without hesitation the instant it becomes proper to place him in a counting house. He was fifteen in february last & has made as great a proficiency in his studies as is usual with boys of that age.[1]

You were so good as to apply for his admission into the counting house of Messrs. Willing & Francis & I understood those gentlemen were willing to receive him.[2] Will you be so obliging as to speak to them once more on this subject & if they are still willing to take him, let me know what are their terms & when they wish him to come. I am willing to bind him & to comply with the terms which those gentlemen may require. I hope they will not be dissatisfied with my son should they take charge of him. I am dear Sir your

J MARSHALL

ALS, Marshall Papers, ViW. Addressed to Washington at Mount Vernon; postmarked Richmond, 16 Mar. Endorsed by Washington.

1. James Keith Marshall entered Harvard College early in 1814 as a member of the class of 1818. His year in Cambridge included being "admonished for breaking a window" and "fined for improper attitude at worship." The last entry in his college records states that he was "consigned," a reference to his apprenticeship to the Philadelphia firm of Willing & Francis (entry for James Keith Marshall, Faculty Records, IX, 1814–1822, MH-Ar; JM to Willing & Francis, 2 May 1815).

2. Washington, whose judicial circuit took him to Philadelphia twice a year, had applied to Willing & Francis on JM's behalf in 1810 (*PJM*, VII, 244–45 and n. 3).

To Bushrod Washington

My dear Sir   [3 April 1815]

On receiving your letter I made the necessary inquiries respecting the lands for which taxes have not been paid.[1] The money can no longer be received in the auditors office but must be paid in the county to the sheriff. If not paid before August they will then be sold. The sooner payment is made the better as the arrears accumulate very fast they carry an interest of ten percent. & I am not sure that it is not compounded.[2]

I have looked alittle into the letters of Genl. Washington. All those to Congress, all the military letters prior to 1780, all the letters to foreign officers & to the Governors of States, all those written subsequent to the adoption of the constitution are in your possession. This will produce some difficulty as I presume they ought to be published, if at all, in the order in which they were written blending letters to different characters together. It will also be necessary to insert a few of those written to Genl. Washington as explanatory of his. Of this however I am not quite sure. If the business proceeds it will be of importance to determine how many volumes shall be published since the letters must be selected with a view to that point. I have gone through the military correspondence in my possession & marked all the letters in my possession. It will be proper to go through them again & exclude many of those which are marked. Should all the interesting letters be inserted they would amount to 10 or 12 large octavos.[3]

I should like to hear from you on this subject.

I must beg the favor of you to settle my account with Mr. Jackson & discontinue his paper.[4] The increased postage has determined me to relinquish all daily papers. I give up the political & commercial Register with the more reluctance from my respect for the Editor. But the advantage to him is very trifling indeed. With much esteem & affection I am dear Sir, Your obedt

J MARSHALL

I send sixteen dollars. Should I owe more which I do not suppose, be so good as to pay it for me. I look with impatience for a letter from you respecting my son James who has again expressed his wish to be bound to Messrs. Will⟨ing & Fran⟩cis.

ALS, Marshall Papers, ViW. Addressed to Washington in Philadelphia; postmarked Richmond, 3 Apr. Endorsed by Washington. MS torn where seal was broken.

1. Letter not found.
2. JM referred to a statute concerning land taxes enacted in Feb. 1814 by the Virginia General Assembly. This legislation instructed the sheriff of each county, beginning in 1815, to collect the previous year's unpaid land taxes plus a penalty of 10 percent of the overdue tax. In cases where the delinquent tax and penalty were not paid, the sheriff was to sell enough of the land to cover these amounts as well as the tax for the current year (*The Revised Code of the Laws of Virginia* . . . [2 vols.; Richmond, Va., 1819], II, 548–49).
3. This is the earliest reference to a proposed edition of George Washington's papers, a project JM and Bushrod Washington ultimately abandoned in 1826 in favor of an edition to be prepared by Jared Sparks (Herbert B. Adams, *The Life and Writings of Jared Sparks* [2 vols.; Boston, 1893], I, 389–413).
4. William Jackson was editor of the *Political and Commercial Register*, a Philadelphia newspaper (see *PJM*, VI, 304 and n. 2).

To [Joseph G. Cogswell?]

Sir   Richmond April 9th. 1815

I received two days past your favor of the 27th. of March.[1] For the communication you have made, and for the interest you take in the fate of my culpable son, I pray you to receive my sincere thanks.[2]

I have been excessively pained at his misconduct, & cannot entirely excuse myself for the unlimited confidence I placed in him. I think myself in some measure accessory to his disgrace.

I am anxious to give him an opportunity to retrieve his reputation & to restore himself to the affection & good opinion of his friends &

connexions. I fear he will not avail himself of any opportunity which may be afforded him. I grieve to percieve in him no mark of sincere penitence, no deep conviction of his faults, no resolute determination to correct them. It is not the unavailing expression of regret unaccompanied by an exemplary performance of duty & a vigorous application to study, that can atone for his errors, or furnish a hope that they will not be repeated. If his conduct in the retirement to which he is sentenced shall be such as perfectly to satisfy the government of the University, if in his studies he shall outstrip the class of which he was a member until he proved himself unworthy of remaining in it, if he shall persevere without relaxation in that course of self improvement which will be the evidence & the sole evidence of real reformation, the past will be forgotten as well as forgiven, & he will be received by his parents & other friends as if no offense had been committed. But every thing depends on himself, & he may rest assured that it will not be in his power to practice imposition on me.[3]

In the wounded feelings of a Father anxious for the welfare of a son of whose unworthiness he is unwilling to be convinced, your goodness will I trust find an apology for the trouble given you by this letter. Allow me to repeat my thanks for the interest you have taken in his affairs & to assur⟨e⟩ you that I am with very much respect, Your Obedt Servt.

J MARSHALL

ALS, Dietrichs Collection, University of Amsterdam, The Netherlands.

1. Letter not found. The recipient was most likely Joseph G. Cogswell (1786–1871), then a tutor in Latin at Harvard, who later became a prominent educator. JM wrote to Cogswell on 23 Apr. and 29 May on the subject of his son's dismissal from Harvard (App. II, Cal.). The addressee might also have been John Thornton Kirkland, president of Harvard from 1810 to 1828.

2. The "culpable son" was John Marshall (1798–1833), a member of the Harvard class of 1817. The faculty had voted to dismiss him on 20 Mar. An entry in the faculty records for that date reads: "Representation being made to the Government, that Marshall of the Sophomore Class had been engaged in a course of immoral & dissolute conduct, which had been long continued & under circumstances that left little hope of his reform, it was voted that he be dismissed from College & not be permitted to return before the expiration of a year, & then only to a degraded standing" (Faculty Records [20 Mar. 1815], IX, 1814–1822, MH-Ar).

3. John Marshall did not return to Harvard. In 1817 he was living at Oak Hill in Fauquier County and trying to bring a schoolmaster into the area. To Charles Prentiss, a 1795 graduate of Harvard who was then editing the *Virginia Patriot* in Richmond, Marshall wrote: "I wish you would prevail on some one who has graduated at Cambridge, provided he be not bigoted in favour of that fat priest, to come among us, but if he be an orthodox Kirkland, unless your son, he will meet with my frown" (John Marshall, Jr., to Charles Prentiss, 10 July 1817, MWA).

To Robert G. Harper

Dear Sir   Richmond Apr. 28th. 1815
   I am much your debtor for the pleasure received from reading the
two pamphlets which you were so good as to transmit to me.¹ Mr.
Livingstone is I think still more the debtor of Mr. Jefferson for having
dragged him & his case before the publick. From that circumstance he
will I think derive one solid advantage in addition to a vast increase of
reputation as a man of talents. Publick sentiment, if it have more than a
nominal existence in the United States, must compel Congress to provide a tribunal for the trial of his cause.² With very much esteem, I am
dear Sir your obedt

J Marshall

ALS, MdHi. Addressed to Harper in Baltimore; postmarked Richmond, 28 Apr. Endorsed by Harper as received 1 May and "no ansr."

   1. The two pamphlets were those by Thomas Jefferson and Edward Livingston concerning the celebrated batture controversy, which were published in successive numbers
of John E. Hall's *The American Law Journal* in 1814. Jefferson's pamphlet, *The Proceedings
of the Government of the United States, in Maintaining the Public Right to the Beach of the
Missisipi, Adjacent to New-Orleans, against the Intrusion of Edward Livingston*, was originally
published in 1812. It was republished "with corrections and additional Notes, by the
Author" in *American Law Journal*, V, no. 17 (1814). Livingston's pamphlet, *An Answer to
Mr. Jefferson's Justification of His Conduct in the Case of the New Orleans Batture*, was published
ibid., V, no. 18 (1814). JM's personal copy of this volume, signed by him three times, was
offered for sale in Sept. 1991 (William Reese Company [New Haven, Conn.], *Catalogue
100* [Sept. 1991], 85–87).
   2. See JM's circuit court opinion in Livingston v. Jefferson (1811), *PJM*, VII, 276–88.

Meade v. Deputy Marshal of Virginia District
Opinion
ca. 1 May 1815

William Meade, a delinquent militiaman from Loudoun County, Virginia,
petitioned to be discharged from custody of the federal marshal under a
writ of habeas corpus. Confined for nonpayment of a fine levied by sentence of court-martial in December 1813, Meade presented his petition to
the chief justice out of term, apparently in April or early May 1815. The
judiciary act empowered federal judges to grant writs of habeas corpus at
any time "for the purpose of an inquiry into the cause of commitment."
Shortly after Marshall rendered his opinion, L. P. W. Balch, a lawyer in
Leesburg (in Loudoun County), obtained a copy, which on 16 May he
submitted for publication in the Leesburg *Washingtonian*. The opinion,
along with Balch's covering letter, was subsequently published in the
Washington *Federal Republican* in early June (*U.S. Statutes at Large*, I, 82;
Harrison Williams, *Legends of Loudoun: An Account of the History and Homes
of a Border Country of Virginia's Northern Neck* [Richmond, Va., 1938], 186;
Federal Republican [Washington, D.C.], 2 June 1815).

William Meade
v
The Depty. Marshal of the Virga. dist.   } Motion to be discharged under a writ of ha. cor.

¶1   By the return of the Deputy Marshal it appears that William Meade the petitioner was taken into custody by him, & is detained in custody on account of the nonpayment of a fine of 48$ assessed upon him by the sentence of a court martial for failing to take the field in pursuance of General orders of the 24th. of March 1814,[1] the Marshal not having found property whereof the said fine might have been made.

¶2   The court martial was convened by the following order.

¶3   Brigade orders   Novr. 8th. 1813
       A general court martial to consist of Lt. Colo. Mason President &c will convene at the court house in Leesburg on friday the third day of next month for the trial of delinquencies which occurred under the late requisitions of the Governor of Virginia & Secretary of war for Militia from the county of Loudoun.
              Signed Hugh Douglass. Brig. Genl. 6th. Brig. of V. M.

¶4   The court being convened the following proceedings were had
       "It appearing to the satisfaction of the court that the following persons of the county of Loudoun were regularly detailed for militia duty & were required to take the field under general orders of March 24th. 1813 but refused or failed to comply therewith, whereupon this court doth order & adjudge that they be each severally fined the sum annexed to their names as follows to wit" "William Mead 48$["]

¶5   On the part of the petitioner the obligation of this sentence is denied
              1st. Because it is a court sitting under the authority of the state & not of the United States.   2d. It has not proceeded according to the laws of the state, nor is it constituted according to those laws. 3d. Because the court proceeded without notice.

¶6   1st. The court was unquestionably convened by the authority of the state & sat as a state court. It is however contended that the marshal may collect fines assessed by a state court for the failure of a militia man to take the field in pursuance of the orders of the President of the United States.

¶7   The constitution of the United States gives power to Congress "To provide for calling forth the militia to execute the laws of the Union &c.["]

¶8   In the execution of this power it is not doubted that Congress may provide the means of punishing those who shall fail to obey the requisitions made in pursuance of the laws of the Union, & may prescribe the mode of proceeding against such delinquents, & the tribunals before which such proceedings should be had. Indeed it would seem reasonable to expect that all the proceedings against delinquents should rest on the authority of that power which had been offended by the delinquency.

This idea must be retained while considering the acts of Congress. ¶9 The first section of the act of 1795[2] authorises the President "whenever the United States shall be invaded or in imminent danger of invasion" "to call forth such number of the militia of the state or states most convenient to the place of danger or scene of action as he may judge necessary to repel such invasion, & to issue his orders for that purpose to such officer or officers of the militia as he shall think proper."

The 5th. section enacts "That every officer non commissioned officer ¶10 or private of the militia who shall fail to obey the orders of the President of the United States in any of the cases before recited shall forfeit a sum not exceeding one years pay, & not less than one months pay to be determined & adjudged by a court Martial."

The 6th. section enacts "That courts martial for the trial of militia ¶11 shall be composed of militia officers only."

Upon these sections depends the question whether courts martial ¶12 for the assessment of fines against delinquent militia men should be constituted under the authority of the United States, or of the state to which the delinquent belongs. The idea originally suggested that the tribunal for the trial of the offence should be constituted by or derive its authority from the government against which the offence had been committed, would seem to require that the court thus referred to in general terms, should be a court sitting under the authority of the United States. It would be reasonable to expect, if the power were to be devolved on the court of a state government, that more explicit terms would be used for conveying it. And it seems also to be a reasonable construction that the legislature, where in the 6 section providing a court martial for the trial of militia, held in mind the offences described in the preceding section & to be submitted to a court martial. If the offences described in the 5th. section are to be tried by a court constituted according to the provisions of the 6th. section, then we should be led by the language of that section to suppose that Congress had in contemplation a court formed of officers in actual service since the provision that it "should be composed of militia officers only" would other wise be nugatory.

This construction derives some aid from the act of 1814.[3] By that act ¶13 courts martial for the trial of offences such as that with which Mr. Meade is charged are to be appointed according to the rules prescribed by the articles of war. The court in the present case is not appointed according to those rules.

The only argument which occurs to me against this reasoning grows ¶14 out of the inconvenience arising from trying delinquent militia men who remain at home by a court martial composed of officers in actual service. This inconvenience may be great, & well deserves the consideration of Congress; but I doubt whether it is sufficient to justify a Judge in so construing a law as to devolve on courts sitting under the authority of the state a power which in its nature belongs to the United States.

¶15   If however this should be the proper construction then the court must be constituted according to the laws of the state.

¶16   On examining the laws of Virginia it appears that no court martial can be called for the assessment of fines or for the trial of privates not in actual service. This duty is performed by courts of enquiry, & a second court must sit to receive the excuses of those against whom a previous court may have assessed fines, before the sentence becomes final or can be executed.[4]

¶17   If it be supposed that the act of Congress has conferred the jurisdiction against delinquent militia privates on courts martial constituted as those are for the trial of officers, still this court has proceeded in such a manner that its sentence cannot be sustained.

¶18   It is a principle of natural justice, with which courts are never at liberty to dispense unless under the mandate of positive law, that no person shall be condemned unheard, or without an opportunity of being heard. There is no law authorising courts martial to proceed against any person without notice. Consequently such proceeding is entirely unlawful. In the case of the courts of enquiry sitting under the authority of the state, the practice has I beleive prevailed to proceed in the first instance without notice; but this inconvenience is in some degree remedied by a second court, & I am by no means prepared for suc⟨h⟩ a construction of the act as would justify rendering the sentence final without substantial notice. But be this as it may. This is a court Martial not a court of enquiry, & no law exists authorizing a court martial to proceed without notice. In this case the court appears so to have proceeded. For this reason I consider its sentences as entirely nugatory & do therefore direct the petitioner to be discharg⟨ed⟩ from the custody of the Marshal.[5]

AD, Marshall Judicial Opinions, PPAmP; printed, John W. Brockenbrough, *Reports of Cases Decided by the Honourable John Marshall . . .* , I (Philadelphia, 1837), 325–28. For JM's deletions and interlineations, see Textual Notes below.

1. The correct year is 1813.

2. *U.S. Statutes at Large*, I, 424.

3. Ibid., III, 134.

4. For Virginia's comprehensive militia law, enacted in 1804, see Shepherd, *Statutes*, III, 3–21. JM referred to sec. 30 of that law (ibid., 13).

5. Meade's case was virtually identical to that of Everard Bolton, a private in the Pennsylvania militia who was imprisoned for nonpayment of a fine assessed by a court-martial sentence. Like Meade, Bolton petitioned for discharge on the ground that the court-martial had no jurisdiction, having acted under state authority and not that of the

U.S. His case came before the Supreme Court for the Western District of Pennsylvania in Pittsburgh in Sept. 1815. In an opinion similar to JM's, Pennsylvania Chief Justice William Tilghman ordered Bolton to be released from imprisonment. Publication of Tilghman's opinion renewed interest in the Meade case, which to this point had not been widely reprinted. The first Richmond publication of the decision was by the *Virginia Argus* in early Nov. 1815, from which *Niles' Weekly Register* picked it up soon thereafter (Pittsburgh *Post Gazette*, 30 Sept. 1815; 3 S & R 177n; Richmond *Virginia Argus*, 18 Oct., 4 Nov. 1815; *Niles' Weekly Register* [Baltimore, Md.], IX [1815], 194–95).

Both the Meade and Bolton decisions were cited in the important case of Houston v. Moore, decided by the Supreme Court in 1820. Like Bolton's case, Houston v. Moore concerned a Pennsylvania militia private who had been tried by a court-martial convened under state authority. However, Houston's court-martial (unlike Bolton's) took place after the enactment of a Pennsylvania law that expressly conferred authority on its own courts-martial to try delinquent militiamen and impose the penalties defined in the 1795 federal militia law. Because the Constitution empowered Congress to govern that part of the militia called into federal service, Houston v. Moore raised the question of whether the Pennsylvania law was repugnant to the Constitution. A divided Supreme Court upheld the state law (5 Wheat. 1, 6, 70; JM to Story, 13 July 1819 and n. 5).

Textual Notes

¶ 2 l. 1	court ~~marshal~~ ↑martial↓ was
¶ 3 l. 3	will ~~convenes~~ ↑convene↓ at
¶ 4 l. 1	↑The court being convened the↓ ~~The~~ following
¶ 5 ll. 3–4	States. ↑2d. It has not proceeded according to the laws of the State, nor is it constituted according to those laws.↓
l. 5	~~2~~ ↑3d.↓ Because
¶ 6 l. 1	court ~~a~~ ↑was↓ unquestionably
l. 4	of ~~an~~ ↑the↓ orders
¶12 l. 11	used ↑for↓ conveying ~~the power.~~ ↑it.↓ And
l. 17	that ~~the~~ Congress
¶13 l. 4	war. ~~This~~ ↑The↓ court
¶14 l. 6	to ~~devolves~~ ↑devolve↓ on
¶15 l. 2	be ~~construed~~ ↑constituted↓ according
¶17 ll. 1–2	jurisdiction ↑against delinquent militia privates↓ on

To Willing & Francis

Gentlemen   Richmond May 2d. 1815

On being informed by my friend Judge Washington that you had consented to receive my son James into your counting house, I directed him to repair immediately from Harvard college to Philadelphia where I hope he will arrive soon after this reaches you. I take the liberty to enclose under your address to your care some letters which I wish him to receive immediately.

As I am extremely anxious respecting the conduct & morals of my son I cannot help feeling some solicitude about the place where he boards & the society to which he may be introduced. I do not know what degree of superintending controul your avocations will allow you to take over the young men in your counting house. Without presuming to ask what may be burdensome, I flatter myself I may say that the more you exercise the authority of a Father a Guardian & a master the more shall I be indebted to you & the more grateful shall I be for your goodness. He will undoubtedly advise with you on every subject & I hope & beleive will follow your advice. His first sliding into bad company, should it happen, will I trust be firmly & sternly corrected. He considers himself as bound to you & I am ready to execute any paper to that effect you may wish, & in all respects to perform whatever is usual or agreeable to yourselves.

My eldest son has given him a letter to Mr. Serjeant—a particular friend, recommending James to his attention.[1] With very great respect, I am your obedt. Servt

J Marshall

ALS, Gratz Collection, PHi. Addressed to Willing & Francis in Philadelphia and marked "private"; postmarked 2 May. Endorsed as received and answered on 5 May.

1. Probably Elihu Spencer Sergeant (1787–1824), a Philadelphia attorney who had graduated from the College of New Jersey (now Princeton University) in 1804, a year after Thomas Marshall. Both were members of the American Whig Society at Princeton (*Pennsylvania Magazine of History and Biography*, II [1878], 442; *Catalogue of the Honorary and Graduate Members of the American Whig Society, Instituted in the College of New Jersey, in 1796* [Princeton, N.J., 1837], 7).

The Fortuna
Opinion
U.S. Circuit Court, North Carolina, 15 May 1815

The *Fortuna* sailed under Russian colors from Riga in September 1813 on a voyage that took her first to London and then to the West Indies. At Havana in February 1814 the *Fortuna* took on a cargo of produce. After leaving Havana bound for Bermuda, the ship was captured in April 1814 by the schooner *Roger*, a privateer out of Norfolk, Virginia, and taken to Wilmington, North Carolina, where the vessel and cargo were condemned at the U.S. District Court in August. An appeal was taken to the U.S. Circuit Court by Henry Behrens, master of the *Fortuna*, on behalf of the claimants, Martin Krause and John Krause of Riga and J. F. Muhlenbruck of Hamburg. The claimants sought restitution on the ground that the captured property belonged to neutrals. The discovery of a concealed parcel of papers, however, raised suspicions of fraud, suggesting that the real owners of the *Fortuna* and cargo were British subjects (U.S. Cir. Ct., N.C., Min. Bk., 15 May 1815; The Fortuna: Krause et al., Claimants, App. Cas. No. 764; *Raleigh Register, and North-Carolina Gazette*, 19 May 1815).

The Fortuna, a vessel sailing under Russian colors, was captured on a voyage from the Havannah to some port in Europe, by the American privateer Roger, and brought into the port of Wilmington, where she was libelled by the captors as enemy's property. The vessel and cargo were claimed as belonging to neutrals. Both were condemned in the district court as prize of war, and from that sentence the claimants have appealed to this Court.

The ship's papers, which were found at the time of capture, represent the vessel as Russian, and the bills of lading and other papers, relative to the cargo, represent that as the property of the neutral claimants. The testimony of the captain and crew comports with these papers. There is, indeed, some apparent contradiction in the affidavits given at different times by the captain. In his claim, and in one of the affidavits, he says that the Fortuna was the property of Martin Krause; in another affidavit he states her to be the property of M. & J. Krause.[1] Now as M. & J. Krause were partners in trade, both Russians, and both residing at Riga, it was perfectly immaterial whether the vessel belonged to one or both of them, and it is entirely probable, as M. & J. Krause were the ostensible owners of the principal part of the cargo, that this inaccuracy of expression in one of the affidavits might escape him inadvertently, or might, as has been stated, be the fault of the translator or person who wrote the affidavit. Although such negligence in those who give testimony in any cause, must be very reprehensible, it would be punishing it rather severely, even if it were certainly committed by the witness, to confiscate a ship in consequence of it. I should, therefore, not lay much stress on that circumstance.

But while the Fortuna lay in the port of Wilmington, a canister containing several papers was found concealed in an old piece of timber. It appears that in the port of Havanna, just before the sailing of the vessel, the carpenter had been taken into the cabin by the captain, who brought in at the same time this piece of wood. They were locked in together, and while there, the canister was let into the timber, and a piece of wood morticed over it for the purpose of concealing it. The timber was then thrown into the hole of the ship. The papers, thus concealed have a material influence on the cause.[2]

The claimants represent Messrs. Bennett & Co. of London, to be the agents of M. & J. Krause of Riga, with respect to the vessel, the voyage, and the cargo. Bennett & Co. are supposed to have empowered a Mr. Muhlenbruck, a German, to purchase a cargo at the Havanna, to which place the Fortuna sailed in ballast, with which she was to return to Riga, touching on her return at Leith or some British port. The concealed papers furnish considerable ground for suspecting, that both the vessel and cargo are, in fact, the property of Bennett & Co.

The first of these secreted papers, contained in the transcript of the record, is a letter of instructions from Bennett & Co. to Captain Behrens, dated London, 18th November, 1813, immediately before the departure of the vessel for the Havanna.[3]

This letter commences thus: "As we have settled your ship's accounts, by paying you a balance of £206 16s. 11d., up to November 13th, we now agree," &c.

The exhibit, No. 40, is an account, (headed, "Dr.—Ship Fortuna,— Cr.,") the balance on which is £206 16s. 11d. The Dr. side of this account charges the ship with an account from Riga, due the captain, with primage going to Riga, the same from Riga, with cabin freight, and with his monthly wages from the 6th of May, to the 13th of November, and credits the ship by account against the captain from Carlscrona, the same from Gottenburg, and account in London, leaving the balance of £206 16s. 11d.

The balance arising against the captain, in London, is taken from exhibit No. 3, which is headed, "expenses in London, on the voyage from Riga, homeward." The account amounts to £202 2s. 10d., and contains a credit of £300, received from Messrs. Bennett & Co., in cash, leaving, against the captain, the balance of £97 17s. 2d., which is carried into the general account for final settlement.[4]

The exhibit No. 1. is headed, "expenses of the ship Fortuna in Riga in the month of July," and amounts to 1602.54 ⅔, Russian currency. A credit is there given in the following words—"From Mr. J. Krause in Riga, I received in cash 1600 roubles, leaving a balance in Russian currency due the captain of 2.54 ⅔ Russian currency." The same exhibit contains the expenses at Carlscrona, amounting to 161.39, and credits cash received from Buhling 180, leaving a balance against the captain of 18.9. Also, expenses in Gottenburg, amounting to 154.7, and credits by cash received from Mr. Wildenberg 150, leaving a balance due the captain of 4.7.

The appearance of these accounts demonstrates that no settlement was made with the captain at Riga, at Carlscrona, or Gottenburg which included them, but that advances were made to him at those places, respectively, to be accounted for by him when his accounts should be finally adjusted by Bennett & Co., and that the account itself was not stated, until after his return to England.

The expenses of the whole voyage appear to be on the same paper, beginning at Riga. There, Mr. Krause is credited with a round sum of 1600 roubles, leaving due the small balance of two roubles and a fraction. This is the natural course of a person directed to make advances to the captain of a ship, but it is not credible that, had the account been settled, the precise balance would not have been paid. Precisely the same thing occurs at Carlscrona and at Gottenburg. At each place a round sum, as a sum in gross, is advanced, nearly the sum due, but never the exact balance. Then, these accounts appear, forming one exhibit, I suppose, drawn upon the same paper, showing that no account had been rendered at either of the foreign ports, but that the whole was received for adjustment with Bennett & Co. This is certainly very natural if Bennett & Co. be the owners of the ship, having agents at Riga, Carlscrona and Gottenburg, but very extraordinary if Krause at Riga was the owner, and Bennett & Co. were their agents in London.

The force of this circumstance is, however, very much impaired by a paper which shows, that on the arrival of the Fortuna in Riga, in June 1813, a settlement of some kind took place, in which the captain's wages, up to the 6th of May, and those of the crew, to the 22d of May, were included. With whom the settlement was made does not appear, but in the subsequent final adjustment with Bennett & Co., the wages of the captain and crew are calculated from the date at which this paper states them to have been paid. It appears then, that a settlement took place on his arrival at Riga on the 7th of June, including his wages to the 6th of May, and those of his crew to the 22d, and that his expenses at Riga, and at other ports, were to be settled in London on his return. There is some difficulty in accounting for the settlement as respects wages, if the vessel arrived at her home port in June. The most rational solution of the difficulty would seem to be, that his voyage commenced in May in London, and was to terminate in London, a circumstance from which it would rather be inferred that London had become her home port, rather than that Riga continued to be so. This is corroborated by the manner in which the account is headed—"Expenses in London on the voyage from Riga homeward." The critique on the word "homeward" is not sustained, for it is the voyage that is homeward, and the meaning is, expenses paid or settled in London, but incurred on the voyage. And we find in the account, the wages of the men from the last settlement. This phraseology might be used by men accustomed to consider London as their home, although the vessel might be chartered from a foreigner, but it could not be expected from a Russian captain, commanding a Russian ship, owned and sailing in the employ of Russians.

The other accounts in the record, relate chiefly to the Ceres, a vessel commanded by Captain Behrens, before he was placed in the Fortuna. They are somewhat mysterious, from the general want of dates, and names; but this may be readily accounted for. In other respects, they are not calculated to dissipate suspicion. That money was paid by Bennett & Co. in London, on account of the Ceres, furnishes strong ground for the opinion, that the account of December 1812, was rendered to Bennett & Co. Now, that account appears, upon the face of it, to have been prepared for final settlement with the owners, or person, who acted as owner.

The Fortuna, and the Ceres, too, would seem to be under the management of the same person. Now, there is proof, that Bennett & Co. were the managers, and most probably, the owners of the Ceres; but we should not be justified by any paper or testimony in the cause, in supposing that the Ceres was owned by Krause, or that Behrens was ever employed by him, or known to him, until he was placed in the Fortuna.

These accounts, taken together, certainly indicate a long connexion between Bennett & Co., and Captain Behrens, and seem to show, that they were in the habit of employing him in their vessels.

After referring to the settlement which had been made, the letter of instructions proceeds thus: "We now agree, that the arrangements," &c. It has been very properly remarked, that this agreeing to confirm the contract made by Krause in Riga, is not the language of an agent, relating to a transaction of his principal; but it is undoubtedly true, that the agreement made by Krause, might terminate on the arrival of the ship in London, when a new contract might be made for the voyage to the Havanna, for the basis of which, the parties took the agreement at Riga.

There are, however, in this contract, expressions which appear somewhat suspicious. It commences thus: "On the following conditions, have I given to Captain Henry Behrens, the command of the ship Fortuna, under Russian colours, lying, at present, at Riga."[5] This contract is dated in August 1813. These words, certainly import, that under this agreement, Captain Behrens took command, for the first time, of the Fortuna. Yet, in fact, he took command of her in London, in 1812, and had sailed in her as commander from London, to the Baltic. This cannot be a confirmation of his previous appointment in London, for it is not the language of approbation or confirmation, but of original appointment. And this appears to be more than two months after the arrival of Behrens at Riga. The language does not appear to be at all fitted to the occasion, and whenever that occurs, there is much cause to suspect that it is uttered with an object, and for a purpose, not avowed. If it be supposed, that this contract was made in contemplation of the voyage to the Havanna, the difficulty is shifted, but not removed. The question recurs, what need had this contract of the confirmation of Bennett & Co.? or of the gratuity of £100? There is too much reason to suspect, that this is a feigned paper, prepared to give the ship the appearance of her being owned by Krause.

It is a little remarkable, too, that Bennett & Co. speak of it, as an arrangement made with M. & J. Krause, whereas it purports to be made with J. Krause only.

The letter proceeds—"We have ordered Mr. J. F. Muhlenbruck to supply you with the cash necessary for your expenses in the Havanna, when arrived out, which we beg may be as little as possible." The letter proceeds to mention persons to whom he may apply for aid, in different ports in England.

It cannot escape observation, that this letter contains no reference to the interests of the Russian merchants. The money is not to be advanced on their account. Mr. Muhlenbruck is not represented as their agent, or as advancing money on their account. The caution to economy, is not for the sake of his owners. This is certainly the language of an actual owner, but is very unlike the language of an agent.

The letter then proceeds to give detailed instructions for the observance of the directions of Mr. Muhlenbruck, in the Havanna, without once alluding to any connexion between Muhlenbruck and Krause.

The next letter is dated Havanna, 24th March, 1814, and is written by Muhlenbruck, to Bennett & Co.[6]

This letter is written with circumspection, and represents the transaction in a manner entirely conforming to the pretensions of the claimants, and is certainly adapted to the inspection of cruisers. It could therefore be concealed only with a hope of keeping Bennett & Co. entirely out of view, if with any fraudulent motive. Taken alone, I should not be inclined to yield to the suspicions it has excited; taken in connexion with the letter of Bennett & Co. to Behrens, I acknowledge it acquires a meaning which might not otherwise be affixed to it. "The Russian ship, Fortuna, &c." This style of communication would rather create the idea, that with respect to the Fortuna, Muhlenbruck was the direct agent of M. & J. Krause, and gave this intelligence to Bennett & Co. as the friends and correspondents of that house; than that he was in fact the agent of Bennett & Co. appointed and instructed by them, with respect to this very vessel. "I enclose you invoice and bill of lading, which you will be pleased to forward by the first opportunity to the above friends."

From this language, it could never be inferred, that Bennett & Co. had the sole management and direction of the vessel, and had employed Muhlenbruck, as a person who would obey and account to them. But if the invoice and bill of lading were intended for M. & J. Krause, why not have sent it in a letter to them? Why through Bennett & Co.?

He then says, that he has given the captain orders to touch at Leith, or some port in the channel, according to winds, and gives as a reason for these orders, that M. & J. Krause may have been induced to countermand the destination to Riga, in some letter to their correspondents Bennett & Co.: thus studiously preserving the idea, that he acted directly for M. & J. Krause, and that the voyage was under their management, not under that of Bennett & Co. He suggests, that the idea of touching at Leith, or in the channel, originates with himself, and yet it appears from a postscript to the instructions given to the captain, by Bennett & Co., that they had ordered him to touch at Leith. "On your arrival at Leith," say they, "apply to Messrs. Ogilvie & Patterson."

The next sentence requests them, should they have received orders from M. & J. Krause, to communicate them immediately to Captain Behrens; a request very proper from the agent of M. & J. Krause to their correspondents, but very extraordinary, if made by the agent of Bennett & Co., who were themselves, the sole managers of the vessel and voyage. The letter proceeds—"Please to inform, also, M. & J. Krause, that I have advanced here the captain $1332 04, for the use of the ship Fortuna." Who, that should collect his knowledge of the fact from this letter, would, or could suppose, that this money had been advanced by the agent of Bennett & Co., and by their express orders?

This letter, so far as it respects the Fortuna, is obviously intended to impress the idea, that Muhlenbruck was employed by M. & J. Krause, and that Bennett & Co. had neither the management of the vessel or cargo, but were written to by him, as the friends and correspondents of the owners at Riga, who might possibly have received instructions from them. Yet the letter of instructions from Bennett & Co. to Behrens, and their letter to the merchants at Charleston demonstrate,[7] that if they were not the owners, they had the sole and exclusive management of the vessel and voyage, and that Muhlenbruck was their agent, appointed to superintend the affairs of the Fortuna, and of other vessels, acknowledged to be owned, or employed, by them. Why thus disguise the truth? If Bennett & Co. were not the owners of the vessel and cargo, but were, in fact, the agents of M. & J. Krause of Riga, with unlimited powers, why not address them in their real character? Why not write to them as the persons having full power over the subject, who had authorized Muhlenbruck to purchase a cargo for their friends, and who were responsible to him for the money he had advanced by their order?

The letter of instructions from Mr. Muhlenbruck, to Captain Behrens, is written precisely in the spirit of that part of the letter to Bennett & Co., which relates to the Fortuna.[8] It is precisely such a letter as would be written by the immediate agents of M. & J. Krause, supposing them to retain in their own hands, the control of the voyage, to their friends and correspondents, who had no certain agency in the business, but might possibly have received letters for the ship, countermanding orders previously given.

I will here notice the letter written by Mr. Muhlenbruck, at the Havanna, to M. & J. Krause.[9] This letter was not secreted, but kept among the ship's papers. Who, that should read this letter, would imagine that Muhlenbruck had been appointed, not by M. & J. Krause, but by Bennett & Co.? Who, that has read the letter of instructions from Bennett & Co. to Behrens, would not expect that this letter would contain some reference to the manner in which the writer became the agent of the persons to whom the letter is addressed? If to this it be said, that this may have been done in a previous letter, I answer, that if any such previous letter had been written, it would, according to mercantile usage, have been referred to in this letter; and the stay of Muhlenbruck, in the Havanna, had been so short, as to diminish the probability of his having written a previous letter to Riga.

I think it almost impossible, that a stranger, slipped by Bennett & Co. into the business of M. & J. Krause, would have written them a letter without hinting at the manner in which he became their agent, or referring to the information they might have received on this subject from Bennett & Co. The proof of any previous letter, or connexion, might diminish, or, perhaps, destroy the impression this letter is calculated to make, but, at present, it has much the appearance of being prepared for the purpose of keeping Bennett & Co. out of view. Such studious concealment always conduces to the opinion, that the person thus kept out of view, is more than a mere agent.

The concealment of the canister, in the piece of timber, cannot, I admit, give to the papers a meaning which their words would not justify. But it shows that the captain, who was much trusted by Bennett & Co., and had, most probably, been long employed by them, believed that these papers contained something which he ought to conceal; what could this be, but the agency of Bennett & Co.? And why should he conceal that, if they were no more than agents? If the letters appeared to be all written with the same view; if Bennett & Co. appeared throughout, as the avowed agents of M. & J. Krause, there would be nothing extraordinary, or suspicious, in the transaction; and there could be no fair reason for attempting to conceal this agency. It would seem as if the original design was to keep them entirely out of view, and the agency was kept in reserve, as the *dernier resort*, if the part they had taken should be discovered. My present impression is, that if the original purchase of the Fortuna was not made by Krause, for Bennett & Co., she was transferred to them before the commencement of this voyage, and that they are to be considered as the owners of the ship, and of that part of the cargo which is claimed for M. & J. Krause.

There is no proof that Muhlenbruck is domiciliated in England, and his property would be restored if he stood in court unimpeached. But he is so deeply concerned in this whole fraud, if it be one, that he must suffer the consequences of fraud. The property claimed by him, is, on that account, condemned also. This cause operates equally against the claim of the captain.

There is, however, a small claim of a Swedish captain, which is not infected with this general contamination, and which, therefore, ought to be restored.

The conduct of the privateer, though justly reprehensible, cannot be punished by this Court in the manner required by the counsel for the complainants.[10] If their case depended, in any degree, on the testimony of the sailors who were taken out of the ship, and might be tampered with, that testimony might be disregarded. Any circumstance in the cause, which could be accounted for by the removal of the persons who ought to have remained in the prize, might be leniently considered; but it is apparent, that the cause rests on testimony in no degree affected by these circumstances, and that the question before the court, appeals, not to its discretion, but to its judgment.

The sentence of the district court is affirmed, with costs, except as to the claim made for Captain Steinmeitz, a Swede, with respect to which, it is reversed, and restitution ordered.

This case might be very much altered by a claim made by M. Krause, in person, or by affidavit, for the vessel, and by M. & J. Krause, for the cargo, by the exhibition of original letters, showing the ownership of the Fortuna, and the plan of this voyage; by the exhibition of letters, showing that Muhlenbruck's appointment was communicated to the house at Riga; by the letter of instruction from Bennett & Co. to Muhlenbruck, showing that he was to act for M. & J. Krause; and by any letter from Muhlenbruck to Krause, communicating his situation to them. I do not suspend the cause, to give time for the production of these papers, because they ought now to be ready; but if an appeal should be prayed, I will make an order for further proof, leaving it to the supreme court, to decide on its admissibility.[11]

Printed, John W. Brockenbrough, *Reports of Cases Decided by the Honourable John Marshall . . .* , I (Philadelphia, 1837), 302–14.

1. The appellate record of this case that was subsequently filed in the Supreme Court contains all the pleadings, testimony, and exhibits presented at the district court trial in Aug. 1814. In addition to his claim and answer, Henry Behrens's testimony consisted of his answers to interrogatories taken by commissioners in admiralty on 9 and 18 Aug. 1814 (The Fortuna: Krause et al., Claimants, App. Cas. No. 764).

2. These facts are based on the testimony of Stephen H. Fling, prize master of the *Roger*, taken on 7 July and 4 Aug. 1814.

3. This letter is marked "265 A." Fling stated that he had collected the *Fortuna*'s papers at three different times. The last parcel contained the concealed papers. Fling noted that he marked these concealed papers with the numbers 265 to 316 with the addition of the letter A. Brockenbrough and Wheaton published the letter in full in their reports (1 Brock. 303–4n; 3 Wheat. 239n).

4. This was actually exhibit "No. 2 B." The figures £202 2s. 10d. and £97 17s. 2d. should be £262 2s. 10d and £37 17s. 2d.

5. The contract of 12 Aug. 1813 is marked "287 A" (printed in 1 Brock. 307n and in 3 Wheat. 237n).

6. The letter of 24 Mar. 1814 is marked "266 A" (printed in 1 Brock. 309–10n and in 3 Wheat. 241–43n [misdated 1815]).

7. Bennett & Co. to Lorent & Steinmetz, 19 Nov. 1813, marked "285 A."

8. Muhlenbruck to Behrens, 24 Mar. 1814, marked "269 A."

9. Muhlenbruck to M. & J. Krause, 24 Mar. 1814, marked "26" (printed in 1 Brock. 312n and in 3 Wheat. 245n).

10. The claimants complained that Captain Behrens and most of the crew of the *Fortuna* were taken from their ship at the time of capture and placed on board the *Roger* until their arrival in Wilmington in Aug. 1814. Such conduct, it was alleged, was contrary to the president's instructions concerning privateers. See the arguments of counsel presented to the Supreme Court in 1817 (2 Wheat. 164–65, 167). For a copy of the instructions, see 2 Wheat., app., 80–81.

11. The claimants appealed to the Supreme Court, where the case was argued at the

1817 term and ordered for further proof. The Court affirmed the circuit court's decree at the 1818 term, Justice William Johnson delivering the opinion (2 Wheat. 161; 3 Wheat. 236).

To Richard Peters

Dear Sir   Richmond July 21st. 1815

In democracies, which all the world confesses to be the most perfect work of political wisdom, equality is the pivot on which the grand machine turns, & equality demands that he who has a surplus of any thing in general demand should parcel it out among his needy fellow citizens. It is therefore not only reasonable & just, but essential to the vital principles of our excellent institutions that celebrity in any thing especially in that which interests the community, should be burthened with the tax of communicating to all who hunt after knowlege, its superabundant stores. Consequently you cannot as a good patriot, be dissatisfied if every person anxious for instruction in the great & useful science of agriculture should be desirous of availing himself of the opportunity given by an occasional visit to Philadelphia, to draw upon your vast stock, & thus enable himself to show away to advantage among the small folks he will on his return find in his own neighborhood eager to receive the lessons he will retail to them.

I hope I have now proved as plainly as a lawyer or rather a politician generally proves a proposition that a visit from & a conversation with every inquisitive traveller is entirely a thing of course, which belongs to your agricultural character & for which your mind is undoubtedly prepared. After this I need make no apology for the liberty I take in introducing to you my friend & neighbor Doctor Adams who is a sensible honorable man & one of our most successful farmers—especially in the cultivation of the grasses.[1] I do this too in the confidence that you will yourself feel some satisfaction in hearing from him something of the practice of this part of the antient dominion. With great & sincere esteem I am dear Sir, Your Obedt

J MARSHALL

ALS, Peters Papers, PHi. Addressed to Peters in Philadelphia and marked "Hond by Doctor Adams" (see n. 1). Endorsed by Peters.

1. Dr. John Adams (1772–1825), a Richmond physician who later served as mayor of the city. His sister, Alice Adams, was the first wife of William Marshall (*Richmond Portraits in an Exhibition of Makers of Richmond, 1737–1860* [Richmond, Va., 1949], 34; Paxton, *Marshall Family*, 53).

To Richard Peters

My dear Sir   Richmond Oct. 12th. 1815

On my return from a tour into the country to visit a plantation productive only of expence & vexation I was gratified by receiving your letter of the 4th. inst.[1] Doctor Adams regretted much his not seeing you for half an hour, on many accounts, but more especially on account of losing a conversation on fioren grass from which he had anticipated pleasure & instruction. His disappointment was occasioned by the failure of more than one who had promised to accompany him to your farm previous to the session of your court.

On the question you propound I shall very freely communicate what occurs to my mind although I have no claims or pretensions to that *redundance* of knowledge on the subject which overflows its banks to the improvement of every thing around.

The setting aside of verdicts is very much within the discretion of the Judge who tries the cause. It must be a very strong case indeed in which his opinion given the one way or the other could be erroneous. Yet a man would wish to exercise this discretion soundly & in conformity with general usage. For a slight irregularity in the party in whose favor a verdict was found I should be disposed to set it aside, because it is important to justice that every attempt of the kind should be prevented, & the invariable rule to set aside a verdict in all such cases, whether it be right or wrong, is perhaps the only means of prevention in the power of the Judge. But for irregularities in the conduct of a juror in which the party does not participate, the necessity of observing this rule is not so obvious. The repetition of the practice may be prevented by a fine which is the appropriate punishment for the offence, & which reaches the guilty without touching the innocent.

There are I think considerable objections to setting aside a verdict where it conforms to the right of the cause. To say nothing of *precious* time consumed in a second trial of the same case, (time which might be so pleasantly employed on the farm) the justice of the case is committed to some hazard by being carried before another jury; &, in any event, a party who has committed no fault, is subjected to costs & delay. It can be of no real utility, if on principle it can be avoided, to send a cause to a new jury where a different verdict would not be received, or if received, would not be as acceptable as that already in possession of the court. I shall terminate these *wise* reflections by observing that if I approved the verdict I would let it stand; if I did not, although my disapprobation might not be sufficient to set it aside had all been perfectly *enregle*, I would avail myself of the irregularity to award a new trial. With much esteem I am dear Sir, Your Obedt

                                                        J MARSHALL

ALS, Peters Papers, PHi. Addressed to Peters in Philadelphia; postmark too faint to read. Endorsed by Peters "Opinion as to setting/aside Verdicts for/Misconduct of/Jurors —or Parties."

1. Letter not found.

To [William H. Crawford?]

Richmond October 20th. 1815[1]
Mr. James K. Duke a Nephew of mine about sixteen or seventeen years of age, whose education has not been neglected, is desirous of entering the military Academy at West Point, & has requested me to name him to you as a candidate for admittance into that institution.[2] I trust you will excuse the liberty I take in naming him to you & beleive to be with much respect, Your obedt. Servt.

J MARSHALL

ALS, RG 94, DNA. Endorsed by clerk.

1. The addressee was apparently Secretary of War William H. Crawford.
2. James K. Duke (1799–1863), son of Charlotte Marshall Duke (1777–1817) and Dr. Basil Duke (1766–1828) of Washington County, Ky. Duke either was not appointed or did not accept his commission. Instead, he attended Yale, graduating in 1818. He was admitted to the bar in 1821 but took up farming in Georgetown, Ky., after his marriage in 1822 (Paxton, *Marshall Family*, 76–77, 179; *Catalogus Collegii Yalensis* [New Haven, Conn., 1847], 55; *Obituary Record of Graduates of Yale College Deceased from July, 1859, to July, 1870* [New Haven, Conn., 1870], 372).

Bond v. Ross
Opinion
U.S. Circuit Court, Virginia, 2 December 1815

The parties to this suit were creditors of David Ross, a wealthy merchant and owner of extensive properties, including the Oxford Iron Works near Lynchburg. Phineas Bond, British consul at Philadelphia, was nominal plaintiff, acting on behalf of the creditors of a British subject. The defendants, besides Ross, were creditors to whom Ross in 1807 had mortgaged some two hundred slaves employed at the ironworks, along with other property. The case arose directly from an earlier suit between Bond and Ross in the federal court, which in 1804 decreed Ross to pay $181,000. On Ross's default of payments under this decree, Bond sued out execution against the slaves and property covered by the mortgage deed. A sale under this execution was prevented, however, by William Mewburn, a party to the mortgage. In December 1810 Bond filed a bill in chancery to set aside the mortgage deed as not having been recorded in the proper court. The defendants filed their answers in 1811, and Marshall gave his opinion on the validity of the deed on 2 December 1815 (*PJM*, VI, 411–20; deed of trust [copy], 21 Oct. 1807; bill in chancery, 1 Dec. 1810; answer of William Mewburn, 22 Nov. 1811, Bond v. Ross, U.S. Cir. Ct., Va., Ended Cases [Unrestored], 1834, Vi; U.S. Cir. Ct., Va., Ord. Bk. VIII, 368; IX, 1, 424–25).

Bond

v

Mewburne & al

¶1   This case depends on the construction of the act of assembly for regulating conveyances which passed in the year 1792.[1]

¶2   It is with much repugnance that this court proceeds to decide any cause dependent on a statute of the state which is extremely vague in its expression, & the construction of which does not appear to have been fully settled by the state tribunals. If the means of avoiding it were perceived those means would be gladly embraced. But were this cause to be postponed until the statute on which it depends should be expounded by the judiciary of Virginia the postponement might be indefinite, as it is not understood that the question is before any of the courts of the state. It is therefore the duty of this court to proceed.[2]

¶3   The first section of the act relates exclusively to lands & declares the conveyance to be void as to subsequent purchasers not having notice thereof & as to all creditors unless it shall be recorded in the General court or court of the district county or corporation in which the lands ly.

¶4   The 2d. sec. relates exclusively to covenants or agreements made in consideration of marriage, & declares that they shall not be valid against a subsequent purchaser without notice or against any creditor unless recorded, if land be charged in the General court or Court of the district county or corporation in which the land lies; or if personal estate only be charged in the court of the district county or corporation in which the party bound by such covenant or agreement resides.

¶5   The 4th. Section relates to conveyances generally & declares all deeds of trust & Mortgages whatsoever to be void as to all creditors & subsequent purchasers unless they shall be proved & recorded according to the directions of the act.

¶6   This section governs the case & the question to be determined is in what court a mortgage of personal property alone is to be recorded.[3] The words of the act are that such mortgage shall be void unless recorded according to the directions prescribing the court in which it is to be recorded. The directions given respect only those conveyances which comprehend lands, or those which are made in consideration of marriage.

In the multiplicity of difficulties growing out of this strange negligence in the legislature, it is not surprising that it should be doubted whether a mortgage containing personalties only may not be recorded in any court whatever. Such a deed being declared to be void unless recorded according to directions which the law does not give, would furnish arguments of almost equal plausibility for the opinion that there was no restriction whatever on the court in which it might be recorded, & for the opinion that it could not be recorded in any court but must be forever void as to creditors & subsequent purchasers without notice. ¶7

Since however the obvious intention of the act is to preserve the validity of a mortgage of a personal thing, & at the same time to prescribe some court in which it may be recorded so as to give notice to the world that the property is incumbered, the court is of opinion that the law must if possible be so construed as to effect this intention. It must be effected too with the least possible violation to the words of the legislature. ¶8

As neither the first nor second section of the act gives directions respecting the court in which a deed mortgaging personalties only shall be recorded, & as the 4th. Section must be understood to refer to those section⟨s⟩ only, it becomes necessary to apply their provisions to such deed, in such manner as to effect in the most rational & convenient way the intention of the law. ¶9

It has been contended that as in a case where personal property is conveyed with real property, the court of the county in which the land lies is that in which the deed must be recorded, it would be reasonable to require that the county in which the personal property resides or is commonly found should furnish the court in which a deed for such property would be looked for. ¶10

For a moment I was struck with this argument which seemed to derive weight from the consideration that had the Oxford iron works themselves been included in this mortgage, it ought to have been recorded in the court for the county of Campbell, & a subsequent purchaser or creditor asserting a claim to the slaves in question would have been bound by such lien upon them recorded in that court. Since the slaves in question if mortgaged together with the lands they worked would have passed by a deed recorded in Campbell it seemed reasonable that creditors should search the records of that court for any incumbrance on them. ¶11

But a very slight examination was sufficient to show the fallacy of this idea. If instead of the Oxford iron works an inconsiderable tract of land in the most remote part of the state had been included in the mortgage the law requires that the deed should be recorded in that county. It is then impossible to argue from the court in which a deed for personalties when mixed with land is to be recorded, to the court in which a ¶12 deed for personalties alone must be recorded. The argument in favor of regulating the place of recording the deed by the locality of the personal thing it may convey, if to be maintained, must rest on other ground.

¶13 The argument urged by the counsel for the defendent on the reasonableness of considering the residence of the property mortgaged as giving the place in which the deed shall be recorded appears to me to be very much weakened by the consideration that in contemplation of law personal property has no locality, & that in fact it has none that is permanent.

¶14 To pass over property the tracing of which would be much more difficult, & to confine my observation to slaves alone, where should a mortgage on slaves usually hired out be recorded? Where if the slave be hired sometimes in one county, sometimes in another? If it be said that in such case the domicil of the master gives locality to the slave, the answer is that if this be true all the locality which a slave can legally have is derived not from his own casual residence, but from the residence of his master on whose will the place he may at any time occupy must entirely depend. The slave shifted according to the caprice of the master from plantation to plantation, or hired sometimes in one county & sometimes in another, has no place of residence sufficiently certain & fixed to furnish a safe guide for the court in which a lien upon him should be recorded. In contemplation of law therefore & in fact slaves & every personal chattel must be considered as transitory; & being fixed to no place they adhere to the person of the owner.

¶15 The 2d. sec. of the act directs the court in which a covenant or agreement in consideration of marriage containing personal estate only shall be recorded. This is to be in the court of the district county or corporation in which the party resides.

¶16 This section it has been already said is not in its terms applicable to conveyances not made in consideration of marriage. But no reason is perceived for directing a lien of personal property remaining in possession of the grantor to be recorded in one court if it be made in consideration of marriage & in a different court if it be made to secure the payment of money. The declaration that deeds of personal property made in consideration of marriage should be recorded in the court of the District county or corporation in which the grantor resides would certainly indicate the opinion of the legislature to be that a lien on the same property made on any other consideration should be recorded in the same court. In the one case & in the other the object of the record is to give notice to the world that the lien exists, & it would seem reasonable that in each case the same notice should be given.

¶17 An argument entitled to great respect has been urged against this construction. It has been said that the legislature certainly intended to provide for every case, & that the law ought to be so construed as to reach every case. That under this construction there would be no court in which a deed for personal property given by a non resident of the state could be recorded.

This objection to the construction contended for by the plf. is certainly not a light one. ¶18

The 5th. Sec. of the act provides that deeds executed by a non resident of the State may be acknowleged or proved at his place of residence in a manner prescribed by that section & recorded in the proper court. This proves that deeds executed by non residents were in contemplation of the legislature & that such deeds were to be recorded somewhere. It is true the section in terms applies only to deeds conveying land, but there would be nothing extraordinary in extending it by construction to chattels also. ¶19

If this act had been drawn in such explicit terms as to provide plainly in other instances for the cases it contemplates the difficulty respecting a mortgage for a personal chattel executed by a nonresident would induce the court to struggle for a construction which would substitute some other place than the residence of the Grantor as that which should designate the court in which the deed should be recorded. But this law is drawn in several of its enacting clauses in such terms as to leave it impracticable to effect the obvious intention without aiding the words. ¶20

I very much incline to the opinion that a deed for personal chattels executed by a non resident would be valid if recorded in the general court. ¶21

It appears to be the general policy of the law to make the general court a place in which all incumbrances on property may be found. For this reason a memorial of the deeds recorded in every county or district is to be transmitted annually to that court. It is also a court of record which is common to the whole state. Its jurisdiction in this respect is universal. It is empowered to receive probat of all deeds whatever. Any deed comprehending personalties & realties may be recorded in that court. It is impossible to find a motive for excluding a deed mortgaging a personal chattel without land. The exclusion cannot have been intended. If in such a case a construction which would give validity to a deed recorded in that court can be supported, it ought to be supported. ¶22

The words are no covenant &c shall be good unless acknowleged &c, if lands be charged, before the general court or the court of that district or county in which the land or part thereof lieth, or if personal estate only be settled &c before the court of that district county city or corporation in which the party shall dwell. ¶23

The mind of the legislature was directed to the designation of the particular court among those whose powers were limited, in which the deeds described might be recorded, & therefore it might not be deemed necessary after naming the general court in the first instance to repeat ¶24 that court in the second. The word General court may be understood & the act construed as if it had been again inserted.

¶25   There are certainly few cases in which this freedom of construction can be justified. If any act will justify it, it is the act for regulating conveyances.

¶26   Altho I at present rather incline to construe the act independent of precedent so as to consider it as requiring that a deed of mortgage for personal estate only must be recorded in the General court or court of the district county or corporation in which the grantor resides I am not sure that I should give this opinion were it not supported by the case of Claiborne v Hill.[4] That case does not decide that a deed of mortgage for slaves recorded in the county where the slaves happen corporeally to reside is void, but it decides that such a deed recorded in the county where the grantor resides, altho the slaves be at the time on a plantation in a different county is good. Either then such deed may be recorded indifferently in the one county or the other, or it can be recorded only in the General court or court of that district county or corporation in which the grantor resides. I can perceive nothing in the act which indicates an intention to allow this alternative, & the policy of the law does not appear to require or admit of it. The decision of the court then on the authority of this case is that this deed is not recorded in the proper county.[5]

AD, Marshall Judicial Opinions, PPAmP; printed, John W. Brockenbrough, *Reports of Cases Decided by the Honourable John Marshall . . .* , I (Philadelphia, 1837), 317–24. For JM's deletions and interlineations, see Textual Notes below.

1. Shepherd, *Statutes*, I, 84.

2. According to sec. 34 of the Judiciary Act of 1789, state laws, "except where the constitution, treaties or statutes of the United States shall otherwise require or provide," were to be the rules of decision in the federal courts (*U.S. Statutes at Large*, I, 92). The Supreme Court interpreted this section to embrace state judicial constructions of state laws. See McKeen v. Delancy's Lessee, 5 Cranch 22 (1809); Polk's Lessee v. Wendell, 9 Cranch 87 (1815).

3. The mortgage deed had been recorded in the court of Campbell County, where the Oxford Iron Works lay. Ross, however, resided in Richmond. The plaintiff contended that the deed should have been recorded either in the General Court or some local court where Ross lived (bill in chancery, 1 Dec. 1810; deed of trust [copy], 21 Oct. 1807, Bond v. Ross).

4. JM had argued this case in the Virginia Court of Appeals in 1793 (1 Wash. 177; *PJM*, V, 501–7).

5. In addition to setting aside the 1807 mortgage deed and upholding the plaintiff's execution upon the property conveyed by the deed, JM's formal interlocutory decree reserved another point raised in the pleadings for future decision. The court also ordered the sale of the slaves and other property, the proceeds of which were to pay off some of the creditors and the remainder of the money to be deposited in the bank subject to the court's future order. This case remained on the court docket until 1834 (U.S. Cir. Ct., Va., Ord. Bk. IX, 424–25; XII, 48–50; U.S. Cir. Ct., Va., Index to Ended Cases, 1790–1860, Vi).

Textual Notes

Title	~~Ross~~ ↑Bond↓ v [erasure] ↑Mewburne↓ & al
¶ 2 l. 6	postponed ~~for~~ until
l. 7	of ~~the State~~ ↑Virginia↓ the postponement might ~~perhaps~~ be
¶ 3 l. 1	first [erasure] ↑section↓ of
l. 2	void ~~unless it be rec~~ as
¶ 4 l. 7	such ~~gover~~ covenant
¶ 5 ll. 1–2	Section ↑relates to conveyances generally &↓ declares all ~~conveyances~~ ↑deeds of trust & Mortgages↓ whatsoever
l. 2	to ~~ere~~ ↑all↓ creditors
¶ 6 l. 1	determined ~~in~~ ↑is↓ in
¶ 7 ll. 2–3	legislature, ~~&~~ ↑it↓ ~~may well occur as a~~ ↑is not surprising that it should be↓ doubted ~~whether the record of~~ ↑whether↓ a
l. 4	whatever. ~~The~~ Such
¶ 8 ll. 1–2	to ~~give~~ ↑preserve the↓ validity ~~to the~~ ↑of a↓ mortgage
l. 2	& ↑at the same time↓ to
l. 6	be ~~affected~~ ↑effected↓ too
¶ 9 l. 3	the [erasure] ↑4th.↓ Section
l. 4	section⟨s⟩ ~~for the court in which such deed must be recorded,~~ ↑only,↓ it becomes necessary to apply ~~the~~ ↑their↓ provisions ~~of those sections~~ to
¶10 l. 2	court ↑of the county↓ in
l. 4	the ~~court ↑of the↓~~ ↑county↓ in
l. 5	should ~~be the~~ furnish
l. 6	property ~~shoul~~ would
¶11 l. 6	by ~~the~~ ↑such↓ lien
¶12 ll. 5–6	which ↑a deed for↓ personalties
ll. 7–10	~~The 2d. section gives a cas~~ ↑The argument in favor of regulating the place of recording the deed by the locality of the personal thing it may convey, if to be maintained, must rest on other ground.↓
¶13 l. 4	be ~~cont~~ ↑very↓ much
¶14 l. 6	that ↑if this be true↓ all
ll. 7–8	but ~~of~~ ↑from↓ the residence of ~~t~~ ↑his↓ master
l. 8	may ↑at any time↓ occupy
l. 10	one ~~place~~ ↑county↓ &
l. 11	no ~~cert~~ place
l. 12	the ~~place~~ ↑court↓ in
ll. 14–15	& ↑being↓ fixed
¶15 l. 1	the ~~manner~~ ↑court↓ in
l. 3	the ↑district↓ county
¶16 l. 3	of ~~one~~ personal property ~~which~~ remaining
l. 6	of [erasure] ↑money.↓ The
l. 11	& ↑in↓ the
ll. 12–13	would ↑seem↓ reasonable
¶17 l. 5	which ~~t~~ ↑a↓ deed
¶19 l. 1	provides [erasure] ↑that↓ deeds

l. 2	the ~~es~~ State
ll. 3–4	section ↑& recorded in the proper court. ↓ This
l. 4	by ~~Stat~~ non
l. 5	& ~~conseq~~ that
ll. 7–8	extending ~~the~~ ↑it by↓ construction
¶20 ll. 1–2	provide ↑plainly↓ in
l. 3	chattel ↑executed by a nonresident↓ would
l. 5	that ~~in~~ which
l. 7	its ~~enating~~ ↑enacting↓ clauses
l. 8	the ↑obvious↓ intention
¶22 l. 4	court. ~~Th~~ It
l. 11	deed ~~which must be~~ recorded
l. 11	supported. ~~The words~~
¶24 l. 2	particular ↑court↓ among
ll. 3–4	therefore ~~after having mentioned~~ ↑it might not be deemed necessary after naming↓ the
¶26 l. 1 beg.	~~It is the opinion of the court~~ Altho
ll. 6–7	deed ↑of mortgage for slaves↓ recorded
ll. 7–8	happen ↑corporeally↓ to
l. 12	the ~~general~~ ↑General↓ court

Marshall and the Fairfax Litigation:
From the Compromise of 1796 to *Martin* v. *Hunter's Lessee*

EDITORIAL NOTE

The 1816 docket of the Supreme Court contained the notable constitutional case of *Martin* v. *Hunter's Lessee*, culminating more than two decades of litigation in the state courts of Virginia and in the U.S. Supreme Court. What began in 1791 as an ejectment to try title to the former Fairfax estate in the Northern Neck of Virginia had been transformed into a contest between the federal high court and the Virginia Supreme Court of Appeals. Chief Justice Marshall's role in *Martin* and its immediate predecessor, *Fairfax's Devisee* v. *Hunter's Lessee* (1813), was that of a private litigant, not official spokesman for the Court. As one of the purchasers of the Fairfax estate, Marshall had long been closely associated with efforts to establish clear legal title to this immense and valuable property.[1]

A quarter century after bringing an ejectment against Denny Martin Fairfax in the state district court at Winchester, David Hunter was still a party of record as the case reached its climax in the Supreme Court. A large-scale investor in Northern Neck lands since the 1780s, Hunter based his title on grants obtained from the commonwealth—in this instance a 1789 patent for a tract in Shenandoah County. His name was linked with the names of Fairfax and Marshall in a number of lawsuits contesting land titles.[2] The other party of record was now General Philip Martin, brother and heir at law of the late Denny Fairfax, who had died in 1800. A British subject, Martin was scarcely more than a nominal party to this litigation, which was directed entirely through his agents in Virginia, the brothers John and James M. Marshall. James Marshall claimed the land in Hunter's patent on the basis of a deed from Denny Fairfax in 1797. He in turn sold this land long before the case came to the Supreme Court.

For fifteen years following the death in 1781 of Thomas, sixth Lord Fairfax, the legal status of the Northern Neck lands remained ambiguous. Lord Fairfax, a resident and citizen of Virginia at the time of his death, had devised his interest in the remaining vacant lands as well as his private estates to his nephew Denny Martin, a British subject who subsequently adopted the Fairfax name as required by the devise. The commonwealth asserted its title to the Northern Neck on the common law principle that an alien was incapable of holding lands in the commonwealth; that the property devised was accordingly escheatable to the state; that various acts of the Virginia General Assembly concerning the Northern Neck were equivalent to escheat proceedings and had perfected the state's title to the lands; that the peace treaty of 1783 between the United States and Great Britain, which stipulated that there should be no future confiscation of estates belonging to British subjects, did not apply to the ordinary laws of escheat by reason of alienage; and that, even if the treaty did apply, title had vested in the commonwealth before the treaty's ratification. The Fairfax interest combated this assertion by contending that if the Northern Neck lands were escheatable, the commonwealth could acquire title only by a formal judicial proceeding known as an inquest of office or by an explicit legislative act; that no title had thereby vested prior to 1783; and that the peace treaty accordingly protected Denny Martin Fairfax's estate from any future confiscation whatever, including proceedings by escheat.

From the outset Marshall believed that Denny Fairfax's title to the Northern Neck was good at law and fully protected by the treaty of 1783. This belief induced him to join with his brother and others in purchasing the Fairfax "manors," those lands within the proprietary that Lord Fairfax had appropriated for himself and his family. In 1793 the Marshall syndicate contracted to buy the two principal manors, Leeds and South Branch, for twenty thousand pounds sterling. Purchase of South Branch was completed in 1797; final payment on Leeds did not occur until 1806. During the 1790s Marshall enjoyed some success in obtaining judicial recognition of the Fairfax title in both the state and federal courts. On the other hand, the commonwealth had obtained judgments on escheat proceedings against the manor lands. The upshot of these inconclusive legal maneuvers was a compromise proposed by Marshall, which the Virginia legislature enacted into law in December 1796. According to the terms of the compromise, the Marshalls relinquished the Fairfax claim to those lands in the Northern Neck that were "waste and unappropriated" at the time of Lord Fairfax's death, and the commonwealth relinquished its claim to lands "specifically appropriated" by Lord Fairfax "to his own use by deed or actual survey."[3]

By the compromise of 1796 the Marshalls gained what they most wanted: clear title in Denny Martin Fairfax to the manor lands. Fairfax could now sell and they could purchase South Branch and Leeds secure in the knowledge that this transaction would meet with no legal challenge. Once the compromise was enacted into law, a definitive Supreme Court ruling upholding the Fairfax title was no longer of crucial importance to Marshall. He might well have preferred to have his title founded on a judicial pronouncement rather than on a legislative enactment, but there is no indication that he was concerned about a possible repeal of the 1796 agreement. In this unlikely event the vested rights acquired under that act would be protected by the contract clause of the Constitution. Yet Marshall had other reasons for continuing to believe that a Supreme Court opinion affirming the Fairfax title on the basis of the peace treaty of 1783 would be desirable.

The compromise was intended to put an end to pending legal cases and forestall future disputes. In this regard, the act was not entirely successful. The commonwealth dropped its attempt to escheat the manor lands, and Hunter did not further prosecute the appeal of a federal court judgment against him. At the same time, however, Hunter's appeal of the Winchester District Court judgment remained on the docket for another fourteen years. After the district court had ruled in favor of the Fairfax title in April 1794, Hunter appealed to the Court of Appeals, where the case was argued in May 1796. It was reargued in October 1809 and finally decided in April 1810, the court reversing the Winchester judgment and confirming Hunter's claim to the land. Why did this appeal remain alive after the compromise? One of the agreed facts in the Winchester case was that the disputed land fell within that part of the Northern Neck designated as waste and ungranted. The compromise conceded title to the waste and ungranted lands to the commonwealth and to those (like Hunter) claiming under patents from the state. Why did not the Court of Appeals, as it did in the case of the escheat judgments against the Marshalls, immediately reverse the Winchester judgment and award the land to Hunter on the basis of the compromise?

To answer this question it is necessary to examine certain features of the compromise of 1796 that have been overlooked or not fully understood in previous accounts of the complex Fairfax litigation.[4] The compromise was carried into effect by two deeds. In the first, dated 30 August 1797, Denny Fairfax conveyed to James M. Marshall his residuary estate in the Northern Neck, excepting Leeds Manor (already under contract to be sold to the Marshalls), quitrents, and one small tract of one hundred acres. The second, dated 10 October 1798 and signed by James M. Marshall and his wife, Hester Marshall, conveyed the waste and ungranted lands to the commonwealth. This transaction was not simply a transfer of title to the unappropriated lands from Fairfax to the commonwealth. In fact, the net result of these two deeds was that James Marshall, on behalf of the syndicate, acquired the remaining Fairfax manor lands, those Lord Fairfax had appropriated for himself "by deed or actual survey." The deed from Denny Fairfax to James Marshall was given for a consideration of £2,625, undoubtedly the price agreed upon for the additional manor lands. By a subsequent deed of partition, dated 24 June 1799, the Marshall brothers—James, John, Charles, and William—and their brother-in-law Rawleigh Colston divided up these lands into four parts.[5] Nearly all of the Marshalls' litigation occurring after the compromise of 1796, including the appeal of Hunter's case, arose from disputes concerning the lands acquired by the deed of August 1797.

The Marshalls must have already known that portions of this newly acquired real estate had previously been granted out by the commonwealth as unappropriated lands to various individuals. Beginning in 1798, they brought suits against holders under the commonwealth whose patents conflicted with their purchase. In each of these cases they contended that the lands in question had been reserved by Lord Fairfax for his personal use and were not grantable by the state. The reserved, or appropriated, lands fell into two categories, those set aside "by deed" and those set aside "by actual survey." Much the greater part of the Marshalls' claim under the Fairfax title, including the principal manors of South Branch and Leeds, belonged to the former category. The boundaries of these tracts were well established by the public records in the state land office and were largely exempt from legal challenge.

Most of the lands sold by Denny Fairfax in 1797 had been appropriated by survey rather than by deed of conveyance. Although confident that their title was good under the compromise and the deed from Denny Fairfax, the Marshalls encountered difficulties in the state courts in proving that a given tract belonged to them on the basis of a survey made on behalf of Lord Fairfax. In some cases the best proof they could offer of a survey was a private memorandum book of the proprietor or of one of his surveyors. Their opponents contended that the only admissible evidence of an appropriation to Lord Fairfax's use was the survey books formerly kept in the proprietor's office and subsequently transferred to the state land office. The compromise, they insisted, was intended to embrace only those surveys that were duly recorded in land office books. The courts were inclined to support this narrow construction of the compromise, as shown by the dismissal of bills in chancery brought by the Marshalls against Abraham Brewbaker and others, David Hunter and Philip Pendleton, and William Janney.[6] In one instance the Court of Appeals did uphold James Marshall's right under the compromise to rents on lots in the town of Winchester. This case, *Marshall* v. *Conrad*, produced a notable dissent from Judge Spencer Roane, whose reference to the Marshalls' "rapacity" reflected his inveterate hostility to their claims under the Fairfax title.[7]

Despite this victory, Marshall was not sanguine that Virginia courts would fully vindicate the Fairfax purchasers' rights under the 1796 compromise. "I begin to fear the event of every suit however clear the merits may be in my estimation," he confided to his brother. Notwithstanding the Conrad decision, James Marshall faced the prospect of continued costly litigation to collect rents from the Winchester townspeople. "If you get once more into the court of appeals your case will I fear be desperate," wrote the chief justice. Referring to a ruling of the Winchester District Court judge in another of his brother's suits, Marshall commented: "I am confident that it is absolutely impossible to make your present case one which can be decided in your favor by the person who has given the opinion which has been rendered." As for his own problems with tenants who refused to pay rent, Marshall concluded he would "have to try in the federal court the validity of our title under the treaty for I am sure that clear as my title is under the compromise the state courts will decide against me."[8]

Marshall evidently believed a federal court decision, preferably by the Supreme Court, declaring the Fairfax title valid under the treaty of 1783 would strengthen the purchasers' cases in the state courts. He had always maintained that this title derived not from the compromise but from the treaty. Under this assumption, the purchasers had voluntarily relinquished title to the unappropriated Northern Neck lands. Having asserted its own title to the Northern

Neck, however, the commonwealth viewed the compromise as its voluntary relinquishment of title to the manor lands. The state courts were accordingly disposed to construe the act of 1796 as if the commonwealth (and those claiming under it) retained every right not explicitly surrendered. Although the Marshalls believed their rights were secure—or should have been secure—under the compromise, a Supreme Court decision might compel the state courts to interpret the compromise more liberally in their favor, placing the burden of proof on claimants under the commonwealth to show a valid title. The Supreme Court's exposition of the treaty would be binding on the state courts, said Marshall, even if the federal tribunal did not possess appellate jurisdiction over them. "The principle is," he explained, "that the courts of every government are the proper tribunals for construing the legislative acts of that government. Upon this principle the Supreme court of the United States, independent of its appellate jurisdiction, is the proper tribunal for construing the laws & treaties of the United States; and the construction of that court ought to be received every where as the right construction." Consequently, if that court upheld the Fairfax title on the basis of the 1783 treaty, the "effect of the principle" was that "we hold not under the compromise but under the treaty, and the question is what does the compromise take from us?"[9]

Among the lands conveyed by Denny Fairfax in the 1797 deed was a tract of 1,000 acres lying on Cedar Creek in northern Shenandoah County, near Strasburg. In the subsequent partition among the syndicate this tract had been allotted to James Marshall. David Hunter's 1789 patent from the commonwealth described a tract containing 739 acres also lying on Cedar Creek. That Hunter's grant fell within the larger tract partitioned to James Marshall can be inferred from this coincidence and is confirmed by the fragment of an argument presented below. Hunter paid taxes on his 739 acres from 1790 through 1805. Thereafter, neither land tax records nor deed books contain any mention of his name in connection with this property, though he continued to be a party to the suit. There is no indication that either Hunter or tenants holding under him ever occupied this tract. As for James Marshall, deed books disclose that he proceeded to sell off the Cedar Creek survey lands soon after acquiring them from Denny Fairfax.[10]

The legal difficulty facing the Marshalls was that in 1793, four years before Denny Fairfax conveyed his residuary estate to James Marshall, the lawyers for Hunter and Fairfax had mutually agreed to a statement of "facts," one of which stated that Hunter's patent embraced lands that were waste and ungranted. This fact was apparently placed on the record to show that the issuing of the patent complied with the 1785 act by which the commonwealth assumed the right to grant the unappropriated lands of the Northern Neck.[11] Neither of the Marshalls was directly concerned with the case at this time, though they were closely associated with Charles Lee, who represented Fairfax in the Winchester proceedings. At the time they were probably unaware that Hunter's patent overlapped with the Cedar Creek survey. In any event, the distinction between granted and ungranted lands was unimportant before the 1796 compromise. Denny Fairfax claimed the entire proprietary in fee simple, manor as well as unappropriated lands. The 1794 decision affirming his title on the basis of the facts agreed in the Winchester ejectment accordingly awarded the Shenandoah tract to Fairfax.

With the enactment of the compromise, Hunter apparently expected to have his title under the commonwealth declared to be good. If his patent truly embraced waste and ungranted lands, then the dispute was at an end, for by the terms of the compromise the purchasers of the Fairfax estate were to relinquish title to these lands to the commonwealth. Soon after the compromise Denny Fairfax deeded his residuary estate, which included the Cedar Creek survey, to James Marshall. At that time, if not before, the Marshalls must have discovered that this survey encompassed Hunter's patent. They accordingly refused to let Hunter take advantage of the compromise to defeat their title acquired through purchase of the residuary Fairfax estate. They believed the appeal of the Winchester judgment should be decided solely on the facts agreed in 1793—as if the compromise adopted three years later had never taken place. Alternatively, the parties could bring a new ejectment and agree to a new statement of facts, one that included both the compromise and facts purporting to show that the disputed land had been reserved by Lord Fairfax. "The offer to try this cause on its real merits in a new ejectment has been repeatedly made by the party claiming the Fairfax title & repeatedly rejected," wrote Marshall. "He may therefore properly say now that the compromise forms no part of this case but will appear in a new ejectment if one should be brought."[12]

Rather than become party to a new suit, Hunter apparently preferred to take his chances with the Court of Appeals, even though that court as constituted in 1796 and for some years thereafter was not likely to support his claim. After the first argument in the spring of 1796, nothing further happened until November 1803, when Hunter revived the appeal, which had abated on Denny Fairfax's death in 1800, against Philip Martin. The formalities of serving process on this new defendant, a resident of Great Britain, consumed another five years. Having attended to the procedural requirements for keeping the appeal alive, Hunter seemed content to let the case continue from term to term.

In the meantime the retirement of one judge and the death of another appeared to brighten Hunter's prospects. When the appeal was reargued in October 1809, the Court of Appeals consisted of three judges: William Fleming, Spencer Roane, and St. George Tucker. Fleming, the aged president, was the sole survivor of the three-judge majority that had decided *Marshall* v. *Conrad* in 1805. Roane, the dissenter in that case, could be counted on to rule in Hunter's favor. Tucker, elevated to the appellate bench in 1804, had decided against Hunter at the district court in 1794. Even so, the Marshalls were not entirely confident of his support. Writing in reference to the approaching argument of the Conrad case, Marshall commented that Tucker's appointment to the court had "bettered" his brother's prospects on one part of the case but that he was "a little afraid of him on some others."[13] Tucker did not sit in this case because his son, Henry St. George Tucker, was a resident of Winchester and interested in the outcome. As it happened, Tucker again disqualified himself in *Hunter* v. *Fairfax's Devisee*, "through motives of delicacy, being nearly related to a person interested." In 1806 Henry St. George Tucker had married Anne Evelina Hunter, daughter of David Hunter.[14]

Roane and Fleming, then, were the two judges who decided *Hunter* v. *Fairfax's Devisee* on 23 April 1810. Roane, as expected, upheld Hunter's claim, principally on the ground that the state, having acquired valid title to the waste

SPENCER ROANE
Oil on canvas by Cephas Thompson, ca. 1809. *Courtesy of the Supreme Court of Virginia*

and ungranted lands of the Northern Neck as a result of Denny Fairfax's alienage, was competent to issue the patent to Hunter. The peace treaty, he said, had "nothing to do with the laws of alienage," but even assuming its application to this case, he contended that the commonwealth had completed its title before the treaty was ratified. As for the compromise, Roane pointed out that it was intended to settle cases of this kind and expressed his surprise that the appellees, having already benefited greatly from that act, would not submit to its terms and give up their claim to this land.[15] Contrary to Roane, Fleming upheld the Fairfax title and said the state's grant to Hunter in 1789 "was an exercise of power, without a right." To the Marshalls' great disappointment, however, Fleming agreed with Roane that the compromise settled the matter in Hunter's favor.[16] The ground of the decision, then, was the compromise act of 1796, the only point on which both judges concurred.

After conferring with Charles Lee, Marshall decided to carry the case to the Supreme Court, personally attending to the forwarding of the record in hopes of having the appeal argued at the ensuing term. *Fairfax's Devisee* v. *Hunter's Lessee* was filed in July 1810, but lack of a quorum in 1811 postponed argument until the 1812 term.[17] Although Marshall saw the appeal as an opportunity to obtain a Supreme Court decision on all the questions relating to the Fairfax title, the case at this stage remained a live dispute over a particular parcel of land in Shenandoah County. In no sense was the appeal contrived to be a test case for determining the extent of the Supreme Court's appellate jurisdiction over the state judiciaries. That it became a landmark case in constitutional law was, so far as Marshall was concerned, an unforeseen and unintended consequence. His primary aim was to secure his brother's title to valuable acreage along a creek in the lower Shenandoah Valley. Nor were the Marshalls trying to execute a legal end run around the compromise of 1796. Taking the case to the Supreme Court did not signify an intention to lay claim to the waste and ungranted lands of the Northern Neck. The real dispute with Hunter was whether the Cedar Creek patent embraced waste and ungranted lands or was part of a larger tract that had previously been appropriated by Lord Fairfax.[18]

Marshall believed the case would also "probably form a precedent" for several long-pending caveat actions (a means of contesting land titles where no patent had issued) originally brought by Denny Fairfax against Hunter and others in 1788. At stake in these cases were titles to more than five thousand acres in Hampshire and Berkeley Counties. Like the tract contested in the principal case, the Marshalls claimed these lands as having been previously set aside for the private use of Lord Fairfax and included in the 1797 deed from Denny Fairfax to James Marshall. "The decision of the supreme court if against us," wrote Marshall, "will save the expence of further litigation on the points decided; if in our favor it will I presume be respected by the state courts or if not, it will ascertain the points on which we may rely on an ultimate determination in favor of our title."[19] As these remarks suggest, Marshall did not count on the Supreme Court's vindication of the Fairfax title as a sure thing; nor was he particularly concerned about an adverse ruling. In his mind, whatever decision might result—one way or the other—was preferable to continuing legal uncertainty. He also appears to have been halfway resigned to the possibility of Virginia's defiance of a decision upholding the title.

Justice Story delivered the opinion in *Fairfax's Devisee* v. *Hunter's Lessee* on

15 March 1813. With Marshall and Thomas Todd not sitting and William Johnson dissenting, the Supreme Court majority consisted of Story, Washington, Brockholst Livingston, and Gabriel Duvall. The Court reversed the decision of the Virginia Court of Appeals and affirmed the original judgment of the Winchester District Court in favor of Fairfax's title. To Marshall's consternation, however, this decision was not based on the peace treaty of 1783. Although counsel Charles Lee and Walter Jones devoted their argument almost entirely to the effect of the peace treaty, Story considered this point unnecessary to decide because Fairfax's estate was fully protected by the Jay Treaty of 1794. That treaty permitted British subjects then holding lands in the United States to continue to enjoy their estates and to dispose of them in the same manner as American citizens. In order to bring the case within the Jay Treaty, Story construed the various acts of Virginia on the subject of the Northern Neck and concluded that none of them vested title in the commonwealth to the vacant lands of the former proprietary.[20]

Such a decision was not likely to be of much use to the Marshalls in the Virginia courts. It not only did not settle the title question to the chief justice's satisfaction but might have introduced greater confusion. Years later he remarked that the 1813 case was "very absurdly put on the treaty of 94."[21] That treaty, he might well have thought, should not have entered into the decision at all, since, like the compromise of 1796, it was not part of the original statement of agreed facts. Moreover, placing the Fairfax title under the protection of the later treaty was risky, for it hinged on the construction of a Virginia act of 1785 "for safe keeping the land papers of the Northern Neck." In addition to transferring the Northern Neck land records to the state land office in Richmond, this act declared that future grants of unappropriated lands of the Northern Neck would be made in the same manner as grants of other unappropriated land belonging to the commonwealth. This was the act under which Hunter obtained his patent.[22] Although admitting that this act "presented some difficulty, if it stand unaffected by the treaty of peace," Story maintained that its terms did not manifest the legislature's intention to vest title to the vacant lands in the commonwealth.[23] Marshall evidently viewed this act in a different light. Either the act was a confiscation barred by the peace treaty, or, if not a confiscation, this construction of the act was plausible only because of the treaty. In short, considered on its own terms independent of the treaty, the 1785 act amounted to a legally valid assumption of title to the Northern Neck. To Marshall, therefore, the treaty of 1783 was essential to establishing the Fairfax title. A Supreme Court opinion embodying this view of the application of the peace treaty to the title question, he believed, would have to be respected by the state courts. On the other hand, those courts would not consider as binding Story's construction of a state legislative act. In this respect, then, *Fairfax's Devisee* v. *Hunter's Lessee* was for Marshall a disappointment, a missed opportunity.

The title dispute now receded to the background as the case assumed the broader dimension of a constitutional controversy concerning the nature and limits of the Supreme Court's appellate jurisdiction. A mandate directing the Virginia Court of Appeals to execute the judgment in *Fairfax's Devisee* v. *Hunter's Lessee* was sent out in August 1813. In the spring of 1814 the Court of Appeals heard six days of arguments on the question of whether it should obey this mandate. Another twenty months elapsed before the court, on 16 December 1815, announced its refusal to carry out the mandate. The reason for the long delay was that the judges (Roane excepted) preferred to wait until the crisis of the War of 1812 and disunion sentiment in New England had passed before announcing their defiance of the Supreme Court.[24]

The formal judgment of the Virginia Court of Appeals in *Hunter* v. *Martin* declared that the Supreme Court's appellate power did not "extend to this court"; that section 25 of the Judiciary Act of 1789, which extended the Supreme Court's appellate jurisdiction to the highest state courts, was unconstitutional; that the Supreme Court's proceedings in this case on the writ of error issued under that act were void; and that the Court of Appeals would accordingly decline obedience to the mandate.[25] The four sitting judges delivered their opinions seriatim, the most elaborate and provocative of which was that by Judge Roane, the dominant voice of the court. Sounding the alarm against "a vortex in the general government" that would "ingulf and sweep away every vestige of the state constitutions," Roane produced a political treatise on the nature of the federal Union as essentially a confederacy of sovereign states whose governments "remain in full force, except as they are impaired by grants of power, to the general government." The general government, by contrast, was strictly limited to exercising powers that were expressly authorized by the compact to which the states were parties or that were incidental and necessary to the execution of an expressed power. From these premises, the Virginia jurist had little difficulty in showing that the Constitution did not extend the appellate jurisdiction of the Supreme Court to the state judiciaries. Roane rehearsed a number of themes and arguments that three years later he would work into his newspaper essays attacking the Supreme Court's decision in *McCulloch* v. *Maryland*.[26]

The Virginia Court of Appeals' challenge to the Supreme Court's appellate jurisdiction produced an application for a second writ of error, this one drawn up by Chief Justice Marshall himself. Unsigned but in his hand, the petition is part of the appellate case file of *Martin* v. *Hunter's Lessee*, as the case was now styled. Marshall probably wrote the petition as soon as he learned of the Court of Appeals' decision, for dispatch was essential to obtain a hearing at the next Supreme Court term. He then forwarded it to Justice Washington, who allowed the writ and signed a citation to David Hunter summoning him to appear. The citation was delivered to Hunter in Berkeley County on 10 January 1816. The record, consisting of a copy of the 1813 mandate and the Court of Appeals judgment of 16 December 1815, was filed in the Supreme Court on 5 February, in good time to put the case on the docket.[27]

The Supreme Court's appellate case records contain another document in Marshall's hand, apparently produced around this time, of which only a tattered fragment has survived. The fragment, damaged by fire, consists of two sheets, with writing on the recto and verso of the first sheet and on the entire recto of the second sheet. At the top left center of the recto of the first sheet Marshall wrote "5." Hence the fragment consists of the fifth, sixth, and seventh pages of the original manuscript. The document must have concluded with the seventh page, since there is no writing on the verso of the second sheet. Enough of the manuscript survives to identify it as an argument relating to the Hunter and Fairfax dispute. Marshall may have drawn it up for the use of his counsel.

The extant portion argues that *Hunter* v. *Fairfax's Devisee* as decided by the

Court of Appeals in 1810 was properly within the Supreme Court's appellate jurisdiction under section 25 of the Judiciary Act. The fragment is presently in the appellate case file of *Fairfax's Devisee v. Hunter's Lessee* (1813), and contextual evidence links it either to that case or to *Martin v. Hunter's Lessee* (1816).[28] According to Cranch's report the applicability of section 25 was not argued by counsel or considered by Justice Story in the 1813 case, although, as indicated by Johnson's separate opinion, this point did arise as a collateral issue.[29] In any event, Story took it up in his 1816 opinion after disposing of the principal question—the constitutionality of section 25. On the basis of similarities with parts of Story's 1816 opinion, the editors have conjectured that Marshall composed his argument sometime between December 1815 and March 1816.[30]

Both the autograph petition for a writ of error and the autograph remnant of an argument testify to Marshall's continuing active involvement in the Fairfax litigation as it was being considered by the Supreme Court. The chief justice obviously did not regard such intervention as inconsistent with prevailing standards of judicial conduct. He was sensitive to the conflict of interest posed by the Fairfax cases and routinely withdrew from hearing them when they came before him either in the high court or on circuit. Indeed, he went even further and refused to sit not only in cases where he or his near relations had a personal interest but in any case where the Fairfax title might be implicated. In the Granville case of 1805, for example, Marshall declined to decide the main question because it involved the same point respecting the treaty of peace as that arising in the Fairfax disputes. So firm was his opinion on this subject, he said, "that he did not believe he could change it; and as that opinion was formed when he was very deeply interested (alluding to the cause of Lord Fairfax in Virginia) he should feel much delicacy in deciding the present question."[31] Similar considerations undoubtedly prevented him from participating in the decision of *Smith v. Maryland* (1810) and *Orr v. Hodgson* (1819) in the Supreme Court.[32] In the spring of 1823 he informed Judge Tucker that the U.S. Circuit Court docket for that term contained "three ejectments in which though neither myself nor any of my connexions are interested I cannot sit because the Fairfax title is implicated on them."[33]

Chief Justice Marshall clearly recognized and scrupulously adhered to a code of appropriate judicial behavior. At the same time this code did not prevent him from taking an active part as a litigant so long as he withdrew from the case in his judicial capacity. In cases where he or his brother were parties (in their own names or as Martin's agent), Marshall, long after becoming chief justice, continued to perform such lawyerly services as preparing pleadings and taking depositions. Although most of these cases were brought in state courts, in at least one instance he drew a bill in chancery on behalf of Philip Martin for presentation in his own U.S. Circuit Court at Richmond.[34] Another Supreme Court case in which the chief justice had a personal interest was *FitzSimons v. Ogden*, decided in 1812. While this case was pending, Thomas FitzSimons sought Marshall's advice about hiring counsel and about when a decision might be expected. He apparently took this liberty on the very assumption that the chief justice would not sit in the case. For his part, Marshall betrayed no hint of awkwardness or impropriety in discussing "our case" with FitzSimons as a fellow party.[35]

As a principal partner with James Marshall in the purchase of the Fairfax manor lands, Chief Justice Marshall was directly interested in the cases of 1813 and 1816. In no sense, however, did the success or failure of his investment in these lands hinge on the Supreme Court's decision. All along he had hoped to get a definitive ruling by the Court that the peace treaty of 1783 protected titles of British subjects. *Fairfax's Devisee v. Hunter's Lessee*, though favorable to the Marshall interest, did not provide a useful precedent in this respect. When in late 1815 he personally intervened to bring the case again before the Supreme Court, Marshall was perhaps less concerned about sustaining the 1813 decision than about upholding the Supreme Court's appellate jurisdiction over the state judiciaries.

After three days of argument Justice Story on 20 March 1816 delivered the Court's opinion in *Martin v. Hunter's Lessee*, reversing the Virginia Court of Appeals' judgment on the mandate and (as in the 1813 case) affirming the 1794 judgment of the Winchester District Court. He firmly established his credentials as a judicial nationalist by arguing that the nature and logic of the Constitution, if not any specific textual provision, conferred upon the Supreme Court the right to review decisions of state courts. Section 25 of the Judiciary Act was therefore constitutional. Years later Story wrote that Marshall "concurred in every word" of his opinion. No doubt the chief justice was in complete agreement with his younger colleague on the issue of appellate jurisdiction, but the notion that he stood over Story's shoulder and dictated the opinion is without foundation. Story was fully capable of composing ringing nationalist pronouncements without assistance from Marshall or anyone else.[36]

Although *Martin v. Hunter's Lessee* yielded a masterly statement on the nature and extent of the appellate jurisdiction of the Supreme Court, the case by no means settled the question of whether appellate supervision of state courts would become a permanent feature of the American constitutional system. As for the question of who had superior title to the Cedar Creek tract in Shenandoah County, the mandate reversing the Court of Appeals and giving judgment for Martin was turned over to James Marshall.[37] Marshall evidently did not have to take any further legal steps, since the effect of the decision was to confirm possession in those who had purchased from him years earlier. For his part, Hunter presumably sought compensation from the state for the money he paid in the purchase of his patent and in paying taxes on the land for fifteen years.

1. For previous editorial notes dealing with the Fairfax purchase and litigation, see *PJM*, II, 140–49; V, 228–36; VI, 94–96.

2. *PJM*, V, 229–56; VI, 94–97, 122–23.

3. Shepherd, *Statutes*, II, 22–23.

4. For detailed discussions of the Fairfax cases, see Albert J. Beveridge, *The Life of John Marshall* (4 vols.; Boston, 1916–19), II, 203–11; IV, 145–66; H. C. Groome, *Fauquier during the Proprietorship* (Richmond, Va., 1927), 218–43; William Winslow Crosskey, *Politics and the Constitution in the History of the United States* (2 vols.; Chicago, Ill., 1953), II, 785–817; John Alfred Treon, "*Martin v. Hunter's Lessee*: A Case History" (Ph.D. diss., University of Virginia, 1970); F. Thornton Miller, "John Marshall versus Spencer Roane: A Reevaluation of *Martin v. Hunter's Lessee*," *VMHB*, XCVI (1988), 297–314. Each of these accounts is flawed by errors of fact and interpretation.

5. Copies of the deeds of 30 Aug. 1797 and 10 Oct. 1798 were entered on the record of Marshall's Lessee v. Foley, Fauquier County Land Causes, III (1833–50), 29–36 (micro-

film) Vi. The former deed is summarized in the report of Marshall v. Conrad, 5 Call 364, 370 (1805). JM's autograph copy of the partition deed, 24 June 1799, is in Martin v. Moffet, U.S. Cir. Ct., Va., Ended Cases (Restored), 1824, Vi.

6. *PJM*, VI, 94–97, 122–24, 202–6.

7. *PJM*, VI, 277, 278 n. 3; 5 Call 364, 393.

8. JM to James M. Marshall, 1 Apr. 1804, 13 Feb. 1806, 21 Nov. 1808 (*PJM*, VI, 277, 426; VII, 186).

9. JM to James M. Marshall, 9 July 1822, Bixby Collection, MoSW.

10. Partition deed, 24 June 1799, Martin v. Moffett; Fairfax's Devisee v. Hunter's Lessee, record on appeal, 13–15, App. Cas. No. 456; Land Tax Books, Shenandoah County, 1790–1805, Vi; Martin v. Hunter's Lessee, Fragment of Argument, [ca. Dec. 1815–Mar. 1816] and n. 10.

11. Hening, *Statutes*, XII, 112.

12. Martin v. Hunter's Lessee, Fragment of Argument, [ca. Dec. 1815–Mar. 1816].

13. JM to James M. Marshall, 1 Apr. 1804 (*PJM*, VI, 277).

14. Hunter v. Fairfax's Devisee, 1 Munf. 223 (1810). Roane was never chief justice of the Virginia Supreme Court of Appeals, which had no such title but designated the senior judge "president." During this period and through the rest of Roane's tenure, the senior judge was William Fleming.

15. 1 Munf. 223–32 (quotation at 226).

16. 1 Munf. 232–38 (quotation at 237).

17. JM to Lee, 7 May 1810 (*PJM*, VII, 246–47 and nn.).

18. Treon misses the real point of the dispute between the Marshalls and Hunter. Miller offers a corrective to Treon but in other respects is off the mark (Treon, "*Martin* v. *Hunter's Lessee*," 118–19; Miller, "John Marshall versus Spencer Roane," *VMHB*, XCVI [1988], 306–8).

19. JM to Charles Lee, 7 May 1810 (*PJM*, VII, 246–47). On the caveat cases, see *PJM*, V, 229–30; VII, 247 n. 11.

20. 7 Cranch 618–28.

21. JM to James M. Marshall, 9 July 1822, Bixby Collection, MoSW.

22. Hening, *Statutes*, XII, 111–13.

23. 7 Cranch 624–26 (quotation at 624).

24. Hunter v. Martin, 4 Munf. 1–3, 26 (1815); Treon, "*Martin* v. *Hunter's Lessee*," 206–8.

25. 4 Munf. 58–59.

26. 4 Munf. 25–54 (quotations at 26, 30); Essays Defending McCulloch v. Maryland, editorial note (at 24 Apr. 1819).

27. Martin v. Hunter's Lessee, App. Cas. No. 793.

28. Fairfax's Devisee v. Hunter's Lessee, App. Cas. No. 456. The fragment's placement in this file may be the result of an archival error (see Martin v. Hunter's Lessee, Fragment of Argument, [ca. Dec. 1815–Mar. 1816] and n. 1).

29. 7 Cranch 631–32.

30. The 1815 opinions of Roane and Fleming also discussed the applicability of section 25. In addition to hearing the Court of Appeals judges deliver their opinions in court, JM could have read the opinions in the pages of the Richmond *Enquirer* (27 Jan., 1, 3 Feb. 1816).

31. Granville's Devisee v. Allen, Remarks, 18 June 1805 (*PJM*, VI, 400).

32. 6 Cranch 286; 4 Wheat. 465.

33. JM to St. George Tucker, 27 May 1823, Tucker-Coleman Papers, ViW.

34. *PJM*, VI, 94–95, 96–98, 122–23, 202–5, 472–75.

35. FitzSimons to JM, 6 Feb. 1809, 31 Jan. 1810, 31 Mar. 1810; JM to FitzSimons, 1 Mar. 1810, 17 Sept. 1810, 28 May 1811 (*PJM*, VII, 188–90, 224–25, 241–42, 261–62, 271).

36. 1 Wheat. 323–62; Story to George Ticknor, 22 Jan. 1831 (Story, *Life and Letters*, II,

48–49; R. Kent Newmyer, *Supreme Court Justice Joseph Story: Statesman of the Old Republic* [Chapel Hill, N.C., 1985], 111–12).
37. U.S. Sup. Ct. Dockets, App. Cas. No. 793.

Martin v. Hunter's Lessee
Petition for Writ of Error

[ca. 16 December 1815]

To the Honble. the Justices of the supreme court of the United States or any one of them the petition of Philip Martin humbly showeth[1]

That a writ of error was heretofore sued out of the Honble. the Supreme court of the United States at the suit of your petitioner to a judgement or final decision of the court of appeals of the Commonwealth of Virginia in a case in which David Hunter was appellant and your petitioner appellee on which such proceedings were had that the judgement or opinion rendered in the court of appeals in favor of the said David Hunter and against your petitioner was reversed and a mandate was awarded to the said court of appeals directing the said court to enter judgement in favor of your petitioner. Your petitioner further shows that the said mandate of the Honble. the supreme court of the United States was filed by your petitioner in the Honble. the court of appeals of Virginia & the said court was prayed to enter judgement in pursuance thereof, whereupon after hearing the arguments of counsel it was on the 16th. of this month of Decr. in the year 1815 adjudged by the said court that their judgement ought not to be varied in conformity with the said mandate it being the opinion of the Honble the said court of appeals for the Commonwealth of Virginia that the act of Congress giving to the supreme court of the United States appelate jurisdiction of causes decided in the courts of a state is unconstitutional & void & that all proceedings in the supreme court of the United States in such case are *coram non judice*.[2] Your petitioner is advised that there is error in the said judgement of the court of appeals of Virginia and assigns for error that the act of Congress giving appellate jurisdiction to the supreme court of the United States in the cases therein specified being constitutional the decision of the supreme court in this case is obligatory & its mandate ought to have been obeyed by the court of appeals of the Commonwealth of Virginia. Your petitioner therefore prays that a writ of error may be awarded & that the record of the proceedings of the court of appeals of Virginia may be removed into the supreme court of the United States & that the error therein may be corrected according to law.

AD, Martin v. Hunter's Lessee, Appellate Case No. 793, RG 267, DNA.

1. In addition to the petition, the file consists of the writ of error, with Bushrod Washington's endorsement allowing the writ; an affidavit of Benjamin W. Leigh, sworn on 31 Jan. 1816, stating that the Va. Court of Appeals had denied a motion to certify the record on presentation of the writ of error; a citation issued to David Hunter, signed by Washington and endorsed by a Frederick County magistrate on 10 Jan. 1816 certifying delivery; a copy of the Supreme Court's mandate of Aug. 1813 along with the Va. Court of Appeals judgment of 16 Dec. 1815, with the clerk's certification dated 19 Dec. 1815 (Martin v. Hunter's Lessee, App. Cas. No 793).

2. *Coram non judice* ("in presence of a person not a judge"), a term applied to a case decided by a court not having jurisdiction in the matter.

Martin v. Hunter's Lessee
Fragment of Argument

[ca. December 1815–March 1816][1]
or affirmed[2] in the supreme court of the United states upon a writ . . .

This case is within the very words of the statute. The construction of a treaty ⟨has?⟩ been drawn in question, & the decision has been against the party claiming ⟨un⟩der the treaty.[3]

But waiving the precise application of the Statute to the ⟨case?⟩ nothing can be more easily demonstrated than that the power given ⟨to the⟩ court by the constitution would be vain, idle, & empty if it did not extend to such cases. ⟨Th⟩at? it would be a meer illusion, holding out the pretext of a tribunal for the ultimate decision of all cases arising under a treaty, without being really ⟨one?⟩ ⟨ . . . ⟩ that must necessarily constitute the component parts of a case arising ⟨un⟩der a treaty. Must not the title of the party at the time the treaty ⟨was⟩ made be examined for the purpose of determining on the appli⟨cability⟩ of the treaty to this case?[4] Must not those laws & acts be examined which ⟨are said⟩ to have defeated that title? If these questions be not answered ⟨ . . . ⟩ shall the court decide on a case arising under a ⟨ . . . ⟩ answered in the affirmative then the decision of the ⟨ . . . ⟩ title is one which the treaty did not protect defeats the op⟨eration of the?⟩ treaty as entirely, & involves as necessarily a construction of th⟨e trea⟩ty as any exposition which can be made. How are we to understand whether a treaty does or does not embrace a particular case? Certainly by understanding that case & by construing the treaty in reference to it. If the state court has decided that a treaty does not protect the ⟨tit⟩le of a party who claims its protection, then the state court must construe ⟨the tre⟩aty & if in the opinion of this court the treaty does protect his title, ⟨then⟩ the state court in deciding otherwise has misconstrued the treaty & has ⟨c⟩ommitted an error which "immediately respects the construction of the treaty."[5] This construction of the constitution equally obvious & necessary has been always ⟨ . . . ⟩ in this court. 5th. Cranch 344.[6] 6th Cranch[7]

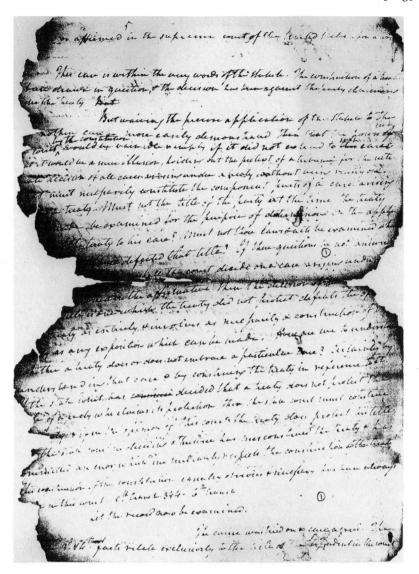

FRAGMENT OF ARGUMENT
From Martin v. Hunter's Lessee, ca. December 1815–March 1816.
Courtesy of the National Archives

Let the record now be examined.

The cause was tried on a case agreed.[8] The ⟨2⟩d. 3d. & 4th. facts relate exclusively to the title of the defendent in the court below. The 5th. fact states the title of the plf in that court. The 6th. ⟨states the charac⟩ter of the then defendent as a British subject. The 8th. states that the ⟨ . . . ⟩ whom the deft. claims left an heir who was a citizen of Virginia ⟨at the time of⟩ the treaty of peace. The 10th. states several acts of Assembly which are said to relate in some manner to the property & finds further that the land ⟨had⟩ never been escheated. The 12th. states also an act of Assembly. The 13⟨th. states⟩ that the plf. is a citizen of Virginia & the 14th. & last states the usual fac⟨ts of⟩ lease entry & ouster.

There is no one fact introduced into this case on ⟨the part?⟩ of the defendent below which does not go directly to sustain his ⟨title?⟩ under the treaty. All those facts which go to sustain his title a⟨re indis⟩pensably necessary for the purpose of showing that it is protecte⟨d by⟩ the treaty. The different acts of assembly passed during the ⟨war and after?⟩ its termination are introduced by the opposite party for the ⟨purpose of?⟩ showing that the treaty does not protect the title, & that the ⟨Commonwealth?⟩ ⟨ . . . ⟩ by the patent issued in 1789. Must not this court ⟨ . . . ⟩ of those laws in order to determine ⟨ . . . ⟩ of the treaty to the title? Certainly the construction of ⟨ . . . ⟩ involved in the question whether it acts on property to which th⟨ . . . ⟩. If the state court has decided that in consequence of those law⟨s the treaty?⟩ does not protect the property in contest, & the opinion of this co⟨urt be?⟩ otherwise, then the error of the state court is one which imme⟨diately⟩ respects the construction of the treaty.

It will be readily admitted that this co⟨urt⟩ can take no notice of errors, if such existed, which do not con⟨cern the⟩ treaty. If, for example, the plf. in the District court had set ⟨ . . . ⟩ obviously defective, if his patent had been without a seal or ⟨ . . . ⟩ any other requisite to its validity, this court could not have ⟨noticed?⟩ such defect. But the court must decide whether the party claiming ⟨under⟩ the treaty has shown a complete title under it, & whether the oppos⟨ing party⟩ has shown any law or fact competent to defeat such title.

The case then is comple⟨tely within the juris⟩diction of this court according to the constitution & the statute.

But I will not pass over unnoticed a fact which is of im⟨port⟩ance to the parties & which has been mentioned elsewhere, though ⟨ . . . ⟩ cannot be seen with legal eyes.

A compromise has taken place ⟨be⟩tween the commonwealth of Virginia & the purchasers of ⟨the⟩ estate of Denny Fairfax.

This compromise is not in the record ⟨and⟩ of course cannot be considered by this court nor ought to have ⟨be⟩en considered by any court. Let the act be produced. It will ⟨be fo⟩und to depend on a condition. That condition is the execution ⟨ . . . ⟩ *in pais*.[9] If the court can open the case so as to let ⟨in the ac⟩t of compromise & this deed will not & ought not th⟨ . . . ⟩ to let Fairfax in also to show that th⟨ . . . ⟩ of this property is such as to bring it within ⟨ . . . ⟩tion. That it was in fact set apart by Lord Fairfa⟨x⟩ for his own use & was at the time occupied by his tenent ⟨to⟩ whom the lands have since been actually conveyed in fee.[10]

The offer to try this cause on its real merits in a new ⟨ej⟩ectment has been repeatedly made by the party ⟨cla⟩iming the Fairfax title & repeatedly rejected. He may therefore properly say now that the compromise forms no part of this case but will appear in a new ejectment if ⟨o⟩ne should be brought.

AD, Fairfax's Devisee v. Hunter's Lessee, Appellate Case No. 456, RG 267, DNA. Jagged edges, particularly in folds, indicating fire damage.

1. In the microfilm publication, the fragment is the penultimate document in the appellate case file of the 1813 case, though it appears to pertain more closely to the 1816 case (see preceding editorial note). It follows the petition, citation, writ, and record on appeal. Between the record and the fragment is an unidentified slip of paper that appears to have no relation to the case. The last document in the file (following immediately after the fragment) is a draft of the court's official judgment in Martin v. Hunter's Lessee, which has obviously been misplaced. The placement of the draft and the fragment in the 1813 file may be owing to an archivist's error committed at the time the Supreme Court's early records were transferred to the National Archives in the 1950s (Fairfax's Devisee v. Hunter's Lessee, App. Cas. No. 456 [M214, reel 18, DNA]; James R. Browning and Bess Glenn, "The Supreme Court Collection at the National Archives," *American Journal of Legal History*, IV [1960], 241–45).

2. JM here wrote "5" in the top margin, indicating that this was the fifth page of the original MS.

3. See the similar remarks by Story (1 Wheat. 357).

4. In Fairfax's Devisee v. Hunter's Lessee (1813), Johnson stated that whenever a case was brought to the Supreme Court under section 25, "the title of the parties litigant must necessarily be enquired into, and that such an enquiry must, in the nature of things, precede the consideration how far the law, treaty, and so forth, is applicable to it; otherwise an appeal to this Court would be worse than nugatory" (7 Cranch 632).

5. See Story's comments on this point (1 Wheat. 357–59).

6. Owings v. Norwood's Lessee, 5 Cranch 344 (1809). In this case the Court (speaking through JM) dismissed the writ of error because the plaintiff in error did "not contend that his right grows out of the treaty." Counsel Robert G. Harper interpreted this opinion to mean that the Supreme Court "had no jurisdiction to revise the decisions of the state courts, in cases where the construction of a treaty was drawn in question *incidentally*." JM replied that Harper "misunderstood" the Court's opinion. "It was not that this court had not jurisdiction if the treaty were drawn in question *incidentally*," he said, adding: "But if the person's title is not affected by the treaty, if he claims nothing under a treaty, his title cannot be protected by the treaty" (5 Cranch 347–48).

7. Smith v. Maryland, 6 Cranch 286 (1810), which Story also cited (1 Wheat. 359). JM did not sit in this case, no doubt because it involved the same questions presented by Fairfax's Devisee v. Hunter's Lessee. In the Smith case, counsel for Maryland argued that the Supreme Court did not have jurisdiction under section 25, because the case turned exclusively on the construction of Maryland's confiscation laws enacted before the treaty of peace and therefore presented no question concerning the construction of the treaty.

Justice Washington, for the Court, contended that the Supreme Court could independently construe those laws to determine whether the confiscation was complete before the treaty. The construction of those laws, he said, was "only a step in the cause leading to the construction and meaning of this article of the treaty; and it is perfectly immaterial to the point of jurisdiction, that the first part of the way is the most difficult to explore." On the merits, the Supreme Court held that the confiscation occurred before the treaty (6 Cranch 304–7 [quotation at 305]).

8. The original trial of this case took place in 1793 in the state district court at Winchester on a case agreed, dated 7 Sept. 1793, which is summarized in the report of Hunter v. Fairfax's Devisee (Fairfax's Devisee v. Hunter's Lessee, record on appeal, 4–18, App. Cas. No. 456; 1 Munf. 219–22).

9. The 1796 compromise was enacted after this suit began in the Winchester District Court and thus did not form part of the case agreed. See the similar passage in Story's opinion: "It has been asserted at the bar that, in point of fact, the court of appeals did not decide either upon the treaty or the title apparent upon the record, but upon a compromise made under an act of the legislature of Virginia. If it be true (as we are informed) that this was a private act, to take effect only upon a certain condition, viz. the execution of a deed of release of certain lands, which was matter *in pais*, it is somewhat difficult to understand how the court could take judicial cognizance of the act, or the performance of the condition, unless spread upon the record" (1 Wheat. 360).

10. Between 1799 and 1807 James Marshall sold the Cedar Creek survey lands to four different purchasers. According to the deeds, the Cedar Creek tract had been laid out and surveyed into five tenements during Lord Fairfax's lifetime. See deeds from James Marshall to Henry Richards, 9 Jan. 1799; to Richard Miller, 31 Mar. 1799; to George W. Timberlake, 6 Jan. 1800; to George Rudolph, 30 Sept. 1807 (Frederick County Superior Court Deed Book, No. 3, 549–50, 602–4; No. 4, 128–31; No. 5, 559–60 [microfilm], Vi).

To [Joseph Story?]

My dear Sir   Washington Feb. 16th. 1816

My brother James of the county of Frederick in Virginia has written to request that I would endeavor to procure the warrant of a midshipman for his son John Marshall.[1] He is a youth for whose character in every respect I am willing to become responsible. His education has been attended to with care & I flatter myself that he will not should he be successful prove unworthy of his profession. May I ask the favor of you to support my application in his behalf to the Secretary of the navy.[2] I am dear Sir, Your

J MARSHALL

ALS, Marshall Papers, DLC. Recipient's identity based on evidence in n. 2.

1. Letter not found. John Marshall (1804–1855) was the son of James Markham Marshall and Hester Morris Marshall (Paxton, *Marshall Family*, 139–41).

2. Joseph Story was apparently JM's intermediary in this matter, as indicated by a letter from Secretary of the Navy Benjamin Crowninshield to Story, 17 Feb. 1816. Crowninshield wrote Story that "the application in behalf of Judge Marshall's Nephew cannot be brought forward under more respectable auspices." He would "comply when the state of the service will admit," but "at present three fourths of our Midshipmen are upon fur-

lough for want of employment in the Navy, and the List of Applicants is still increasing over the number of one thousand, with the best recommendations in the U. States" (Crowninshield to Story, 17 Feb. 1816, Miscellaneous Letters Sent by the Secretary of the Navy, RG 45, DNA). JM's nephew ultimately received a commission in 1818. See JM to Crowninshield, 21 Feb. 1818 and n. 1.

To John Randolph

Dear Sir   March 4th. 1816

When you asked me to dine with you on wednesday next the inclination I felt to gratify myself with the pleasure of your company was so strong that I was incapable of declining the invitation. But the Judges have pledged themselves to each other to continue at home for the purpose of conferring on the causes under consideration, & I cannot absent myself from our daily consultation without interupting the course of the business & arresting its progress. This, in the present state of things, would be peculiarly unfortunate, as we have several cases before us which remain undecided. That you saw us yesterday at Mrs. Dowsons was no breach of the rule, because we have not applied it to sundays.[1] That day is passed by three of the Judges with their families, & our conferences are of course broken up. I regret very sincerely that official duties compel me to deny myself a gratification for which I feel the strongest inclination. With very much respect & esteem, I am dear Sir your Obedt.

J MARSHALL

ALS, Collection of Carl A. Przyborowski, McHenry, Ill. Addressed to Randolph and endorsed "The great Lord Chief."

1. Elizabeth Dowson ran a boardinghouse on Capitol Hill in Washington, D.C. from 1807 until her death in Sept. 1816. Her son, Alfred R. Dowson, then took over the business. Dowson's establishment was popular with Southerners, especially Virginians (*Daily National Intelligencer* [Washington, D.C.], 20 Sept. 1816; *The Washington Directory, Showing the Name, Occupation, and Residence . . .* [Washington, D.C., 1822], vii–xiv, 31); George Rothwell Brown, *Washington: A Not Too Serious History* [Baltimore, Md., 1930], 136–37).

The Commercen
Opinion
U.S. Supreme Court, 22 March 1816

The *Commercen*, a Swedish ship carrying barley and oats (the produce of Great Britain) to British troops in Spain, was captured by the American privateer *Lawrence* in April 1814. Brought into Portland, in the District of

Maine, the *Commercen* and her cargo were libeled as prize of war. By a decree of June 1814 the U.S. District Court condemned the cargo as enemy property but restored the vessel to her owners with an allowance for freight—the compensation paid for transporting goods. In October, however, the U.S. Circuit Court at Boston, composed of Judges Story and John Davis, reversed that part of the decree allowing freight. The claimants thereupon took an appeal to the Supreme Court, where the case was argued on 16 March 1816 by Francis Scott Key and Robert G. Harper for the appellants and Samuel Dexter and William Pinkney for the captors. Justice Story delivered the Court's opinion on 22 March 1816, repeating in substance his circuit decree disallowing freight. While admitting the general rule of international law that allowed freight to a neutral carrier of enemy property, Story contended that in carrying provisions for British troops the *Commercen* "must, to all intents and purposes, be deemed a British transport." That Great Britain was engaged in distinct wars with France and with the United States at the time made no difference in this case. British "armies are everywhere our enemies, and every assistance offered to them must, directly, or indirectly, operate to our injury." Marshall, joined by Justices Johnson and Livingston, dissented from this opinion (The Commercen, record on appeal, 2, 17–20, 22–25, App. Cas. No. 749; U.S. Sup. Ct. Minutes, 16 Mar. 1816; U.S. Sup. Ct. Dockets, App. Cas. No. 749; 1 Wheat. 387–95 [quotations at 393, 394]).

The Ship Comercen

¶1   As a principle which I think new & which may certainly in future be very interesting to the United States has been decided in this case, I trust I may be excused for stating the reasons which have prevented my concurring in the opinion that has been delivered.

¶2   In argument this sentence of the circuit court has been sustained on two grounds.

> 1st. That the exportation of grain from Ireland is generally prohibited & therefore that a neutral cannot lawfully engage in it during war.
>
> 2d. That the carriage of supplies to the army of the enemy is to take part with him in the war & consequently to become the enemy of the United States so far as to forfeit the right to freight.

The first point has been maintained on its supposed analogies to certain principles which have been at different times avowed by the great maritime & belligerent powers of Europe, respecting the colonial & coasting trade; & which are generally known in England & in this country by the appellation of the rule of 1756.[1]

¶3   Without professing to give any opinion on the correctness of those principles, it is sufficient to observe that they do not appear to me to apply to this case.

¶4   The rule of 1756 prohibits a neutral from engaging in time of war in a trade in which he was prevented from participating in time of peace, because that trade was by law exclusively reserved for the vessels of the belligerent state.

This prohibition stands upon two reasons. ¶5

1st. That a trade, such as the coasting or colonial trade, which by the permanent policy of a nation is reserved for its own vessels, if opened to neutrals during war, must be opened under the pressure of the arms of the enemy, & be opened to obtain releif from that pressure. The neutral who interposes to releive the belligerent under such circumstances, rescues him from the condition to which the arms of his enemy has reduced him, restores to him those resources which have been wrested from him by the arms of his adversary, & deprives that adversary of the advantages which successful war has given him. This the opposing belligerent pronounces a departure from neutrality & an interference in the war to his prejudice which he will not tolerate, or if the trade be not opened by law.

2dly. That a neutral employed in a trade thus reserved by the enemy for his own vessels, identifies himself with that enemy, and by performing functions exclusively appertaining to the enemy character, assumes that character.

Neither the one nor the other of these reasons applies to the case under consideration. The trade was not a trade confined to British vessels during peace, & opened to neutrals during war under the pressure created by the arms of the enemy. It was prohibited for political reasons entirely unconnected with the interests of navigation, & thrown open on motives equally unconnected with maritime strength.

Neither did the neutral employed in it, engage in a trade then or at ¶6
any time reserved for British vessels; & therefore did not identify himself with them. He was not performing functions exclusively appertaining to the enemy; &, consequently in performing them did not assume that character.

The second point presents a question of much more difficulty. That a ¶7
neutral carrying supplies to the army of the enemy does, under the mildest interpretation of national law, expose himself to the loss of freight, is a proposition too well settled to be controverted. That it is a general rule, admitting of few if of any exceptions, is not denied by the counsel for the appellants. But he contends that this case is withdrawn from that rule by its peculiar circumstances.

The late war between the United States & Great Britain was declared ¶8
at a time when all Europe including our enemy was engaged in a war with which ours had no connection, & in which we professed to take no interest. The allies of our enemy, engaged with him in a common war, the most tremendous & the most vitally interesting to the parties that has ever desolated this earth, were our friends. We kept up with them the mutual interchange of good offices, & declared our determination

to stand aloof from that cause which was common to them & Great Britain. They too considered this war as entirely distinct from that in which they were engaged. Although at a most critical period we had attacked their ally, they did not view it as an act of hostility to them. They did not ascribe it to any wish to affect in any manner the war prosecuted in Europe, but solely to the desire of asserting our violated rights. They seemed almost to consider the Britain who was our enemy, as a different nation from that Britain who was their ally.

¶9   How long this extraordinary state of things might have continued it is impossible to say; but it certainly existed when the commercen was captured. What its effect on that capture ought to be, must depend more on principle than on precedent.

¶10   It has been said & truely said by the counsel for the captors that we were at war with great Britain in every part of the world. We were enemies every where. Her troops in Spain or elsewhere as well as her troops in America, were our enemies. It was a conflict of nation against nation. This is conceded; & therefore the cargo of the commercen being British property, was condemned as prize of war. But although this must be conceded, the corollary which is drawn from it, that those who furnish their armies in spain with provisions, aid them to our prejudice; & therefore take part against us in the war, & are guilty of unneutral conduct; must be examined before it can be admitted.

¶11   It is not true that every species of aid given to the enemy is an act of hostility which will justify our treating him who gives it, or his vessels as hostile to us. The history of all europe, & especially of Swisserland, furnishes many examples of the truth of this proposition. Those examples need not be quoted particularly, because they stand on principles not entirely applicable to this case. It is the peculiarity of this war which requires the adoption of rules peculiar to a new state of things, in adopting which we must examine the principle on which a nation is justified in treating a neutral as an enemy.

¶12   That a neutral is friendly to our enemy, & continues to interchange good offices with him, can furnish no subject of complaint; for then all commerce with one belligerent would be deemed hostile by the other. The effect of commerce is to augment his resources & enable him the longer to prosecute the war; but this augmentation is produced by an act entirely innocent on the part of the neutral & manifesting no hostility to the opposing belligerent. It cannot therefore be molested by him while the same good offices are allowed to him; although he may not be enabled to avail himself of them to an equal degree. It would seem then that a remote & consequential effect of an act is not sufficient to give it a hostile character; its tendency to aid the enemy in the war must be direct & immediate. It is also necessary that it should be injurious to us: for a meer benefit to another which is not injurious to us, cannot convert a friend into an enemy.

If these principles be correct, & they are believed to be so, let us ¶13
apply them to the present case.

When hostilities commenced between the United States & Great ¶14
Britain, that nation was carrying on a war with France in which all the
great powers of Europe were combined. We did not expect, & certainly
had no right to expect that our declaration of war against one of the
allies would in any manner affect the operations of their common war
in europe. The armies of Portugal & Spain were united to those of
Britain, & unquestionably aided & assisted our enemy; but they did not
aid & assist him against us, &, therefore, did not become our enemies.
Had any other of the combined powers equipped a military expedition
for the purpose of reinforcing the armies of Britain in any part of
Europe, or had a new ally engaged in the war, that would have been no
act of hostility against the United States, altho it would have aided our
enemy. But if a military expedition to the United States had been undertaken, the case would have assumed a different aspect. Such expedition would be hostile to this country, & the power undertaking it
would become our enemy. It would have been an interference operating directly to our prejudice.

So the declaration of war against Great Britain had without doubt a ¶15
remote & consequential effect on the war in Europe. The force employed against the United States must be subducted from that employed in support of the common cause in Europe; or greater exertions must be made which might sooner exhaust those resources which
enabled her to continue her gigantic efforts in their common war. Consequently the declaration of war by the United States remotely affected
the war in Europe to the advantage of one party & the injury of the
other. Yet no one of the allies considered this declaration as taking part
in that war & placing America in the condition of an enemy. But had
the United States employed their force on the peninsula against the
British troops, or had they interfered in the operations of the common
war, it may well be doubted whether they might not have been rightfully considered a[s] taking part against the allies & arranging themselves on the side of the common enemy.

In answer to arguments of this tendency made at the bar it was said ¶16
that nations are governed by political considerations, & may chuse
rather to overlook conduct at which they might justly take offence,
than unnecessarily to increase the number of their enemies, or provoke increased hostility; but that courts are bound by the law & must
inflexibly adhere to its mandate.

While this is conceded, it is deemed equally true that those acts which ¶17
will justify the condemnation of a neutral as an enemy would also
justify the treating his nation as an enemy if they were performed or
defended by the nation. There is a tacit compact that the hostile act of
the individual shall not be ascribed to his government, & that in turn

the government will not protect the individual from being treated as an enemy. But if the government adopts the act of the individual, & supports it by force, the government itself may be rightfully treated as hostile. Thus contraband of war though belonging to a neutral is condemned as the property of an enemy, & his government takes no offence at it; but should his government adopt the act & insist upon the right to carry articles deemed contraband & support that right, he would furnish just cause of war. The belligerent might chuse to overlook this hostile act, but the act would be in its nature hostile. The enquiry then whether the act in which this individual Swede was employed, would if performed by his government, have been an act of hostility to the United States & might rightfully be so considered, is material to the decision of the question whether the act of the individual is to be treated as hostile.

¶18   Great Britain & Sweden were allies in the war against France. Consequently the King of Sweden might have ordered his troops to cooperate with those of Britain in any place against the common enemy. He might have ordered a reinforcement to the British army on the peninsula, & this reinforcement might have been transported by sea. An attempt on the part of the United States to intercept it, because it was aiding her enemy, would certainly have been an interference in the war in Europe, which would have provoked, & would have justified the resentment of all the allied powers. It would then have been an interference not to be justified by our war with Britain, because those troops were not to be employed against us.

¶19   If instead of a reinforcement of men a supply of provisions were to be furnished to that part of the allied army which was British, would this alter the case? Could an American squadron intercept a convoy of provisions, or of military stores of any description, going to an army engaged in a war common to Great Britain & Sweden, & not against the United States? Could this be done without interfering in that war, & taking part in it against all the allies? If it could not then any supplies furnished by the government of Sweden promoting the operations of their common war, whether intended immediately for the British or any other division of the allied armies had a right to pass unmolested by American cruizers.

¶20   It is not beleived that any act which, if performed by the government, could not rightfully be deemed an act of hostility, is to be so deemed if performed by an individual. Had the provisions then on board the comercen been swedish property the result of this reasoning is that it could not have been confiscated as prize of war. Being British property it is confiscable; but the Swede is guilty of no other offence than carrying enemy property, an offence not enhanced in this particular case by the character of that property. He is therefore as much entitled to freight as if his cargo had been of a different description. His trade was not more illicit than the carriage of enemy goods for common use would have been.

If the cases in which neutrals have been condemned for having on ¶21 board articles the transportation of which cloath him with the enemy character, be attentively considered; it is beleived that they will not be found to contravene the reasoning which has been urged.

To carry dispatches to the government has been considered as an act ¶22 of such complete hostility as to communicate the hostile character to the vessel carrying them.[2] But this decision was made in a case where the dispatches could only relate to the war between the government of the captors & that to which the dispatches were addressed. They were communications between a colonial government in danger of being attacked & the mother country. In a subsequent case, it was determined that a neutral vessel might bear dispatches to a belligerent government without assuming the Belligerent character, if they were from an Ambassador residing in the neutral state.[3] Yet such dispatches might contain inteligence material to the war. But this is a case in which the belligerent right to intercept all communications addressed to its enemy by the officers of that enemy, is modified & restrained by the neutral right to protect the diplomatic communications which are necessary to the political intercourse between belligerents & neutrals. It is a case in which the right of a belligerent is narrowed & controlled by the positive rights of a neutral; still more reasonably may they be narrowed & controlled by the positive rights of a belligerent engaged in a war in which we have no concern & in which we ought not to interfere.

To transport troops or military personages belonging to the enemy ¶23 from one place to another, has also been determined to subject the vessel to condemnation; but in those cases, the service in which it was supposed the persons so conveyed were to be employed, was against the government of the captors.[4] The transportation of these personages was to aid the views of one belligerent against the other, & was therefore to take part in the war against that other. It is an act the operation of which is direct & immediate.

It may be said that this reasoning would go to the protection of ¶24 British troops passing to the peninsula; & of British supplies transported in British vessels for their use. That it therefore proves too much, & must consequently be unsound.

It is admitted that, pressed to its extreme point, the argument would ¶25 go to this extent—an extent which cannot be maintained: but it does not follow that it is unsound in every stage of its progress. In every case of conflicting rights each must cede some thing to the other. The pretensions of neither party can be carried to the extreme. They meet, they check, they limit each other. The precise line which neither can pass, but to which each may advance, is not easily to be found & marked; yet such a line must exist whatever may be the difficulty of discerning it.

¶26   To attack our enemy & to take his property if either can be done without violating the sovereignty of a friend, is of the very essence of war. None can be offended at the exercise of this right who may not be offended at the declaration of war itself. The injury which the allies of our enemy in a war common to them but in which we are not engaged, sustain by this occasional interuption is incidental, while on our part it is the exercise of a direct & essential right.

¶27   But when we attack a friend who is carrying on military operations conjointly with our enemy but not against us, we are not making direct war, but are using those incidental rights which war gives us, against those direct rights which are exercised by a belligerent not our enemy, & which constitute war itself. In either case it would seem to me that the incidental must yield to the direct & essential right.

¶28   Upon this view of the subject, I have at length, not, it is confessed, without much doubt & difficulty, come to the conclusion that the comercen being a swede whose nation was engaged in a war common to Great Britain & Sweden against France, & to which the United States was not a party; might convey military stores for the use of the British armies engaged in that war, as innocently as she could carry British property of any other description; & is therefore as much entitled to freight as she would be had the property belonged to the enemy but been destined for ordinary use.[5]

AD, The Commercen, Appellate Opinions, RG 267, DNA; printed, Henry Wheaton, *Reports of Cases Argued and Adjudged in the Supreme Court of the United States . . .* , I (Philadelphia, 1816), 395–406. For JM's deletions and interlineations, see Textual Notes below.

1. The so-called Rule of 1756 was a British doctrine formulated during the Seven Years' War in response to France's opening its colonial trade to the ships of neutral powers. Great Britain contended that allowing neutrals to engage in such trade was a direct interference with her maritime rights. Wheaton, with Story's assistance, prepared a long note on this subject, which he appended to his first volume (1 Wheat. 507–34; Story, *Life and Letters*, I, 285–89).

2. JM alluded to the case of The "Atalanta," 6 C. Rob. 440, 165 Eng. Rep. 991 (Adm., 1808), which Story cited in his opinion (1 Wheat. 391 and n.).

3. The "Caroline," 6 C. Rob. 461, 165 Eng. Rep. 999 (Adm., 1808), decided shortly after The "Atalanta" and distinguished from the earlier case.

4. The "Carolina," 4 C. Rob. 256, 165 Eng. Rep. 604 (Adm., 1802); The "Friendship," 6 C. Rob. 420, 165 Eng. Rep. 985 (Adm., 1807); The "Orozembo," 6 C. Rob. 430, 165 Eng. Rep. 988 (Adm., 1807). Story cited these cases (1 Wheat. 391 and n.).

5. In their brief concurrences Livingston and Johnson held that the Swedish government and its subjects had a right to transport provisions for British troops engaged in the Peninsular War without violating Sweden's neutral character in respect to the United States (1 Wheat. 406–7).

Textual Notes

¶ 1 l. 1 beg. ~~The Ship Commercen Lingren & al claimants~~

v

~~Vezey & others &c of the privatier Lawrence~~
~~This is an appeal from a sentence of the circuit court for~~
~~the District of Massachusetts, rejecting a claim of the~~
~~appellants for freight.~~
~~The Ship commercen is a swedish vessel captured by an~~
~~American cruizer in a voyage from ———— in Ireland to~~
~~Bilboa in Spain, with a cargo of grain for the use of the~~
~~British troops on the peninsula. The cargo, being the~~
~~property of British subjects, was condemned as prize of war.~~
~~The vessel was liberated but her claim for freight was~~
~~rejected, & it is on an appeal from~~ ↑so much of↓ ~~the~~
~~sentence as rejects this claim that the case is now before this~~
~~court.~~
↑The Ship Commercen
As a principle which I think new & which may certainly in
future be very interesting to the United States has been
decided in this case, I trust I may be excused for stating the
reasons which have prevented my concurring in the opinion
that has been delivered. ↓

¶ 2 ll. 10–11   times ~~by the principal~~ ↑avowed by the great↓ maritime
ll. 12–13   trade; ↑& which are generally known in England & in this
country by the appellation of the rule of 1756.
¶ 3 l. 2   appear ↑to me↓ to
¶ 4 l. 2   trade ~~from into~~ ↑in↓ which
¶ 5 l. 10   adversary of ~~those~~ ↑the↓ advantages
ll. 13–14   tolerate, ↑or if the trade be not opened by law.↓
l. 23   unconnected with ~~maritime strength~~ the
¶ 6 ll. 2–3   vessels; ↑& therefore did not identify himself with them. ↓
He was not ~~engaged in a voyage~~ ↑performing functions↓
exclusively
¶ 7 l. 6   appellants. [erasure] ↑But↓ he
l. 7   by ~~a concurrence of~~ ↑its peculiar↓ circumstances. ~~which~~
¶ 8 l. 1   & ~~our enemy~~ Great
ll. 14–15   Britain ~~with whom we were engaged in Britain~~ ↑who was
our enemy, as a different nation↓ from
¶10 ll. 4–5   enemies. ~~& was~~ ↑It was↓ a conflict of nation against nation.
~~Altho~~ This
l. 5   the ~~property~~ ↑cargo↓ of the
ll. 9–10   of ~~anti neutral~~ ↑unneutral↓ conduct;
¶11 ll. 2–3   him ↑who gives it,↓ or his vessels as [erasure] ↑hostile↓ to
l. 4   proposition. ~~Perhaps the cases which have occurred in~~
~~Europe The Swiss even furnish troops to our belligerent~~
~~who serve in the very war remotely, without being~~
~~considered as becoming parties to the war; but those troops~~
~~are not employed directly against the friends of Swisserland.~~

"Since France has been mistress of Alsace, says Vattel, the Switzers who serve in her armies never cross the Rhine to attack the empire."

It will not be contended that this practice can be depended if carried beyond the obligation of treaties ↑existing↓ previously to the war; but it shows Those

l. 6	not ↑entirely↓ applicable
l. 7	to this ↑a↓ new
¶12 ll. 7–8	molested ↑by him↓ while the same good offices are in the power of the other somewhat allow allowed
l. 11	character; but its
ll. 12–13	be an injury injurious
¶14 l. 1	When the war ↑hostilities↓ commenced
l. 5	of the ↑their common↓ war
ll. 8–9	enemies. Had Had
ll. 9–10	expedition to for
l. 11	Europe, ↑or had a new ally engaged in the war,↓ that would
ll. 16–17	enemy. ↑It would have been an interference operating directly to our prejudice.↓
¶15 ll. 1–2	So when the United States declared ↑the declaration of↓ war against Great Britain there can be no ↑had without↓ doubt that a remote
l. 2	Europe. Either The
l. 3	United ↑States↓ must
ll. 10–11	condition of th ↑an↓ enemy. But if ↑had↓ the
ll. 14–15	themselves against ↑on the side of↓ the
¶16 l. 1	to these observations when ↑arguments of this tendency↓ made
l. 3	which it ↑they↓ might
¶17 l. 3	his governed nation as an enemy if those they
l. 4	nation. If therefore There
ll. 8–9	government ↑itself↓ may be rightfully treated as an enemy ↑hostile.↓ Thus a neutral captured in the act of transporting ↑carrying↓ ↑Thus↓ contraband of war to an enemy though
l. 16	government, be ↑have been↓ an act
¶18 ll. 9–10	interference which not
¶19 l. 8	Sweden tow furthering ↑promoting↓ the
l. 10	armies must ↑had a right to↓ pass
¶20 l. 3	performed by a neutral ↑an individual.↓ Had
ll. 7–8	enhanced ↑in this particular case↓ by
ll. 9–11	description. ↑His trade was not more illicit than the carriage of enemy goods for common use would have been.↓
¶21 l. 4	reasoning in the case ↑which has been urged.↓
¶22 ll. 6–7	government near the seat of war ↑in danger of being attacked↓ & the
l. 9	if those dispatches ↑they↓ were

	l. 14	protect ↑the↓ diplomatic
¶23	l. 7	against ~~their captors~~ ↑that other.↓ It is
¶24	l. 1	It may ~~certainly~~ be
¶25	l. 2	extent ~~to~~ which
	l. 3	in ~~any~~ ↑every↓ stage
¶26	ll. 1–2	if ~~not protect~~ ↑either can↓ be done without violating the ~~rights or~~ sovereignty
	l. 4	itself. ~~The capture of a neu~~ The
	ll. 5–6	them ↑but in which we are not engaged,↓ sustain
¶27	l. 1	attack a ~~neutral~~ friend
	l. 5	seem ↑to me↓ that
¶28	l. 1	subject, ~~the court has~~ ↑I have↓ at
	ll. 2–3	that ~~the trade in which was engaged~~ the comercen ↑being a swede whose↓ nation
	l. 8	enemy ~~but~~ but
	l. 9	~~T So much of the sentence therefore ↑of the circuit court↓ as reverses that part of the sentence of the district court which allows freight to the claimant is reversed, & annulled, & the cause is to be remanded to the district ↑circuit↓ court with directions to affirm that part of the sentence of the District court & to allow freight to the claimant.~~
		~~Judge Livingston concurs in this opinion~~

To St. George Tucker

My dear Sir   [25 May 1816]

I sincerely regret your indisposition & should much regret your increasing it by exposing yourself to day. My poor brother is I think on the eve of breathing his last. I shall adjourn the court in an hour.[1] Your

J MARSHALL

ALS, Tucker-Coleman Papers, ViW. Endorsed by Tucker. Date supplied by information in n. 1.

1. William Marshall, clerk of the U.S. Circuit Court for Virginia, died on 27 May 1816. JM and Tucker both attended court on 24 May; JM presided alone on 25 and 27 May (Saturday and Monday). Tucker returned on 28 May (Richmond *Enquirer*, 29 May, 1 June 1816; U.S. Cir. Ct., Va., Ord. Bk. IX, 444, 452–58).

To [Thomas Willing, Jr.]

Dear Sir   Richmond Aug. 16th. 1816

I have had the pleasure of receiving your favor of the 6th. & am highly gratified at the favorable opinion you entertain of my son.[1]

I certainly did wish to render his education more complete, but as he is destined for commerce I am much more anxious to complete his knowledge of his profession & fit him in every respect for entering it with capacity & character than I am to bestow on him acquirements which tho certainly desirable, are not so essential as is everything by which he may be rendered a more complete merchant. Understanding your letter rather as indicating an opinion that his professional talents would be improved by his continuing in the counting house though an absence from it for two years might be compensated by application to business afterwards, I shall leave him with you in the hope that he will employ to advantage in the improvement of his mind any liesure which may be on his hands. With very much respect & esteem, Your Obedt. Servt

J MARSHALL

ALS, Marshall Papers, NcD. Identity of recipient based on context and on subsequent correspondence (see JM to Willing, 5 Nov. 1817).

1. Letter not found. After leaving Harvard, James K. Marshall had begun an apprenticeship in Willing's countinghouse in May 1815 (JM to Willing & Francis, 2 May 1815).

To Martin Marshall

My dear Nephew[1]   Richmond Septr. 10th. 1816
On the preceding half sheet is a copy of the paper I mention'd to you. I find I was mistaken in supposing it to be a list of the lands in which my brothers were interested. It is merely a memorandum from the Auditors office.[2] It may however be of some use to you & therefore I send it. Inclosed is a letter to my sister Taylor which I wish you to put in the post office should any thing prevent your going to Kentucky. She had written to request that I would ask you to engage a house for her at Fauquier court house but I have advised her to defer any step of that kind till she comes in herself.[3] I mention it that you may consult with your mother on the subject & if you or ⟨she?⟩ can think of a suitable house you may m⟨ention?⟩ it to your aunt.

I wish you an agreeable & successful journey & am my dear Nephew your affectionate

J MARSHALL

ALS, Breckenridge-Marshall Papers, KyLoF. Addressed to Martin Marshall at "Fauquier Court house." Endorsed. Angle brackets enclose words obscured by tear in MS.

1. Martin P. Marshall (1798–1883), son of Charles Marshall and Lucy Pickett Marshall, had joined JM's household in Richmond after Charles Marshall died in 1805. At the time of this letter he was at his mother's home in Warrenton (Fauquier Court House), preparing to leave for Kentucky. Late in life Martin recalled that JM had offered to send him to college but that he chose instead to move to Kentucky to make his fortune. After study-

JANE MARSHALL TAYLOR
Miniature watercolor on ivory by E. Deane, ca. 1800–1810. *Courtesy of
the Association for the Preservation of Virginia Antiquities*

ing law with another uncle, Alexander Keith Marshall (1770–1825), Martin obtained his license in 1818 and soon after married his cousin, Eliza Colston Marshall (1801–1874). He led a distinguished career as a lawyer and state legislator and opposed secession in 1861 (Paxton, *Marshall Family*, 54, 58–59, 125–27).

2. The enclosure concerned the lands of Charles and William Marshall in Mason and Franklin Counties, noting that certain tracts had been sold for payment of taxes. Martin recollected that he went to Kentucky to find his father's "wild lands" (Paxton, *Marshall Family*, 125).

3. Letters not found. Jane Marshall Taylor (1779–1866) was the widow of George Keith Taylor, who had died in Nov. 1815. Her home was in Petersburg, but she evidently was visiting family in Kentucky at this time. In 1817 she opened a school for young women in Petersburg, which operated successfully for some years (Paxton, *Marshall Family*, 77–78; Richmond *Enquirer*, 11 Nov. 1815; James G. Scott and Edward A. Wyatt, IV, *Petersburg's Story: A History* [Petersburg, Va., 1960], 116).

To Bushrod Washington

My dear Sir   Richmond Septr. 10th. 1816

I had the pleasure of receiving on my return from the upper country your letter dated in August.[1] I had not seen Brown & had formed an opinion of the civil admiralty jurisdiction from the character of a case of piracy not from precedent.[2] A pirate being an enemy of the human race & at war with the civilized world I had considered a libel for the condemnation of his vessel as partaking rather of the character of a prize cause than of one belonging to the civil admiralty side of the court. But I bow to precedent.[3]

I should have deferred any communication respecting a revision of "The life" till I see you in Washington if I did not wish you to have some particular conversation with Mr. Wayne on the subject for which there may be an opportunity while you are in Philadelphia.[4] I do not think a new edition ought to be hurried. It cannot be pressed on the publick. We must wait till it is required. I wish you to present this idea to Mr. Wayne & know what evidence he possesses if any that the work is really demanded.

The idea which presents itself to me as eligible is that the introduction be so much abridged as to comprehend the two chapters now inserted in the 2d. vol. respecting the controversies which preceded hostilities & the military operations anterior to the organization of a continental Army & the appointment of a commander in chief. The war may readily be comprized in two volumes. I mentioned to you formerly & I mention it again that I think the introduction may in a new edition be subscribed for distinctly from the residue of the work. That any person at his option subscribe for the whole, or for the introduction solely, or for the life of Washington exclusive of the introduction. If it is contemplated to bring the war within less than two volumes

I could wish to know it. The volume respecting the civil administration may be somewhat reduced, particularly by excluding so much of the transactions of the government during Mr. Adams's Presidency as is unconnected with General Washington personally. I give you my ideas & should like to possess yours & Mr. Waynes.[5]

As the alterations I presume will be considerable it would very much aid Mr. Wayne for me to mark them in the work itself. If Mr. Wayne has a set not bound it will be desirable that you should bring it with you to be applied in this manner. You can let me have it at Washington this winter or at any other time. It is a work which must be perfo⟨rmed⟩ at liesure & I repeat my conviction that ⟨the⟩ edition ought not to be offered till it is really demanded. I am my dear Sir with much esteem, Your Obedt. Servt

J MARSHALL

ALS, Marshall Papers, ViW. Addressed to Washington at Mount Vernon; postmarked Richmond, 12 Sept. Endorsed by Washington. Angle brackets enclose letters obscured by tears in MS.

1. Letter not found.

2. Arthur Browne, *A Compendious View of the Civil Law, and of the Law of the Admiralty* (2d ed.; 2 vols.; London, 1802).

3. The reference is apparently to Browne's discussion of "civil droits" of admiralty, "as distinguished from those arising in the course of war." Among the former were the "ships and goods of pirates," even "though the pirate should be subdued and brought in by the king's own ships; for besides that these goods are in the lord admiral's patent, there are precedents very full and apposite to this effect" (ibid., II, 45, 54).

4. Caleb P. Wayne of Philadelphia, publisher of JM's *The Life of George Washington* . . . (5 vols.; Philadelphia, 1804–7). Washington was unable to see Wayne during his autumn circuit but left JM's letter for him in Philadelphia. On his return to Mount Vernon, Washington wrote to Wayne on the subject of a second edition (Washington to Wayne, 26 Nov. 1816, Dreer Collection, PHi).

5. A second edition was eventually published in 1832 by James Crissy of Philadelphia. The "introduction" was published separately in 1824 by Abraham Small as *A History of the Colonies Planted by the English on the Continent of North America*. . . . Small, a Philadelphia printer and bookseller, had purchased Wayne's remaining copies of the first edition in 1817 (agreement, 3 Jan. 1817, Dreer Collection, PHi; *Robinson's Original Annual Directory for 1817* . . . [Philadelphia, 1817], 399).

To [Gouverneur Morris]

Dear Sir   Richmond October 3d 1816

I received too much pleasure from reading your "inaugural discourse to the New York Historical society" not to return you my thanks for it. Your question "what is History?" leads to serious reflection. It is mortifying to join in the answer that it is too often "an entertaining novel with the ornament of real names." This would not be the case did not "great minds disdain to tell their own good deeds."[1] To the same cause Baron Grimm ascribes the inferiority of modern to antient history.[2] The last he says was, & the first is not written by practical statesmen. How much is it to be regretted that some one of those who has been engaged in the great & interesting events of our country & who has talents as well as leisure, will not devote a part of that leisure to the useful object of transmitting to posterity the knowledge he possesses. But I must not forget that I write only to express the double gratification I have felt in reading your oration & in the recollection that it is transmitted by yourself,[3] and to assure that I remain with respectful esteem, Your Obedt.

J MARSHALL

ADfS, Marshall Papers, ViW. Addressee identified by internal evidence (see n. 1).

1. *An Inaugural Discourse, Delivered before the New-York Historical Society, by the Honourable Gouverneur Morris. (President,) 4th September, 1816* (New York, 1816; S #38292), 4–5.

2. Frederick Melchior Grimm (1723–1807), an influential Enlightenment publicist and man of letters. A native of Bavaria, Grimm at age twenty-five moved to Paris, where for forty years he engaged in literary pursuits and served as a diplomat. He was editor of *La correspondence littéraire*, a semimonthly newsletter that circulated among enlightened aristocrats and monarchs (*Historical & Literary Memoirs and Anecdotes, Selected from the Correspondence of Baron de Grimm and Diderot...*, I [2d ed.; London, 1815], vii–xiv; Joseph Royall Smiley, *Diderot's Relations with Grimm* [Urbanna, Ill., 1950], 1–3, 8–10).

3. This was JM's last communication with Morris, who died on 6 Nov.

To [Henry Wheaton]

Dear Sir   Richmond October 27th. 1816

I have received in sheets the 7th. & 8th. volumes of Cranch's reports for which I believe myself to be indebted to you & beg you to receive my thanks for the attention.[1] I have looked cursorily into them & am in general pleased with the manner in which the work is executed as well as with the promptness with which it has been carried on after the delay of its commencement.[2] I have not received your page of *errata* for the 8th. vol. & although it may be unnecessary, take the liberty to call your attention to a few typographical errors in my opinion in the case of the Venus. In page 298. l. 37. or 39—for "facts" read "parts." p 311. l 20. for "permanent," read "prominent." p 313 l 5. for "a" read "as."[3]

As the opinion is a very long one these mistakes may perhaps escape the reviser of the press; & as it is one on a subject of great interest on which I have differed from the court I wish it to be correctly printed. I am dear Sir with much regard & esteem, Your Obedt.

J MARSHALL

ALS, Wheaton Papers, NNPM.

1. The last three volumes of Cranch's reports (covering the 1812, 1813, 1814, and 1815 terms) were brought out by Wheaton in 1816 and 1817.

2. Cranch had been under increasing criticism for the tardiness of his reports, his last published volume (vol. VI) having appeared in 1812. See G. Edward White, *The Marshall Court and Cultural Change, 1815–35*, the Oliver Wendell Holmes Devise History of the Supreme Court of the United States, III–IV (New York, 1988), 385–89.

3. The errata sheet printed only the last of the three corrections; see The Venus, Opinion, 12 Mar. 1814 and nn. 11 and 29.

Thompson v. Marshall
Answer in Chancery

[9 December 1816]

The answer of John Marshall to the bill of complaint exhibited against him by Joseph Thompson in the Honble. the superior court of chancery holden at Winchester.

This respondent saving to himself every just exception to the bill of the complainant for answer thereto saith

That he admits the contract annexed to the bill of the complainant, & refers to it as containing the true & real agreement made & intended to be made between the parties.[1] It was drawn by this respondent at the request of the complainant, he not then expecting that it would be impracticable to obtain payment otherwise than by proceedings at law; but he does not admit or beleive that any material stipulation favorable to the complainant which was in contemplation of the parties has been omitted.

If the complainant means to state that the contract was made at one time & reduced to writing at another, the fact is denied. This respondent had sold to the complainant & his two brothers a survey made for the use of Lord Fairfax on one of the streams in Hampshire or Hardy county, & has a confused & uncertain impression on his mind that subsequent to this sale he received from the complainant a letter expressing his wish to purchase this survey also which comprehended high lands adjoining the survey previously sold to the three brothers, but he is not certain whether such letter was received or whether the impressions relative to the motives of the complainant for wishing to make the purchase were made on the day of the contract. He understood that the complainant expected by the acquisition of this property to influence the partition of the land purchased in common. However this may be he is confident that no contract was made until they met at Washington & that it was immediately reduced to writing & executed.

If the complainant means to say that the quantity of land is totally uncertain, or that the respondent claims "for any quantity of land he might think proper to name," the fact is certainly otherwise. This respondents claim was a survey of two hundred acres of land made by order of Lord Fairfax for his own use. This survey immediately adjoined a larger survey purchased from him not long before by the complainant & his two brothers, & on which he understands & beleives they had long resided.[2] The survey was well known to the complainant who came to Washington & visited this respondent as he said for the purpose of purchasing it. His application to this respondent was to purchase this survey of two hundred acres. And the contract, as will appear by a reference thereto expressly states that the respondent sells "his survey adjoining the tract sold to the said Joseph & his brothers." The plat of this survey however was at Richmond, not in Washington; and, although the quantity was he beleives perfectly in the recollection of the complainant who resided in its neighborhood & who came to purchase it, it was not in the recollection of this respondent. The sale therefore was not for a gross sum nor was the quantity mentioned, but for ten shillings per acre neither party suggesting so far as this respondent recollects or beleives that the quantity expressed in the survey was inaccurate, but each as he also beleives, being willing to rely on the survey made by order of Lord Fairfax. There is therefore no stipulation, nor does he recollect any conversation respecting a resurvey. He does not however hesitate to admit that he had no objection to a resurvey, & would at any time have assented to it had the complainant signified his wish for one.

The complainant knew perfectly well that the title of this respondent to the land sold was the same as his title to the survey previously sold to the complainant & his brothers. They were two surveys made by order of Lord Fairfax in his life time for his own use, & by his last will devised to Denny Martin afterwards Denny Martin Fairfax who sold & conveyed them with other property to James M. Marshall who purchased in his own name for himself & others.[3] On a partition these surveys were allotted to this respondent, & the deed conveying them is recorded in the General court of this commonwealth.[4] It is this survey which the complainant has purchased & which the defendent has bargained & sold. He is of course bound to convey it, & he is ready & willing to convey it, & always has been ready & willing to convey it with a general warranty on receiving the purchase money. Until he does receive it, he is not willing, nor is he, as he concieves, bound to convey.

This respondent does not beleive that the complainant has felt any difficulty or ought to feel any respecting title. In the long course of time between the contract & the filing of his bill, he has never suggested to this respondent his fears respecting a conveyance; had he done so, he would have been informed that on his paying the purchase money the conveyance would be executed. If he ever wrote the letter mentioned in the bill it has not been received. Had it been received, the conveyance would not have been executed until the purchase money was paid, it being expressly stipulated that the land should remain a security therefor.

This respondent is informed by his counsel that the order for survey was made at a time when he was not in possession of the original plat. On receiving it he supposed a resurvey to be unnecessary & proceeded to trial without making one.

The respondent does not recollect ever to have heard it suggested that there is a deficiency in the quantity of land; nor does the complainant in his bill suggest it. This respondent rather supposes there is a surplus; but of this he knows nothing. He submits it to the consideration of this Honble. court whether in a case like this where an actual survey has been made & land sold which is claimed under it, a judgement at law ought to be injoined and a resurvey ordered on a bill which does not even suggest a suspicion that the survey on which the contract was made is erroneous. At any rate, he trusts that the delay, the expence & the inconvenience of a resurvey will not be incurred unless the complainant will enter into a bond obliging himself to pay for any excess in the quantity; the bond to be delivered to this respondent should the survey show that the tract contains more than two hundred acres of land. This defendent denies all combination & prays to be dismissed with and he will ever pray &c.[5]

City of Richmond to wit

John Marshall appeared before me a magistrate for the City aforesaid this 9th. day of December 1816 & made oath that the allegations of the foregoing answer are true so far as they are stated to be of his own knowledge & so far as they are stated to be of the knowledge of others he beleives them to be true.

WM. H. FITZWHYLSONN

AD, ViU. Entirely in JM's hand except for magistrate's signature and insertion of "City of Richmond" and "City" in affidavit. Endorsed by JM, with clerk's notations below endorsement.

1. The contract, drawn up early in 1804, was for the sale of a tract of land in Hampshire County (now W. Va.). Thompson's bill in chancery, filed in the Superior Court of Chancery at Winchester, has not been found. For the contract, see *PJM*, VI, 268–69 and nn.

2. The land in question, along with the remaining Fairfax manor lands, had been conveyed by Denny Martin Fairfax to James M. Marshall on 30 Aug. 1797. By a deed of partition of 24 June 1799 between James M. Marshall of the first part, JM of the second part, Rawleigh Colston of the third part, and Charles and William Marshall of the fourth part, these lands were divided up. Among the lands allotted to JM were 872 acres on the Cacapon River in Hampshire County, of which 672 acres were then "in the occupation of certain persons of the name of Thompson." JM sold the 672 acres to the Thompsons in Aug. 1802. The contract giving rise to this suit was for the other two hundred acres (copy of deed, Denny M. Fairfax to James M. Marshall, 30 Aug. 1797, Marshall's Lessee v. Foley, record, Fauquier County Land Causes, III [1833–50], 29–31 [microfilm], Vi; copy

of partition deed [in JM's hand], 24 June 1799, Martin v. Moffet, U.S. Cir. Ct., Va., Ended Cases [Restored], 1824, Vi; *PJM*, VI, 269 n. 2).

3. The deed of 30 Aug. 1797 (see n. 2).

4. The partition deed of 24 June 1799 (see n. 2).

5. According to the clerk's endorsement, this answer was filed at the Jan. 1817 rules of the court. The bill was ultimately dismissed in Apr. 1818. After the Thompsons made final payments in 1819 and 1822, JM executed deeds for the land (Frederick County Superior Court of Chancery, Ord. Bk., I [1812–19], 295, 313, 444 [microfilm], Vi; *PJM*, VI, 269 n. 2).

To [Louis Marshall]

My dear brother   Richmond Decr. 23d. 1816

Our Nephew the son of our Sister Taylor leaves us to day for Kentucky for the purpose of being educated under your superintendence.[1] His mother was very desirous of committing him to your care & I have entirely approved her determination. His Father when dying requested me to supply his place as far as should be in my power & I accepted the trust with an earnest wish to fulfil the engagement. Had the state of my family allowed of my taking him into my own house I should still have preferred his being brought up in the country under your eye.[2] This town is a dangerous place for youth & our seminaries are far from being respectable. I imagine my sister will write to you respecting the funds for his support & I will myself attend to the necessary arrangements. I have not conversed with her on the subject but will do so as soon as I see her. There will probably be no difficulty in your drawing on me; but if it should be more convenient the necessary funds shall be placed in a bank at this place, or Baltimore or Philadelphia or elsewhere as may be prescribed by yourself.

My wife continues in wretched health. Her nervous system is so affected that she cannot set in a room while a person walks across the floor. I am now preparing to convey her out of town in order to escape the noisy rejoicings of the season which is approaching.

Our legislature is entirely occupied with banks & conventions. But I am so withdrawn from the busy active world that I seldom know much of what is passing.

It would give me great pleasure to see you here, but it is a pleasure which I scarcely expect. My Kentucky friends when they visit Virginia seldom take Richmond in their tour. With the best wishes for Mrs. Marshall[3] & your family, I am my dear brother, Your affectionate

J MARSHALL

ALS, Collection of Margaret Cardwell Higonnet, Cambridge, Mass.

1. Thomas M. Taylor (d. 1820), son of Jane Marshall Taylor and the late George Keith Taylor, was also the subject of JM's letters to Louis Marshall of 7 Dec. 1817 and 19 May

1818. In a note to his account as George Keith Taylor's executor, JM later recalled that Thomas Taylor went to Kentucky late in 1816 and died in 1820 (Petersburg City, Hustings Court Will Book No. 2, [1804–26], p. 121; Account Book No. 2, [1826–31], f. 110, 111 [microfilm], Vi).

2. Louis Marshall operated a classical school for boys at Buckpond, his home in Woodford County, Ky.

3. Agatha Smith Marshall (1782–1844) (Paxton, *Marshall Family*, 69).

To St. George Tucker

My dear Sir   [December 1816]

    I regret your indisposition extremely. You will of course take care of yourself. I always regret your absence but should regret much more your being present to your own injury. Your

J M

ALS, Tucker-Coleman Papers, ViW. Addressed to Tucker. Endorsed by Tucker as dated Dec. 1816.

To John Randolph

Dear Sir[1]   Richmond Jany. 13th. 1817

    I had the pleasure a few days past of receiving a letter from you with the bill establishing an uniform system of Bankruptcy throughout the United States.[2] I thank you for both.

    Our legislature is engaged in debating the question respecting a convention. The prevailing opinion seems to be that a convention with limited powers will be recommended. But on this subject you have correspondents much better informed than myself. I will therefore only say that under the present or any other constitution I am & shall remain with much respect & esteem, Your obedt

J Marshall

ALS, ViHi. Addressed to Randolph in Washington and franked; postmarked Richmond, 15 Jan. Endorsed by Randolph: "The chief Justice/of Human nature" (see n. 1).

1. On the verso of an undated (ca. Dec. 1816) dinner invitation from JM, Randolph wrote: "From the Chief Justice of Human Nature, as Lord Somers was called it's Chancellor by Horace Walpole. If a clearer head & sounder heart than Mr. Justice M. possessed be on earth, I have never found them" (Tucker-Coleman Papers, ViW).

2. Letter not found. The bankruptcy bill, reported by the House Judiciary Committee on 13 Dec. 1816, was published as *H.R. 9, A Bill to Establish an Uniform System of Bankruptcy throughout the United States, December 13, 1816* (Washington, D.C., 1816; S #39328). The bill was postponed indefinitely on 24 Feb. 1817 (*Annals of Congress*, XXX, 276, 1025).

To Dudley Chase

Sir   Washington Feby. 7th. 1817

Your letter inclosing a copy of the bill "To provide for reports of the decisions of the Supreme court," in which you do me the honour to request, for the Committee, my views relative to ["]the object and utility of the proposed act" was yesterday received & communicated to the Judges.[1]

We all concur in the opinion that the object of the bill is in a high degree desirable.

That the cases determined in the Supreme court should be reported with accuracy & promptness is essential to correctness & uniformity of decision in all the courts of the United States. It is also to be recollected that from the same tribunal the public receives that exposition of the constitution laws & treaties of the United States as applicable to the cases of individuals, which must ultimately prevail. It is obviously important that a knowledge of this exposition should be attainable by all.

It is a minor consideration, but not perhaps to be entirely overlooked, that even in cases where the decisions of the Supreme court are not to be considered as authority except in the courts of the United States, some advantage may be derived from their being known. It is certainly to be wished that independent tribunals having concurrent jurisdiction over the same subject, should concur in the principles on which they determine the causes coming before them. This concurrence can be obtained only by communicating to each the judgements of the other, & by that mutual respect which will probably be inspired by a knowledge of the grounds on which their judgements respectively stand. On great commercial questions especially it is desirable that the judicial opinions of all parts of the Union should be the same.

From experience, the Judges think there is much reason to apprehend that the publication of the decisions of the Supreme court will remain on a very precarious footing, if the Reporter is to depend solely on the sales of his work for a reimbursement of the expenses which must be incurred in preparing it, & for his own compensation. The patronage of the government is beleived to be necessary to the secure & certain attainment of the object.

Law Reports can have but a limited circulation. They rarely gain admission into the libraries of other than professional gentlemen. The circulation of the decisions of the Supreme court will probably be still more limited than those of the courts of the states, because they are useful to a smaller number of the profession. Only a few of those who practise in the courts of the United States, or in great commercial cities, will often require them. There is therefore much reason to beleive that no Reporter will continue to employ his time & talents in preparing those decisions for the press, after he shall be assured that the government will not countenance his undertaking.² With very great respect, I am Sir your obedt. Servt

J MARSHALL

ALS, RG 46, DNA. Addressed to Chase. Endorsed (by Chase?): "Judge Marshall's/ Accompanying the bill from the Senate for the publication of the decisions of the Supreme Court." MS torn where seal was broken.

1. Letter not found. Chase (1771–1846) of Vermont was chairman of the Senate Judiciary Committee. He resigned from the Senate in Nov. 1817 to become chief justice of the Vermont Supreme Court. A bill to provide for publication of the Supreme Court's decisions was introduced in the Senate on 31 Jan., following defeat of a similar bill by the House in December. It was referred to the Judiciary Committee on 3 Feb. and approved by the Senate on 19 Feb. After amending the bill, the House adopted it on 1 Mar. (*Annals of Congress*, XXX, 90, 96–97, 108, 132–33, 357, 366–67, 1019, 1042–43, 1044).

2. The act provided $1,000 annual compensation for the Supreme Court reporter on condition that he publish the decisions within six months of delivery and that he deliver eighty copies of the publication to the secretary of state for distribution among federal judicial and administrative officials (*U.S. Statutes at Large*, III, 376).

To Mary W. Marshall

My dearest Polly   Washington Feb. 14th. 1817

Since my being in this place I have been more in company than I wish & more than is consistent with the mass of business we have to go through. I have been invited to dine with the President with our own secretaries & with the minister of France & tomorrow I dine with the British minister.¹ I have been very much pleased with the French minister & with his Lady.² She is among the most simple & domestic women I ever saw. Speaks of the comfortable habits of our country with great approbation & with regret of the increasing luxury of those who possess but moderate fortunes. In the midst of these gay circles my mind is carried to my own fire side & to my beloved wife. I conjecture where you are sitting & who is with you to cheer your solitary moments. I am most anxious to know how you do but no body is kind enough to gratify my wishes. Mr. Wirt I understand came yesterday & I looked eagerly for a letter to day—but no letter came.³ I still retain some hope of receiving one tomorrow when I shall certainly see him.

Our weather continues intensely cold & I am the more grieved at it because I am sure it must prevent your riding out. You must not fail when you go to chiccahominy on the 21st. to carry out blankets enough to keep you comfortable. I am very desirous of hearing what is doing there but as no body is good enough to let me know how you do & what is passing at home I could not expect to hear what is passing at the farm.⁴ I am my dearest Polly, Your ever affectionate

J MARSHALL

Feb. 15th.
I have kept my letter open till to day in the hope that Mr. Wirt would bring me a letter. I have the extreme mortification to find that he has brought none.

ALS, Marshall Papers, ViW. Addressed to Mrs. Marshall in Richmond; postmarked Washington, 16 Feb.

1. On 5 Feb. JM accepted an invitation to dine with President and Mrs. Madison on "Saturday next at four"—that is, Saturday, 15 Feb. Assuming he dated his letter correctly, the dinner with the Madisons was to take place "tomorrow." His invitation to dine with British minister Charles Bagot was perhaps for Sunday, 16 Feb. (JM to Madison, 5 Feb. 1817, Collection of Joseph Z. Willner, Chicago, Ill.).

2. Jean-Guillaume Hyde de Neuville (1776–1857) was the French minister to the U.S. He and the Baroness Anne-Marguerite Hyde de Neuville were a popular couple in Washington society. An amateur artist, the Baroness de Neuville painted watercolors depicting scenes of early Washington (Edgar Leon Newman and Robert Lawrence Simpson, *Historical Dictionary of France from the 1815 Restoration to the Second Empire* [New York, 1987], 503–4; Thomas Froncek, ed., *An Illustrated History of the City of Washington* [New York, 1980], 128–30).

3. William Wirt arrived in Washington on 13 Feb. to argue a case before the Supreme Court (Wirt to Elizabeth W. Wirt, 14, 17 Feb. 1817, Wirt Papers, MdHi; The Fortuna, 2 Wheat. 161, 165–66).

4. JM's farm on the Chickahominy River in Henrico County, northeast of Richmond (*Inventory of Early Architecture and Historic and Archeological Sites, County of Henrico, Virginia* [Richmond, Va., 1976], 126).

To John Wickham

Dear Sir   Washington Feb. 17th. 1817
I have forborne to write to you since my arrival because it was not in my power to give you any satisfactory information respecting the subject on which I was to write. That uncertainty still remains. I have conversed with Mr. Wirt & the conclusion is that after his return he will, if you & he can arrange with the court of appeals, write to some gentleman of the bar here to fix the cause to a certain day.[1] I am dear Sir your obdt.

J MARSHALL

ALS, Collection of Mrs. W. C. Wickham, Jr., Ashland, Va. Addressed to Wickham in Richmond; postmarked Washington, 18 Feb. Endorsed by Wickham.

1. The reference is to the cases of Craig v. Leslie and Nicholas v. Craig, which had been filed in the Supreme Court on 10 Jan. 1817 on a certificate of division from the U.S. Circuit Court for Virginia. These cases were to be argued by Wickham and Wirt, which meant they would have to miss part of the concurrent session of the Virginia Court of Appeals. Argument was accordingly postponed until Feb. 1818, with Washington giving the opinion for the Supreme Court on 11 Mar. JM's notes of Wirt's argument are in the

appellate case file (Wirt to Elizabeth W. Wirt, 17 Feb. 1817, Wirt Papers, MdHi; Craig v. Leslie, App. Cas. No. 834; Nicholas v. Craig, App. Cas. No. 835; U.S. Sup. Ct. Minutes, 20–21 Feb. 1818; 3 Wheat. 563).

From James Monroe

Sir   Washington March 1st 1817

I propose to take the oath which the constitution prescribes to the President of the United States, before he enters on the execution of his office, on tuesday next, at 12 oClock, in the chamber of the House of Representetives; and have to request, that you will have the goodness, to meet me there for the purpose of administering it. I have the honor to be, with the greatest respect, Sir, your most obt. servant.

JAS. MONROE

LS, Marshall Papers, ViW. Inside address to JM.

To James Monroe

Sir   Washington March 1st. 1817

I have just received your letter of this morning & shall certainly do myself the honor to attend in the house of Representatives on tuesday next for the purpose of administering the oath prescribed by the constitution to the President of the United States. With the greatest respect, I am Sir your obedt. Servt

J MARSHALL

ALS, RG 59, DNA. Endorsed by Monroe.

From Marquis de Lafayette

My dear Sir   La grange[1] April 22d 1817

Permit me to introduce to You My friend M. descaves Who is on the point of Returning to the U.S. and Who Expects to go to Virginia Where I much Wish to obtain for Him the Honour and pleasure of Your Acquaintance.[2] I Regret Not to Have it in My power to Accompany Him and personally to Repeat How much I Have Enjoy'd the Historical Monument You Have Raised to the Memory of My paternal friend; How Sensible I Have been of Your Benevolent disposition in My Behalf.

Our friend Mr. Bushrod Washington Has Been pleased to intend for me a present the Most precious I Could Receive. My Correspondence With the General Has Been Lost in the Revolutionary Storms of france. The Misfortune May be Retrieved By the possession of that part of the papers Which Contain My own letters and Copies of those I Have to Regret, the Better So as You Know that the Respected Author often Copied With His own Hand Such of His letters as Were Wholly Confidential.

Had His Nephew or Yourself Any farther occasion for those writings, Any intention to publish the Epistolary Correspondence of the General, I Would not Hasten to avail Myself of Mr. Bushrod's Good intentions, as in those Very Letters, particularly the Confidential ones, You Would find New Specimens of our Venerable friend's Amiable Sentiments and illustrious Virtues. But if You Have No Need of the papers, I am Sure You Will See With pleasure they are transmitted by Mr. Bushrod Washington to the Man Who So Well feels their Value and Whom You Honour With Your friendship.[3]

Whatever Assistance M. descaves May Give in the Business I am Sure He Will offer With a Sincere and Well informed Zeal. I am Happy in the Opportunity to Repeat to You the Sentiments of High and Grateful Regard I Have the Honour to Be With, Yours

LAFAYETTE

ALS, Marshall Papers, ViW. Addressed to JM as "The Hon. John Marshall Chief Justice of the/United States/Virginia" and marked "To the Care of M. descaves"; enclosed in Mark L. Descaves to JM, ca. 31 Mar. 1818.

1. Lagrange-Bléneau, Lafayette's estate in Seine-et-Marne, France.
2. Mark L. Descaves, described by Lafayette as "a Gallo American Merchant," had a place of business in Baltimore at this time (Gilbert Chinard, ed., *The Letters of Lafayette and Jefferson* [Baltimore, Md., 1929], 385–88; *The Baltimore Directory and Register, for the Year 1816* [Baltimore, Md., 1816; S #36798], 53; *The Baltimore Directory, for 1817–18* . . . [Baltimore, Md., 1817], 49).
3. This correspondence was returned to Lafayette and remained in the family archives at Lagrange until after World War I. The letters are now at Lafayette College in Easton, Pa. (Descaves to JM, [ca. 31 Mar. 1818]; Louis Gottschalk, ed., *The Letters of Lafayette to Washington, 1777–1799* [2d ed., rev.; Philadelphia, 1976], xxiv–xxv).

Marshall v. Lee
Bill in Chancery

[ca. 30 April 1817][1]

To the Honble. the Judge of the superior court of Chancery holden at Fredericksburg humbly complaining showeth to your honor your orator, John Marshall.

That James M. Marshall the brother of your orator purchased for himself and others of whom your orator was one, the landed estate of Denny Martin Fairfax devised to him in the last will and testament of Thomas Lord Fairfax deceased. That the conveyance of what was denominated the residuary estate, a term comprehending all the lands of the said Denny M. Fairfax except the Leeds manor & the south branch manor & a small tract adjacent to the south branch manor called the resurvey, was made to James M. Marshall. The parties really interested in this purchase agreed on a partition of the property agreeably to which conveyances were made to each individual by James M. Marshall.[2] In the part of your orator was one tract of land containing two hundred acres surveyed for Lord Fairfax on the 31st. day of July in the year 1776 lying in the county of Hampshire[3] adjoining his Lordships six hundred & seventy two acre survey on the North river of Cacapon; also one other tract of land containing four hundred & thirty acres lying in the county of Hampshire on the Allegheny mountain between the land surveyed for Richard Houghland Richard Lane & his Lordships meadow.[4] These tracts being in the part allotted to your orator were conveyed to him by the said James M. Marshall by deed recorded in the General court of this commonwealth.

Your orator further shows that previous to the conveyance of the said estate to the said James M. Marshall doubts were entertained respecting the validity of the title of the said Denny M Fairfax, he being a British subject, in consequence of which land warrants were laid by sundry individuals on parts of the said land. To avoid as far as in his power the danger to be apprehended from the continuance of such locations Thomas Bryan Martin a citizen of Virginia, the brother & agent of Denny M. Fairfax was advised to assign the plats of surveys made for Lord Fairfax to persons friendly to his brother who might obtain patents therefor in their own names as assignees. The two tracts herein before mentioned were assigned by the said Thomas Bryan Martin to Charles Lee who obtained patents therefor.[5] The said Charles Lee had an interest in the purchase herein before stated to have been made by James M Marshall & was a party to the partition herein before mentiond, & has received a conveyan[ce] for the lands which in the said partition were allotted to him.[6] As he set up no claim to the two tracts of land before mentioned although the patents issued in his name he transmitted to your orator a conveyance for both tracts which were never recorded & which he has carelessly mislaid or lost. Some decisions not expected by your orator induced him to suppose that the title under the patents might be convenient to him in consequence of which he prepared other deeds of conveyance & requested Mr. Lee execute them. He took them for consideration & afterwards declined executing them because as he said they were defectively drawn; but he gave your orator the most positive assurance that he would prepare others himself & execute them & either transmit them to your orator or deliver them to him at the succeeding term of the supreme court. Before the succeeding term Mr. Lee departed this life intestate not having executed the deeds to your orator according to his promise & intention.[7]

Your orator humbly states that[8] Margarett C. Lee is the widow & relict of the said Charles Lee & that Ann Lucinda who has intermarried with Walter Jones and Alfred Lee Robert C Lee Elizabeth Lee are his children & hiers at law of whom Alfred, Robert C. and Elizabeth are infants under the age of twenty one years. To the end therefore that Margarett C. Lee the widow of the said Charles Lee and Walter Jones & Ann L Lee his wife and Alfred Lee who is an infant under the age of twenty one years by Edmund J. Lee his guardian appointed by this Honble. court to defend them in this suit and Robe[r]t C. Lee Elizabeth Lee who are also infants under the age of twenty one years by John Scott their guardian appointed by this Honble court to defend them in this suit may be made defendents hereto & may on oath or otherwise true answer make to the premises & that the defendents may be decreed to release or otherwise convey the lands herein before mentioned to your orator without warranty & that your orator may have such other relief as is proper MAY it please your Honor &c AND your orator will ever pray &c.[9]

AD, Marshall v. Lee, File 184, Office of the Clerk, Fredericksburg Circuit Court, Fredericksburg, Va. Entirely in JM's hand except for names of defendants (see n. 8, below). Endorsed by clerk "967 words." Markings in margin to indicate word count.

1. The editors have assigned this approximate date on the basis of James M. Marshall's deposition, in JM's hand, sworn in Frederick County on 30 Apr. 1817 (Marshall v. Lee).

2. The residuary Fairfax estate had been conveyed to James M. Marshall by deed of 30 Aug. 1797. The lands comprehended by this deed were subsequently divided up by a deed of partition, dated 24 June 1799, to which James M. Marshall, JM, Rawleigh Colston, William Marshall, and Charles Marshall were parties. (Thompson v. Marshall, Answer in Chancery, 9 Dec. 1816 and n. 2).

3. This was the same two-hundred-acre tract that JM had contracted to sell to Joseph Thompson in 1804 and for which Thompson later brought suit (ibid.).

4. The 1799 partition deed noted that a patent for this tract had been issued to Charles Lee (copy of partition deed [in JM's hand], 24 June 1799, Martin v. Moffet, U.S. Cir. Ct., Va., Ended Cases [Restored], 1824, Vi).

5. These patents had been issued to Charles Lee on 26 Oct. 1793. James M. Marshall deposed that the patents had been issued "in the name of Charles Lee in trust for Denny Martin Fairfax or those who might be entitled under him." He further stated that he had "seen a written declaration of the trust" in Lee's handwriting and had "always understood from himself that he claimed no beneficial interest for himself" (deposition of James M. Marshall, 30 Apr. 1817, Marshall v. Lee; Fredericksburg Superior Court of Chancery, Ord. Bk. [Rec. Bk.], 1815–20, 224–25 [microfilm], Vi).

6. Lee, who appeared frequently as counsel for the Marshalls in their Fairfax lands litigation, was not an original party to the partition deed drawn up in 1799. He apparently acquired an interest in the lands at a later time. See JM to Lee, 7 May 1810 (PJM, VII, 246–47).

7. Lee died on 24 June 1815.

8. Here and below the names of Margaret C. Lee, Ann Lucinda, Alfred Lee, Robert E. Lee, and Elizabeth Lee were inserted in an unknown hand. The correct middle initial for Robert Lee is "E" (Eden).

9. The answers of the several defendants stated ignorance of the facts concerning this transaction. On 29 Apr. 1818 the court ordered the defendants to convey all right and interest in the two tracts of land to JM (Fredericksburg Superior Court of Chancery, Ord. Bk. [Rec. Bk.], 1815–20, 223–25 [microfilm], Vi).

To Martin Marshall

My dear Nephew   Richmond May 24th 1817

I have received several letters from you since your arrival in Kentucky, the last of which gave the afflicting inteligence of the death of my brother & the illness of my sister Duke.[1] In this country too our wide spreading family encounters new distresses. My brother James has lost his wife & the whole family is plunged in deep distress.[2]

I am much inclined to believe that your determination to study the law in Kentucky & to remain there is a wise one. Your Fathers interest in that country is I doubt not considerable if it can be discovered & will require all your care. I have no doubt that he is concerned in many tracts where his name does not appear & in some about which I fear you will be able to get no information. My brother Alexander will probably be able to give you much useful inteligence and to put you on the track of obtaining more from others. He will tell you whether you are in danger of losing your property by the non payment of taxes & what it will be necessary to do to save it. I think it will be advisable not to let the taxes accumulate. They are loaded I presume there as well as here with a very heavy interest.[3]

William has just been here & seems determined to take a trip to Kentucky this summer for the purpose of examining into his Fathers affairs. Perhaps you & he may be useful to each other. I gave him two papers found among those of my brother which have some memoranda respecting land but they cannot be of much importance.[4] I shal rejoice to hear of your doing well & am my dear Nephew, Your affectionate

J MARSHALL

Tr (typed), supplied by owner of ALS, Herbert E. Klingelhofer, Bethesda, Md., 1967; Tr (typed, dated 21 May), Marshall Papers, DLC; Tr (typed, dated 21 May), Collection of Thomas W. Bullitt, Louisville, Ky.

1. Letters not found. Thomas Marshall died in Washington, Ky., on 19 Mar. 1817; Charlotte Marshall Duke died less than a month later, on 17 Apr., also in Washington, Ky. (*Reporter* [Lexington, Ky.], 2 Apr. 1817; Paxton, *Marshall Family*, 47, 50, 76).

2. Sources consistently list the date of Hester Morris Marshall's death as 18 Apr. 1816, but JM's comments here and in his letter to Louis Marshall, 30 Aug. 1817, establish that she died in 1817 (Paxton, *Marshall Family*, 51–52; Duane L. Borden, *Tombstone Inscrip-*

tions: *Prospect Hill Cemetery, Front Royal, Virginia, and Other Warren County Vicinities* [Ozark, Mo., 1985], 327).

3. See JM to Martin Marshall, 10 Sept. 1816 and n. 2. In Kentucky, as in Virginia, 10 percent interest was added to the principal sum of unpaid land taxes (William Littell, *The Statute Laws of Kentucky* ... [5 vols.; Frankfort, Ky., 1809–19], II, 327–29; *The Revised Code of Virginia* ... [2 vols.; Richmond, Va., 1819], II, 548–49).

4. Presumably William Marshall (d. 1824). He and Martin Marshall were first cousins, sons of the twin brothers William and Charles Marshall. Their late fathers had extensive holdings of Kentucky lands (Paxton, *Marshall Family*, 53, 145).

To Lucy Marshall

My dear Sister   Aug. 26th.[1] 1817

On my return to Richmond I found two letters, one from Martin & the other from my brother Louis urging me strongly to write to you respecting Charles & to advise his immediate resignation & withdrawal from the school at West Point.[2] The reasons they urge in favor of this proposition appear to me to be conclusive. The prospects of a young man in the military line in this country are unfavorable & I have always thought it more advisable that Charles should rely on his exertions in a civil character either at the bar or otherwise; but I did hope that he would receive such an education as would fit him for a military or civil profession as future circumstances might render most eligible. I am now induced to fear that his situation is unfavorable to his education & that there is danger of his acquiring very pernicious habits. He is at a time of life when it is extremely dangerous to trust him to such a place without a prudent & experienced person who will in some measure superintend his education. Both Louis & Martin urge strongly that he should come immediately to Kentucky where he may be placed in an excellent & cheap school among friends who will attend both to his education & morals. I am convinced that they advise for the best & would strongly recommend that Charles should immediately resign his commission as cadet & withdraw from the school at West Point. If he can go out this fall to Kentucky I think it desirable that he should do so.[3] I am my dear Sister Your affectionate

J MARSHA⟨LL⟩

ALS, RG 94, DNA. Addressed to Lucy Marshall at "Fauquier Ct house"; postmarked Richmond, 29 Aug. MS torn where seal was broken.

1. JM apparently misdated this letter, which was probably written on 28 or 29 Aug. According to his letter to Louis Marshall of 30 Aug., JM did not return to Richmond until 28 Aug.

2. Letters not found. On Charles C. Marshall's appointment to West Point, see JM to [James Monroe?], 10 Mar. 1815 and n. 2. Martin P. Marshall was Charles's older brother.

3. Charles Marshall resigned his commission on 29 Oct. 1817. Two years later he

appears to have considered returning to West Point, as indicated in a letter from Sylvanus Thayer, superintendent of the academy: "The cause of his resignation was, I believe, his unfavorable prospects at the Academy. As a student he was inattentive & made but little progress. In other respects his conduct was generally correct. At the time of his Resignation he belonged to the 3d now the first Class & may be appointed with that Class in July next under the existing Regulations of the Academy." In Nov. 1821 he married Judith Steptoe Ball (1805–1865) and settled with her first in Lancaster County, Va., later moving to Kentucky and finally to Mississippi (Charles C. Marshall to Thayer, 29 Oct. 1817; Thayer to George Graham, 8 Nov. 1817; Thayer to Maj. C. Van De Venter, 14 Dec. 1819 [misfiled in the file of Charles R. Marshall], RG 94, DNA; Paxton, *Marshall Family*, 147).

To Louis Marshall

My dear brother   Richmond Aug. 30th. 1817

I received two days past on my return from Oakhill your letter of the 1st. of August.[1] I concur entirely in the opinions you express respecting our Nephew Charles, & have written to his mother to that effect. She will I am persuaded feel no difficulty in removing him from west point. I hope Martin has written to her on this subject.

In obtaining for Charles a situation in the military school I was influenced by the hope & expectation that his education would be useful & his morals attended to. The enquiries I had made led me to beleive that the institution was conducted with talent & integrity; but I fear there is no place in our country to which a young man may be safely confided unless superintended by the vigilant & anxious eye of a near & inteligent friend. I hope the mischief is not irreparable & that Charles may derive some advantage from the recollection of his indiscretion. Martin I hope will enter on his professional career with zeal & resolution enough to carry him through its first difficulties.

We have had in this lower country a summer of incessant rain which has almost inundated our flat lands. I hope it will not be followed by a sickly autumn.

I have just returned from a visit to the upper country where I passed a few days with our brother James. He struggles against the melancholy produced by his late heavy loss, & directs his whole attention to his family his farm & his library. My sister Taylor is at present with him. She will be much gratified at hearing your favorable opinion of her son. I hope the grand *desideratum*—application—will not long be wanting. I am my dea⟨r brother⟩, Your affectionate

J Marshall

ALS, Collection of Thomas W. Bullitt, Louisville, Ky. Addressed to Louis Marshall at Buckpond, Woodford County, Ky. MS torn where seal was broken.

1. Letter not found.

Nathaniel Pendleton

Dear Sir   Richmond Septr. 13th. 1817

Your letter of the 27th. of August did not reach me till two or three days past.[1] I cordially wish that you may succeed in the application you purpose making to the President, & shall be much gratified if I can be of any service to you.[2] My power to be useful to you does not I fear equal my inclination. I shall not however decline the attempt. When you suppose circumstances make it proper for me to mention you to the President, I will do so on your giving me the necessary information.

I have no right to ask any thing from Colo. Monroe. I can only state to him my opinion of your fitness for the office you solicit. The recommendation of Judge Livingston will I hope avail you. Mine I fear will not be of much use.[3] With great regard I am dear Sir, Your obedt.

J MARSHALL

ALS, Miscellaneous Manuscripts, NHi. Addressed to Pendleton at "Hyde Park/Dutchess County/New York." Endorsed (by Pendleton?).

1. Letter not found.
2. Pendleton sought appointment as U.S. district judge for Southern New York, which he was informed would soon become vacant. Formerly U.S. district judge for Georgia, Pendleton had moved to New York City in 1796, practicing law there until ill health forced him "to retire into the Country" and to relinquish much of his business (Pendleton to John Quincy Adams, 8 Jan. 1818, RG 59, DNA).
3. This judgeship did not become vacant again before Pendleton's death in 1821. William P. Van Ness held the post from 1812 to 1826 (*Journal of the Executive Proceedings of the Senate* . . . [Washington, D.C., 1828], II, 272; III, 549).

To Thomas Willing, Jr.

Dear Sir   Richmond Novr. 5th. 1817

As my son will probably settle in this place, I have supposed that it would be desirable for him to acquire some knowledge of the nature of business here, & of the mode of transacting it, before he engages in it. Under this impression, I have beleived that it would be advantageous to him to leave Philadelphia. I do not however think it proper to take any step of this kind, without consulting you, & obtaining your approbation. If your opinion concurs with mine, & his leaving your counting house is agreeable to you, I shall make arrangements for his continuance in Richmond when he takes leave of you this fall or winter.[1] However this may be, I pray you to accept my thanks for your kind attentions to him & beleive me to be with great respect, Your Obedt. Servt

J MARSHALL

ALS, Gratz Collection, PHi. Addressed to Willing in Philadelphia. Endorsed (by Willing?).

1. James K. Marshall had moved to Richmond by Feb. 1818 (see JM to Jaquelin A. Marshall, [16 Feb. 1818]).

To Louis Marshall

My dear Brother   Richmond Decr. 7th. 1817.

I received this instant the enclosed letter from our sister which will best speak for itself.[1] It was occasioned by one from her son complaining of harsh treatment. I greatly fear that Tom has been to blame, & has drawn upon himself your displeasure by some misconduct. You will greatly releive his mother, & oblige me by letting us know what has really happened, (for Tom's letter contains no particulars), and what is his conduct. I have written to him by post reproving him for his supposed faults, & telling him that he is under your authority.[2] Tom is unfortunately unused to discipline, & submits to it, no doubt, very unwillingly. Early indulgence has very probably given him ideas of self importance which render him less tractable than boys ought to be. You my dear brother are the best judge of what the occasion may require, & will I doubt not mingle as much mildness with authority as the state of things will justify. My anxiety respecting him on his own account, as well as on account of his Father who was a most estimable man, & of his mother, is very great. I shall indulge the hope of soon hearing from you that things are not so bad as my fears suggest.

We have no news in this country, nor any political events on which to speculate, except those which are furnished by the Presidents message.[3] You will percieve that he thinks with his predecessors on the subject of internal improvements, & is of opinion that to expend money on roads or canals requires amendments to our constitution, which, most assuredly, will never be made. You will percieve too that he casts a longing eye on Florida, & wishes this *arondissement* of our territory to take place during his administration. I wish it also very sincerely, but think we ought to act by Spain in the business rather more liberally than we have done. I sometimes fear that by wishing to get it for nothing we may lose it altogether. Our proposition to cede for the Floridas the country west of the Colorado, & to make that river the boundary between us, is proposing worse than nothing, & is asking them to give not only the Floridas but also a portion of country to which we have I believe no pretext of right. The affairs of Spain wear an aspect that is wretched in the extreme, & it is not improbable that they may lose entirely their possessions on this continent. Should the event be otherwise we may regret that we have not been content with making a good bargain, having in it some reciproc⟨i⟩ty.

My poor wife continues in wretched health. I am entirely excluded from society by her situation. Your's I hope is well & happy.

Farewell. I am my dear brother, Your affectionate

J MARSHALL

I have thought it most advisable to enclose my letter to Tom open to you. You will determine whether he ought to know that it has past through your hands.

ALS, Collection of Stimson Bullitt, Seattle, Wash. Addressed to Louis Marshall at Buckpond, Woodford Co., Ky.

1. The letter from Jane Marshall Taylor has not been found.
2. Letter not found.
3. Monroe's first annual address to Congress, 2 Dec. 1817, was published in the Richmond *Enquirer* of 4 Dec. See James D. Richardson, ed., *A Compilation of the Messages and Papers of the Presidents, 1789–1897* (11 vols.; Washington, D.C., 1896–99), II, 11–20.

Wormeley v. Wormeley
Opinion and Decree
U.S. Circuit Court, Virginia, 16 December 1817

This was a suit in equity to enforce the trusts of a marriage settlement, filed in April 1814 on behalf of Mary Wormeley (then of Kentucky) and her children, against Hugh Wallace Wormeley (Mary's husband), Thomas Strode, and others. Hugh Wallace Wormeley was a nominal defendant, joined with the other defendants only because of the formalities of equity pleading. The principal defendant was Strode, brother of Mary Wormeley and trustee of the property conveyed in the marriage settlement. The other defendants were purchasers of the trust property. By the marriage settlement deed of trust, executed in August 1807, Hugh Wallace Wormeley conveyed all his real and personal estate to Strode upon several trusts stipulating how the property was to be held in the event of various contingencies. The trust lands consisted of 350 acres in Frederick County, which Wormeley had inherited from his father. According to the bill, the object of the trust was to protect Mary and any children she might have from indiscreet or imprudent acts of her intended husband, then a young man recently returned from eight years at sea and presumably "somewhat deficient" in worldly knowledge. The deed empowered Strode to sell the Frederick land and reinvest the proceeds in other lands subject to the same trusts. In 1810 Strode sold the Frederick property to Richard Veitch, who in turn conveyed the land to David Castleman and Charles McCormick. In the meantime Wormeley and his family, after first settling in Frederick, moved to Fauquier County and then to Kentucky. After the filing of answers and the taking of depositions in 1815 and 1816, Marshall delivered the following opinion on 16 December 1817. The questions for the court were whether Strode committed a breach of trust in selling the land and whether the purchasers had notice of the facts constituting the breach (bill in chancery, [Apr. 1814], Wormeley v. Wormeley, U.S. Cir. Ct., Va., Ended Cases [Unrestored], 1830, Vi; U.S. Cir. Ct., Va., Rec. Bk. XIX, 28–41).

Wormley & al
    v
Wormley & al }

The plfs in this cause are a wife & a mother with her three infant children. They apply to this court for its aid to restore them to the possession of property conveyed in contemplation of marriage by a deed of which they are the principal objects. ¶1

The defendents are the husband, the trustee (& that trustee a brother), and the purchasers of the trust estate. ¶2

The defendent Hugh Wallace Wormley being about to intermarry with the plf. Mary, executed a deed dated the 5th. of August 1807, the day on which the marriage took effect, by which he conveyed, in lieu of dower his paternal estate consisting of a small tract of land in the county of Frederick & some slaves, to Thomas Strode the brother of his intended wife, in trust principally for her & her children.[1] ¶3

This property is gone. The trust is totally defeated and the first enquiry is whether this effect has been produced by the regular execution of any power inserted in the deed. ¶4

The deed contains this uncommon clause: "And it is further covenanted bargained & agreed by & between the said contracting partie[s] that whenever in the opinion of the said Thomas Strode the said landed estate can be sold & conveyed and the money arising from the sale thereof laid out in the purchase of other lands advantageously for those concerned or interested therein, that then in that case he the said Thomas Strode is hereby authorized and by these presents fully empowered to sell and by proper deeds of writing convey the same, and the lands so by him purchased shall be in every respect subject to all the provisions uses trusts & contingencies as those were by him sold & conveyed." ¶5

I term this an uncommon clause because it authorizes the trustee to sell on his own judgement, without consulting those who trust. ¶6

The power which has been read is great, but not unlimited. The trustee is not to exercise his will, but his judgement. Whenever, in his opinion the trust estate can be sold, & the money invested in other land advantageously for the parties interested, then & then only may he sell & make this reinvestment. The standard by which he is to act is invis- ¶7 ible, yet it is an actually existing standard, and one by which the conduct of the trustee must be measured. To determine whether he has been regulated by it or not, his actions must be examined.

¶8   In enquiring whether a party has acted according to his best judgement or not, allowance must be made for the fallibility of the human mind, & for difference of opinion. But there are strong cases in which all will unite in saying that the judgement has not been fairly exercised. If under such a power as is in this deed, a tract of land notoriously worth $10000 should be sold & invested in a tract not worth 1000$—it would be in vain for the trustee to say that in his opinion the sale & reinvestment was an advantageous operation. He could not have entertained such an opinion. The case is certainly not less strong where he makes no reinvestment whatever. He could not be of opinion that it was advantageous to the parties to sell the land & get nothing for it.

¶9   But further. Where there is no reinvestment of the money the very letter of the power is disregarded. He is to sell only when the money can be advantageously laid out in the purchase of other lands, "and the lands *so purchased* are to be held in trust for the same objects with those sold.["] There must be other lands purchased or the power is not executed. The sale & purchase are different links of the same chain; though the parts are distinct, they seem to be parts of one operation, which is incomplete if either be wanting. These parts too, it would seem, must be in execution at the same time. I do not well comprehend how the judgement can be fairly exercised on the advantageousness of a sale & purchase, without comparing the tract to be sold with that to be purchased. The words of the power, & the situation of the parties, are equally opposed to the idea of selling first, & then searching for other lands on which to place the Wormley family.

¶10   Having premised these general observations on the nature of the power under which the trustee acted, the court will proceed to consider more particularly the facts of the case; in order to decide whether c'estuis que trust[2] have still a remedy against the land, or only against the person of the trustee or purchaser.

¶11   Wormley & his wife resided for a short time either on the trust estate or with his mother. Their situation seems not to have been comfortable; &, in little more than a year after the marriage, both the Father & brother of Mrs. Wormley expressed a strong desire to remove her into their neighborhood; and an agreement was made between the defendents Strode & Wormley, with the approbation as it appears of the friends of Wormley; for the exchange of the trust land for a tract lying in the county of Fauquier.[3] To this tract Wormley removed and soon afterwards Thomas Strode sold the land in Frederick to Richard Veitch one of the defendents in this cause, & conveyed it to him by deed dated in September 1810 to which deed Wormley was a party. Veitch was the holder of a Mortgage on the estate of Strode in Culpeper, which had been foreclosed, & on which something more than $3000 were due. This sum was discounted in part payment for the trust estate.[4]

The Fauquier lands were never conveyed to the same uses with the ¶12 Frederick lands, nor have any others been substituted in their place. In about twelve months Wormley became dissatisfied with this estate, & some arrangements were made for furnishing him with lands in Kentucky, which are not further noticed because they have terminated in nothing, & do not affect this part of the case. Subsequent to those arrangements Strode sold the land in Fauquier.[5]

Excluding from our view the rights of the purchaser, & considering ¶13 the case as between the plfs. & the trustee, can it be doubted whether this transaction would in any manner affect the Frederick lands?

We will not enquire into the relative value of the two tracts; We will ¶14 not enquire whether the approbation given by the friends of Wormley to this exchange arose from a knowledge of this relative value, or from the hope that he might derive other advantages from living in the neighborhood of his wifes Father which would more than compensate for any small loss in the exchange; We will not enquire whether at the time Strode intended to execute the contract; We will suppose this transaction to have originated in the causes which have been assigned for it: still the policy & the wise policy of courts of equity forbids trustees to bargain with themselves. In the execution of trusts, especially such as this, no unworthy ingredient respecting self ought to be intermingled. It is wisely held to vitiate the whole transaction. A trustee conscious of the utmost purity & fairness of intention, who makes a contract with himself for the trust property, performs a most perilous act. He exposes himself to every hazard which can befal the estate.

It does not in point of law alter the case, that Wormley assented to ¶15 this exchange. He had no power to assent. The deed was executed to secure the land against him & his indiscretions.

If then the Fauquier lands had been actually settled in trust, the title ¶16 of Strode to the Frederick land could not be secure. But the Fauquier lands have not been, nor can they be settled on the Wormley Family. That part of the power which respects the reinvestment of the money in other lands remains totally unexecuted. Can it then be doubted that Strode, if he now held the Frederick lands, if he had conveyed them & taken back a reconveyance to himself, would hold them under the trusts created by the deed of 1807? Beleiving this point to be perfectly clear, the court will proceed to enquire

2d Whether the land in the hands of purchasers remains liable to the ¶17 same trusts.

It is beleived to be unquestionable that by conveying the lands in ¶18 Frederick to his own purposes, without settling other lands to the same trusts, the trustee committed a breach of trust.

It is equally clear that a purchaser of the trust property, with notice ¶19 of the trust & its violation, is himself a trustee. This principle is too familiar with the profession to require that cases should be cited in its support.[6]

¶20   Had the purchasers in this case notice? and first had Veitch notice? I do not mean to enquire meerly whether he had notice of the trust; because claiming title under the trust deed he is of course acquainted with its contents; but whether he had also notice of the breach of trust?

¶21   Strode violated his duty as a trustee probably in bargaining with himself or with Wormley whom he knew to be incapable of making a contract respecting this property; & in selling the Frederick land for his own purposes; certainly in not immediately executing a proper deed for the Fauquier lands. He ought not to have permitted this duty to remain a day unperformed. He ought not to have exposed the Fauquier lands to the hazard of remaining apparently his property without any deed declaring the trusts by which he held them. Had he purchased other lands for the Wormley family & taken a conveyance to himself without specifying the trusts, his conduct would certainly not have comported with his duty; As little did it accord with his duty to hold this land without a declaration of trust. I speak of the state of things at the time of the sale to Veitch, not of the state of things afterwards.

¶22   Were these facts known to Veitch?

¶23   With the application of the purchase money in discharge of his own decree he was of course acquainted. That Wormley relied on receiving the Fauquier land instead of the Frederick land was probably equally well known to him. The character of the title & the situation of the parties, Wormley being no longer residing on the Frederick land, and having removed to Fauquier, would lead to enquiries which must explain the transaction. Wormleys certificate too given a few days before the deed to Veitch was executed shows that some specific land was substituted for that in Frederick, & shows further that the tract so substitu[te]d, was acquired by an exchange of property with the trustee.[7] Veitch then knew from this certificate that the land was not to be sold to him by Strode in execution of his power, but that Strode had already appropriated the trust estate to his own use, & was selling for himself. Whether he knew that the land in Fauquier was the tract alluded to or not, he knew the character of the transaction, & took upon himself the risk of its validity. But it is not to be beleived that he did not know everything which it was material to know. The certificate itself points to the tract, for it is dated at Roseville in Fauquier.

¶24   He must also be considered in this court as having notice that a deed was not executed declaring the trusts on which the newly acquired land was held. He had a right to see this deed, and was bound to see it. Its non production was proof of its non existence. But this is not all. If he knew that the Fauquier land was substituted for the Frederick land, as we think he did, then the deed he received of those lands as collateral security proves his knowledge in fact that no conveyance of them in trust had been made.[8]

He probably relied on the certificate of Wormley as his security; and ¶25 certainly that certificate would go far in protecting him from any claim made by Wormley. But he ought to have been advised that Mrs. Wormley & her children could not be affected by it.

There is a circumstance growing out of the deed from Strode to ¶26 Veitch which is not entirely unworthy of notice. That deed is apparently drawn by counsel before whom the papers were laid.[9] We should expect it to state the transaction truely, was there nothing in the transaction which there was a wish to conceal. We should expect it to refer to the exchange between Wormley & Strode if that exchange was beleived to be a fair execution of the trust. Such a reference would have secured that land from many casualties. But the deed declares that Strode sold the trust land to Veitch "with *an intention* of investing the proceeds of such sale in other lands of equal or greater value."[10] This untruth which was known to Veitch, betrays a consciousness that the transaction required some other shape than its own.

But could Veitch even have supposed that the money was to be in- ¶27 vested in other lands to be purchased in future, he knew that a large portion of it was diverted to his own debt; & he must have known that a trustee whose embarassments could induce him to seize a trust fund in order to relieve his own estate from being sold under a mortgage that was foreclosed, could not come into the market without money, to purchase other lands, under very advantageous circumstances.

Add to this consideration that the power given by the deed of trust to ¶28 Strode was not to sell with the *intention* of vesting the money in other lands at some future time, but to sell & invest, when in his opinion it could be done to advantage.

Veitch then had notice of all the material facts which constituted the ¶29 breach of trust committed by Strode & is consequently to be considered in this court as holding the land subject to the trusts created by the deed of August 1807.

Are Castleman & MCormack in a different situation? ¶30

The answer to this question depends on their having notice of the ¶31 transactions which constitute the breach of trust.

Purchasing a title depending on the deed of August 1807 they would ¶32 of course inspect that deed, & would percieve that Strodes power to sell was coupled with the duty of investing the money in other lands. They would percieve that this was not a case where a sale is the object of the trust; where it is the duty of the trustee to sell in any event, and afterwards to dispose of the trust money; but a case in which the great object of the trust was the security of the estate; & the power to sell was limited to the case when "in the opinion of Strode the land can be sold and the money laid out in the purchase of other lands advantageously for those interested." And that in such case, the lands so purchased were to be held for the same trusts &c. The very deed under which they claim then informed them that their title originated in a trust, & that it behoved them to enquire how that trust had been executed. The parties were all within the reach of enquiry, & the difficulty of making it was inconsiderable. The deed to Veitch was dated the 16th. of September 1810 and the deed to Castleman & MCormack was certified for the purpose of being recorded on the 25th. day of June 1811. They say in their answer that they purchased in 1810.[11] Previous to this time Wormley had become dissatisfied with the Fauquier land & they knew it. Had they not been informed of this they must have known that the title to those lands still remained in Strode; &, consequently that he had not performed his duty as a trustee. With this knowledge they enable Strode to sell the Fauquier land.[12]

¶33   If the case rested on these facts the court would feel much difficulty in allowing to these defendants the protection they claim as purchasers without notice. But the case does not rest on these facts.

¶34   The answer of these defendants say they cannot doubt the fairness of the transaction "because they are well satisfied that Mr. Strode never received more from Mr Veitch than what he has given the c'estui que trust credit for."[13]

¶35   Is it a fair execution of this trust & power to sell the trust estate & give the c'estui que trust credit for the amount of sales?

¶36   The defendants proceed to deny all fraud in themselves & all knowledge of fraud in Strode or Veitch.

¶37   This is not sufficient. Fraud is an inference of law from facts, & this answer denies no fact alledged in the bill, nor does it deny knowledge of those facts with which knowledg⟨e⟩ they are charged; but states their opinion that no fact which has come to their knowledge is fraudulent. The answer then though it does not confess, does not controvert notice of the facts which prove a breach of trust. Is that notice otherwise proved?

¶38   Benjamin Barnet deposes that they were in treaty with Strode for the land before the sale to Veitch, & were to have paid a part of the purchase money to Veitch in discharge of a debt due to him from Strode, & that they endeavored to make an arrangement with Veitch but failed.[14]

¶39   When afterwards this land was sold to Veitch, these defendants must have known that it was sold not for the purposes of the trust, but on Strodes own account. Their answer avers the opinion that such a sale was lawful.

¶40   George Tacket proves that in May 1811, prior to the execution of the deed from Veitch while the Wormly family were in Frederick on their way to Kentucky, where some doubt was expressed of continuing their journey the deft Castleman expressed great uneasiness lest the journey should not be prosecuted, because he expected they would receive lands in that country in lieu of the lands he had purchased from Veitch.[15]

Still further. It is well known that to be a purchaser without notice ¶41 not only the contract must be made but the purchase money paid before notice—and this should be averred in the answer. Now there is no such averment, and the fact is otherwise. It is proved by Mr. Powell that upwards of $3000 part of the purchase money was paid in the fall of 1813 & spring of 1814 not only after the full notice acknowledged in May 1811, but after the institution of this suit.[16]

What material fact then was unknown to those defendents? Not one. ¶42 They were not ignorant of the facts but of the law arising on those facts. Either there has been no breach of trust, & the original contract is valid, or the defendents are trustees. The court is of opinion that they are trustees.

But although trustees they are not to be considered as meer squat- ¶43 ters—the light in which they are viewed by the counsel for the plfs. They beleived their title to be good & acted on the conviction that it was so. They trusted to the full power of Strode. They do not appear to have placed Veitch between them & danger, but probably could not raise the money. While compelled to do equity they are entitled to equity. They are entitled to the benefit of the incumbrances from which the land has been releived, and of the permanent improvements they have made on it, & to the advances to Wormley for the use of his family. At the same time they are accountable for profits. The advances are properly chargeable against the profits, but the incumbrances which have been taken up & the improvements, if not absorbed by the profits constitute a charge upon the lands.

[Decree]
Wormley & others by their next friend
  vs
Wormly & others[17]

This cause came on to be heard on the bill answers exhibits & depositions of witnesses and arguments of counsel which being fully considered the court is of opinion that the exchange of land made between the defendents Hugh Wallace Wormley & Thomas Strode is not valid in equity, and that the defendent Thomas Strode has committed a breach of trust in selling the land conveyed to him by the deed of the 5th. of August 1807 for purposes not warranted by that deed, in misapplying the money produced by the said sale, & in failing to settle other lands to the same trusts as were created by the said deed: The court is further of opinion that the defendents Richard Veitch   Castle-

man &   MCormack are purchasers with notice of the facts which
constitute the breach of trust committed by the said Thomas Strode
& are therefore in equity considered as trustees; and that the defendents   Castleman and   MCormack do hold the land conveyed by Hugh Wallace Wormley to Thomas Strode by deed bearing
date the 5th. day of August in the year 1807 charged with the trusts in
the said deed mentioned until a court of equity shall decree a conveyance thereof. And this court is further of opinion that the said
defendents are severally accountable for the rents & profits arising out
of the said trust property while in possession thereof, and that the
defendents   Castleman and   McCormack are entitled to
the amount of the incumbrances from which the land has been releived
by any of the defendents, and of the value of the permanent improvements made thereon, and of the advances which have been made to the
said Hugh Wallace Wormley by any of the defendents for the support
of his family. The said advances to be credited against the rents &
profits, and the value of the said permanent improvements & of the
incumbrances which have been discharged, & which may not be absorbed by the rents & profits, to be charged on the land itself. And it is
referred to one of the Commissioners of this court to take accounts
according to the directions herein given & report the same to this court
in order to a final decree.[18]

AD, Marshall Judicial Opinions, PPAmP; printed, John W. Brockenbrough, *Reports of Cases Decided by the Honourable John Marshall . . .* , I (Philadelphia, 1837), 335–45. En-dorsed in unknown hand: "Quære. Where is my manuscript copy of this opinion?/July 21st 1832." For JM's deletions and interlineations, see Textual Notes below.

1. The original deed of trust, dated 5 Aug. 1807, is in the voluminous case file of this suit. Copies of the suit papers were also entered in the record book (Wormeley v. Worme-ley; U.S. Cir. Ct., Va., Rec. Bk. XIX, 28–203 [deed of trust at 130–32]).

2. *Cestui que trust* (he for whom is the trust), the beneficiary who possesses the equitable right to property, the legal title to which is vested in a trustee.

3. In his answer Hugh Wallace Wormley stated that two years after his marriage, Thomas Strode proposed to give him a tract of land in Fauquier County and money in exchange for the trust lands in Frederick. As a further inducement, John Strode (father of Mary Wormeley and Thomas Strode) promised to build the Wormeleys a house on the Fauquier tract. Other testimony established that John Strode, who lived in Culpeper County, wanted his daughter (his favorite child) close by him in neighboring Fauquier County. The land in Fauquier was known as Marshfield Farm (U.S. Cir. Ct., Va., Rec. Bk. XIX, 35–40, 81–82, 88–89).

4. Wormeley stated that at the time he believed this sale was "genuine and original" but subsequently learned that its true purpose was to prevent foreclosure on lands in Cul-peper, which had been mortgaged as a security for a debt owed to Richard Veitch, an Alexandria merchant (ibid., 36). On Veitch, see T. Michael Miller, comp., *Artisans and Merchants of Alexandria, Virginia, 1780–1820*, II (Bowie, Md., 1992), 206.

5. Marshfield Farm contained valuable land but was difficult to cultivate and liable to flooding. Wormeley lost his entire corn crop because of floods. Wormeley and Strode then made an arrangement that the former should move with his family to Kentucky,

settling on a tract belonging to the trustee. The Kentucky lands, if a price could be agreed upon, were to be a compensation for the Frederick lands. Wormeley, however, believed Strode's price for the Kentucky lands was too high and that his title was defective (U.S. Cir. Ct., Va., Rec. Bk. XIX, 31, 37–38, 79, 88).

6. For citation of cases illustrating this principle, see counsel's argument in the appeal of this case in 1823 (8 Wheat. 435 and n.).

7. The deed from Strode to Veitch was executed on 16 Sept. 1810. Wormeley's certificate, dated Roseville, Fauquier, 5 Sept. 1810, stated that the lands given him by Strode were in his "estimation worth one Thousand Pounds more than the Land I got from the Estate of my Father and which I gave him in exchange." (U.S. Cir. Ct., Va., Rec. Bk. XIX, 119–21, 134). According to Wormeley, Strode told him that he (Strode) could not sell the Frederick land unless Wormeley certified that he had received an equivalent. Strode provided the form of the certificate, which Wormeley, not suspecting anything was amiss, willingly signed. Wormeley subsequently came to believe that the certificate was "a mere finesse to bolster up a fraudulent transaction" (ibid., 36–37).

8. The day after executing the deed to the Frederick property to Veitch, Strode mortgaged to Veitch the Fauquier land designated for Wormeley. The purpose of the mortgage was to warrant the title to the Frederick estate (ibid., 31, 121–22).

9. The deed was drawn by John W. Green, who gave a deposition in this suit (ibid., 74–77).

10. Ibid., 119–20.

11. The answer of Castleman and McCormick and the deed from Veitch to them are ibid., 32–34, 122–24.

12. Strode made an agreement with Castleman and McCormick that the mortgage to Veitch on the Fauquier lands would be released and that the guarantee of the title to the Frederick lands would be secured by a deed of trust on Kentucky lands. The deed of release and the deed of trust were executed in Apr. 1813 (ibid., 31, 125–29).

13. Ibid., 32.

14. Barnett's deposition was taken on 5 July 1817 in Culpeper (ibid., 89).

15. Tackett's deposition was also taken on 5 July 1817 in Culpeper (ibid., 90).

16. Cuthbert Powell gave his deposition in Loudoun County on 27 June 1817. Powell had received by assignment two bonds given by Castleman and McCormick to Veitch as payment for the Frederick lands (ibid., 92).

17. In the space to the right of this heading someone (Brockenbrough?) wrote: "(Decree entered the 16th. Dec: 1817)."

18. After receiving the commissioners' report, dated Sept. 1818, JM issued a second decree in this suit on 8 Dec. 1818, ordering the sale of the Frederick lands. The proceeds of the sale, after deducting the amount due Castleman and McCormick, were to be invested in lands in the state of Mississippi, where the Wormeleys had recently decided to move. The decree also appointed another trustee in place of Strode, who was declared to be "an unfit person" for this purpose. The defendants then took an appeal to the Supreme Court, which confirmed the circuit court's decree at the Feb. 1823 term. The circuit court issued further decrees relating to the sale of the lands in 1824, 1829, and 1830 (U.S. Cir. Ct., Va., Rec. Bk. XIX, 41–74; 8 Wheat. 421).

Textual Notes

¶ 1 ll. 2–3	the ~~possessive~~ ↑ possession ↓ of	
¶ 3 l. 6	trust ↑ principally ↓ for	
¶ 7 l. 1	power ~~conveyed granted by~~ ↑ which has been read ↓ is	
l. 5	The ~~the~~ standard	
¶ 8 l. 2	fallibility ~~& for the~~ of	
l. 6	worth [erasure] ↑ $10000 ↓ should	

¶ 9 l. 3   advantageously ~~reinvested in~~ ↑laid out in the purchase of↓ other

l. 6   different [*erasure*] ↑links↓ of

l. 8   either ~~part~~ be

l. 11   & ~~his investment~~ ↑purchase,↓ without

l. 12   purchased. ~~If we consider either the~~ ↑The↓ words of the power, ~~or~~ ↑&↓ the

¶10 ll. 3–5   case ~~:~~ ↑; in order to decide whether c'estuis que trust have still a remedy against the land, or only against the person of the trustee or purchaser.↓

¶11 ll. 6–7   of ~~his~~ ↑the↓ friends

l. 9   afterwards ~~to wit on the   day of   in the~~ Thomas

ll. 10–11   cause, ~~to whom the estate of Strode in Culpeper had been mortgaged, a decree for th~~ ↑& conveyed it to him by deed dated in September 1810 to which deed Wormley↓ was

l. 13   which ~~about~~ ↑something more than↓ $3000

l. 14   was ~~received~~ ↑discounted↓ in part payment ~~of~~ for

¶12 ll. 6–7   case. ↑Subsequent to those arrangements Strode sold the land in Fauquier.↓

¶14 l. 1 beg.   ~~There are certain~~ We

ll. 4–5   the ~~vicinity~~ neighborhood

ll. 6–7   small ~~inferiority~~ loss in the exchange; ↑We will not enquire whether at the time Strode intended to execute the contract;↓ We

l. 15   estate. ~~Had the land in Fauquier then been conveyed in trust exchange then been executed the~~

¶17 l. 1 beg.   [*erasure*] 2d

¶20 ll. 3–4   he ~~has~~ ↑is↓ of course ~~notice of~~ ↑acquainted with↓ its

¶21 l. 3   property; ~~certainly~~ ↑&↓ in selling the ↑Frederick↓ land

l. 6   day ~~in~~ unperformed. He ought ↑not↓ to

l. 11   little ~~does~~ ↑did↓ it

l. 13   to ~~Veith~~ ↑Veitch,↓ not

¶23 ll. 3–4   was ~~equally~~ ↑probably↓ ↑equally well↓ known

l. 8   executed ~~& dated at Roseville in Fauquier~~ shows

ll. 9–10   that ~~this specific~~ ↑the↓ tract ↑so substitu[t]ed,↓ was

ll. 17–18   know. ↑The certificate itself points to the tract, for it is dated at Roseville in Fauquier.↓

¶24 l. 6   of ~~the Fauquier~~ those

l. 7   conveyance ↑of them↓ in

¶25 l. 1 beg.   ~~It is argued that~~ ↑He probably relied on↓ the

¶26 l. 3   counsel ↑before↓ whom

l. 4   the ~~case~~ ↑transaction↓ truely,

ll. 7–8   trust. ↑Such a reference would have secured that land from many casualties.↓ But

¶29 l. 4   of ~~Sep~~ ↑August↓ 1807.

¶30 l. 1   ~~well known to him. It appears from his answers from the certificate of Wormeley on which he relies. That he ought to have known the Fauquier lands were not conveyed to since no deed of coveyance was produced cannot be denied, and~~

~~that he did in fact know it is proved by his taking a deed of collateral security on those lands from Strode.~~
    ~~Veitch then purchased with full notice of everything committed & admitted by~~ ↑that the commissions comissions ~~of Strode were such as to vitiate &↓ Strode, & is~~ ↑was↓ ~~of consequence trustee in this court to be considered as holding the lands subject to all the trusts of the deed of September 1807.~~ ↑. . . .t does not appear from any expression of the deed. The conveyance [*erasure*] from Strode to Veitch of the 16th. of September 1810 professes to sell not with a view to purchase any particular tract but to purchase some tract of equal or greater value. Veitch knew that Strode disabled himself from doing this imme. by this application of the purchase money to the mortgage. If he understood from Wormly's certificate or otherwise that an exchange had actually been made he knew all the material circumstances of that exchange. If he believed that no purchase had been made, he knew the impropriety of such a sale & that the↓~~

¶31 l. 1 beg.   ~~This de~~ The
¶32 l. 1   Purchasing ↑a title↓ depending
     l. 1   of ~~September~~ ↑August↓ 1807
     l. 3   lands. ~~; and if they did not know that he could not sell for his own benefit, or that he could not divest the↓~~ ↑land of the↓ ~~trust & turn the trustees to a personal claim upon himself their ignorance was not of the fact but of the law. In any view of the case sufficient time had intervened for the settlement of other lands to the purposes of the trust & they ought to have enquired whether such settlement had been made~~ They
     l. 4   a [*erasure*] sale↓ is
     l. 6   the ↑great↓ object
     l. 11   held ~~by~~ ↑for↓ the
     l. 12   that ~~his~~ ↑their↓ title
     ll. 19–20   land ↑& they knew it.↓ ~~Whether this was known to them on~~ ↑Had they not been informed of this↓ they
¶33 l. 1 beg.   ↑If↓ the case rested on ~~this simple~~ ↑these↓ facts
     l. 3   these ~~single~~ facts.
¶36 l. 1 beg.   The ~~answer~~ ↑defendents↓ proceed
¶37 l. 5   then ↑though it↓ does not ↑confess, ~~but~~ does not↓ controvert
¶38 l. 1   Barnet ~~proves~~ ↑deposes↓ that
     l. 3   Veitch ~~on~~ ↑in↓ discharge
     l. 5   failed. ~~, in cor~~
¶40 l. 2   while ~~he was~~ ↑the↓ Wormly family were ~~on~~ ↑in↓ Frederick
     l. 4   journey ↑the deft↓ Castleman
¶42 ll. 1–3   one. ↑They were not ignorant of the facts but of the law arising on those facts.↓ Either
     l. 4   of ~~the last~~ opinion

¶43 l. 1   although ~~of this~~ trustees
 ll. 4–6   so. ↑They trusted to the full power of Strode. They do not
     appear to have placed Veitch between them & danger, but
     probably could not raise the money.↓ While
 ll. 9–10   it, ↑& to the advances to Wormley for the use of his
     family.↓ At

Prentiss v. Barton
Opinion
U.S. Circuit Court, Virginia, [17? December 1817]

This suit began in 1806, when Charles Prentiss, trustee of William Prentiss, filed a bill in chancery against Seth Barton, a merchant residing in
Fredericksburg. Both William Prentiss (1754–1831) and Charles Prentiss
(1774–1820), nephew of William, were members of a prominent Massachusetts family. While in London in 1784, the elder Prentiss formed a
partnership with Barton, then of Baltimore. The partners subsequently
had a falling out, with Prentiss claiming a large account balance against
Barton. Pursued by creditors, Prentiss during the 1790s lived in various
places on the eastern seaboard, including Baltimore, Georgia, Philadelphia, and Boston. Appointed trustee of his insolvent uncle in the early
1800s, Charles Prentiss, a 1795 graduate of Harvard, also lived a peripa-
tetic life as a newspaper editor and printer in Massachusetts, the District of
Columbia, Maryland, and Virginia. In his original bill and in an amended
bill, filed in 1816, he stated that he was a resident and citizen of Maryland.
In their answer to the amended bill, the executors of Barton (who had died
in 1814) denied that Prentiss was a citizen of Maryland and insisted that he
was a resident either of the District of Columbia or of Richmond, Virginia.
They accordingly entered a plea to the court's jurisdiction, to which Marshall in December 1817 (see n. 1, below) gave the following opinion (bill in
chancery [filed 26 Nov. 1806]; amended bill in chancery [filed 29 June
1816], Prentiss v. Barton's Executors, U.S. Cir. Ct., Va., Ended Cases [Un-
restored], 1817 Vi; U.S. Cir. Ct., Va., Rec. Bk. XII, 107–125; *The History
and Genealogy of the Prentice, or Prentiss Family, in New England* . . . [Boston,
1883], 21–22, 56–57, 60, 97–98).

Prentis Trustee &c ⎫
   v   ⎬
Barton exr. &c ⎭

¶1 The jurisdiction of the court in this case depends on the citizenship
of the plf.[1] If he was a citizen of the District of Columbia or of the
Commonwealth of Virginia, this suit cannot be maintained; if he was a
citizen of any other state, he may sue in this court.[2]

¶2 Before I proceed to examine the facts of the case I will consider the
principle which must govern it.

The constitution of the United States gives the courts of the union ¶3
jurisdiction over controversies "between citizens of different states."
And the judicial act gives this court jurisdiction "where the suit is between a citizen of the state where the suit is brought and a citizen of
another state."[3]

The constitution as well as the law clearly contemplates a distinction ¶4
between citizens of different states; and altho the 4th. article declares
that "the citizens of each state shall be entitled to all privileges and
immunities of citizens in the several states" yet they cannot be in the
sense of the judicial article or the judicial act, citizens of the several
states. There is still a distinction between them, if in no other respect, in
their right to sue in the courts of the Union. This distinction, although
it may be clear enough in theory, cannot always be easily drawn in fact.
In a government composed, like ours, of distinct governments, & containing the principle which has been stated, it cannot depend entirely
on birth. A citizen living in a state, with all the privileges & immunities
of a citizen of that state, ought to share its burthens also, & will be
considered to every purpose as a citizen. Accordingly the universal
understanding & practice of America is, that a citizen of the United
states residing permanently in any state, is a citizen of that state. Otherwise, a citizen by statute, could never belong to any state & could never
maintain a suit in the courts of the United States. In the sense of the
constitution and of the judicial act, he who is incorporated into the
body of the state by permanent residence therein so as to become a
member of it, must be a citizen of that state although born in another.
Or to use a phrase more familiar in the books, A citizen of the United
States must be deemed a citizen of that state in which his domicil is
placed.[4] This question what is permanent residence? must in some
cases, depend on a great variety of considerations; and, as in all mixed
and doubtful questions of fact, each circumstance must be allowed its
due weight. Birth alone, undoubtedly gives a man permanent rights as
a citizen; and although those rights so far as respects suits in the courts
of the United States, may be changed by a change of residence, yet, in
doubtful cases, birth will always have great influence.

This question has never come directly, so far as I can discover before ¶5
the supreme court of the United States. The cases rather prove that the
jurisdiction of the court must be shown, than determine what constitutes citizenship.

The first is that of Bingham v Cabot & al which was decided in 1798.[5] ¶6
"The declaration was in the nam⟨e o⟩f John Cabot of Beverly in the
district of Massachussetts merchant & in the names of other plaintiffs
described in the same manner. The court were clearly of opinion that it
was necessary to set forth the citizenship or alienage of the respective
parties in order to bring the case within the jurisdiction of the circuit
court.["]

¶7   In the argument the Attorney General observed "A citizen of one state may reside for a term of years in another state of which he is not a citizen; for citizenship is clearly not coextensive with inhabitancy.["][6]

¶8   Mr. Dexter, in support of the jurisdiction contended that citizenship of a particular state may be changed without going through the forms & solemnities required in case of an alien; that, on the principles of the constitution, a citizen of the United States is to be considered more particularly as a citizen of that state in which he has his house & family, is a permanent inhabitant, and is, in short domiciliated.[7]

¶9   This question came on again in 1803 in the case ⟨of?⟩ Abercrombie v Dupuis & another.[8] The suit was brought in the d⟨is⟩trict of Georgia & the plaintiffs averred "that they do severally reside without the limits of the district of Georgia aforesaid, to wit in the state of Kentucky, therefore they have a right to commence their said action &c. ["]

¶10   The judgement was reversed on the authority of the case of Bingham v Cabot & al.

¶11   The question came on again in 1804 in the case of Wood v Wagnon also from the district of Georgia.[9] The de[c]laration in that case stated the plaintiff to be a citizen of Pennsylvania & the defendent to be "of Georgia.["]

¶12   The judgement in this case also was reversed.

¶13   These cases all show that the jurisdiction of the court must appear on the record; but the last shows that jurisdiction is not given by averring a party to be of a particular state. The plf. was a citizen of Pennsylvania & had consequently a right to sue either an alien or a citizen of Georgia in the circuit court of Georgia. The defendent must have been either an alien or a citizen. If an alien, the court had jurisdiction. The judgement then must have been reversed because the defendent might be "of Georgia" & yet a citizen of another state. This certainly does not prove what residence will constitute domicil or citizenship, but I think it does prove that it is not constituted by every residence.

¶14   By the general laws of the civilized world, the domicil of the parents at the time of birth, or what is termed the domicil of origin, constitutes the domicil of an infant, and continues until abandoned, according to some law or by the acquisition of a new domicil in a different place. As it gives political rights which are not lost by a meer change of domicil it is recovered by any manifestation of a disposition to resume the native character; perhaps by a surrender of the new domicil. In fact it may be considered rather as suspended than as annihilated.

¶15   All agree that a new domicil is not acquired by a residence for temporary purposes. It must be a permanent residence. Vattel defines it to be "a habitation fixed in any place with an intention of always staying there."[10] The existence of this intention must be manifested by overt acts, in explanation of which if doubtful, the declarations of the party will undoubtedly be received.

Let this rule be applied to the case at bar. Charles Prentis was born in ¶16
Massachussetts, of which state his parents were citizens, & there he re-
ceived his education & married a wife. He appears to have continued to
reside in Massachussetts until the year 1801 when he came to George
Town in the district of Columbia & joined Mr. Rind in editing a paper
published in that place.[11] In 1802 he sold his interest in that paper to
Mr. Caldwell & removed to Baltimore with his family, where he con-
tinued for some time as the editor of a paper.[12] In 1803 he returned to
Massachussetts & leaving his wife with her Father, went himself to
England. After his return in 1804, he was frequently in the district
where he was employed to take the debates of Congress for a printer in
Philadelphia.[13]

I think there is not much difficulty in d⟨e⟩termining that Mr. Prentis ¶17
w⟨as not a citizen of the district of⟩ Col⟨um⟩bia. If he acquired a domicil in that pl⟨ace in⟩ 1801 he certainly abandoned it in 1802 when he
sold his property & removed with his family to Baltimore. ⟨What⟩ever
might have been his character while residing in Baltimore with his
family, he certainly ⟨resumed⟩ his original domicil when he returned
with his wife to Massachussetts, & there is no ground for saying that his
afterwards residing in the district for the purpose of taking the debates
was an abandonment of it.

It remains to enquire whether at the emanation of this writ he was a ¶18
citizen of Virginia?

It appears that he came to Richmond in March 1805 & engaged ¶19
generally with Mr. Davis as the editor of his paper. On the 18th. of July
he returned to Massachussetts where he continued until the latter end
of September when he came to Virginia & resumed his employment
with Mr. Davis. About the last of November he left Mr. Davis finally &
has since been occasional⟨ly⟩ in Massachussetts where his family resides
& occasionally in other states.[14]

I cannot think this residence in Richmond was a "habitancy with an ¶20
intention of staying here always." It continued for only a few months, a
considerable part of which was passed in his native state, and his employment was one which he could abandon at any time. Had he acquired any property in the paper the case would have been more doubtful; or had he remained in Richmond to this time or until this question
occurred—his residence would have assumed the appearance of permanence—as to ⟨3 pls.?⟩ The cases of the Nereid, & Wood v wagnon.[15]

AD, Marshall Judicial Opinions, PPAmP; printed, John W. Brockenbrough, *Reports of
Cases Decided by the Honourable John Marshall . . .* , I (Philadelphia, 1837), 390–95. Words in
angle brackets supplied from Brockenbrough. For JM's deletions and interlineations, see
Textual Notes below.

1. Although Brockenbrough places this opinion at the Nov. 1819 term, the record
clearly shows this case to have ended with the court's decree of 17 Dec. 1817 dismissing

the bill. On the same day Augustine Davis testified in open court concerning Prentiss's residence in Richmond, an indication that the jurisdictional question was still under consideration. It is possible that JM's opinion was given prior to the argument on the plea of the statute of limitations, which according to Tucker's notes took place on 9 Dec. (U.S. Cir. Ct., Va., Rec. Bk. XII, 107, 193; notes of argument, 9 Dec. 1817, Prentiss v. Barton, Tucker-Coleman Papers, ViW).

2. In Hepburn and Dundas v. Ellzey, decided in 1805, the Supreme Court held that residents of the District of Columbia were not to be considered citizens of a "state" for the purpose of giving federal courts jurisdiction in diversity of citizenship cases (2 Cranch 445; *PJM*, VI, 371–72).

3. *U.S. Statutes at Large*, I, 78.

4. JM wrote the preceding two sentences on a separate sheet and marked the passage "A," indicating that it was to be inserted at this point.

5. 3 Dall. 382.

6. Charles Lee, U.S. attorney general (3 Dall. 383).

7. Samuel Dexter (3 Dall. 383).

8. 1 Cranch 343.

9. 2 Cranch 9.

10. Vattel, *Law of Nations* (1805 ed.), Bk. I, chap. xix, sec. 218, p. 163.

11. The depositions of William Cranch, William A. Rind, and Elias B. Caldwell, taken in Nov. 1816, establish that Prentiss resided in Georgetown in 1801 and 1802, where he was associated with Rind in editing the *Washington Federalist* (U.S. Cir. Ct., Va., Rec. Bk. XII, 143–45).

12. The depositions of William Gwynn and John Cole, taken in Nov. 1816, show that Prentiss resided in Baltimore in 1802 and 1803, where he edited *The Republican, or Anti-Democrat* (ibid., 140, 142).

13. See Coles's deposition (ibid., 140).

14. Augustine Davis, publisher of the *Virginia Gazette, and General Advertiser*, gave his deposition on 7 Dec. 1816. Davis invited Prentiss to join his paper as editor or partner. In Nov. 1805 Prentiss announced his resignation, citing poor financial prospects owing to an insufficient number of subscribers. Davis also testified in court on 17 Dec. 1817 that Prentiss returned to Richmond in Mar. 1816 and lived with him until July 1817, assisting in editing the *Virginia Patriot* (ibid., 193, 195; Richmond *Virginia Gazette*, 27 Nov. 1805).

15. On Wood v. Wagnon, see JM's discussion in the text at n. 9 above. In The Nereide, decided in 1815, JM rejected the contention that a Buenos Aires merchant acquired an English domicile and an English "commercial character" by temporary residence in London. "Whatever facility may be given to the acquisition of a commercial domicil," he wrote, "it has never heretofore been contended that a merchant having a fixed residence, and carrying on business at the place of his birth, acquires a foreign commercial character by occasional visits to a foreign country" (Opinion, 11 Mar. 1815; 9 Cranch 413, 414).

In its decree of 17 Dec. 1817, the court "being divided in opinion on sundry material questions" dismissed the bill pro forma so that an appeal could be taken to the Supreme Court. Shortly thereafter Prentiss agreed not to prosecute an appeal in consideration of receiving $4,500 from Barton's executors (U.S. Cir. Ct., Va., Rec. Bk. XII, 139–40, 253–54).

Textual Notes

¶ 1	l. 3	Commonwealth ↑of Virginia,↓ this
	l. 4	other ~~suit~~ state,
¶ 2	l. 1 beg.	~~Charles Prentis was born in the state~~ Before
	l. 2	which ~~forms the law of the case.~~ ↑must govern it.↓
¶ 3	l. 1 beg.	~~By the~~ ↑The↓ constitution

¶ 4 l. 1 beg.   ~~The con~~ The
    l. 9   government ~~posed~~ ↑composed,↓ like
    ll. 17–24   States. ↑In the sense of the constitution and of the judicial act, he who is incorporated into the body of the state by permanent residence therein so as to become a member of it, ~~is~~ must be a citizen of that state although born in another. Or to use a phrase more familiar in the books, A citizen of the United States must be deemed a citizen of that state in which his domicil is placed.↓ ~~The~~ ↑This↓ question ↑what is permanent residence?↓ must ↑in some cases,↓ depend
    l. 26   Birth ~~alone cannot be decisive~~ ↑alone, undoubtedly↓ gives
    l. 27   rights ~~may be~~ so
    l. 29   influence. [erasure] ⌐
¶ 5 ll. 1–4   never ~~been so fully decided in the courts of the United States as to give a rule already applicable to this case; but several decisions have been made, which bear strongly on it.~~ ↑come directly, so far as I can discover before the supreme court of the United States. The cases rather ~~show~~ prove that the jurisdiction of the court must be shown, than determine what constitutes citizenship.↓
¶ 6 l. 4   manner. ~~and the defendent was stated to be.~~ The
¶13 ll. 1–3   that ~~a party does not give the court jurisdiction by stating himself to be of a particular state although the cause would be properly brought were he a citizen of that place.~~ ↑the jurisdiction of the court must appear on the record; but the last shows that jurisdiction is not given by ~~stating~~ averring a party to be of a particular state. The↓ plf.
    l. 5   Georgia. ~~If the~~ ↑The↓ defendent
    l. 10   that ~~domicil~~ ↑it↓ is
¶14 ll. 3–4   abandoned, ~~or until a new domicil is acquired~~ ↑according to some law or by the acquisition of a new domicil↓ in
¶15 l. 2   a ↑permanent↓ residence. ~~with~~ Vattel
    l. 5   which ↑if doubtful,↓ the
¶16 ll. 8–9   to ~~New Engla~~ Massachusetts
    l. 10   England. ~~On~~ ↑After↓ ~~his~~ his
¶17 ll. 7–8   afterwards ~~atten~~ residing
¶20 l. 2   It ~~was~~ ↑continued↓ for
    l. 3   in ~~New E~~ ↑his↓ native
    l. 6   Richmond ~~for~~ to
    l. 8   The ~~case~~ ↑cases↓ of

To St. George Tucker

My dear Sir   Richmond Decr 27th. 1817
    Enclosed is a letter which I received a few days past & which will best explain itself.[1] I have only to say that the writer[2] is one of the kindest

hearted men in the world, & that I am convinced the letter is written at the instance of that heart & not of Mr. Ogden. I had never heard that Mrs. Morris intended the publication alluded to.[3] If she does you will yourself be the best judge of the course which you as her most esteemed friend ought to pursue.

I hope your health has improved since your escape from the court & its labors & am my dear Sir with much regard & esteem, your obedt

J MARSHALL

ALS, Tucker-Coleman Papers, ViW. Addressed to Tucker in Williamsburg; postmarked Richmond, 27 Dec. Endorsed by Tucker: "John Marshall esqr/Decr: 27. 1817./ Enclosing letter from Mr./B: Livingston of N.York./with/my Answer—and/a Copy of my Letter to/Mrs. Ann C: Morris." Tucker wrote draft of his reply of 30 Dec. 1817 on verso.

1. Brockholst Livingston's letter to JM has not been found.

2. Here Tucker inserted "+" and noted at the bottom of the page, "+B: Livingston of New York."

3. Ann Cary Randolph Morris (called Nancy), widow of Gouverneur Morris, had become involved in a protracted financial dispute with David B. Ogden (1775–1849), Morris's nephew and a prominent New York attorney. Ogden and other relatives of Morris had opposed his marriage to Nancy Randolph in 1809, and their animosity toward her intensified after the birth of a son in 1813. Nancy Morris claimed that Ogden, heavily indebted, had "swindled" Morris's estate by taking out an undisclosed second mortgage on property previously mortgaged to Morris. According to rumors circulating in New York, Nancy was preparing to publish a pamphlet concerning her dispute with Ogden. Tucker strongly advised her against resorting either to the press or to the courts in seeking redress against Ogden (Ann C. Morris to St. George Tucker, 2 Dec. 1816; St. George Tucker to Ann C. Morris, 30 Dec. 1817, Tucker-Coleman Papers, ViW; Howard Swiggett, *The Extraordinary Mr. Morris* [Garden City, N.Y., 1952], 417–18, 424–28, 443–45).

From St. George Tucker

My dear Sir,   Wmsburg. Decr. 30th. 1817.

By the last Evenings Mail I recieved your favor of the 27th. and in consequence of it, enclose you a Letter to Mrs. Morris which you will be pleased to peruse and forward as directed.[1] I beg you will request your friend Mr. Livingston, let what will be the result, not to mention my name to any human Being, as having anything to do with the subject of his Letter to you. If my advice should have any good Effect I shall most sincerely rejoice in the Event. I am &c. &c.

S: G: T:

P:S: I have thought it best to enclose my Letter to Mrs. M. to her Brother (T. M. R.)[2] and leave both open for your perusal; be pleased Seal both.

ADfS, Tucker-Coleman Papers, ViW. On verso of JM to Tucker, 27 Dec. 1817. In top margin Tucker wrote "*Answer*."

1. Tucker's copy of his letter to Ann C. Randolph, 30 Dec. 1817, is filed with this letter. See JM to Tucker, 27 Dec. 1817 and n. 3.
2. Thomas Mann Randolph, Jr.

To Mary W. Marshall

My dearest Polly   Washington Feby. 16th. 1818

Yesterday I received Jaquelin's letter of the 12th. informing me that your health was at present much the same as when I left Richmond but that you had just recovered from a cold.[1] The weather has been so very cold as to fill me with apprehensions for you. Indeed my dearest Polly as we grow older we suffer more from the cold & ough[t] to use more precautions against it. Your fears of being too warm push you into the other extreme & you expose yourself to more cold than is consistent with your health or safety. Let me entreat you to be more careful in this particular.

I am as usual in good health for an old man & very busily employed. No resolution is taken respecting the time of our rising but I conjecture that it will be about the middle of March. Farewell my dearest Polly. That you may be the happy is the fervent prayer of, your affectionate

J MARSHALL

ALS, Marshall Papers, ViW; Tr, Claudia Hamilton Mason Notebook, Collection of H. Norton Mason, Richmond, Va. On verso of JM to Jaquelin A. Marshall, [16 Feb. 1818].

1. Letter not found.

To Jaquelin A. Marshall

My dear Son   [16 February 1818]

I have received your letter of the 12th. & thank you for the information it contains.[1] I do not wish the overseer to attempt ploughing when the ground is unfit for it, but I am anxious to know what he is doing. I gave him explicit instructions to prepare a great deal of plaister & I wish to know whether he has observed them. I also directed him to avail himself of the first hard weather to draw in the stalks & hay that was in the low grounds & intended for the farm pen. I am anxious to know how the grubbing & cutting advances & where the people are now at work, also whether this dry windy weather has enabled him to burn any of the places which I directed. It will perhaps be well to direct him to write me an account of everything & to give you the letter.

I do not wish the packages you mention to be sent by post. Should a private conveyance offer, send them. If that indorsed Thos. P. Devereux can come free from postage send it—not otherwise.[2]

I do not recollect how my account stands in the bank & therefore send you a note to indorse & negotiate & pay Mr. Cocke for his corn.[3] 20 barrels would amount to 90$. I have advanced him 30$ consequently you are to pay him 60$. What is James doing? I hope he has engaged in a course of reading. I am your affectionate Father

J MARSHALL

ALS, Marshall Papers, ViW. On verso of JM to Mary W. Marshall, 16 Feb. 1818.

1. Letter not found.

2. Thomas P. Devereux (1793–1869), an 1813 graduate of Yale, was then practicing law in New Bern, N.C. He moved to Raleigh upon being appointed U.S. attorney for North Carolina in 1822. He later became reporter for the North Carolina Supreme Court of Appeals (William S. Powell, ed., *Dictionary of North Carolina Biography* [Chapel Hill, N.C., 1979–], II, 59–61; *Journal of the Executive Proceedings of the Senate . . .* , III [Washington, D.C., 1828], 257, 270, 448, 457).

3. Probably John Cocke, who owned land adjacent to JM's Chickahominy farm (deed, JM to John Adams, 15 Apr. 1815, Collection of Robert W. Clifton, Old Church, Va.; Ronald Vern Jackson et al., eds., *Virginia 1810 Census Index* [Bountiful, Utah, 1976], 64).

To Benjamin W. Crowninshield

Dear Sir   Washington Feb. 21st. 1818

I received a few days past a letter from my brother whose son has been lately appointed a midshipman, informing me that his son had understood that he was nominated to the senate & was extremely anxious to ascertain the fact.[1] There has not been an opportunity of hearing from him since your letter was forwarded, as the mail reaches him but once a weak. I can however say with confidence that he will accept & therefore take the liberty now to make an application to you which I had purposed to make so soon as his acceptance shall be received. It is that he may be placed in the Independence, Commodore Bainbridge, which I understand is in actual service.[2]

I am anxious to place my nephew in a situation which may give him the fairest chance of making himself master of his profession & advancing himself in it, & shall feel myself much obliged by his being placed in the Independence if in your opinion it can be done consistently with justice & the good of the service.[3] Very respectfully I am Sir your obedt

J MARSHALL

ALS, RG 45, DNA. Addressed to "The Honble./The Secretary of the Navy." Endorsed.

1. The letter from James M. Marshall has not been found. JM's nephew John Marshall was issued a midshipman's warrant on 1 Jan. 1818 (abstract of service record, John Marshall, RG 24, DNA).

2. William Bainbridge (1774–1833) was then commandant of the Boston Navy Yard. There he supervised construction of the *Independence*, which was launched in 1814 and served as his flagship until 1820.

3. Midshipman Marshall arrived in Boston on 24 Apr. 1818 for duty on the *Guerrière*. Rising to the rank of lieutenant, Marshall resigned from the navy in 1838 and settled into a life of farming in Fauquier County (abstract of service record, John Marshall, RG 24, DNA; Paxton, *Marshall Family*, 139–41).

United States v. Bevans
Opinion
U.S. Supreme Court, 21 February 1818

William Bevans, a marine serving on the U.S. warship *Independence*, was indicted in the U.S. Circuit Court at Boston for murdering a cook's mate on 6 November 1816 while the ship lay at anchor in the main channel of Boston Harbor. A jury found Bevans guilty, but upon a motion for a new trial, the judges were divided on the questions of whether Bevans's offense was within the jurisdiction of the state of Massachusetts or within the cognizance of the federal circuit court. The case was accordingly certified to the Supreme Court, where it was argued on 14 and 16 February 1818 by Daniel Webster for Bevans and by Henry Wheaton and Attorney General Wirt for the United States. Marshall delivered the opinion of the Court on 21 February (U.S. v. Bevans, App. Cas. No. 866; U.S. Sup. Ct. Minutes, 14, 16 Feb. 1818; *Daily National Intelligencer* [Washington, D.C.], 25 Feb. 1818).

The question proposed by the circuit court, which will be first considered, is,

Whether the offence charged in this indictment was, according to the statement of facts which accompanies the question, "within the jurisdiction or cognizance of the circuit court of the United States for the district of Massachusetts?"[1]

The indictment appears to be founded on the 8th sec. of the "act for punishment of certain crimes against the United States."[2] That section gives the courts of the union cognizance of certain offences committed on the high seas, or in any river, haven, basin, or bay, out of the jurisdiction of any particular state.

Whatever may be the constitutional power of congress, it is clear that this power has not been so exercised, in this section of the act, as to confer on its courts jurisdiction over any offence committed in a river, haven, basin or bay; which river, haven, basin, or bay, is within the jurisdiction of any particular state.

What then is the extent of jurisdiction which a state possesses?

We answer, without hesitation, the jurisdiction of a state is co-extensive with its territory; co-extensive with its legislative power.

The place described is unquestionably within the original territory of Massachusetts. It is then within the jurisdiction of Massachusetts, unless that jurisdiction has been ceded by[3] the United States.

It is contended to have been ceded by that article in the constitution which declares, that "the judicial power shall extend to all cases of admiralty and maritime jurisdiction." The argument is, that the power thus granted is exclusive; and that the murder committed by the prisoner is a case of admiralty and maritime jurisdiction.

Let this be admitted. It proves the power of congress to legislate in the case; not that congress has exercised that power. It has been argued, and the argument in favour of, as well as that against the proposition deserves great consideration, that courts of common law have concurrent jurisdiction with courts of admiralty, over murder committed in bays, which are inclosed parts of the sea; and that for this reason the offence is within the jurisdiction of Massachusetts. But in construing the act of congress, the court believes it to be unnecessary to pursue the investigation which has been so well made at the bar respecting the jurisdiction of these rival courts.[4]

To bring the offence within the jurisdiction of the courts of the union, it must have been committed in a river, &c out of the jurisdiction of any state. It is not the offence committed, but the bay in which it is committed, which must be out of the jurisdiction of the state. If, then, it should be true that Massachusetts can take no cognizance of the offence; yet, unless the place itself be out of her jurisdiction, congress has not given cognizance of that offence to its courts. If there be a common jurisdiction, the crime cannot be punished in the courts of the union.

Can the cession of all cases of admiralty and maritime jurisdiction be construed into a cession of the waters on which those cases may arise?

This is a question on which the court is incapable of feeling a doubt. The article which describes the judicial power of the United States is not intended for the cession of territory or of general jurisdiction. It is obviously designed for other purposes. It is in the 8th section of the 2d article,[5] we are to look for cessions of territory and of exclusive jurisdiction. Congress has power to exercise exclusive jurisdiction over this district, and over all places purchased by the consent of the legislature of the state in which the same shall be, for the erection of forts, magazines, arsenals, dock yards, and other needful buildings.

It is observable, that the power of exclusive legislation (which is jurisdiction) is united with cession of territory, which is to be the free act of the states. It is difficult to compare the two sections together, without feeling a conviction, not to be strengthened by any commentary on them, that, in describing the judicial power, the framers of our constitution had not in view any cession of territory, or, which is essentially the same, of general jurisdiction.

It is not questioned, that whatever may be necessary to the full and unlimited exercise of admiralty and maritime jurisdiction, is in the government of the union. Congress may pass all laws which are necessary and proper for giving the most complete effect to this power. Still, the general jurisdiction over the place, subject to this grant of power, adheres to the territory, as a portion of sovereignty not yet given away. The residuary powers of legislation are still in Massachusetts. Suppose for example the power of regulating trade had not been given to the general government. Would this extension of the judicial power to all cases of admiralty and maritime jurisdiction, have devested Massachusetts of the power to regulate the trade of her bay? As the powers of the respective governments now stand, if two citizens of Massachusetts step into shallow water when the tide flows, and fight a duel, are they not within the jurisdiction, and punishable by the laws of Massachusetts? If these questions must be answered in the affirmative, and we believe they must, then the bay in which this murder was committed, is not out of the jurisdiction of a state, and the circuit court of Massachusetts is not authorized, by the section under consideration, to take cognizance of the murder which had been committed.

It may be deemed within the scope of the question certified to this court, to inquire whether any other part of the act has given cognizance of this murder to the circuit court of Massachusetts?

The third section enacts, "that if any person or persons shall, within any fort, arsenal, dockyard, magazine, or in any other place, or district of country, under the sole and exclusive jurisdiction of the United States, commit the crime of wilful murder, such person or persons, on being thereof convicted, shall suffer death."

Although the bay on which this murder was committed might not be out of the jurisdiction of Massachusetts, the ship of war on the deck of which it was committed, is, it has been said, "a *place* within the sole and exclusive jurisdiction of the United States," whose courts may consequently take cognizance of the offence.[6]

That a government which possesses the broad power of war; which "may provide and maintain a navy"; which "may make rules for the government and regulation of the land and naval forces," has power to punish an offence committed by a marine on board a ship of war, wherever that ship may lie, is a proposition never to be questioned in this court. On this section, as on the 8th, the inquiry respects, not the extent of the power of Congress, but the extent to which that power has been exercised.

The objects with which the word "*place*" is associated, are all, in their nature, fixed and territorial. A fort, an arsenal, a dock-yard, a magazine, are all of this character. When the sentence proceeds with the words, "or in any other place or district of country under the sole and exclusive jurisdiction of the United States," the construction seems irresistible that, by the words "other place" was intended another place of a similar character with those previously enumerated, and with that which follows. Congress might have omitted, in its enumeration, some similar place within its exclusive jurisdiction which was not comprehended by any of the terms employed to which some other name might be given; and, therefore, the words "other place," or "district of country," were added; but the context shows the mind of the legislature to have been fixed on territorial objects of a similar character.

This construction is strengthened by the fact that at the time of passing this law, the United States did not possess a single ship of war. It may, therefore, be reasonably supposed, that a provision for the punishment of crimes in the navy might be postponed until some provision for a navy should be made. While taking this view of the subject, it is not entirely unworthy of remark, that afterwards, when a navy was created, and congress did not proceed to make rules for its regulation and government, no jurisdiction is given to the courts of the United States, of any crime committed in a ship of war, wherever it may be stationed.[7] Upon these reasons the court is of opinion, that a murder committed on board a ship of war, lying within the harbour of Boston, is not cognizable in the circuit court for the district of Massachusetts; which opinion is to be certified to that court.[8]

The opinion of the court, on this point, is believed to render it unnecessary to decide the question respecting the jurisdiction of the state court in the case.[9]

Printed, Henry Wheaton, *Reports of Cases Argued and Adjudged in the Supreme Court of the United States . . .* , III (New York, 1818), 386–91.

1. This was the second of the two questions certified to the Supreme Court. The first was whether the offense "was within the jurisdiction of the state of Massachusetts, or of any court thereof" (3 Wheat. 339).

2. *U.S. Statutes at Large*, I, 113–14.

3. Should be "to."

4. Webster devoted much of his argument to showing that the common law courts of Massachusetts had concurrent jurisdiction in this case and that Congress had made no provision for extending federal admiralty jurisdiction to cases in which state courts had concurrent common law jurisdiction. He contended that the admiralty jurisdiction conferred by the Constitution was to be understood as limited and defined by English common law. By this definition Bevans's case was not one of exclusive admiralty jurisdiction but one in which common law courts in England and America had historically exercised concurrent jurisdiction. Wheaton and Wirt argued that the framers intended the federal courts to have a broad and exclusive admiralty jurisdiction, not one "frittered down by the illiberal jealousy, and unjust usurpations of the common law courts" (3 Wheat. 344–75 [quotation at 362]).

5. The correct reference is to Article I of the Constitution.

6. See Wirt's argument (3 Wheat. 375).

7. Wheaton here subjoined the following footnote: "This, it is conceived, refers to the

ordinary courts of the United States, proceeding according to the law of the land. The crime of murder, when committed by any officer, seaman, or marine, belonging to any public ship or vessel of the United States, *without the territorial jurisdiction of the same*, may be punished with death by the sentence of a court martial. Act. of 1803 for the better government of the navy, ch. 187 (33,) sect. 1, art. 21. But the case at bar was not cognizable by a navy court martial, being committed within the territorial jurisdiction of the United States" (ibid., 391–392).

8. JM's draft of the certificate is in the appellate case file (U.S. v. Bevans, App. Cas. No. 866).

9. Story prepared an opinion in this case but did not deliver or publish it, for reasons explained in a letter to Henry Wheaton of 10 Apr. 1818: "According to your request I enclose you my opinion in United States *v*. Bevans. I have never changed my mind as to its legal accuracy, but as the case was a capital offence, I yielded to the opinion of my brethren. If it had been of another nature, I should have adhered to it. . . . The truth is, that after the decision, I put the opinion by with a view at some future day perhaps to publish it, and I should have delivered it in Court, if I had not felt a delicacy in respect to the Chief Justice, especially as I acquiesced in the opinion he delivered; though I think it is not drawn up with his usual precision and accuracy. You will please therefore to keep my opinion *confidential*, though, if you think it worth preservation, I have no objection to your taking a copy of it, as corrected, for your own *private* use, but by no means for the public use. Upon the point as to exemption of a public ship of war from State jurisdiction, a majority of the Court held the same opinion as myself, although, as the decision of the other point settled the cause, that opinion was suppressed from motives of delicacy" (Story, *Life and Letters*, I, 305).

From Benjamin W. Crowninshield

Sir,   Navy Department. Feby 23d. 1818.
    In compliance with the request in your letter of the 21st. inst. I have the pleasure to enclose an order for your Nephew Midsn. Marshall, and would beg the favor of your forwarding it to his address, which you will be pleased to communicate to this Department. Very respectfully, &c.

                                       B. W. CROWNINSHIELD.

Letterbook copy, RG 45, DNA.

To Unknown

Sir   Washington March 12th. 1818
    Mr. Lamb did me the favor some days past to call & deliver me your letter together with two publications containing the British Colonial Slave laws for which I return you my thanks.[1]
    Have the goodness to make my acknowledgements to Sir R. Phillips for this polite mark of attention & to Mr. Busby for forwarding it.[2] If

you do not correspond with Sir R Phillips, I must hope to pass my acknowlegements to him through Mr. Busby. With very great respect, I am Sir your Obedt

J MARSHALL

ALS, Park Collection, CtY. Endorsed as received on 23 Mar. 1818 "in answer to mine by Major John Lamb."

1. The publications were two collections of British colonial slave laws which the House of Commons had ordered printed in 1816 and 1817, respectively: *Colonial Laws respecting Slaves* (London, 1816–17) and *Additional Colonial Laws respecting Slaves: 1816–1817 . . .* (London, 1817).

2. Presumably Sir Richard Phillips (1767–1840), a British author, bookseller, and publisher, who published the English edition of Marshall's *Life of Washington* (*PJM*, VI, 220, 324 n. 8).

To Benjamin W. Crowninshield

Dear Sir   Washington March 13th. 1818

I trust you will excuse my putting on paper as a memorandum the request I took the liberty to make when I had last the pleasure of seeing you. My Nephew John Marshall will repair to Boston & report himself to Commodore Bainbridge. He could not be placed under an officer of whom I think more highly; but as his friends are extremely desirous of his becoming master of his profession, & suppose that he would derive advantages from being on board a vessel in actual service which could not be acquired in a vessel lying in port, they would be highly gratified with his being placed in any frigate which may be ordered to sea. Permit me sir to ask, should any of our Frigates be ordered into actual service, that you will direct my nephew to be one of the Midshipmen that goes in her. With very much respect, I am your Obedt

J MARSHALL

ALS, RG 45, DNA. Addressed to "The Honble./The Secretary of the Navy." Endorsed: "Present, March 13, 1818./Wishes his nephew Mid. John/Marshal, to be ordered to some vessel/about going to sea."

To Joseph Delaplaine

Sir[1]   Richmond March 22d. 1818.

I received while at Washington your letters requesting me to sit for my portrait to be taken first by Mr. Wood & afterwards by Mr. Lawrence.[2] The first gentleman I could not see & the last did not reach Washington during my stay in the city. At your request my portrait was formerly taken by Mr. Wood, & I did suppose it was in your possession.[3]

His price I presume as well as that of Mr. Lawrence is forty dollars. If it is, & you can receive from him that which he has already painted, & you direct me to remit the money to him or yourself, I will do so.

I have also received your letter requesting some account of my birth parentage &c.[4] I believe I answered the same or nearly the same queries two years past—but suppose my letter is mislaid. I shall again comply with your request. It is not however my wish to appear in your next half volume, nor is it my opinion that persons who are still in the view of the public ought to be placed in it.[5] But I do not pretend to interfere with any mode of conducting your great work which to yourself shall seem eligible.

I was born on the 24th. of September 1755, in the county of Fauquier in Virginia.[6] My Father Thomas Marshall was the eldest son of John Marshall who intermarried with a Miss Markham, & whose parents migrated from Wales, & settled in the county of Westmoreland in Virginia, where my Father was born. My mother was named Mary Keith. She was the daughter of a clergyman of the name of Keith who migrated from Scotland & intermarried with a Miss Randolph on James River. I was educated at home, under the direction of my Father, who was a planter, but was often called from home as a surveyor. From my infancy I was destined for the bar; but the contest between the mother country & her colonies drew me from my studies & my Father from the superintendence of them; & in September 1775, I entered into the service as a subaltern. I continued in the army until the year 1781, when, being without a command, I resigned my commission, in the interval between the invasions of Virginia by Arnold & Phillips. In the year 1782 I was elected into the legislature of Virginia, & in the fall session of the same year, was chosen a member of the Executive counsel of that state. In Jany. 1783 I intermarried with Mary Willis Ambler, the second daughter of Mr. Jaquelin Ambler, then Treasurer of Virginia, who was the third son of Mr. Richard Ambler a gentleman who had migrated from England, & settled at York Town in Virginia. In April 1784 I resigned my seat in the Executive counsel, & came to the bar, at which I continued, declining any other public office than a seat in the legislature, until the year 1797, when I was associated with General Pinkney & Mr. Gerry in a mission to France. In 1798 I returned to the United States, & in the spring of 1799 was elected a member of Congress, a candidate for which much against my inclination, I was induced to become by the request of General Washington. At the close of the first session I was nominated first to the Department of war, & afterwards to that of state, which last office I accepted, & in which I continued until the beginning of the year 1801; when, Mr. Ellsworth having resigned, & Mr. Jay having declined his appointment, I was nominated to the office of Chief Justice, which I still hold.

I am the oldest of fifteen children all of whom lived to be married & of whom nine are now living. My Father died when about seventy four years of age & my mother who survived him about seven years, died about the same age. I do not recollect all the societies to which I belong, though they a[re] very numerous. I have written no book except the Life of Washington which was executed with so much precipitation as to require much correction.

I received also a letter from you requesting some expression of my sentiments respecting your repository, & indicating an intention to publish in some conspicuous manner, the certificates which might be given by Mr. Wirt & myself.[7]

I have been ever particularly unwilling to obtain this kind of distinction, & must insist on not receiving it now. I have however no difficulty in saying that your work is one in which the nation ought to feel an interest, & I sincerely wish it may be encouraged, & that you may receive ample compensation for your labor & expence. The execution is I think in many respects praiseworthy. The portraits, an object of considerable interest, are, so far as my acquaintance extends, good likenesses; & the printing is neatly executed with an excellent type. In the characters there is of course some variety. Some of them are drawn with great spirit & justice—some are perhaps rather exaggerated. There is much difficulty in giving living characters—at any rate until they shall have withdrawn from the public view. The plan might perhaps have been improved by introducing a greater number of persons who were distinguished for their exertions in [illegible] settling & discovering our country. Sir Walter Raleigh & Capt Smith for example might have been added with advantage to Columbus & Americas.[8] Many of those distinguished individuals who took an early part in our revolutionary contest & whose portraits might probably be obtained in their families or in Peales Museum, would have been most desirable precursors to the lives of those who are still in being.[9] But as it is, we behold in it a great national undertaking, & I cordially wish it success. Very respectfully I am Sir, your obedt. Servt

J MARSHAL[L]

ALS, Marshall Papers, DLC; copy (facsimile), NHi; copy (facsimile), NN. ALS addressed to Delaplaine in Philadelphia; postmarked Richmond, 23 Mar. Endorsed by Delaplaine as answered on 26 Mar. Additional endorsements: "Facts of his life" and "Portrait." Facsimiles reproduce dateline, salutation, third paragraph (containing autobiographical sketch), and signature.

1. Joseph Delaplaine (1777–1824), the Philadelphia publishing entrepreneur, engaged in several business ventures between 1810 and 1818. His most ambitious project was *Delaplaine's Repository of the Lives and Portraits of Distinguished Americans* (2 vols.; Philadelphia, 1816–18; S #34554). The *Repository* combined finely engraved portraits with

short biographies based, whenever possible, on material provided by the subjects themselves. Although Delaplaine expected the *Repository* to be a continuing series, financial problems prevented publication of any additional volumes after vol. II, pt. 1, appeared in 1818. JM's biography, along with his portrait and facsimiles of his handwriting, was intended for a volume that never appeared. His portrait, however, was exhibited in Delaplaine's "National Panzographia for the Reception of the Portraits of Distinguished Americans," which opened in Philadelphia in Jan. 1819 (Gordon M. Marshall, "The Golden Age of Illustrated Biographies: Three Case Studies," in Wendy Wick Reaves, ed., *American Portrait Prints: Proceedings of the Tenth Annual American Print Conference* [Charlottesville, Va., 1984], 32–45; *Delaplaine's Repository*, vol. II, pt. 1; [Joseph Delaplaine], *Prospectus of Delaplaine's National Panzographia for the Reception of the Portraits of Distinguished Americans* [Philadelphia, 1818], 15–16).

2. Letters not found. Joseph Wood (ca. 1778–1830), who specialized in cabinet-sized and miniature paintings, had moved to Washington in 1816 after earlier stints in New York and Philadelphia. Charles B. Lawrence was a portrait and landscape painter in Philadelphia (Andrew Oliver, *The Portraits of John Marshall* [Charlottesville, Va., 1977], 35–37; George C. Groce and David H. Wallace, *The New-York Historical Society's Dictionary of Artists in America, 1564–1860* [New Haven, Conn., 1957], 387).

3. This is apparently a reference to Wood's portrait, taken around 1816. It has not been found, but an engraving produced from this painting by Francis Kearny was published in the Feb. 1817 issue of the *Analectic Magazine and Naval Chronicle* (Oliver, *Portraits of Marshall*, 35–37). Wood's portrait was presumably the one Delaplaine later exhibited in his Panzographia.

4. Letter not found.

5. In a letter to Delaplaine of 5 Nov. 1818, William Wirt quoted JM as saying, "I hope to God they [biographers] will let me alone till I am dead" (John P. Kennedy, *Memoirs of the Life of William Wirt* . . . [rev. ed.; 2 vols.; Philadelphia, 1850–54], II, 78).

6. This is the earliest extant autobiographical account composed by JM. He prepared a longer one for Joseph Story in 1827, which has been published in John Stokes Adams, ed., *An Autobiographical Sketch by John Marshall* (Ann Arbor, Mich., 1937), 3–32. In 1814 John Wickham wrote a biographical sketch of JM that was published anonymously in the *Port Folio* (a Philadelphia magazine) for Jan. 1815 (Bushrod Washington to Wickham, 25 May 1814 [filed with Wickham's autograph draft of the sketch], ViHi; *The Port Folio*, 3d ser., V [1815], 1–6).

7. Letter not found. Delaplaine often used favorable correspondence from public figures in his publicity for the *Repository* (Marshall, "Golden Age," in Reaves, ed., *American Portrait Prints*, 42).

8. The first half-volume of *Delaplaine's Repository* presented biographies of Columbus, Amerigo Vespucci, Benjamin Rush, Fisher Ames, Alexander Hamilton, and George Washington. The second half-volume contained sketches of Peyton Randolph, Thomas Jefferson, John Jay, Rufus King, DeWitt Clinton, and Robert Fulton. Samuel Adams, George Clinton, Henry Laurens, Benjamin Franklin, Francis Hopkinson, and Robert Morris were the subjects of the second volume (*Delaplaine's Repository*, I, II; Marshall, "Golden Age," in Reaves, ed., *American Portrait Prints*, 72).

9. Charles Willson Peale (1741–1827), the American portraitist, opened a museum in his home in Philadelphia in July 1786. The museum, which featured "Natural Curiosities" and also contained a portrait gallery, moved to the American Philosophical Society in 1794 and then to Independence Hall in 1802. In 1810 Peale transferred control over the museum to his son Rubens (1784–1865) and retired. Peale's museum eventually became the Philadelphia Museum (Lillian B. Miller et al., eds., *The Selected Papers of Charles Willson Peale and His Family* [New Haven, Conn., 1983–], I, xlvi, lii, 448; II, pt. 2, pp. 1245–46 and n.).

From Mark L. Descaves

Sir   [ca. 31 March 1818]

I have the honour to inclose a letter from our mutual friend General Lafayette who desired me to deliver it myself to you: but having been disappointed in the hope I had of meeting you at Washington I am afraid you'll think I should have much sooner, forwarded it by mail.[1] You will, I flatter myself be so good as to excuse this delay the motives of it having originated from a wish to comply with Gen. L's desires & particular Instructions.

I had the pleasure of seeing, a few months ago Juge Washington who told me you had sent, by Mr. Graham I think, the original letters and other papers our worthy friend so eagerly anticipated the repossession of: I should have been happy to offer you my services in any thing I could have done to promote Genl. L's views as nothing would make me happier than being agreeable or usefull at the same time to you, Sir, and to So Dear and So good a friend. I have the honour to be respectfully, Sir, Yr. hble devoted Servt.

MARK L DESCAVES.
OF BALTIMORE

ALS, Marshall Papers, ViW. Addressed to JM as chief justice; "Richmond/Va" added in unknown hand. Noted on cover: "Forwarded by his very humble servt/Washington City 31 March 1818/Eugene A Vache[?]."

1. Lafayette to JM, 22 Apr. 1817.

To Louis Marshall

My dear Brother   Richmond May 19th. 1818

I had yesterday the pleasure of receiving your letter by Mr. Alexander.[1] He sat with me an hour or two & I was much pleased with his manners & conversation. I should have felt much pleasure in contributing all in my power to render his stay in Richmond agreeable to him, but he arrived while I was on my circuit at Raleigh in North Carolina. I returned only yesterday & some short time after my reaching home Mr. Alexander came in & gave me your letter. To my enquiries respecting his continuance with us, he answered that he should leave town this morning early for Philadelphia, & did not expect to return this way. I should have been much gratified had it been in my power to bestow the proper attentions on a young gentleman of merit who is your friend.

I have never my dear brother entertained a doubt of the propriety of your conduct to our nephew T. Taylor. My only fear was that his idle habits & head strong temper, spoiled or at any rate greatly injured by indulgence, might disappoint your best exertions for his improvement, & disgust you with him. I am gratified in beleiving that this fear is unfounded. I approve highly the course you have taken with him, & am truely rejoiced that he is under your protection.

I had expected that you would draw on Mr. Leigh or myself for the money which is required for him but suppose there may be some difficulty in drawing on this place & have therefore sent you a check on Philadelphia for 200$.[2] My sister informs me that she inclosed a note for $100 in a letter to our sister. If you will let me know whether this mode of remittance is agreeable to you & what remittances ought to be made I will take care that this business shall not be neglected. I indorse the check particularly to you that, in the event of its miscarriage it may perhaps be stopped at the bank. You will indorse it as you please & will I presume find no difficulty in negotiating it. I am my dear Brother your affectionate

J MARSHALL

ALS, Owned by John Marshall Bullitt, Cambridge, Mass., 1973. Addressed to Louis Marshall at Buckpond, Woodford County, Ky., and postmarked Richmond, 22 May.

1. Letter not found. Alexander may have been Andrew Jonathan Alexander (1796–1833), John Regis Alexander, or Charles Alexander, sons of William Alexander by his second wife, Agatha De La Porte. The Alexander and Marshall families of Woodford County, Ky., were closely associated. William Alexander, a Scots merchant who had settled in Richmond in 1784 and moved to Kentucky in 1811, had been associated with Robert Morris during the 1780s in a tobacco contract with the French Farmers-General. JM served as Morris's counsel in Morris v. Alexander, a case that grew out of this contract (William E. Railey, *History of Woodford County, Kentucky* [1938; Baltimore, 1975 reprint], 207–9; Margaret R. Cardwell, ed., "A Web of Family: Letters from a Kentucky Family, 1816–1865," 12–13 [typescript in office of The Papers of John Marshall]; *PJM*, V, 93–116; VI, 277, 279 n. 5, 497, 498 n. 2).

2. JM and Benjamin Watkins Leigh (1781–1849) were executors of George Keith Taylor, father of Thomas Taylor. Born in Chesterfield County, Leigh studied briefly at the College of William and Mary and was admitted to the bar in 1802. He practiced law in Petersburg until he moved to Richmond in 1813. He subsequently achieved professional distinction, supervising preparation of the Code of 1819, representing Virginia in a land dispute with Kentucky, and serving as reporter for the state Court of Appeals. His second wife, Susanna Colston, was JM's niece—daughter of Rawleigh Colston and Elizabeth Marshall Colston (Paxton, *Marshall Family*, 111).

United States v. Schooner Little Charles
Opinion and Decree
U.S. Circuit Court, Virginia, 27 May 1818

The schooner *Little Charles* was seized at the port of Norfolk in April 1808 for violating the embargo laws of December 1807 and January 1808. U.S. Attorney George Hay filed his libel in the U.S. District Court in June

1808. The libel alleged that the vessel, which sailed from Camden, North
Carolina, "on or about" 19 January 1808, proceeded to a foreign place,
namely, the island of Antigua in the British West Indies. On arrival in
Norfolk, James Corrmatt, master of the *Little Charles*, made a report and
manifest, signed and sworn on 31 March 1808, proving that the schooner
had stopped at Antigua and taken on a cargo of rum, molasses, and other
West India produce. In December 1809 District Court Judge Cyrus Griffin dismissed the libel on the ground that the "ex parte affidavit" of the
master "could not be read as evidence in this cause to which he is no
party." Although Hay filed an appeal in the U.S. Circuit Court in June
1810, a complete and certified record of the lower court's proceedings was
not sent up until November 1815. Marshall rendered his opinion and
decree on 27 May 1818 (proceedings in U.S. District Court [copy], 26 Dec.
1809; decree, 27 May 1818 [newspaper clipping], U.S. v. Schooner Little
Charles, U.S. Cir. Ct., Va., Ended Cases [Unrestored], 1819, Vi; U.S. Cir.
Ct., Va., Ord. Bk. VIII, 176–77; IX, 228, 234, 268, 306, 336).

The first point made in this case, respects the pleadings. It is contended, on the part of the claimants, that the libel is insufficient to
support a sentence confiscating the vessel.

The libel is supposed to be defective, because it does not state the
character of the vessel. The Court is not informed whether the Little
Charles was a foreign vessel, an American registered, or a coasting
vessel.

If the embargo acts omitted in their prohibitions any vessels of either
description, the failure to aver the character of the vessel would certainly be fatal to the libel. The evidence in the cause, showing, that in
point of fact, the Little Charles had incurred the penalty of the law,
would not supply the want of a case stated in the libel. Nor would the
averment, that the vessel had departed contrary to the provisions of
the acts of congress, aid the libellants. The libel must contain a substantial statement of the offence, or it will not sustain a sentence of confiscation. These principles were, after mature deliberation, settled in the
supreme court, in the case of the schooner Hoppet.[1] But in the same
case it is laid down, "that all those technical niceties which are unimportant in themselves, and which stand only on precedents, of which the
reason cannot be discerned, are not to be transplanted from the courts
of common law into the courts of admiralty."[2] All, then, that is required
is, that the offence created by the law should be stated substantially, and
with reasonable precision.

The libel charges, that the schooner Little Charles, did on or about
the 19th day of January, in the year 1808, depart from the port of
Camden, in the state of North Carolina, a port of the United States,
and proceed to a foreign place, to wit, to the island of Antigua, with a
cargo on board.

The act of December 1807, declares, "that an embargo be, and hereby is, laid on all ships and vessels in the ports and places, within the limits or jurisdiction of the United States, cleared or not cleared, bound to any foreign port or place."[3]

This prohibitory clause extends to vessels of every description. Foreign and domestic, registered and coasting vessels, are equally included in it. No vessel of either character could proceed from an American to a foreign port, without violating this part of the law. Suppose it pleaded, that this was a coaster, would this excuse? It cannot, therefore, be necessary, in reason, or under the decision in the case of the Hoppet, so far as respects this part of the law, to aver the particular character of the vessel. The defence does not depend on her character.

The only part of the description found in the law, and not in the libel, is, "bound to any foreign port or place." These words are supplied by the charge that she did proceed to a foreign port. The fact charged in the libel, then, is a violation of the prohibitory part of the act of 1807. It remains to inquire whether the law contains any other provision which requires a more particular description of the vessel, or of the offence.

The section provides "That nothing herein contained, shall be construed to prevent the departure of any foreign ship, or vessel, either in ballast, or with goods, wares, and merchandize, on board of such foreign ship or vessel when notified of this act."

The whole section amounts to this. A general clause for forbidding the departure of all vessels, from a port in the United States, to a foreign port, or place, is followed by an exception in favour of a foreign ship, departing in ballast, or with the cargo she had on board, when notified of the prohibition. If it be necessary in the libel to assert, that the Little Charles is not within the exception, then this libel is defective, otherwise it is sufficient.

This point, also, has been considered in the supreme court. In the case of the Aurora, it is said by the Court, "That in no case can it be necessary to state, in a libel, any fact which constitutes the defence of the claimant, or a ground of exception to the operation of the law on which the libel is founded."[4]

The third section of the supplemental act declares that, "if any ship or vessel shall, during the continuance of the act to which this act is a supplement, depart from any port of the United States without a clearance or permit, or if any ship, or vessel, shall, contrary to the provisions of this act, or of the act to which this act is a supplement, proceed to a foreign port or place, such ship, &c., shall be wholly forfeited."[5]

This act expressly annexes the penalty of forfeiture to any ship or vessel which shall violate either the original or the supplemental act. It is, therefore, unimportant, so far as respects the sufficiency of the libel, which act is violated.

If, as has been argued, different penalties were imposed by the act, on different descriptions of vessels, the Court would certainly require that the libel should describe the vessel. But so far as the Court can understand the law, forfeiture is inflicted on every vessel, of every description, which shall commit the offence charged in the libel. Consequently, it is not necessary, for the instruction of the Court, that the vessel should be described.

The Court is fully satisfied that the libel, in this case, is sufficient to sustain a sentence of condemnation, should the testimony prove the offence charged in it to have been committed.

2. The Court will next proceed to examine that testimony. In doing so, the caption which the clerk has prefixed to the documents in the record, will certainly be disregarded, and only the documents themselves be considered as testimony.

The offence is, departing from a port in the United States, after the passage of the first and second embargo acts, and proceeding to Antigua, which is a foreign port, or place.

That the Little Charles was in the port of Camden, in North Carolina, in December, 1807, and January, 1808, when both those acts passed, is not controverted. That she was in the port of Norfolk, on the 8th of April, 1808, while they were in force, is equally clear, because she was then seized in that port. The inquiry is, had she, in the mean time, proceeded to a foreign port?

The report and manifest, with the affidavit, made by the captain, before the collector of the port, at Norfolk, if admissible, in the form in which they appear in the record, are certainly, in the absence of all exculpatory testimony, sufficient to satisfy the mind that the Little Charles took on board, at Antigua, the cargo which was imported into Norfolk, and, consequently, that she had violated the embargo laws.[6]

The objections to the admissibility of this document, are 1. That it is only part of a transaction.

2. That, in a criminal case, the declarations of the captain cannot affect the owner.

It will be unnecessary to inquire whether, in any case, part of a transaction may be received as testimony. The general principle, that it may not, is certainly correct; but it might be improper to say, that this general rule admits of no possible exception. The inquiry is, at present, unnecessary, because the Court is clear in its opinion, that this is not a part of, but is an entire transaction.

The document is a report and manifest, as required by law, with the affidavit annexed, which is also required.[7] Had the report and manifest been offered without the affidavit, or the affidavit without the report and manifest, it would have been part of a transaction. But offered together, they form one entire transaction, requiring nothing for its completion.

It has been argued, that the entry ought to be produced. But the entry is a distinct and independent act, which must be preceded by, but may not follow the report and manifest. It is to be made by a different person, and if made, may be deferred fifteen days after the report.[8] In the meantime, a seizure, as in this case, may prevent an entry. The validity of this objection cannot be admitted.

The Court will next inquire, whether this document can affect the vessel.

The argument, that in criminal cases no authority can be given, that the character of principal and agent disappears, and the parties become accomplices, will not be controverted. If this was a prosecution against the owner personally, and the confession of the master was adduced, to prove that he acted under the authority of the owner, the argument would be entitled to great consideration. But this is not a proceeding against the owner; it is a proceeding against the vessel, for an offence committed by the vessel, which is not less an offence, and does not the less subject her to forfeiture, because it was committed without the authority, and against the will of the owner.

It is true, that inanimate matter can commit no offence. The mere wood, iron, and sails of the ship, cannot, of themselves, violate the law. But this body is animated and put in action by the crew, who are guided by the master. The vessel acts and speaks by the master. She reports herself by the master. It is, therefore, not unreasonable, that the vessel should be affected by this report.

But this vessel is the property of another; and his property, it is said, ought not to be wrested from him by evidence, which would be inadmissible in an ordinary question, concerning property.

The Court thinks otherwise.

The master is selected by the owner, as his agent, for the purpose, among others, of reporting the vessel on her coming into port. The report is not a criminal act, but one prescribed by law. It must state, truly, the voyage, and however criminal that voyage may be, in reporting it, the master is in the precise line of his duty, and in the execution of an authority, inseparable from his character as master. This report, then, which is in the very terms prescribed by law, contains, according to the mandate of the law, an averment of the place from which the vessel last sailed. This averment, then, the owner has authorized the master to make for him; and although he may certainly be permitted to controvert it, the Court deems it *prima facie* evidence of the fact. Such evidence has often been considered, in the supreme court, sufficient to warrant a forfeiture in the absence of that testimony, which would be in the power of the claimant, if innocent, and was so considered in the case of the Aurora, already cited.

But admitting the sufficiency of the libel, and the proof, it is contended, that the Court has lost its jurisdiction, by losing possession of the thing to be condemned. The stipulation which is substituted for the vessel was, it is said, irregularly taken, and, consequently, cannot be considered as a substitute.[9]

That possession of the thing is necessary, as a foundation for the jurisdiction of the court, is, in general, true. There must be seizure to vest the jurisdiction. But it is not believed that the continuance of possession, is necessary to continue the jurisdiction. It is a general principle, that jurisdiction, once vested, is not divested, although a state of things should arrive in which original jurisdiction could not be exercised. No authority has been found, nor is any reason perceived, for making this case an exception to the general rule.

If, in proceedings *in rem*, the vested jurisdiction of the Court could be divested by the loss of the thing, the reason must be, that as the thing could neither be delivered to the libellants, nor restored to the claimants, the sentence would be useless, and courts will not render judgments which can operate on nothing. But this reason will not apply to any case where the judgment will have any effect whatever: if, for example, the liability of the officer for making the seizure, to damages, be dependent on it, or if the parties have, by consent, substituted other property to abide the fate of the suit. However this may be, the Court is not satisfied that its jurisdiction is lost by the circumstance that has occurred, and is of opinion, that the sentence of the district court be reversed, and the Little Charles be condemned and forfeited.

[Decree]

The United States

v

The Schooner Little Charles

This cause came on to be heard on the transcript of the record of the district court and was argued by counsel on consideration whereof this court is of opinion that there is error in the sentence of the District court dismissing the libel and doth reverse the same and this court proceeding to give such sentence as the District court ought to have given is of opinion that the Schooner Little Charles her rigging tackle apparel & furniture was forfeited to the United States; and it appearing in the proceedings that the Schooner the Little Charles had been restored to Charles Grice the claimants by order of the Judge of the District court on his giving bond with security in the value thereof and in one hundred dollars in addition thereto which said bond in the penalty of nineteen hundred dollars was executed & filed among the papers of the said cause whereupon the vessel was by the Marshal restored to the claimant, it is farther ordered that unless the claimant Charles Grice do on or before the first day of July next pay to the use of the United States the sum of $1900 the amount of the penalty of the said bond, that a monition issue to the said Charles Grice & to Warren

Ashly the surety to the said obligation requiring them to appear on the first day of the next term of this court to show cause why a decree should not be rendered against them for the sum of money expressed in the said obligation, and it appearing that the said charles Grice is not an inhabitant of this state it is directed that this order be published for two weeks successively in one of the papers printed in the town of Norfolk, and the cause is continued to the next term.[10]

Printed, John W. Brockenbrough, *Reports of Cases Decided by the Honourable John Marshall* . . . , I (Philadelphia, 1837), 350–55. Decree, AD, U.S. v. Schooner Little Charles, U.S. Cir. Ct., Va., Ended Cases (Unrestored), 1819, Vi.

1. Schooner Hoppet v. U.S., 7 Cranch 389 (1813).

2. JM quoted (with minor variations) from the opinion he delivered for the Court (7 Cranch 394).

3. *U.S. Statutes at Large*, II, 451–52.

4. The quotation is from Justice Johnson's opinion for the Court in Brig Aurora v. U.S. (7 Cranch 382, 389 [1813]).

5. *U.S. Statutes at Large*, II, 453–54.

6. The report and manifest of Capt. James Corrmatt, sworn on 31 Mar. 1808, was entered on the record (proceedings in U.S. District Court [copy], 26 Dec. 1809, U.S. v. Schooner Little Charles).

7. JM referred to provisions of the 1799 act to regulate the collection of duties (*U.S. Statutes at Large*, I, 645, 649–50).

8. Ibid., I, 655.

9. By an order of District Court Judge Griffin, dated 12 Apr. 1808, the vessel was directed to be released, pending a final decree of the court, on the owner's giving bond for the full amount of its value. The bond was accordingly executed on 14 Apr. 1808 by Charles Grice, with Warren Ashley as security (proceedings in U.S. District Court [copy], 26 Dec. 1809, U.S. v. Schooner Little Charles).

10. See the further opinion in this case under date of ca. 22 Nov. 1819.

From William Wirt

Dear Sir,   Washington July 4. 1818

An application has been made by the Governor of Georgia to the president of the U.S. to direct a trial of captn Wright, charged with the murder of certain friendly Indians, before the courts of the U.S.[1] Wright was at the head of a company of militia, acting under the orders of the governor of Georgia, and not in the service of the U.S. when he made the attack in question, on the Chehaw village. He alledges that he had the governor's express orders for attacking and destroying this particular village, which was confessedly friendly: the Governor on the other hand denies this assertion and contends that his orders pointed out other Indians who were confessedly hostile. If the courts of the U S have jurisdiction over this case, it is presumed they must take it under an act of the 30th March 1802 entitled "an act to regulate trade and intercourse with the Indian tribes and to procure peace on the frontiers" 3d Vol Laws U.S. page 460 of the new edition. The 6th. section of this act, you will observe makes the killing of a friendly Indian (within their own territory) murder: and the 15th. section gives the U.S. courts jurisdiction over all offences committed against this act: the same section also authorizes the president of the U.S. to issue a commission to any one or more judges of the Supreme court of the U.States, and the judge of the district within which such offender may be apprehended to try the offence when capital: a provision which it is supposed was intended to ensure a speedy trial, where the next session of the regular court was distant.[2]

The president is disposed to exercise the authority given him by this law, if it applies to the case so as to found the jurisdiction of the courts of the U.S. and if any two judges of the Supreme court will attend. The decision to proceed, civilly, under this law (in preference to a court martial of the State of Georgia) was taken before the president left Washington. But in a conference, since that, with the secretary of State, he suggests the two doubts as to the jurisdiction and the probability of procuring the attendance of any two judges of the Supreme court.[3]

In relation to the jurisdiction of the court he is under the impression, that the law did not contemplate a military movement and that the moment Wright produces his commission, the court will disclaim jurisdiction: that the law meant to punish private and individual assassination only: and that Wright's offence (if it be one) having been committed under a commission, at the head of an armed body, regularly armed and marched for war, is a military offence, only, and can be tried by no other tribunal than a court-martial: that a civil tribunal can neither examine his commission nor his orders, so as to try the fact, whether he has or has not acted in obedience to them, but that the commission the orders and the execution of the orders are purely military affairs, with which a civil tribunal has nothing to do. On the other hand, it is said, that the case of Wright is within the 6th section of the law, and that his commission his orders and the execution are matters of defence as completely examinable before the civil court as any other matters of defence: that neither his commission nor his orders afford him any more protection against his responsibility for this murder, than they would against the murder of one of our citizens, on whom he should direct his company to fire, and that even admitting his commission and his orders to be, as he alleges, they neither oust the jurisdiction of the court nor constitute a justification of the act.

The doubt whether any two judges of the Supreme court can be prevailed upon to attend, depends in a great degree on yourself. The court under the commission cannot be held earlier than the first of October; it will be held at Milledgville in Georgia; and you and Judge Johnston are the Judges in view, as being most convenient to that place.

The Secretary of state being extremely engaged with other affairs, has requested me to write you—first to inquire (if it be not improper, as we hope it is not) whether you think the courts of the U.S. have jurisdiction of the offence: and secondly, whether it will be in your power to attend at the time and place appointed to execute the commission in conjunction with Judge Johnson & the Judge of the District. Be pleased to favor us with an answer at your earliest convenience.[4] I have the honour to be Sir with res &.

WM. WIRT

Letterbook copy, RG 60, DNA.

1. On 1 June 1818 Gov. William Rabun wrote to Secretary of War John C. Calhoun concerning the recent attack on Chehaw, an Indian village on the west side of the Flint River in what was then the Creek Nation, by Capt. Obed Wright of the Georgia militia. This incident gave rise to a spirited clash between state civil authority and federal military authority personified by Governor Rabun and Gen. Andrew Jackson. Wright had been arrested on Jackson's orders and then ordered to be released by state authorities on habeas corpus proceedings. At the time of the governor's communication with Calhoun, Wright was in state custody (*ASP, Military Affairs*, I, 774–78; *Niles' Weekly Register* [Baltimore, Md.], XIV [1818], 218–19, 236, 267–69, 292–93, 416).

2. *U.S. Statutes at Large*, II, 139, 142, 144.

3. For cabinet deliberations on this incident, see Charles Francis Adams, ed., *Memoirs of John Quincy Adams, Comprising Portions of His Diary from 1795 to 1848* (11 vols.; Philadelphia, 1874–76), IV, 104; Worthington Chauncey Ford, ed., *Writings of John Quincy Adams* (7 vols.; New York, 1913–17), VI, 358–59.

4. Although no written reply has been found, JM may have privately advised against a special court. In his diary entry of 28 July Adams noted: "There are new difficulties suggested to the appointment of a special Court for the trial of Captain Obed Wright, and Mr. Calhoun agreed with me in opinion that the best course would be to refer the trial to the ordinary Circuit Court which is to sit in Georgia next December" (Adams, ed., *Memoirs*, IV, 118–19).

On 27 July Wright escaped confinement and was subsequently reported to be in St. Augustine (now Fla.) under Spanish protection and intending to proceed to Havana. Governor Rabun issued a proclamation on 30 July offering a reward of five hundred dollars for Wright's apprehension. President Monroe considered issuing a similar proclamation, but his cabinet advised against this step as being of doubtful constitutionality. There is no record that Wright was ever tried in the U.S. Circuit Court for Georgia (*Niles' Weekly Register* [Baltimore, Md.], XIV [1818], 439–40; XV, 63; W. Edwin Hemphill, ed., *The Papers of John C. Calhoun*, III [Columbia, S.C., 1967], 65, 112).

To James M. Marshall

My dear Brother   July 22d. 1818

I received some time past a letter from Mr. Hopkins informing me that propositions had been made to him for the purchase of part of our Washington property, & that he had asked the principal advanced by us with compound interest from the time of the advance.[1] I received another letter from him this morning desiring to know whether I would sell on these terms. I have written to him expressing my assent, provided you approve the sale.[2] Should you not hear from him, it will be in consequence of the difficulty & delay of your communication, & I wish you would write to him mentioning this letter & saying what you think of selling & of the terms.[3] Your affectionate

J MARSHALL

Photostat of ALS, Marshall Papers, DLC. Addressed to James Marshall "near Front Royal/Frederick county"; postmarked Richmond, 22 July. Marked "missent & forwd/ from Fred[ricksbur]g." Note in left margin: "Given to me by/Miss Mary M. Marshall of Fairfield Fauquier Co. Va./Octo. 24. 1854."

1. Letter not found. In 1799 JM, James Marshall, and John Hopkins had purchased seven lots in Washington, D.C., near what is now Lafayette Park (Herbert A. Johnson, "The Tribulations of Conway Robinson, Jr.: John Marshall's 'Washington Lotts,'" *VMHB*, LXXIX (1971), 427–28).

2. Letters not found.

3. This property remained unsold at the time of JM's death. On the disposition of the lots after his death, see Johnson, "Tribulations of Conway Robinson," *VMHB*, LXXIX (1971), 428–35.

To Bushrod Washington

My dear Sir   Richmond October 28th. [1818]

I have this instant received yours of the 24th.[1]

The court I beleive was of opinion that the particular act for the releif of Oliver Evans varies the general patent law in this particular case.[2] Under that act, the court was, so far as I can recollect, of opinion that the patent might issue for the general result—the combination of the whole machinery for the purpose of manufacturing flour, & also for the improvement in each machine and for the invention of any one of the machines invented by him. It is considered under the act as a patent with a double aspect. There is I beleive no error of the reporter in stating the opinion, though on this point I cannot speak positively as I have not retained the original.[3]

I am a little puzzled to say what is the extent of the declaration in p 518. I rather think the court meant to decide that the specification was sufficient & enabled O.E. to prove under it at the trial that his improvement had been violated.[4] In all proceedings under this particular patent you will observe my dear Sir that the act for the releif of O.E. is understood by the court as authorising a much greater latitude than is authorized by the general patent law.[5] Yours affectionately

J MARSHALL

O. E. certainly cannot be the inventor & improver of the same machine, but he may the inventor of one & improver of another employed in the general man[u]factory.

ALS (advertised for sale by Houlé Gallery & Bookshop, Los Angeles, Cal., 1992). Addressed to Washington in Philadelphia; endorsed by Washington. Words in brackets supplied by transcript from Houlé.

1. Letter not found.
2. The reference is to the case of Evans v. Eaton, which had been decided at the Feb. 1818 term of the Supreme Court. The Court reversed an 1816 judgment of the U.S. Circuit Court for Pennsylvania, remanding the case to the lower court for a new trial. The case came again before Judge Washington on circuit at the Oct. 1818 term. Oliver Evans, the Philadelphia inventor, had obtained a private act of Congress in 1808 extending his patent on flour-milling machinery and improvements. He then sued numerous individuals in Pennsylvania and in other states for patent infringement (3 Wheat. 454; 8 Fed. Cas. 846, 856; *PJM*, VII, 404–11).
3. JM's opinion for the Supreme Court declared that Evans under his 1808 patent could claim "exclusive use of his inventions and improvements in the art of manufacturing flour and meal, and in the several machines which he has invented, and in his improvements on machines previously discovered." The Court's official judgment was that Judge Washington's instructions to the jury were erroneous in expressing the opinion that Evans's patent conveyed "only an exclusive right to his improvement in manufacturing flour and meal, produced by the general combination of all his machinery, and not to his improvement in the several machines applied to that purpose" (3 Wheat. 517, 519).
4. The passage referred to reads: "In all cases where his [Evans's] claim is for an improvement on a machine, it will be encumbent on him to show the extent of his improvement, so that a person understanding the subject may comprehend distinctly in what it consists" (3 Wheat. 518).
5. After the second trial in 1818, the case again went to the Supreme Court, which in 1822 upheld the circuit court's judgment (7 Wheat. 356).

To Peter Minor

Sir[1]   Richmond Novr. 7th. 1818
    Your letter of the   day of   with its enclosure was laid before the society which convenes at this place at its last meeting.[2] We are instructed to express the thanks of the society for the communication it contains, and the pleasure derived from the very valuable address delivered by your President.[3]

    The agriculture of our country will, we trust, soon manifest the advantages to be derived from the inteligence now devoted to its improvement.

    Allow us to assure you that as individuals not less than as members of our society, we have been much gratified by your communication, and feel much pleasure in executing the enclosed resolution. With great respect we are Sir your obed

JOHN MARSHALL
W. C. NICHOLAS
J. COALTER
J. WICKHAM
JOHN ADAMS
COMMITTEE OF CORRESPONDENCE[4]

ALS, Vi. In JM's hand except for other signatures and "Committee of correspondence." Endorsed: "Judge Marshall & others—Committee of/Correspondence of Richmond Society,/or rather Agl. Socy. of Virginia/Nov.7th. 1818."

1. Peter Minor was secretary of the Agricultural Society of Albemarle, which had been formed in 1817. James Madison was elected first president of the society (Rodney H. True, "Early Days of the Albemarle Agricultural Society," *Annual Report of the American Historical Association for the Year 1918* [3 vols., Washington, D.C., 1921], I, 243–59).

2. Letter not found. The enclosure was Madison's address to the Albemarle society, given in May 1818: *An Address Delivered before the Agricultural Society of Albemarle . . .* (Richmond, Va., 1818).

3. JM and the other signatories were members of the Virginia Society for Promoting Agriculture, which had been organized in 1811 as the first state agricultural society (Charles W. Turner, "Virginia State Agricultural Societies, 1811–1860," *Agricultural History*, XXXVIII [1964], 167–77; A. J. Morrison, "Note on the Organization of Virginia Agriculture," *WMQ*, 1st ser., XXVI [1918], 169–73).

4. The words "Committee of correspondence" were written (by John Adams?) in the right margin at a right angle to the signatures.

Schooner Thomas & Henry v. United States
Opinion
U.S. Circuit Court, Virginia, [ca. 1 December 1818]

The schooner *Thomas & Henry* was seized by customs officers on Virginia's Eastern Shore in March 1811, shortly after returning from a voyage to the West Indies. The vessel was subsequently libeled in the U.S. District Court at Norfolk for violating the 1799 act regulating the collection of duties. The specific charges were that the schooner unloaded a portion of her cargo of rum and limes without a permit and that her master failed to make a written report to the inspector of the revenue within forty-eight hours of arriving. For these violations U.S. Attorney Hay sought to have the vessel and cargo condemned and forfeited to the United States. Thomas Fletcher and Henry Parker, residents of Accomack County and joint owners of the schooner and cargo, denied the charges and sought restoration of their property. Trial of the cause was delayed until November 1815. Two years later District Court Judge St. George Tucker pronounced his decree condemning the vessel and cargo. An appeal was then taken to the U.S. Circuit Court and further evidence submitted. Marshall heard the appeal at the

November 1818 term and gave the following decree (proceedings in U.S. District Court [copy], 10 Nov. 1817, Schooner Thomas & Henry v. U.S., U.S. Cir. Ct., Va., Ended Cases [Unrestored], 1820, Vi; *U.S. Statutes at Large*, I, 627, 650, 665).

Much of the testimony found in the record, has been objected to, and to these objections, the first attention of the Court has been directed.

The depositions of Lewis Gordon and John York, the persons on whose information the seizure was made, were taken *de bene esse*, and are offered as evidence.[1] Two objections are made to their being read: 1st. That it does not appear, that they might not have been produced in the district court.

2d. That they are interested, and, therefore, incompetent witnesses.

According to the judicial act, a deposition taken *de bene esse* cannot be read at the trial, unless it appear to the court, that the witness is dead, or has removed out of the United States, or to a greater distance from the place of trial, than one hundred miles, or that he is unable to attend the court. No one of these requisites appear on the record to have been complied with. But, it is said by the attorney for the United States, very correctly, that if a deposition be read without objection, all objections to it are understood to be waived, and if particular exceptions are taken, all others are waived. To these depositions, he insists, a particular objection was made in the district court, which is not valid.

The objection is, "that the deposition was not taken and returned according to law."[2]

I must understand this objection as being, that that deposition is not taken and returned, according to law, as a deposition *in chief*. It does not appear, that the attorney for the United States, offered to prove those circumstances, which would entitle him to read it, as a deposition taken *de bene esse*. This he ought to have done, when the objection was taken to it, as a deposition *in chief*. Although the attorney for the claimants might have explained himself more fully, he was not bound so to do; and the party offering the deposition, was bound to show, that it was admissible. Even if this reasoning were incorrect, the certificate of the magistrate is insufficient. That is, that the deposition was taken, because the witness was a transient person.

The deposition of John York was also objected to, because, "it did not appear to have been duly taken, according to the act of congress."

This objection was overruled, because notice was given to the persons in possession of the property.

This reason is certainly sufficient for overruling the objection, if taken to it as a deposition *de bene esse*. But if offered, unaccompanied by the evidence, which would justify its being read as a deposition *de bene esse*, it must be supported as a deposition, taken *in chief*, or it cannot be read.

I think it not improbable, that the objections on the part of the claimant were understood to be made to the regularity of the depositions, as taken *de bene esse*, and that the fact of the witnesses having left the United States, or having removed to a distance of more than one hundred miles from the place of trial, was neither controverted, or controvertible. But I deem it proper, in cases where depositions are taken under the act of congress, that the requisition of the act should be observed, and should appear to have been observed.

On the part of the United States, it is contended, that so far as respects the deposition of York, these requisites are dispensed with, by the appearance of the attorney of the claimants, under an express declaration, that he waived all objections to the proceedings.[3]

But I understand this general waiver, as extending to the deposition, in the character in which it was intended to be taken, not as giving it a new character, not intended by the party taking it. It was not taken under a commission, issued by the court, and is, consequently, taken *de bene esse*. The waiver of all objection to the proceeding, therefore, is a waiver of objection to the deposition, as one *de bene esse*, and cannot be understood to make it a deposition *in chief*.

The objection to the competency of these witnesses, is also entitled to serious consideration. The law certainly is, that the witness must be competent, when his testimony is given, and if he be not then competent, his testimony is inadmissible. If these witnesses were competent, it must be, because the very act of giving their depositions amounted to a release of their interest.[4] Is this so? Had the depositions not been offered at the trial, but been shown to defeat a claim to their share of the forfeiture, would the attempt have succeeded? Had the depositions been rejected for any cause whatever, could they have extinguished the rights of the informers? I am not prepared to answer these questions in the affirmative.

The language of the law would seem to justify these doubts. If any person, entitled to a share of the forfeiture, "shall be necessary as a witness on the trial," says the act, "such person may be a witness upon the said trial," &c. Who is to judge of this necessity? Certainly not the collector. It is not for him to oust the informer for his own benefit. Then the Court must judge of this necessity, and must judge of it, after hearing the other testimony. Such person "may be a witness on the trial." This language, I think, is not applicable to a deposition, taken before the trial. Gordon and York were not witnesses at the trial. They were witnesses before the trial, at the time when these depositions were taken by a magistrate. The act of congress does not speak of depositions, and it seems to me, that such persons can be rendered competent to give depositions, only by releasing their interest.

On both grounds, therefore, I think these depositions inadmissible. Indeed their testimony was either rejected or disregarded in the district court.[5]

The direct testimony of the informers being discarded, the case turns on the other proofs in the cause.

The act under which this seizure was made, declares that "in actions, suits, or informations to be brought, where any seizure shall be made pursuant to this act, if the property be claimed by any person, in every such case the *onus probandi* shall be upon such claimant."[6]

In this case, then, the United States are not required to establish guilt, but the claimants must prove innocence.

It is not the duty of the judge to justify the legislature, but surely, if, in any case, such a legislative provision be proper, it is in this. The fact is generally premeditated, and is perpetrated under all the precautions and in all the secrecy which ingenuity can suggest, and the means of proving innocence, at least, to a reasonable extent, which is all that can be required, are in possession of the accused. In such a case, he may, without a violation of principle, be required to prove his innocence.

In such a case, the absence of testimony, clearly in the power of the claimants, if not supplied by other equivalent testimony, must be fatal. It is impossible to smuggle so large a part of a cargo, as is charged to have been smuggled in this case, without the knowledge of the master and crew. Consequently, their testimony against the fact, if believed, would be nearly conclusive. Why is it not produced? The master, being himself liable to a fine under one of the charges in this libel, was perhaps not admissible as a witness; but to the crew, no objection existed. Why were they not examined? If they were unattainable, this fact ought to have been shown, and might have excused their non-production. The deposition of one of them only was offered, and his was taken so irregularly, as to be rejected. No attempt appears to have been made to take it again, or to take the depositions of other mariners.

The documentary papers which usually accompany a cargo, and show its amount, are not produced. There is no testimony to prove, and no reason to believe, that the thirty-four puncheons of rum, and twenty barrels of limes, mentioned in the paper called a report and manifest, if we add the barrel of sugar, and of coffee found on board, and not included in the paper, constituted a full cargo for the vessel; nor is there any testimony, of any description, to show that she sailed with less than a full cargo.

To the absence of important testimony in the power of the claimants, is to be added, the testimony on the part of the United States. The mate of the revenue cutter found a lighter by the side of the vessel, the use of which, it is fair to presume, was to receive goods from her, although no permit had been granted.[7] I say none was granted, because none is produced: nor is any circumstance proved, to create a presumption that one was granted.

The arrangement of the cargo forms a strong presumption, that a part of it had been taken out. A large vacancy was found in the place which would have been filled in preference; and the cargo, which did not appear to have been moved, was so disposed, that the vessel could not have been navigated.

No evidence was offered to do away these causes of suspicion. I do not term the claims evidence, although they are sworn to, because the law does not allow to the affidavit made to them the dignity of testimony. If they amount to any thing, it is to no more, if I may use the phrase of Lord Coke, than "the exclusion of a conclusion."

Such are the circumstances under which this case appeared in the district court. The judge of that court was, I think very properly, of opinion, that they do not establish the innocence of the transaction.

In this Court, the depositions of Robert Pitts, George P. Barnes, and Wm. Pitts, are offered.[8]

To the reading of these depositions, the attorney for the United States objects, because,

They are taken *de bene esse*, and it does not appear, that the two Pitts have gone out of the United States, or to a greater distance from this place than one hundred miles.

This objection is, undoubtedly, conclusive; but as I have no doubt of the fact, I should allow the counsel for the claimants now to prove it, if these depositions would alter the case. I shall, therefore, consider them as if they were admitted. They are intended to meet the testimony of Butler, the officer of the revenue cutter, and to disprove the strong circumstances stated by him.

Before examining the testimony particularly, I will notice some general circumstances attending it, which seem to me to be worthy of observation.

The testimony of Butler was in the cause, long before it was tried. Why was not this explanatory or conflicting evidence offered in the district court? It must have been within the knowledge of the claimants; why was it not taken? why have they now taken it *ex-parte*? If it be true that the law authorizes this proceeding, it is not less true, that testimony, acquired under such circumstances, ought to be critically examined, and not carried beyond the plain meaning of the words of the witness; that material omissions justify the conclusion, that the facts omitted to be noticed, could not be noticed satisfactorily. With these observations, I shall examine these depositions.

Robert Pitts states, that he was on board of the vessel when she was seized; that they had to move the hogsheads out of the hatchway to get at the cargo, and there was no appearance of any thing having been moved when he went on board.

He does not say how many hogsheads were removed. Two hogsheads were on the deck and one on the slings, according to the testimony of Butler, who also says, that appearances indicated the recent removal of three hogsheads. When the witness says, there was no appearance of any having been moved, he states his own conclusion, which may have been drawn from the appearance of the hogsheads he saw. He does not say, that there was not a large vacancy in the centre of the vessel, nor that the disposition of the cargo was compatible with the navigation of the vessel.

George P. Barnes has, at least, sworn carelessly in saying, that he went on board the vessel immediately on her arrival. He says, he did not discover any particular deficiency of cargo midships of said schooner, nor that there appeared to be any particular breakage of the cargo in the midships.

This testimony is entirely negative, and instead of stating facts from which his conclusions are drawn, states the conclusion of the witness. He does not say that the midships were full; that the large vacancy, described by Butler, did not exist. He does not say that the hogsheads were there; but that no particular breakage of the cargo appeared. He may not have considered this vacancy, if he observed it, as evidence of the breakage of the cargo; and if he did not so consider it, the vacancy may have made no impression on him.

William Pitts says, that the floor of the schooner, from main to fore-mast, was covered, when she was seized, with hogsheads of rum and barrels of limes, and that there was no appearance of the cargo having been broken in any part.

This testimony is certainly more explicit than any other. Had it been taken in the district court, or were any satisfactory reasons assigned for its not having been taken; or had an opportunity been given to cross-examine the witness, I will not say, that his testimony would have out-weighed the conflicting and more explicit testimony of Butler; but I will say, that it would have had much more influence on my mind than it now has.

I come now to consider the second charge in the libel, the omission to make the report required by law.[9]

The claimants, contend that the allegation of this offence in the libel, is too defective to sustain a sentence of condemnation, whatever the testimony may be.

My opinion on this point depends on the construction of the act of congress. If, by that act, the rum is forfeited for the omission of any thing required, although the report may be perfect so far as respects the rum, then I rather think the libel is not so totally insufficient as to be incapable of sustaining the sentence. It alleges, in substance, that such a report as is required by the act, was not made.

But if the forfeiture of the rum depends on some omission respecting that article, then I presume the attorney for the United States, would not hazard an argument in support of this count in the libel.

On the best consideration I can give to this section of the act of congress, I am of opinion that the rum is not forfeited, unless something respecting that article be omitted in the report. The act requires that a certain report shall be made, and does not forfeit the cargo, if the report be not made in the form prescribed, but the rum which is omitted. If no rum be omitted, the article to be forfeited, does not exist. Let us vary the phraseology and read it thus, "on pain of five hundred dollars, and the article so omitted." All, I presume, will admit, that only so much of the cargo as was omitted, would be forfeited, and that it would be indispensable to the validity of the libel, that it should specify the omitted article. When, instead of saying that the omitted article shall be forfeited, the law says that the omitted rum shall be forfeited, I construe the law as equally requiring, to produce the forfeiture, that rum should be omitted, and consequently that the omission should be charged in the libel.[10]

Printed, John W. Brockenbrough, *Reports of Cases Decided by the Honourable John Marshall . . .* , I (Philadelphia, 1837), 371–79.

1. A deposition taken *de bene esse* was provisional and could be offered as evidence only upon proof that the witness was dead, lived more than one hundred miles from the place of trial, or was otherwise unable to attend the trial. Gordon and York, seamen serving on the *Thomas & Henry* during the voyage to the West Indies, both testified that the schooner, without making any entry or report, unloaded twenty hogsheads of rum under cover of darkness. These witnesses were described in the record as being "transients" (*U.S. Statutes at Large*, I, 88–90; proceedings in U.S. District Court [copy], 10 Nov. 1817, 24–25, 29–30, Schooner Thomas & Henry v. U.S.).

2. Counsel for the claimants objected to the reading of these depositions at the district court trial. When the court overruled the objection, the claimants filed a bill of exceptions (proceedings in U.S. District Court [copy], 10 Nov. 1817, 5–6, 14–15, Schooner Thomas & Henry v. U.S.).

3. Robert B. Taylor appeared as counsel for the claimants at the taking of York's deposition "under an express understanding and declaration that he waved all objections to the proceedings" (proceedings in U.S. District Court [copy], 10 Nov. 1817, 29–30, Schooner Thomas & Henry v. U.S.).

4. The act to regulate the collection of duties, sec. 91, provided for the distribution of fines, forfeitures, and penalties among the revenue officers and informants. Anyone who was entitled to a share could serve as a witness at the trial but in that case would no longer be entitled to a share (*U.S. Statutes at Large*, I, 697).

5. Judge Tucker stated that he did not rely on the depositions of York and Gordon in condemning the vessel and cargo (proceedings in U.S. District Court [copy], 10 Nov. 1817, 11–12, Schooner Thomas & Henry v. U.S.).

6. JM quoted from sec. 71 of the collection act (*U.S. Statutes at Large*, I, 678).

7. JM referred to the testimony of Thomas V. Butler, second mate on the revenue cutter *Jefferson*, which was taken in the district court in Nov. 1817 (proceedings in U.S. District Court [copy], 10 Nov. 1817, 32–33, Schooner Thomas & Henry v. U.S.).

8. These witnesses, residents of Accomack County, testified on behalf of the claimants. Their depositions were taken in Accomack in Apr. and May 1818 and opened in the circuit court on 23 May 1818. Barnes was the inspector of customs for the district of Folly Landing. He, along with his assistants Robert Pitts and William Pitts, was on board the *Thomas & Henry* at the time the schooner was boarded by customs officers from Norfolk (deposition of Robert Pitts, 7 May 1818; deposition of George P. Barnes, 6 Apr. 1818; deposition of William Pitts, 12 May 1818, Schooner Thomas & Henry v. U.S.).

9. The libel charged that the master of the *Thomas & Henry* "did not within forty-eight hours after his arrival and the arrival of the said schooner . . . make any report in writing to the Surveyor or officer acting as inspector of the revenue . . . of the facts or circumstances required by law to be so reported." As prescribed by sec. 30 of the collection law, this report was required of all vessels arriving from a foreign port carrying distilled spirits, wines, or teas. The report was to include such information as the foreign port from which the vessel arrived and the kinds and quantities of spirits, wines, and teas on board. The penalty for failing to comply with these requirements was five hundred dollars and "the loss of the spirits so omitted" (proceedings in U.S. District Court [copy], 10 Nov. 1817, 2, Schooner Thomas & Henry v. U.S.; *U.S. Statutes at Large*, I, 650).

10. In its decree of ca. 1 Dec. 1818, the circuit court reversed that part of the district court's sentence condemning the cargo of rum on the ground that the libel was insufficient for this purpose. The U.S. attorney was allowed to amend the libel, however, and the case was retained for further proceedings. On the basis of the amended libel, filed on 2 Dec. 1818, the circuit court at the May 1819 term affirmed the lower court's sentence (1 Brock. 379; proceedings in U.S. District Court [copy], 10 Nov. 1817 [clerk's notations on wrapper]; amended libel [filed 2 Dec. 1818], Schooner Thomas & Henry v. U.S.).

Ronald's Heirs v. Barkley
Opinion and Decree
U.S. Circuit Court, Virginia, 9 December 1818

This complicated suit began in May 1807 with a bill in chancery on behalf of Elizabeth Ronald and Anne Ronald, children and coheirs of the late William Ronald. The bill sought to enjoin the sale of land in Goochland County and to obtain a conveyance of the land to the plaintiffs. The principal defendant was Ann Barkley, a British subject, who had obtained a judgment for debt against the heirs at the November 1799 term of the U.S. Circuit Court. In execution of this judgment two writs were levied in August 1800 upon tracts of land descending to the heirs, one in Goochland, the other in Powhatan County. These lands were accordingly "extended"—that is, their annual value was assessed by inquisition of a jury—and then turned over to Barkley until her debt was satisfied. Evidently as a result of a compromise between William Bentley, the children's guardian, and John Wickham, Barkley's agent, the extended lands were allowed to remain in the heirs' possession for several years. In 1805 Wickham brought ejectments to obtain possession, which he subsequently dismissed on Bentley's executing a deed of trust in January 1806 conveying a six-hundred-acre tract in Goochland (not part of the extended lands) to secure payment of the balance of Barkley's debt. The heirs claimed that this tract belonged to them in equity and that their guardian had no authority to execute the deed of trust. In the meantime the extended lands had been sold in 1807 in consequence of a decree in another suit in the federal court. The purchasers bought these lands subject to the lien arising from Barkley's debt and were subsequently made parties to this suit. The issue for the court to decide was the respective liabilities of the heirs and of the purchasers for the unpaid portion of Barkley's debt. The filing of amended bills, the taking of answers and depositions, and the preparation of commissioner's reports delayed a final decree in this suit until 9 December 1818 (U.S. Cir. Ct., Va., Rec. Bk. XIII, 582–628).

1st. The Court will first consider the claim of Anne Barkley on the purchasers.[1]

It seems well settled, in modern practice, that the officer who executes an elegit does not put the creditor in actual possession of the land, but gives him only a legal possession, which he must enforce by ejectment.[2]

It seems, also, to be settled, that if the actual possession be withheld by the owner of the land, without the fault of the tenant by elegit, he will have a right to hold over;[3] but if, from the act of the creditor himself, or of a third person, the rents and profits of the extended lands be not received, the creditor cannot hold over, but his estate expires when his debt might have been satisfied.

How do these principles apply to the facts of this case?

From August 1800, when the inquest was taken, to some time in the year 1805, when the ejectment was brought, the creditor appears to have acquiesced entirely in the possession of Ronald's heirs.[4] There is no reason to suspect, that their possession was not with her full assent other than is furnished by the ejectment brought in 1805. It will not be denied, that an ejectment brought within a reasonable time may amount to *prima facie* evidence, that the possession, thus adversarily maintained, was originally adversary; but it cannot be admitted, that the creditor, after this long and quiet acquiescence, can be allowed to say, the[5] she has been held out against her will. In this case, the creditor does not say it. She says, she was not bound to bring her ejectment. If, by this, her counsel intends to say, that she might, for an unlimited time, leave Ronald's heirs in the perception of the profits, and keep her elegit in force, I answer, that I think the law is otherwise. It has been adjudged and settled, that the estate by elegit continues, not until the debt be actually satisfied, but until it might have been satisfied. This principle is entitled to peculiar respect, where third persons are interested. The creditors of Ronald had rights which could not be suspended or impaired by these arrangements.

Nor can it avail Mrs. Barkley, as against the purchasers, that they received the possession from Ronald's heirs, subject, as they held it, to the elegit. They received a right to the possession, whenever the elegit should, in law, expire, from the creditors at whose suit the lands were sold; and their taking immediate possession, could not alter or postpone the right, unless by special contract.

I think it, then, too clear from controversy, that the profits for the time between the inquest and the service of the ejectment, are to be deducted from the debt, so far as respects the purchasers, in like manner as if they had been actually received. The time between the service of the ejectment, and the deed of January 1806, may admit of more doubt.[6]

The non-delivery of possession, when demanded by the tenant by elegit, does not appear to me to be a tort, for which the guardian is alone personally responsible. The possession being the possession of the infants, continued for them by their guardian, I rather incline to the opinion, that it is such a holding by the infants, as prolongs the term of the elegit. I have felt, and do feel, great doubts on this part of the case. But it must be decided, and I think the objections to this, less weighty than those to the contrary opinion.

If the term might have been prolonged, this is the legal effect of the ejectment on the estate by elegit, and by that legal effect the purchasers are bound. I doubted, whether the purchasers could be required to take notice of an ejectment, which was dismissed; but, be this as it may, they are bound by the elegit, according to its legal extent, of which they must take notice.

I come next, to consider the claim of Mrs. Barkley, on the lands on the tract of 600 acres in Goochland, which is contained in the deed of January 1806. This claim is rendered one of peculiar hardship, by the waste and havoc committed by this guardian, on the estate entrusted to his care. To determine, whether any part of the loss, and if any, what part, ought to fall on Mrs. Barkley, requires an attentive consideration of the transactions which have taken place.

When the judgment in question was obtained, and the writ of elegit was issued, the land on which it was served, was in possession of Ronald's heirs. This possession was not changed by the service of the writ. If, as has been already decided in considering the rights of the purchasers, they remained in possession, with the assent of Anne Barkley, they must be considered, unless the contrary appear, as retaining that possession, under an agreement to pay the annual value, at which the land was estimated in the inquest. As infants, they could not themselves make this contract. Could their guardian legally make it for them?

The power of guardians does not seem to be precisely defined. They may certainly do many acts, which bind the estate of their wards; and among others, they may remove encumbrances and make leases, especially if such acts are for the benefit of the infants. This elegit was an encumbrance, which I am not satisfied, the guardian might not contract to remove, in whole, or in part. Nor do I perceive, if he may make a lease of the lands of his ward, why he may not get in a lease, or an encumbrance, in the nature of a lease, of that estate.

It is, I believe, not to be controverted, that these acts may be directed by a court of chancery, and would be directed, on being satisfied, that the proposed contract was for the interest of the infants. And, I think, few will deny, that had an application to that court, been made in this case by the guardian, its sanction would have been given to the acquisition of this estate by elegit, unless some suspicion existed of his unfaithfulness, in the performance of his trust. The infants were in possession of a number of slaves, and of a large landed estate. There are few, who would not think it more advisable, to retain both in their own possession, if practicable, than to let the lands be cultivated by a tenant by elegit, and the slaves, composed as they are, of men, breeding women, and children, to pass into the hands of the highest bidder. No court, in a common case of this description, would refuse its sanction to a contract, by which the infants retained possession of the property.

The great objection, generally, to the exercise of the power of a guardian to purchase, is, that he changes thereby the nature of the estate, by converting personal into real estate. Even this might be sometimes allowed, as would appear from the opinion of the chancellor, in the case of Inwood *v.* Twine, Ambler, 407.[7] But, in this case, there is no change in the nature of the estate. The whole operation is, the taking in an encumbrance, in the nature of a lease for years.

If I was of opinion, that this was a case in which a previous application to a court was necessary, I should be much inclined to say, that a contract, which the court would certainly have directed, ought to be protected, as far as respects a third person. But I do not think an application was necessary. The general power of a guardian, in my opinion, extends to it; and, as an application to a court must be attended with expense, there is no reason why it should be made. Had the guardian honestly applied the profits of the term, this transaction could not have been shaken in any court; and for his misapplication of them, the creditor cannot be responsible.

I am, therefore, of opinion, that the occupation of the extended lands by the infants, must, under the circumstances of this case, be considered as an occupation under an implied contract, which the guardian had a right to make for them, and that the perception of the profits by him, is, in this suit, to be considered as a perception by them.

If this principle be correct, not much difficulty remains in the case.

The land conveyed in trust by Bently for the use of Barkley, was purchased by him in his own name, under a verbal declaration that he bid for the plaintiffs.[8] In consequence of this declaration, he purchased the lands at about half their value, and the infants have the benefit of this purchase. As the commissioners could not have sold to the infants and returned them as the purchasers, Bently was necessarily the legal purchaser, and was so returned, and must have been so returned, to the court of chancery. The right of the infants is an equity growing out of the conduct of Bently, which is extrinsic of the regular proceedings, and forms no part of them. The commissioner of the court, acting in strict conformity with his power, is, I think, so far as this question goes, not to be distinguished from a person holding the legal estate.[9] All the rights of those who were parties to the decree are in him. Bently is, therefore, to be considered as purchasing from the person holding the legal estate. If this be correct, the right of a person holding Bently's title, were he a mere purchaser from or creditor of Bently, would be very much in the situation of Williamson, in the case decided in the court of appeals.[10] But Mrs. Barkley presents herself in a still more favourable point of view. A part of her debt is for money received for the plaintiffs, by a person who had a right to receive it. If it was diverted from its proper course, and wasted, it is in no degree the fault of Barkley. Hard then as it is on the infants, to bear the losses consequent on the misconduct of the guardian, I cannot relieve them from it, by throwing it upon Barkley.

So far as the money of Barkley was received by Bently, for the use of the plaintiffs, her equity appears to me, to be still superior to theirs; and if the conveyance of January 1806, should be construed to make the grantees, trustees for Ronald's heirs, still I think their equity stands charged with the rights of Barkley on them.

The result of this opinion is, that the trust estate is bound to Barkley for the balance remaining unpaid, of the value of the extended lands, from the date of the inquest, until the institution of the ejectment, and from the 28th day of January, 1806, until August 1807, when the extended lands were purchased under a decree of this court. That the purchasers under that decree, ought to pay the annual value of the lands by them severally purchased, as estimated in the inquest, until the debt of Anne Barkley might have been made, adding thereto, the time during which the ejectment, brought by Anne Barkley for those lands, was depending.

If any loss has been sustained, by the rents of the extended lands, since they were rented out by the officer of the court; that loss must be borne by the owners, unless there be particular circumstances, which should place it elsewhere.

The result of the best consideration the Court can give this subject, is, that upon receiving what remains due to Anne Barkley, according to the judgment of the Court, and the inquest of the jury, for the time that the extended lands were held by the plaintiffs, with the acquiescence of the said Barkley, John Wickham, the surviving trustee in the deed of January 1806, ought to convey to the plaintiffs, and that James Pleasants, the surviving commissioner, acting under the decree of that court, ought to be considered as a trustee for Anne Barkley, until so much of her debt as, according to this opinion, the plaintiffs ought to pay, be satisfied, and then to the use of the plaintiffs.

[Decree]

Ronalds heirs

v

Barklay & others

The bill having been taken for confessed against William Bently. This cause came on to be heard on the original bill & amended bills & answers of the other defendents the depositions of witnesses exhibits & report of the Commissioner and was argued by counsel on consideration whereof this court is of opinion that the tract of land containing six hundred acres which was purchased by William Bently in July 1797 at the sale thereof made under a decree of the high court of chancery, & was afterwards conveyed by him to Edward Carrington & John Wickham by deed bearing date the 28th. of January in the year 1806 was purchased in trust for the plaintiffs & ought to be conveyed to them. This court is farther of opinion that the Defendent Anne Barkly has a lien on the said land for so much of her judgement under which the lands of the plfs in Powhatan & Goochland were extended as remains unpaid and is equal to the annual value of the said land while they remained in possession of the plfs with the assent of that defendent, which amounts by an estimate made by the parties to $1143.46; and that the other defendents ought to pay to the said Ann Barkly the annual value of the extended lands respectively purchased by them, from the date of their purchase until the judgement might have been satisfied adding these to the value for the time that the ejectment brought by Ann Barkly against Wm. Bently was depending, and are still liable for so much thereof as remains unpaid, which according to an estimate made by the parties amounts to $47.14 due from the defendents William Fenwick & Edward Johnson and to $883.32 due from Neil McCoul. The court doth therefore decree and order that William Fenwick &   Johnson do pay to the defendent Ann Barkley the sum of $47.14 and that Niel McCoul pay to the said Defendant Ann Barkley the sum of $883.32.

And doth farther order that on the plaintiffs paying to the defendent Ann Barkly the sum of $1143.46 with interest at the rate of 6 per cent. per annum from this 8th. day of December 1818 John Wickham do convey to the plfs. without warranty the tract of land conveyed to Edward Carrington and the said John Wickham by deed bearing date the 28th. of January 1806 in the proceedings mentioned and that the defendent James Pleasant do also convey to the plfs the said tract of land on their producing to him the receipt of Ann Barkly or her attorney showing that the sum of $1143.46 has been paid, and on his receiving evidence that the money has also been paid for which the said land was sold to William Bently. And the court doth farther direct that on the payment of the said sum of $1143.46 the plaintiffs be permitted by the said Ann Barkly to use her name for the purpose of enforcing the judgement obtained by her against the said William Bently liberty being reserved.[11] And the court doth further decree that the plaintiffs and the defendant Ann Barkley pay equally as between them—the plts one half & the said deft the other half & the costs of the reports of comrs. made in this cause and that the defendant William Bentley pay to the plaintiff, the said moiety of the costs of the said reports & all the other costs by them expended in the prosecution of this suit against him and that he pay to the defendant Ann Barkley the other moiety of the costs the said reports, and liberty, is reserved to the defendant Ann Barkley in the event that the plfs should not pay the sum of money to be paid by them under this decree on or before the 1st. of June next to apply to this court for a dismission of the bill or for such order as to the court may seem proper to enforce the payment thereof.

Printed, John W. Brockenbrough, *Reports of Cases Decided by the Honourable John Marshall . . .* , I (Philadelphia, 1837), 359–66. Decree, AD, Ronald's Heirs v. Barkley, U.S. Cir. Ct., Va., Ended Cases (Unrestored), 1818, Vi.

1. The extended lands were sold in Aug. 1807 as a result of a decree in the case of Corbet v. Johnson, to which the heirs of William Ronald had become parties. The purchasers, William Fenwick, Edward Johnson, and John Martin, Jr., were made parties to this suit in 1816 (*PJM*, VI, 383–84, 389 n. 12; amended bill in chancery, 17 Dec. 1816, Ronald's Heirs v. Barkley; U.S. Cir. Ct., Va., Rec. Bk. XIII, 613–15).

2. Strictly speaking, the execution that issued on Barkley's judgment was not the statutory writ of elegit but the common law writ of extent. The latter writ applied to special judgments in debt against an heir or devisee on an obligation in which the ancestor expressly bound his heirs. Such judgments were recoverable by writ of extent on all the lands descended or devised. On an elegit the creditor could choose between the personal estate or one-half the lands to satisfy his judgment. Both writs put the creditor in possession of the land for the time necessary to satisfy the debt out of the annual profits (*PJM*, V, 133 n. 3).

3. A "holdover tenant" retains possession after the expiration of a lease—or, as in the case of a tenant by elegit or extent, after the time when the debt might have been satisfied.

4. The inquisitions were held in Powhatan and Goochland, respectively, on 6 and 8 Aug. 1800. According to a chancery commissioner's report, Wickham stated that he brought ejectments to obtain possession of the extended lands and dismissed them upon the execution of the deed of trust in Jan. 1806 (U.S. Cir. Ct., Va., Rec. Bk. XIII, 623–27).

5. Should be "that."

6. Wickham, as attorney for Barkley, contended that the writs should not begin to run until the sale of the extended lands in Aug. 1807. This would place the liability for Barkley's debt entirely upon the purchasers. The purchasers insisted that their liability should cease at the time the judgment might have been discharged had the writs run from Aug. 1800 (U.S. Cir. Ct., Va., Rec. Bk. XIII, 605–6, 613–15).

7. Inwood v. Twyne, Amb. 417, 27 Eng. Rep. 279 (Ch., 1762). The lord chancellor was Robert Henley, earl of Northington.

8. The land conveyed by the trust deed of 28 Jan. 1806, once owned by William Ronald, was purchased by Bentley in 1797 at a sale decreed by the state High Court of Chancery in a suit brought by Thomas Jefferson against Ronald's representatives. At the sale Bentley announced to the assembled bidders that he wished to purchase the land for the benefit of Ronald's children. The result was that no other bid was made, and Bentley was able to

purchase for the amount of the debt and interest owed Jefferson—amounting to about one-half the value of the land (U.S. Cir. Ct., Va., Rec. Bk. XIII, 609–10, 619–23).

9. James Pleasants, surviving commissioner to sell the land under the High Court of Chancery foreclosure decree, was made a defendant in this case in 1810. He testified that no deed for the land sold Bentley in 1797 had been conveyed. The legal estate accordingly remained in the hands of the surviving commissioner (amended bill in chancery, 6 Apr. 1810, Ronald's Heirs v. Barkley; U.S. Cir. Ct., Va., Rec. Bk. XIII, 609–10).

10. Williamson v. Gordon's Executors, 5 Munf. 257, decided in the Virginia Court of Appeals in Nov. 1816.

11. The rest of the decree is in a different hand.

To William Gaston

My dear Sir   Richmond Decr. 11th. 1818

Your letter of the 5th. reached me only this morning, & I now give with pleasure the information you request.[1] The allusion which you wish explained is to a state of things which was thought probable by the Judges, but which, I now understand, does not exist. It was supposed by the court that Williams might claim the land by some other title than possession, which might possibly, in Tenessee, be consummated by a patent. In such an event, as the court had sustained the equitable title of Burton, it could afford him a remedy against one who with less equity might obtain the legal title.[2]

In this case the court was unanimous on every point but one. I thought the agreement between the two states had never taken effect, because it dependend on the passage of an act of Congress which should give its sanction to the whole, not to a part of the contract; & I could not concur in that astute reasoning which construes the act of Congress into a sanction of the whole.[3] As however, I did & do beleive that the decision is much more beneficial to the claimants under North Carolina than one which would have continued the conflict, I was secretly gratified that my opinion did not prevail, & took no pains to support it. We all understood that there would be no difficulty, if not created by North Carolina, in obtaining an act of Congress which would enable her citizens to derive titles from the State of Tennessee; and we all thought that though she lost the point of honour, she gained substantially the point of interest.[4]

You will of course consider this communication as intended only for yourself.

I rejoice that you are in the legis⟨lature⟩ of your state, since you determined to withdraw fro⟨m⟩ that of the union; & I rejoice too that the time is a⟨r⟩riving when the spirit of party prejudice, though still intolerant, is not so totally blind, nor so fiercely vindictive, as it has been. With much respect & esteem, I am dear Sir your obedt

J MARSHALL

ALS, William Gaston Papers, Southern Historical Collection, NcU. Addressed to Gaston in Raleigh, N.C.; postmarked Richmond, 11 Dec. MS torn where seal was broken.

1. Letter not found. Gaston (1778–1844) was a North Carolina lawyer and politician who later became a distinguished jurist. A Federalist, he had served in both houses of the state legislature before he entered the U.S. House of Representatives in 1813. He left Congress in 1817 and the following year was elected to the North Carolina Senate. After additional terms in the state legislature, Gaston was elected a judge of the North Carolina Supreme Court in 1833. He held this position until his death.

2. The reference is to the case of Burton's Lessee v. Williams, an ejectment action for land lying in Tennessee, which had been decided at the Feb. 1818 term of the Supreme Court. The Court affirmed an 1816 judgment of the U.S. Circuit Court for East Tennessee in favor of Jacob Williams and others, citizens of Tennessee, who claimed under a Tennessee grant. Robert Burton, of North Carolina, claimed under a grant of that state. Gaston sought information on this case in connection with a report he was preparing for the North Carolina Senate (Burton's Lessee v. Williams, App. Cas. No. 826; 3 Wheat. 529; J. Herman Schauinger, *William Gaston, Carolinian* [Milwaukee, Wis., 1949], 106–8).

3. The case hinged on the construction of an 1806 act of Congress authorizing the state of Tennessee to issue grants within the territory ceded by North Carolina and to settle claims to unappropriated lands within that territory. A North Carolina act of 1803 had ceded that state's right to issue grants to the state of Tennessee, with the assent of Congress. Counsel for Burton contended that the 1806 act of Congress contained conditions that in effect rendered the North Carolina law inoperative. Johnson, who gave the opinion for the court, rejected this argument (*U.S. Statutes at Large*, II, 381–83; 3 Wheat. 530–31, 533–40).

4. Although the Supreme Court concluded that North Carolina had "parted with the power to issue this grant, and could not resume it," Johnson added that "it must not be inferred that we think unfavourably of his [Burton's] right to the land." The United States had an obligation "to make provision for issuing a grant in his favour; and in the mean time the courts of the United States are not without resources in their equity jurisdiction to afford him relief" (3 Wheat. 540).

Dartmouth College v. Woodward
Opinion
U.S. Supreme Court, 2 February 1819

EDITORIAL NOTE

The first of the great decisions rendered at the 1819 term of the Supreme Court was *Dartmouth College* v. *Woodward*, which had come up by writ of error to a November 1817 judgment of the New Hampshire Superior Court. Argued at the close of the 1818 term, the appeal was continued when the justices could not agree on an opinion. On the second day of the next term, 2 February, Marshall delivered the Supreme Court's opinion, holding that the charter incorporating Dartmouth College was a contract protected by the Constitution from legislative infringement. The immediate effect of the decision was to prevent the state of New Hampshire from seizing control of a small New England college and turning it into a public institution. The principle of constitutional law announced in *Dartmouth* applied not only to "eleemosynary" (charitable and benevolent) corporations but also to business corporations. By creating a wide scope for unfettered entrepreneurial activity, this principle facilitated development of the business corporation and stimulated the economic growth of the new nation. Yet the case had broader significance than the carving out of an extensive zone of legal immunity for corporations. In essence, *Dartmouth* was a statement about the inviolability of private rights in the exercise of governmental power. This concern, rather than the welfare of corporations as such, was foremost in Marshall's mind at the time he wrote the opinion.[1]

Before taking the form of a judicial dispute, the Dartmouth College controversy was mired in the political and religious factionalism of early nineteenth-century New Hampshire. The college was incorporated by royal charter in 1769, largely through the efforts of the Reverend Eleazar Wheelock, who served as the institution's first president until his death in 1779. The charter established a trust fund that was to be administered by a self-perpetuating board of trustees. During the administration of John Wheelock (who had succeeded his father as president in 1779), petty quarrels between the president and trustees eventually thrust the college into partisan politics, with Federalists and Congregationalists supporting the trustees and Republicans siding with the Presbyterian president. The college issue dominated the 1816 state elections, which gave Republicans control of the legislature and the governorship. In the same year the legislature adopted statutes that radically revised the Dartmouth charter, in effect transforming the college into a state institution. Not only was the number of trustees increased from twelve to twenty-one, with new members appointed by the governor, but the trustees were placed under the control of a board of overseers also appointed by the governor. Henceforth, the institution was to be known as Dartmouth University.

Claiming that this legislation was an unlawful deprivation of property rights, the college trustees sued for recovery of the college records, books, and seal, asking damages of $50,000.[2] Lawyers for the trustees carefully adopted a strategy of contending that the state laws were invalid not only as beyond the scope of legislative power and against the New Hampshire constitution and bill of rights but also as contrary to the contract clause of the United States Constitution. In this way, a loss in the state court (which was anticipated) could be appealed under section 25 of the Judiciary Act to the federal Supreme Court. The case proceeded by a previously agreed upon special verdict that recited the 1769 charter and the 1816 statutes, leaving to the court to decide whether the latter unconstitutionally revoked the former.

In arguments presented to the New Hampshire Superior Court in September 1817, the contract clause played a distinctly subordinate role. The trustees' lawyers relied principally on the ground that the New Hampshire legislature, even without specific constitutional restrictions on its powers, was incompetent to abolish private vested rights of property. The vested rights argument in turn depended on the classification of the Dartmouth College corporation. Was it a public institution and therefore subject to legislative control, or was it a private institution immune from state interference? This distinction was crucial to the outcome of the case, whether the New Hampshire laws were challenged as violating vested rights or whether they were contested as being contrary to specific state and federal constitutional restrictions. The trustees contended that Dartmouth College belonged to the class of eleemosynary corporations that originated in private bounty and whose privileges were granted to perpetuate and secure application of the bounty to its charitable objects. Such corporations were always private, having no concern with the civil government of the state, and possessed rights entitled to the same protection as those of individuals. Opposing counsel maintained that Dartmouth had been founded for the benefit of the province of New Hampshire and that its extensive public purposes properly classified it as a public corporation.

On 6 November 1817 Chief Justice William M. Richardson delivered the court's unanimous opinion, which not unexpectedly came down against the college trustees. While conceding that the property and privileges of private corporations should be accorded the same protection as the private rights of individuals, Richardson ruled that Dartmouth was a public corporation and that no question of private right was involved in the case. The restrictions and prohibitions in the state and federal constitutions, he said, were designed to protect private rights. The contract clause was not intended "to limit the power of the states, in relation to their own publick officers and servants, or to their own civil institutions." Significantly, Richardson's opinion implicitly endorsed the notion that private corporate charters could be considered contracts under the Constitution.[3]

Once the case came to the Supreme Court, the provisions of section 25 restricted the justices to the single issue of whether the New Hampshire acts violated the contract clause. Arguments began on 10 March 1818 and extended over the next three days. Representing the college were Daniel Webster, then engaged in private law practice after serving two terms in Congress, and Joseph Hopkinson, a distinguished lawyer and member of Congress from Pennsylvania. On the other side were Representative John Holmes (1773–1843) of Massachusetts and Attorney General William Wirt. Ignoring the jurisdictional restriction to the contract clause, Webster presented a broadly conceived and elaborately argued attack on the New Hampshire laws similar to that made in the state court. He stated the issue as essentially a taking of private property and giving it to another, a deprivation of vested rights, which the New Hampshire legislature was prohibited from doing either by general limitations on legislative power or by specific restrictions found in the state constitution. In an argument filling nearly fifty printed pages, Webster devoted only a dozen to the contract clause. The other advocates confined their remarks to the constitutional question. Holmes and Wirt reiterated Judge Richardson's holding that Dartmouth was a public institution and that its charter was not a contract protected by the Constitution. Hopkinson agreed that colleges and other eleemosynary institutions were public in a "popular sense" because they benefited the public; but in a "legal and technical sense" they remained private charities whose property and privileges were private.[4]

Arguments concluded on 12 March. The next day Chief Justice Marshall ordered the cause continued to the next term, observing that some of the judges had "not come to an opinion on the case" and that those who had "formed opinions do not agree."[5] Some justices might have been uncertain about bringing the case within the purview of the contract clause. Webster clearly believed that framing the issue as a taking of private property without due process of law put the college's case on more solid ground than relying on the contract clause would. Bringing the New Hampshire acts within reach of the contract clause was a "strong" point, he admitted, but "not perhaps stronger than that derived from the character of these acts, compared with the Constitution of N. Hampshire." Joseph Story, one of the undecided justices, likewise expressed regret "that we were so stinted in jurisdiction in the Supreme Court, that half the argument could not be met and enforced." To avoid the jurisdictional limits imposed on section 25 appeals, Webster proposed commencing new actions in the federal circuit court. An appeal from this court could raise the broader question "whether, by the general principles of our government, the state legislatures be not restrained from divesting vested rights."[6] Accordingly, soon after the 1818 argument, three "cognate" suits were brought in Story's circuit court and then quickly certified to the Supreme Court in time to be argued with the expected rehearing of *Dartmouth College* v. *Woodward* at the 1819 term. The opposing side cooperated with these legal maneuvers in the hope of getting new facts before the Supreme Court.[7]

Chief Justice Marshall confounded these expectations when he announced on 2 February 1819 that the Court had come to a decision in the college case. By a vote of five to one—Duvall alone silently dissenting—the Court upheld the Dartmouth trustees. Along with Marshall, whose opinion was that of the Court, Washington and Story wrote separate concurring opinions; Johnson joined Marshall's opinion, and Livingston concurred with the opinions of Marshall, Washington, and Story. Although the Court was not unanimous, the chief justice did succeed in persuading the justices that the case could be satisfactorily resolved under the contract clause. Adapting the arguments and reasoning of counsel, he set forth his own distinctive reading of that clause, finding in its general language ample protection for vested property rights. Webster, for his part, was pleased with the result: "The Chief Justice's opinion was in his own peculiar way. He reasoned along from step to step; and not referring to the cases, adopted the principle of them, and worked the whole into a close, connected and very able argument." Hopkinson, too, praised the opinion for placing the decision for the college "upon principles broad and deep, and which secure corporations of this description from legislative despotism and party violence for the future."[8]

As Webster noted, the chief justice argued from principle rather than authority. Except for a couple of citations to Blackstone and a brief allusion to the Court's previous contract decisions, the opinion was uncluttered with references to cases and precedents. In a case where lawyers' arguments and the opinions of Washington and Story were replete with citations to the English common law of corporations, the conspicuous omission of such references by Marshall is to be attributed not to ignorance or carelessness but to deliberate decision. Clearly, the chief justice concluded that these English cases were either irrelevant or of dubious precedential value and that his argument would be more effective by not placing it upon such a foundation.

Stating the case exclusively in terms of contract, Marshall assumed without argument that the 1769 charter incorporating Dartmouth College constituted a "contract." This assumption was scarcely controversial in 1819, for it accorded with natural and common law principles that a grant of property was a contract and with the holding in *Fletcher* v. *Peck* that a grant by the state was as much a contract as a grant between private individuals. And because at common law corporations were classified as franchises, that is, as a kind of private property, it reasonably followed that a corporate charter granted by the state was as much a contract as a grant of land.[9] This point, indeed, was not seriously disputed even by opponents of the college. Their principal contention was that the Dartmouth charter was a grant of political power, not of private property rights, and therefore was not a contract meant to be protected by the Constitution.

Marshall agreed with Judge Richardson that the contract clause was never intended "to restrain the states in the regulation of their civil institutions, adopted for internal government." He likewise believed the clause was restricted to contracts that concern private property and that "confer rights which may be asserted in a court of justice."[10] The pivotal issue was the nature of the 1769 charter. If it created a civil institution of government, or if it granted powers or property in trust to be administered for purely public purposes, then the charter was a proper subject for state legislation of the kind enacted by New Hampshire. If, however, the charter created a private, eleemosynary institution, then the question of whether the rights conferred by the charter were of a kind that came within the protection of the contract clause presented itself. Examining the charter, the chief justice had no difficulty in concluding that Dartmouth College in both its origins and funds was "purely private and eleemosynary" and that it retained this character despite the application of those funds to broad public purposes such as education. Moreover, the fact of incorporation was immaterial in determining an institution's character. A charter of incorporation was merely a legal device that enabled a perpetual succession of individuals to act "like one immortal being" for the promotion of some object. But such an act did not transform a private into a public institution, did not confer any political power or character upon this artificial being. "The character of civil institutions does not grow out of their incorporation," Marshall observed, "but out of the manner in which they are formed, and the objects for which they are created."[11] Institutions created for the purposes of government, whether incorporated or not, were subject to legislative control. An incorporating act neither gave nor prevented this control.

The most difficult problem in assimilating this case to the law of contract was identifying whose rights were protected under the 1769 charter. While strongly implying that the trustees personally had a beneficial interest "as the law may respect," the chief justice avoided deciding this point by making the corporation itself the possessor of private rights deserving constitutional protection.[12] The corporation was the "assignee" of the rights of the original founders and donors; it "stands in their place, and distributes their bounty, as they would themselves have distributed it, had they been immortal."[13] The charter, in short, was a continuing contract with a continuing obligation, the same in 1819 as it was in 1769. The chief justice admitted that the protection of corporate rights was probably not contemplated by the framers of the Constitution, but he could find no authority or reason to justify excepting this case from the reach of the contract clause.

Unlike Story and Washington, Marshall did not found his argument on an alleged common law distinction between private and public corporations. He relied on the English law of charitable corporations only to the extent of identifying Dartmouth College as a private, eleemosynary institution. He did not get bogged down in a discussion of such technical doctrines as the visitatorial power, though he was conversant with the cases on this subject.[14] The chief justice largely ignored the English law of corporations because he recognized the problems it posed. The doctrine of visitation, for instance, was not strictly relevant to the circumstances of the Dartmouth case. For another, the cases could be manipulated to support contradictory results, either that legislative immunity should extend to all corporate charters, public and private, or that the state should have superintending power over both public and private corporations. Neither conclusion was consistent with American practice.[15] Marshall's omission of English precedents enabled him to make a stronger case for the college than did Washington and Story with all their splendid learning and array of citations. In selecting his opinion as that of the Court, the other justices signified their agreement with this assessment.

A NOTE ON THE TEXT

The text of Marshall's opinion in *Dartmouth* is from Timothy Farrar's *Report of the Case of the Trustees of Dartmouth College against William H. Woodward* (Portsmouth, N.H., 1819). Farrar (1788–1874), an 1807 graduate of Dartmouth, was Webster's law partner.[16] His work contains the most complete record of the case, including the arguments and opinion in the state court as well as those in the Supreme Court. Both this publication and Henry Wheaton's fourth volume, which reported all the Supreme Court cases decided at the 1819 term, were published at about the same time. Wheaton, however, used the proof sheets of Farrar's book in preparing his own report of *Dartmouth*.[17]

Farrar stated that "in most instances" he took the arguments and opinions "from the original minutes of their authors, and corrected by themselves." In compiling the Supreme Court arguments and opinions, he had close cooperation from Webster and Story. On his return to New England from Washington in March, Webster brought with him the opinions of Marshall, Washington, and Story.[18] That Webster had Marshall's original manuscript is indicated by a comment to Story, written in late March. Concerned that Farrar's report might not be finished in time for Wheaton's use, Webster intended to have "the opinions copied immediately. But, before they are copied, I wish to go over the Chief's [Marshall's] & Judge [Bushrod] W[ashington]'s *with you*, & to see that every word & letter be right." After reviewing Marshall's opinion, Story wrote the chief justice suggesting that a passage be deleted. Marshall readily assented; hence to that extent his published opinion reflects Story's editing.[19]

1. Francis N. Stites, *Private Interest and Public Gain: The Dartmouth College Case, 1819* (Amherst, Mass., 1972); Bruce A. Campbell, "*Dartmouth College* as a Civil Liberties Case: The Formation of Constitutional Policy," *Kentucky Law Journal*, LXX (1981–82), 643–706.

2. The nominal defendant, William H. Woodward, had been secretary-treasurer of the college but was now loyal to the university.

3. Timothy Farrar, *Report of the Case of the Trustees of Dartmouth College against William H. Woodward* (Portsmouth, N.H., 1819), 229; Stites, *Private Interest and Public Gain*, 52–54.

4. 4 Wheat. 551–600 (Webster), 600–6 (Holmes), 606–15 (Wirt), 615–24 (Hopkinson, quotations at 616–17).

5. *Daily National Intelligencer* [Washington, D.C.], 16 Mar. 1818.

6. Webster to Charles Marsh, 8 Dec. 1817, quoted in John M. Shirley, *The Dartmouth*

College Causes and the Supreme Court of the United States (1895; New York, 1971 reprint), 5; Story to Jeremiah Mason, 6 Oct. 1819, in Story, *Life and Letters*, I, 323; Webster to Jeremiah Mason, 28 Apr. 1818, in Fletcher Webster, ed., *The Private Correspondence of Daniel Webster* (2 vols.; Boston, 1857), I, 282–83.

7. Stites, *Private Interest and Public Gain*, 89–95.

8. Webster to Mason, 2 Feb. 1819, quoted in Charles Warren, *The Supreme Court in United States History* (rev. ed.; 2 vols.; Boston, 1926), I, 483; Hopkinson to Francis Brown, in Webster, ed., *Private Correspondence of Webster*, I, 301.

9. Warren B. Hunting, *The Obligation of Contracts Clause of the United States Constitution* (1919; New York, 1977 reprint), 64–93; Stites, *Private Interest and Public Gain*, 78–79.

10. Opinion, 2 Feb. 1819 (225, 226, below). Compare with Richardson's opinion (Farrar, *Report*, 229).

11. Opinion, 2 Feb. 1819 (230, below).

12. Ibid. (238, below).

13. Ibid. (232–33, below).

14. See JM's argument in *Bracken v. College of William and Mary* (3 Call 577–79, 589–97; *PJM*, II, 72–81).

15. Hunting, *Obligation of Contracts Clause*, 72–75; Stites, *Private Interest and Public Gain*, 83–86; Campbell, "*Dartmouth College* as a Civil Liberties Case," 661–66.

16. Charles M. Wiltse and Harold D. Moser, eds., *The Papers of Daniel Webster: Correspondence*, I, (Hanover, N.H., 1974), 52.

17. Wheaton to Story, 25 July, 2, 24 Aug. 1819, Wheaton Papers, NNPM. Farrar took out his copyright on 9 Aug., Wheaton on 26 Aug.

18. Farrar, *Report*, "Advertisement"; Webster to Francis Brown, 25 Feb. 1819; Webster to Timothy Farrar, Jr., 12 Mar. 1819, Wiltse and Moser, eds., *Papers of Webster: Correspondence*, I, 248–49, 250–51.

19. Webster to Story, 25 Mar. 1819, Wiltse and Moser, eds., *Papers of Webster: Correspondence*, I, 254; JM to Story, 28 Apr. 1819.

OPINION

This is an action of trover, brought by the Trustees of Dartmouth College against William H. Woodward, in the state court of New-Hampshire, for the book of records, corporate seal, and other corporate property, to which the plaintiffs allege themselves to be entitled.

A special verdict, after setting out the rights of the parties, finds for the defendant, if certain acts of the legislature of New-Hampshire, passed on the 27th of June, and on the 18th of December, 1816, be valid, and binding on the trustees without their assent, and not repugnant to the constitution of the United States; otherwise, it finds for the plaintiffs.[1]

The superiour court of judicature of New-Hampshire rendered a judgment upon this verdict for the defendant, which judgment has been brought before this court by writ of error. The single question now to be considered is, Do the acts, to which the verdict refers, violate the constitution of the United States?

This court can be insensible neither to the magnitude nor delicacy of this question. The validity of a legislative act is to be examined; and the opinion of the highest law tribunal of a state is to be revised; an opinion, which carries with it intrinsic evidence of the diligence, of the ability, and the integrity, with which it was formed. On more than one occasion, this court has expressed the cautious circumspection, with which it approaches the consideration of such questions; and has declared, that, in no doubtful case, would it pronounce a legislative act to be contrary to the constitution. But the American people have said in the constitution of the United States, that "No state shall pass any bill of attainder, *ex post facto* law, or law impairing the obligation of contracts." In the same instrument they have also said, "that the judicial power shall extend to all cases in law and equity arising under the constitution." On the judges of this court, then, is imposed the high and solemn duty of protecting from even legislative violation those contracts, which the constitution of our country has placed beyond legislative controul; and however irksome the task may be, this is a duty, from which we dare not shrink.

The title of the plaintiffs originates in a charter dated the 13th day of December, in the year 1769, incorporating twelve persons therein mentioned, by the name of "The Trustees of Dartmouth College," granting to them and their successors the usual corporate privileges and powers, and authorizing the trustees, who are to govern the college, to fill up all vacancies, which may be created in their own body.

The defendant claims under three acts of the legislature of New-Hampshire, the most material of which was passed on the 27th of June 1816, and is entitled, "an act to amend the charter, and enlarge, and improve the corporation of Dartmouth College." Among other alterations in the charter, this act increases the number of trustees to twenty-one, gives the appointment of the additional members to the executive of the state, and creates a board of overseers with power to inspect and controul the most important acts of the trustees. This board consists of twenty-five persons. The president of the senate, the speaker of the house of representatives of New-Hampshire, and the governour and lieutenant-governour of Vermont, for the time being, are to be members *ex officio*. The board is to be completed by the governour and council of New-Hampshire, who are also empowered to fill all vacancies, which may occur. The acts of the 18th and 26th of December are supplemental to that of the 27th of June, and are principally intended to carry that act into *effect*.

The majority of the trustees of the college have refused to accept this amended charter, and have brought this suit for the corporate property, which is in possession of a person holding by virtue of the acts, which have been stated.

It can require no argument to prove, that the circumstances of this case constitute a contract. An application is made to the crown for a charter to incorporate a religious and literary institution. In the application it is stated, that large contributions have been made for the object which will be conferred on the corporation, as soon as it shall be created. The charter is granted, and on its faith the property is conveyed. Surely in this transaction every ingredient of a complete and legitimate contract is to be found.

The points for consideration are,

1st. Is this contract protected by the constitution of the United States?

2d. Is it impaired by the acts, under which the defendant holds?

1st. On the first point it has been argued, that the word "contract" in its broadest sense would comprehend the political relations between the government and its citizens, would extend to offices held within a state for state purposes, and to many of those laws concerning civil institutions, which must change with circumstances, and be modified by ordinary legislation, which deeply concern the publick, and which, to preserve good government, the publick judgment must controul. That even marriage is a contract, and its obligations are affected by the laws respecting divorces. That the clause in the constitution, if construed in its greatest latitude, would prohibit these laws. Taken in its broad unlimited sense, the clause would be an unprofitable and vexatious interference with the internal concerns of a state, would unnecessarily and unwisely embarrass its legislation, and render immutable those civil institutions, which are established for purposes of internal government, and which, to subserve those purposes, ought to vary with varying circumstances. That as the framers of the constitution could never have intended to insert in that instrument a provision so unnecessary, so mischievous and so repugnant to its general spirit, the term "*contract*" must be understood in a more limited sense. That it must be understood as intended to guard against a power of at least doubtful utility, the abuse of which had been extensively felt; and to restrain the legislature in future from violating the right to property. That anterior to the formation of the constitution, a course of legislation had prevailed in many, if not in all of the states, which weakened the confidence of man in man, and embarrassed all transactions between individuals, by dispensing with a faithful performance of engagements. To correct this mischief by restraining the power, which produced it, the state legislatures were forbidden "to pass any law impairing the obligation of contracts," that is, of contracts respecting property, under which some individual could claim a right to something beneficial to himself; and that since the clause in the constitution must in construction receive some limitation, it may be confined, and ought to be confined, to cases of this description; to cases within the mischief, it was intended to remedy.

The general correctness of these observations cannot be controverted. That the framers of the constitution did not intend to restrain the states in the regulation of their civil institutions, adopted for internal government, and that the instrument they have given us, is not to be so construed, may be admitted. The provision of the constitution never has been understood to embrace other contracts, than those, which respect property, or some object of value, and confer rights, which may be asserted in a court of justice. It never has been understood to restrict the general right of the legislature to legislate on the subject of divorces. Those acts enable some tribunal, not to impair a marriage contract, but to liberate one of the parties because it has been broken by the other. When any state legislature shall pass an act annulling all marriage contracts, or allowing either party to annul it without the consent of the other, it will be time enough to enquire, whether such an act be constitutional.

The parties in this case differ less on general principles, less on the true construction of the constitution in the abstract, than on the application of those principles to this case, and on the true construction of the charter of 1769. This is the point, on which the cause essentially depends. If the act of incorporation be a grant of political power, if it create a civil institution to be employed in the administration of the government, or if the funds of the college be publick property, or if the state of New-Hampshire, as a government, be alone interested in its transactions, the subject is one, on which the legislature of the state may act according to its own judgment, unrestrained by any limitation of its power imposed by the constitution of the United States.

But if this be a private eleemosynary institution, endowed with a capacity to take property for objects unconnected with government, whose funds are bestowed by individuals on the faith of the charter; if the donors have stipulated for the future disposition and management of those funds in the manner prescribed by themselves; there may be more difficulty in the case, although neither the persons, who have made these stipulations, nor those, for whose benefit they were made, should be parties to the cause. Those, who are no longer interested in the property, may yet retain such an interest in the preservation of their own arrangements, as to have a right to insist, that those arrangements shall be held sacred. Or, if they have themselves disappeared, it becomes a subject of serious and anxious inquiry, whether those, whom they have legally empowered to represent them forever, may not assert all the rights, which they possessed, while in being; whether, if they be without personal representatives, who may feel injured by a violation of the compact, the trustees be not so completely their representatives in the eye of the law, as to stand in their place, not only as respects the government of the college, but also as respects the maintenance of the college charter.

It becomes then the duty of the Court most seriously to examine this charter, and to ascertain its true character.

From the instrument itself, it appears, that about the year 1754, the Rev. Eleazer Wheelock established at his own expense, and on his own estate a charity school for the instruction of Indians in the christian religion. The success of this institution inspired him with the design of soliciting contributions in England for carrying on, and extending, his undertaking. In this pious work he employed the Rev. Nathaniel Whitaker, who, by virtue of a power of attorney from Dr. Wheelock, appointed the Earl of Dartmouth and others, trustees of the money, which had been, and should be, contributed; which appointment Dr. Wheelock confirmed by a deed of trust authorizing the trustees to fix on a site for the college. They determined to establish the school on Connecticut river, in the western part of New-Hampshire; that situation being supposed favourable for carrying on the original design among the Indians, and also for promoting learning among the English, and the proprietors in the neighbourhood having made large offers of land on condition that the college should there be placed. Dr. Wheelock then applied to the crown for an act of incorporation; and represented the expediency of appointing those, whom he had by his last will named, as trustees in America, to be members of the proposed corporation. "In consideration of the premises," "for the education and instruction of the youth of the Indian tribes, &c." "and also of English youth, and any others," the charter was granted, and the trustees of Dartmouth College were by that name created a body corporate, with power, *for the use of the said college*, to acquire real and personal property, and to pay the president, tutors, and other officers of the college such salaries as they shall allow.

The charter proceeds to appoint Eleazer Wheelock, "the founder of said college," president thereof, with power by his last will to appoint a successor, who is to continue in office, until disapproved by the trustees. In case of vacancy, the trustees may appoint a president, and in case of the ceasing of a president, the senior professor or tutor, *being one of the trustees*, shall exercise the office, until an appointment shall be made. The trustees have power to appoint and displace professors, tutors and other officers, and to supply any vacancies, which may be created in their own body by death, resignation, removal or disability; and also to make orders, ordinances, and laws, for the government of the college, the same not being repugnant to the laws of Great Britain, or of New-Hampshire, and not excluding any person on account of his speculative sentiments in religion, or his being of a religious profession different from that of the trustees.

This charter was accepted, and the property both real and personal, which had been contributed for the benefit of the college, was conveyed to, and vested in the corporate body.

From this brief review of the most essential parts of the charter, it is apparent, that the funds of the college consisted entirely of private donations. It is perhaps not very important, who were the donors. The probability is, that the Earl of Dartmouth and the other trustees in England were, in fact, the largest contributors. Yet the legal conclusion from the facts recited in the charter, would probably be, that Dr. Wheelock was the founder of the college.

The origin of the institution was, undoubtedly, the Indian charity school, established by Dr. Wheelock at his own expense. It was at his instance, and to enlarge this school, that contributions were solicited in England. The person soliciting these contributions was his agent; and the trustees, who received the money, were appointed by, and acted under his, authority. It is not too much to say, that the funds were obtained by him, in trust to be applied by him to the purposes of his enlarged school. The charter of incorporation was granted at his instance. The persons named by him in his last will, as the trustees of his charity school, compose a part of the corporation, and he is declared to be the founder of the college, and its president for life. Were the enquiry material, we should feel some hesitation in saying, that Dr. Wheelock was not, in law, to be considered as the founder (1) of this institution, and as possessing all the rights appertaining to that character.[2] But be this as it may, Dartmouth college is really endowed by private individuals, who have bestowed their funds for the propagation of the christian religion among the Indians, and for the promotion of piety and learning generally. From these funds the salaries of the tutors are drawn; and these salaries lessen the expense of education to the students. It is then an eleemosynary, (2) and, as far as respects its funds, a private corporation.[3]

Do its objects stamp on it a different character? Are the trustees and professors publick officers, invested with any portion of political power, partaking in any degree in the administration of civil government, and performing duties, which flow from the sovereign authority?

That education is an object of national concern, and a proper subject of legislation, all admit. That there may be an institution founded by government, and placed entirely under its immediate controul, the officers of which would be publick officers, amenable exclusively to government, none will deny. But is Dartmouth College such an institution? Is education altogether in the hands of government? Does every teacher of youth become a publick officer, and do donations for the purposes of education necessarily become publick property, so far that the will of the legislature, not the will of the donor, becomes the law of the donation? These questions are of serious moment to society, and deserve to be well considered.

Doctor Wheelock, as the keeper of his charity school, instructing the Indians in the art of reading, and in our holy religion; sustaining them at his own expense, and on the voluntary contributions of the charitable, could scarcely be considered, as a publick officer, exercising any

(1) 1 Black. Comm. 481.
(2) 1 Black. Comm. 471.

portion of those duties, which belong to government; nor could the legislature have supposed that his private funds, or those given by others, were subject to legislative management, because they were applied to the purposes of education. When, afterwards, his school was enlarged, and the liberal contributions made in England and in America enabled him to extend his cares to the education of the youth of his own country, no change was wrought in his own character, or in the nature of his duties. Had he employed assistant tutors with the funds contributed by others, or had the trustees in England established a school with Dr. Wheelock at its head, and paid salaries to him and his assistants, they would still have been private tutors; and the fact, that they were employed in the education of youth, could not have converted them into publick officers, concerned in the administration of publick duties, or have given the legislature a right to interfere in the management of the fund. The trustees, in whose care that fund was placed by the contributors, would have been permitted to execute their trust uncontrouled by legislative authority.

Whence, then, can be derived the idea, that Dartmouth College has become a publick institution, and its trustees publick officers, exercising powers conferred by the publick for publick objects? Not from the source, whence its funds were drawn, for its foundation is purely private and eleemosynary. Not from the application of those funds, for money may be given for education, and the persons receiving it do not by being employed in the education of youth, become members of the civil government. Is it from the act of incorporation? Let this subject be considered.

A corporation is an artificial being, invisible, intangible, and existing only in contemplation of law. Being the mere creature of law, it possesses only those properties, which the charter of its creation confers upon it, either expressly, or as incidental to its very existence. These are such as are supposed best calculated to effect the object, for which it was created. Among the most important are immortality, and, if the expression may be allowed, individuality; properties, by which a perpetual succession of many persons are considered as the same, and may act as a single individual. They enable a corporation to manage its own affairs, and to hold property without the perplexing intricacies, the hazardous and endless necessity of perpetual conveyances for the purpose of transmitting it from hand to hand. It is chiefly for the purpose of clothing bodies of men, in succession, with these qualities and capacities, that corporations were invented, and are in use. By these means, a perpetual succession of individuals are capable of acting for the promotion of the particular object, like one immortal being. But this being does not share in the civil government of the country, unless that be for the purpose, for which it was created. Its immortality no more confers on it political power, or a political character than immortality would confer such power or character on a natural person. It is no more a state instrument, than a natural person exercising the same powers would be. If then a natural person employed by individuals in the education of youth, or for the government of a seminary, in which youth is educated, would not become a publick officer, or be considered as a member of the civil government, how is it, that this artificial being, created by law, for the purpose of being employed by the same individuals for the same purposes, should become a part of the civil government of the country? Is it because its existence, its capacities, its powers are given by law? Because the government has given it the power to take and to hold property in a particular form, and for particular purposes, has the government a consequent right substantially to change that form, or to vary the purposes, to which the property is to be applied? This principle has never been asserted, or recognized, and is supported by no authority. Can it derive aid from reason?

The objects for which a corporation is created, are universally such, as the government wishes to promote. They are deemed beneficial to the country; and this benefit constitutes the consideration, and in most cases, the sole consideration of the grant. In most eleemosynary institutions, the object would be difficult, perhaps unattainable, without the aid of a charter of incorporation. Charitable, or publick spirited individuals, desirous of making permanent appropriations for charitable or other useful purposes, find it impossible to effect their design securely, and certainly, without an incorporating act. They apply to the government, state their beneficent object and offer to advance the money necessary for its accomplishment, provided the government will confer on the instrument, which is to execute their designs, the capacity to execute them. The proposition is considered and approved. The benefit to the publick is considered as an ample compensation for the faculty it confers, and the corporation is created. If the advantages to the publick constitute a full compensation for the faculty it gives, there can be no reason for exacting a further compensation by claiming a right to exercise over this artificial being, a power which changes its nature, and touches the fund, for the security and application of which it was created. There can be no reason for implying in a charter, given for a valuable consideration, a power, which is not only not expressed, but is in direct contradiction to its express stipulations.

From the fact then, that a charter of incorporation has been granted, nothing can be inferred, which changes the character of the institution or transfers to the government any new power over it. The character of civil institutions does not grow out of their incorporation, but out of the manner in which they are formed, and the objects for which they are created. The right to change them, is not founded on their being incorporated, but on their being the instruments of government, created for its purposes. The same institutions, created for the same objects, though not incorporated, would be publick institutions and, of course, be controulable by the legislature. The incorporating act, neither gives, nor prevents, this controul. Neither, in reason can the incorporating act change the character of a private eleemosynary institution.

We are next led to the enquiry, for whose benefit the property given to Dartmouth College was secured? The counsel for the defendant have insisted, that the beneficial interest is in the people of New-Hampshire. The charter, after reciting the preliminary measures, which had been taken, and the application for an act of incorporation, proceeds thus. "Know ye therefore, that we, considering the premises, and being willing to encourage the laudable and charitable design of spreading christian knowledge, among the savages of our American wilderness, and also that the best means of education be established, in our province of New-Hampshire, for the benefit of said province, do of our special grace, &c." Do these expressions bestow on New-Hampshire any exclusive right to the property of the college, any exclusive interest in the labours of the professors? Or do they merely indicate a willingness, that New-Hampshire should enjoy those advantages, which result to all from the establishment of a seminary of learning in the neighbourhood? On this point we think it impossible to entertain a serious doubt. The words themselves, unexplained by the context, indicate, that the "benefit intended for the province" is that, which is derived from "establishing the best means of education therein;" that is, from establishing in the province Dartmouth College, as constituted by the charter. But, if these words considered alone, could admit of doubt, that doubt is completely removed by an inspection of the entire instrument.

The particular interests of New-Hampshire never entered into the mind of the donors, never constituted a motive for their donation. The propagation of the christian religion among the savages, and the dissemination of useful knowledge among the youth of the country, were the avowed and the sole objects of their contributions. In these New-Hampshire would participate; but nothing particular or exclusive, was intended for her. Even the site of the college was selected, not for the sake of New-Hampshire, but because it was "most subservient to the great ends in view," and because liberal donations of land were offered by the proprietors, on condition, that the institution should be there established. The real advantages from the location of the college, are, perhaps, not less considerable to those on the west, than to those on the east side of Connecticut river. The clause which constitutes the incorporation, and expresses the objects, for which it was made, declares those objects to be the instruction of the Indians, "and also of English youth, and any others." So that the objects of the contributors, and the incorporating act were the same; the promotion of christianity, and of education generally, not the interests of New-Hampshire particularly.

From this review of the charter, it appears that Dartmouth College is

an eleemosynary institution, incorporated for the purpose of perpetuating the application of the bounty of the donors to the specified objects of that bounty; that its trustees or governours, were originally
named by the founder, and invested with the power of perpetuating
themselves; that they are not publick officers, nor is it a civil institution, participating in the administration of government; but a charity
school, or a seminary of education, incorporated for the preservation
of its property and the perpetual application of that property to the
objects of its creation.

Yet a question remains to be considered, of more real difficulty on
which more doubt has been entertained, than on all that have been
discussed. The founders of the college, at least those, whose contributions were in money, have parted with the property bestowed upon it,
and their representatives have no interest in that property. The donors
of land are equally without interest, so long as the corporation shall
exist. Could they be found, they are unaffected by any alteration in its
constitution, and probably regardless of its form, or even of its existence. The students are fluctuating and no individual among our youth
has a vested interest in the institution, which can be asserted in a court
of justice. Neither the founders of the college, nor the youth, for whose
benefit it was founded, complain of the alteration made in its charter, or
think themselves injured by it. The trustees alone complain, and the
trustees have no beneficial interest to be protected. Can this be such a
contract, as the constitution intended to withdraw from the power of
state legislation? Contracts, the parties to which have a vested beneficial
interest, and those only, it has been said, are the objects about which the
constitution is solicitous, and to which its protection is extended.

The court has bestowed on this argument the most deliberate consideration, and the result will be stated. Dr. Wheelock acting for himself, and for those, who at his solicitation, had made contributions to
his school, applied for this charter, as the instrument which should
enable him, and them to perpetuate their beneficent intention. It was
granted. An artificial, immortal being, was created by the crown, capable of receiving and distributing forever, according to the will of the
donors, the donations, which should be made to it. On this being, the
contributions, which had been collected, were immediately bestowed.
These gifts were made not indeed to make a profit for the donors or
their posterity, but for something in their opinion of inestimable value;
for something which they deemed a full equivalent for the money, with
which it was purchased. The consideration for which they stipulated, is
the perpetual application of the fund to its object, in the mode prescribed by themselves. Their descendants may take no interest in the
preservation of this consideration. But in this respect their descendants
are not their representatives. They are represented by the corporation.
The corporation is the assignee of their rights, stands in their place and

distributes their bounty, as they would themselves have distributed it, had they been immortal. So with respect to the students, who are to derive learning from this source. The corporation is a trustee for them also. Their potential rights, which taken distributively, are imperceptible, amount collectively to a most important interest. These are in the aggregate, to be exercised, asserted and protected, by the corporation. They were as completely out of the donors, at the instant of their being vested in the corporation, and as incapable of being asserted by the students as at present.

According to the theory of the British constitution, their parliament is omnipotent. To annul corporate rights might give a shock to publick opinion, which that government has chosen to avoid; but its power is not questioned. Had parliament immediately after the emanation of this charter, and the execution of those conveyances, which followed it, annulled the instrument, so that the living donors would have witnessed the disappointment of their hopes, the perfidy of the transaction would have been universally acknowledged. Yet then as now, the donors would have had no interest in the property; then, as now, those, who might be students, would have had no rights to be violated; then as now, it might be said, that the trustees, in whom the rights of all were combined, possessed no private, individual, beneficial interest in the property confided to their protection. Yet the contract would at that time, have been deemed sacred by all. What has since occurred to strip it of its inviolability? Circumstances have not changed it. In reason, in justice, and in law, it is now what it was in 1769.

This is plainly a contract to which the donors, the trustees and the crown (to whose rights and obligations New-Hampshire succeeds) were the original parties. It is a contract made on a valuable consideration. It is a contract for the security and disposition of property. It is a contract, on the faith of which, real and personal estate has been conveyed to the corporation. It is then a contract within the letter of the constitution; and within its spirit also, unless the fact, that the property is invested by the donors in trustees for the promotion of religion and education, for the benefit of persons, who are perpetually changing, though the objects remain the same, shall create a particular exception, taking this case out of the prohibition contained in the constitution.

It is more than possible, that the preservation of rights of this description was not particularly in the view of the framers of the constitution, when the clause under consideration was introduced into that instrument. It is probable, that interferences of more frequent recurrence, to which the temptation was stronger, and of which the mischief was more extensive, constituted the great motive for imposing this restriction on the state legislatures. But although a particular, and a rare case may not, in itself, be of sufficient magnitude to induce a rule, yet it must be governed by the rule, when established, unless some plain and strong reason for excluding it can be given. It is not enough to say, that this particular case was not in the mind of the convention, when the article was framed, nor of the American people, when it was adopted. It is necessary to go farther, and to say that, had this particular case been suggested, the language would have been so varied, as to exclude it, or it would have been made a special exception. The case being within the words of the rule, must be within its operation likewise, unless there be something in the literal construction so obviously absurd, or mischievous, or repugnant to the general spirit of the instrument, as to justify those, who expound the constitution in making it an exception.

On what safe and intelligible ground can this exception stand. There is no expression in the constitution, no sentiment delivered by its contemporaneous expounders, which would justify us in making it. In the absence of all authority of this kind, is there in the nature and reason of the case itself that, which would sustain a construction of the constitution, not warranted by its words? Are contracts of this description of a character to excite so little interest, that we must exclude them from the provisions of the constitution, as being unworthy of the attention of those, who framed the instrument? Or does publick policy so imperiously demand their remaining exposed to legislative alteration, as to compel us, or rather permit us to say, that these words, which were introduced to give stability to contracts, and which in their plain import comprehend this, must yet be so construed, as to exclude it?

Almost all eleemosynary corporations, those which are created for the promotion of religion, of charity or of education, are of the same character. The law of this case is the law of all. In every literary or charitable institution, unless the objects of the bounty be themselves incorporated, the whole legal interest is in trustees, and can be asserted only by them. The donors, or claimants of the bounty, if they can appear in court at all, can appear only to complain of the trustees. In all other situations, they are identified with, and personated by the trustees; and their rights, are to be defended and maintained by them. Religion, charity, and education, are in the law of England legatees, or donees, capable of receiving bequests, or donations in this form. They appear in court, and claim or defend by the corporation. Are they of so little estimation in the United States, that contracts for their benefit must be excluded from the protection of words, which in their natural import include them? Or do such contracts so necessarily require new modelling by the authority of the legislature, that the ordinary rules of construction must be disregarded in order to leave them exposed to legislative alteration?

All feel, that these objects are not deemed unimportant in the United States. The interest, which this case has excited proves, that they are not. The framers of the constitution did not deem them unworthy of its care and protection. They have, though in a different mode, manifested their respect for science, by reserving to the government of the Union the power, "to promote the progress of science and useful arts, by securing for limited times to authors and inventors, the exclusive right to their respective writings and discoveries." They have so far withdrawn science, and the useful arts, from the action of the state governments. Why then should they be supposed so regardless of contracts made for the advancement of literature, as to intend to exclude them from provisions, made for the security of ordinary contracts between man and man? No reason for making this supposition is perceived.

If the insignificance of the object does not require, that we should exclude contracts respecting it from the protection of the constitution; neither, as we conceive, is the policy of leaving them subject to legislative alteration so apparent, as to require a forced construction of that instrument in order to effect it. These eleemosynary institutions do not fill the place, which would otherwise be occupied by government, but that which would otherwise remain vacant. They are complete acquisitions to literature. They are donations to education; donations, which any government must be disposed rather to encourage than to discountenance. It requires no very critical examination of the human mind to enable us to determine, that one great inducement to these gifts is the conviction felt by the giver, that the disposition he makes of them is immutable. It is probable, that no man ever was, and that no man ever will be, the founder of a college, believing at the time, that an act of incorporation constitutes no security for the institution; believing, that it is immediately to be deemed a publick institution, whose funds are to be governed, and applied, not by the will of the donor, but by the will of the legislature. All such gifts are made in the pleasing, perhaps, delusive, hope, that the charity will flow forever in the channel, which the givers have marked out for it. If every man finds in his own bosom strong evidence of the universality of this sentiment, there can be but little reason to imagine, that the framers of our constitution were strangers to it, and that, feeling the necessity and policy of giving permanence and security to contracts, of withdrawing them from the influence of legislative bodies, whose fluctuating policy, and repeated interferences produced the most perplexing and injurious embarrassments, they still deemed it necessary to leave these contracts subject to those interferences. The motives for such an exception must be very powerful to justify the construction, which makes it.

The motives suggested at the bar grow out of the original appointment of the trustees, which is supposed to have been in a spirit hostile to the genius of our government, and the presumption, that if allowed to continue themselves, they now are, and must remain forever, what they originally were. Hence is inferred the necessity of applying to this corporation, and to other similar corporations, the correcting, and improving hand of the legislature.

It has been urged repeatedly, and certainly with a degree of earnestness, which attracted attention, that the trustees deriving their power from a regal source, must, necessarily partake of the spirit of their origin; and that their first principles, unimproved by that resplendent light, which has been shed around them, must continue to govern the college, and to guide the students. Before we enquire into the influence which this argument ought to have on the constitutional question, it may not be amiss to examine the fact, on which it rests. The first trustees were undoubtedly named in the charter by the crown; but at whose suggestion were they named? By whom were they selected? The charter informs us. Dr. Wheelock had represented, "that for many weighty reasons it would be expedient, that the gentlemen whom he had already nominated in his last will to be trustees in America, should be of the corporation now proposed." When afterwards, the trustees are named in the charter, can it be doubted, that the persons mentioned by Dr. Wheelock in his will were appointed? Some were probably added by the crown with the approbation of Dr. Wheelock. Among these is the Dr. himself. If any others were appointed at the instance of the crown, they are the governour, three members of the council, and the speaker of the house of representatives of the colony of New-Hampshire. The stations filled by these persons ought to rescue them from any other imputation, than too great a dependence on the crown. If in the revolution, that followed, they acted under the influence of this sentiment, they must have ceased to be trustees; if they took part with their countrymen, the imputation, which suspicion might excite, would no longer attach to them. The original trustees then, or most of them, were named by Dr. Wheelock, and those, who were added to his nomination, most probably with his approbation, were among the most eminent, and respectable individuals in New-Hampshire.

The only evidence, which we possess of the character of Dr. Wheelock, is furnished by this charter. The judicious means employed for the accomplishment of his object, and the success, which attended his endeavours, would lead to the opinion, that he united a sound understanding to that humanity and benevolence, which suggested his undertaking. It surely cannot be assumed, that his trustees were selected without judgment. With as little probability can it be assumed, that while the light of science and of liberal principles pervades the whole community, these originally benighted trustees remain in utter darkness, incapable of participating in the general improvement; that while the human race is rapidly advancing, they are stationary. Reasoning *a priori*, we should believe, that learned, and intelligent men selected by its patrons for the government of a literary institution, would select learned and intelligent men for their successors; men as well fitted for the government of a college, as those, who might be chosen by other means. Should this reasoning ever prove erroneous in a particular case, publick opinion, as has been stated at the bar, would correct the institution. The mere possibility of the contrary would not justify a construction of the constitution, which should exclude these contracts from the protection of a provision, whose terms comprehend them.

The opinion of the court after mature deliberation, is, that this is a contract, the obligation of which cannot be impaired without violating the constitution of the United States. This opinion appears to us to be equally supported by reason, and by the former decisions of this court.

2d. We next proceed to the enquiry—whether its obligation has been impaired by those acts of the legislature of New-Hampshire, to which the special verdict refers.

From the review of this charter, which has been taken, it appears, that the whole power of governing the college, of appointing and removing tutors, of fixing their salaries, of directing the course of study to be pursued by the students, and of filling up vacancies created in their own body, was vested in the trustees. On the part of the crown it was expressly stipulated, that this corporation, thus constituted should continue forever; and that the number of trustees should forever consist of twelve, and no more. By this contract the crown was bound, and could have made no violent alteration in its essential terms, without impairing its obligation.

By the revolution the duties, as well as the powers, of government devolved on the people of New-Hampshire. It is admitted, that among the latter, was comprehended the transcendent power of parliament, as well as that of the executive department. It is too clear to require the support of argument, that all contracts and rights respecting property remained unchanged by the revolution. The obligations then, which were created by the charter to Dartmouth College, were the same in the new, that they had been in the old government. The power of the government was also the same. A repeal of this charter at any time prior to the adoption of the present constitution of the United States, would have been an extraordinary and unprecedented act of power, but one, which could have been contested only by the restrictions upon the legislature, to be found in the constitution of the state. But the constitution of the United States has imposed this additional limitation, that the legislature of a state, shall pass no act "impairing the obligation of contracts."

It has been already stated, that the act "to amend the charter, and enlarge and improve the corporation of Dartmouth College," increases the number of trustees to twenty-one, gives the appointment of the additional numbers to the executive of the state, and creates a board of overseers, to consist of twenty-five persons, of whom twenty-one are also appointed by the executive of New-Hampshire, who have power to inspect and controul the most important acts of the trustees.

On the effect of this law, two opinions cannot be entertained. Between acting directly, and acting through the agency of trustees and overseers, no essential difference is perceived. The whole power of governing the college is transferred from trustees appointed according to the will of the founder, expressed in the charter, to the executive of New-Hampshire. The management and application of the funds of this eleemosynary institution, which are placed by the donors, in the hands of trustees named in the charter, and empowered to perpetuate themselves, are placed by this act under the controul of the government of the state. The will of the state is substituted for the will of the donors, in every essential operation of the college. This is not an immaterial change. The founders of the college contracted not merely for the perpetual application of the funds which they gave to the objects, for which those funds were given; they contracted also to secure that application by the constitution of the corporation. They contracted for a system, which should, as far as human foresight can provide, retain forever the government of the literary institution, they had formed, in the hands of persons approved by themselves. This system is totally changed. The charter of 1769 exists no longer. It is reorganized; and reorganized in such a manner, as to convert a literary institution, moulded according to the will of its founders, and placed under the controul of private literary men, into a machine entirely subservient to the will of government. This may be for the advantage of this college in particular, and may be for the advantage of literature in general; but it is not according to the will of the donors, and is subversive of that contract on the faith of which their property was given.

In the view which has been taken of this interesting case, the court has confined itself to the rights possessed by the trustees, as the assignees and representatives of the donors and founders, for the benefit of religion and literature. Yet it is not clear, that the trustees ought to be considered as destitute of such beneficial interest in themselves, as the law may respect. In addition to their being the legal owners of the property and to their having a freehold right in the powers confided to them, the charter itself countenances the idea, that trustees may also be tutors with salaries. The first president was one of the original trustees; and the charter provides that in case of vacancy, in that office "the senior professor or tutor, *being one of the trustees*, shall exercise the office of president, until the trustees shall make choice of, and appoint a president." According to the tenor of the charter, then, the trustees might without impropriety appoint a president and other professors from their own body. This is a power not entirely unconnected with an interest. If the proposition of the counsel for the defendant were sustained, if it were admitted, that those contracts only are protected by the constitution, a beneficial interest in which is vested in the party, who appears in court to assert that interest; yet it is by no means clear, that the trustees of Dartmouth College, have no beneficial interest in themselves.

But the court has deemed it unnecessary to investigate this particular point, being of opinion on general principles that in these private eleemosynary institutions, the body corporate, as possessing the whole legal and equitable interest, and completely representing the donors, for the purpose of executing the trust, has rights which are protected by the constitution.

It results from this opinion, that the acts of the legislature of New-Hampshire, which are stated in the special verdict found in this cause, are repugnant to the constitution of the United States; and that the judgment on this special verdict ought to have been for the plaintiffs. The judgment of the state court must therefore be reversed.

Printed, Timothy Farrar, *Report of the Case of the Trustees of Dartmouth College against William H. Woodward* (Portsmouth, N.H., 1819), 306–30; Henry Wheaton, *Reports of Cases Argued and Adjudged in the Supreme Court of the United States . . .* , IV (New York, 1819), 624–54.

1. For the voluminous special verdict, which embodied the texts of the 1769 charter and the 1816 New Hampshire acts, see 4 Wheat. 519–51.

2. In the cited passage, Blackstone noted that the English law pertaining to eleemosynary corporations distinguished "two species of foundation; the one *fundation incipiens*, or the incorporation, in which sense the king is the general founder of all colleges and hospitals; the other *fundation perficiens*, or the dotation of it, in which sense the first gift of the revenues is the foundation, and he who gives them is in law the founder: and it is in this last sense that we generally call a man the founder of a college or hospital" (Blackstone, *Commentaries*, I, 480–81).

3. Blackstone discussed two classes of lay corporations, civil and eleemosynary: "The eleemosynary sort are such as are constituted for the perpetual distribution of the free alms, or bounty, of the founder of them to such persons as he has directed. Of this kind are all hospitals for the maintenance of the poor, sick, and impotent; and all colleges, both *in* our universities and *out* of them" (ibid., 470–71).

Sturgis v. Crowninshield
Opinion and Certificate
U.S. Supreme Court, 17 February 1819

EDITORIAL NOTE

Two weeks after the *Dartmouth* decision, Marshall again expounded the contract clause in *Sturgis* v. *Crowninshield*.[1] This case brought into question the power of the states to enact bankruptcy legislation, an issue the Supreme Court had not yet addressed and one that had become a matter of great urgency. Coinciding with a financial and business panic and the onset of a severe economic depression, the case attracted great public interest, for the extent to which the states could respond to the crisis hinged on the Court's decision. Although Congress was empowered by the Constitution to establish "uniform Laws on the subject of Bankruptcies," there was no federal bankruptcy statute in force at the time.[2]

In *Sturgis* and in earlier cases heard in federal circuit courts, state bankruptcy laws were challenged as repugnant both to the contract clause and to the clause authorizing Congress to legislate on this subject. The circuit cases revealed sharply opposing opinions among Supreme Court justices concerning the applicability of these clauses to state legislation. Judge Washington in 1814 applied the contract clause to void a Pennsylvania statute that operated retrospectively upon an existing contract. At the same time he declared that a prospective law, enacted before the parties entered into the contract, "would be clearly constitutional," a position that ultimately became the law of the land in 1827. Washington also set forth his "unhesitating opinion" that the Constitution vested Congress with exclusive power to pass bankruptcy laws, effectively withdrawing this subject from the state governments.[3] Judge Livingston in 1817 emphatically rejected the exclusive power doctrine in upholding a New York statute subsequently overturned in *Sturgis*. Livingston also denied that bankruptcy or insolvency laws that discharged a debtor from future liability, whether retrospective or prospective, were intended to be embraced by the contract clause. Such laws, he contended, must be presumed constitutional from the long practice of enacting them in New York and in other states without any complaints that they violated the obligation of contracts. In a South Carolina case, Judge Johnson expressed an opinion that the states shared concurrent power with Congress over bankruptcy legislation.[4]

An underlying difficulty presented by these cases was the proper definition of a "bankrupt" law as distinct from an "insolvent" law. In America these terms were employed almost interchangeably in referring to debtor-relief legislation, resulting in much confusion. The distinguishing feature of an insolvent law was said to be the liberation of the debtor from imprisonment on assignment of his assets to creditors, leaving future assets still liable for his debts. Laws of this kind had routinely been adopted in the American states since the colonial period. The defining characteristic of a bankrupt law, on the other hand, was said to be the release not only of the person of the debtor but also of his liability for his debts, enabling him to get a fresh start free from the crushing burden of past obligations. Such laws were not unknown in the colonial period, and since the adoption of the Constitution several states had passed laws discharging debts.[5] Although lawyers could point out other differences between bankruptcy and insolvency legislation, "the line of partition between them," Marshall astutely observed in *Sturgis*, "is not so distinctly marked as to enable any person to say, with positive precision, what belongs exclusively to the one, and not to the other class of laws."[6] The New York and Pennsylvania laws discharging debtors from future liability were entitled acts "for the relief of insolvent debtors."

In an 1814 letter to Judge Washington, Marshall doubted that the bankruptcy clause conferred exclusive power on Congress, foreshadowing the opinion he adopted in *Sturgis* five years later. Hence there is no reason to suppose the chief justice sacrificed a private conviction that Congress's bankruptcy power was exclusive in order to achieve unanimity in *Sturgis*.[7] As for the contract clause, Marshall leaned to the opinion that "on a fair & necessary construction" its words would apply to bankruptcy laws, though such laws were probably not among the obnoxious and mischievous legislative acts the framers had specifically in mind in restricting state power. Here was the genesis of the important distinction he formulated in *Sturgis* between those clauses prohibiting particular laws—paper-money legislation, for example—and the contract clause, which was aimed not at specific acts but intended "to establish a great principle, that contracts should be inviolable."[8] As of 1814 Marshall doubted that a general prospective bankruptcy law could "fairly be termed a law impairing the obligation of contracts" and was inclined to accept the validity of such a law. Yet he acknowledged "very great doubts whether I shall retain that opinion."[9] The chief justice did not consider this question judicially until 1827, when in dissent he contended that the contract clause prohibited both prospective and retrospective bankruptcy laws—a conclusion that he most likely had reached by 1819.[10]

The contract giving rise to the 1819 case consisted of two promissory notes given by Richard Crowninshield to Josiah Sturgis in New York City in March 1811. A member of a prominent political and merchant family of Salem, Massachusetts, Crowninshield then resided in New York, having earlier moved his shipping business to that city. By November 1811 he had become insolvent and submitted a petition under a New York statute, enacted in April 1811, enabling debtors to be discharged from their debts on assigning their property for the benefit of creditors. Crowninshield obtained his discharge in February 1812 over Sturgis's protest and subsequently returned to Massachusetts, where he established a prosperous textile business. In 1816 Sturgis sued to recover his debt in the United States Circuit Court at Boston. After hearing arguments in October 1817, Judge Story and District Court Judge John Davis divided in order to certify the case to the Supreme Court.[11]

The Supreme Court heard the appeal on 8 and 9 February 1819, David Daggett and Joseph Hopkinson arguing for the plaintiff and William Hunter and David B. Ogden for the defendant. Daggett devoted most of his presentation to demonstrating that Congress had exclusive power over bankruptcy and that the New York act for the relief of insolvent debtors was indeed a bankruptcy law.[12] Hopkinson concentrated on the contract clause in an argument similar to that adopted by the chief justice. Contending that prospective as well as retrospective laws discharging debts were unconstitutional, he read the contract clause as signifying the framers' intention "to incorporate into the constitution a provident principle which should apply to every possible case that might arise." As Marshall was to do, Hopkinson posited a sharp distinction between bankruptcy laws and laws that regulate the remedy for recovering debts such as statutes of limitation—the latter being clearly constitutional because they left intact the obligation of contract.[13]

Hunter, for the defendant, dwelled at length on the distinction between bankruptcy and insolvency, contending that Congress's power was narrowly confined to the former and that the states were left fully in possession of their ancient power over insolvency. The New York statute was an insolvent law and therefore constitutional; moreover, though it discharged debts as well as the person, the law did not impair the obligation of contract. Ogden, taking a different line of argument, maintained that whether the New York law was a bankruptcy or insolvent law did not matter, for the states had concurrent power to pass the former. If the Constitution left the states free to enact bankruptcy laws, then the contract clause could not have been intended to prohibit them.[14]

Marshall crafted an opinion incorporating arguments employed by both sides. He agreed with Ogden that the states possessed concurrent power with Congress over the subject of bankruptcies, a construction whose soundness he largely attributed to convenience. The concurrent power construction, he pointed out, obviated the vexing difficulty of discriminating between bankruptcy and insolvency laws, making it unnecessary to determine whether the New York statute belonged to the former class. The only question to decide, then, was whether the state law impaired the obligation of contract. On this point Marshall found Hopkinson's reasoning persuasive. For all his reliance on counsel, however, the chief justice wove their arguments into a broad statement that was characteristically his own, notably in expounding the meaning of the contract clause and in formulating a rule for interpreting the Constitution.

As in *Dartmouth*, Marshall had to meet the objection that the contract clause did not cover the particular case—corporate charters in the one and bankruptcy and insolvency laws in the other. If such cases seemed to come within the plain meaning of the words, yet it was insisted that the framers never contemplated such cases and therefore to include them within the prohibition would violate the spirit of the Constitution. Marshall agreed that "the spirit of an instrument, especially of a constitution, is to be respected not less than its letter, yet the spirit is to be collected chiefly from its words. It would be dangerous in the extreme to infer from extrinsic circumstances, that a case for which the words of an instrument expressly provide, shall be exempted from its operation."[15] The particular intentions of particular framers, in short, should not be confused with the intention of the instrument itself. The intention of the Constitution was embodied in its words, which had to be interpreted literally, unless such a construction produced a manifestly absurd or unjust result. For Marshall the general language of the contract clause clearly evinced an intention to establish an enduring principle of the sanctity of contracts, one that would apply to all cases within its words, not merely those foreseen at the time.

Although Marshall wrote for a purportedly unanimous Court, the justices remained divided over the reach of the contract clause with respect to bankruptcy legislation. As Johnson later remarked, the *Sturgis* judgment partook "as much of a compromise, as of a legal adjudication."[16] He characterized the compromise as one in which the minority acquiesced in the voiding of the New York law only so long as the decision was understood to embrace laws applying to prior contracts. Yet the opinion itself left some doubt as to the scope of the Court's holding. Nowhere did Marshall expressly confine his reading of the contract clause to retrospective bankruptcy laws. Indeed, public reaction to the decision appeared to assume that all state bankruptcy laws were prohibited by that clause. True, Marshall in a cryptic penultimate paragraph did say the opinion was "confined to the case actually under consideration." Presumably, these words restricted the authority of *Sturgis* to retrospective legislation, since in that case the New York law had been enacted after the contract. Yet in the very passage that restricted the opinion "to the case actually under consideration," Marshall's recital of the particular circumstances of the case did not include the circumstance that the act was passed subsequent to the contract.

Compounding the perplexity was the Court's judgment in *McMillan* v. *McNeill*, another bankruptcy case, announced the day after *Sturgis*. In a brief opinion for the Court, Marshall said the "case was not distinguishable in principle from . . . Sturges v. Crowninshield. That the circumstance of the State law, under which the debt was attempted to be discharged, having been passed before the debt was contracted, made no difference in the application of the principle."[17] Although this language seemed to bring prospective as well as retrospective bankruptcy laws within the meaning of the contract clause, the facts of *McMillan* v. *McNeill* precluded using it as authority to extend the contract clause's reach to prospective laws. In this case the defendant pleaded a discharge under a Louisiana law to a contract executed in South Carolina. As Justice Washington later explained, a bankruptcy law of one state could not operate extraterritorially to affect contracts executed in another, whether the law preceded or followed the date of the contract. Suggesting that the reporter might have misunderstood Marshall's *McMillan* pronouncement, Washington said he understood that decision "to go no farther than to intimate that there was no distinction between the cases as to the constitutional objection, since it professed to discharge a debt contracted in another state, which, at the time it was contracted, was not within its operation, nor subject to be discharged by it."[18] Both 1819 bankruptcy cases, then, left open the question whether a state law discharging a debtor from a subsequent contract made within the same state was constitutional. When this question did come before the Supreme Court in the 1827 case of *Ogden* v. *Saunders*, a majority upheld the state law. Chief Justice Marshall was not among this majority, and for the first and only time in his career, he was compelled to register a dissent in a major constitutional case.[19]

1. In the minutes, docket, and appellate case file, the appellant's name is correctly spelled "Sturgis." In entering the official judgment, however, the clerk wrote "Sturgess." Both the *Daily National Intelligencer* and Henry Wheaton rendered the name as "Sturges" (U.S. Sup. Ct. Minutes, 8, 9 Feb. 1819; U.S. Sup. Ct. Dockets, App. Cas. No. 896; Sturgis v. Crowninshield, App. Cas. No. 896; *Daily National Intelligencer* [Washington, D.C.], 18 Feb., 16 Mar. 1819).

2. Such a law existed from 1800 to 1803; Marshall served on the committee that prepared the bill. Another federal bankruptcy statute was not enacted until 1841 (*PJM,* IV, 52; Charles Warren, *Bankruptcy in United States History* [Cambridge, Mass., 1935], 19–79).

3. Golden v. Prince, U.S. Cir. Ct., Pa. (1814), 10 Fed. Cas. 542, 544, 545; JM to Washington, 19 Apr. 1814 and nn.

4. Adams v. Storey, U.S. Cir. Ct., N.Y. (1817), 1 Fed. Cas. 141; Hannay v. Jacobs, U.S. Cir. Ct., S.C. (cited by counsel in Sturgis v. Crowninshield, 4 Wheat. 135).

5. Peter J. Coleman, *Debtors and Creditors in America: Insolvency, Imprisonment for Debt, and Bankruptcy, 1607–1900* (Madison, Wis., 1974), 6–15, 31–36.

6. Opinion, 17 Feb. 1819 (245, below).

7. JM to Washington, 19 Apr. 1814; G. Edward White, *The Marshall Court and Cultural Change, 1815–35,* the Oliver Wendell Holmes Devise History of the Supreme Court of the United States, III–IV (New York, 1988), 635–36.

8. JM to Washington, 19 Apr. 1814; Opinion, 17 Feb. 1819 (252, below).

9. JM to Washington, 19 Apr. 1814.

10. Ogden v. Saunders, 12 Wheat. 332.

11. Gerald T. Dunne, *Justice Joseph Story and the Rise of the Supreme Court* (New York, 1970), 158; Coleman, *Debtors and Creditors*, 32–33; Sturgis v. Crowninshield, App. Cas. No. 896.

12. 4 Wheat. 123–35.

13. 4 Wheat. 180–91 (quotation at 191).

14. 4 Wheat. 135–80.

15. Opinion, 17 Feb. 1819 (249–50, below).

16. Ogden v. Saunders, 12 Wheat. 272–73.

17. 4 Wheat. 212–13.

18. 12 Wheat. 255.

19. 12 Wheat. 332.

OPINION

This case is adjourned from the Court of the United States, for the first circuit and the district of Massachusetts, on several points on which the judges of that Court were divided, which are stated in the record for the opinion of this Court.[1] The first is,

Whether, since the adoption of the constitution of the United States, any State has authority to pass a bankrupt law, or whether the power is exclusively vested in the Congress of the United States?

This question depends on the following clause, in the 8th section of the 1st article of the constitution of the United States.

"The Congress shall have power," &c. to "establish a uniform rule of naturalization, and uniform laws on the subject of bankruptcies throughout the United States."

The counsel for the plaintiff contend, that the grant of this power to Congress, without limitation, takes it entirely from the several States.

In support of this proposition they argue, that every power given to Congress is necessarily supreme; and, if, from its nature, or from the words of grant, it is apparently intended to be exclusive, it is as much so as if the States were expressly forbidden to exercise it.

These propositions have been enforced and illustrated by many arguments, drawn from different parts of the constitution. That the power is both unlimited and supreme, is not questioned. That it is exclusive, is denied by the counsel for the defendant.

In considering this question, it must be recollected that, previous to the formation of the new constitution, we were divided into independent States, united for some purposes, but, in most respects, sovereign. These States could exercise almost every legislative power, and, among others, that of passing bankrupt laws. When the American people created a national legislature, with certain enumerated powers, it was neither necessary nor proper to define the powers retained by the States. These powers proceed, not from the people of America, but from the people of the several States; and remain, after the adoption of the constitution, what they were before, except so far as they may be abridged by that instrument. In some instances, as in making treaties, we find an express prohibition; and this shows the sense of the Convention to have been, that the mere grant of a power to Congress, did not imply a prohibition on the States to exercise the same power. But it has never been supposed, that this concurrent power of legislation extended to every possible case in which its exercise by the States has not been expressly prohibited. The confusion resulting from such a practice would be endless. The principle laid down by the counsel for the plaintiff, in this respect, is undoubtedly correct. Whenever the terms in which a power is granted to Congress, or the nature of the power, require that it should be exercised exclusively by Congress, the subject is as completely taken from the State Legislatures, as if they had been expressly forbidden to act on it.

Is the power to establish uniform laws on the subject of bankruptcies, throughout the United States, of this description?

The peculiar terms of the grant certainly deserve notice. Congress is not authorized merely to pass laws, the operation of which shall be uniform, but to *establish* uniform laws on the subject throughout the United States. This *establishment* of *uniformity* is, perhaps, incompatible with State legislation, on that part of the subject to which the acts of Congress may extend. But the subject is divisible in its nature into bankrupt and insolvent laws; though the line of partition between them is not so distinctly marked as to enable any person to say, with positive precision, what belongs exclusively to the one, and not to the other class of laws. It is said, for example, that laws which merely liberate the person are insolvent laws, and those which discharge the contract, are bankrupt laws. But if an act of Congress should discharge the person of the bankrupt, and leave his future acquisitions liable to his creditors, we should feel much hesitation in saying that this was an insolvent, not a bankrupt act; and, therefore, unconstitutional. Another distinction has been stated, and has been uniformly observed. Insolvent laws operate at the instance of an imprisoned debtor; bankrupt laws at the instance of a creditor. But should an act of Congress authorize a commission of bankruptcy to issue on the application of a debtor, a Court would scarcely be warranted in saying, that the law was unconstitutional, and the commission a nullity.

When laws of each description may be passed by the same Legislature, it is unnecessary to draw a precise line between them. The difficulty can arise only in our complex system, where the Legislature of the Union possesses the power of enacting bankrupt laws; and those of the States, the power of enacting insolvent laws. If it be determined that they are not laws of the same character, but are as distinct as bankrupt laws and laws which regulate the course of descents, a distinct line of separation must be drawn, and the power of each government marked with precision. But all perceive that this line must be in a great degree arbitrary. Although the two systems have existed apart from each other, there is such a connection between them as to render it difficult to say how far they may be blended together. The bankrupt law is said to grow out of the exigencies of commerce, and to be applicable solely to traders; but it is not easy to say who must be excluded from, or may be included within, this description. It is, like every other part of the subject, one on which the Legislature may exercise an extensive discretion.

This difficulty of discriminating with any accuracy between insolvent and bankrupt laws, would lead to the opinion, that a bankrupt law may contain those regulations which are generally found in insolvent laws; and that an insolvent law may contain those which are common to a bankrupt law. If this be correct, it is obvious that much inconvenience would result from that construction of the constitution, which should deny to the State Legislatures the power of acting on this subject, in consequence of the grant to Congress. It may be thought more convenient, that much of it should be regulated by State legislation, and Congress may purposely omit to provide for many cases to which their power extends. It does not appear to be a violent construction of the constitution, and is certainly a convenient one, to consider the power of the States as existing over such cases as the laws of the Union may not reach. But be this as it may, the power granted to Congress may be exercised or declined, as the wisdom of that body shall decide. If, in the opinion of Congress, uniform laws concerning bankruptcies ought not to be established, it does not follow that partial laws may not exist, or that State legislation on the subject must cease. It is not the mere existence of the power, but its exercise, which is incompatible with the exercise of the same power by the States. It is not the right to establish these uniform laws, but their actual establishment, which is inconsistent with the partial acts of the States.

It has been said, that Congress has exercised this power; and, by doing so, has extinguished the power of the States, which cannot be revived by repealing the law of Congress.

We do not think so. If the right of the States to pass a bankrupt law is not taken away by the mere grant of that power to Congress, it cannot be extinguished; it can only be suspended, by the enactment of a general bankrupt law. The repeal of that law cannot, it is true, confer the power on the States; but it removes a disability to its exercise, which was created by the act of Congress.

Without entering farther into the delicate inquiry respecting the precise limitations which the several grants of power to Congress, contained in the constitution, may impose on the State Legislatures, than is necessary for the decision of the question before the Court, it is sufficient to say, that until the power to pass uniform laws on the subject of bankruptcies be exercised by Congress, the States are not forbidden to pass a bankrupt law, provided it contain no principle which violates the 10th section of the first article of the constitution of the United States.

This opinion renders it totally unnecessary to consider the question whether the law of New-York is, or is not, a bankrupt law.[2]

We proceed to the great question on which the cause must depend. Does the law of New-York, which is pleaded in this case, impair the obligation of contracts, within the meaning of the constitution of the United States?

This act liberates the person of the debtor, and discharges him from all liability for any debt previously contracted, on his surrendering his property in the manner it prescribes.

In discussing the question whether a State is prohibited from passing such a law as this, our first inquiry is into the meaning of words in common use, What is the obligation of a contract? and what will impair it?

It would seem difficult to substitute words which are more intelligible, or less liable to misconstruction, than those which are to be explained. A contract is an agreement in which a party undertakes to do, or not to do, a particular thing. The law binds him to perform his undertaking, and this is, of course, the obligation of his contract. In the case at bar, the defendant has given his promissory note to pay the plaintiff a sum of money on or before a certain day. The contract binds him to pay that sum on that day; and this is its obligation. Any law which releases a part of this obligation, must, in the literal sense of the word, impair it. Much more must a law impair it which makes it totally invalid, and entirely discharges it.

The words of the constitution, then, are express, and incapable of being misunderstood. They admit of no variety of construction, and are acknowledged to apply to that species of contract, an engagement between man and man for the payment of money, which has been entered into by these parties. Yet the opinion that this law is not within the prohibition of the constitution has been entertained by those who are entitled to great respect, and has been supported by arguments which deserve to be seriously considered.

It has been contended, that as a contract can only bind a man to pay to the full extent of his property, it is an implied condition that he may be discharged on surrendering the whole of it.[3]

But it is not true that the parties have in view only the property in possession when the contract is formed, or that its obligation does not extend to future acquisitions. Industry, talents, and integrity, constitute a fund which is as confidently trusted as property itself. Future acquisitions are, therefore, liable for contracts; and to release them from this liability impairs their obligation.

It has been argued, that the States are not prohibited from passing bankrupt laws, and that the essential principle of such laws is to discharge the bankrupt from all past obligations; that the States have been in the constant practice of passing insolvent laws, such as that of New-York, and if the framers of the constitution had intended to deprive them of this power, insolvent laws would have been mentioned in the prohibition; that the prevailing evil of the times, which produced this clause in the constitution, was the practice of emitting paper money, of making property which was useless to the creditor a discharge of his debt, and of changing the time of payment by authorizing distant instalments. Laws of this description, not insolvent laws, constituted, it is said, the mischief to be remedied; and laws of this description, not insolvent laws, are within the true spirit of the prohibition.

The constitution does not grant to the States the power of passing bankrupt laws, or any other power; but finds them in possession of it, and may either prohibit its future exercise entirely, or restrain it so far as national policy may require. It has so far restrained it as to prohibit the passage of any law impairing the obligation of contracts. Although, then, the States may, until that power shall be exercised by Congress, pass laws concerning bankrupts; yet they cannot constitutionally introduce into such laws a clause which discharges the obligations the bankrupt has entered into. It is not admitted that, without this principle, an act cannot be a bankrupt law; and if it were, that admission would not change the constitution, nor exempt such acts from its prohibitions.

The argument drawn from the omission in the constitution to prohibit the States from passing insolvent laws, admits of several satisfactory answers. It was not necessary, nor would it have been safe, had it even been the intention of the framers of the constitution to prohibit the passage of all insolvent laws, to enumerate particular subjects to which the principle they intended to establish should apply. The principle was the inviolability of contracts. This principle was to be protected in whatsoever form it might be assailed. To what purpose enumerate the particular modes of violation which should be forbidden, when it was intended to forbid all? Had an enumeration of all the laws which might violate contracts been attempted, the provision must have been less complete, and involved in more perplexity than it now is. The plain and simple declaration, that no State shall pass any law impairing the obligation of contracts, includes insolvent laws and all other laws, so far as they infringe the principle the Convention intended to hold sacred, and no farther.

But a still more satisfactory answer to this argument is, that the Convention did not intend to prohibit the passage of all insolvent laws. To punish honest insolvency by imprisonment for life, and to make this a constitutional principle, would be an excess of inhumanity which will not readily be imputed to the illustrious patriots who framed our constitution, nor to the people who adopted it. The distinction between the obligation of a contract, and the remedy given by the legislature to enforce that obligation, has been taken at the bar, and exists in the nature of things. Without impairing the obligation of the contract, the remedy may certainly be modified as the wisdom of the nation shall direct. Confinement of the debtor may be a punishment for not performing his contract, or may be allowed as a means of inducing him to perform it. But the State may refuse to inflict this punishment, or may withhold this means, and leave the contract in full force. Imprisonment is no part of the contract, and simply to release the prisoner does not impair its obligation. No argument can be fairly drawn from the 61st section of the act for establishing a uniform system of bankruptcy, which militates against this reasoning. That section declares, that the act shall not be construed to repeal or annul the laws of any State *then in force* for the relief of insolvent debtors, except so far as may respect persons and cases clearly within its purview; and in such cases it affords its sanction to the relief given by the insolvent laws of the State, if the creditor of the prisoner shall not, within three months, proceed against him as a bankrupt.[4]

The insertion of this section indicates an opinion in Congress, that insolvent laws might be considered as a branch of the bankrupt system, to be repealed or annulled by an act for establishing that system, although not within its purview. It was for that reason only that a provision against this construction could be necessary. The last member of the section adopts the provisions of the State laws so far as they apply to cases within the purview of the act.

This section certainly attempts no construction of the constitution, nor does it suppose any provision in the insolvent laws impairing the obligation of contracts. It leaves them to operate, so far as constitutionally they may, unaffected by the act of Congress, except where that act may apply to individual cases.

The argument which has been pressed most earnestly at the bar, is, that although all legislative acts which discharge the obligation of a contract without performance, are within the very words of the constitution, yet an insolvent act, containing this principle, is not within its spirit, because such acts have been passed by Colonial and State Legislatures from the first settlement of the country, and because we know from the history of the times, that the mind of the Convention was directed to other laws which were fraudulent in their character, which enabled the debtor to escape from his obligation, and yet hold his property, not to this, which is beneficial in its operation.

Before discussing this argument, it may not be improper to premise that, although the spirit of an instrument, especially of a constitution, is to be respected not less than its letter, yet the spirit is to be collected chiefly from its words. It would be dangerous in the extreme to infer from extrinsic circumstances, that a case for which the words of an instrument expressly provide, shall be exempted from its operation. Where words conflict with each other, where the different clauses of an instrument bear upon each other, and would be inconsistent unless the natural and common import of words be varied, construction becomes necessary, and a departure from the obvious meaning of words is justifiable. But if, in any case, the plain meaning of a provision, not contradicted by any other provision in the same instrument, is to be disregarded, because we believe the framers of that instrument could not intend what they say, it must be one in which the absurdity and injustice of applying the provision to the case, would be so monstrous, that all mankind would, without hesitation, unite in rejecting the application.

This is certainly not such a case. It is said the Colonial and State Legislatures have been in the habit of passing laws of this description for more than a century; that they have never been the subject of complaint, and, consequently, could not be within the view of the general Convention.

The fact is too broadly stated. The insolvent laws of many, indeed, of by far the greater number of the States, do not contain this principle. They discharge the person of the debtor, but leave his obligation to pay in full force. To this the constitution is not opposed.

But, were it even true that this principle had been introduced generally into those laws, it would not justify our varying the construction of the section. Every State in the Union, both while a colony and after becoming independent, had been in the practice of issuing paper money; yet this practice is in terms prohibited. If the long exercise of the power to emit bills of credit did not restrain the Convention from prohibiting its future exercise, neither can it be said that the long exercise of the power to impair the obligation of contracts, should prevent a similar prohibition. It is not admitted that the prohibition is more express in the one case than in the other. It does not indeed extend to insolvent laws by name, because it is not a law by name, but a principle which is to be forbidden; and this principle is described in as appropriate terms as our language affords.

Neither, as we conceive, will any admissible rule of construction justify us in limiting the prohibition under consideration, to the particular laws which have been described at the bar, and which furnished such cause for general alarm. What were those laws?

We are told they were such as grew out of the general distress following the war in which our independence was established. To relieve this distress, paper money was issued, worthless lands, and other property of no use to the creditor, were made a tender in payment of debts; and the time of payment, stipulated in the contract, was extended by law. These were the peculiar evils of the day. So much mischief was done, and so much more was apprehended, that general distrust prevailed, and all confidence between man and man was destroyed. To laws of this description therefore, it is said, the prohibition to pass laws impairing the obligation of contracts ought to be confined.

Let this argument be tried by the words of the section under consideration.

Was this general prohibition intended to prevent paper money? We are not allowed to say so, because it is expressly provided, that no State shall "emit bills of credit"; neither could these words be intended to restrain the States from enabling debtors to discharge their debts by the tender of property of no real value to the creditor, because for that subject also particular provision is made. Nothing but gold and silver coin can be made a tender in payment of debts.

It remains to inquire, whether the prohibition under consideration could be intended for the single case of a law directing that judgements should be carried into execution by instalments?

This question will scarcely admit of discussion. If this was the only remaining mischief against which the constitution intended to provide, it would undoubtedly have been, like paper money and tender laws, expressly forbidden. At any rate, terms more directly applicable to the subject, more appropriately expressing the intention of the Convention, would have been used. It seems scarcely possible to suppose that the framers of the constitution, if intending to prohibit only laws authorizing the payment of debts by instalment, would have expressed that intention by saying "no State shall pass any law impairing the obligation of contracts." No men would so express such an intention. No men would use terms embracing a whole class of laws, for the purpose of designating a single individual of that class. No court can be justified in restricting such comprehensive words to a particular mischief to which no allusion is made.

The fair, and, we think, the necessary construction of the sentence, requires, that we should give these words their full and obvious meaning. A general dissatisfaction with that lax system of legislation which followed the war of our revolution undoubtedly directed the mind of the Convention to this subject. It is probable that laws such as those which have been stated in argument, produced the loudest complaints, were most immediately felt. The attention of the Convention, therefore, was particularly directed to paper money, and to acts which enabled the debtor to discharge his debt, otherwise than was stipulated in the contract. Had nothing more been intended, nothing more would have been expressed. But, in the opinion of the Convention, much more remained to be done. The same mischief might be effected by other means. To restore public confidence completely, it was necessary not only to prohibit the use of particular means by which it might be effected, but to prohibit the use of any means by which the same mischief might be produced. The Convention appears to have intended to establish a great principle, that contracts should be inviolable. The constitution, therefore, declares, that no State shall pass "any law impairing the obligation of contracts."

If, as we think, it must be admitted that this intention might actuate the Convention; that it is not only consistent with, but is apparently manifested by, all that part of the section which respects this subject; that the words used are well adapted to the expression of it; that violence would be done to their plain meaning by understanding them in a more limited sense; those rules of construction, which have been consecrated by the wisdom of ages, compel us to say, that these words prohibit the passage of any law discharging a contract without performance.

By way of analogy, the statutes of limitations, and against usury, have been referred to in argument; and it has been supposed that the construction of the constitution, which this opinion maintains, would apply to them also, and must therefore be too extensive to be correct.

We do not think so. Statutes of limitations relate to the remedies which are furnished in the courts. They rather establish, that certain circumstances shall amount to evidence that a contract has been performed, than dispense with its performance. If, in a State where six years may be pleaded in bar to an action of assumpsit, a law should pass declaring that contracts already in existence, not barred by the statute, should be construed to be within it, there could be little doubt of its unconstitutionality.

So with respect to the laws against usury. If the law be, that no person shall take more than six per centum per annum for the use of money, and that, if more be reserved, the contract shall be void, a contract made thereafter, reserving seven per cent., would have no obligation in its commencement; but if a law should declare that contracts already entered into, and reserving the legal interest, should be usurious and void, either in the whole or in part, it would impair the obligation of the contract, and would be clearly unconstitutional.

This opinion is confined to the case actually under consideration. It is confined to a case in which a creditor sues in a Court, the proceedings of which the legislature, whose act is pleaded, had not a right to control, and to a case where the creditor had not proceeded to execution against the body of his debtor, within the State whose law attempts to absolve a confined insolvent debtor from his obligation. When such a case arises, it will be considered.[5]

It is the opinion of the Court, that the act of the State of New-York, which is pleaded by the defendant in this cause, so far as it attempts to discharge this defendant from the debt in the declaration mentioned, is contrary to the constitution of the United States, and that the plea is no bar to the action.

[Certificate]

Sturgis

v

Crowninshield

This cause came on to be heard on the transcript of the record of the court of the United States for the first circuit & the District of Massachussetts & on the questions on which the Judges of that court were divided in opinion and was argued by counsel, on consideration whereof this court is of opinion that since the adoption of the constitution of the United States, a state has authority to pass a bankrupt law, provided such law does not impair the obligation of contracts within the meaning of the constitution, & provided there be no act of Congress in force to establish an uniform system of bankruptcy, conflicting with such law.

This court is farther of opinion that the act of New York which is pleaded in this case, so far as it attempts to discharge the contract on which this suit was instituted is a law impairing the obligation of contracts within the meaning of the constitution of the United States, & that the plea of the defendent is not a good & sufficient bar of the plaintiffs action.

All which is directed to be certified to the said circuit Court.

Printed, Henry Wheaton, *Reports of Cases Argued and Adjudged in the Supreme Court of the United States* . . . , IV (New York, 1819), 191–208. Certificate, AD, Sturgis v. Crowninshield, App. Cas. No. 896, RG 267, DNA.

1. The circuit court certified four questions to be decided: (1) whether the bankruptcy power was concurrent, or exclusively vested in Congress; (2) whether the New York act was a bankruptcy law; (3) whether the New York act impaired the obligation of contract; (4) whether the plea of this act was a sufficient bar to the plaintiff's action. For the certificate of division, see Sturgis v. Crowninshield, App. Cas. No. 896 (also summarized in 4 Wheat. 123).

2. This was the second question on the certificate of division.

3. "Insolvent laws," said Hunter, "are based upon the confessed and physical inability of a party to perform a pecuniary contract, otherwise than by a surrender of all he has. How idle, then, to make a provision in respect to such laws, guarding against the impairing a contract; that is, providing for its strict, adequate, and undiminished performance, when the impossibility of any performance is pre-supposed. The total, physical inability of the individual is his exemption, and this is tacitly and necessarily reserved and implied in every contract" (4 Wheat. 152).

4. JM referred to the federal bankruptcy law, in force from 1800 to 1803. Both Hunter and Ogden cited this provision to support the validity of state insolvent laws that discharged the debtor's liability (*U.S. Statutes at Large*, II, 19, 36; 4 Wheat. 144–45, 176).

5. Between Sturgis and Ogden v. Saunders in 1827, the Supreme Court heard one other bankruptcy case, Farmers and Mechanics' Bank of Pennsylvania v. Smith, decided in 1821. This case came by writ of error to an 1817 decision of the Pennsylvania Supreme Court upholding the same state insolvency statute that Judge Washington had declared unconstitutional in Golden v. Prince. In this case, as in Golden v. Prince and in Sturgis v. Crowninshield, the act operated on a previously existing contract. The Supreme Court reversed the state court, JM declaring in a brief opinion that this case "was not distin-

guishable" from Sturgis or McMillan, except that the parties were citizens of the same state: "But . . . these facts made no difference in the cases. The constitution of the United States was made for the whole people of the Union, and is equally binding upon all the Courts and all the citizens" (3 S & R 63; 6 Wheat. 131, 134).

To Gulian C. Verplanck

Sir   Washington Feby. 27th. 1819
    I received a few days past your anniversary discourse delivered before the New York Historical Society in December last, & hav[e] deferred making my acknowledgements for this polite & gratifying mark of attention until I should be able to read it through.[1] I have at length stolen time enough from my other avocations for its perusal, & beg leave to assure you that it has afforded me real pleasure. It is a specimen of chaste style & lucid arrangement which authorizes the expectation of something farther from the author, & the public will certainly not be content should this expectation be disappointed. With great respect, I am Sir your obedt

                                                        J MARSHALL

ALS, PP. Addressed to Verplanck.

1. *An Anniversary Discourse, Delivered before the New-York Historical Society, December 7, 1818* (New York, 1818; S #46648). A New York politician and man of letters, Verplanck (1786–1870) was the author of numerous works on literature, art, architecture, theology, and law. He also wrote biographical sketches, poems, and political satire. A Federalist in his younger years, he was later associated with both the Democratic and Whig parties. He served in Congress from 1824 to 1833, where he was a leading opponent of high tariffs. The *Anniversary Discourse*, an early expression of cultural nationalism, was a celebration of American national character. For a bibliography and sketch, see John W. Rathbun and Monica M. Grecu, eds., *American Literary Critics and Scholars, 1800–1850* (Detroit, Mich., 1987), 317–23.

McCulloch v. Maryland
Opinion
U.S. Supreme Court, 6 March 1819

EDITORIAL NOTE

The most controversial decision handed down by the Supreme Court at the 1819 term upheld the power of Congress to incorporate the Second Bank of the United States. At the same time the Court denied the right of a state to tax the bank. *McCulloch* v. *Maryland*, "the great bank case," was an arranged case brought to challenge a Maryland act laying a stamp tax on all banks "not chartered" by the state legislature. The Second Bank, chartered by act of Congress in 1816, had opened for business in 1817, establishing branches at various locations throughout the country. When James McCulloch, cashier of the Baltimore branch, circulated bank notes that had not been issued on special stamped paper as prescribed by the state law, the state sued him in the local county court. Judgment against McCulloch was subsequently affirmed by the Maryland Court of Appeals in June 1818. The cashier then obtained a writ of error in time to have his case entered on the Supreme Court docket for the February 1819 term.[1]

Both the timing of *McCulloch* and the issues it raised guaranteed widespread public attention to the Supreme Court's hearing of this case. The immediate question was the validity of the state tax, which in turn called into question the legitimacy of the national bank. Yet the constitutionality of a federally chartered national bank was not, in 1819, a matter of great moment. For an institution that had been around for most of the preceding thirty years, this was scarcely an "open question," as Marshall observed at the outset of his opinion. Congress had first chartered the Bank of the United States in 1791, when the constitutionality of the measure was fully aired in both the legislature and the cabinet. The question arose again in 1811 when Congress, then under Republican control, refused to renew the bank's charter. Within five years, however, financial disarray resulting from the War of 1812 produced a change of mind among many Republicans, enough of whom put aside their constitutional scruples to secure passage of the bill creating the Second Bank of the United States. The bill was signed by President James Madison, who as a congressman in 1791 had been a leading opponent of the bank.

McCulloch's case thus called upon the Supreme Court to determine the validity of a measure whose constitutionality had been debated and affirmed by the other departments of government. In these circumstances a holding that Congress had no authority to charter a bank would have been extraordinary. Why, then, did the decision provoke such prolonged and vehement public controversy in the months following its announcement? The impassioned denunciations of *McCulloch* can be attributed in part to the unpopularity of the Second Bank, particularly in the southern and western sections of the country. Having initially encouraged expansion by extending liberal credit, the bank in the summer of 1818 abruptly shifted to a policy of contraction that proved ruinous to many state banks. At the same time investigation into the practices of several branch banks revealed mismanagement and corrupt speculation. In the ensuing financial panic and economic depression, the bank became the focus of blame and resentment as the cause of this misery. The tax levied by Maryland was but one example of hostile legislation enacted against the bank in various states in 1818 and 1819.[2]

Any decision in favor of the bank at this juncture was bound to engender criticism of the Supreme Court. Yet the intensity of the reaction to *McCulloch* is better explained in terms of issues that transcended the Second Bank of the United States. The case's abiding importance lay in its being the occasion of an inquiry concerning the extent of federal power, the limits on state sovereignty, the nature of the federal Union, and the principles of constitutional interpretation. These topics formed the core of a recurrent national debate that had been going on since the inception of the Constitution—a debate between Federalists and Antifederalists in 1787 and 1788, Federalists and Republicans in the 1790s, and between national and states' rights Republicans in the early nineteenth century. Before 1819 this constitutional dialogue had taken place mainly within the executive cabinet or in the halls of Congress. Most recently it had arisen during deliberations over a proposed federal program of internal improvements and, ominously, over a proposal to prohibit the introduction of slavery into the territories. The implications of *McCulloch* for these controversial measures were not lost on contemporaries. With the bank case, the Supreme Court was for the first time drawn directly into the debate, provoking such harsh public censure that Chief Justice Marshall took the extraordinary step of publishing anonymous essays defending the Court's decision.[3]

In deference to the case's extraordinary public significance, the Supreme Court dispensed with its customary rule restricting the number of lawyers to no more than two for each party. The argument of *McCulloch*, which extended over nine days beginning on 22 February, employed the talents of six distinguished Supreme Court practitioners. Appearing for the bank were Daniel Webster, Attorney General William Wirt, and the legendary William Pinkney (a former attorney general). Representing the state of Maryland were Joseph Hopkinson; Walter Jones, United States attorney for the District of Columbia; and Luther Martin, attorney general of Maryland, making one of his final appearances at the bar. The ablest advocate on this occasion was Pinkney, of whose forensic effort Story remarked that he had "never, in my whole life, heard a greater speech. . . . All the cobwebs of sophistry and metaphysics about State rights and State sovereignty he brushed away with a mighty besom."[4] Pinkney's powerful arguments on behalf of implied powers, broad construction, and national supremacy left their mark on the opinion delivered a few days later by the chief justice. The combined efforts of Maryland's counsel could not match Pinkney's effectiveness. Hopkinson only feebly contested the constitutionality of the bank, concentrating instead on upholding the state's right to tax the institution. Jones presented a capable brief for strict construction and state sovereignty based on the theory of the Constitution as a "compact" entered into by the states as parties. Martin, in a reprise of his Antifederalist role of 1787 and 1788, contended that the doctrine of implied powers was repugnant to the contemporaneous exposition of the Constitution. Although Martin spoke more than two days, Wheaton's report of his performance covers a mere five pages. This circumstance may explain why certain references in Marshall's opinion to arguments by Maryland's counsel cannot be documented in the published report.[5]

Three days after arguments concluded, Marshall delivered the Court's opinion. Much the greater part considered the question of Congress's power to incorporate a bank. As a prelude to this inquiry, the chief justice discussed the nature of the Constitution, the sources of its authority, and the rules for expounding the instrument. The Constitution, he affirmed, was the constituent act of the American people, not a compact among sovereign states; the powers it conferred on the general government were delegated not by the states but by conventions elected by the people. In so acting in their highest sovereign capacity, the people not only established a general government of enumerated powers but also restricted the state sovereignties. Although limited to specified powers, the general government was "supreme within its sphere of action," a proposition supported by general reasoning and Constitutional text.[6] There was nothing in the Constitution, moreover, that precluded implied powers arising from those expressly delegated to the government of the Union. As evidenced by its nature and language, the Constitution was not intended to prescribe in minute detail either the multiplicity of subordinate powers or the means of executing the principal powers. Such an instrument, marking only the "great outlines," was therefore to be construed to allow Congress ample discretion to select the means of carrying out its designated objects and powers.[7] This principle of construction was founded not only in reason but in that clause granting Congress power to pass all laws "necessary and proper" for executing its enumerated powers.

Marshall expounded this clause at length to prove that the word "necessary" was to be understood not as restricting Congress only to those means "absolutely" or "indispensably necessary" but as enabling Congress to select means that were "convenient" or "conducive" to the beneficial exercise of its express powers. "Let the end be legitimate," he wrote, "let it be within the scope of the constitution, and all means which are appropriate, which are plainly adapted to that end, which are not prohibited, but consist with the letter and spirit of the constitution, are constitutional."[8] Applying this criterion, the chief justice had little difficulty in showing that the act incorporating the bank was within the scope of Congress's constitutional powers. Having set forth the doctrine of implied powers of Congress, Marshall in the briefer second part of his opinion formulated a corollary doctrine of implied restrictions on state powers. Although the Constitution expressly limited state taxing power only in prohibiting duties on imports, exports, and tonnage, the principle of national supremacy in effect prohibited any state tax that conflicted with Congress's exercise of a constitutional power. Maryland's tax on the bank was therefore unconstitutional.

In *McCulloch* Chief Justice Marshall restated principles that had enjoyed a long currency in American constitutional discourse. As early as 1791, for example, Alexander Hamilton had offered a classic defense of implied powers in advising President Washington to sign the bank bill. Marshall was thoroughly familiar with Hamilton's opinion, having published a lengthy extract of it (along with Jefferson's opinion) in a note to his *Life of Washington*. His construction of the "necessary and proper" clause also closely followed Hamilton's.[9] Scarcely a passage in the first part of *McCulloch* could not be traced to Hamilton's advisory opinion or to some earlier writing, speech, or legal argument. Yet the enduring fame of *McCulloch* does not rest on the originality of its ideas but in the way its author gathered up various familiar strands of interpretation and wove them together into a masterly exposition of the Constitution.

McCulloch came down emphatically in favor of reading the Constitution as conferring on Congress wide latitude in determining the extent of its express powers. Such a reading also abridged state powers more stringently than did the express prohibitions contained in the Constitution. In its uncompromising theory of national supremacy, its expansive view of federal powers, and its restrictive view of state sovereignty, the opinion has often been cited as the exemplifying statement of the Marshall Court's "nationalism." Subsequent events ultimately ratified the nationalizing principles of *McCulloch*, confirming its standing as an eminent landmark of American constitutional development.

Later generations of legislators and jurists frequently invoked its eloquent phrases to justify the great expansion of national power that occurred in the late nineteenth and the twentieth centuries. Nationalism, indeed, irresistibly emerges as a dominant theme of *McCulloch*, whether viewed in its immediate context or from the broader perspective of constitutional history.

As an expression of constitutional nationalism, however, *McCulloch* is not to be understood as a prescient anticipation of the modern liberal state, in which a federal government of vastly augmented powers has assumed primary responsibility for regulating the economy and promoting social welfare. Neither praise nor blame for this development is properly ascribed to the Marshall Court. Despite contemporary fulminations against the "consolidating" doctrines of *McCulloch*, the nationalism endorsed by that opinion is more accurately defined in negative or defensive terms—concerned primarily with preserving the Union against powerful centrifugal tendencies that constantly threatened its dissolution. The intention of *McCulloch* was not so much to enhance the powers of the federal government as to enable that government to exercise its powers effectively and to prevent state encroachments upon its legitimate operations.[10] The argument did not so much affirm a "liberal" or "loose" (terms Marshall did not use) construction of Congress's powers as reject the restrictive construction adopted by Maryland's counsel. The latter construction, he contended, would emasculate the general government, preventing it from carrying out the important objects entrusted to it by the Constitution. A government so tightly tethered would scarcely be more effective than Congress under the former Confederation. His overriding concern was that strict construction would inexorably transform the Union into a league of sovereign states—a belated triumph for Antifederalism.

McCulloch dealt not only with "federalism," the division of sovereignty between the general and state governments, but no less importantly with establishing the boundary between judicial and legislative power. In upholding Congress's power to charter a bank, Marshall reaffirmed the limited conception of judicial review he had first invoked sixteen years earlier in *Marbury v. Madison*. This "departmental" theory confined the Court's power of review to "legal" disputes, to the adjudication of individual rights, and renounced all claim to decide "political" questions or to interfere with the discretionary authority vested in the legislative and executive departments. The Supreme Court was not the exclusive interpreter of the Constitution but deferred to the constructions established by Congress and the executive in cases falling within their respective spheres.[11] Although in *Marbury* the Court pronounced an act of Congress unconstitutional, most of that opinion was an inquiry into the extent to which the judiciary could take cognizance over acts of the executive. In *McCulloch*, more so than in *Marbury*, the chief justice sought to establish an intelligible standard for reviewing acts of Congress. According to the rule he formulated, implied powers were constitutional so long as they were "plainly adapted" to carrying out a delegated power, were not prohibited by the Constitution, and were consistent with the letter and spirit of the Constitution. In applying this standard to a legislative act, a judge would not have to "inquire into the degree of its necessity." Such an inquiry would require him "to pass the line which circumscribes the judicial department, and to tread on legislative ground. This court disclaims all pretensions to such a power."[12]

Just as in *Marbury* Marshall admitted the existence of a wide range of executive actions and conduct that could not be reviewed by judicial authority, so in *McCulloch* he conceded a broad measure of unreviewable discretion to Congress to choose means for carrying into effect its delegated powers. To make this concession was simply to recognize that judicial power was incompetent to decide questions involving the extent of an affirmative grant of power. Questions of this kind could not be adjudicated according to any intelligible *legal* standards. The chief justice assuredly did not mean to suggest that this admission was equivalent to giving Congress a blank check to do whatever it deemed expedient. His point, rather, was that the limits on the powers of the federal legislature were to be principally defined and enforced by the political process. To forswear judicial interference in political matters was not merely a prudent act of self-denial but, more fundamentally, an acquiescence to the will of the majority as expressed through the people's elected representatives. In short, *McCulloch* placed on Congress—and, ultimately, the American people—much of the burden and responsibility for settling the meaning of the Constitution, for adapting that instrument "to the various *crises* of human affairs."[13]

1. McCulloch v. Maryland, App. Cas. No. 938.

2. Charles Warren, *The Supreme Court in United States History* (rev. ed.; 2 vols.; Boston, 1926), I, 499–507; Charles Grove Haines, *The Role of the Supreme Court in American Government and Politics, 1789–1835* (1944; New York, 1973 reprint), 351–53.

3. See Essays Defending McCulloch v. Maryland, editorial note, at 24 April 1819.

4. Story to Stephen White, 3 Mar. 1819, Story, *Life and Letters*, I, 325.

5. Soon after the McCulloch decision, Martin was reportedly preparing his argument for press. No such publication has been found, however. A few months later Martin suffered an incapacitating stroke (Paul S. Clarkson and R. Samuel Jett, *Luther Martin of Maryland* [Baltimore, Md., 1970], 301n, 302).

6. Opinion, 6 Mar. 1819 (262, below).

7. Ibid. (263, below).

8. Ibid. (270–71, below).

9. See *The Life of George Washington* . . . (5 vols.; Philadelphia, 1804–7), V, app., 3–11. JM had briefly expounded the "necessary and proper" clause in U.S. v. Fisher (1805): "In construing this clause it would be incorrect and would produce endless difficulties, if the opinion should be maintained that no law was authorised which was not indispensably necessary to give effect to a specified power" (2 Cranch 396; *PJM*, VI, 369).

10. G. Edward White, *The Marshall Court and Cultural Change, 1815–35*, the Oliver Wendell Holmes Devise History of the Supreme Court of the United States, III–IV (New York, 1988), 486–87.

11. Kermit L. Hall, *The Supreme Court and Judicial Review in American History* (Washington, D.C., 1985), 1–16.

12. Opinion, 6 Mar. 1819 (272, below).

13. Ibid. (267, below). The opinion and the scholarly commentary it has generated are discussed in A. I. L. Campbell, " 'It is *a constitution* we are expounding': Chief Justice Marshall and the 'Necessary and Proper' Clause," *Journal of Legal History*, XII (1991), 190–245.

OPINION

In the case now to be determined, the defendant, a sovereign state, denies the obligation of a law enacted by the Legislature of the Union, and the plaintiff, on his part, contests the validity of an act which has been passed by the Legislature of that state. The Constitution of our country, in its most interesting and vital parts, is to be considered; the conflicting powers of the government of the Union and of its members, as marked in that Constitution, are to be discussed; and an opinion given, which may essentially influence the great operations of the government. No tribunal can approach such a question without a deep sense of its importance, and of the awful responsibility involved in its decision. But it must be decided peacefully, or remain a source of hostile legislation, perhaps of hostility of a still more serious nature; and if it is to be so decided, by this tribunal alone can the decision be made. On the Supreme Court of the United States has the Constitution of our country devolved this important duty.

The first question made in the cause is, Has Congress power to incorporate a Bank?

It has been truly said, that this can scarcely be considered as an open question, entirely unprejudiced by the former proceedings of the nation respecting it. The principle now contested was introduced at a very early period of our history, has been recognized by many successive legislatures, and has been acted upon by the judicial department, in cases of peculiar delicacy, as a law of undoubted obligation.[1]

It will not be denied, that a bold and daring usurpation might be resisted, after an acquiescence still longer and more complete than this. But it is conceived that a doubtful question, one on which human reason may pause and the human judgment be suspended, in the decision of which the great principles of liberty are not concerned, but the respective powers of those who are equally the representatives of the people, to be adjusted, if not put at rest by the practice of the government, ought to receive a considerable impression from that practice. An exposition of the Constitution, deliberately established by legislative acts, on the faith of which an immense property has been advanced, ought not to be lightly disregarded.[2]

The power now contested was exercised by the first Congress elected under the present Constitution. The bill for incorporating the Bank of the United States did not steal upon an unsuspecting legislature and pass unobserved. Its principle was completely understood, and was opposed with equal zeal and ability. After being resisted first in the fair and open field of debate, and afterwards in the executive cabinet, with as much persevering talent as any measure has ever experienced, and being supported by arguments which convinced minds as pure and as intelligent as this country can boast, it became a law. The original act was permitted to expire, but a short experience of the embarrassments to which the refusal to revive it exposed the government, convinced those who were most prejudiced against the measure of its necessity, and induced the passage of the present law. It would require no ordinary share of intrepidity to assert that a measure adopted under these circumstances was a bold and plain usurpation, to which the Constitution gave no countenance.

These observations belong to the cause; but they are not made under the impression that, were the question entirely new, the law would be found irreconcileable with the Constitution.

In discussing this question, the counsel for the State of Maryland have deemed it of some importance in the construction of the Constitution, to consider that instrument not as emanating from the people, but as the act of sovereign and independent states.[3] The powers of the general government, it has been said, are delegated by the states, who alone are truly sovereign, and must be exercised in subordination to the states, who alone possess supreme dominion.

It would be difficult to sustain this proposition. The Convention which framed the Constitution was indeed elected by the state legislatures. But the instrument, when it came from their hands, was a mere proposal, without obligation, or pretensions to it. It was reported to the then existing Congress of the United States, with a request that it might "be submitted to a Convention of Delegates, chosen in each state by the people thereof, under the recommendation of its Legislature, for their assent and ratification." This mode of proceeding was adopted; and by the Convention, by Congress, and by the State Legislatures, the instrument was submitted to the people. They acted upon it in the only manner in which they can act safely, effectively, and wisely on such a subject, by assembling in Convention. It is true, they assembled in their several states—and where else should they have assembled? No political dreamer was ever wild enough to think of breaking down the lines which separate states, and of compounding the American people into one common mass. Of consequence, when they act they act in their states. But the measures they adopt do not, on that account, cease to be the measures of the people themselves, or become the measures of the state governments.[4]

From these Conventions the Constitution derives its whole authority. The government proceeds directly from the people; is "ordained and established" in the name of the people; and is declared to be ordained "in order to form a more perfect union, establish justice, ensure domestic tranquility, and secure the blessings of liberty to themselves and to their posterity." The assent of the states, in their sovereign capacity is implied in calling a Convention, and thus submitting that instrument to the people. But the people were at perfect liberty to accept or reject it; and their act was final. It required not the affirmance, and could not be negatived, by the state governments. The Constitution, when thus adopted, was of complete obligation, and bound the state sovereignties.

It has been said, that the people had already surrendered all their powers to the state sovereignties, and had nothing more to give. But surely the question whether they may resume and modify the powers granted to government does not remain to be settled in this country. Much more might the legitimacy of the general government be doubted, had it been created by the states. The powers delegated to the state sovereignties were to be exercised by themselves, not by a distinct and independent sovereignty, created by themselves. To the formation of a league such as was the confederation, the state sovereignties were certainly competent. But when "in order to form a more perfect union," it was deemed necessary to change this alliance into an effective government, possessing great and sovereign power and acting directly on the people, the necessity of referring it to the people, and of deriving its powers directly from them, was felt and acknowledged by all.

The government of the Union, then, whatever may be the influence of this fact on the case, is, emphatically and truly, a government of the people. In form and in substance it emanates from them. Its powers are granted by them, and are to be exercised directly on them, and for their benefit.

This government is acknowledged by all to be one of enumerated powers. The principle that it can exercise only the powers granted to it, would seem too apparent to have required to be enforced by all those arguments which its enlightened friends, while it was depending before the people, found it necessary to urge. That principle is now universally admitted. But the question respecting the extent of the powers actually granted, is perpetually arising, and will probably continue to arise as long as our system shall exist.

In discussing these questions, the conflicting powers of the general and state governments must be brought into view, and the supremacy of their respective laws, when they are in opposition, must be settled.

If any one proposition could command the universal assent of mankind, we might expect it would be this—that the government of the Union, though limited in its powers, is supreme within its sphere of action. This would seem to result necessarily from its nature. It is the government of all; its powers are delegated by all; it represents all, and acts for all. Though any one state may be willing to control its operations, no state is willing to allow others to control them. The nation, on those subjects on which it can act, must necessarily bind its component parts. But this question is not left to mere reason: the people have, in express terms, decided it, by saying, "this constitution, and the laws of the United States, which shall be made in pursuance thereof," "shall be the supreme law of the land," and by requiring that the members of the state legislatures, and the officers of the executive and judicial departments of the states shall take the oath of fidelity to it.

The government of the United States, then, though limited in its powers, is supreme; and its laws, when made in pursuance of the con-

stitution, form the supreme law of the land, "any thing in the constitution or laws of any state to the contrary notwithstanding."

Among the enumerated powers, we do not find that of establishing
a bank or creating a corporation. But there is no phrase in the instrument which, like the articles of confederation, excludes incidental
or implied powers; and requires that every thing granted shall be expressly and minutely described. Even the 10th amendment, which was
framed for the purpose of quieting the excessive jealousies which had
been excited, omits the word "expressly," and declares only that the
powers "not delegated to the United States, nor prohibited to the
states, are reserved to the states or to the people"; thus leaving the
question, whether the particular power which may become the subject
of contest has been delegated to the one government, or prohibited to
the other, to depend on a fair construction of the whole instrument.
The men who drew and adopted this amendment had experienced the
embarrassments resulting from the insertion of this word in the articles
of confederation, and probably omitted it to avoid those embarrassments.[5] A constitution, to contain an accurate detail of all the subdivi-
sions of which its great powers will admit, and of all the means by which
they may be carried into execution, would partake of the prolixity of a
legal code, and could scarcely be embraced by the human mind. It
would probably never be understood by the public. Its nature, therefore, requires that only its great outlines should be marked, its important objects designated, and the minor ingredients which compose
those objects be deduced from the nature of the objects themselves.
That this idea was entertained by the framers of the American constitution, is not only to be inferred from the nature of the instrument, but
from the language. Why else were some of the limitations, found in the
ninth section of the 1st article, introduced? It is also, in some degree,
warranted by their having omitted to use any restrictive term which
might prevent its receiving a fair and just interpretation. In considering this question, then, we must never forget that it is *a constitution* we
are expounding.

Although, among the enumerated powers of government, we do not
find the word "bank" or "corporation," we find the great powers to lay
and collect taxes, to borrow money, to regulate commerce, to declare
and conduct a war, and to raise and support armies and navies. The
sword and the purse, all the external relations, and no inconsiderable
portion of the industry of the nation, are entrusted to its government.
It can never be pretended that these vast powers draw after them
others of inferior importance, merely because they are inferior. Such
an idea can never be advanced. But it may with great reason be contended, that a government, entrusted with such ample powers, on the
due execution of which the happiness and prosperity of the nation so
vitally depends, must also be entrusted with ample means for their

execution. The power being given, it is the interest of the nation to facilitate its execution. It can never be their interest, and cannot be presumed to have been their intention, to clog and embarrass its execution by withholding the most appropriate means. Throughout this vast republic, from the St. Croix to the Gulph of Mexico, from the Atlantic to the Pacific, revenue is to be collected and expended, armies are to be marched and supported. The exigencies of the nation may require that the treasure raised in the north should be transported to the south, *that* raised in the east conveyed to the west, or that this order should be reversed. Is that construction of the constitution to be preferred which would render these operations difficult, hazardous, and expensive? Can we adopt that construction, unless the words imperiously require it, which would impute to the framers of that instrument, when granting these powers for the public good, the intention of impeding their exercise by withholding a choice of means? If, indeed such be the mandate of the constitution, we have only to obey; but that instrument does not profess to enumerate the means by which the powers it confers may be executed, nor does it prohibit the creation of a corporation, if the existence of such a being be essential to the beneficial exercise of those powers. It is, then, the subject of fair enquiry, how far such means may be employed.

It is not denied, that the powers given to the government imply the ordinary means of execution. That, for example, of raising revenue and applying it to national purposes, is admitted to imply the power of conveying money from place to place, as the exigencies of the nation may require, and of employing the usual means of conveyance. But it is denied that the government has its choice of means; or that it may employ the most convenient means, if, to employ them, it be necessary to erect a corporation.

On what foundation does this argument rest? On this alone: The power of creating a corporation is one appertaining to sovereignty, and is not expressly conferred on Congress.[6] This is true. But all legislative powers appertain to sovereignty. The original power of giving the law on any subject whatever, is a sovereign power; and if the government of the Union is restrained from creating a corporation as a means for performing its functions, on the single reason, that the creation of a corporation is an act of sovereignty; if the sufficiency of this reason be acknowledged, there would be some difficulty in sustaining the authority of Congress to pass other laws for the accomplishment of the same objects.

The government which has a right to do an act, and has imposed on it the duty of performing that act, must, according to the dictates of reason, be allowed to select the means; and those who contend that it may not select any appropriate means, that one particular mode of effecting the subject is excepted, take upon themselves the burden of establishing that exception.

The creation of a corporation, it is said, appertains to sovereignty. This is admitted. But to what portion of sovereignty does it appertain? Does it belong to one more than to another? In America, the powers of sovereignty are divided between the government of the Union and those of the states. They are each sovereign, with respect to the objects committed to it, and neither sovereign with respect to the objects committed to the other. We cannot comprehend that train of reasoning which would maintain that the extent of power granted by the people is to be ascertained, not by the nature and terms of the grant, but by its date. Some state constitutions were formed before, some since that of the United States. We cannot believe that their relation to each other is in any degree dependent upon this circumstance. Their respective powers must, we think, be precisely the same as if they had been formed at the same time. Had they been formed at the same time, and had the people conferred on the general government the power contained in the constitution, and on the states the whole residuum of power, would it have been asserted that the government of the Union was not sovereign with respect to those objects which were entrusted to it, in relation to which its laws were declared to be supreme? If this could not have been asserted, we cannot well comprehend the process of reasoning which maintains, that a power appertaining to sovereignty cannot be connected with that vast portion of it which is granted to the general government, so far as it is calculated to subserve the legitimate objects of that government. The power of creating a corporation, though appertaining to sovereignty, is not, like the power of making war, of levying taxes, or of regulating commerce, a great substantive and independent power, which cannot be implied as incidental to other powers, or used as a means of executing them. It is never the end for which other powers are exercised, but a means by which other objects are accomplished. No contributions are made to charity for the sake of an incorporation, but a corporation is created to administer the charity; no seminary of learning is instituted in order to be incorporated, but the corporate character is conferred to subserve the purposes of education. No city was ever built with the sole object of being incorporated, but is incorporated as affording the best means of being well governed. The power of creating a corporation is never used for its own sake, but for the purpose of effecting something else. No sufficient reason is, therefore, perceived why it may not pass as incidental to those powers which are expressly given, if it be a direct mode of executing them.

But the constitution of the United States has not left the right of Congress to employ the necessary means for the execution of the powers conferred on the government, to general reasoning. To its enumeration of powers is added that of making "all laws which shall be necessary and proper for carrying into execution the foregoing powers, and all other powers vested by this constitution, in the government of the United States, or in any department thereof."

The Counsel of the State of Maryland have urged various arguments, to prove that this clause, though in terms a grant of power, is not so in effect; but is, really, restrictive of the general right, which might otherwise be implied, of selecting means for executing the enumerated powers.

They[7] have found it necessary to contend that this clause was inserted for the purpose of conferring on Congress the power of making laws. That, without it, doubts might be entertained, whether Congress could exercise its powers in the form of legislation.[8]

But could this be the object for which it was inserted? A government is created by the people, having legislative, executive, and judicial powers. Its legislative powers are vested in a Congress, which is to consist of a Senate and House of Representatives. Each House may determine the rules of its proceedings; and it is declared that every bill which shall have passed both houses, shall, before it become a law, be presented to the President of the United States. The 7th section describes the course of proceedings, by which a bill shall become a law, and, then, the 8th section enumerates the powers of Congress. Could it be necessary to say, that a legislature should exercise legislative powers, in the shape of legislation? After allowing each house to prescribe its own course of proceeding, after describing the manner in which a bill should become a law, would it have entered into the mind of a single member of the convention, that an express power to make laws was necessary, to enable the legislature to make them? That a legislature, endowed with legislative powers, can legislate, is a proposition too self-evident to have been questioned.

But the argument on which most reliance is placed, is drawn from the peculiar language of this clause. Congress is not empowered by it to make all laws which may have relation to the powers conferred on the government, but such only as may be "*necessary and proper*" for carrying them into execution. The word "*necessary*" is considered as controlling the whole sentence, and as limiting the right to pass laws for the execution of the granted powers, to such as are indispensable, and without which the power would be nugatory. That it excludes the choice of means, and leaves to Congress, in each case, that only which is most direct and simple.

Is it true, that this is the sense in which the word "necessary" is always used? Does it always import an absolute physical necessity, so strong, that one thing, to which another may be termed necessary, cannot exist without that other? We think it does not. If reference be had to its use, in the common affairs of the world, or in approved authors, we find that it frequently imports no more than that one thing is convenient, or useful, or essential to another. To employ the means necessary to an end, is generally understood as employing any means calculated to produce the end, and not as being confined to those single means, without which the end would be entirely unattainable. Such is the character of human language, that no word conveys to the mind, in all situations, one single definite idea; and nothing is more common than to use words in a figurative sense. Almost all compositions contain words, which, taken in their rigorous sense, would convey a meaning different from that which is obviously intended. It is essential to just construction that many words which import something excessive, should be understood in a more mitigated sense—in that sense which common usage justifies. The word 'necessary' is of this description. It has not a fixed character peculiar to itself. It admits of all degrees of comparison, and is often connected with other words which increase or diminish the impression the mind receives of the urgency it imports. A thing may be necessary, very necessary, absolutely or indispensably necessary. To no mind would the same idea be conveyed by these several phrazes. This comment on the word is well illustrated by the passage cited at the bar, from the 10th section of the 1st article of the constitution. It is, we think, impossible to compare the sentence which prohibits a state from laying "imposts, or duties on imports or exports, except what may be *absolutely* necessary for executing its inspection laws," with that which authorises Congress "to make all laws which shall be necessary and proper for carrying into execution" the powers of the general government, without feeling a conviction that the convention understood itself to change materially the meaning of the word "necessary" by prefixing the word "absolutely." This word, then, like others, is used in various senses, and, in its construction, the subject, the context, the intention of the person using them, are all to be taken into view.[9]

Let this be done in the case under consideration. The subject is the execution of those great powers, on which the welfare of a nation essentially depends. It must have been the intention of those who gave these powers, to ensure, as far as human prudence could ensure, their beneficial execution. This could not be done by confiding the choice of means to such narrow limits as not to leave it in the power of Congress to adopt any which might be appropriate, & which were conducive to the end. This provision is made in a constitution intended to endure for ages to come, and, consequently, to be adapted to the various *crises* of human affairs. To have prescribed the means by which government should, in all future time, execute its powers, would have been to change, entirely, the character of the instrument, and give it the properties of a legal code. It would have been an unwise attempt to provide, by immutable rules, for exigencies which, if foreseen at all, must have been seen dimly, and which can be best provided for as they occur.[10] To have declared that the best means shall not be used, but those alone without which the power given would be nugatory, would have been to deprive the legislature of the capacity to avail itself of experience, to exercise its reason, and to accommodate its legislation to circumstances. If we apply this principle of construction to any of the powers of the government, we shall find it so pernicious in its operation that we shall be compelled to discard it. The powers vested in Congress may certainly be carried into execution, without prescribing an oath of office. The power to exact this security for the faithful performance of duty, is not given, nor is it indispensably necessary. The different departments may be established, taxes may be imposed and collected, armies and navies may be raised and maintained, and money may be borrowed, without requiring an oath of office. It might be argued, with as much plausibility as other incidental powers have been assailed, that the convention was not unmindful of this subject. The oath which might be exacted—that of fidelity to the constitution, is prescribed, and no other can be required. Yet, he would be charged with insanity who should contend, that the legislature might not superadd, to the oath directed by the constitution, such other oath of office as its wisdom might suggest.

So, with respect to the whole penal code of the United States; whence arises the power to punish in cases not prescribed by the constitution? All admit that the government may, legitimately, punish any violation of its laws; and yet, this is not among the enumerated powers of Congress. The right to enforce the observance of law, by punishing its infraction, might be denied with the more plausibility, because it is expressly given in some cases.

Congress is empowered "to provide for the punishment of counterfeiting the securities and current coin of the United States," and "to define and punish piracies and felonies committed on the high seas, and offences against the laws of nations." The several powers of Congress may exist, in a very imperfect state to be sure, but they may exist, and be carried into execution, although no punishment should be inflicted in cases where the right to punish is not expressly given.

Take, for example, the power "to establish post offices and post roads." This power is executed by the single act of making the establishment. But, from this has been inferred the power and duty of carrying the mail, along the post road, from one post office to another. And, from this implied power, has again been inferred the right to punish those who steal letters from the post office, or rob the mail. It may be said, with some plausibility, that the right to carry the mail, and to punish those who rob it, is not indispensably necessary to the establishment of a post office and post road. This right is indeed essential to the beneficial exercise of the power, but not indispensably necessary to its existence. So, in the punishment of the crimes of stealing or falsifying a record or process of a court of the United States, or of perjury in such court. To punish these offences is certainly conducive to the due administration of justice. But courts may exist, and may decide the causes brought before them, though such crimes escape punishment.

The baneful influence of this narrow construction on all the operations of the government, and the absolute impracticability of maintaining it without rendering the government incompetent to its great objects, might be illustrated by numerous examples drawn from the constitution and from our laws. The good sense of the public has pronounced, without hesitation, that the power of punishment appertains to sovereignty, and may be exercised whenever the sovereign has a right to act, as incidental to his constitutional powers. It is a means for carrying into execution all sovereign powers, and may be used, although not indispensably necessary. It is a right incidental to the powers, and conducive to its beneficial exercise.

If this limited construction of the word "necessary" must be abandoned in order to punish, whence is derived the rule which would reinstate it, when the government would carry its powers into execution by means not vindictive in their nature? If the word "necessary" means "needful," "requisite," "essential," "conducive to," in order to let in the power of punishment for the infraction of law, why is it not equally comprehensive when required to authorise the use of means which facilitate the execution of the powers of government without the infliction of punishment?

In ascertaining the sense in which the word "necessary" is used in this clause of the constitution, we may derive some aid from that with which it is associated. Congress shall have power "to make all laws which shall be necessary and *proper* to carry into execution" the powers of the government. If the word "necessary" was used in that strict and rigorous sense for which the counsel for the State of Maryland contend, it would be an extraordinary departure from the usual course of the human mind, as exhibited in composition, to add a word, the only possible effect of which is to qualify that strict and rigorous meaning; to present to the mind the idea of some choice of means of legislation not straightened and compressed within the narrow limits for which gentlemen contend.

But the argument which most conclusively demonstrates the error of the construction contended for by the Counsel of Maryland, is founded on the intention of the convention, as manifested in the whole clause. To waste time and argument in proving that, without it, Congress might carry its powers into execution, would be not much less idle than to hold a lighted taper to the sun. As little can it be required to prove that, in the absence of this clause, Congress would have some choice of means. That it might employ those which in its judgment, would most advantageously effect the object to be accomplished. That any means adapted to the end, any means which tended directly to the execution of the constitutional powers of the government, were in themselves constitutional. This clause, as construed by the State of Maryland, would abridge and almost annihilate this useful and necessary right of the Legislature to select its means. That this could not be intended is, we should think, had it not been already controverted, too apparent for controversy. We think so for the following reasons.

1. The clause is placed among the powers of Congress, not among the limitations in those powers.

2nd. Its terms purport to enlarge, not to diminish the powers vested in the government. It purports to be an additional power, not a restriction on those already granted. No reason has been or can be assigned for thus concealing an intention to narrow the discretion of the national legislature under words which purport to enlarge it. The framers of the constitution wished its adoption, and well knew that it would be endangered by its strength, not by its weakness. Had they been capable of using language which would convey to the eye one idea, and, after deep reflection, impress on the mind another, they would rather have disguised the grant of power, than its limitation. If then their intention had been, by this clause, to restrain the free use of means which might otherwise have been implied, that intention would have been inserted in another place, and would have been expressed in terms resembling these. "In carrying into execution the foregoing powers and all others," &c. "no laws shall be passed but such as are necessary and proper." Had the intention been to make this clause restrictive, it would unquestionably have been so in form as well as in effect.

The result of the most careful and attentive consideration bestowed upon this clause is that, if it does not enlarge, it cannot be construed to restrain the powers of Congress, or to impair the right of the legislature to exercise its best judgment in the selection of measures to carry into execution the constitutional powers of the government. If no other motive for its insertion can be suggested, a sufficient one is found in the desire to remove all doubts respecting the right to legislate on that vast mass of incidental power which must be involved in the constitution, if that instrument be not a splendid bauble.

We admit, as all must admit, that the powers of the government are limited, and that its limits are not to be transcended. But we think the sound construction of the constitution must allow to the national legislature that discretion, with respect to the means by which the powers it confers are to be carried into execution, which will enable that body to perform the high duties assigned to it, in the manner most beneficial to the people. Let the end be legitimate, let it be within the scope of the constitution, and all means which are appropriate, which are plainly adapted to that end, which are not prohibited, but consist with the letter and spirit of the constitution, are constitutional.

That a corporation must be considered as a means not less usual, not of higher dignity, not more requiring a particular specification than other means, has been sufficiently proved. If we look to the origin of corporations, to the manner in which they have been framed in that government from which we have derived most of our legal principles and ideas, or to the uses to which they have been applied, we find no reason to suppose that a constitution, omitting, and wisely omitting, to enumerate all the means for carrying into execution the great powers vested in government, ought to have specified this. Had it been intended to grant this power as one which should be distinct and independent, to be exercised in any case whatever, it would have found a place among the enumerated powers of the government. But being considered merely as a means, to be employed only for the purpose of carrying into execution the given powers, there could be no motive for particularly mentioning it.

The propriety of this remark would seem to be generally acknowledged by the universal acquiescence in the construction which has been uniformly put on the 3rd sec. of the 4th article of the constitution. The power to "make all needful rules and regulations respecting the territory or other property belonging to the United States" is not more comprehensive, than the power "to make all laws which shall be necessary and proper for carrying into execution" the powers of the government. Yet all admit the constitutionality of a territorial government, which is a corporate body.

If a corporation may be employed indiscriminately with other means to carry into execution the powers of the government, no particular reason can be assigned for excluding the use of a bank if required for its fiscal operations. To use one, must be within the discretion of Congress, if it be an appropriate mode of executing the powers of government. That it is a convenient, a useful, and essential instrument in the prosecution of its fiscal operations, is not now a subject of controversy. All those who have been concerned in the administration of our finances, have concurred in representing its importance and necessity; and so strongly have they been felt, that statesmen of the first class, whose previous opinions against it had been confirmed by every circumstance which can fix the human judgment, have yielded those opinions to the exigencies of the nation. Under the confederation, Congress, justifying the measure by its necessity, transcended perhaps its powers to obtain the advantage of a bank; and our own legislation attests the universal conviction of the utility of this measure. The time has passed away when it can be necessary to enter into any discussion in order to prove the importance of this instrument as a means to effect the legitimate objects of the government.

But were its necessity less apparent, none can deny its being an appropriate measure; and if it is, the degree of its necessity, as has been very justly observed, is to be discussed in another place. Should Congress, in the execution of its powers, adopt measures which are prohibited by the constitution; or should Congress under the pretext of executing its powers, pass laws for the accomplishment of objects not entrusted to the government; it would become the painful duty of this tribunal, should a case requiring such a decision come before it, to say that such an act was not the law of the land. But where the law is not prohibited, and is really calculated to effect any of the objects entrusted to the government, to undertake here to enquire into the degree of its necessity, would be to pass the line which circumscribes the judicial department, and to tread on legislative ground. This court disclaims all pretensions to such a power.

After this declaration it can scarcely be necessary to say that the existence of state banks can have no possible influence on the question. No trace is to be found in the constitution of an intention to create a dependence of the government of the union on those of the states, for the execution of the great powers assigned to it. Its means are adequate to its ends; and on those means alone was it expected to rely for the accomplishment of its ends. To impose on it the necessity of resorting to means which it cannot controul, which another government may furnish or withold, would render its course precarious, the result of its measures uncertain, and create a dependence on other governments which might disappoint its most important designs, and is incompatible with the language of that constitution. But were it otherwise, the choice of means implies a right to choose a national bank in preference to state banks, and Congress alone can make the election.

After the most deliberate consideration it is the unanimous and decided opinion of this court that the act to incorporate the Bank of the United States, is a law made in pursuance of the constitution, and is a part of the supreme law of the land.

The branches proceeding from the same stock, and being conducive to the complete accomplishment of the object, are equally constitutional. It would have been unwise to locate them in the charter, and it would be unnecessarily inconvenient to employ the legislative power in making those subordinate arrangements. The great duties of the bank are prescribed; those duties require branches; and the bank itself may, we think, be safely trusted with the selection of places where those branches shall be fixed; reserving always to the government the right to require that a branch shall be located where it may be deemed necessary. It being the opinion of the court that the act incorporating the bank is constitutional; and that the power of establishing a branch in the State of Maryland might be properly exercised by the bank itself we proceed to enquire.

2. Whether the State of Maryland may, without violating the constitution, tax that branch?

That the power of taxation is one of vital importance; that it is retained by the states; that it is not abridged by the grant of a similar power to the government of the union; that it is to be concurrently exercised by the two governments; are truths which have never been denied. But, such is the paramount character of the constitution, that its capacity to withdraw any subject from the action of even this power, is admitted. The states are expressly forbidden to lay any duties on imports or exports, except what may be absolutely necessary for executing their inspection laws. If the obligation of this prohibition must be conceded—if it may restrain a state from the exercise of its taxing power on imports and exports, the same paramount character would seem to restrain, as it certainly may restrain, a state from such other exercise of this power as is in its nature incompatible with, and repugnant to the constitutional laws of the Union. A law absolutely repugnant to another as entirely repeals that other, as if express terms of repeal were used.

On this ground the counsel for the bank place its claim to be exempted from the power of a state to tax its operations. There is no express provision for the case, but the claim has been sustained on a principle which so entirely pervades the constitution, is so intermixed with the materials which compose it, so interwoven with its web, so blended with its texture, as to be incapable of being separated from it, without rending it into shreds.

This great principle is, that the constitution and the laws made in pursuance thereof, are supreme; that they control the constitution and laws of the respective states, and cannot be controlled by them. From this, which may be almost termed an axiom, other propositions are deduced as corrollaries, on the truth or error of which, and on their application to this case, the cause has been supposed to depend. These are—1st. that a power to create implies a power to preserve. 2nd. that a power to destroy, if wielded by a different hand, is hostile to, and incompatible with these powers to create and to preserve. 3d. that where the repugnancy exists, that authority which is supreme must control, not yield to that over which it is supreme.

These propositions, as abstract truths, would, perhaps, never be controverted. Their application to this case, however, has been denied; and, both in maintaining the affirmative and the negative, a splendor of eloquence, and strength of argument, seldom, if ever, surpassed, have been displayed.

The power of Congress to create, and of course to continue, the bank, was the subject of the preceding part of this opinion, and is no longer to be considered as questionable.

That the power of taxing it by the States may be exercised so as to destroy it, is too obvious to be denied. But taxation is said to be an absolute power which acknowledges no other limits than those expressly prescribed in the constitution, and like sovereign power of every other description, is trusted to the discretion of those who use it. But the very terms of this argument admit that the sovereignty of the state, in the article of taxation itself, is subordinate to, and may be controlled by, the constitution of the United States. How far it has been controlled by that instrument must be a question of construction. In making this construction, no principle not declared, can be admissable, which would defeat the legitimate operations of a supreme government. It is of the very essence of supremacy to remove all obstacles to its action within its own sphere, and so to modify every power vested in subordinate governments, as to exempt its own operations from their own influence. This effect need not be stated in terms. It is so involved in the declaration of supremacy, so necessarily implied in it, that the expression of it could not make it more certain. We must, therefore, keep it in view while construing the constitution.

The argument on the part of the State of Maryland is not that the states may directly resist a law of Congress, but that they may exercise their acknowledged powers upon it, and that the constitution leaves them this right in the confidence that they will not abuse it.

Before we proceed to examine this argument, and to subject it to the test of the constitution, we must be permitted to bestow a few considerations on the nature and extent of this original right of taxation, which is acknowledged to remain with the states. It is admitted that the power of taxing the people and their property is essential to the very existence of government, and may be legitimately exercised on the objects to which it is applicable, to the utmost extent to which the government may chuse to carry it. The only security against the abuse of this power, is found in the structure of the government itself. In imposing a tax the legislature acts upon itself and upon[11] its constituents. This is in general a sufficient security against erroneous and oppressive taxation.

The people of a state, therefore, give to their government a right of taxing themselves and their property, and as the exigencies of government cannot be limited, they prescribe no limits to the exercise of this right, resting confidently on the interest of the legislator, and on the influence of the constituents over their representative, to guard them against its abuse. But the means employed by the government of the union have no such security, nor is the right of a state to tax them sustained by the same theory. Those means are not given by the people of a particular state, not given by the constituents of the legislature which claim the right to tax them, but by the people of all the states. They are given by all, for the benefit of all—and upon theory, should be subjected to that government only which belongs to all.

It may be objected to this definition that the power of taxation is not confined to the people and property of a state. It may be exercised upon every object brought within its jurisdiction.

This is true. But to what source do we trace this right? It is obvious that it is an incident of sovereignty, and is co-extensive with that to which it is an incident. All subjects over which the sovereign power of a state extends are objects of taxation; but those over which it does not extend, are, upon the soundest principles, exempt from taxation. This proposition may almost be pronounced self-evident.

The sovereignty of a state extends to every thing which exists by its own authority, or is introduced by its permission, but does it extend to those means which are employed by Congress to carry into execution powers conferred on that body by the people of the U. States? We think it demonstrable that it does not. Those powers are not given by the people of a single state. They are given by the people of the United States to a government whose laws made in pursuance of the constitution are declared to be supreme—consequently, the people of a single state cannot confer a sovereignty which will extend over them.

If we measure the power of taxation residing in a state, by the extent of sovereignty which the people of a single state possess, and can confer on its government, we have an intelligible standard applicable to every case to which the power may be applied. We have a principle which leaves the power of taxing the people and property of a state unimpaired: which leaves to a state the command of all its resources: and which places beyond its reach, all those powers which are conferred by the people of the United States on the government of the Union, and all those means which are given for the purpose of carrying those powers into execution. We have a principle which is safe for the states, and safe for the Union. We are relieved, as we ought to be, from clashing sovereignty, from interfering powers: from a repugnancy between a right in one government to pull down, what there is an acknowledged right in another to build up; from the incompatibility of a right in one government to destroy what there is a right in another to preserve. We are not driven to the perplexing enquiry, so unfit for the judicial department, what degree of taxation is the legitimate use, and what degree may amount to the abuse, of the power. The attempt to use it on the means employed by the governments of the Union, in pursuance of the Constitution, is itself an abuse, because it is the usurpation of a power which the people of a single state cannot give.

We find then, on just theory, a total failure of this original right to tax the means employed by the government of the Union for the execution of its powers. The right never existed, and the question whether it has been surrendered, cannot arise.

But, waving this theory for the present, let us resume the enquiry whether this power can be exercised by the respective states, consistently with a fair construction of the constitution?

That the power to tax involves the power to destroy; that the power to destroy may defeat and render useless the power to create; that there is a plain repugnance in conferring on one government a power to controul the constitutional measures of another, which other, with respect to those very measures, is declared to be supreme over that which exerts the controul, are propositions not to be denied. But all inconsistencies are to be reconciled by the magic word *confidence*. Taxation, it is said, does not necessarily and unavoidably destroy. To carry it to the excess of destruction, would be an abuse, to presume which would banish that confidence which is essential to all government. But is this a case of confidence? Would the people of any one state trust those of another with a power to controul the most insignificant operations of their state government? We know they would not. Why then should we suppose that the people of any one state should be willing to trust those of another with a power to controul the operations of a government to which they have confided their most important and most valuable interests? In the Legislature of the Union alone, are all represented. The Legislature of the Union alone, therefore, can be trusted by the people with the power of controuling measures which concern all, in the confidence that it will not be abused. This, then, is not a case of confidence, and we must consider it as it really is.

If we apply the principle for which the state of Maryland contends, to the constitution generally, we shall find it capable of changing totally the character of that instrument. We shall find it capable of arresting all the measures of the government, and of prostrating it at the foot of the states. The American people have declared their Constitution, and the laws made in pursuance thereof, to be supreme; but this principle would transfer the supremacy in fact to the states.

If the states may tax one instrument employed by the government in the execution of its powers, they may tax any and every other instrument. They may tax the mail, they may tax the mint, they may tax patent rights, they may tax the papers of the custom house, they may tax judicial process, they may tax all the means employed by the government, to an excess which would defeat all the ends of government. This was not intended by the American people. They did not design to make their government dependent on the states.

Gentlemen say, they do not claim the right to extend state taxations to these objects. They limit their pretentions to property. But on what principle is this distinction made? Those who make it have furnished no reason for it, and the principle for which they contend denies it. They contend that the power of taxation has no other limit than is found in the 10th section of the 1st article of the constitution; that, with respect to every thing else, the power of the state is supreme, and admits of no control. If this be true, the distinction between property and other subjects to which the power of taxation is applicable, is merely arbitrary, and can never be sustained. This is not all. If the controling power of the states be established, if their supremacy as to taxation be acknowledged, what is to restrain their exercising this control in any shape they may please to give it? Their sovereignty is not confined to taxation. That is not the only mode in which it might be displayed. The question is, in truth, a question of supremacy; and if the right of the states to tax the means employed by the general government be conceded, the declaration that the constitution, and the laws made in pursuance thereof, shall be the supreme law of the land, is empty and unmeaning declamation.

In the course of the argument, the Federalist has been quoted; and the opinions expressed by the authors of that work have been justly supposed to be entitled to great respect in expounding the constitution. No tribute can be paid to their worth[12] which exceeds their merit; but in applying their opinions to the cases which may arise in the progress of our government, a right to judge of their correctness must be retained; and, to understand the argument, we must examine the proposition it maintains and the objections against which it is directed. The subject of those numbers, from which passages have been cited, is the unlimited power of taxation which is vested in the general government.

The objection to this unlimited power, which the argument seeks to remove, is stated with fullness and clearness. It is, "that an indefinite power of taxation in the latter (the government of the Union) might, and probably would, in time, deprive the former (the government of the states) of the means of providing for their own necessities; and would subject them entirely to the mercy of the national legislature. As the laws of the Union are to become the supreme laws of the land; as it is to have power to pass all laws that may be necessary for carrying into execution the authorities with which it is proposed to vest it; the national government might at any time abolish the taxes imposed for state objects, upon the pretence of an interference with its own. It might allege a necessity for doing this, in order to give efficacy to the national revenues; and thus all the resources of taxation might, by degrees, become the subjects of federal monopoly, to the entire exclusion and destruction of the state governments."[13]

The objections to the constitution which are noticed in these numbers, were to the undefined power of the government to tax, not to the incidental privilege of exempting its own measures from state taxation. The consequences apprehended from this undefined power, were: that it would absorb all the objects of taxation, "to the exclusion and destruction of the state governments." The arguments of the Federalist are intended to prove the fallacy of these apprehensions; not to prove that the government was incapable of executing any of its powers, without exposing the means it employed to the embarrassments of state taxation.

Arguments urged against these objections, and these apprehensions, are to be understood as relating to the points they mean to prove. Had the authors of those excellent essays been asked, whether they contended for that construction of the constitution, which would place within the reach of the states those measures which the government might adopt for the execution of its powers; no man, who has read their instructive pages, will hesitate to admit, that their answer must have been in the negative.

It has also been insisted, that, as the power of taxation in the general and state governments is acknowledged to be concurrent, every argument which would sustain the right of the general government to tax banks chartered by states, will equally sustain the right of the states to tax banks chartered by the general government.

But the two cases are not on the same reason. The people of all the States have created the general government; and have conferred upon it the general power of taxation. The people of all the States, and the States themselves, are represented in Congress, and by their Representatives exercise this power. When they tax the chartered institutions of the States, they tax their constituents; and these taxes must be uniform. But, when a state taxes the operations of the government of the United States, it acts upon institutions created, not by their own constituents, but by people, over whom they claim no control. It acts upon the measures of a government created by others, as well as themselves, for the benefit of others in common with themselves. The difference is that which always exists, and always must exist, between the action of the whole, or a part, and the action of a part and the whole—between the laws of a government declared to be supreme, and those of a government which, when in opposition to those laws, is not supreme.

But if the full application of this argument could be admitted, it might bring into question the right of Congress to tax the State Banks, and could not prove the right of the States to tax the Bank of the United States.

The court has bestowed on this subject its most deliberate consideration. The result is a conviction that the States have no power, by taxation, or otherwise, to retard, impede, burden, or in any manner control the operations of the constitutional laws enacted by Congress to carry into execution the powers vested in the general government. This is, we think, the unavoidable consequence of that supremacy, which the Constitution has declared.

We are unanimously of opinion, that the law passed by the Legislature of Maryland, imposing a tax on the Bank of the United States, is unconstitutional, and void.

This opinion does not deprive the states of any resources which they originally possessed. It does not extend to a tax paid by the real property of the bank, in common with the other real property within the state, nor to a tax imposed on the interest which the citizens of Maryland may hold in this institution, in common with other property of the same description throughout the state. But this is a tax on the operations of the bank, and is consequently a tax on the operation of an instrument employed by the government of the Union, to carry its powers into execution. Such a tax must be unconstitutional.

The[14] judgment of the court of appeals of the state of Maryland, is therefore erroneous, and must be reversed; and a mandate be issued to that court, directing a judgment to be entered for the plaintiff in error.

Printed, *Daily National Intelligencer* (Washington, D.C.), 13 March 1819.

1. JM apparently had in mind criminal prosecutions of persons indicted for counterfeiting or forging notes of the Bank of the U.S. For examples of cases heard by him on circuit, see U.S. v. Logwood (U.S. Cir. Ct., Va. [1804]), U.S. v. Holtsclaw (U.S. Cir. Ct., N.C. [1806]), and U.S. v. Twitty (U.S. Cir. Ct., N.C. [1811]), in *PJM*, VI, 290–91, 422–23; VII, 274–75.

2. In argument, Pinkney stated: "A legislative construction, in a doubtful case, persevered in for a course of years, ought to be binding upon the Court" (4 Wheat. 378).

3. JM alluded to Jones's argument: "It is insisted, that the constitution was formed and adopted, not by the people of the United States at large, but by the people of the respective States. To suppose that the mere proposition of this fundamental law threw the American people into one aggregate mass, would be to assume what the instrument itself does not profess to establish. It is, therefore, a compact between the States, and all the powers which are not expressly relinquished by it, are reserved to the States" (4 Wheat. 363). Martin might have also elaborated upon the compact theory in his inadequately reported argument.

4. The Constitution, Pinkney observed, "springs from the people, precisely as the State constitutions spring from the people, and acts on them in a similar manner. It was adopted by them in the geographical sections into which the country is divided. The federal powers are just as sovereign as those of the States. The State sovereignties are not the authors of the constitution of the United States" (4 Wheat. 377–78).

5. Pinkney had called attention to the omission of "expressly" in the Tenth Amendment (4 Wheat. 384).

6. Jones: "The power of creating corporations is a distinct sovereign power, applicable to a great variety of objects, and not being expressly granted to Congress for this, or any other object, cannot be assumed by implication" (4 Wheat. 368).

7. In Wheaton this paragraph begins, "In support of this proposition, they."

8. Jones: "Now, we insist, that this clause shows that the intention of the Convention was, to define the powers of the government with the utmost precision and accuracy. The creation of a sovereign legislature implies an authority to pass laws to execute its given powers. This clause is nothing more than a declaration of the authority of Congress *to make laws*, to execute the powers expressly granted to it, and the other departments of the government" (4 Wheat. 366).

9. This "philological analysis" (as Pinkney called it) was employed by each of the bank's counsel, who along with JM no doubt drew upon Hamilton's 1791 opinion (4 Wheat. 324, 354–56, 387–88).

10. Pinkney: "How unwise would it have been to legislate immutably for exigencies

which had not then occurred, and which must have been foreseen but dimly and imperfectly!" (4 Wheat. 385).

11. Wheaton omitted "itself and upon."

12. In Wheaton "their worth" is omitted and "them" inserted.

13. *The Federalist* No. 31 (Hamilton), Rossiter, *Federalist Papers*, 195–96. This passage is a quotation of an objection meant to be answered by "Publius."

14. This paragraph is not in Wheaton.

To Joseph Story

Dear Sir   Richmond March 24th. 1819

Since my return to Washington[1] I mentioned to a very near friend who owns an extensive nail factory that I had understood that some machinery was in use in & about Boston which greatly facilitated the making of nails. He was anxious to have some account of the machine which I was totally unable to give.[2]

I have some idea that the subject was mentioned by you—at any rate it was mentioned in your presence. I understood that there were two machines—one very expensive—the other almost equally valuable & costing only about one hundred dollars. If you have leisure will you have the goodness to mention in a letter to me what these machines are called, what is their operation, & what they cost? You can probably say something about their advantages.[3]

Our opinion in the bank case has roused the sleeping spirit of Virginia—if indeed it ever sleeps. It will I understand be attacked in the papers with some asperity; and as those who favor it never write for the publick it will remain undefended & of course be considered as *damnably heretical*. Yours truely

J MARSHALL

ALS, Story Papers, MHi. Note beneath JM's signature in hand of Daniel Webster (see n. 3).

1. JM meant either "from Washington" or "to Richmond."

2. The "near friend" was Jaquelin B. Harvie, JM's son-in-law. JM sent Harvie an extract of Story's reply of 15 May (Story to JM, [15 May 1819]).

3. Story forwarded JM's letter to Daniel Webster (Story to JM, [15 May 1819]), who returned it with the following note written beneath JM's signature:

"Mr Baldwin & Mr. May referred me to Mr./Geo: Odiorne. I have seen him—he says/he will find *one*, all fitted for use, for/*200 Dlls*—Altho. that is below/his usual price, & he would not engage to/fill another at that rate—The machine/can be shipped here, for Richmond, on request./I believe this to be the least expen[s]ive, &/is the Machine which is in sucessfull/operation in various places./D.W."

To Bushrod Washington

My dear Sir   Richmond March 27th. [1819]

I have a nephew a son of Major Taylor who is at school in Kentucky under the direction of my brother Doctor Marshall. He has written to me for some books which I cannot procure here, & which if I had them could not without much difficulty be conveyed from this place.[1] I take the liberty to ask the favor of you to purchase them for me in Philadelphia & leave them with the bookseller packed up to be delivered to the order of Doctor Marshall.[2] The books I wish to purchase are Terence & Livy in latin, Longinus Thucydides & Demosthenes in Greek, also Xenophons retreat of the 10,000.

Be so good as to send the booksellers receipt for the money as it is to be inserted in an executors account. Should the inclosed be insufficient I will immediately remit the residue. I will thank you also to pay Delaplaine four dollars for me & take his receipt for that sum for the last half volume, I beleive it is the third.[3]

Great dissatisfaction has been given to the politicians of Virginia by our opinion on the bank question. They have no objection to a decision in favor of the bank, since the good patriots who administer the government wished it, & would probably have been seriously offended with us had we dared to have decided otherwise, but they required an obsequious, silent opinion without reasons. That would have been satisfactory, but our heretical reasoning is pronounced most damnable. We shall be denounced bitterly in the papers & as not a word will be said on the other side we shall undoubtedly be condemned as a pack of consolidating aristocratics. The legislature & executive who have enacted the law but who have power & places to bestow will escape with impunity, while the poor court who have nothing to give & of whom nobody is afraid, bears all the obloquy of the measure.

We are in great distress here for money. Many of our merchants stop—a thing which was long unknown & was totally unexpected in Richmond. Farewell, I am dear Sir yo⟨ur⟩

J Marsh⟨all⟩

ALS, Marshall Papers, ViW. Addressed to Washington in Philadelphia; postmarked Richmond, 27 Mar. Endorsed by Washington: "27 March 1819/Chf Jus. Marshall/Sam A. Bascom—Corner 6 & Carpenter Street." MS torn.

1. JM's nephew was Thomas Taylor (JM to Louis Marshall, 13 Dec. 1816 and n. 1). The letter referred to by JM, presumably from Louis Marshall, has not been found.

2. As indicated by Washington's endorsement, the Philadelphia bookseller was Samuel A. Bascom (John Adams Paxton, *The Philadelphia Directory and Register, for 1819* . . . [Philadelphia, 1819; S #49079]).

3. Vol. II, pt. I, of [Joseph Delaplaine], *Delaplaine's Repository of the Lives and Portraits of Distinguished Americans* (2 vols.; Philadelphia, 1816–18; S #43830). See JM to Delaplaine, 22 Mar. 1818 and n. 1.

Essays Defending McCulloch v. Maryland

EDITORIAL NOTE

Nowhere was *McCulloch* v. *Maryland* more vehemently denounced than in Virginia, with such a degree of intensity that the chief justice of the United States was provoked into writing a series of anonymous newspaper articles in defense of the opinion. As a Federalist partisan in the 1790s, Marshall had engaged in newspaper polemics, but these 1819 essays constitute his only direct foray into the sphere of public controversy while he sat on the Supreme Court. That he took up his pen on this occasion is a measure of how seriously he regarded the attack on the Supreme Court, which he came to perceive as nothing less than an attack on the federal Union as established by the Constitution of 1787.

Although the chief justice provided sufficient clues in his correspondence, for years biographers and other scholars had failed to uncover the full dimensions of Marshall's counterattack. Then in 1969 Professor Gerald Gunther published the results of his research in preparing a history of the Marshall Court. Gunther was the first to make the connection between Marshall's comments in letters to Bushrod Washington and Joseph Story and the publication of a dozen essays (now known to have been written by Marshall) in an Alexandria, Virginia, newspaper. Previous to Gunther's discoveries, Marshall was thought to have written only two pieces in defense of *McCulloch*, the two numbers of "A Friend to the Union," published in the Philadelphia *Union* in April 1819. This publication was so hopelessly botched, however, that the chief justice arranged to have the essays reprinted in Alexandria. Gunther's research in the files of the *Gazette and Alexandria Daily Advertiser* unearthed not only the reprinting of "A Friend to the Union" (now divided into three numbers instead of two) but also nine previously unknown essays written by Marshall under the nom de plume "A Friend of the Constitution."[1]

Delivered on 6 March and first published a week later in the Washington *Daily National Intelligencer*, the *McCulloch* opinion was subsequently reprinted in newspapers throughout the country. During the spring and summer the Court's decision was a leading topic of newspaper and pamphlet commentary. While the opinion initially generated its share of extravagant praise, impassioned denunciations soon made their appearance. As early as 13 March, Hezekiah Niles, editor of *Niles' Weekly Register* in Baltimore, launched a series of attacks on the decision as a "deadly blow" to the "*sovereignty of the states*" and as the "first grand step towards a *consolidation of the states*, or a *separation of them*."[2] On 23 March the Richmond *Enquirer* published the opinion, accompanied by editor Thomas Ritchie's appeal to "those firm Republicans of the Old School" to "rally round the banners of the constitution, defending the rights of the states against federal usurpation." Recalling Virginia's role in 1798 and 1799 in opposing the Alien and Sedition laws, Ritchie continued: "This opinion must be controverted and exposed. Virginia has proved herself the uniform friend of state rights—again, she is called to come forth!"[3]

Soon after Ritchie's editorial appeared, Marshall remarked that the bank opinion "has roused the sleeping spirit of Virginia—if indeed it ever sleeps" and predicted the Court would "be denounced bitterly in the papers."[4] This prediction was borne out on 30 March, when the first number of "Amphictyon," heartily recommended by Ritchie as a "most satisfactory" exposition of

THOMAS RITCHIE
Oil on canvas by Thomas Sully, ca. 1845. *Courtesy of the Muscarelle Museum of Art, College of William and Mary in Virginia*

the Supreme Court's "alarming errors," was published in the *Enquirer*. A second number followed on 2 April. Scarcely mentioning the bank, Amphictyon undertook to refute two principles adopted by the Supreme Court that "endanger the very existence of state rights": (1) the denial that the Constitution was a compact to which the states as parties delegated powers to the federal government, and (2) the rule that federal powers, particularly those granted under the "necessary and proper" clause, should "be construed in a liberal, rather than a restricted sense."[5]

These pieces were long attributed to Spencer Roane, the undoubted author of the later "Hampden" essays, but Marshall himself identified Amphictyon as William Brockenbrough (1778–1838), a judge of the Virginia General Court, law reporter, and Roane's first cousin. Along with Roane and Ritchie, Brockenbrough was a member of the "Richmond Junto," the powerful Republican organization that controlled politics in the Old Dominion. These Virginia Republicans were animated by fear of a resurgent Federalist party led by the Supreme Court. Not only *McCulloch* but also *Dartmouth*, *Sturgis*, and the earlier decision in *Martin* v. *Hunter's Lessee* were cited as evidence of the federal judiciary's scheme to overthrow the state governments and revive the principles of a supposedly moribund Federalism. To combat this alarming trend, the junto (with Thomas Jefferson's blessing) used the pages of the *Enquirer* and other imprints to disseminate orthodox Virginia constitutional doctrine—the principles of 1798 and 1799, compact theory, and state rights.[6]

Throughout April Ritchie directed a steady barrage of articles and editorials opposing the bank opinion.[7] Marshall began writing "A Friend to the Union" soon after reading Amphictyon's critique, motivated by his growing apprehension that the animosity generated by *McCulloch* was merely the entering wedge of a broader assault on the Constitution and the Union itself, aimed at the government's "weakest department," the federal judiciary.[8] His overriding fear was that the unleashing of the "antifederal spirit of Virginia," which had been agitating with increasing fury since *Martin* v. *Hunter's Lessee* in 1816, would produce defiant resolutions by the Virginia General Assembly similar to those of 1798 and 1799. The consequence might be the emasculation of the Supreme Court and other measures that would effectively dismantle the federal government. If the principles of "the democracy in Virginia" prevailed, he fretted, "the constitution would be converted into the old confederation." Indeed, Hampden would soon confirm Marshall's suspicions by claiming that the present general government was "as much a federal government, or a 'league,' as was the former confederation."[9]

Through no fault of his own, Marshall's initial effort to defend *McCulloch* fell flat. He sent his "Friend to the Union" pieces to Bushrod Washington, then attending circuit in Philadelphia. Washington arranged for their publication in the *Union* published by Enos Bronson. The first number appeared on 24 April, the second on 28 April; they were reprinted in the "country" edition of that paper on 28 April and 1 May. Much to his chagrin, the chief justice, a subscriber to the country paper, discovered that his replies to Amphictyon had been mutilated in the printing. Bronson had "cut out the middle of the first number to be inserted into the middle of the second; & to show his perfect impartiality, has cut out the middle of the second number to be inserted in the first." The resulting mixture was "rather nauseous to the intellectual palate."

Undaunted by this contretemps, Marshall believed the situation too urgent to quit the field at this point. He instructed Washington to have the essays reprinted in their "true shape" in Alexandria, which would also have the added benefit of making his side of the debate more accessible in the state where it was most needed.[10] "A Friend to the Union" was accordingly published as three separate numbers in the *Gazette and Alexandria Daily Advertiser* on 15, 17, and 18 May.

Three weeks later the *Enquirer* carried the first number of Hampden, whose identity virtually everyone conversant with this controversy knew to be Spencer Roane, eminent judge of Virginia's Court of Appeals. An opponent of the Constitution in 1788, Roane had distinguished himself as an outspoken champion of state rights in resisting the Supreme Court's mandate in the case of *Fairfax's Devisee v. Hunter's Lessee* (1813).[11] Roane produced four installments of Hampden, which ran in the *Enquirer* between 11 and 22 June. Covering much the same ground as Amphictyon, Hampden exceeded his predecessor in the asperity and bitter invective that characterized his indictment of the Supreme Court. The sarcastic tone of his commentary was revealed at the outset, when he remarked that judicial power, "which, in England, has only invaded the constitution in the worst of times, and then, always, on the side of arbitrary power, has also deemed its interference necessary, in our country."[12]

The essential charge against *McCulloch* was that it manifested a sinister design to overthrow the Constitution, prostrate the rights of the states and the people, and establish a consolidated general government of unlimited powers—-confirming the worst fears voiced by Antifederalists in 1788 and Republicans in the crisis of 1798 and 1799. This "warfare" against the states and people, heretofore carried on with varying success in Congress, was now to be directed by the "bolder" hands of the federal judiciary, who "by a judicial *coup de main*" would "give a *general* letter of attorney to the future legislators of the union" and "tread under foot" all constitutional limits upon federal legislative powers. Like John Hampden, the celebrated seventeenth-century opponent of arbitrary monarchical power, and the American patriots who resisted the claims of Parliament, Roane would take his stand as "a freeman" at this present "crisis," which "portends destruction to the liberties of the American people."[13]

Reading such inflammatory rhetoric, Marshall found himself "more stimulated on this subject than on any other because I believe the design to be to injure the Judges and impair the constitution."[14] In Hampden the chief justice recognized a bold and formidable opponent who went far beyond Amphictyon in impeaching the integrity and legitimacy of the judiciary department. What must have particularly rankled him was Hampden's contention that the Supreme Court had not merely "gone out of the record" to grant Congress "this *general* power of attorney" but in fact had no jurisdiction to decide cases involving a clash of powers between the state and general governments. This court, declaimed Hampden, "had no power to adjudicate away the *reserved* rights of a sovereign member of the confederacy, and vest them in the general government."[15] Tedious as it might be to recapitulate many of the same points previously advanced to refute Amphictyon, Marshall resolved to answer Hampden—again through the medium of the Alexandria newspaper. He sent off his replies to Washington, instructing him not to begin publication until "I shall have seen the last of Hampden." Working at a furious pace during the last two weeks of June, Marshall ultimately produced nine numbers of "A Friend of the Constitution," with publication in the *Gazette and Alexandria Daily Advertiser* commencing on 30 June and continuing through 15 July. As before, his motive in writing was not the pleasure to be derived from intellectual engagement but anxiety lest the erroneous principles of Amphictyon and Hampden work their noxious influence upon the General Assembly. To make sure his own message got across to the right people, he directed that his essays be placed "in the hands of some respectable members" of the Virginia legislature.[16]

In addition to Amphictyon and Hampden, one other *Enquirer* essayist caught the chief justice's attention during the summer of 1819. "Hortensius," identified by Marshall as United States attorney George Hay, weighed in with three numbers in late July and early August.[17] Although highly critical of the Court's reasoning in *McCulloch*, particularly its "boundless . . . latitude of construction" in defining the Constitution's "necessary and proper" clause, Hortensius adopted a moderate tone that "implicitly admitted" the Court's "purity of . . . motives" and expressed "high respect" for its "abilities and learning." Professing himself to be "the advocate *of constitutional rights*," whether vested in the general or state governments, Hortensius sought to distance himself from the extreme state-sovereignty views of Amphictyon and Hampden.[18] He accepted the challenge thrown out by "A Friend to the Union" defying "any man, to furnish an argument which shall, at the same time, prove the Bank to be constitutional, and the reasoning of the court to be erroneous." Hortensius in turn invited the author of "A Friend to the Union" to respond to his exposition of the Constitution.[19] But the chief justice, undoubtedly eager to escape to the mountains for a belated summer holiday, was done with newspaper polemics.

The sequel to the great debate provoked by *McCulloch* was played out in the Virginia General Assembly, which met in December. As Marshall feared, resolutions condemning the bank decision were introduced in the House of Delegates, the first of which instructed the state's senators and representatives in Congress to procure a constitutional amendment creating a separate tribunal for deciding all questions involving a conflict between the powers of the federal and state governments. Another instructed them "to resist on every occasion" legislation that attempted to exercise any power not "expressly given" to the national government or that was not "*necessary and proper*," which phrase was to be construed in the more restricted sense approved by the state legislature. Following the precedent of 1798 and 1799, a third resolution requested the governor to transmit copies of these resolutions to each of the other states.[20] The first resolution was eventually dropped and replaced by one urging a "declaratory amendment" prohibiting Congress from incorporating a bank anywhere except in the District of Columbia. As amended, these resolutions were adopted by a large majority in the House of Delegates. The Senate, however, "contrary to every expectation," declined to take up the resolutions, reportedly for lack of time "to consider and digest" them. "It is with the profoundest regret we have to give this information," wrote the disappointed editor of the *Enquirer*.[21]

Chief Justice Marshall was undoubtedly relieved, if not partially vindicated, when the legislature closed its session without taking any official action. The attack against the Supreme Court had subsided only for the moment, however, to be renewed with greater intensity scarcely a year later with the announcement of the opinion in *Cohens* v. *Virginia*. Marshall had not heard the last of Judge Roane.

1. Gerald Gunther, "John Marshall, 'A Friend of the Constitution': In Defense and Elaboration of *McCulloch v. Maryland*," *Stanford Law Review*, XXI (1969), 449–55. An expanded version of the article and documents was published as *John Marshall's Defense of McCulloch v. Maryland* (Stanford, Calif., 1969).

2. *Niles' Weekly Register* [Baltimore, Md.], XVI (1819), 41, 103, 145. For a sampling of newspaper reaction, see Charles Warren, *The Supreme Court in United States History* (rev. ed.; 2 vols.; Boston, 1926), I, 511–25.

3. Richmond *Enquirer*, 23 Mar. 1819.

4. JM to Story, 24 Mar. 1819; JM to Washington, 27 Mar. 1819.

5. Gunther, *Marshall's Defense*, 54–55.

6. W. Hamilton Bryson, ed., *The Virginia Law Reporters before 1880* (Charlottesville, Va., 1977), 7–10. On the Richmond Junto, see Harry Ammon, "The Richmond Junto, 1800–1824," *VMHB*, LXVI (1953), 395–418; Joseph H. Harrison, Jr., "Oligarchs and Democrats: The Richmond Junto," ibid., LXXVIII (1970), 184–98. Brockenbrough's son, John W. Brockenbrough, later published Marshall's circuit court opinions.

7. Amphictyon was followed by three numbers of "Franklin" and one by "A Virginian" (Richmond *Enquirer*, 13, 16, 20, 23, 30 Apr. 1819).

8. "A Friend to the Union," 24 Apr. 1819 (288, below); see also "A Friend of the Constitution," 30 June 1819 (318, below).

9. JM to Story, 28 Apr., 27 May 1819; Gunther, *Marshall's Defense*, 146.

10. JM to Washington, 6 May 1819.

11. See Martin v. Hunter's Lessee, editorial note, at ca. 16 Dec. 1816.

12. Gunther, *Marshall's Defense*, 108.

13. Ibid., 110, 111–12.

14. JM to Washington, 17 June 1819.

15. Gunther, *Marshall's Defense*, 110–11.

16. JM to Washington, 17 June, [ca. 28 June], 3 Aug. 1819.

17. JM to Washington, 3 Aug. 1819; Richmond *Enquirer*, 23, 27 July, 3 Aug. 1819.

18. Richmond *Enquirer*, 23 July 1819.

19. "A Friend to the Union," 28 Apr. 1819 (307, below); "Hortensius," Richmond *Enquirer*, 27 July 1819.

20. Richmond *Enquirer*, 23, 25 Dec. 1819.

21. Ibid., 12, 15, 29 Feb. 1820; Charles Grove Haines, *The Role of the Supreme Court in American Government and Politics, 1789–1835* (1944; New York, 1973 reprint), 364–67.

A Friend to the Union
No. I

MR. EDITOR, [24 April 1819][1]

My attention has been a good deal attracted by some essays which have appeared lately in one of the Virginia papers which seem to have for their object the infliction of deep wounds on the constitution through a misrepresentation of the opinion lately delivered by the Supreme Court on the constitutionality of the act incorporating the bank of the United States. I have bestowed a few leisure moments on the refutation of some of the mischievous errours contained in these essays; and, if you think what I have written worth publishing you will give this answer to Amphyction a place in your useful paper.

A spirit which was supposed to have been tranquillized by a long possession of the government, appears to be resuming its original activity in Virginia. The decision of the Supreme Court in the case of McCullough against the state of Maryland has been seized as a fair occasion for once more agitating the publick mind, and reviving those unfounded jealousies by whose blind aid ambition climbs the ladder of power.

The bill for incorporating the bank of the United States had become a law, without exciting a single murmur. The reason is obvious. Those who fill the legislative and executive departments are elected by the people, and are of course popular. In addition, they possess great power and great patronage. Had they been unjustly attacked, champions would have arisen on every side, who would with equal zeal and ability have presented the truth to a publick not unwilling to perceive it. But the Judges of the Supreme Court, separated from the people by the tenure of office, by age, and by the nature of their duties, are viewed with respect, unmingled with affection, or interest. They possess neither power not patronage. They have no sops to give; and every coffeehouse furnishes a Cerberus,[2] hoping some reward for that watchfulness which his bark proclaims; and restrained by no apprehension that any can be stimulated by personal considerations to expose the injustice of his attacks. We ought not, therefore, to be surprised if it should be deemed criminal in the judicial department to sustain a measure, which was adopted by the legislature, and by the executive with impunity. Hostility to the Union, must cease to be guided by its usual skill, when it fails to select the weakest department as that through which a breach may be effected.

The Inquirer, the leading paper of Virginia, abounds with hostile attacks on this opinion. That which is written with most talent, most system, and most design, appears under the signature of Amphyction. The Editor assures his readers that it contains "a most satisfactory exposition" "of the alarming errours of the Supreme Court of the United States" in their interpretation of the constitution; and Amphyction himself does not leave his object to conjecture. "Most ardently" does he "hope that this decision of the Supreme Court will attract the attention of the state legislatures, and that Virginia will, as heretofore, do her duty."

The avowed object being of so serious a nature, it behoves not only the friends of the Bank, but the friends of the constitution, the friends of Union, to examine well the principles which are denounced as heretical, and those which are supported as orthodox.

The objections of Amphyction are to that part of the opinion which declares the act incorporating the bank to be constitutional. He intro-

WILLIAM BROCKENBROUGH
Oil on canvas by unknown artist, ca. 1830s. *Courtesy of the Virginia State Library and Archives*

duces them with expressing his disapprobation of that mode of transacting their official duties which the Supreme Court has adopted. He
would prefer *seriatim* opinions, to the combined opinion of the bench
delivered by a single Judge.

On the justness of this criticism in general, or on its peculiar application to this particular case, I shall make no observation; because the
principles expressed in this single opinion are neither more nor less
vulnerable than they would have been if expressed in six separate opinions. But the criticism was made for the purpose of conveying an insinuation which marks the spirit in which the discussion is conducted. "We
are not," says Amphyction, "informed whether the whole court united
in the course of reasoning adopted by the Chief Justice, nor whether
they all accorded in the various positions and principles he advanced."

Now I humbly conceive this is a subject on which we are informed.
The opinion is delivered, not in the name of the chief justice, but in the
name of the whole court. This observation applies to the "reasoning
adopted," and "to the various positions and principles which were advanced" as entirely as to the conclusions drawn from "those positions
and principles." Throughout the whole opinion, the chief justice never
speaks in the singular number, or in his own person, but as the mere
organ of the court. In the presence of all the judges, and in their names
he advances certain propositions as their propositions, and certain reasoning as their reasoning. I appeal to Amphyction himself, I appeal to
every man accustomed to judicial proceedings, to determine whether
the judges of the Supreme Court, men of high & respectable character,
would sit by in silence, while great constitutional principles of which
they disapproved, were advanced in their name, and as their principles. I appeal to the usage of the Supreme Court itself. Their decisions
are reported, and are in possession of the publick. It has often happened that a judge concurring in the opinion of the court, but on
reasons peculiar to himself, has stated his own reasoning. The great
case of the Nereid is one among many examples, of this course of
proceeding.[3] In some instances too it has occurred, that the judge delivering the opinion of the court has stated the contrariety of reasoning
on which the opinion was formed. Of this, the case of Olivera v. the
Union Ensurance Co. is an example.[4] The course of every tribunal
must necessarily be, that the opinion which is to be delivered as the
opinion of the court, is previously submitted to the consideration of all
the judges; and, if any part of the reasoning be disapproved, it must be
so modified as to receive the approbation of all, before it can be delivered as the opinion of all. Amphyction himself thinks so; for he says:
"We are driven, however reluctantly, to the conclusion that each judge
approves of each argument and position advanced by the chief justice."

Why then has he suggested a contrary idea? He leaves us in no
uncertainty for the answer to this question.

After stating that the subject is one "which has employed his (the chief justice's) thoughts, his tongue, and his pen, as a politician and as an historian for more than thirty years," he adds that it "is one which has, perhaps more than any other, heretofore drawn a broad line of distinction between the two great parties in this country, in which line no one has taken a more distinguished and decided rank than the judge who has thus expounded the supreme law of the land."

The chief justice then is a federalist; who was a politician of some note before he was a judge; and who with his tongue and his pen, supported the opinions he avowed. To expose the reasoning of the court to still greater odium, if it be possible, we are told that "the liberal and latitudinous construction" he has attached to a term in the constitution, had been ["]attached to it" before him, "by Mr. Secretary Hamilton." The reasoning, then, of the court is, dexterously enough, ascribed to Mr. Secretary Hamilton and the chief justice, two inveterate federalists. This question cannot be trusted, by Amphyction, to his exposition of the constitution, unless the spirit of party be introduced into the cause, and made its judge. How favourable this spirit is to truth, and to a fair exercise of the human judgement, Amphyction well knows. Had he admitted his opinion, including the reasoning, to be what it professes to be—what it must be—the opinion and reasoning of all the judges—four of whom have no political sin upon their heads—who in addition to being eminent lawyers, have the still greater advantage of being sound republicans; of having been selected certainly not for their federalism, by Mr. Jefferson, and Mr. Madison, for the high stations they so properly fill, his argument would have been stripped of one powerful recommendation, and must have depended rather more on its intrinsick merit. We need not then be surprised that this improbable suggestion is made, although a sense of propriety has compelled the writer to abandon it as soon as its effect was produced.

Having thus prepared his readers for the dangerous errours contained in the opinion of the Supreme Court, Amphyction proceeds to inform them what those errours are.

"The first is the denial that the powers of the federal government were delegated by the states; and the second is that the grant of powers to that government, and particularly the grant of powers *necessary and proper* to carry the other powers into effect, ought to be construed in a liberal rather than a restricted sense."

But before Amphyction can permit himself to enter on his first point, he deems it necessary to cast a little more odium on the opinion he is about to examine. "For what purpose" he asks, "did the federal court decide that question?" After stating that it was totally unnecessary, that the opinion on it "is obiter and extrajudicial"; he adds that "whether the powers of the federal government were delegated to it by the states in their sovereign capacity, or by the people, can make but little difference in the extent of those powers. In either case it is still true that the powers of that government are limited by the charter that called it into existence" &c.

I shall not controvert the proposition that the constitution ought to receive the same construction, whether its powers were delegated by the people or the states. That Amphyction entertains the same opinion, is brought into some doubt by the extreme importance he attaches to his theory.

If the powers of the general government were to be in no degree affected by the source from which they were derived, it is not easy to comprehend how the liberty of the American people can depend on the adoption of the one opinion or of the other. The origin of the government would seem to be[5] a mere historical fact, which it would be desirable to settle correctly, but for the settlement of which it could scarcely be necessary to call on the legislatures of the respective states or to express so earnest a hope that "Virginia would, as usual, do her duty." If it be possible for Amphyction to persuade himself that the right of the state legislatures "to canvass" or "remonstrate against the publick measures of the Congress or of the President," depended on their having delegated to the general government all its powers, it would prove only with what facility the most intelligent mind may impose on itself, when pursuing a favourite and dominant idea. Surely nothing can be more obvious, nothing better established, than that the right to canvass the measures of government, or to remonstrate against the abuse of power, must reside in all who are affected by those measures, or over whom that power is exercised, whether it was delegated by them or not. Were this allegation of Amphyction true, it would follow that the people have no right to canvass the measures of government, or to remonstrate against them. The right to canvass and remonstrate resides, according to his argument, in those only who have delegated the powers of the government. Those powers were delegated, not by the people, but by the states in their sovereign capacity. It follows that the states in their sovereign capacity, not the people, have the right to canvass publick measures. If this conclusion be false, as it must be, the premises are false also; and that a man of Amphyction's intelligence should have advanced them, only proves that he is too little accustomed to political opposition, and is too confident of the prejudices he addresses, to be very attentive to the correctness of his positions, or to the accuracy of his reasoning.

But if Amphyction had not been more anxious to throw obloquy on the court than to ascertain its justice, he might have spared this unnecessary charge of travelling out of the case for the purpose of delivering, extrajudicially, a doctrine so dangerous as he represents this to be. The principles he now maintains, appear to have been advanced, and relied on at the bar. "The counsel for the state of Maryland," we are told in the opinion, "have deemed it of some importance in the construction of the constitution to consider that instrument, not as emanating from the people; but, as the act of sovereign and independent states. The powers of the general government, it has been said, are delegated by the states who alone are truly sovereign, and must be exercised in subordination to the states, who alone possess supreme dominion.["] It is in consequence of this argument that the subject is introduced into the opinion.

His eagerness to censure must be much stronger than his sense of justice, who will criminate a court for noticing an argument advanced by eminent counsel, as one of leading importance in the cause.

But waving any further discussion of these incidental observations, I will proceed to consider the first objection made to the opinion of the Supreme Court. It is stated to be "the denial that the powers of the federal government were delegated by the states."

This assertion is not literally true. The court has not, in terms, denied "that the powers of the federal government were delegated by the states," but has asserted affirmatively that it "is emphatically and truly a government of the people," that it, "in form and in substance emanates from them."

If Amphyction chuses to construe the affirmative assertion made by the court into a negative assertion that "the powers of the government were not delegated by the states," I shall not contest the point with him unless he uses the word "states" in a different sense from that which great part of his argument imports. In what sense, let me ask, does he use the word? Does he mean the people inhabiting that territory which constitutes a state? Or does he mean the government of that territory? If the former, the controversy is at an end. He concurs with the opinion he arraigns. The Supreme Court cannot be mistaken. It has said, not indeed in the same words, but in substance precisely what he says. The powers of the government were delegated, according to that opinion, by the people assembled in convention in their respective states, and deciding, as all admit, for their respective states.

If Amphyction means to assert, as I suppose he does, that the powers of the general government were delegated by the state legislatures, then I say that his assertion is contradicted by the words of the constitution, and by the fact; and is not supported even by that report, on which he so confidently relies.

The words of an instrument, unless there be some sinister design which shuns the light, will always represent the intention of those who frame it. An instrument intended to be the act of the people, will purport to be the act of the people. An instrument intended to be the act of the states, will purport to be the act of the states. Let us then examine those words of the constitution, which designate the source whence its powers are derived. They are: "We the people of the United

States, in order to form a more perfect union, &c. do ordain and establish this constitution for the United States of America."

The constitution then proceeds in the name of the people to define the powers of that government which they were about to create.

This language cannot be misunderstood. It cannot be construed to mean, "We the states, &c."

If still more complete demonstration on this point could be required, it will be furnished by a comparison of the words just recited from the constitution, with those used in the articles of confederation.

The confederation was intended to be the act of the states, and was drawn in language comporting with that intention. The style is: "Articles of confederation and perpetual union between the states of New Hampshire, Massachusetts Bay, &c." The 3d article is completely descriptive of the character of the instrument. It is in these words: "The said states hereby severally enter into a firm league of friendship with each other for their common defence, the security of their liberties, and their mutual and general welfare; binding themselves to assist each other against all force offered to, or attacks made upon them, or any of them, on account of religion, sovereignty, trade, or any other pretence whatever."

The confederation was a mere alliance offensive and defensive, and purports to be, what it was intended to be, the act of sovereign states. The constitution is a government acting on the people, and purports to be, what it was intended to be, the act of the people.

The fact itself is in perfect consonance with the language of the instrument. It was not intended to submit the constitution to the decision of the state legislatures, nor was it submitted to their decision. It was referred to conventions of the people "for their assent or ratification," whose decision thereon was not to be reported to the state legislatures but to Congress. Had the legislature of every state in the Union been hostile to the constitution, it would still have gone into operation, if assented to and ratified by the conventions of the people. With what propriety, then, can it be denied to be the act of the people?

On this part of the question also, a comparison with the mode of proceeding for the adoption of the constitution, which was the act of the people, with that observed in adopting the confederation, which was the act of the states, may not be altogether useless.

We have seen that the constitution was submitted to the people themselves, assembled in convention.

The confederation was submitted to the state legislatures, who adopted or rejected it; and who expressed their adoption by empowering their members in Congress, who were their ministers plenipotentiary, to subscribe it in their behalf.

I cannot be mistaken when I say that no political proposition was ever more fully demonstrated than that maintained by the Supreme

Court of the United States, respecting the source from which the government of the Union derives its powers.

I will now show that the very report cited by Amphyction, admits the proposition contained in the opinion he reprobates.

Certain resolutions he informs us had been adopted by the legislature of Virginia in 1798, one of which contained the assertion that the assembly viewed "the powers of the federal government as resulting from the compact to which the states are parties." "Those resolutions" he says "having been disapproved of by most of the other state legislatures, became the subject of examination at the succeeding session, and produced that remarkable commentary which has generally been known by the name of Madison's report."[6] The language of this commentary on this part of that resolution is; "It is indeed true that the term 'states,' is sometimes used in a vague sense and sometimes in different senses, according to the subject to which it is applied. Thus it sometimes means the separate sections of territory occupied by the political societies within each; sometimes the particular governments established by those societies; sometimes those societies as organized into those particular governments; and lastly, it means the people in their highest sovereign capacity."

In which of these senses does the committee assert that the states are parties to the constitution or compact? In that sense in which the term is used to designate the government established by the particular society within the territory? No. The chairman of that committee had too much self respect, too much respect for the opinions of intelligent men out of Virginia as well as in it, to advance a proposition so totally untrue. The report continues: "Whatever different constructions of the term 'states' in the resolution may have been entertained, all will at least concur in that last mentioned" (the people composing those political societies in their highest sovereign capacity) "because," the report proceeds, "in that sense the constitution was submitted to the 'states.' In that sense the states ratified it; and in that sense they are consequently parties to the compact from which the powers of the federal government result."

This celebrated report, then, concurs exactly with the Supreme court, in the opinion that the constitution is the act of the people.[7]

I will now examine the facts on which those arguments are founded, with which Amphyction attempts to support his most extraordinary dogma.

The first is that "the federal convention of 1787, was composed of delegates appointed by the respective state legislatures."[8]

This fact is stated in the opinion of the court; and the inference drawn from it is completely refuted by the observation that the constitution, when it came from the hands of that convention, was a mere proposal without, any obligation. Its whole obligation is derived from the assent and ratification of the people afterwards assembled in state conventions. Had Amphyction confined himself to the assertion that the constitution was proposed to the people by delegates appointed by the state legislatures, he would have accorded with the Supreme Court, and would have asserted a fact which I believe no person is disposed to deny.

His second proposition is: "That the constitution was submitted to conventions elected by the people of the several states; that is to say, to the states themselves in their highest political and sovereign authority; by those separate conventions, representing, not the whole mass of the people of the United States, but the people only within the limits of the respective sovereign states, the constitution was adopted and brought into existence. The individuality of the several states was still kept up, &c."

It surely cannot escape Amphyction himself, that these positions accord precisely with the opinion he pronounces so mischievously erroneous. He admits in terms the whole subject in controversy. He admits that the powers of the general government were not delegated by the state governments, but by the people of the several states. This is the very proposition advanced by the Supreme Court, and advanced in terms too plain to be mistaken. The argument on the part of the state of Maryland was, as we learn from the opinion, that the constitution did not emanate from the people, but was the act of sovereign and independent states: clearly using the term "states" in a sense distinct from the term "people." It is this argument which is denied by the court; and in discussing it, after stating that the constitution was submitted to conventions of the people in their respective states, the opinion adds: "From these conventions the constitution derives its whole authority."

Were it possible to render the views of the court on this subject more clear, it is done in that part of the opinion which controverts the proposition advanced by the counsel for the state of Maryland, "that the people had already surrendered all their power to the state sovereignties and had nothing more to give;" and which, in opposition to this doctrine, maintains that the legitimacy of the general government would be much more questionable had it been created by the states. It is impossible to read that paragraph and retain a single doubt, if indeed a doubt could ever have been created, of the clear understanding of the court that the term people was used as designating the people of the states, and the term "states" as designating their government.

Amphyction adds, that those conventions represented "not the whole mass of the people of the United States, but the people only within the limits of the respective sovereign states." "The individuality of the several states was still kept up, &c."

And who has ever advanced the contrary opinion? Who has ever said that the convention of Pennsylvania represented the people of any other state, or decided for any other state than itself? who has ever been so absurd as to deny that "the individuality of the several states was still kept up?" Not the Supreme Court certainly. Such opinions may be imputed to the judges, by those who, finding nothing to censure in what is actually said, and being predetermined to censure, create odious phantoms which may be very proper objects of detestation, but which bear no resemblance to any thing that has proceeded from the court.

Nothing can be more obvious than that in every part of the opinion, the terms "state" and "state sovereignties" are used in reference to the state governments, as contradistinguished from the people of the states. The words of the federal convention, requesting that the constitution might "be submitted to a convention of delegates chosen in each state by the people thereof," are quoted; and it is added, "This mode of proceeding was adopted; and by the convention, by congress, and by the states legislatures, the instrument was submitted to the people." That is, to the people of the respective states; for that is the mode of proceeding said to have been recommended by the convention, and to have been adopted. After noticing that they assembled in their respective states, the opinion adds: "And where else should they have assembled? No political dreamer was ever wild enough to think of breaking down the lines which separate the states, and of compounding the American people into one mass."

Yet Amphyction affects to be controverting the reasoning of the supreme court when he says that the convention of our state did not represent all the people of the United States, that "the individuality of the several states was still kept up." Disregarding altogether the language of the court, he ascribes to the judges an opinion which they "say no political dreamer was ever wild enough to think of."

The next proposition advanced by Amphyction is that "the President is elected by persons who are, as to numbers, partly chosen on the federal principle"; and that the senators are chosen by the states legislatures.

If these facts are alleged for the purpose of proving that the powers of the general government were delegated by the state legislatures, he has not shown us, and I confess I do not perceive, their bearing on that point. If they are alleged to prove the separate existence of the states, he has very gravely demonstrated what every body knows, and what no body denies. He would be about as usefully employed in convincing us that we see with our eyes and hear with our ears.

The last fact on which the argument of Amphyction is founded is, that the constitution is to be amended by the legislatures of three fourths of the states, or by conventions of the same number of states, in the manner provided by the 5th article.

It is not true that the legislatures of the states can of themselves amend the constitution. They can only decide on those amendments which have previously been recommended to them by Congress. Or they may require Congress to call a convention of the people to propose amendments, which shall, at the discretion of Congress, be submitted to the state legislatures, or to conventions to be assembled in the respective states.

Were it untrue that the constitution confers on the state legislatures the power of making amendments, that would not prove that this power was delegated to them by themselves. The amendments would indeed be the act of the states, but the original would still be the act of the people.

I have now reviewed the first number of Amphyction; and will only add my regrets that a gentleman whose claims to our respect appear to be by no means inconsiderable should manifest such excessive hostility to the powers necessary for the preservation of the Union, as to arraign with such bitterness the opinion of the supreme court on an interesting constitutional question, either for doctrines not to be found in it, or on principles totally repugnant to the words of the constitution, and to the recorded facts respecting its adoption.

A FRIEND TO THE UNION.

Printed, *The Union. United States' Gazette and True American* (Philadelphia), 24 [and 28] Apr. 1819 (see nn. 5, 8); reprinted in *Gazette and Alexandria Daily Advertiser*, 15, 17 May 1819.

1. This and the following piece are responses to the two numbers of "Amphictyon" (William Brockenbrough), published in the Richmond *Enquirer* on 30 Mar. and 2 Apr. 1819. Amphictyon's essays are reprinted in Gunther, *Marshall's Defense*, 52–77.

2. In Greek mythology, a three-headed dog that guards the gates of Hades.

3. The Nereide, Opinion, 11 Mar. 1815 (9 Cranch 388). JM delivered the opinion of the Court, with Justices Johnson and Story giving separate concurring opinions.

4. Olivera v. Union Insurance Company, 3 Wheat. 183 (1818). In delivering the opinion of the Court, JM noted that "much diversity of opinion has prevailed" among the judges, whose positions he then summarized. Story, though convinced the decision was wrong, was persuaded by Washington not to dissent in this case. He agreed "that the habit of delivering dissenting opinions on ordinary occasions weakens the authority of the Court, and is of no public benefit" (3 Wheat. 195; Story to Wheaton, 8 Apr. 1818, Story, *Life and Letters*, I, 303–4).

5. At this point the *Union* editor transposed JM's manuscript, inserting a section of the second "Friend to the Union" essay. The continuation of the first number was inserted in the midst of the second number, published in the 28 Apr. issue.

6. Amphictyon concluded his first number with a long extract from James Madison's *Report of the Committee to Whom Was Committed the Proceedings of Sundry of the Other States, in Answer to the Resolutions of the General Assembly* . . . (Richmond, Va., [1800]; Evans #38961). Much of this report is reproduced in Marvin Meyers, ed., *The Mind of the Founder: Sources of the Political Thought of James Madison* (rev. ed.; Hanover, N.H., 1981), 229–73.

7. In the Alexandria *Gazette* reprint, the first number ends here.

8. At this point the text of the first number picks up again in the 24 Apr. issue of the *Union*.

A Friend to the Union
No. II

MR. EDITOR,   [28 April 1819]

The second errour supposed by Amphyction to be contained in the opinion of the Supreme Court is: "That the grant of powers to Congress which may be *necessary and proper* to carry into execution, the other powers granted to them or to any department of the government, ought to be construed in a liberal rather than a restricted sense."

For the sake of accuracy I will observe that the Supreme Court has not said that this grant ought to be construed in a "liberal sense"; although it has certainly denied that it ought to be construed in that "restricted sense" for which Amphyction contends. If by the term "liberal sense" is intended an extension of the grant beyond the fair and usual import of the words, the principle is not to be found in the opinion we are examining.

There is certainly a medium between that restricted sense which confines the meaning of words to narrower limits than the common understanding of the world affixes to them, and that extended sense which would stretch them beyond their obvious import. There is a fair construction which gives to language the sense in which it is used, and interprets an instrument according to its true intention. It is this medium, this fair construction that the Supreme Court has taken for its guide. No passage can, I think, be extracted from the opinion, which recognises a different rule; and the passages are numerous which recognise this. In commenting on the omission of the word "expressly" in the 10th amendment, the court says: "Thus leaving the question whether the particular power which may become the subject of contest, has been delegated to the one government or prohibited to the other, to depend on a fair construction of the whole instrument.["] So too, in all the reasoning on the word "necessary," the court does not, in a single instance, claim the aid of a "latitudinous," or "liberal" construction; but relies, decided and confidently, on its true meaning, "taking into view the subject, the context, and the intention of the framers of the constitution."

Ought any other rule to have been adopted?

Amphyction answers this question in the affirmative. This word, he contends, and indeed all the words of the constitution, ought to be understood in a restricted sense; and for not adopting his rule, the Supreme Court has drawn upon itself his heaviest censure.

The contest, then, so far as profession goes, is between[1] the fair sense of the words used in the constitution, and a restricted sense. The opinion professes to found itself on the fair interpretation. Amphyction professes to condemn that opinion because it ought to have adopted the restricted interpretation.

The counsel for the state of Maryland had contended that the clause authorizing Congress "to pass all laws *necessary and proper* to carry into execution" the various powers vested in the government, restrained the power which Congress would otherwise have possessed; and the reasoning of Amphyction would seem to support the same proposition.

This question is of real importance to the people of the United States. If the rule contended for would not absolutely arrest the progress of the government, it would certainly deny to those who administer it the means of executing its acknowledged powers in the manner most advantageous to those for whose benefit they were conferred.

To determine whether the one course or the other be most consistent with the constitution, and with the public good, let the principles laid down by the counsel for the state of Maryland, as stated in the opinion of the court, and the principles of Amphyction as stated by himself, be examined, and compared with the reasoning which has been so bitterly execrated.

The counsel for the state of Maryland, as we are informed, contended that the word "necessary" limits the right of Congress to pass laws for the execution of the specifick powers granted by the constitution "to such as are indispensable, and without which the power would be nugatory, that it excludes the choice of means, and leaves to Congress in each case that only which is most direct and simple."

Amphyction contends that necessary means "are those means *without which* the end *could not* be obtained." "When a law is about to pass, the inquiry," he says, "which ought to be made by Congress is, does the constitution expressly grant the power? If not, then, is this law one *without which* some power *cannot* be executed? If it is not, then it is a power reserved to the states, or to the people, and we may not use the means, nor pass the law."

With some variety of expression, the position maintained in the argument of the cause, and that maintained by Amphyction, are the same. Both contend that Congress can pass no laws to carry into execution their specifick powers, but such as are *indispensably* necessary; that they can employ no means but those *without which* the end *could not* be obtained.

Let us apply this rule to some of the powers delegated to the government.

Congress has power to lay and collect taxes.

According to the opinion of the Supreme Court, Congress may exercise this power in the manner most beneficial to the people, and may adopt those regulations which are adapted to the object, and will best accomplish it. But according to Amphyction, the inquiry must always be, whether the particular regulation be one *without which* the power *could not* be executed. If the power could be executed in any other way, the law is, in his opinion, unconstitutional.

Look at our tax laws. Observe their complex and multifarious regulations. All of them, no doubt, useful and conducing directly to the end; all of them essential to the beneficial exercise of the power. But how many may be indispensably necessary; how many may be such that without them the tax *could not* be collected, it is probable that neither Amphyction nor myself can say. In some of the laws imposing internal taxes, the collector is directed to advertise certain places of meeting, at which certain acts are to be performed; and those who do not attend and perform those acts are subject to an increased tax. Is this regulation indispensable to the collection of the tax? It is certainly proper and convenient; but who will deny that the tax may be collected without it?

In almost every conceivable case, there is more than one mode of accomplishing the end. Which, or is either, indispensable to that end? Congress, for example, may raise armies; but we are told they can execute this power only by those means which are indispensably necessary; those without which the army could not be raised. Is a bounty proposed? Congress must inquire whether a bounty be absolutely necessary? Whether it be possible to raise an army without it? If it be possible, the bounty, on this theory, is unconstitutional.

Undoubtedly there are other means for raising an army. Men may enlist without a bounty; and if they will not, they may be drafted. A bounty, then, according to Amphyction, is unconstitutional, because the power may be executed by a draft; and a draft is unconstitutional, because the power may be executed by a bounty.

So too, Congress may provide for calling out the militia; and this power may be executed by requisitions on the governours, by direct requisitions on the militia, or, perhaps, by receiving volunteers. According to the reasoning of Amphyction, no one of these modes can be constitutional, because no one of them is indispensably necessary.

Every case presents a choice of means. Every end may be attained by different means. Of no one of these means can it be truly said, that, "*without it*, the end *could not* be attained."

The rule then laid down by Amphyction is an impracticable, and consequently an erroneous rule.

If we examine the example he has adduced for its illustration, we shall find that, instead of sustaining, it disproves his proposition. The example is this: "Where lands are let by one man to another at the will of the lessor, and the lessor[2] sows the land, and the lessee,[3] after it is sown and before the corn is ripe, put him out, yet the lessor[4] shall have the corn, and shall have *free entry ingress, and regress, to cut, and carry away the corn.*"[5]

The right to the crop growing on the land when the lessor determines the estate, is an incident which the law, with much justice, annexes to a tenancy at will, but is not indispensable to its existence. To this right is annexed as a necessary incident, the power of carrying away the crop. The transportation of the crop then becomes the end for which entry into the land is allowed, and the mode of transportation, the means by which that end is to be accomplished. Has the tenant the choice of means, or can he use that mode of conveyance only without which the crop cannot be carried away? A crop may be removed by employing men only, by employing men and horses, by employing horses and carts, or by employing wagons. In some instances it may be removed by land or by water. Has the person entitled to the crop, and exercising this power of conveyance, his choice of means? or may the landlord say to him, whatever mode of conveyance he may adopt, this is not indispensably necessary; you might have conveyed away the crop by other means? Undoubtedly the person allowed to carry away his crop, would not be permitted to throw down the fences, trample the enclosed fields, and trespass at will on the landholder. But he has the choice of "appropriate" means for the removal of his property, and may use that which he thinks best.

This example then might very well have been put by the court, as an apt illustration of the rule avowed in their opinion.

The rule which Amphyction gives us, for the construction of the constitution, being obviously erroneous, let us examine that which is laid down by the Supreme Court.

The Court concludes a long course of reasoning which completely demonstrates the falacy of the construction made by the counsel for the state of Maryland, and now adopted by Amphyction, by stating its own opinion in these words: "We think the sound construction of the constitution must allow to the national legislature that discretion with respect to the means by which the powers it confers are to be carried into execution, which will enable that body to perform the high duties assigned to it, in the manner most beneficial to the people. Let the end be legitimate, let it be within the scope of the constitution, and all means which are appropriate, which are plainly adapted to that end, which are not prohibited, but consistent with the letter and spirit of the constitution, are constitutional."

To this rule of construction, unless it be itself grossly misconstrued, I can perceive no objection. I think, as the Supreme Court has thought, that it would be the proper rule, were the grant which has been the subject of so much discussion, expunged from the constitution.

It is a palpable misrepresentation of the opinion of the court to say, or to insinuate that it considers the grant of a power "to pass all laws necessary and proper for carrying into execution" the powers vested in the government, as augmenting those powers, and as one which is to be construed "latitudinously," or even "liberally."

It is to be recollected that the counsel for the state of Maryland had contended that this clause was to be construed as restraining and limit-

ing that choice of means which the national legislature would otherwise possess. The reasoning of the court is opposed to this argument,
and is concluded with this observation: "The result of the most careful
and attentive consideration bestowed upon this clause is, that, if it does
not enlarge, it cannot be construed to restrain the powers of congress,
or to impair the rights of the legislature to exercise its best judgement
in the selection of measures to carry into execution the constitutional
powers of the government. If no other motive for its insertion can be
suggested, a sufficient one is found in the desire to remove all doubt
respecting the right to legislate on that vast mass of incidental powers
which must be involved in the constitution, if that instrument be not a
splendid bauble."

The court then has not contended that this grant enlarges, but that it
does not restrain the powers of Congress; and I believe every man who
reads the opinion will admit that the demonstration of this proposition
is complete. It is so complete that Amphyction himself does not venture directly to controvert the conclusion, although the whole course of
his reasoning seems intended to weaken the principles from which it is
drawn. His whole argument appears to be intended to prove that this
clause does restrain congress in the execution of all the powers conferred by the constitution, to those "means *without which* the end *could
not* be obtained." Thus converting an apparent grant of power into a
limitation of power.[6]

The court has said, and I repeat it, that the constitution and laws of
the United States abound with evidence demonstrating the erreour of
this construction. I have already stated some instances in which this
rule must be discarded; and I will now refer to others which were
selected by the court, the aptness of which Amphyction denies.

I will pass over the acts requiring an oath of office, because Amphyction seems half disposed to admit there is something in that particular
example, and will proceed to some of those which he pronounces totally inapplicable.

Congress possesses power "to establish post offices, and post roads."
Amphyction says that the right to carry the mail, and to punish those
who rob it, are necessary incidents to this power. I admit it. But who
does not perceive that, in making this assertion, he abandons his own
interpretation of the word "necessary" and adopts that of the supreme
court? Let us apply his rule to the case. Let us suppose a bill before
congress to punish those who rob the mail. The inquiry is, he says:
"Does the constitution expressly grant the power?" The answer must
be in the negative. There is no express power to carry the mail, nor to
punish those who rob it. The member is next to ask: "Is this law one
without which the power cannot be executed?" That is, can a post office
and a post road be established, without an act of Congress for the
punishment of those who rob the mail? The plain common sense of

every man will answer this question in the affirmative. These powers were divided under the confederation. Then the conclusion of the member must be, this right to punish those who rob the mail "is a power reserved to the states, or to the people, and we may not use the means, nor pass the law. Then the state legislature may pass laws to punish those who rob the mail, but congress cannot. Post offices and post roads may be established without such a law, and therefore the power to pass it is reserved to the states." Adopt the construction of Amphyction, and this conclusion is inevitable.

Let the question be on the right of Congress to pass an act for the punishment of those who falsify a record.

The power is to ordain and establish inferior courts, the judges of which shall hold their offices during good behaviour, and receive as a compensation for their services, salaries which shall not be diminished during their continuance in office. The second section defines the extent of the judicial power.

Is a law to punish those who falsify a record, one without which a court cannot be established, or one without which a court cannot exercise its functions? We know that under the confederation Congress had the power to establish, and did establish certain courts, and, had not the power to pass laws for the punishment of those who should falsify its records. Unquestionably such a law is "needful," "requisite," "essential," "conducive to," the due administration of justice; but no man can say it is one without which courts cannot decide causes, or without which it is physically impossible for them to perform their functions. According to the rule of Amphyction then, such a law cannot be enacted by Congress, but may be enacted by the state legislatures.

It would be tedious to go through all the examples put by the supreme court. They are all of the same character, and show, conclusively, that the principles maintained by the counsel for the state of Maryland, and by Amphyction, would essentially change the constitution, render the government of the Union incompetent to the objects for which it was instituted, and place all its powers under the control of the state legislatures. It would, in a great measure, reinstate the old confederation.

It cannot escape any attentive observer that Amphyction's strictures on the opinion of the supreme court, are founded on a total and obvious perversion of the plain meaning of that opinion, as well as on a misconstruction of the constitution. He occasionally substitutes words not used by the court, and employs others, neither in the connexion, nor in the sense, in which they are employed by the court, so as to ascribe to the opinion sentiments which it does not merely not contain, but which it excludes. The court does not say that the word "necessary" means whatever may be 'convenient,' or 'useful.' And when it uses "conducive to," that word is associated with others plainly showing that no remote, no distant conduciveness to the object, is in the mind of the court.

With as little remorse as the Procrustes of ancient fable stretched and lopped limbs in order to fit travellers to his bed does Amphyction extend and contract the meaning of words in the constitution, and in the opinion of the court, in order to accommodate those papers to his strictures. Thus, he says, if Congress should impose a tax on Land, "it would be extremely *convenient*, and a very *appropriate* measure, and very *conducive* to their purpose of collecting this tax speedily, and promptly, if the state governments could be prohibited during the same year from laying & collecting a land tax. Were they to pass such a law and thereby directly encroach on one of the most undoubted rights of the states, the present liberal and sweeping construction of the clause by the Supreme court would justify the measure."

Now I deny that a law prohibiting the state legislatures from imposing a land tax would be an "appropriate" means, or any means whatever, to be employed in collecting the tax of the United States. It is not an instrument to be so employed. It is not a means "plainly adapted," or "conducive to" the end. The passage of such an act would be an attempt on the part of Congress, "under the pretext of executing its powers, to pass laws for the accomplishment of objects not intrusted to the government." So far is the construction given to this clause by the supreme court from being so "liberal & sweeping" as to "justify the measure" that the opinion expressly rejects it. Let its language be quoted. "That the power of taxation is one of vital importance; that it is retained by the states; that it is to be concurrently exercised by the two governments, are truths, says the opinion, which have never been denied." The court afterwards quotes a passage from the Federalist in which this construction is urged vehemently as an objection to the constitution itself, and obviously approves the argument against it.

Many laborious criticisms would be avoided; if those who are disposed to condemn a paper, would take the trouble to read, with a disposition to understand, it.

I shall not notice the various imaginary and loose opinions which Amphyction has collected, or suggested, because they are not imputable to the supreme court. I content myself with exposing *some* of his errours in construing the constitution, and in ascribing to the opinion he condemns, doctrines which it does not contain.

I cannot however avoid remarking that Amphyction himself, as soon as he has closed his stricture on the supreme court, seems to desert his own construction and take up their's. "I think it clear," he says, "that the intention of the constitution was to confer on Congress the power of resorting to such means as are incidental to the express powers; to such means as directly and necessarily tend to produce the desired effect." How much more, let me ask, has been said by the supreme court?

That court has said: "Let the end be legitimate, let it be within the scope of the constitution, and all means which are appropriate, which are plainly adapted to that end, which are not prohibited," "are constitutional." The word "appropriate," if Johnson be authority, means "peculiar," ["]consigned to some particular use or person,"—"belonging peculiarly."

Let the constructive words used by the supreme court, in this their acknowledged sense, be applied to any of the powers of Congress. Take for example, that of raising armies. The court has said that "all means which are appropriate," that is "all means which are peculiar" to raising armies, which are "consigned to that particular use," which "belong peculiarly" to it, all means which are, "plainly adapted" to the end, are constitutional.

If Amphyction is better pleased with his own language, I shall not contest its right to the preference; but what essential difference is there between "means which directly and necessarily tend to produce the desired effect," and means which "belong peculiarly" to the production of that effect? I acknowledge that I perceive none. Means which are "appropriate," which are "plainly adapted" to the end, must "directly and necessarily tend to produce" it. The difference however between these means, and those *without which* the effect *cannot* be produced, must be discerned by the most careless observer.

Let us apply these different definitions of the words, to any the most common affairs of human life. A leases to B a mill for a number of years on a contract that A shall receive half the profits, and shall pay half the expenses of all the machinery which B may erect therein, and which shall be *"necessary and proper"* for the manufacture of flower. Pending this lease, the elevator and hopper boy are invented, and applied, with great advantage, to the manufacture of flower. B erects them in his mill. A is very well satisfied with receiving the increased profits, but is unwilling to pay half the expense of the machinery, because, as he alleges, it was not *"necessary"* to the manufacture of flower. All will admit that this machinery is "appropriate, and plainly adapted to the end"; or, in the words of Amphyction, that it "directly and necessarily tends to produce the desired effect." But none can think it so indispensably necessary that the end *cannot* be produced *without* it. The end was produced, flower was manufactured, before the elevator and hopper boy were invented.

The same may be observed of the cotton machine of the south, of the use of Gypsum on a farm, of many things which occur in the ordinary transactions of human life.

It will be readily perceived in every case, that this rule of construction, which seems to have escaped Amphyction in a moment when the particular object of his essay was out of view, and that contained in the opinion he condemns, are precisely the same; and are both in direct opposition to that other restricted rule by which he tries the reasoning of the supreme court.

If, as I think all will admit, that construction of the words in which Amphyction and the court concur, furnish the true rule for construing the words "*necessary and proper*" in a contract between man & man, how much more certainly must it be the true rule for construing a constitution—an instrument the nature of which excludes the possibility of inserting in it an enumeration of the means of executing its specifick powers. If this rule be applicable to the relations between individuals, how much more applicable must it be to the relations between the people and their representatives, who are elected for the very purpose of selecting the best means of executing the powers of the government they are chosen to administer.[7]

I have confined my observations to the reasoning of the Supreme Court, and have taken no notice of the conclusion drawn from it, because the essays I am reviewing make no objections to the latter, but denounce the former as false and dangerous. I think, on the contrary, I hazard nothing when I assert that the reasoning is less doubtful than the conclusion. I myself concur in the conclusion; but I do not fear contradiction from any fair minded and intelligent man when I say that the principles laid down by the court for the construction of the constitution may all be sound, and yet the act for incorporating the Bank be unconstitutional. But if the act, be constitutional, the principles laid down by the court must be sound. I defy Amphyction, I defy any man, to furnish an argument which shall, at the same time, prove the Bank to be constitutional, and the reasoning of the court to be erroneous. Why then is Amphyction so delicate on the constitutionality of the law, while he is vehement and strenuous in his exertions to rouse the nation against the court? If we do not account for this by saying that the court is less popular, and therefore more vulnerable, than the executive and the legislature, how shall we account for it?

Before I conclude let me ask this gentleman and those who think with him, what train of reasoning would have satisfied him and them? The court did not volunteer in this business. The question was brought before them, and they could not escape it. What course then does Amphyction think they ought to have adopted? Does he think they ought to have declared the law unconstitutional and void? He does not say so; and we are not permitted to draw this inference from what he does say. After lamenting that *seriatim* opinions were not delivered, he supposes what might have been the opinions of Judges concurring in the decision, but dissenting from the reasoning, delivered by the Chief Justice. "Some of them" he says, "may have believed that it was for Congress to have judged of that necessity and propriety, and having exercised their undoubted functions in so deciding, that it was not consistent with judicial modesty to say there was no such necessity, and thus to arrogate to themselves a right of putting their *veto* upon a law.["]

Again, he says: "It may however be asked, whether I can at this day pretend to argue against the constitutionality of a bank established by Congress? In answer, I reply that it is not my intention by these remarks to bring that subject into discussion. I am willing to acquiesce in this particular case, so long as the charter continues without being violated—because it has been repeatedly argued before Congress, and not only in 1791 but in 1815, was solemnly decided in favour of the measure."

Let us suppose that the court had supported its decision by the reasoning which Amphyction conjectures may have influenced some of the Judges whom he does not appear inclined to censure, or by that which he adopts for himself. Suppose the court had said: "Congress has judged of the necessity and propriety of this measure, and having exercised their undoubted functions in so deciding, it is not consistent with judicial modesty to say there is no such necessity, and thus to arrogate to ourselves the right of putting our *veto* upon a law."

Or suppose the court, after hearing a most elaborate and able argument on the constitutionality of the law, had said: "It is not our intention to bring that subject into discussion. We are willing to acquiesce in this particular case so long as the charter continues without being violated—because it has been repeatedly argued before Congress, and not only in 1791, but in 1815, was solemnly decided against the measure."

Would this reasoning have satisfied, or ought it to have satisfied the publick? Would Amphyction himself be content with the declaration of the Supreme Court that, on any question concerning the constitutionality of an act, it is enough to say, "it is not consistent with judicial modesty" to contradict the opinion of Congress, and "thus to arrogate to themselves the right of putting their *veto* upon a law" or that "they are willing to acquiesce" in the particular act, "because it has been repeatedly argued before Congress, and not only in 1791, but in 1815," or at some other time since 1801, "was solemnly decided in favour of the measure?"

But if, as we must believe was the fact in this case, because it was so stated by the Judges, the court should be "unanimously and decidedly of opinion that the law is constitutional," would it comport with their honour, with their duty, or with truth, to insinuate an opinion that Congress had violated the constitution? If it would not, then was it incumbent on the court in this case, to pursue, not the course marked out by Amphyction but that which he censures. It was incumbent on them to state their real opinion and their reasons for it. Those reasons, I am persuaded, require only to be read with fairness and with attention to be approved.

A FRIEND TO THE UNION.

Printed, *The Union. United States' Gazette and True American* (Philadelphia), 28 [and 24] Apr. 1819 (see nn. 1, 5); reprinted in *Gazette and Alexandria Daily Advertiser*, 17, 18 May 1819.

1. Because of the erroneous transposing of JM's manuscript, the following section of the second number appeared in the 24 Apr. issue, inserted in the middle of the first number.

2. This should be "lessee."

3. This should be "lessor."

4. This should be "lessee."

5. The quotation is based on a passage from Edward Coke, *The First Part of the Institutes of the Laws of England; or, A Commentary upon Littleton . . .* , I, (16th ed.; London, 1809), 56a.

6. In the Alexandria *Gazette* reprint, the second number ends here. The remainder of the second number as published in the Philadelphia *Union* constitutes the third number of the reprint.

7. At this point the text of the second "Friend of the Union" essay picks up again in the 28 Apr. issue.

To Joseph Story

My dear Sir   Richmond Apl. 28th. 1819.
To day on my return from a tour to our upper country I had the pleasure of receiving your favor of the 16th. inst.[1] I thank you very sincerely for the attention you have paid to the opinion in the case of the Dartmouth College & shall be obliged by your making the correction you propose. I would myself prefer that it should stand as you suggest; but were it otherwise, your opinion in a case on which I felt no particular solicitude, would be decisive with me.

Although I entirely approve the erasure of the words you propose to omit I will state to you, meerly as an excuse for having inserted them the thought which passed over my mind at the time.

The expression that a legislature might perform some judicial functions was carelessly introduced, but was introduced with a view to the prohibitions on the states contained in the constitution of the United States, not with a view to the interior regulations made by state constitutions. My idea was that it was entirely a subject for state regulation with which the courts of the United States could have no concern. I had understood that in Rhode Island & Connecticut the legislature or some branch of it exercised certain judicial powers, & I knew that in New York their senate was like the House of Lords in England a court of Dernier resort. Be this as it may I am happy that you have adverted to the subject & hope it will not be too late to omit the words to which you object.[2]

The opinion in the Bank case has brought into operation the whole antifederal spirit of Virginia. Some latent feelings which have been working ever since the decision of Martin & Hunter have found vent on this occasion, & are working most furiously. The sin of the court is thought much more hienou[s] than that of Congress or the President. The offence would have been equally great had we pronounced the law unconstitutional. They would have been more merciful had we said simply that it was for the legislature to decide on the necessity & not for the court &c.

I condole with you sincerely on the severe affliction with which you have been visited.[3] It is one of those wounds which time will heal & for which, while green, occupation furnishes the best salve. I speak from repeated experience.

Farewell. With much esteem & rega⟨rd⟩, I am dear Sir your obed⟨t⟩

J MARSHALL

ALS, Berg Collection, NN. Addressed to Story in Salem, Mass.; postmarked Richmond, 29 Apr. MS stained where seal was placed.

1. Letter not found.

2. In the absence of the original draft, the precise line of argument in the omitted passage cannot be recovered. These remarks might have been inserted in an early section of the opinion, in which JM conceded that the contract clause was not intended to restrict the states from regulating their civil institutions.

3. Story's six-year-old daughter, Caroline Wetmore Story, had died on 1 Apr. (Story, *Life and Letters*, I, 332).

To Bushrod Washington

My dear Sir   Richmond Apl. 28th 1819

I left this place the day after I wrote to you & did not return till to day. I cannot account for the inaccuracy you state otherwise than by supposing that I read the latter part of the sentence under an impression that instead of the word "*deny*" in the former part some affirmative word had been used & the correction was made in a hurry without taking time to examine the whole sentence. Undoubtedly the alteration you mention ought to be made. I hope you have made it. If not I wish Mr. Bronson to publish the correction. If you have left Philadelphia write to him.

I have received the receipts you mention & thank you for your attention. Your

J M

ALS, Marshall Papers, ViW. Addressed to Washington in Alexandria, Va., "care of Mr Herbert" and marked "If Mr. Washington has not returned/from Philadelphia the post master/will please to forward this immediately/to that place"; postmarked Richmond, 28 Apr. Endorsed by Washington.

To Bushrod Washington

My dear Sir   Richmond May 6th. 1819

I have given you a great deal of trouble to very little purpose, & am now about to add to it, perhaps to as little. Our friend Mr. Bronson has made a curious piece of work of the essays he was requested to publish. He has cut out the middle of the first number to be inserted into the middle of the second; & to show his perfect impartiality, has cut out the middle of the second number to be inserted in the first. He has thrown these disrupted parts together without the least regard to their fitness & made a curious mixture—a sort of Olla podrida,[1] which, however good the ingredients may be, when compounded as he has compounded them, are rather nauseous to the intellectual palate.

It is understood that this subject is not to drop. A very serious effort is undoubtedly making to have it taken up in the next legislature. It is said that some other essays written by a very great man are now preparing & will soon appear.[2] On this account I am desirous that the answer to Amphyction should appear in its true shape & will be obliged to you to have it republished in the Alexandria paper.[3] I will give the instructions which I will thank you to copy & furnish with the papers I now send containing those essays marked—to the editor.

Without any remark on the errors committed in the original publication—state it as taken from the union.[4] Omit the letter to the editors & begin where the essay No. 1 begins. Continue to the mark in the third column of the first page of No. 1 (paper of Apl. 28) to the words "would seem to be," inclusive, in about the 13th. line of that column. Then proceed with what is misplaced in the second number (paper May 1st.) at the mark in the first column in the 6th. paragraph with the words "a meer historical fact" &c. & continue to the mark in the third column & end of the 10th. paragraph at the words "states legislatures" inclusive. Then return to the paper of Apl. 28 to the mark in the second column of the second page the beginning of the fifth paragraph & proceed with the words "This fact is stated in the opinion" &c to the end of the essay. These pieces form the first number.

The second number begins properly in the paper of the first of May. Continue it to the mark in the sixth paragraph of the first column to the words "goes, is between," inclusive. Then return to the first number to the mark in the 3d. column of the first page the second paragraph & proceed with the words "the fair sens⟨e of⟩ the words used in the constitution" &c & continue ⟨to the⟩ word "administer" at the end of the 4th. parag⟨raph⟩ in the second column of the second page. Then go to the mark in the 3d. column of the second number & begin at that mark with the words "I have confined" &c which commence the 11th. paragraph of that column. Continue to the end. These disjointed parts form the second number.

These directions are formed from the country paper. Your

J M

ALS, Marshall Papers, DLC. Addressed to Washington in Alexandria, Va., and marked "To remain till Judge/Washington returns from Philadelphia"; postmarked Richmond, 7 May. Endorsed by Washington. MS torn where seal was broken.

1. A highly seasoned stew of meat and vegetables, a traditional Spanish dish.

2. Roane's "Hampden" essays appeared in the Richmond *Enquirer* on 11, 15, 18, and 22 June.

3. The corrected "A Friend to the Union" essays were republished as three numbers in the *Gazette and Alexandria Daily Advertiser* on 15, 17, and 18 May.

4. The two numbers of "A Friend to the Union" were published in the daily edition of the Philadelphia *Union* on 24 and 28 Apr. and in the semiweekly "country" edition on 28 Apr. and 1 May. JM's instructions refer to the country edition.

From Joseph Story

[15 May 1819]

Extract of a letter from Mr Story

I have waited some time with the hope to obtain a specific description of the machines used in this state for making nails & to accompany it with the prices of each for the exact information of your friend.[1] I have been disappointed thus far, not from any difficulty in communicating the information, but from that natural tendency to postpone business that possesses no interest to the parties, which prevails here as every where else. I have therefore thought it best to state to you the machines in use here with the prices which are now usually paid for them.

The nail machines invented by Mr. Perkins are used very extensively at the Amesbury Factory in this neighborhood & are adapted to large establishments.[2] They cost about $1000 a piece. The nail machines of Mr. Reed are in more general use. He has two patents for different machines.[3] The most perfect can be bought for about $400; but Mr. Reed has no authority as I understand to sell one for use in the southern states as he has disposed of the patent right for the southern states to some gentleman there. The other machine invented by Mr. Reed is very good & cuts very good nails & I understand can now be bought for $200, although until recently the price was much higher. Each of these machines can be adapted to cut nails of any size; but they are liable to get out of order, & require a skilful hand to manage & repair them—At least this is the information that I derive from two gentlemen who have been superintendents of two factories for several years with which they are however no longer connected. I cannot learn that there are any other nail machines in use among us; and none are spoken of as lower in price than that I have stated. There are machines for making brads which however are generally used on a large scale.

I am sorry that this information is so imperfect but it is as exact as I could get after some considerable enquiries. Mr. Webster, through whom I have made some enquiries in Boston, writes me that a Mr. Odiorne who is possessed of Reeds patent in Boston will sell one machine fit for use for $200.[4] This is the least expensive machine as he writes me, & is below the usual price, & is the machine in powerful operation in various places. It could be shipped direct from Boston to Richmond.

Copy (in JM's hand), Marshall Papers, ViW. Addressed by JM to Jaquelin B. Harvie. Date established by JM to Story, 27 May 1819.

1. See JM to Story, 24 Mar. 1819 and n. 2.

2. Jacob Perkins (1766–1849) of Newburyport, Mass., had invented a machine to cut and head nails, obtaining his first patent in 1794. A prolific inventor, Perkins moved to England in 1818, where he set up an engraving business and conducted experiments to improve steam engines. On Perkins and the Amesbury Nail Factory, see J. Leander Bishop, *A History of American Manufacturers from 1608 to 1800* (3 vols.; 1868; New York, 1966 reprint), I, 492–93; Greville Bathe and Dorothy Bathe, *Jacob Perkins, His Inventions, His Times, and His Contemporaries* (Philadelphia, 1943), 13–21.

3. On Jesse Reed of Bridgewater, Mass., see Bishop, *History of American Manufacturers*, I, 488; Bathe and Bathe, *Jacob Perkins*, 177–78; Odiorne v. Amesbury Nail Factory, 18 Fed. Cas. 578 (U.S. Cir. Ct., Mass., 1819).

4. See JM to Story, 24 Mar. 1819 and n. 3. George Odiorne was a partner in a Boston nail store and held one of Reed's patents. Webster advised him in a lawsuit against the Amesbury Nail Factory concerning that patent. As it happened, this suit was heard by Story at the term of the federal circuit court in Boston commencing the day he wrote this letter (Charles M. Wiltse and Harold D. Moser, eds., *The Papers of Daniel Webster: Correspondence*, I [Hanover, N.H., 1974], 89, 90; *The Boston Directory*... [Boston, 1820], 159; Andrew J. King, ed., *The Papers of Daniel Webster: Legal Papers*, III [Hanover, N.H., 1989], pt. 2, p. 826; Odiorne v. Amesbury Nail Factory, 18 Fed. Cas. 578 [U.S. Cir. Ct., Mass., 1819]).

To Joseph Story

My dear Sir   Richmond May 27th. 1819

I had the pleasure of receiving a few days past your favour of the 15th. & thank you very sincerely for the information you have given respecting the nail machines in use in your country. The information will be valuable to my friend.

I am much obliged by the alterations you have made in the opinion in the Dartmouth college case, & am highly gratified by what you say respecting it. The opinion in the Bank case continues to be denounced by the democracy in Virginia. An effort is certainly making to induce the legislature which will meet in December to take up the subject & to pass resolutions not very unlike those which were called forth by the alien & sedition laws in 1799. Whether the effort will be successful or not may perhaps depend in some measure on the sentiments of our sister states. To excite this ferment the opinion has been grossly misrepresented; and where its argument has been truely stated it has been met by principles one would think too palpably absurd for inteligent men. But prejudice will swallow anything. If the principles which have been advanced on this occasion were to prevail, the constitution would be converted into the old confederation. The piece to which you allude was not published in Virginia. Our patriotic papers admit no such political heresies. It contained I think a complete demonstration of the fallacies & errors contained in those attacks on the opinion of the court which have most credit here & are supposed to proceed from a high source, but was so mangled in the publication that those only who had bestowed close attention to the subject could understand it. There were two numbers & the Editor of the Union in Philadelphia the paper in which it was published, had mixed the different numbers together so as in several instances to place the reasoning intended to demonstrate one proposition under another. The points & the arguments were so separated from each other & so strangely mixed as to constitute a labyrinth to which those only who understood the whole subject perfectly could find a clue.

I wish to consult you on a case which to me who am not versed in admiralty proceedings has some difficulty. The Little Charles was libelled for a violation of the first embargo act in 1808. She was acquitted in the District but condemned in the circuit court. After a thousand delays a question is now before the circuit court as a court of Admiralty for judgement on the bond given on the property being restored. Several objections are made, two of which deserve consideration. The first is that the order for restitution w⟨as⟩ made, not in court, but by the Judge out of court not at a called cou⟨rt and⟩ second that the bond was taken by the marsh⟨al⟩ to himself & not the U.S. Upon this order the vessel was delivered & this bond has been returned to court but has not been acted on, Nor is there any act of the court approving the proceeding. It is contended to be a meer act *in pais* not sanctioned by the court. That it is the unauthorized act of the marshal who might release the bond or sue upon it; and that the court cannot consider it as in the place of the vessel & so act upon it.[1] With great regard & esteem I am dear Sir your Obedt

J MARSHALL

ALS, Story Papers, MHi. MS torn where seal was broken.

1. See JM's two opinions in U.S. v. Schooner Little Charles, 27 May 1818 and [ca. 22 Nov. 1819].

To Bushrod Washington

My dear Sir   May 31st. 1819

I received a few days past your letter inquiring whether the defence of the opinion had been correctly republished in the Alexandria paper.[1] I went to the coffee house for the purpose of reading it but the papers had been mislaid & I was disappointed. I cannot therefore say whether they have appeared in an inteligible shape or not & therefore am not desirous that any further effort should be made to get them before the public.

I have a case before me which depends entirely on the question whether the master of a vessel belonging to one port can hypothecate her in the port of a different state.[2] Is the port of one state a foreign port with respect to the vessel of a citizen of another state? Will you give me your opinion on this point? Your

J MARSHALL

ALS, Spencer Library, KU. Addressed to Washington at Mount Vernon; postmarked Richmond, 31 May. Endorsed by Washington.

1. Letter not found.
2. See Selden v. Hendrickson & Pryor, Opinion, [ca. 22 Nov. 1819].

To Basil Duke

Dear Sir:[1]   Richmond, June 8th., 1819

I have just returned from a visit to my sister Taylor in Petersburg who expressed a strong desire to see me respecting her affairs.[2] All her property was in bank stock and the difficulties which our Banks experience are such that they will probably make no dividends for some time to come. She looks anxiously for relief to her property in the western country and complains heavily of being unable to receive any satisfactory intelligence respecting it. She says some money has been for several years in the hands of Mr. Marshall[3] and she knows not how to get it from him. She told me some time past that after permitting her to leave Kentucky without suggesting anything to her on the subject, he required some security respecting the purchase money, in the event of a better title appearing, before he could part with it. I wrote to him and to you offering to become security and declaring my readiness to execute any writing which might be deemed necessary.[4] As I do not know what instrument is required, and am not well enough acquainted with the subject to prepare one, and as that letter bound me as much as any bond, I did hope all difficulty would be removed, or at any rate that such a bond as would be satisfactory would be sent to me. I have never heard a syllable on the subject and my sister informs me that she cannot receive her money nor hear anything respecting it. Will you, my dear sir, have the goodness to explain this affair to me and to say what is wanting? If the money can be received my sister could wish that 3 or 400$ might be paid to Doctor Marshall for the use of Tom Taylor.[5] If anything further from me is necessary you will greatly oblige my sister by sending in the bond which is to be executed, that I may put an end to this business. I beg you to give me explicit information.

She also says that she has some other property in that country which she wishes to sell and that you say it has not been sold because a division has not taken place. Will you have the goodness to say what is necessary to be done on her part to procure a division? or whether the undivided interest might be sold?

My sister says a Colonel or Major Bullock has some business of hers in his hands. Can you tell me where he resides?

Excuse this trouble. My sister's situation is such as to require that she should speedily command her resources, which ought not to have been so long with-held from her. I am, dear Sir, with much esteem, Your obed't

J. MARSHALL

Tr (typescript), Collection of Thomas W. Bullitt, Louisville, Ky; Marshall Papers, DLC. Inside address to Duke in Washington, Ky.

1. Duke was the widowed husband of JM's sister Charlotte (JM to Martin Marshall, 24 May 1817 and n. 1).
2. Jane Marshall Taylor, widow of George Keith Taylor.
3. Apparently Humphrey Marshall, JM's cousin and brother-in-law.
4. Letters not found.
5. Dr. Louis Marshall was overseeing Thomas Taylor's education.

To Bushrod Washington

My dear Sir   Richmond June 17th 1819
The storm which has been for some time threatening the Judges has at length burst o⟨n⟩ their heads & a most serious hurricane it is. The author is spoken of with as much confidence as if his name was sub-

scribed to his essays. It is worth your while to read them. They are in the Enquirer under the signature of Hampden.

I find myself more stimulated on this subject than on any other because I beleive the design to be to injure the Judges & inpair the constitution. I have therefore thought of answering these essays & sending my pieces to you for publication in the Alexandria paper. I shall send them on in successive numbers but do not wish the first to be published till I shall have seen the last of Hampden. I will then write to you & request you to have the publications made immediately. As the numbers will be marked I hope no mistake will be made by the printer & that the manuscript will be given to the flame. I wish two papers of each number to be directed to T. Marshall, Oak hill Fauquier. I do not wish them to come to me lest some suspicion of the author should be created.

I send you a check for 30$ on account of my subscription to your society for colonization. I am not sure that Mr. Caldwell is in the city or I should send it to him.[1] Your

J MARSHALL

ALS, NHi. Addressed to Washington in Alexandria, Va.; postmarked Richmond, 17 June. Endorsed by Washington.

1. Washington was first president of the American Colonization Society, which was formed in Dec. 1816. Elias B. Caldwell, clerk of the Supreme Court, was secretary (P. J. Staudenraus, *The African Colonization Movement* [New York, 1961], 27–30).

To Bushrod Washington

[ca. 28 June 1819]

I expected These numbers would have concluded my answer to Hampden but I must write two others which will follow in a few days. If the publication has not commenced I could rather wish the signature to be changed to "A Constitutionalist." A Friend of the Constitution is so much like a Friend of the Union that it may lead to some suspicion of identity. It is however of no great consequence. I hope the publication has commenced unless the Editor should be unwilling to devote so much of his paper to this discussion. The letters of Amphyction & of Hampden have made no great impression in Richmond but they were designed for the country & have had considerable influence there. I wish the refutation to be in the hands of some respectable members of the legislature as it may prevent some act of the assembly ⟨that is?⟩ silly & wicked. If the publication be made I should ⟨wish?⟩ to have two or three sets of the papers to be used if necessary. I will settle with you for the printer.

AL, Marshall Papers, DLC. Addressed to Washington in Alexandria, Va.; postmarked Richmond, 28 June. Endorsed by Washington. MS torn where seal was broken.

A Friend of the Constitution
No. I

[30 June 1819]

If it be true that no rational friend of the constitution can wish to expunge from it the judicial department, it must be difficult for those who believe the prosperity of the American people to be inseparable from the preservation of this government, to view with indifference the systematic efforts which certain restless politicians of Virginia have been for some time making, to degrade that department in the estimation of the public.[1] It is not easy to resist the conviction that those efforts must have other and more dangerous objects, than merely to impair the confidence of the nation in the present judges.

The zealous and persevering hostility with which the constitution was originally opposed, cannot be forgotten. The deep rooted and vindictive hate, which grew out of unfounded jealousies, and was aggravated by defeat, though suspended for a time, seems never to have been appeased. The desire to strip the government of those effective powers, which enable it to accomplish the objects for which it was created; and, by construction, essentially to reinstate that miserable confederation, whose incompetency to the preservation of our union, the short interval between the treaty of Paris and the meeting of the general convention at Philadelphia, was sufficient to demonstrate, seems to have recovered all its activity. The leaders of this plan, like skilful engineers, batter the weakest part of the citadel, knowing well, that if that can be beaten down, and a breach effected, it will be afterwards found very difficult, if not impracticable, to defend the place. The judicial department, being without power, without patronage, without the legitimate means of ingratiating itself with the people, forms this weakest part; and is, at the same time, necessary to the very existence of the government, and to the effectual execution of its laws. Great constitutional questions are unavoidably brought before this department, and its decisions must sometimes depend on a course of intricate and abstruse reasoning, which it requires no inconsiderable degree of mental exertion to comprehend, and which may, of course, be grossly misrepresented. One of these questions, the case of McCullough against the state of Maryland, presents the fairest occasion for wounding mortally, the vital powers of the government, thro' its judiciary. Against the decision of the court, on this question, weighty interests & deep rooted prejudices are combined. The opportunity for the assault was too favorable not to be seized.

A writer in the Richmond Enquirer, under the signature of "Hampden," who is introduced to us by the editor, as holding "a pen equal to the great subject he has undertaken to discuss," after bestowing upon Congress in general, and some of its most respectable members in particular, language not much more decorous than that reserved for the judges, says, "The warfare waged by the judicial body has been of a bolder tone and character. It was not enough for them to sanction, in former times, the detestable doctrines of Pickering & Co. as aforesaid; it was not enough for them to annihilate the freedom of the press, by incarcerating all those who dared, with a manly freedom, to canvass the conduct of their public agents; it was not enough for the predecessors of the present judges to preach political sermons from the bench of justice, and bolster up the most unconstitutional measures of the most abandoned of our rulers; it did not suffice to do the business in detail, and ratify, one by one, the legislative infractions of the constitution. That process would have been too slow, and perhaps too troublesome. It was possible also, that some *Hampden* might make a stand against some ship money measure of the government, and, although he would lose his cause with the court, might ultimately gain it with the *people*. They resolved, therefore, to put down all discussions of the kind in future, by a judicial *coup de main*; to give a general letter of attorney to the future legislators of the union; and to tread under foot all those parts and articles of the constitution, which had been heretofore deemed to set limits to the power of the federal legislature."

Without stopping to enquire whether this ranting declamation, this rash impeachment of the integrity, as well as opinions of all those who have successively filled the judicial department, be intended to illustrate the diffidence with which this modest gentleman addresses his fellow citizens, and the just comparison he has made between "the smallness of his means and the greatness of his undertaking"; or to demonstrate his perfect possession of that temperate, chastened, and well disciplined mind, which is so favorable to the investigation of truth, and which so well fits him who instructs the public, for tasks in which he engages, I shall endeavor to follow him, and to notice the evidence and the arguments with which he attempts to justify this unqualified arraignment of all those who have been selected for the great duty of expounding our constitution and our laws.

But before I proceed to discuss the principles for which Hampden contends, I must be permitted to bestow a few moments on some other of his preliminary observations.

After representing the "legislative power" as "every where extending the sphere of its activity, and drawing all power into its impetuous vortex," he adds, "That judicial power, which, according to Montesqueiu, is, in some measure, next to nothing, &c." "That judiciary, which, in Rome, according to the same writer, was not entrusted to decide questions which concerned the interest of the state, in the relation which it bears to the citizens; and which, in England, has only invaded the constitution in the worst of times, and then always on the side of arbitrary power, has also deemed its interference necessary in our country."

I do not quote this passage for the purpose of noticing the hostility of Hampden to those American principles, which, in confiding to the courts, both of the union and of the states, the power, have imposed on them the duty, of preserving the constitution as the permanent law of the land, from even legislative infractions: nor for the purpose of enquiring why he has thought it necessary to inform us that "the judiciary in England has only invaded the constitution in the worst of times, and then always on the side of arbitrary power." I mean only to mark the unjust and insidious insinuation, that the court had thrust itself into the controversy between the United States and the state of Maryland, and had unnecessarily volunteered its services. "The judiciary" he says, "has also deemed its interference necessary in our country."

If Hampden does not know that the court proceeded in this business, not because "it deemed its interference necessary," but because the question was brought regularly before it by those who had a right to demand, and did demand, its decision, he would do well to suspend his censures until he acquires the information which belongs to the subject; if he does know it, I leave it to himself to assign the motives for this insinuation.

With as little regard to the real state of the transaction, he represents the judges as going out of the case, and giving opinions on extrinsic matter. "The supreme court of the United States," he says, "have not only granted this general power of attorney to congress, but they have gone out of the record to do it in the present question. It was only necessary in that case to decide whether or not the bank law was necessary and proper within the meaning of the constitution, for carrying into effect some of the granted powers; but the court have in effect expunged those words from the constitution."

It is scarcely necessary to say that this charge of "in effect expunging those words from the constitution," exists only in the imagination of Hampden. It is the creature of his own mind. But let us see how he makes good his assertion, that the court "has gone out of the record." "It was necessary," he admits, "to decide whether or not the bank law was necessary and proper, within the meaning of the constitution, for carrying into effect some of the granted powers." And, how, let me ask, was the court to decide this question? Does it not plainly involve an enquiry into the meaning of those words as used in the constitution? The court is required to decide whether a particular act is inhibited by certain words in an instrument: yet if the judges examine the meaning of the words, they are stopped by Hampden, and accused of travelling out of the record. Their construction may be erroneous. This is open to argument. But to say that in making the construction they go out of the record, may indeed show the spirit in which these strictures originate; but can impose on no intelligent man.

I must also be permitted to remark that, in discussing a question concerning the power of congress to pass a particular act, it is not allowable to assume as a postulate that the interests of the people are necessarily on the side of the state which contests that power, or that the cause of liberty must be promoted by deciding the question against the government of the union. When the right to call out the militia was solemnly denied, and the right to lay an unlimited embargo was seriously questioned, Hampden himself, perhaps, was not of opinion that the interest or liberty of the public required the decision of those points to be against the claims of the United States.[2] In fact, the government of the union, as well as those of the states, is created by the people, who have bestowed upon it certain powers for their own benefit, and who administer it for their own good. The people are as much interested, their liberty is as deeply concerned, in preventing encroachments on that government, in arresting the hands which would tear from it the powers they have conferred upon it, as in restraining it within its constitutional limits. The constitution has defined the powers of the government, and has established that division of power which its framers, and the American people, believed to be most conducive to the public happiness and to public liberty. The equipoise thus established is as much disturbed by taking weights out of the scale containing the powers of the government, as by putting weights into it. His hand is unfit to hold the state balance who occupies himself entirely in giving a preponderance to one of the scales.

If it be possible that congress may succeed "in seeing the constitution expounded by the *abuses* committed under it"; if "a new mode of amending the constitution" may be "added to the ample ones provided in that instrument, and the strongest checks established in it" may be "made to yield to the force of precedents"; if the time may soon arrive ["]when the constitution may be expounded without even looking into it—by merely reading the acts of a renegado congress, or adopting the outrageous doctrines of Pickering, Lloyd, or Sheffy": It is not less possible that the constitution may be so expounded by its enemies as to become totally inoperative, that a new mode of amendment, by way of report of committees of a state legislature, and resolutions thereon, may pluck from it power after power in detail, or may sweep off the whole at once by declaring that it shall execute its acknowledged powers by those scanty and inconvenient means only which the states shall prescribe, and without which the power cannot exist. Thus, "by this new mode of amendment," may that government which the American "people have ordained and established," "in order to form a more perfect union, establish justice, ensure domestic tranquility, provide for the common defence, promote the general welfare, and secure the blessings of liberty to themselves and their posterity," become an inanimate corpse, incapable of effecting any of these objects.

The question is, and ought to be considered, as a question of fair construction. Does the constitution, according to its true sense and spirit, authorize Congress to enact the particular law which forms the subject of enquiry? If it does, the best interests of the people, as well as the duty of those who decide, require that the question should be determined in the affirmative. If it does not, the same motives require a determination in the negative.

A FRIEND OF THE CONSTITUTION.

Printed, *Gazette and Alexandria Daily Advertiser* (Alexandria, Va.), 30 June 1819.

1. This was a reply to "Hampden" No. 1, published in the Richmond *Enquirer* on 11 June (reprinted in Gunther, *Marshall's Defense*, 107–14).

2. JM referred to the protest in New England against the embargo enforcement act of 1809 and accompanying instructions from the Jefferson administration to the state governors directing them to call out the militia if necessary. For an account of this episode, see Dumas Malone, *Jefferson and His Time*, V: *Jefferson the President: Second Term, 1805–1809* (Boston, Mass., 1974), 649–55.

A Friend of the Constitution
No. II

[1 July 1819]

I gladly take leave of the bitter invectives which compose the first number of Hampden, and proceed to a less irksome task—the examination of his argument.[1]

These are introduced by laying down these propositions which he declares to be incontrovertible in themselves, and which he seems to suppose, demonstrate the errors of the opinion he censures.

I do not hazard much when I say that these propositions, if admitted to be true, so far from demonstrating the error of that opinion, do not even draw it into question. They may be all true, and yet every principle laid down in the opinion be perfectly correct.

The first is that the constitution conveyed only a limited grant of powers to the general government, and reserved the residuary powers to the government of the states and to the people.

Instead of controverting this proposition, I beg leave to add to the numerous respectable authorities quoted by Hampden in support of it, one other which, in this controversy at least, is entitled to some consideration, because it is furnished by the opinion he condemns. The supreme court say, ["]The government (of the United States) is acknowledged by all to be one of enumerated powers. The principle that it can exercise only the powers granted to it, would seem too apparent to have required to be enforced by all those arguments which its enlightened friends, while it was depending before the people, found it necessary to urge. That principle is now universally admitted. But the question respecting the extent of the powers actually granted, is perpetually arising, and will probably continue to arise, as long as our system shall exist.["]

The supreme court then has affirmed this proposition in terms as positive as those used by Hampden. The judges did not indeed fortify it by authority, nor was the necessity of doing so very apparent, as mathematicians do not demonstrate axioms, neither do judges or lawyers always deem it necessary to prove propositions, the truth of which "is universally admitted."

2d. The second proposition is that the limited grant to congress of certain enumerated powers, only carried with it such additional powers as were *fairly incidental* to them; or in other words, were necessary and proper for their execution.

I will here remark, merely for the sake of perspicuity, that the second branch of this proposition, which seems to be intended as explanatory of the first, introduces I think a distinct idea. The power to do a thing, and the power to carry that thing into execution, are I humbly conceive, the same power, and the one cannot be termed with propriety "additional" or "incidental" to the other. Under the confederation congress could do scarcely any thing, that body could only make requisitions on the states. The passage of a resolution requiring the states to furnish certain specified sums of money, was not an "additional" or "incidental" power, but a mode of executing that which was granted. Under the constitution, the powers of government are given in terms which authorise and require congress to execute them. The execution is of the essence of the power. Thus congress can lay and collect taxes. A law to lay and collect taxes, and making all the provisions to bring the money into the treasury, is not the exercise of an "additional power" but the execution of one expressly granted. The laws which punish those who resist the collection of the revenue, or which subject the estates of collection[2] in the first instance to the claim of the United States, or which make other collateral provisions, may be traced to incidental powers. Not to those laws which simply execute the granted power. They are a part of the original grant.

The proposition itself, I am perfectly willing to admit, and should pass it over without a comment as one in no degree controverting the principles contained in the opinion of the supreme court, did I not suppose that some attention to the quotation made by Hampden, might conduce to a more clear and distinct understanding of those quotations themselves, and of their application to the subject under consideration.

The object of making them is, I presume, to show that a general grant of a specific power or thing, does not carry with it those incidents, or those means for giving the grant full and complete effect, which the opinion of the supreme court contends for.

His first quotation from Vattel contains words which might easily mislead a careless reader. "Since" says that author, "a nation is obliged to preserve itself, it has a right to every thing necessary for its preservation. For the law of nature gives us a right to every thing, without which we could not fulfil our obligation; otherwise it would oblige us to do impossibilities, or rather would contradict itself, in prescribing a duty, and prohibiting at the same time the only means of fulfilling it."[3]

Hampden has been caught by the words "necessary," "without which," and "only means," in the foregoing passage, which he has marked in italics or capitals, so as to give them a weight not given by the author, and has inferred from them, and other passages in the same book, that what he denominates the incidental power, is limited to things strictly "necessary," or "without which" the obligation could not be fulfilled; and in no case, he says, "is a latitude allowed, as extensive as that claimed by the supreme court."

The great and obvious error of Hampden consists in this. He converts an affirmative into a negative proposition. He converts a declaration of Vattel, that a nation has a natural right to do certain things, into a declaration that a nation has no natural right to do other things. But for this, I could not ask a stronger passage to show that the terms on which Hampden relies, are employed in a very different sense from that in which he understands them. "A nation" says Vattel, "has a right to every thing *necessary* for its preservation." Will any man seriously contend that the rights of a nation are limited to those acts which are necessary for its preservation, in the sense affixed by Hampden to the term "necessary"? May it not pass the bounds of strict necessity, in order to consult or provide for its happiness, its convenience, its interest, its power? "The law of nature," says Vattel, "gives a right to every thing without which we could not fulfil an obligation." But does it inhibit every thing else? If it does, then our obligations are sufficiently broad and latitudinous to cover the whole extent of human policy and human action.

"A nation," says Vattel, in the same page, speaking of the destruction of a state, "has a right to every thing which can secure it from such a threatening danger, and to keep at a distance whatever is capable of causing its ruin."[4] There is plainly no difference between that which a nation may do for its preservation, and that which it may do to prevent its ruin. It is a continuation of the same subject; the author means to convey the same sentiment; the change of phraseology is merely casual; and it is obvious that the restrictive terms used in the passage quoted by Hampden, are employed in such a mitigated sense, as to have the same signification with the broader words subsequently used on the same subject. In the whole, the author plainly recognizes the right acknowledged and acted upon by all the world, of a nation to exercise all its foresight, its policy, and its means, for its own security; and of the necessity of resorting to those means, it is the sole judge.

I certainly do not perceive the application of these paragraphs, but they are pressed into the service by Hampden.

We are also referred to a passage in Vattel, which respects tacit or implied engagements. I shall quote it rather more at large than we find it in Hampden. "Tacit faith," says that author, "is founded on a tacit consent, and tacit consent is that which is deduced by a just consequence from the steps taken by any one. Thus all that is included, as Grotius says, in the nature of certain acts on which an argument[5] is made, is tacitly comprehended in the convention; or, in other words, every thing without which what is agreed cannot take place, is tacitly granted.["][6] Several examples of the rule are then given; as, the allowance of provisions to an army which has stipulated for permission to return home in safety; and the security which is tacitly promised to an enemy who demands or accepts an interview.

I acquiesce implicitly in the rule as laid down by Vattel and by Grotius. I wish to extend tacit consent no farther than to that which is deduced by a just consequence from the steps taken by any one; nor to comprehend, by implication, more in a convention than "is included in the nature of certain acts on which an agreement is made." If the supreme court goes farther, I do not understand their opinion.

The case put by Vattel, and quoted by Hampden, of the grant of a free passage, is one on which I should particularly rely, as strongly supporting that liberal and just construction for which I contend.

The grant of a free passage seems, necessarily, to imply no more than that the sovereign who makes the grant shall remain passive, and to include only "every particular connected with the passage of troops," "such as the liberty of carrying whatever may be necessary to an army, that of exercising military discipline on the officers and soldiers, and that of buying at a reasonable rate every thing that an army may want."[7] Yet it is construed to go much further, and to stipulate for something active on the part of the sovereign making it. "He who grants the passage," says Vattel, "is, as far as lies in his power, to take care that it should be safe."[8] That is, he is not only not to injure, but to protect the army while in his territory.

This is certainly a reasonable construction of the grant; but if the implication be necessary, the necessity cannot be absolute or indispensable.

The case of a grant of a house to one man, and of a garden to another, which could be entered only through the house, is put by Vattel as an example of the *restrictive*, in opposition to the *extensive* interpretation.[9] Hampden cannot mean to give this example as forming a general rule—that construction is always *restrictive*, and never *extensive*; and never even reasonable.

In truth, the only principle which can be extracted from Vattel, and safely laid down as a general independent rule is, that parts[10] are to be understood according to the intention of the parties, and shall be construed liberally, or restrictively, as may best promote the objects for which they were made. For this I refer to his whole chapters on the faith, and on the interpretation of treaties. "The uncertainty of the sense," he observes, (b. 2. sec. 282) "that ought to be given to a law or a treaty, does not proceed from the obscurity, or any other fault in the expression, but also from the narrow limits of the human mind, which cannot foresee all cases and circumstances, or include all the consequences of what is appointed or promised; and, in short, from the impossibility of entering into the immense detail. We can only make laws or treaties in a general manner, and the interpretation ought to apply them to particular cases conformably to the intention of the legislature and of the contracting powers."[11] "Again," (sec. 283) he says, "we do not presume that sensible persons had nothing in view in treating together, or in forming any other serious agreement. *The interpretation which renders a treaty null, and without effect cannot then, be admitted. It ought to be interpreted in such a manner as that it may have its effect, and not be found vain and illusive.* It is necessary to give the words that sense which ought to be presumed most conformable to the intention of those who speak. If many different interpretations present themselves, proper to avoid the nullity or absurdity of a treaty, we ought to prefer that which appears most agreeable to the intention for which it was dictated."[12]

I trust then Hampden will not charge me, as he has charged the supreme court, with using "*high sounding words*," when, in his own language, I say that "I take it to be a clear principle of universal law—of the law of nature, of nations, of war, and of reason," that all instruments are to be construed fairly, so as to give effect to their intention, and I appeal with confidence to the authority to which Hampden has introduced us, to support my proposition.[13]

A FRIEND OF THE CONSTITUTION.

Printed, *Gazette and Alexandria Daily Advertiser* (Alexandria, Va.), 1 July 1819.

1. JM here begins his reply to "Hampden" No. 2, published in the Richmond *Enquirer* on 15 June (reprinted in Gunther, *Marshall's Defense*, 114–24).
2. This should be "collectors."
3. Vattel, *Law of Nations* (1805 ed.), Bk. I, ch. ii, sec. 18, p. 64.
4. Ibid., sec. 19.
5. This should be "agreement."

6. Vattel, *Law of Nations* (1805 ed.), Bk. II, ch. xv, sec. 234, p. 300.

7. Ibid., Bk. III, ch. vii, sec. 130, p. 412.

8. Ibid., sec. 131.

9. Ibid., Bk. II, ch. xvii, sec. 293, p. 326. Vattel here discusses the restrictive interpretation of treaties.

10. This should be "pacts."

11. Ibid., sec. 282, p. 319.

12. Ibid., sec. 283, p. 320.

13. This was a twist on a passage from Hampden, which reads: "I take it to be a clear principle of universal law—of the law of nature, of nations, of war, of reason, and of the common law—that the general grant of a thing or power, carries with it all those means (and those only) which are necessary to the perfection of the grant, or the execution of the power" (Gunther, *Marshall's Defense*, 117).

A Friend of the Constitution
No. III

[2 July 1819]

I now proceed to enquire how the principles of the common law apply to the case.[1] Although I might cite from that code, examples of the extended construction of the words of a grant for the purpose of implying what is not expressed. As that "by the grant of a house, an orchard, and curtilage, may pass"; (*a*)[2] or might cite from it the most complete evidence that the *intention* is the most sacred rule of interpretation.[3] I am content to limit my observations to the phrases quoted by Hampden.

I admit it to be a principle of common law, "that when a man grants any thing, he grants also that without which the grant cannot have its effect"; and, by this word "effect," I understand, not a stinted, halfway effect, but full and complete effect, according to the intention of the parties, and to their mutual accommodation. Thus, a right of way over the land of another for a particular purpose, whether given expressly or by implication, is to be so exercised as to effect that purpose completely, with convenience to the grantee, and with as little injury to the landholder as is compatible with the full enjoyment of the right. The same principle is laid down by Lord Coke in the passage also quoted by Hampden. "For," says that great lawyer, "when the law doth give any thing, it giveth, impliedly whatsoever is necessary for the taking and enjoying of the same. And, therefore, the law giveth all that which is convenient; viz. free entry, egress, and regress, as much as is necessary."[4] Hampden says the word "convenient" is here convertible with "necessary." This is true. But it is not less true that the word "necessary" is here convertible with "convenient." Lord Coke uses both words, as

(*a*) Ch. 5. b. 3 Ba. abr. 396 c. b. 6 Ba. abr. 384 title statute.

they are often used, in nearly the same sense. When so used, they signify neither a feigned convenience, nor a strict necessity; but a reasonable convenience, and a qualified necessity; both to be regulated by the state of the parties, and the nature of the act to be done. In this case, according to Lord Coke, the party having ingress, egress, and regress, in order to bring away his own, is not obliged to take it away at once; or before it is ready; he may use a reasonable convenience.

I admit also, "that the incident is to be taken *in a reasonable and easy sense*, and not strained to comprehend things remote, unlikely, or unusual."⁵ By which I understand, that no strained construction, either to include or exclude the incident, is admissible; but that the natural construction is the true one. This is "taking the incident in a reasonable and easy sense."

The doctrines of the common law then on this subject, are not at variance with those more general principles which are found in the laws of nature and nations. The rules prescribed by each are subjected to that great paramount law of reason, which pervades and regulates all human systems.

The object of language is to communicate the intention of him who speaks, and the great duty of a judge who construes an instrument, is to find the intention of its makers. There is no technical rule applicable to every case, which enjoins us to interpret instruments in a more restricted sense than their words import. The nature of the instrument, the words that are employed, the object to be effected, are all to be taken into consideration, and to have their due weight.

Although I have demonstrated, as I trust, that the quotations of Hampden contradict, instead of proving the principle he would extract from them, I should not do justice to the subject, were I to dismiss it without further comment.

The difference between the instruments in the examples taken from Vattel, or from the books of the common law, and the constitution of a nation, is, I think, too apparent to escape the observation of any reflecting man.

Take that of an invading army, which, after advancing far into the country of its enemy, stipulates for a safe return home.

The parties to this contract are enemies endeavoring to accomplish the ruin of each other. The contract relates to a single operation, the material circumstances connected with which may be, and therefore ought to be, foreseen, and minutely provided for. There is no reason for including in this stipulation, things which it does not clearly reach. Yet even in this case, the words are so construed as to comprehend more than is clearly expressed, in order to give full effect to the manifest intention of the parties. The same observations apply to the case of an interview between enemies.

So, the cases put in the books of the common law, are, all of them, cases of contract between individuals. Having only a single object to provide for, the provisions respecting that object might be explicit and full. It is not to be supposed that any essential circumstance will be omitted, which the parties intended to include in the grant, and there is consequently the less propriety in implying such circumstance. They are all likewise cases of property; and the terms of the grant cannot be enlarged in favor of one man, without impairing the rights of another. Yet, even in these cases, we have seen that every thing necessary to give full effect to the grant, every thing essential to the perfect enjoyment of the thing granted, passes by implication. Hampden himself is compelled to admit it to be "a clear principle of universal law"—"That the general grant of a thing, or power, carries with it all those means (and those only) which are necessary to the perfection of the grant, or the execution of the power." And he admits also, that by necessary means, he does not intend "in all cases, a sheer necessity"; which I understand to be equivalent to *an absolute or indispensable* necessity.

It can scarcely be necessary to say, that no one of the circumstances which might seem to justify rather a strict construction in the particular cases quoted by Hampden, apply to a constitution. It is not a contract between enemies seeking each other's destruction, and anxious to insert every particular, lest a watchful adversary should take advantage of the omission. Nor is it a case where implications in favor of one man impair the vested rights of another. Nor is it a contract for a single object, every thing relating to which, might be recollected and inserted. It is the act of a people, creating a government, without which they cannot exist as a people. The powers of this government are conferred for their own benefit, are essential to their own prosperity, and are to be exercised for their good, by persons chosen for that purpose by themselves. The object of the instrument is not a single one which can be minutely described, with all its circumstances. The attempt to do so, would totally change its nature, and defeat its purpose. It is intended to be a general system for all future times, to be adapted by those who administer it, to all future occasions that may come within its own view. From its nature, such an instrument can describe only the great objects it is intended to accomplish, and state in general terms, the specific powers which are deemed necessary for those objects. To direct the manner in which these powers are to be exercised, the means by which the objects of the government are to be effected, a legislature is granted. This would be totally useless, if its office and duty were performed in the constitution. This legislature is an emanation from the people themselves. It is a part chosen to represent the whole, and to mark, according to the judgement of the nation, its course, within those great outlines which are given in the constitution. It is impossible to construe such an instrument rightly, without adverting to its nature, and marking the points of difference which distinguish it from ordinary contracts.

The case which comes nearest to it, is a treaty regulating the future intercourse between two nations. If in such a treaty "it is impossible from the narrow limits of the human mind," to foresee all cases and circumstances, or include all consequences of what is appointed or promised, if, "from the impossibility of entering into this immense detail," the terms of a treaty must be general, and must be applied by interpretation to particular cases, so as to effect the intention of the parties; how much more impossible is it for a constitution to enter into this immense detail, and how much more necessary is it that its principles be applied to particulars by the legislature.[6]

A still more decisive objection to the exact application of the cases put by Hampden, is, that a rule applicable to powers, which may, strictly speaking, be denominated incidental, is not equally applicable to all the means of executing enumerated powers.

An "incident," Hampden tells us, "is defined, in the common law, to be a thing appertaining to, or following another, as being more worthy or principal"; and is defined by Johnson, to be means falling in beside the main design.[7] In his second proposition, he considers "an incident as an additional power."

I am content with these definitions. In applying them to the subject under consideration, I shall show conclusively that the means by which a power expressly granted is to be executed, would, most generally, be improperly classed with incidental powers.

Congress has power "to raise and support armies." Will any man contend that an act for raising an army of ten thousand men, for appointing the proper officers, for enlisting the troops, for allowing them pay and rations, proceeds from a power *appertaining to or following* the principal power to raise and support armies? Can such an act, with any propriety, be denominated, "means falling in beside the main design"? or "an additional power"?

Is it not too clear for controversy that such an act would be the direct execution of the principal power, and not of one appertaining to or following it? That it would be the main design itself, and not "means falling in beside it"? That it would be the primary, and not "an additional power"?

Had the right "to make rules for the government of the land and naval forces" not been expressly granted, a law made for that purpose would have rested, for its support, on the incidental or implied powers of congress, and to a question respecting its constitutionality, the doctrines of implication would have applied. But, the constitution having expressly given this power, the law enacting the articles of war is the instrument, or the means by which congress has chosen to execute it. With these means the doctrine of incidents has nothing to do. No court has a right to enquire whether the punishments inflicted by the articles of war are necessary or unnecessary. The means are appropriate, and congress may, constitutionally, select and vary them at will.

So congress has power "to establish post offices and post roads."

The law designating post offices and post roads, with all the provisions relating to that subject, is made in execution of this power. Such laws are the means which congress chuses to employ. But the right to punish those who rob the mail is an incidental power, and the question whether it is fairly deducible from the grant is open for argument. Under the confederation, congress possessed no implied powers, and was therefore unable to punish those who robbed the mail, but was capable of regulating the post office. These regulations were means, not incidents.

Thus too congress has power "to constitute tribunals inferior to the supreme court."

An act constituting these tribunals, defining their jurisdiction, regulating their proceedings, &c. is not an incident to the power, but the means of executing it. The legislature may multiply or diminish these tribunals, may vary their jurisdiction at will. These laws are means, and the constitution creates no question respecting their necessity. But a law to punish those who falsify a record, or who commit perjury or subornation of perjury, is an execution of an incidental power; and the question whether that incident is fairly deduced from the principal, is open to argument. Under the confederation congress could establish certain courts; but, having no incidental powers, was incapable of punishing those who falsified the records, or committed perjury within those courts.

In the exercise of an incidental power, we are always to enquire whether "it appertains to or follows the principal"; for the power itself may be questioned; but in exercising one that is granted, there is no question about the power, and the very business of a legislature is to select the means. It is not pretended that this right of selection may be fraudulently used to the destruction of the fair land marks of the constitution. Congress certainly may not, under the pretext of collecting taxes, or of guaranteeing to each state a republican form of government, alter the law of descents; but if the means have a plain relation to the end—if they be direct, natural and appropriate, who, but the people at the elections, shall, under the pretext of their being unnecessary, control the legislative will, and direct its understanding?

The distinction then between a power which is "incidental" or "additional" to another, and the means which may be employed to carry a given power into execution, though not perceived by Hampden, is most obvious. I have been the more particular in stating it, not only because his attention to it produces errors which pervade his whole argument, but because also it has led him to the application of language of the most unbecoming as well as unmerited asperity, to the judges of the supreme court. He is excessively displeased with them for not having used the word "incident" when speaking of "means." The term "means," he says, "started up on the present occasion, is not only undefined, but is general; and *guile*," he has permitted himself to add, *"covers itself under general expressions.* Why should the supreme court," he continues, "trump up a term on this occasion, which is equally novel, undefined, and general? Why should they select a term which is broad enough to demolish the limits prescribed to the general government by the constitution?"

All this irritation is excited by the heinous offence of using, when, speaking on one subject, words directly applicable to that subject, instead of employing those Hampden chuses to prescribe, but which belong to another, and a totally different subject. All must admit that there are *means* by which a legislature may carry its powers into execution; and Hampden is, I believe, the only man in the United States who will deny that the word *means* expresses that idea more accurately, and with more precision, than the word *incidents*.

It is certainly a piece of information which must surprise if it does not instruct us, that the word *means* has been "trumped up on this occasion" by the supreme court, that it is "equally novel, undefined and general," and that it is "broad enough to demolish the limits prescribed to the general government."

These strange positions are not in themselves more curious than the manner in which they are supported. We might reasonably expect to find that this favorite term "incidental," which must be dragged into use, not only where it is appropriate, but where it is inappropriate also, was employed in the constitution, and might thence derive some pretensions to this preference over every other word. It is not however to be found in that instrument—and one would therefore suppose, might be used or rejected with impunity, according to its fitness to the subject discussed.

But Hampden tells us that the terms "necessary" and "incidental" powers "were those uniformly used at the outset of the constitution; while the term means is entirely of modern origin." In support of this assertion he immediately quotes a passage from the Federalist, which contains the word *means*, and does not contain the word *incidental*. "A power," says the Federalist in the passage referred to, "is nothing but the ability or faculty of doing a thing, and that ability includes the means necessary for its execution."[8]

If, instead of this general reference to the terms "uniformly used at the outset of the constitution" we go to particulars, we find the words *incidental* and *means*, employed equally, as either in the opinion of the speaker or writer was best adapted to the occasion.

In the debates in the first congress on the bank bill, we find the opponents of that measure continually using the word *means*—and some gentlemen said "the true exposition of a necessary mean to produce a given end, was that mean without which the end could not be produced."[9]

The friends of the bill also employed the same term. They maintained the sound construction of the clause granting to congress the right "to make all laws necessary and proper" for carrying into execution the powers vested in the government, to be a recognition of an authority in the national legislature to employ all the known usual *means* for executing those powers. They farther contended that a bank was a known and usual instrument by which several of them were exercised.[10]

In the opinions afterwards given on this subject by the cabinet ministers, as stated to us in the life of Washington, this term is repeatedly used. The secretary of state and the attorney general, observe in substance, that "the constitution allows only the means which are necessary, not those which are convenient." And, after stating the dangerous consequences of such a latitudinous construction as they suppose was contended for by the friends of the bill, these gentlemen add ["]therefore it was that the constitution restrained them to *necessary means*, that is to say, to those *means* without which the grant of power must be nugatory."

The secretary of the treasury commences his argument with the general proposition. "That every power vested in a government, is, in its nature, *sovereign*, and includes, by *force* of the *term* a right to employ all the *means* requisite and *fairly applicable* to the attainment of the *ends* of such power.["][11]

It would be tedious to cite from this masterly argument, every passage in which we find this word *means*. It is used whenever the occasion requires it. It is used too in all the papers of the day which have fallen within my observation. How then can Hampden justify his assertion that this word is "trumped up" by the supreme court, that it is "novel, undefined, and general"?

The third & last proposition of Hampden is, "that the insertion of the words *necessary and proper* in the last part of the 8th section of the 1st article, did not enlarge powers previously given, but were inserted only through abundant caution."

To the declaration that I do not mean to controvert this proposition, I will only add the following extract from the opinion of the supreme court. "The result of the most careful and attentive consideration bestowed upon this clause is that, if it does not enlarge, it cannot be construed to restrain the powers of congress, or to impair the rights of the legislature to exercise its best judgement in the selection of measures to carry into execution the constitutional powers of the government. If no other motive for its insertion can be suggested, a sufficient one is found in the desire to remove all doubts respecting the right to legislate on that vast mass of incidental powers which must be involved in the constitution, if that instrument be not a splendid bauble."

The court then does not give to these words any greater extension than is allowed to them by Hampden.

The three general propositions laid down by this writer as containing those great and fundamental truths which are to convict the supreme court of error, have now been examined. The first is directly affirmed, & the last admitted, in the opinion so much reprobated. The second contains in itself, no principle, which that opinion controverts. Yet the quotations arranged under it, and the aspersions, alike unjust and injurious on the supreme court of our country, which are intermingled with those quotations, have been noticed in some detail, because this was necessary to the correct understanding of this application to the subject under discussion.

A FRIEND OF THE CONSTITUTION.

Printed, *Gazette and Alexandria Daily Advertiser* (Alexandria, Va.), 2 July 1819.

1. This is a continuation of the reply to "Hampden" No. 2.

2. The quotation is based on a passage from Edward Coke, *The First Part of the Institutes of the Laws of England; or, A Commentary upon Littleton* . . . , (16th ed.; London, 1809), 5b, and cited by Matthew Bacon, *A New Abridgment of the Law* (1st. Am. ed. from 6th London ed.; 7 vols.; Philadelphia, 1811), III, 396.

3. Bacon, *Abridgment*, VI, 384: "The Intention of the Makers thereof must, in the Construction of an Act of Parliament, be attended to."

4. Coke, *First Part of the Institutes*, 56a.

5. JM quoted Hampden quoting Bacon, *Abridgment*, III, 395 (Gunther, *Marshall's Defense*, 120–21).

6. Vattel, *Law of Nations* (1805 ed.), Bk. II, ch. xvii, sec. 282, p. 319 (passage quoted by JM in the second "Friend of the Constitution" essay).

7. Hampden quoted Coke, *First Part of the Institutes*, 151b, and Samuel Johnson's *Dictionary* (Gunther, *Marshall's Defense*, 123).

8. The quotation is Hampden's paraphrase of *The Federalist* No. 33 (Hamilton): "What is a power but the ability or faculty of doing a thing? What is the ability to do a thing but the power of employing the *means* necessary to its execution?" (Rossiter, *Federalist Papers*, 202).

9. JM quoted from his discussion of the bank bill debate of 1791 in *The Life of George Washington* . . . ([5 vols.; Philadelphia, 1804–7], V, 295).

10. This is a close paraphrase of another passage from the *Life of Washington* (ibid., 296).

11. Ibid., App., 4–6, in which JM paraphrased at length the opinions of Jefferson, Edmund Randolph, and Hamilton on the constitutionality of the bank bill.

To [Peter V. Daniel]

Sir[1]   July 2d. 1819

The Prisoners charged with Piracy who are to be tried at the special court of the United States to be held on tuesday next are here in custody of the Marshal & cannot be got into the jail.² May I ask you for permission to lodge them in the Penitentiary?³ With great respect I have the honor to be, Your Obedt. Servt

J MARSHALL

ALS, Vi. Addressed to Lt. Governor of Virginia. Endorsed "rejected."

1. Peter V. Daniel (1784–1860), a future justice of the Supreme Court, served as lieutenant governor of Virginia from 1818 to 1831 (John P. Frank, *Justice Daniel Dissenting: A Biography of Peter V. Daniel, 1784–1860* [Cambridge, Mass., 1964], 38).

2. See U.S. v. Smith, Charge to Jury, 27 July 1819.

3. As indicated by the endorsement, the executive council rejected this request.

A Friend of the Constitution
No. IV

[3 July 1819]

In his third number, Hampden states those specific objections to the opinion of the supreme court, which are to justify the virulent invectives he has, so unsparingly bestowed on the judicial department.¹

Before noticing these objections, I must be allowed to observe that, in recapitulating what he supposes himself to have established in his preceeding numbers, he entirely misrepresents what he has himself attempted to prove.

After stating that the clause containing the words necessary and proper was "tautologous and redundant," he adds, "I have also shown that, in that case, such means were implied, and such only, as were essential to effectuate the power; and that this is the case in all the codes of the law of nature, of nations, of war, of reason, and the common law. The means, and the only means, admitted by them all, and especially by the common law, are laid down emphatically to be such, *without which*, the grant cannot have its effect."

Can Hampden possibly believe that he has even attempted to show these things? Can he possibly have so far misunderstood himself? Or does he shift his ground to impose on his readers? Can he already have forgotten that all his quotations and all his arguments apply to "incidental" or "additional" powers, not to the *means* by which powers are to be executed? Can it have escaped his recollection that, so far from even making an effort to show that by any law whatever, it is "laid down emphatically" that those means only may be used in the execution of the power "*without which* the grant cannot have its effect," he has proscribed the term itself, as one "broad enough to demolish the limits prescribed to the general government by the constitution"? "As one which might cover the latent designs of ambition and change the nature of the general government"? Does he not remember, or does he suppose his readers will not remember, the motives he ascribes to the supreme court for "trumping up this equally novel, undefined, and general term"? I will not retort on Hampden the charge of *"guile"* on this occasion, but I cannot leave him the advantage he claims, of having proved that which he has not even suggested. I have not controverted his real proposition "that the limited grant to congress of certain enumerated powers, only carried with it such additional powers as were *fairly incidental* to them." But I utterly deny that when a power is granted, "those means *only* may be used in its execution, *without which* the grant cannot have its effect.["] I utterly deny that this proposition is maintained in any code whatever. When the attempt to establish it shall be made it will be time enough to show that it is totally unsustainable.

I now proceed to the errors ascribed by Hampden, to the opinion of the supreme court.

The first is that the court has agreed in favor of an enlarged construction of the clause authorizing congress "to make all laws necessary and proper for carrying into execution" the powers vested in the government.

Hampden does not venture to assert in express terms that the court has ascribed to that clause the quality of enlarging the powers of congress, or of enabling the legislature to do that which it might not have done had the clause been omitted. He knows well that such an assertion would have been unfounded, for he says "the supreme court itself admits that these terms were used & *only used*, to remove all doubts of the implied powers of the national legislature in relation to the great mass of concerns entrusted to it. This is an admission by the court that they were not used for the purpose of enlargement."

Why then does he seek indirectly to impress on the minds of his readers this idea known to himself to be incorrect?

But I will advert to the particular instances of this error, which he has selected in support of his charge.

The first is that the supreme court has said that this clause "is placed among the powers of the government, and not among the limitations on those powers."

That it is so placed, is acknowledged. But the court is supposed to be highly culpable for stating this truth, because it was stated for a purpose which this writer condemns.

To demonstrate that this argument was not used for the purpose, or in the manner alleged by Hampden, it is only necessary to advert to the opinion itself.

The court has laid down the proposition that "the government which has a right to do an act, and has imposed upon it the duty of performing that act must, according to the dictates of reason, have a right to select the means." Having reasoned on this proposition, the court adds, but the constitution of the United States has not left the right of congress to employ the necessary means for the execution of the powers conferred on the government to general reasoning. To its enumeration of powers is added that of making "all laws which shall be necessary and proper."

The meaning of the court cannot be mistaken. It is that this clause expresses what the preceding reasoning shewed must be implied.

The court then proceeds, "The counsel for the state of Maryland have urged various arguments to prove that this clause, tho' in terms a grant of power, is not so in effect; but is really restrictive of the general right, which might otherwise be implied, of selecting means for executing the enumerated powers."

The court then proceeds to combat these arguments of counsel— and combats them so successfully as to draw from Hampden himself the acknowledgement that "the words prohibit nothing to the general government." "It is only contended," he says, "That they create no enlargement of the powers previously given." Yet after thus explicitly yielding the point which was really in contest, he attempts to turn this total defeat into a victory, by contending that those arguments which were urged to prove that this clause did not restrain the powers of congress were brought forward to prove that it enlarges them, and fails of doing so.

No man, I think, who will even glance at the opinion, will fall into the error into which Hampden would lead him. The court, after reasoning at some length upon the clause, says, "To waste time and argument to prove that, without it, congress might carry its powers into execution, would be not much less idle than to hold a lighted taper to the sun. As little can it be required to prove that, in the absence of this clause, congress would have some choice of means," &c. "This clause," the court adds, "as construed by the state of Maryland, would abridge, and almost annihilate this useful and necessary right of the legislature to select its means. That this could not be intended, is, we should think, had it not been already controverted, too apparent for controversy. We think so for the following reasons: The clause is placed among the powers of congress, and not among the limitations on those powers."

The court proceeds to state several other reasons, to show that the clause could not have been intended by the convention to abridge those powers which congress would otherwise have possessed, and concludes with expressing the entire conviction that it could not be construed "to impair the right of the legislature to exercise its best judgement in the selection of measures to carry into execution the constitutional powers of the government." Hampden himself refers to that part of this conclusion which assigns to the clause the office of removing all doubt respecting the right "to legislate on that vast mass of incidental powers, which must be involved in the constitution," and approves it. Yet he has mentioned this argument, "that the clause is placed among the powers of congress, and not among the limitations on those powers," as his first objection to the opinion of the court; and he objects to it, not because the statement is untrue, but because the court urged it to establish an enlarged construction, an "extension" of the powers of congress.

I appeal to any man of the most ordinary understanding, when I ask if Hampden can possibly have misunderstood the opinion of the supreme court on this point? If he has not, why has he misrepresented it?

The second reason assigned by the court to prove that this clause could not be intended to abridge the powers of congress, is, "That its terms purport to enlarge, not to diminish the powers vested in the government."

Its terms are, "Congress shall have power to make all laws which may be necessary and proper for carrying into execution the foregoing powers."

I ask, with much confidence, whether these words *purport* to be words of grant, or of limitation? If the answer must be that they are words of grant, then the court stated them correctly. Hampden cannot controvert this; but he censures the argument, because it was urged to prove an extension of the powers of government. It was not so urged. The court states it explicitly as the second reason for believing that this clause did not *abridge* the powers of congress; and adds "no reason has been, or can be assigned, for thus concealing an intention to narrow the discretion of the national legislature, under words which purport to enlarge it."

Why, again let me ask, why has Hampden thus plainly misrepresented the opinion he condemns?

"The supreme court," he says, "has also claimed such an enlargement, on the ground that our constitution is one of a vast republic, whose limits they have pompously swelled, and vastly exaggerated."

The supreme court has not *claimed* "such enlargement" on the ground stated by this very inaccurate writer, or on any other ground.

After stating truly the extent of our great republic, the court says, "The exigencies of the nation may require that the treasure raised in the north should be transported to the south, *that* raised in the east conveyed to the west, or that this order should be reversed. Is that construction of the constitution to be preferred which would render these operations difficult, hazardous, and expensive?["] &c.

I refer to this whole paragraph in the opinion; and aver that not a syllable uttered by the court, applies to an enlargement of the powers of congress. The reasoning of the judges is opposed to that restricted construction which would embarrass congress, in the execution of its acknowledged powers; and maintains that such construction, if not required by the words of the instrument, ought not to be adopted of choice; but make no allusion to a construction enlarging the grant beyond the meaning of its ends. The charge of having "pompously swelled, and greatly exaggerated" the limits of the United States, would be too paltry for notice, were it not to remark, that, even in the most unimportant circumstances, Hampden delights to cast unmerited censure. The court had said, "From the St. Croix to the Gulph of Mexico, from the Atlantic to the Pacific, revenue is to be collected and expended, armies are to be marched and supported." And is not the St. Croix our north-eastern boundary? Is not Louisiana bounded by the Gulph of Mexico on the south? Does not our late treaty with England establish a line between the territory of the two governments, to the Pacific? And do we not, independent of our unratified treaty with Spain, claim the mouth of the Columbia, which empties into that ocean?

"The supreme court," says Hampden, "also claimed favor in this particular, on account of the magnitude of the trust confided to the general government."

This charge, like every other, is totally unfounded. The language of the court is, "the sword and the purse, all the external relations, and no inconsiderable portion of the industry of the nation, are entrusted to its government. It can never be pretended that such vast powers draw after them others which are inferior, merely because they are inferior. Such an idea can never be advanced. But it may with great reason be contended that a government entrusted with such ample powers, on the due execution of which the happiness and prosperity of the nation so vitally depend, must also be entrusted with ample means for their execution. The power being given, it is the interest of the nation to facilitate its execution. It can never be their interest, and cannot be presumed to have been their intention, to clog and embarass its execution."

And I ask if every sentiment here advanced be not strictly true? Congress has power to raise armies. Whatever doubts Hampden may entertain of the propriety of granting this power, can he seriously contend that its execution should be so clogged and embarrassed as that the troops cannot be raised in the manner most economical and most convenient to the people? So congress has power to levy taxes, with this only limitation, that direct taxes shall be proportioned to numbers, and indirect taxes shall be uniform. Does he so construe the constitution as to impose other limitations, or to inhibit congress from raising taxes by the means least burthensome to the people?

But be this as it may, it is most obvious that the opinion does not even hint the idea ascribed to it by Hampden. So far from suggesting that an enlarged construction is to be inferred from the magnitude of the trust, it expressly rejects this inference by saying, "It can never be pretended that such vast powers draw after them others which are inferior, merely because they are inferior." The argument is plainly advanced by the court in opposition to that unnaturally restrained construction which had been pressed by the counsel for the state of Maryland; and contends only that the government should be allowed, for the execution of its powers, means co-extensive with them.

I ask if Hampden himself can deny the correctness of this reasoning? I ask if he can discern any thing in the proposition that means for the execution of powers should be proportioned to the powers themselves, which contends that those powers ought to be enlarged by construction or otherwise?

A FRIEND OF THE CONSTITUTION.

Printed, *Gazette and Alexandria Daily Advertiser* (Alexandria, Va.), 3 July 1819.

1. "Hampden" No. 3 was published in the Richmond *Enquirer* on 18 June 1819 (reprinted in Gunther, *Marshall's Defense*, 125–38).

A Friend of the Constitution
No. V

[5 July 1819]

With as little regard to the text on which he comments as was shown in the instances mentioned in the preceding number, Hampden says, "The court is pleased to remind us with the same view" (that is with a view to a construction that shall extend the powers of congress) "that it is a constitution we are expounding."[1]

He is so very reasonable as not to deny that it is a constitution. Consequently he does not, on this occasion, charge the court with using an inaccurate expression. Its offensiveness consists only in the intention with which it is used. This criminal intention exists only in the fertile imagination of Hampden. The court makes no allusion whatever to that enlarged construction which he ascribes to it.

In answer to the argument that the clause under consideration so narrowed the powers of congress as to prohibit, the passage of any law *without which* any given power could be executed, the court, after showing that the word *necessary* did not always import the last degree of necessity, or that "*sheer* necessity" of which Hampden speaks, adds, "in its construction, the subject, the context, the intention of the person using it, are all to be taken into view." And I stop to ask if any fair mind can reject this rule of exposition? This "provision," continues the court, "is made in a constitution intended to endure for ages to come—and, consequently, to be adapted to the various crises of human affairs. To have prescribed the means by which government should, in all future time, execute its powers, would have been to change entirely the character of the instrument, and to give it the properties of a legal code."

The passage is too long to be quoted entire, but I say with confidence that it does not contain the most distant allusion to any extension, by construction of the powers of congress. Its sole object is to remind us that a constitution cannot possibly enumerate the means by which the powers of government are to be carried into execution.

The correctness of this position, Hampden does not venture to deny. He distinctly admits it; but thinks it necessary to add, (as if the contrary had been insinuated by the supreme court) "that the constitution establishes a *criterion* in relation to them, and that criterion should be the *law* to the several departments in making the selection.["]

The whole opinion of the court proceeds upon this basis, as on a truth not to be controverted. The principle it labors to establish is, not that congress may select means beyond the limits of the constitution, but means within those limits.

The grand objection made to the opinion so bitterly inculpated is, that it construes the clause which has been so frequently repeated, as an enlargement of the enumerated powers of congress, and contends, throughout, for an extension of these powers beyond the import of the words. To support this objection, various passages are selected from it. I have reviewed them all; and have, I think demonstrated that no one of them will bear the construction for which Hampden contends. I do not fear to be contradicted by any rational man who will read the opinion with a real desire to understand it, when I say that it contains not a single sentence in support of these doctrines. In form and in substance, it is a refutation of the argument that this clause narrows the right of congress to execute its powers; and it claims only that, in ascertaining the true extent of those powers, the constitution should be fairly construed.

Why has Hampden attempted thus plainly to pervert this opinion, and to ascribe to it doctrines which it clearly rejects? He knows well that prejudices once impressed on the public mind, are not easily removed; and that the progress of truth and reason is slow.

I should perhaps trespass too much on the patience of the public, were I to advert with the same minuteness to every thing said by Hampden on the subject of the means by which congress may constitutionally exercise its enumerated powers, or to cite from the opinion of the court the several passages to which he alludes with disapprobation, and which he mistates either directly or by insinuation. I have examined them all with attention, and I say, without fear of contradiction, that the general principles maintained by the supreme court are, that the constitution may be construed as if the clause which has been so much discussed, had been entirely omitted. That the powers of congress are expressed in terms which, without its aid, enable and require the legislature to execute them, and of course, to take means for their execution. That the choice of these means devolve on the legislature, whose right, and whose duty it is, to adopt those which are most advantageous to the people, provided they be within the limits of the constitution. Their constitutionality depends on their being the natural, direct, and appropriate means, or the known and usual means, for the execution of the given power.

In no single instance does the court admit the unlimited power of congress to adopt any means whatever, and thus to pass the limits prescribed by the constitution. Not only is the discretion claimed for the legislature in the selection of its means, always limited in terms, to such as are appropriate, but the court expressly says, "should congress under the pretext of executing its powers, pass laws for the accomplishment of objects, not entrusted to the government, it would become the painful duty of this tribunal, should a case requiring such a decision come before it, to say that such an act was not the law of the land."

How then can Hampden justify to his country, or even to himself, the declarations "that the court had resolved to put down all discussions respecting the powers of the government in future, by a judicial *coup de main*; to give a general letter of attorney to the future legislators of the union; and to tread under foot all those parts and articles of the constitution which had been heretofore deemed to set limits to the power of the federal legislature.["] That in fact "the court had granted to congress unlimited powers under the pretext of a discretion in selecting means"?

In a grand effort to impair the constitution of our country by construction, the doctrine "that the end will justify the means," seems not to be entirely exploded.

Hampden is much dissatisfied with the declaration of the court "that the general government, though limited in its powers, is supreme within the sphere of its action." He "does not understand this jargon. This word supreme," he says, "does not sound well in a government which acts under a limited constitution."

This writer, the least of whose charges against the supreme court is inaccuracy of language, would seem to have confounded *supremacy* with *despotism*. The word "supreme" means "highest in authority"; and there must be a highest in authority under a limited, as well as under an unlimited constitution. Is not the government of the union, "within its sphere of action," "supreme," or "highest in authority"? This is certainly the fact, and is as certainly the language of the constitution. That instrument declares, that "This constitution and the laws of the United States, made in pursuance thereof," &c. "shall be the supreme law of the land." The states, the state judges, and the people, are bound by it, "any thing in the constitution or laws of any state to the contrary notwithstanding." Is not that power supreme which can give the supreme law?

The constitution may be changed, any constitution may be changed. But while it remains what it is, the government "while moving within its proper sphere," is supreme. What authority is above it?

This "jargon" may grate harshly on the ears of Hampden, and he may be unaccustomed to it; but it is the language of truth, and of the constitution, and his displeasure will not banish it. The language of nature and of truth would grate harshly on the ears of an Eastern despot, unaccustomed to its words. He would not like "such jargon." But it would not be, on that account, inaccurate or improper.

In the continued spirit of misrepresentation, Hampden says, "The court is of opinion, that the right to establish a bank stands on the same foundation with that to exact oaths of office"; and also, that "the denial of a right to establish banks" "carries with it the denial of that of annexing punishments to crimes."

I do not deny that the cases bear a strong analogy to each other; but I do deny that the court has made the statement ascribed to it; and therefore, I do not deem it incumbent on me, in this mere justification of a judicial opinion, to show the fallacy of Hampden's distinctions between them, or to prove propositions, however true they may be, which that opinion does not assert.

The counsel for the state of Maryland, we are told, had contended that the clause which Hampden asserts to be "tautologous and redundant," "limits the right of congress to make laws for the execution of the powers granted by the constitution, to such as are indispensable, and *without which* the power would be nugatory."

The court rejects this construction, and in reasoning against it, says, "If we apply this principle to any of the powers of the government, we shall find it so pernicious in its operation, that we shall be compelled to discard it." The court then proceeds to show that this principle, if recognized, would prove many of those acts, the constitutionality of which, are universally acknowledged, such as the act prescribing the oaths of office, &c. to be usurpations. The argument is, avowedly, urged to disprove a proposition supported by counsel in the cause, as all essential in the construction of the constitution, but which Hampden expressly abandons as unsustainable.

He is equally incorrect when he says, "The supreme court is farther of opinion, that the power of incorporating banks is justified by the admitted right of congress to establish governments for the vacant territories of the United States."

The court had shown by a long, and, I think, an accurate course of reasoning, that, "if the end be within the scope of the constitution, all means which are appropriate, which are plainly adapted to that end, which are not prohibited, but consist with the letter and the spirit of the constitution, are constitutional."

But it had been urged that a bank, should it even be a measure of this description, is placed beyond the reach of congress, because the legislature of the union has no power to erect a corporation.

The court proceeds to consider this argument; and, in order to show its fallacy, proves incontestably, that the act of incorporation is the mere annexation of a quality to a measure, to the doing which, if the measure itself be proper, the constitution creates no objection. In illustration of this argument, reference is made to the territorial governments which are corporations. This reference is not made for the purpose of showing that a bank is as absolutely necessary to the union, as a government to a territory; but of showing that if an instrument be proper in itself, the circumstance that an act of incorporation is essential to its efficacy, creates no constitutional objection to it.

After a long and perspicuous review of the arguments which had been urged against the act of congress which was under consideration, the court proceeds to the act itself, and places its constitutionality simply on the ground, that a bank is "a convenient, a useful, and an essential instrument in the prosecution of the fiscal operations of the government." "That all those who have been concerned in the administration of the finances, have concurred in representing its importance and necessity."

The court may be mistaken in the "propriety and necessity" of this instrument. I do not think so; but others may honestly entertain this opinion. Be this as it may, the grand objection to the opinion, the reason assigned for all the malignant calumnies which have been heaped upon the judicial department, is, not that the court has decided erroneously, but that its decision is placed on principles which prostrate all the barriers to the unlimited power of the general government. That it "has made a declaratory decision that congress has power to bind us in all cases whatsoever."

We had before seen how totally untrue this allegation is, so far as it relies for support on the general reasoning of the court; and we now see how untrue it is, so far as it relies on the particular reason expressly given for the decision. That particular reason is, that a bank "is a convenient, a useful, an essential instrument in the prosecution of the fiscal operations of the government, the importance and necessity of which" is so strong that the best judges of that importance and necessity have concurred in representing; and the most intelligent original enemies of the measure have admitted it.

Hampden himself seems half inclined to make this admission. He says, "there is no doubt but many of those who voted for the bank, did it under what was supposed the peculiar pressure of the times. It was not adopted in relation to ordinary times, nor on the ground of its being a constitutional measure."

If "the pressure of the times" when this bill passed, rendered it neces-

sary, I am at a loss to conceive how it can be repugnant to that constitution which was made for all times. The peculiar circumstances of the
moment may render a measure more or less wise, but cannot render it
more or less constitutional.

I have claimed too much of the public attention already, to be equally
minute on the remaining observations of Hampden. On his argument
therefore respecting the necessity of the bank, I will make only one
remark, the correctness of which will be perceived by all who read that
argument. He requires that a measure, to be constitutional, must be so
indispensable that without it the power cannot be executed. This principle, if at all sustainable, can only be sustained by contending that the
clause in which the word "necessary" is found, abridges the powers
congress would otherwise have possessed. This construction he has
expressly surrendered. He cannot be permitted to avail himself of a
construction which he, in terms, abandons.

A FRIEND OF THE CONSTITUTION.

Printed, *Gazette and Alexandria Daily Advertiser* (Alexandria, Va.), 5 July 1819.

1. JM continues his reply to "Hampden" No. 3.

A Friend of the Constitution
No. VI

[6 July 1819]

Hampden has deemed it proper to introduce his objections to the
jurisdiction of the court, in the case of McCulloch against the state of
Maryland, with a long dissertation on the nature of our government.[1]
On so much of this dissertation as labors to prove that it is not a consolidated one, I will only remark, that it is a truth universally known and
universally admitted. No person in his senses ever has, ever will, or ever
can controvert it. Any writer who pleases, may certainly amuse himself
with the demonstration of this political axiom but he adds just as much
to our political knowledge, as he would to our geographical, were he to
tell us, and produce a long train of authorities to prove it, that the
United States lie on the western, and not on the eastern side of the
atlantic.

But when Hampden says that however "indistinct" may be the language of the court, on this point, "their doctrines admit of no controversy. They show the government to be, in the opinion of the court, a
consolidated, and not a federal government." His assertion is neither
equally true, nor equally innocent.

The question whether our government is consolidated or federal,
does not appear to have been stirred in the argument of the cause. It

does not appear to have occurred to counsel on either side, that any question respecting the existence of the state governments, as a part of the American system, could any where be made. The motion of such a point would probably have excited not much less surprize, than if any gentleman had thought proper seriously to maintain that there was a bench and a bar, and judges on the one, and lawyers at the other. It is not wonderful then, that the court should have omitted to state such a question in terms, or formally to decide it. But the principles laid down, and the language used, presuppose the existence of states as a part of our system, too clearly to be misunderstood by any person.

The court says, that "the defendant is a sovereign state"; that "the conflicting powers of the government of the union, and of its members, as marked in the constitution, are to be discussed"; "that the government of the union is one of enumerated powers"; "that it can exercise only the powers which are granted to it"; that "no political dreamer was ever wild enough to think of breaking down the lines which separate states, and of compounding the American people into one mass"; "that the assent of the states in their sovereign capacity" to the constitution, "is implied in calling a convention, and thus submitting that instrument to the people"; "that in discussing the questions" "respecting the extent of the powers actually granted", "the conflicting powers of the general and state governments, must be brought into view"; "that the constitution requires" that "the members of the state legislatures, and the officers of the executive and judicial departments of the states, shall take the oath of fidelity to it."

If Hampden can reconcile these passages with his assertion, he will, I doubt not, also reconcile the following, as preliminary to discussing the right of a state to tax the bank; the court says, "That the power of taxation is one of vital importance; that it is retained by the states; that it is not abridged by the grant of a similar power to the government of the union; that it is to be concurrently exercised by the two governments; are truths which have never been denied."

The whole opinion is replete with passages such as these. They demonstrate, as conclusively as words can demonstrate, the incorrectness of the assertion, imputing to it the doctrine that the government of the United States is a consolidated one.

Without making, at this time, farther quotations from that opinion, I will proceed to examine the reasons given for the assertions, that this plain language is "indistinct"; & that it conveys "*doctrines*" directly the reverse of what the words import. I shall do so the more readily, because, in treating this part of the subject, this gentleman, though he rarely states correctly the opinion he professes to quote, discloses still more clearly than heretofore, his real sentiments, and real objects; and because those sentiments and that object ought, I think, to receive the most serious attention of the people.

Hampden frequently uses, for what purpose let him say, the word "national" as synonimous with "consolidated." Thus he says, "It is not easy to discern how a government whose members are sovereign states, and whose powers conflict with those of such states, can be a national or consolidated government."

I deny that these terms are convertible. The government of the United States is almost universally denominated the national government, or the government of the nation. It is repeatedly so termed in the Federalist, and in other political treatises, and has never been termed a consolidated government.

Hampden defines a consolidated government to be "one which acts only on individuals, and in which other states and governments are not known." What name will he give us for a government "which acts only on individuals," but "in which other states and governments are known"? Such is the government of the United States; and, in a work (a) now acknowledged by all to be a clear and a just exposition of the constitution, we are told, that, according to the definitions of those terms given by its opponents, "it is neither a national, nor a federal constitution; but a composition of both."[2]

But waving, for the present, any controversy about terms, I will proceed to the evidence adduced in support of the charge that the language of the court, on the question of consolidation, is indistinct.

The first is, that "They use the word *people* in a sense seeming clearly to import the people of the United States, as contradistinguished from the people of the several states; from which the inference would arise, that the states were not known in the establishment of the constitution." As no particular passage in the opinion is referred to, it is not in my power, by quoting the words of the court, to give a precise refutation to this allegation. I must content myself with the more general, and less pointed observations.

The counsel for the state of Maryland, we are told, contended that the constitution was the act of sovereign states, as contradistinguished from the people. In opposition to this proposition, the court maintained that the constitution is not the act of the state governments, but of the people of the states. In the course of this argument, the term— *the people*—without any annexation, is frequently used; but never in a sense excluding the idea that the people were divided into distinct societies, or indicating the non-existence of states. It is positively denied that this use of the term, even unaccompanied by those passages with which the opinion abounds, would afford any countenance to the inference "that the states were not known in the establishment of the constitution." Still less can such an inference arise in opposition to the express and repeated declarations of the court.

(a) Federalist, No. 39.

If instead of using the word "*people*" generally, and in a sense avowedly contradistinguished from their governments, the court had used the words "*people of the United States*," not even this language would have had any tendency to warrant the inference which is said to arise.

Will Hampden deny that there is such a people as the people of the United States? Have we no national existence? We were charged by the late emperor of France with having no national character, or actual existence as a nation; but not even he denied our theoretical or constitutional existence. If congress declares war, are we not at war as a nation? Are not war and peace national acts? Are not all the measures of the government national measures? The United States is a nation; but a nation composed of states in many, though not in all, respects, sovereign. The people of these states are also the people of the United States. The two characters, so far from being incompatible with each other, are identified. This is the language of the constitution. In that instrument, the people of the states term themselves "the people of the United States." A senator must have been nine, a representative seven years "a citizen of the United States." ["]No person except a natural born citizen, or a citizen of the United States at the time of the adoption of the constitution," is eligible to the office of president. The oath taken by every adopted citizen, is as a citizen of the United States; and we are all citizens, not only of our particular states, but also of this great republic.

The constitution then does not recognize, but rejects, this incompatibility of our existence and character as a nation, with the existence of the several states. Hampden himself says that the words, "we the people of the United States," in the constitution, do ["]not necessarily import the people of *America*, in exclusion of those of the *several states*." And I insist that, so far from excluding, they include, "those of the several states." Surely then the term "the people," used generally by the supreme court, and expressly applied to the people acting in their several states, cannot justify the inference "that the states were not known in the establishment of the constitution."

"The opinion of the supreme court," says Hampden, "seems farther to incline to the side of consolidation, from their considering the government as no alliance or league, and from their seeming to say that a federal government must be the offspring of state governments."

I admit explicitly that the court considers the constitution as a government, and not "a league." On this point I shall make some farther observations hereafter. But I deny "their seeming to say that a federal government must be the offspring of state governments." They have expressly said the very reverse. In answer to the argument, that the people had already conferred all the powers of government on the state authorities, ["]and had nothing left to give," the court says, "much more might the legitimacy of the general government be doubted, had it been created by the states." When Hampden contends that state governments had no power to change the constitution, and represents himself as opposing, in this respect, the opinion he condemns, he is in fact reurging the very argument which had been previously advanced in that opinion. "The powers delegated to the state sovereignties," says the court, "were to be exercised by themselves, not by a distinct independent sovereignty created by themselves."

A FRIEND OF THE CONSTITUTION.

Printed, *Gazette and Alexandria Daily Advertiser* (Alexandria, Va.), 6 July 1819.

1. JM begins his consideration of "Hampden" No. 4, published in the Richmond *Enquirer* on 22 June 1819 (reprinted in Gunther, *Marshall's Defense*, 138–54).
2. *The Federalist* No. 39 (Madison), in Rossiter, *Federalist Papers*, 246.

A Friend of the Constitution
No. VII

[9 July 1819]

I proceed now to those doctrines, which, according to Hampden, "show the government to be, in the opinion of the court, a consolidated, and not a federal government."

"Differing from the court entirely," he says, "on this subject, he will give his own view of it."

We must, of course, suppose his view to be in proportion to that from which he differs.

In stating this difference, he tells us, "The constitution of the United States was not adopted by the people of the United States as one people, it was adopted by the several states," &c. And he then proceeds to show that the constitution was adopted by the people of the several states acting in separate conventions.

This is precisely what the court had previously said. It is to be recollected that the question discussed by the court, was, not whether the constitution was the act of the people in mass, or in states; but whether it was the act of the people, or of the state governments? In discussing this question, the court says, "The constitution was reported to the then existing congress of the United States, with a request that it might be submitted to a convention of delegates, chosen in each state by the people thereof, under the recommendation of its legislature, for their assent and ratification. This mode of proceeding was adopted."

Language, I think, cannot be more explicit than this; nor more entirely repugnant to the idea that the people acted in one body, and not by states.

Hampden also alleges in support of this plain perversion of the language and meaning of the court, the stress laid on the words "We, the people of the United States," in the preamble of the constitution.

The opinion cannot be inspected without perceiving that these words are not quoted, as "importing" in the constitution, "the people of America in exclusion of those of the *several* states," but as importing the people, in exclusion of their governments.

The court then has not denied, but has affirmed, that the constitution was adopted by the people acting as states.

Were it even otherwise, this error respecting the origin of the government, would not have proved it "to be in the opinion of the court, a consolidated, and not a federal government."

The character of a government depends on its constitution; not on its being adopted by the people acting in a single body, or in single bodies. The kingdom of Great Britain and Ireland is a consolidated kingdom. Yet it formerly consisted of three distinct kingdoms—England, Scotland, & Ireland; and this union was effected by their several parliaments, acting separately in each kingdom.

The convention of France, which was assembled in 1792, consisted of a single body elected by the people of the whole nation. Had the faction of the Gironde prevailed, and a federal republic been established, it would not have been the less a federal republic, because it was adopted by the representatives of the whole people, acting in mass.

If then the judges had made the assertion ascribed to them, they would have advanced a doctrine equally untrue and absurd, but not one which would "show that, in their opinion, our government is consolidated, and not federal."

The fact alleged then, and the conclusion drawn from it, are equally erroneous.

Hampden states many arguments which he supposes the court might urge in favor of consolidation, all of which he ingeniously refutes; but as the court has not itself urged one of these arguments, and has not, in the most distant manner, suggested a single idea in favor of consolidation, I shall be excused for passing them over without a comment.

I cannot, however, pass over, in like manner, his idea that the ligament which binds the states together, is "an alliance, or a league."

This is the point to which all his arguments tend. To establish this fundamental principle, an unnatural or restricted construction of the constitution is pressed upon us, and a fair exercise of the powers it confers, is reviled as an infraction of state rights. We need no longer be surprised at finding principles supported which would reduce the constitution to a dead letter, at the irritation excited by a course of reasoning which puts down those principles, at the effort to render the terms *American people* and *national government*, odious; at hearing that the supremacy of the whole within its sphere of action, over the parts is "jargon"; or at the exaggerated description of the power of the states to make amendments. All this is the necessary consequence of the doctrine that the constitution is not a national government, but a league, or a contract of alliance between the states, sovereign and independent.

But our constitution is not a league. It is a government; and has all the constituent parts of a government. It has established legislative, executive, and judicial departments, all of which act directly on the people, not through the medium of the state governments.

The confederation was, essentially, a league; and congress was a corps of ambassadors, to be recalled at the will of their masters. This corps could do nothing but declare war or make peace. They could neither carry on a war nor execute the articles of peace. They had a right to propose certain things to their sovereigns, and to require a compliance with their resolution; but they could, by their own power, execute nothing. A government, on the contrary, carries its resolutions into execution by its own means, and ours is a government. Who ever heard of sovereigns in league with each other, whose agents assembled in congress, were authorized to levy or collect taxes on their people, to shut up and open ports at will, or to make any laws and carry them into execution? Who ever heard of sovereigns taking the oath of fidelity to their agents? Who ever heard of sovereigns in league with each other, stripping themselves of all the important attributes of sovereignty, and transferring those attributes to their ambassadors?

The people of the United States have certainly a right, if they choose to exercise it, to reduce their government to a league. But let them act understandingly. Let them not be impelled to destroy the constitution, under the pretext of defending state rights from invasion. Let them, before they proceed too far in the course they are invited to take, look back to that awful and instructive period of our history which preceded the adoption of our constitution. These states were then truly sovereign, and were bound together only by a league. Examine with attention, for the subject deserves all your attention, the consequences of such a system. They are truly depicted in the Federalist, especially in the 15th No. of that work. The author thus commences his catalogue of the ills it had brought upon us. "We may indeed, with propriety, be said to have reached almost the last stage of national humiliation. There is scarcely any thing that can wound the pride, or degrade the character, of an independent people, which we do not experience." And he concludes his long and dark detail of those ills with saying, "To shorten an enumeration of particulars which can afford neither pleasure nor instruction, it may in general be demanded, what indication is there of national disorder, poverty, and insignificance, that could befal a community so peculiarly blessed with natural advantages as we are, which does not form a part of the dark catalogue of our public misfortunes."[1]

Such was the situation to which these states were brought, in four

years of peace, by their league. To change it into an effective government, or to fall to pieces from the weight of its constituent parts, & the
weakness of its cement, was the alternative presented to the people of
the United States. The wisdom and patriotism of our country chose the
former. Let us not blindly and inconsiderately replunge into the difficulties from which that wisdom and that patriotism have extricated us.

A FRIEND OF THE CONSTITUTION.

Printed, *Gazette and Alexandria Daily Advertiser* (Alexandria, Va.), 9 July 1819.

1. *The Federalist* No. 15 (Hamilton), Rossiter, *Federalist Papers*, 106–7.

To Joseph Story

My dear Sir   Richmond July 13th. 1819
    I had the pleasure this morning of receiving your letter of the 7th. by
which I am greatly obliged.[1] I shall at the next term decide the case of
the Little Charles in conformity with your reasoning.[2] It is I think
perfectly sound; & were this even questionable, the practice of the
courts ought to be uniform.
    Another admiralty question of great consequence has occurred at
the last term which I would carry before the supreme court if I could,
but as I have not the privilege of dividing the court when alone & as the
sum is only about 1800$ it must abide by my decision. It is however one
of general importance & I must ask the favor of you to give me your
views of it.[3]
    A vessel belonging to the port of Richmond in Virginia was hypothe-
cated for necessary repairs in New York & has been libelled in the
district court of this state. The district Judge condemned her & the case
is before me on an appeal.
    It has been argued that New York is as much foreign to Virginia
as Ireland or Guernsey to England. It has also been argued that the
power of hypothecation on simple interest is not so strictly guarded as
the power of pledging the ship on bottomree for usurious interest.
    From a consideration of this case I have been led to doubt what rule
ought to be adopted in the United States, & to question the propriety of
applying the rule in England to our situation. The foundation of the
rule is that in a foreign port this exercise of ownership on the part of
the master may be necessary, where as in a domestic port it cannot be
presumed to be so. Now let the ports of one state be considered as
foreign or domestic with respect to the vessels of another & cases may
arise in which the literal application of the rule would violate its principle. It would be absurd that a vessel belonging to Amboy should be
hypothecated in New York. But the same vessel at New Orleans or in

the mouth of Columbia would be completely out of the reach of the owner. The necessity for exercising this power by the master would be much stronger than in the case of a vessel belonging to one side of the bay of Passimiquoddy hypothecated in a port on the other.

I do not think a republication of the piece you mention in the Boston papers to be desired as the antifederalism of Virginia will not I trust find its way to New England.[4] I should also be sorry to see it in Mr. Wheatons appendix because that circumstance might lead to suspicions respecting the author & because I should regret to see it republished in its present deranged form with the two centres transposed.

I am highly gratified by the sentiments you express, & shall always feel a grateful recollection of them. The esteem of those we esteem is among the most delightful sensations of the human heart.

I had never thought of preparing an opinion in the militia case. That is committed to you & cannot be in better hands. I shall just sketch my ideas for the purpose of examining them more closely but shall not prepare a regular opinion. As at present disposed I do not think we shall differ.[5] With very much esteem & regard, I am dear Sir your obedt

J MARSHALL

ALS, Story Papers, MHi. Addressed to Story in Salem, Mass; postmarked Richmond, 14 July.

1. Letter not found.

2. See U.S. v. Schooner Little Charles, Opinion, [ca. 22 Nov. 1819].

3. See Selden v. Hendrickson & Pryor, Opinion, [ca. 22 Nov. 1819].

4. A reference to JM's "A Friend to the Union" essays.

5. Houston v. Moore, which had been argued at the 1819 term, brought into question the constitutionality of a Pennsylvania act of 1814 providing for state courts-martial to try militiamen neglecting or refusing to serve when called into federal service. At the 1820 term Washington delivered the Court's opinion upholding this act. Johnson gave a separate concurring opinion and Story dissented, remarking that his opinion had "the concurrence of one of my brethren." JM probably joined Story's dissent (5 Wheat. 1, 12, 32, 47, 76 [quotation]). See also Meade v. Deputy Marshal of Virginia, Opinion, ca. 1 May 1815; G. Edward White, *The Marshall Court and Cultural Change, 1815–35*, the Oliver Wendell Holmes Devise History of the Supreme Court of the United States, III–IV (New York, 1988), 535–41.

A Friend of the Constitution
No. VIII

[14 July 1819]

The last accusation brought against the supreme court, is, a violation of the constitution, by deciding a cause not within its jurisdiction.

Grave as is this charge, the question is still more important to the people than to the judges. It more deeply concerns the prosperity of the union, the due execution of its laws, and even its preservation, that its courts should possess the jurisdiction Hampden denies them, than it does the character of the judges, to stand acquitted of usurpation.

Before I proceed to examine this question, I must be allowed to express some surprize at its not having occurred to the counsel for the state of Maryland. The talents of those gentlemen are universally acknowledged; and, if we may judge of their zeal by the specimens of their arguments given in the opinion of the court, they made every point which judgment, ingenuity, or imagination could suggest, on which a decent self respect would permit them to insist. How happened it, then, that this point of jurisdiction escaped them?

A brief consideration of the subject will, I am persuaded, solve this difficulty.

The reasoning on which this objection seems to be founded, proceeds from the fundamental error, that our constitution is a mere league, or a compact, between the several state governments, and the general government. Under the influence of this unaccountable delusion, he makes some quotations from Vattel, favorable to the choice of a foreign government as an umpire to decide controversies which may arise between the government of the union and those of the states. "The princes of Neufchatel" we are informed, "established in 1406, the canton of Berne, the judge and perpetual arbitrator of their disputes."[1]

Were the petty princes of Neufchatel united under one paramount government having a constitutional power to adjust their differences, or were they only in alliance with each other? Was there any analogy between their situation and that of the United States? This at least ought to be shown by him who holds up to us their example for imitation.

He tells us also, on the same authority, "that among sovereigns who acknowledge no superior, treaties form the only mode of adjusting their several pretensions"; and "that *neither* of the contracting parties has a right to interpret the *pact* or treaty, at his pleasure."[2]

There is no difficulty in admitting this doctrine. The only difficulty consists in discerning its application to the United States. It applies to independent sovereigns, who stand in no relation to each other, but that which is created by the general law of nations, and by treaty. Has Hampden succeeded in convincing his fellow citizens that this is the condition of the American states?

Without pressing further the total inapplicability of these historical facts, and general principles, to our situation; or urging the weakness and danger of introducing into our system, a foreign potentate as the arbiter of our domestic disputes, I will proceed to examine the question of jurisdiction on its real grounds.

I will premise that the constitution of the United States is not an alliance, or a league, between independent sovereigns; nor a compact between the government of the union, and those of the states; but is itself a government, created for the nation by the whole American people, acting by convention assembled in and for their respective states. It does not possess a single feature belonging to a league, as contradistinguished from a government. A league is formed by the sovereigns who become members of it; our constitution is formed by the people themselves, who have adopted it without employing, in that act, the agency of the state legislatures. The measures of a league are carried into execution by the sovereigns who compose it; the measures of our national government are carried into execution by itself, without requiring the agency of the states. The representatives of sovereigns in league with each other, act in subordination to those sovereigns, and under their particular instruction; the government of the union, "within its sphere of action," is "supreme"; and, although its laws should be in direct opposition to the instructions of every state legislature in the union, they are "the supreme law of the land, any thing in the constitution or laws of any state to the contrary notwithstanding." This government has all the departments, and all the capacities for performing its various functions, which a free people is accustomed to bestow on its government. It is not then, in any point of view a league.

As little does it resemble a compact between itself and its members.

A contract is "an agreement on sufficient consideration to do or not to do a particular thing."

There must be parties. These parties must make an agreement, and something must proceed to and from each.

The government of the United States can certainly not be a party to the instrument by which it was created. It cannot have been concerned in making that by which it was brought into existence.

Neither have the state governments made this instrument. It is the act of the people themselves, and not the act of their governments.

There is then no agreement formed between the government of the United States and those of the states. Our constitution is not a compact. It is the act of a single party. It is the act of people of the United States, assembling in their respective states, and adopting a government for the whole nation. Their motives for this act are assigned by themselves. They have specified the objects they intended to accomplish, and have enumerated the powers with which those objects were to be accomplished.

All arguments founded on leagues and compacts, must be fallacious when applied to a government like this. We are to examine the powers actually conferred by the people on their government; and the capacities bestowed upon it for the execution of those powers.

This government possesses a judicial department; which, like the others, is erected by the people of the United States. It is not a partial, local tribunal, but one which is national.

For what purpose was this department created?

Before we look into the constitution for an answer to this question, let any reasonable man ask himself what must have been the primary motive of a people forming a national government for endowing it with a judicial department? Must it not have been the desire of having a tribunal for the decision of all national questions? If questions which concern the nation might be submitted to the local tribunals no motive could exist for establishing this national tribunal. Such is the language of reason. What is the language of the constitution?

"The judicial power shall extend to all cases in law and equity, arising under this constitution, the laws of the United States & treaties made or to be made under their authority."

Cases then arising under the constitution, and under the laws and treaties of the U. States, are, as was to be expected, the objects which stood first in the mind of the framers of the constitution.

Is the case of M'Cullough against the state of Maryland of this description?

Only two points appear to have been made by the defendant in the argument.

1st. That the act of congress establishing the bank is unconstitutional and void.

2d. That the act of the legislature of Maryland is constitutional, and consequently obligatory.

It was then a case arising under the constitution. Let us hear how Hampden contrives to withdraw it from the jurisdiction of the court.

He relies first on certain authorities which he quotes as being favorable to his opinion. In the Federalist, he says, "the supremacy of either party in such cases" ("these clashings between the respective governments") "seems to be denied."

If he seems to say no more than that the positive supremacy of an act of Congress, until it shall be tried by the standard of the constitution, is denied, he is undoubtedly correct. But the application of this opinion to the jurisdiction of the court cannot readily be perceived.

If he means to say that the jurisdiction of the supremacy of the judicial department, in cases of this description, "seems to be denied" by the Federalist, he is as certainly incorrect.

The writers of that valuable treatise allow a concurrent jurisdiction in such cases, except so far as that of the state courts may be restrained by congress; but the supremacy of the courts of the United States, is expressly recognized. In the 80th No. they are full and explicit to the point, that the courts of the Union have, and ought to have jurisdiction, in all cases, arising under the constitution and laws of the United States. After laying down a[s] political axioms, the propositions that the judicial department should be co-extensive with the legislative, and with the provisions of the constitution, the Federalist says "thirteen independent courts of final jurisdiction over the same causes, arising upon the same laws, is a hydra in government from which nothing but contradiction and confusion can proceed.["]

["]Still less may be said in regard to the third point. Controversies between the nation and its members, or citizens, can only be properly referred to the national tribunals."[3]

In the 82d No. speaking of the concurrent jurisdiction of the different courts, he adds, "here another question occurs—what relation would subsist between the national and state courts, in these instances of concurrent jurisdiction? I answer that an appeal would certainly lie to the supreme court of the United States."[4] The writer then proceeds to give his reasons for this opinion.

It is then most certain that the Federalist, does not "seem to deny," but does expressly affirm, that the jurisdiction and supremacy of the courts of the United States, in "all cases arising under the constitution"; which jurisdiction may be applied in the appellate form to those decided in the state courts.

Hampden refers also to two judicial decisions, which, he says, "are in full accordance with his principles." These are the case of Hunter *v.* Fairfax, and the case of the commonwealth of Pennsylvania *v.* Cobbett.[5] In the first case he says the court of appeals of Virginia declared "an act of congress unconstitutional, although it had been sanctioned by the opinion of the supreme court of the United States."

This is true; and it is the only example furnished by any court in the union of a sentiment favorable to that "hydra in government, from which," says the Federalist, "nothing but contradiction and confusion can proceed." But it is also true that this decision was reversed by the unanimous opinion of the supreme court,[6] and has, notwithstanding the acknowledged respectability of the court of appeals of Virginia, been disapproved by every state court, and they are not a few, which has had occasion to act on the subject. The supreme court, as we perceive in the reports, has reversed the decisions of many state courts founded on laws supported by a good deal of state feeling. In every instance, except that of Hunter and Fairfax, the judgment of reversal has been acquiesced in, and the jurisdiction of the court has been recognized. If the most unequivocal indications of the public sentiment may be trusted, it is not hazarding much to say, that, out of Virginia, there is probably not a single judge, nor a single lawyer of eminence, who does not dissent from the principles laid down by the court of appeals in Hunter and Fairfax.

Hampden's representation of the case of the commonwealth and Cobbett is entirely inaccurate. In that case, the supreme court of Pennsylvania did not come to the resolutions he recapitulates, nor, "go on to render a judgment bottomed on those principles, and in opposition to the provisions of an act of congress."

The case, as reported in the 3d Dal. is this: Cobbett had been guilty of an offence against the criminal code of Pennsylvania, and had been bound in a recognizance to be of good behaviour. His recognizance having been put in suit, he endeavored to remove the cause into the federal court on an affidavit that he was an alien. This motion was opposed, not on the unconstitutionality of the act of congress, but on its construction. The counsel for the commonwealth contended that the case was not within the act, 1st because it gave the circuit court no jurisdiction in a cause where a state was a party; and 2dly because it was not, properly speaking, "a civil suit"; but was incidental to, and in the nature of, a criminal action.

On these grounds the court decided that the act of congress did not embrace the case.

When the decision was about to be made, chief justice McKean, who was, not long afterwards, elected governor of Pennsylvania, whether in his character as a candidate or a judge, I submit to every intelligent reader, thought proper to deliver a political disquisition on the constitution of the United States. "Previous to the delivery of my opinion," he says, "in a cause of so much importance, as to the consequences of the decision, I will make a few preliminary observations on the constitution and laws of the United States of America." He then proceeds with the political disquisition stated by Hampden. But this is so far from being a part of the opinion of the court, that it was neither understood, nor stated, even by himself, as belonging in any manner to the cause. After having finished this dissertation, he says, "I shall now consider the case before us."[7] The opinion of the court is then delivered, in which not one syllable indicating the unconstitutionality of the act of congress is to be found. It was held not to comprehend the case.

This decision then, so far from questioning the validity of an act of congress, clearly recognizes its authority. The construction given to the act was, I presume, tho't correct by Mr. Cobbett's counsel, or he would have brought the question before the Federal courts.

A FRIEND OF THE CONSTITUTION.

Printed, *Gazette and Alexandria Daily Advertiser* (Alexandria, Va.), 14 July 1819.

1. Vattel, *Law of Nations* (1805 ed.), Bk. I, ch. iv, sec. 52, p. 79.
2. Ibid., Bk. II, ch. xv, sec. 219, p. 295; ch. xvii, sec. 265, p. 311.
3. *The Federalist* No. 80 (Hamilton), in Rossiter, *Federalist Papers*, 476.
4. *The Federalist* No. 82 (Hamilton), ibid., 493.
5. Hunter v. Martin, Devisee of Fairfax, 4 Munf. 58 (1815); Republica v. Cobbet, 3 Dall. 467 (1798).
6. Martin v. Hunter's Lessee, 1 Wheat. 304 (1816).
7. For Judge Thomas McKean's "political disquisition," see 3 Dall. 473–74.

A Friend of the Constitution
No. IX

[15 July 1819]

Hampden is not more successful in his reasoning against the jurisdiction of the court, than in his authorities.

Having finished his quotations, he exclaims—How after all this, in this contest between the head, and one of the members of our confederacy, in this vital contest for power between them, can the supreme court assert its exclusive right to determine the controversy?

The court has itself answered this question. It has said—"On the supreme court of the United States, has the constitution of our country devolved this important duty."

Such a question cannot assume a form for judicial investigation, without being "a case arising under the constitution"; and to "all" such cases "the *judicial power*" is expressly extended. The right asserted by the court, is then, expressly given by the great fundamental law which unites us as a nation.

If we were now making, instead of controversy, a constitution, where else could this important duty of deciding questions which grow out of the constitution, and the laws of the union, be safely or wisely placed? Would any sane mind prefer to the peaceful and quiet mode of carrying the laws of the union into execution by the judicial arm, that they should be trampled under foot, or enforced by the sword? That every law of the United States should be resisted with impunity, or produce a civil war? If not, what other alternative presents itself? Hampden suggests the arbitration of some foreign potentate—Britain, France, or Russia, for example. Is he sure that the parties could agree on an arbiter? Is he sure that such arbiter would be influenced entirely by the principles of right and not at all by those of policy? Is he sure that such arbiter would understand the constitution and laws of the United States? Is he sure that this intrusion of a foreign potentate into our domestic "vital contests for power" would not give that potentate an undue influence over the weaker party, and lead to intrigues which might foment divisions, animate discord, and finally produce dismemberment? If he is not certain on these and many other points which suggest themselves, and ought to be considered, how can he think the submission of these controversies to such an arbiter, preferable to the submission of them to a domestic tribunal, composed of American citizens, selected by the man in whom the American people have reposed their highest confidence, approved by the representatives of the state sovereignties, and placed by the people themselves in a situation which exempts them from all undue influence?

But this is not now a question open for consideration. The constitution has decided it.

After expressing some doubts respecting the propriety of that great American principle, the judicial right to decide on the supremacy of the constitution, a right which is inseparable from the idea of a paramount law, a written constitution, he adds, "but the present claim on the part of the judiciary is to give unlimited powers to a government only clothed by the people with those which are limited. It claims the right, in effect, to change the government, to convert a federal into a consolidated government.["]

Hampden leaves us to search for that part of the opinion in which this claim is asserted. Is it in the following? "This government is acknowledged by all to be one of enumerated powers. The principle that it can exercise only the powers granted to it, would seem too apparent," &c.

If not in this, or in such as this, for the opinion abounds with them, is it inseparable from the power of deciding in the last resort, all questions "arising under the constitution and laws" of the United States? If he contends that it is, I answer that the constitution has expressly given the power, and the exercise of it, cannot be the assertion of a right to change that instrument.

Hampden again demands the clause in the constitution which grants this jurisdiction, "The necessity," he says, "of showing an express provision for a right claimed by one of the contracting parties to pass finally on the rights or powers of another" "is increased when the right is claimed for a deputy or department of such contracting party. The supreme court is but a department of the general government."

I am not sure that I comprehend the meaning of these sentences. The words "one of the contracting parties" and "general government," appear to be used in the same sense, as designating the same object. So the words "deputy" and "department of such contracting party." If they are not to be understood so, I am unable to construe them. If they are, then let me ask what is meant by the word "general government"? Is it Congress? Is it the whole government? If the former, whence does he derive his authority for saying that the judicial department is the "deputy" of congress? Certainly, not from the constitution. According to that instrument, the judicial, is a co-ordinate department, created at the same time, and proceeding from the same source, with the legislative and executive departments.

If the latter, the whole government consists of departments. Neither of these is the deputy of the whole, or of the other two. Neither can perform the duties, or exercise the powers assigned to another; nor can all of them together participate in those duties and powers, or perform them jointly. Each is confined to the sphere of action prescribed to it by the people of the United States, and within that sphere, performs its functions alone. The legislature and executive can no more unite with the judiciary in deciding a cause, than the judiciary can unite with them in making a law, or appointing a foreign minister. On a judicial question then, the judicial department is the government, and can alone exercise the judicial power of the United States.

Can Hampden have been so inattentive to the constitution of his country as not to have made these observations; or does his hostility to this department lead him to indulge in expressions which his sober judgement must tell him are totally misapplied?

But he denies that there exists in the government a power to decide this controversy. He says—"They cannot do it unless we tread under foot the principle which forbids a party to decide his own cause."

Let us temperately examine how far this principle applies to the case.

The government of the Union was created by, and for, the people of the United States. It has a department in which is vested its whole legislative power, and a department in which is vested its whole judicial power. These departments are filled by citizens of the several states.

The propriety and power of making any law which is proposed must be discussed in the legislature before it is enacted. If any person to whom the law may apply, contests its validity, the case is brought before the court. The power of Congress to pass the law is drawn into question. But the courts of the union, Hampden says, cannot decide this question "without treading under foot the principle that forbids a man to decide his own cause."

What would be the condition of the world should this principle be deemed applicable to the exercise of the judicial authority by the regular tribunals of the country?

Any individual of Virginia, for example, chooses to deny the validity of a law, and proceedings for its enforcement are instituted. But, according to this new doctrine the court of the state is incapable of deciding a question involving the power of the legislature, without treading under foot this sacred principle. Let the state itself be a nominal party as in prosecutions for crimes, or suits against its debtors, and the violation of the sacred principle would be still more apparent. How are these questions to be settled without the intervention of a court? Or are they to remain for ever suspended?

It is the plain dictate of common sense, and the whole political system is founded on the idea, that the departments of government are the agents of the nation, and will perform, within their respective spheres, the duties assigned to them. The whole owes to its parts the peaceful decision of every controversy which may arise among its members. It is one of the great duties of government, one of the great objects for which it is instituted. Agents for the performance of this duty must be furnished, or the government fails in one of the great ends of its creation.

To whom more safely than to the judges are judicial questions to be referred? They are selected from the great body of the people for the purpose of deciding them. To secure impartiality, they are made perfectly independent. They have no personal interest in aggrandizing the legislative power. Their paramount interest is the public prosperity, in which is involved their own and that of their families. No tribunal can be less liable to be swayed by unworthy motives from a conscientious performance of duty. It is not then the party sitting in his own cause. It is the application to individuals by one department of the acts of another department of the government. The people are the authors of all; the departments are their agents; and if the judge be personally disinterested, he is as exempt from any political interest that might influence his opinion, as imperfect human institutions can make him.

To the demand that the words which give the jurisdiction should be stated, I answer—they have already been stated. The jurisdiction is expressly given in the words "the judicial power shall extend to all cases arising under this constitution." How does Hampden elude this provision? Not by denying that the case "arises under the constitution." That, not even he can venture to deny. How then does he elude it? He says that "these words may be otherwise abundantly satisfied.["] But how "otherwise satisfied," he has not told us; nor can he. I admit there are other cases arising under the constitution. But the words are "all cases" and I deny that the word "some," can be substituted for "all," or that the word "all," can be satisfied if any one case can be withdrawn from the jurisdiction of the court. But the same reason may be assigned for withdrawing any or every other case. As each occurs, Hampden may say "these words may be otherwise abundantly satisfied." What peculiar reason has he assigned for this case which is not equally applicable to any and every other? His reason is that the case involves an enquiry, into the extent of the powers of the general government, and of a state government. And I ask what case can arise under the constitution which does not involve one or both of these enquiries? Let Hampden, if he can, state the case.

These words then cannot be otherwise satisfied. Hampden does not merely contract, he annihilates them.

But suppose him to succeed in excluding from the federal courts, all cases in which a question respecting the powers of the government of the union, or of a state can arise, are they to remain for ever undecided? Hampden does not say so. They must of course be decided in the state courts. He quotes, as sustaining his principles, a decision of the court of appeals in Virginia overruling an act of congress; and a decision of the supreme court of Pennsylvania, (though in this he is mistaken) to the same effect. It follows then that great national questions are to be decided, not by the tribunal created for their decision by the people of the United States, but by the tribunal created by the state which contests the validity of the act of congress, or asserts the validity of its own act. Thus, in the language of the Federalist, (No. 45)[1] presenting to the world "for the first time, a system of government founded on an inversion of the fundamental principles of all government"; "the authority of the whole society every where subordinate to the authority of the parts"; ["]a monster in which the head is under the direction of the members."[2]

Hampden is not more fortunate in the second principle with which he attempts to sustain this strange construction of the constitution, although he is pleased to term it "conclusive." "The rank of this controversy," he says, "between the head and one of the members of the confederacy, may be said to be superior to those depending between two of the members; and the lawyers well know that a specification beginning with a person or thing of an inferior grade, excludes those of a superior."

If I could be surprized at any argument found in the essays of Hampden, I should be surprised at this.

The jurisdiction of the federal courts, as described in the constitution, is dependent on two distinct considerations. The first is the character of the cause; the second, the character of the parties. All cases arising under the constitution, laws, and treaties of the United States; all cases affecting public ministers; and all cases of admiralty and maritime jurisdiction; are cognizable in those courts, whoever may be the parties. The cases of the second class depend entirely on the character of the parties, without regard to the nature of the cause. It is not necessary that these two properties should be combined in the same cause, in order to give the court jurisdiction. If a case arise under the constitution, it is immaterial who are the parties; and if an alien be a party, it is not requisite that the case should arise under the constitution.

But McCullough, not the United States, is the party on the record; and were it otherwise, that circumstance would bring the case within, not exclude it from, the jurisdiction of the court. The constitution expressly gives jurisdiction to the courts of the union in "cases to which the United States shall be a party."

There is then no one objection made to the opinion of the supreme court which fails more entirely than this to its jurisdiction.

I have been induced to review these essays the more in detail, because they are intended to produce a very serious effect; and because they advance principles which go, in my judgment, to the utter subversion of the constitution. Let Hampden succeed, and that instrument will be radically changed. The government of the whole will be prostrated at the feet of its members; and that grand effort of wisdom, virtue, and patriotism, which produced it, will be totally defeated.

A FRIEND OF THE CONSTITUTION.

Printed, *Gazette and Alexandria Daily Advertiser* (Alexandria, Va.), 15 July 1819.

1. Possibly a printer's error (see n. 2).
2. *The Federalist* No. 44 (Madison), Rossiter, *Federalist Papers*, 287.

To Basil Duke

Dear Sir: Richmond, July 24th, 1819
    I received a few days ago your letter of the 3rd. and thank you for
the trouble you have taken in giving me a statement of my sister Taylor's affairs.[1] I did not know when I wrote to you that you had previously made a communication to my sister giving her the information
I requested.[2]
    Your letter has surprised and grieved me. That my sister should
have sustained such heavy losses is truly afflicting, and that these losses
should be occasioned by the negligence of such near connections adds
to the affliction. By the law of Virginia, to which I had supposed that of
Kentucky was assimilated, twenty years possession is a bar to an ejectment, but not to a writ of right. Your legislature, I presume, has short-
ened the time.[3] It is indeed cause of deep regret if your property has
been lost from a failure to assert your title.
    I am a little surprised at the charge made by Mr. Marshall for his
services. Being, however, unacquainted with their nature and with the
usual allowance for such services, I can form no opinion on its reasonableness; but I should hope that his sense of justice will be strong
enough to induce him to pay interest on money he has received for
others and applied to his own use.
    I thank you for your undertaking to become responsible for my
sister should she be required to refund the money she has received. I
have formerly assured you that I will be responsible to you and this
letter repeats the assurance.
    The mode of remittance you had adopted was, I doubt not, the most
eligible, and will, I hope, place the money in the hands of my sister
Taylor who greatly needs it. What remains she wishes should be paid to
Doctor Marshall on account of her son. On this subject we wish to hear
from you, particularly because arrangements ought to be immediately
made to remit to my brother such farther sum as may be necessary.
    Present me affectionately to your family and believe me to be dear
Sir, With much esteem and regards, Your obedient
                                                        J. MARSHALL

Tr (typescript), Collection of Thomas W. Bullitt, Louisville, Ky; Marshall Papers, DLC.
Inside address to Duke in Washington, Ky.

    1. Letter not found.
    2. See JM to Duke, 8 June 1819.
    3. By the Virginia act of limitations, rights of entry on lands were barred after twenty
years. On writs of right, the limitation was fifty years. Kentucky's act of limitations was
copied from that of Virginia (*The Revised Code of Virginia* . . . [2 vols.; Richmond, Va.,
1819], I, 487–88; William Littell, *The Statute Laws of Kentucky* . . . [5 vols.; Frankfort, Ky.,
1809–19], I, 380–81).

From Joseph Story

Dear Sir   Salem July 26. 1819.

I have the pleasure to acknowlege the receipt of your letter of the 13th instant. It affords me great satisfaction that the views taken by me of the case formerly stated have in any degree approved themselves to your mind.

In respect to the case of the hypothecation at New York, which is very important in its principles, I will most readily give you my present impressions.[1]

The authority of the master to *contract for repairs* of the ship & to bind the owner *personally*, as well where the repairs are made in *domestic* ports as *foreign* ports, is no where in our law questioned. It seems generally conceded that it grows out of his general authority & agency, & is not suspended even in the *home* port of the owner. His authority to hypothecate the ship for repairs in *foreign* ports seems also universally admitted. And I take it now to be settled, notwithstanding some early doubts, that material men have a lien, independent of any instrument of hypothecation, upon a *foreign ship* for repairs in *our ports* & upon *our ships* for repairs in *foreign ports*. At least I have considered this doctrine so well established that I find it so stated by me in delivering the opinion of the Court in the Aurora 1 Wheaton. R. 105 & in the Ship Genl. Smith at the last February Term, where the question was directly in judgment.[2] And recent cases in England, particularly 13 Ves. 594 & 3 Ves. & Beame 483. seem to proceed upon an admission of the same doctrine.[3] In respect to the right of hypothecation, I know of no difference in the construction of it, whether simple or extraordinary interest be reserved. The only question on this head is whether the money be at risk on the vessel; if so, extraordinary or usurious interest may be taken; if not, then the hypothecation is not void, but the party cannot recover more than simple interest.

I take the rule too to be established in the Ship Genl. Smith's case, that where the maritime law or the municipal law gives a lien for repairs of a Ship, the Court of Admiralty will enforce it by a process in rem.

The question then is reduced to this, whether the ports of the different states are to be deemed foreign ports in respect to the right of hypothecation or of implied lien. If New York be foreign in respect to Richmond, then the repairs were an implied lien, & the master had complete authority to make them an express lien by an hypothecation. In *practice* I have for a long time supposed this question settled. By analogy to the cases of repairs of an English ship in Ireland & Jersey, the ports of different states in the union have been supposed to be foreign. This has certainly been the doctrine in my circuit; & I gather also from cases that it is the doctrine in South Carolina, Maryland,

Pennsylvania, & New York. I have certainly understood also from Judge Johnson that it is his opinion. And in New York, there is an express statute which gives a lien for repairs on all ships, where the owners do *not reside* within the State. I understand the ground of this doctrine in England to be that the jurisdictions being different, the process of the Courts against the owner can not run into them, & therefore though in some respects under the same sovereignty, they are foreign for the purpose of remedies. This reasoning applies with greater force in the United States, where each state is really a distinct sovereignty, governed by its own laws, & confined in its process to its own territorial limits. So strong has been my impression as to this question, that I shall not be surprised if it shall [be] found that in delivering the opinion in the case of the Genl Smith, I put the case & affirmed the right of the master to hypothecate in case of repairs in a port of a different State from that where the owner resides.

I agree with you that the reason assigned in the books for allowing an hypothecation & implied lien in cases of repairs in *foreign ports* is not entirely satisfactory. It does not apply to all cases. The reason assigned is that in the absence of the owner in another jurisdiction, the master cannot be supposed to be able to consult him, & the owner cannot be supposed in a condition to order the repairs, or to remit funds for the purpose, & therefore from the necessity of the case the master as the general agent of the owner is at liberty to pledge the personal credit of the owner, & the ship also, as a security for the repairs. In the cases which you put of foreign ports contiguous to each other, where the owner resides in one & the ship is repaired in the other the reason certainly fails; & yet the law in such cases is, I presume, settled, that the master has authority to hypothecate the ship.

I do not however think that the reason usually given for the universality of the rule in cases of repairs in *foreign ports*, is the true reason. The rule itself was borrowed from the civil law & incorporated into the maritime law of the continent & thence imported into England. The true foundation of it appears to me to be that the Owner is without the reach of the jurisdiction of the Courts where the repairs are made & cannot be made personally responsible there for the payment of the debt; & therefore unless the master were under such circumstances at liberty to hypothecate the ship, there would be no *certain* remedy for the repairs except against the master himself. The laws of different states differ as to rights & remedies. In some there may be no remedy against the person; in others none against the goods or property, or there may be special exemptions or priorities of payment in respect to debts. The ownership of foreign ships & the residence of the owners may not be easily known & imposition is practicable. There may be trust & usufructuary interests recognised by the local law, materially affecting the question of ownership & the remedy of the person against

JOSEPH STORY
Oil on canvas by Gilbert Stuart, 1819. *Courtesy of the Harvard Law Art Collection*

whom the actions will lie. This is not all. The law of the foreign country, though contiguous, may be entirely different from ours. It may not allow & we know in fact that the laws of some countries do not allow, the master to pledge the personal credit of his owner, but the ship only for repairs. Persons, in one country, & artisans & merchants in particular, cannot be supposed to be conusant of foreign laws, or bound to take notice of them at their peril. The law therefore from motives of policy to procure repairs upon the best & safest terms gives an implied lien on the ship for such repairs, as the best security for the repayment, & binding the interests of all, who receive the benefit of the repairs. It will not drive the party to a foreign jurisdiction to hunt up his debtor, & enforce his remedy against him. Under this aspect, it appears to me, that the rule is founded upon an enlarged maritime policy, & all the cases, which it governs are within its principle.

If however all the ports of the United States are to be considered as domestic ports, (which I can admit only for the sake of argument) I am of opinion that the English rule in this Subject is inapplicable to our situation & ought not to be adopted here. It cannot be disguised that the English rule grew up in very narrow times; & was adopted with the express view to cripple & destroy the admiralty jurisdiction. It had no higher or purer source than hostility to all but common law courts. And I do not doubt if the thing were res integra[4] a very different course would now be pursued in the English courts. It was perceived that the admiralty claimed jurisdiction in all cases of repairs of ships as a maritime contract, & that if an implied lien on the ship for repairs in England were admitted, that jurisdiction would be established in the most popular manner. The Courts of common law felt themselves bound to admit the right of hypothecation by the master, as it was held in the maritime law; & that law gave it in all cases except in the "*place* of the owner's residence," where for manifest reasons the power might be properly held to be suspended, or to be exercised by the owner only. The English Courts affecting to follow the rule with its limitation, violated both its letter & spirit. They construed "the place of residence" to be, not the home port of the owner, but the whole kingdom. And I do not perceive why they might not in the same manner have extended it to all places with in the British dominions & Sovereignty. The reason of the exception in the rule of the maritime law, might well apply to cases, not only, where the repairs were done in the *home* port of the ship, but also in ports so *near*, as that the Owner might be consulted, or might readily supply funds or credit, without delay or injury to the voyage, or where the necessity of repairs was not pressing. But the *reason usually* given for the right of hypothecation in a *foreign* port applies with equal force to a *remote domestic* port. Suppose a Russian ship owned in St Petersburgh wants repairs in Odessa, or Archangel? Or a French ship owned in Dunkirk wants repairs in Marseilles? Or a ship owned in

Eastport in the District of Maine wants repairs in Savannah or New Orleans? In such remote ports it is extremely difficult to know the real situation of the owner, or to communicate with him without great loss of time, or to procure funds upon his personal credit. Yet the master in such a port has a right to order repairs upon the personal credit of the owner because he acts as his *general* agent in respect to the ship; & for the same reason in a case of necessary repairs it seems to me, he must have a right, where the personal credit of the owner will not procure the funds, to hypothecate the ship. It is to prevent a greater loss, perhaps a total loss to the owner; & the authority may be fairly inferred from the master's duty to do all in his power to preserve the ship. In short it may be as fairly inferred in a remote domestic as in a foreign port.

If I have made myself understood, my opinion goes to these propositions 1. That the right of the master to hypothecate in a foreign port is founded not merely on the difficulty of communication with the owner to procure a remittance of funds, but chiefly & mainly on the fact that the owner is in a foreign jurisdiction to which the process of the Courts of the place of repairs cannot reach so as to enforce a *personal* remedy against the owner. 2. That the right of the master to hypothecate exists when the ship is in a remote domestic port from the necessity of avoiding a greater loss, & for the reasons which are usually given in the books for the right in a foreign port. 3. That ⟨the⟩ ports of the different States in the Union are in practice deemed *foreign* ports as to this right, being ports in different jurisdictions & sovereignties. 4 That if they were to be deemed *domestic* ports, the right would not be suspended, unless those ports were contiguous to the residence of the owner, or so near that his funds might be remitted or his wishes consulted without delay to the voyage or injury to the ship.

I have gone into the point generally with a view to express my sentiments at large. But there is a short ground upon which I should not hesitate to support the hypothecation in the case before you. It is this. By the Statute of New York the repairs were expressly made a lien on the ship itself; & if so by the lex loci, I think the lien is not lost by a mere departure from the port, but may be enforced in the admiralty in any other State. The hypothecation by the master was only an express recognition of the prior lien; & if the lex loci gave the implied lien, he must have the authority to continue that lien after a departure from the port, other wise the ship would never be allowed to depart on the voyage, & it would be completely frustrated.

I hope you will excuse my going so much at large into my views of this subject, as I felt an anxiety on a topic of such general interest to give you some of the grounds, upon which I have formed my opinions. I have done this the more cheerfully, because I think we are at liberty to adopt a rule in the United States which shall be consistent in its application & of general convenience. The maritime law of the continent appears to me better adapted to the general interests of the commercial world, than a narrow adoption of the municipal law of England on this subject. And the authorities are not so stringent that we have no discretion left. Probably your decision will form a leading case for our future government.

After all I may be very wrong in my opinion; & if so, I am open to argument, & will follow in a better path. And as the advancement of the law, & not merely of our private opinions should be the great ambition of all judges, I am quite content to yield to the judgment of others.

It will give me great pleasure if you will send me a copy of the opinion you may ultimately deliver on this case. And if in the meantime there are any further explanations wished of my views I shall be most happy to give them. With the highest respect & esteem, I am Dear Sir, your most obliged friend & Servant,

JOSEPH STORY

ALS, Marshall Papers, ViW. Addressed to JM in Richmond; postmarked Salem, Mass., 2 Aug.

1. Selden v. Hendrickson & Pryor, Opinion, [ca. 22 Nov. 1819].
2. The Aurora, 1 Wheat. 96, 105 (1816); The General Smith, 4 Wheat. 438, 443. Story gave the Court's opinion in both cases.
3. Hussey v. Christie, 13 Ves. 594, 33 Eng. Rep. 417 (Ch., 1807); Halket, Ex parte, 3 Ves. & Bea. 135, 35 Eng. Rep. 430 (Ch., 1814). The page citation for Halket, Ex parte, is from the second edition of the reports of Vesey and Beame, the edition reprinted in *English Reports*.
4. *Res integra* (a whole thing; a new or unopened thing). The term is applied to points of law not yet decided.

United States v. Smith
Charge to Jury
U.S. Circuit Court, Virginia, 27 July 1819

Thomas Smith was one of twenty-one crewmen of the *Irresistible* tried for piracy at a special term of the U.S. Circuit Court in the summer of 1819. Piracy cases were common in the federal courts at this time, many of them brought against crewmen serving on privateers fitted out in United States ports and commissioned for service on behalf of Latin American governments in revolt against Spain and Portugal. Because privateering was often a convenient pretext for plundering Spanish and Portuguese commerce, the United States government encountered increasing diplomatic pressure to put an end to this activity. Smith and his mates had originally served on the *Creola*, a privateer out of Baltimore in the service of the government of Buenos Aires. In March 1819 the crew of the *Creola* (then lying in the port of Margarita) mutinied, left the vessel, and forcibly seized the *Irresistible*, a privateer also out of Baltimore that had been commissioned by a rival rebel government. On a subsequent cruise the *Irresistible* committed several acts of plunder, including the robbery of a Spanish vessel off the coast of Cuba. Shortly after the privateer arrived in the Chesapeake Bay, the crewmen were taken prisoner and sent to Richmond for trial. The indictment was brought under a recently enacted law to punish piracy, which prescribed death upon conviction for anyone who committed piracy "as defined by the law of nations." The trial, which began on 26 July, attracted a large audience that filled the House of Delegates chamber in the Capitol. After two days of hearing evidence and arguments, the court delivered its charge to the jury (Richmond *Enquirer*, 9, 30 July 1819; special verdict, U.S. v. Smith, U.S. Cir. Ct., Va., Ended Cases [Unrestored], 1820, Vi; *U.S. Statutes at Large*, III, 513–14).

The Court[1] then charged the jury in substance that the prisoner at the bar was indicted for cruizing on the high seas without any commission & boarding and plundering a Spanish vessel or vessels belonging to some power[2] to the jurors unknown, and piratically taking out of such vessel a sum of money, which the crew divided among themselves. The essential objects of enquiry were, whether the prisoner at the bar was engaged in such cruize without a commission, whether the robbery charged in the indictment was committed by him and others so cruizing as aforesaid, and whether the fact amounted to piracy under the act of Congress.

The fact of cruizing and plundering the Spanish vessel was proved by the testimony of accomplices, and it was contended by the counsel for the prisoner that they were totally unworthy of credit.

It is undoubtedly true that the testimony of accomplices is to be heard with suspicion; and if their testimony should be improbable or contradicted by circumstances, or by other testimony; the jury might justifiably discredit it: but if all the circumstances of the case, circumstances which could not be mistaken or misrepresented, corroborated the testimony of the accomplice, and in fact were merely connected by that testimony, it would be going too far to say that the facts supplied by the witness were to be disregarded because he was an accomplice. But in this case one of the witnesses—Donald, had been acquitted by the Grand Jury, because he was forced on board the vessel, and his testimony concurred with that of the other witnesses in all that was material.[3]

If the robbery was committed, their next enquiry would be, whether the vessel committing it, sailed under a lawful commission.

There was not only no testimony whatever of a commission, but all the facts given in evidence were totally incompatible with the idea of sailing under any authority whatever. The crew of one vessel had mutinied, seized another vessel, and proceeded on a cruize under officers elected by themselves.

The question whether the case came within the act of Congress was one of more difficulty.[4] It was impossible that the act could apply to any case if not to this. The case was undoubtedly piracy according to the understanding and practice of all nations. It was a case in which all nations surrendered their subjects to the punishment which any government might inflict upon them, and one in which all admitted the right of each to take and exercise jurisdiction. Yet the standard referred to by the act of Congress, as expressed in that act, must be admitted, to be so vague as to allow of some doubt. The writers on the law of nations give us no definition of the crime of piracy.[5] Under the doubts arising from this circumstance, the court recommended it to the jury to find a special verdict which might submit the law to the more deliberate consideration of the court.[6]

Printed, *Enquirer* (Richmond, Va.), 30 July 1819.

1. The charge is extracted from the full report of the case published in the *Enquirer*.

2. "Person" probably meant.

3. John Donald, of the *Creola*, testified that another crewman "threatened to blow out his brains if he did not join them in going against the Irresistable" (Richmond *Enquirer*, 30 July 1819).

4. The central question was whether the act of Mar. 1819 punishing piracy "as defined by the law of nations" could support an indictment for that crime. Counsel for the prisoners contended that the act was too vague; that piracy was not clearly and sufficiently defined by the law of nations; and that Congress had failed to do its constitutional duty by making "a rule which might be understood by the judiciary of the country." U.S. Attorney Robert Stanard replied that the designation of pirates by authorities on the law of nations as "enemies of the human race" provided a sufficient standard. Admitting that writers differed in their definitions of piracy, there was no definition that would not embrace this particular case. He urged the jury to uphold the honor of the country by enforcing the law "against brigands who not only sallied from its waters, to collect plunder, but returned to them as the scene for its partition, and as a sanctuary where they expected to escape the punishment of their crimes" (ibid.).

5. JM privately expressed the same doubts in letters to Bushrod Washington. In piracy cases he was disposed to construe acts of Congress strictly, as, for example, in U.S. v. Palmer, decided at the 1818 term of the Supreme Court (JM to Washington, 3 Aug. and 31 Oct. 1819; 3 Wheat. 626–35).

6. The special verdict left the decision to the court. On 30 July JM and Tucker (probably by prior agreement) divided in opinion on whether the offense committed by Smith and others amounted to the crime of piracy so as to be punishable under the 1819 act. The case then went by certificate of division to the Supreme Court, which at the 1820 term certified its opinion that the offense was piracy. Story gave the opinion for the Court, with Livingston dissenting. Accordingly, at the ensuing term of the circuit court, JM sentenced Smith and the other convicted pirates to death by hanging. Before the executions (set for 19 June 1820) were carried out, however, two of the prisoners received a full pardon from President Monroe and the rest were indefinitely reprieved. In an entry on the Smith case, dated 12 Dec. 1820, Tucker noted that the pirates' "Execution has hitherto been respited." Congress in the meantime amended the law by specifying precisely the offenses to be adjudged piracy (Richmond *Enquirer*, 3 Aug. 1819, 26, 30 May, 16 June 1820; 5 Wheat. 153, 157–83; Tucker, "Cases in the Courts of the United States, 25 February 1813–November 1824," No. 2, p. 136, Tucker-Coleman Papers, ViW; *U.S. Statutes at Large*, III, 600–1).

To Bushrod Washington

My dear Sir   Richmond Aug. 3d. 1819
   You will receive with this some printed reports which are all that I
can get on the subject of your enquiries.¹ I learn that the affairs of the
society, so far as respects the country, are in a very deranged state; but I
have no personal knowledge from which I can speak. The fact however
is generally beleived, & is supposed to be notorious. I have heard that
applications on account of losses have been made without success, but I
know of no particular case.
   In the enquirer you have probably seen before this, a full & fair statement of the case of the pirates.² It is adjourned to the supreme court. I
have serious doubts of the sufficiency of the law to authorize the infliction of punishment in a case of as notorious piracy as ever occurred.
   If you have an opportunity of sending the reserved sets of "a friend
to the constitution" to oak hill in Fauquier during the month of August
by any waggon, I shall receive them. Perhaps I may direct a waggoner
to call on you. Should there be no opportunity to oak hill, perhaps you
may send them by some opportunity to this place. My object is to put
them in the hands of some member of assembly should an attempt be
made to move the subject in the legislature. Keep them till they may be
sent without any very considerable expence.
   Amphyction is Judge Brockenbrough.
   Hampden is Judge Roane.
   Hortensius is G. Hay.³

AL, Marshall Papers, DLC. Endorsed by Washington above salutation.

   1. Letter not found. The context indicates that the inquiries concerned the solvency of
the Mutual Assurance Society. JM was a founding member of the company in 1794 but
resigned sometime after 1805 in response to a law that created separate funds to be
applied to losses on town and country properties. See *PJM*, VII, 217–18 and nn.
   2. U.S. v. Smith, Charge to Jury, 27 July 1819.
   3. The essays of "Hortensius" (George Hay) appeared in the Richmond *Enquirer* on 23,
27 July, and 3 Aug. 1819. It is uncertain whether there was an additional page of this
letter with JM's signature. If the letter did in fact end at this point, JM might have
deliberately omitted his signature to lessen the possibility of being identified as the
author of "A Friend of the Constitution."

To Bushrod Washington

Dear Sir   Richmond Oct. 31st. 1819
   I received this morning yours of the 26th.¹ The cases which will come
before you in Philadelphia, if the indictments are drawn on the last act
of Congress, must depend, if the accused are guilty, on the very point I
have adjourned to the supreme court because that question [is] whether

in any case what ever a conviction can take place under that act.² In the trials at Richmond the evidence was perfectly clear & the case was unequivocally a case of piracy according to the laws of every civilized nation. The doubt I entertain is whether there is any such thing as Piracy as "defined by the law of nations." All nations punish robbery committed on the high seas by vessels not commissioned to make captures yet I doubt seriously whether any nation punishes otherwise than by force of its own particular statute.

The account given by the editor of the union is not correct. The subscription was four dollars per annum instead of five unless the subscriber was in arrears & I was in advance. I had paid to Colo. Gamble³ the authorized agent of Mr. Bronson. When the Gazette of the United States became the Union it was advertized that in future the paper would be five dollars, but that this change would not affect those who were in advance for the paper until the time for which they had paid should elapse.⁴ I was then in advance to last June. Consequently I only owe from that time. I am not however disposed to squabble about it. Mr. Bronson I presume has sold out his accounts with his paper & has credited me only from the time his agent has settled with him in consequence of which he has charged me five instead of four dollars. I request you therefore to pay the account. I am dear Sir you⟨r⟩

J MARS⟨HALL⟩

ALS, Marshall Papers, DLC. Addressed to Washington in Philadelphia; postmarked Richmond, 31 Oct. Endorsed by Washington. MS torn where seal was broken.

1. Letter not found.

2. See U.S. v. Smith, Charge to Jury, 27 July 1819, and nn.

3. Possibly Robert Gamble (1754–1810), a Revolutionary War veteran and prominent Richmond merchant (*Richmond Portraits in an Exhibition of Makers of Richmond, 1737–1860* [Richmond, Va., 1949], 74).

4. In Mar. 1818 Enos Bronson's *United States' Gazette* merged with the *True American* to become the *Union. United States Gazette and True American*. Bronson sold the *Union* to William Henry Sanford sometime in 1819 (Clarence S. Brigham, *History and Bibliography of American Newspapers, 1619–1820* [2 vols.; Worcester, Mass., 1947], II, 957).

From Daniel Webster

Sir   Boston Nov. 19. 1819

May I beg permission to introduce to you Mr Gilbert, a very respectable Gentleman of the New Hampshire Bar.¹ He has occasion to be at Richmond, & would be particularly happy to make an acquaintance with you. He is a Gentleman of excellent character, & of respectability in his profession. I have the honor to be, with great respect, Your Ob. Serv

DANIEL WEBSTER

ALS, NhD. Addressed to JM in Richmond.

1. Probably Benjamin J. Gilbert (Charles M. Wiltse and Harold D. Moser, eds., *The Papers of Daniel Webster: Correspondence*, I [Hanover, N.H., 1974], 112).

United States v. Schooner Little Charles
Opinion
U.S. Circuit Court, Virginia, [ca. 22 November 1819]

After the circuit court in May 1818 reversed the district court's decree in this case, the United States moved for execution on a bond given by Charles Grice, owner of the *Little Charles*, in April 1808. This bond was executed in consequence of District Court Judge Griffin's order releasing the vessel pending a final decree of the court. In December 1818 the circuit court issued a writ of monition (a summons in admiralty proceedings) to Warren Ashley, Grice's security, to show cause why a decree should not be rendered against him and Grice for the penalty of the bond. Before deciding this case, Marshall sought Story's advice on some troublesome objections raised by the defendant, which he discussed in the opinion below (U.S. v. Schooner Little Charles, Opinion, 27 May 1818; proceedings in U.S. District Court [copy], 26 Dec. 1809; monition, 1 Dec. 1818, U.S. v. Schooner Little Charles, U.S. Cir. Ct., Va., Ended Cases [Unrestored], 1819, Vi; JM to Story, 27 May, 13 July 1819).

The United States		on motion for execution on bond
v	}	given on delivery of the Little
The Schooner Little Charles		Charles

This is a motion for an execution against Warren Ashly who signed a ¶1 bond with Charles Grice the owner of the Little Charles then libelled for a breach of the embargo laws, on receiving which the vessel was restored to the owner. In the district court the vessel was acquitted; that sentence was on appeal reversed, & the vessel was condemned by the sentence of this court. On the return of the monition which has been issued to the party who signed the bond, Mr. Ashly contends that the proceedings in the case have been so irregular, informal, & defective, that no execution can be issued on the bond, against him.

The objections are ¶2

1st. That the order for release is a nullity & all the consequent proceedings void, because the order was made by the Judge at his chambers, & not in court.[1]

The judicial act appoints certain stated terms of the District court, & ¶3 gives the Judge the power to hold special courts at his discretion either at the place appointed by law, "or at such other place in the District as the nature of the business & his discretion shall direct."[2]

¶4   No power, it is contended, is given to the Judge, except when sitting as a court, & therefore the form of declaring himself to be a court, is indispensable to the validity of his acts.

¶5   This objection seems rather technical than substantial. By law the District Judge alone composes the court. He is a court wherever & whenever he pleases. No notice to parties is required; no previous order is necessary. The various ex parte orders which admiralty proceedings require, renders this informal mode of acting essential to justice & expedition. The Judge will take care that neither party shall be injured by the orders which he makes ex parte, & where they are of course, it is convenient that they should be made without the formality of summoning the parties to attend. It does not seem to be a violent construction of such an act to consider the Judge as constituting a court whenever he proceeds on judicial business. Such seems to have been the practice in this & in other Districts of the United States. Had the Judge prefixed to his order such words as these—"At a special court held at   on this   day of   it is ordered &c.["] the proceeding would have been regular for the law does not, in terms at least, require that the order for a special court should be made in court or made any given time previous to its session. To every purpose of justice the order of the Judge made in his character as a Judge is made by him as a court whether he declares himself in words to be a court or not. This order is in its nature judicial. It is such an order as may be made exparte; it is signed by the Judge in his official character & is directed to the officer of the court. Under such circumstances I cannot overturn a practice which is convenient, which is not liable to abuse, on a meer technical objection.

¶6   2d. The 2d. objection is that the condition of the bond has not been broken. It is to perform the decree of the court which must mean the district court; & by that decree the libel was dismissed.

¶7   This objection too must search for other supp⟨ort⟩ than is furnished by the merits of the cause. The bond was intended to be substituted for the vessel; & to be acted upon as the vessel would have been acted upon had it remained in the power of the court. I think myself justified then by authority & by reason in construing the general term, "the court"— which is used in the condition, as meaning the court which shall ultimately decide the cause.

¶8   3d. An objection which I felt most difficulty in removing was that the bond was executed to the Marshal & that the valuation ought to have been made by commissioners appointed by the court.[3]

¶9   I beleive there is no special act of Congress prescribing the form of the bond or the mode of valuing the property. The act for regulating process in the courts of the United States directs that in causes in equity & in those of Admiralty & maritime jurisdiction the proceedings shall be "according to the principles, rules & usages which belong to courts of equity & to courts of admiralty respectively, as contradistinguished from courts of common law."[4]

The courts of the United States have never doubted their right to proceed under their general powers as courts of Admiralty where they were not restrained from the use of those powers by statute. ¶10

It may be that the proceedings in this case have not conformed strictly to the usages of Admiralty; But I do not think the defendent can be permitted to avail himself of an irregularity to which he is himself a party & which could only affect the libellants. ¶11

The bond is executed voluntarily to the marshal for the purpose of being substituted for the vessel & with full knowledge of the valuation. The libellants might have objected that the valuation was informal & insufficient. But they have not objected. The stipulation as it is was filed in court & has remained there in place of the vessel. I do not think that those who with full knowledge have made this stipulation, have placed it in the stead of the vessel & thereby obtained restitution thereof can be permitted to allege any unimportant informalitie⟨s⟩ in their own act. ¶12

The execution is to be awarded. ¶13

AD, Marshall Judicial Opinions, PPAmP; printed, John W. Brockenbrough, *Reports of Cases Decided by the Honourable John Marshall . . .* , I (Philadelphia, 1837), 381–83. For JM's deletions and interlineations, see Textual Notes below.

1. This order, which Judge Griffin signed and sealed at Yorktown on 12 Apr. 1808, contained no words indicating that it was an official order of the U.S. District Court (proceedings in U.S. District Court [copy], 26 Dec. 1809, U.S. v. Schooner Little Charles).

2. *U.S. Statutes at Large*, I, 74.

3. The order of release directed that the bond should be taken for the value of the schooner, "to be made by three disinterested Merchants or Shipwrights." The valuation, dated Norfolk, 14 Apr. 1808, is in these words: "We the subscribers being called upon by Mr. Cary Selden to value the Schooner Little Charles . . . are of opinion that she is worth Eighteen Hundred Dollars." The bond was executed to Joseph Scott, then U.S. marshal for Virginia (proceedings in U.S. District Court [copy], 26 Dec. 1809, U.S. v. Schooner Little Charles).

4. JM quoted from the 1792 act (*U.S. Statutes at Large*, I, 276).

Textual Notes

¶ 1 l. 1	who ~~executed~~ ↑signed↓ a	
l. 3	for ~~the~~ ↑a↓ breach	
l. 3	on ↑receiving↓ which	
¶ 2 l. 1 beg.	~~The asser~~ ↑The objections↓ are	
l. 2	order ~~of release~~ was	
¶ 5 l. 9	It [erasure] ↑does↓ not	
l. 11	seems ↑to↓ have	
ll. 13–14	court ~~of Admiralty~~ held	
l. 16	order ↑for a special court↓ should	
l. 18	made ↑in his character↓ as	
l. 21	his ~~judicial~~ official	

¶ 7 l. 1   too ~~is~~ ↑ must ↓ search
    l. 6   as ↑ meaning ↓ the
¶ 8 l. 2   that ~~va~~ ↑ the ↓ valuation
¶11 l. 3   of ~~this~~ ↑ an ↓ irregularity
    l. 4   could ~~af~~ ↑ only ↓ affect
¶12 ll. 7–8   obtained ~~th~~ ↑ restitution ↓ ~~e~~ ↑ thereof ↓ can be permitted to
                    [*erasure*] ↑ allege ↓ any

Selden v. Hendrickson & Pryor
Opinion
U.S. Circuit Court, Virginia, [ca. 22 November 1819]

This was an appeal from an admiralty sentence of the U.S. District Court, sitting at Richmond in October 1818. John Hendrickson and George Pryor, New York merchants, brought a libel in the district court against the schooner *Richmond* to recover the amount of a bottomry bond given by the master of the vessel to the libelants. In February 1816 the *Richmond*, owned by Cary Selden of Richmond and commanded by Joseph P. Colvin, put in for repairs and refitting in the port of New York. Colvin "hypothecated" the vessel, executing a bottomry bond that pledged her as security for repayment of money lent by Hendrickson & Pryor for supplying and fitting out the schooner for the return voyage to Richmond. In answer to the libel Selden denied Colvin's right to hypothecate the vessel in a domestic port, contending that the right of hypothecating in a foreign port arose from necessity (the inability of the master to apply to the owner for money) and that no such necessity existed in this case. He also insisted that the amount advanced was far greater than was necessary to repair and refit the schooner. District judge Tucker upheld the libel, ordering Selden to pay the balance and interest due on the bottomry bond. The appeal was argued at the May 1819 term of the circuit court, but Marshall postponed giving an opinion until after he had consulted with Washington and Story about the difficult points arising from the case (proceedings in U.S. District Court [copy], 22 Oct. 1818, Selden v. Hendrickson & Pryor, U.S. Cir. Ct., Va., Ended Cases [Unrestored], 1827, Vi; JM to Washington, 31 May 1819; JM to Story, 13 July 1819; Story to JM, 26 July 1819).

Selden
v   ⎫   appeal from the district court in
Hendrickson &   ⎬   Admiralty.
Prior   ⎭

¶1   This case arises on a Bottomree bond given by the master of the Schooner Richmond to the appellee for repairs done on that vessel. The vessel belonged to the port of Richmond at which place the owner resided, & the repairs were made & the money advanced in New York.

The question whether the master of an American vessel may hypoth-   ¶2
ecate her for necessary repairs in a port of the United States, is one of
considerable importance to commerce, which has never yet, I beleive,
been directly decided. In considering it, the relative situation of the
owner & master must be taken into view.

The owner remains generally on land, engaged in those occupations   ¶3
to which his interest or his inclination may lead him. The care & management of his vessel, while navigating the ocean, is entrusted to the
Master: It is generally of much importance that the voyage should be
prosecuted; & that it should be prosecuted without great delays. A ship
navigating the ocean is exposed to perils which frequently disable her
from prosecuting her voyage without repairs, or necessary supplies.
When these circumstances are taken into consideration, & when it is
recollected that the master is appointed by the owner, it would seem
reasonable to expect that every power necessary for the performance
of the voyage should be vested in him by his appointment; & might
be exercised wherever the owner himself, or his known & authorized
agent, could not be consulted without endangering or retarding the
voyage.

In conformity with this principle of reason is the maritime law of all   ¶4
nations. It is stated to be the law, not only in Valin, Emerigon[1] & other
foreign writers but is expressly laid down to be the law of the Admiralty
& the law of England in Bridgemans case reported by Hobart,[2] is admitted in the case of Justin v Ballam reported in Lord Raymond[3] as
well as in several modern cases, & is recognized by Parke, Marshall,
Jacobson, Abbot, Livermore, & other modern compilers.[4] Upon this
point there is no doubt. In the absence of the owner the master is in the
place of the owner, & is, by his appointment, impliedly clothed with
power to do all that is necessary for the success of the voyage; & to bind
the vessel, or the owners, or both, by his engagements. The difficulty is
to decide in what situations the absence of the owner is such as to
authorize the master to act independently of his special orders. Must
the vessel, if belonging to an American, be without the territory &
jurisdiction of the United States? Or is it enough that she be without
the state in which the owner resides?

As the same motives exist every where for empowering the master to   ¶5
act in the absence of the owner during the voyage, the laws of the different nations of Europe on this subject, resemble each other very nearly;
& indeed on all maritime questions, the decisions of one country have
been very much respected in the courts of every other. They originate
in the same source, & have preserved considerable uniformity.

There is scarcely any thing on the subject which is entitled to more   ¶6
respect than the marine ordinance of Louis 14th. It was compiled with
great care, by the ablest civilians of the nation, & with a view, as we are
told, not only to all the antient codes which are extant, but also to the

customs & laws of all the maritime states of Europe. By that ordinance, the master is not allowed to hypothecate the vessel "in the place where the owner resides["]; and these expressions are construed in France to comprehend the whole district, but not the whole country. In his treatise on agencies, Mr. Livermore says "And upon the construction of these words *le lieu de la demeure des proprietaires*, the place of residence of the owners, Emerigon observes, that the whole district or bailiwick, is to be considered the owners place of residence; but that, if the vessel puts into a neighboring port, in another district, this is not the owners place of residence. Therefore where the master of a vessel from Toulon gave a bottomry bond at Marseilles, it was determined that he had authority to do so."[5] Valin says the master may hypothecate the ship when on her voyage & in a place where neither the owner nor his correspondents reside.[6]

¶7   This decision seems consonant to the principles of reason. The power of the master to act in the absence of the owner is a rule of convenience founded on the necessity of the case. This necessity depends not meerly on the vessel's being within the same jurisdiction with the owners; but on its being so near them, that application may be made to them without material injury to the voyage. In small territories, the whole country may, without inconvenience, be considered as the place of residence of the owners, but in large territories, as in Russia, the rule would often be defeated by encumbering it with such a condition. In such countries, the power of the master must commence with his voyage, or must commence after passing some line within the limits of the empire, or the success of the voyage must be greatly endangered.

¶8   In England the same principle has been adopted, but has been so modified as to suit the situation of that country. The master has power to hypothecate the vessel or to bind the owners personally for necessary repairs abroad, but not at home. This is the general principle of English law, & is precisely the same with that which is contained in the marine ordinance of Louis the 14th. When the vessel is abroad, & when at home, has been, in England, as well as in France, a question for construction. This question has arisen in cases where the repairs were actually made beyond the seas & generally in a foreign country; & the language used by the court is adapted to the case. It has never arisen, I beleive, in a case where an English vessel was hypothecated by the master in a distant port of England; and it has never I beleive been decided that such hypothecation would not be valid. Those writers who lay down the English law understand the principle to be, but do not say expressly that it is, that every port in England is to an English vessel a home port. That principle however is not expressly affirmed by any writer, nor by any Judge, so far as the cases have come under my inspection. Marshall after stating the practice of allowing the master to hypothecate the ship in a foreign country, says "And it is essential to the safety of the ship & the success of the voyage, that the master in the absence of the owners, should have this power, which is, indeed, by the marine law, implied in his appointment.

["]But as the owners are presumed to give entire authority to the master, only in their absence, and for such affairs as they cannot themselves conveniently transact, he is not in fact master till after he sets sail. Till then he is subject to their orders, & they have the power of dismissing him at pleasure; til then therefore he can transact no business of importance but under their immediate directions. Hence if the master borrow money on bottomry in the place where the owners reside, without there express authority, it can only affect his own interest on board."[7]   ¶9

Nothing in this passage, or in any other part of Marshall so far as I have examined him, would indicate that the power of the master commences only when he leaves England, & can not be exercised even in a port of England, other than the home port of the vessel.   ¶10

Mr. Abbot says "It is obvious that a loan of money upon bottomry, while it releives the owner from many of the perils of maritime adventure, deprives him also of a great part of the profits of a successful voyage"; (This I presume alludes to those cases of bottomry where more than legal interest is reserved.) "and therefore" continues Mr. Abbot, "in the place of the owners residence, where they may exercise their own judgement upon the propriety of borrowing money in this manner, the master of the ship is by the maritime law of all states precluded from doing it, so as to bind the interest of the owners, without their consent.["]   ¶11

["]The meaning of the words place of residence (*la de meure des proprietaires*) has given occasion to some questions in France. With us I apprehend the whole of England is considered, for this purpose, as the residence of an English man; at least before the commencement of a voyage."   ¶12

Mr. Abbot cites no authority for supposing that the whole of England would for this purpose be considered as the residence of an Englishman. Nor have I been able to find any express authority for it. He gives it as his own speculative opinion, & he gives it with considerable doubt, for he adds, "at least before the commencement of a voyage."[8]   ¶13

In the case of Watkinson v Bernardiston 2. P. W. 367. it is said "But it is true that if at sea, where no treaty or contract can be made with the owner, the master employs any person to do work on the ship, or to new rig or repair the same, this, for necessity & encouragement of trade, is a lien upon the ship; and in such case, the master, by the maritime law, is allowed to hypothecate the ship."[9] The⟨se⟩ words would rather seem ⟨to⟩ include a port in England into which an English vessel   ¶14 damaged during her voyage might put for repairs. Our countryman Mr. Livermore takes the same view of this subject with Mr. Abbot.

¶15   I am inclined to beleive that on this subject the courts of Admiralty in England would proceed according to the general principles of maritime law. The cases in the books where they have been restrained by prohibition would seem to justify the inference that, if not so restrained, they would have granted the releif which was sought, & in no case that I have seen, has a prohibition been awarded to a court of Admiralty proceeding on a bottomry bond given by the master in a distant English port after the commencement of the voyage. In fact I can concieve no reason why a master may not for the success of the voyage hypothecate the vessel to secure a debt carrying only legal interest, in any place where he might bind the owners personally, & it has been determined that he may bind them personally by his contracts for repairs made in England at a port where they do not reside.

¶16   Although it has never been decided affirmatively that every port in England is for this purpose the residence of an English owner, it has been decided negatively that a colonial port, or a port in Ireland, or a port in Jersey, is not a home port.

¶17   On the same reason I think it would be held that a port in Scotland is not a home port for an English vessel. That this is the prevailing opinion with legal men in England I infer from the language of Mr. Abbott who says that he apprehends "the whole of England" not the whole of Britain, "is considered for this purpose as the residence of an Englishman." I infer it too from the general language of other cases & particularly of Wood & others against Hamilton which was a case from Scotland decided in the house of Lords & is mentioned by Abbot.[10]

¶18   These cases show conclusively that in the law of England, it is not necessary that a vessel should be without the realm in order to authorize the master to hypothecate her for repairs, or other necessaries, to enable her to prosecute her voyage. The same principle, applied to the United States, requires, I think that a port in one state should not be considered as the place of residence of owners who live in another state. This rule of maritime law originates in the principle that in the absence of the owner, the master is by himself substituted for him, that he is entrusted with the vessel for the purpose of performing the voyage, & must necessarily act for the owner in all cases where he is incapable of acting for himself. The rule has no connexion with territory or with jurisdiction. In reason then the power should exist whenever the necessity exists: And where there is positive law modifying a rule thus originating, it would seem strange to insist that the power of the master to act because the owner is absent, should not commence with his voyage, but should commence only on his passing the limits of the nation however wide or however narrow those limits might be. It would be strange if a vessel belonging to Eastport might be hypothecated by the master in the port of St. Andrews, because the owner was absent & yet might not be hypothecated at New Orleans, St. Louis, or the mouth of Columbia.[11]

The reason of the case then concurs with the practice of maritime nations in declaring that the owner cannot be considered as present in every port belonging to the nation, but that some subdivisional line, as the districts in France, must be taken, on passing which the power of the master commences. If every port, except that in which the owner actually resides, be not for this purpose, a foreign port, I percieve no rule more proper in this country, no rule better adapted to our situation & to the reason of the thing, than to say that the power of the master to hypothecate exists in every port out of the state in which the owner resides, where he has no agent. I am therefore of opinion that a vessel belonging to the port of Richmond in Virginia may be hypothecated in the Port of New York by the master, for necessary repairs, if the owner have no agent in New York. ¶19

This power is unquestionably limited by the necessity in which it originates. The money for which the bond is taken must be advanced on the faith of the bottom & must be necessary to enable the vessel to prosecute her voyage. Both these circumstances are proved in this case if the witness is to be beleived. ¶20

I do not think myself at liberty to discredit him. His character is unimpeached, & I do not percieve any intrinsic impossibility in his statement. He might know all that he asserts himself to know.[12] ¶21

I cannot resist the suspicion that these expenses were too considerable & that the Master has not been faithful to his owner. But this case presents no testimony which will authorize a court to indulge this suspicion. There is no testimony whatever which questions any one item of the account on which the hypothecation was made & every item of that account is proved. ¶22

It has been argued that the owner might have had an agent in New York. I should rather think that proof on this point ought not to be required from the person who advances the money; but if it ought Mr. Seldens letter of the 24th. of Feby. states it expressly.[13] ¶23

It is said that the vessel remained in New York long enough to have consulted the owner. ¶24

The time of her arrival is not mentioned. The first advance was made on the 10th. of Feby. & the instrument of hypothecation is dated on the 17th. The evidence is that the advance was made on a contract of hypothecation; & this is supported by Mr. Seldens letter of the 24th. in which he acknowledges a letter of the 16th. giving notice of the fact. That letter too contains an express assumpsit of the debt. ¶25

I do not percieve any just objection in law to the account & as the proof establishes both the necessity of the repairs & the fact that the a⟨dv⟩ance was made on the credit of the bottom the sentence must be affirmed with costs.[14] ¶26

AD, Marshall Judicial Opinions, PPAmP; printed, John W. Brockenbrough, *Reports of Cases Decided by the Honourable John Marshall* . . . , I (Philadelphia, 1837), 398–406. For JM's deletions and interlineations, see Textual Notes below.

1. René Josué Valin, *Nouveau commentaire sur l'ordonnance de la marine, du mois d'Août 1681* . . . (2 vols.; La Rochelle, Fr., 1760); Balthazard Marie Emérigon, *An Essay on Maritime Loans* . . . , trans. John E. Hall (Baltimore, Md., 1811).

2. Bridgeman's Case, Hob. 11, 80 Eng. Rep. 162 (K.B., n.d.). Henry Hobart was chief justice of the Court of Common Pleas from 1613 to 1625.

3. Justin v. Ballam, 2 Raym. Ld. 805, 92 Eng. Rep. 38 (K.B., 1702).

4. James Allan Park, *A System of the Law of Marine Insurances* (1787; 7th ed.; London, 1817); Samuel Marshall, *A Treatise on the Law of Insurance* (1st Am. ed.; Boston, 1805; S #8837); Friedrich Johann Jacobsen, *Laws of the Sea, with Reference to Maritime Commerce, during Peace and War* . . . (Baltimore, Md., 1818; S #44450); Charles Abbott, *A Treatise of the Law Relative to Merchant Ships and Seamen: In Four Parts* (2d Am. ed.; Newburyport, Mass., 1810; S #19295); Samuel Livermore, *A Treatise on the Law of Principal and Agent; and of Sales by Auction* (2 vols.; Baltimore, Md., 1818; S #44599).

5. Livermore, *Principal and Agent*, I, 171.

6. Ibid., 164.

7. Marshall, *Treatise on the Law of Insurance*, 638.

8. Abbott, *Treatise relative to Ships and Seamen*, 171.

9. Watkinson v. Bernardiston, 2 P.Wms. 367, 24 Eng. Rep. 769 (Ch., 1726). JM copied this passage on a separate sheet for insertion here.

10. Wood v. Hamilton, cited by Abbott, *Treatise relative to Ships and Seamen*, 159.

11. Eastport, Maine, and St. Andrews, New Brunswick, lie on Passamaquoddy Bay.

12. JM referred to the deposition of John H. Watson, clerk in Hendrickson & Pryor's store, taken on 21 Sept. 1816. Watson testified that all the articles charged in an annexed account were delivered to the master of the *Richmond*, which was then in New York port and unfit for sea without repairs (proceedings in U.S. District Court [copy], 22 Oct. 1818, Selden v. Hendrickson & Pryor).

13. In his letter to Hendrickson & Pryor of 24 Feb. 1816, Selden stated he "had but one acquaintance in New York" (ibid.).

14. The appeal remained on the docket until June 1827, when it was dismissed on the libelants' acknowledging full satisfaction of their demand (U.S. Cir. Ct., Va., Ord. Bk. XII, 159).

Textual Notes

¶ 1 l. 2	Schooner ↑Richmond↓ to th ↑the↓ appellee	
ll. 2–3	vessel. ~~in the port of New York~~ The	
l. 3	of ~~Norfolk~~ ↑Richmond↓ at	
l. 4	in ~~the port of~~ New York.	
¶ 2 l. 1	of ~~a~~ ↑an American↓ vessel	
¶ 3 l. 1	land, ~~pursuing~~ engaged	
ll. 2–3	The ↑care &↓ management	
l. 4	of ~~great~~ ↑much↓ importance	
ll. 6–7	disable [*erasure*] ↑her↓ from	
ll. 9–10	would ~~b~~ ↑seem↓ reasonable	
l. 11	voyage ~~was~~ ↑should be↓ vested in ~~the master~~ ↑him↓ by	
l. 12	his ↑known &↓ authorized	
¶ 4 ll. 2–3	nations. ↑It is stated to be the law, not only in Valin, Emerigon & other foreign writers but↓ ~~It~~ is	
ll. 3–4	Admiralty ↑& the law of England↓ in	

ll. 5–6		Raymond ↑as well as in several modern cases,↓ &
l. 7		& m̶ ↑other↓ modern
l. 9		impliedly e̶l̶ ↑clothed↓ with
ll. 13–16		orders. ↑Must the vessel, if belonging to an American, be without the territory & jurisdiction of the United States? Or is it enough that she be without the state in which the owner resides?↓
¶ 5 l. 6		same c̶o̶d̶e̶ source,
¶ 6 l. 2		Louis X̶I̶I̶I̶I̶t̶h̶ 14th.
l. 4		told, ↑not only to all the antient codes which are extant, but also↓ to
l. 5		maritime n̶a̶t̶i̶o̶n̶ states
ll. 10–11		*demeure* p̶ ↑*des*↓ *proprietaires*, ↑the place of residence of the owners,↓ Emerigon
ll. 16–18		so." ↑Velin says the master may hypothecate the ship when on her voyage & in a place where neither the owner nor his correspondents reside.↓
¶ 7 l. 2		the o̶w̶n̶e̶r̶ ↑master↓ to act in the absence of the m̶a̶s̶t̶e̶r̶ ↑owner↓ is
¶ 8 l. 8		construction. I̶t̶ ̶h̶a̶s̶ ̶b̶e̶e̶n̶ ̶d̶e̶t̶e̶r̶ This
l. 9		the s̶e̶a̶l̶ ↑seas↓ & i̶n̶ ↑generally↓ in
l. 11		where a̶ ̶B̶r̶ ↑an English↓ vessel
l. 14		understand i̶t̶ ↑the principle↓ to
l. 18		the p̶r̶ practice
¶10 l. 3		exercised ↑even↓ in
¶14 ll. 1–8		↑In the case of Watkinson v Bernardiston 2. P. W. 367. it is said "But it is true that if at sea, where no treaty or contract can be made with the owner, the master employs any person to do work on the ship, or to new rig or repair the same, this, for necessity & encouragement of trade, is a lien upon the ship; and in such case, the master, by the maritime law, is allowed to hypothecate the ship." The⟨se⟩ words would rather seem ⟨to⟩ include a port of England into which an English vessel damaged during her voyage might put for repairs.↓ Our
¶15 l. 2		general l̶a̶w̶ ↑principles of↓ maritime
l. 3		have ↑been↓ restrained
l. 6		been g̶r̶a̶n̶t̶e̶d̶ ↑awarded↓ to
l. 8		voyage. I̶t̶ ̶h̶a̶s̶ ̶b̶e̶e̶n̶ ̶d̶e̶t̶e̶r̶m̶i̶n̶e̶d̶ In
ll. 9–10		not ↑for the success of the voyage↓ hypothecate
ll. 11–13		personally ⁒ ↑, & it has been determined that he may bind them personally by his contracts for repairs made in England at a port where they do not reside.↓
¶16 l. 1		decided ↑affirmatively↓ that
l. 2		is ↑for this purpose↓ the
l. 3		decided ↑negatively↓ that
¶17 l. 2		port ↑for an English vessel.↓ That
l. 5		"w̶o̶u̶l̶d̶ ↑is considered↓ for
l. 7		of w̶o̶o̶d̶ ↑Wood↓ &

ll. 7–8	case ~~of~~ ↑from↓ Scotland
¶19 l. 1 beg.	~~These~~ The
ll. 10–11	a [*erasure*] ↑vessel↓ belonging
l. 12	master, ↑for necessary repairs,↓ if
¶25 l. 2	the ~~bond~~ ↑instrument↓ of hypothecation ~~w~~ ↑is↓ dated

To Thomas Morris

Dear Sir[1]   Richmond Decr. 20th. 1819

I have received your letter transmitting me a check on the Mechanicks bank of New York which I negotiated without any difficulty.[2] This remittance releived me from some embarassment which was unpleasant.

I am far from wishing you to make any sacrifice in order to take up the mortgage on the Genessee land; but I am at the same time desirous that it should be done as soon as is practicable without a sacrifice.[3] A mortgage on property which we are selling is disagreeable & I am particularly solicitous to close this transaction because we have a suit in Philadelphia against the Land company for some shares from which we hope to raise nearly the residue of our debt; & I fear that suit may produce some difficulty as respects our claim on the trust fund. For both these reasons I wish an adjustment with Mr. Higbee[4] as soon as it can be made without loss.

I am much gratified both on your account & my own at your prospect of receiving next spring so considerable a sum as you mention. I have been guilty of the folly of indorsing for a particular friend who has failed two notes of 5000$ each, one of which I have borrowed money to settle, & the other I expect to be under the necessity of settling next spring. This unexpected demand added to the claims of my sons who are marrying in great haste really presses me beyond my resources, & our banks can give no aid.[5] You will oblige me by letting me know how far I may rely on you in the spring. I am dear Sir with great regard & esteem, Your Obedt

J Marshall

ALS, NhHi. Addressed to Morris in New York; postmarked Richmond, 20 Dec. Endorsed by Morris "acknowledging Rct of $4000."

1. Son of Robert Morris, Thomas Morris (1771–1849) was a New York lawyer who had served in the Seventh Congress (1801–1803). He was then U.S. marshal for the southern district of New York. JM had corresponded with him in 1813 about the Genesee lands (*PJM*, VII, 414).

2. Letter not found. As indicated by the endorsement, the amount of the check was $4,000.

3. Morris was acting on behalf of JM and James Marshall in regard to the sale of Robert

Morris's Genesee lands. Robert Morris had conveyed these lands to trustees in 1798 for the purpose of securing his numerous creditors. This deed of trust gave rise to the case of FitzSimons v. Ogden, decided by the Supreme Court in 1812. For the background to this case, see *PJM*, VII, 188–89, 190 nn.

4. Joseph Higbee, a Philadelphia merchant, was one of the trustees under the deed of 1798.

5. Jaquelin A. Marshall had been married the preceding January; John Marshall was to be married in Feb. 1820, and James K. Marshall in Dec. 1821 (Paxton, *Marshall Family*, 99, 101).

APPENDICES

Appendix I
Opinions Delivered by Chief Justice John Marshall in the U.S. Supreme Court
1814–1819

The calendar below lists in chronological order all the opinions delivered by Chief Justice Marshall from the 1814 term through the 1819 term of the Supreme Court. All 105 opinions were cases of appellate jurisdiction, seven of which came up by certificate of division and the rest by appeal or by writ of error. For a brief discussion of federal appellate procedure under the judicial statutes of 1789, 1802, and 1803, see *The Papers of John Marshall*, VI, 537–38.

In addition to the date of the opinion and the name of the case, the calendar provides the following information: the citation to the printed report; the type of appeal; the name of the court of origin; the appellate case number; and the date(s) of arguments by counsel. This information has been compiled from the printed reports and the Supreme Court minutes, dockets, and appellate case files belonging to Record Group 267 in the National Archives. The style of the case is that used by the reporters William Cranch and Henry Wheaton, unless other sources indicate that they were mistaken. The existence of an original manuscript opinion in Marshall's hand is also noted.

1814

15 February	Griffith v. Frazier, 8 Cranch 19–30. Error to U.S. Circuit Court, S.C. Appellate Case No. 563. Argued 9–10 Feb. 1814.
15 February	Van Ness v. Forrest, 8 Cranch 33–35. Error to U.S. Circuit Court, D.C. Appellate Case No. 562. Argued 8 Feb. 1814.
16 February	Bank of Alexandria v. Herbert, 8 Cranch 38–39. Appeal from U.S. Circuit Court, D.C., Alexandria. Appellate Case No. 582. Argued 14 Feb. 1814.
19 February	Clementson v. Williams, 8 Cranch 73–74. Error to U.S. Circuit Court, D.C., Alexandria. Appellate Case No. 583. Argued 14 Feb. 1814.
19 February	Gracie v. Marine Insurance Co. of Baltimore, 8 Cranch 81–84. Error to U.S. Circuit Court, Md. Appellate Case No. 589. Argued 16–17 Feb. 1814.
2 March	Brown v. United States, 8 Cranch 121–29. Appeal from U.S. Circuit Court, Mass. Appellate Case No. 650. No oral arguments.
7 March	The Alexander, 8 Cranch 179–80. Appeal from U.S. Circuit Court, Mass. Appellate Case No. 643. Argued 5 Mar. 1814.
8 March	Pratt v. Carroll, 8 Cranch 471–78. Appeal from U.S. Circuit Court, D.C. Appellate Case No. 535. Argued 9–10 Mar. 1813.
9 March	Alexander v. Pendleton, 8 Cranch 468–70. Appeal from U.S. Circuit Court, D.C., Alexandria. Appellate Case No. 558. Argued Feb. 1813 term.

12 March   The Venus, 8 Cranch 288–317. Appeal from U.S. Circuit Court, Mass. Appellate Case Nos. 633, 634. Argued 23–24, 26 Feb. 1814.

12 March   The Merrimack, 8 Cranch 327–28. Appeal from U.S. Circuit Court, Md. Appellate Case No. 596. Argued 26, 28 Feb. 1814.

12 March   The Frances (Thompson and others, claimants), 8 Cranch 347–48. Appeal from U.S. Circuit Court, R.I. Appellate Case No. 610. Argued 28 Feb., 1, 7 Mar. 1814.

12 March   The Frances (Graham's claim), 8 Cranch 348–53. Appeal from U.S. Circuit Court, R.I. Appellate Case No. 631. Argued 1 Mar. 1814.

12 March   The Frances (Dunham & Randolph's claim), 8 Cranch 357–58. Appeal from U.S. Circuit Court, R.I. Appellate Case No. 611. Argued 2 Mar. 1814.

12 March   The Frances (Kennedy's claim), 8 Cranch 358–59. Appeal from U.S. Circuit Court, R.I. Appellate Case No. 613. Not argued.

12 March   The Frances (Gillespie's claim), 8 Cranch 371. Appeal from U.S. Circuit Court, R.I. Appellate Case No. 632. Argued 7 Mar. 1814.

1815

9 February   Mandeville v. Union Bank of Georgetown, 9 Cranch 11. Error to U.S. Circuit Court, D.C., Alexandria. Appellate Case No. 580. Argued 8 Feb. 1815.

13 February   Meigs v. McClung's Lessee, 9 Cranch 16–18. Error to U.S. Circuit Court, E. Tenn. Appellate Case No. 622. Argued 11 Feb. 1815.

14 February   Simms v. Guthrie, 9 Cranch 23–27. Error to U.S. Circuit Court, Ky. Appellate Case No. 606. Argued 8–9 Feb. 1815.

15 February   Taber v. Perrott and Lee, 9 Cranch 41–43. Error to U.S. Circuit Court, R.I. Appellate Case No. 559. Argued 14 Feb. 1815.

16 February   Speake v. United States, 9 Cranch 39. Error to U.S. Circuit Court, D.C. Appellate Case No. 617. Argued 10 Feb. 1815.

17 February   Brig Short Staple and Cargo v. United States, 9 Cranch 59–64. Appeal from U.S. Circuit Court, Mass. Appellate Case No. 594. Argued 13 Feb. 1815.

18 February   Parker v. Rule's Lessee, 9 Cranch 67–71. Error to U.S. Circuit Court W. Tenn. Appellate Case No. 626. Argued 11 Feb. 1815.

21 February   Polk's Lessee v. Wendell, 9 Cranch 94–102. Error to U.S. Circuit Court, W. Tenn. Appellate Case No. 511. Argued 7 Feb. 1815.

22 February   The Ship Richmond v. United States, 9 Cranch 102–4. Appeal from U.S. Circuit Court, Ga. Appellate Case No. 621. Argued 15 Feb. 1815.

25 February   The Mary, 9 Cranch 139–51. Appeal from U.S. Circuit Court, R.I. Appellate Case No. 647. Argued 8–9 Mar. 1814; 18, 20–21 Feb. 1815.

27 February   Doe, Lessee of Lewis and Wife v. McFarland, 9 Cranch 151–53. Error to U.S. Circuit Court, Ky. Appellate Case No. 641. Argued 17 Feb. 1815.

28 February	Clark's Executors v. Van Riemsdyk, 9 Cranch 154–63. Appeal from U.S. Circuit Court, R.I. Appellate Case No. 651. Argued 22–23 Feb. 1815.
28 February	Finley v. Williams, 9 Cranch 165–71. Appeal from U.S. Circuit Court, Ky. Appellate Case No. 490. Argued 22 Feb. 1813.
1 March	McIver's Lessee v. Walker, 9 Cranch 177–79. Error to U.S. Circuit Court, E. Tenn. Appellate Case No. 616. Argued 9–10 Feb. 1815.
1 March	Owens v. Hanney, 9 Cranch 180. Error to U.S. Circuit Court, Ga. Appellate Case No. 560. Argued 8 Feb. 1815.
4 March	Thirty Hogsheads of Sugar v. Boyle, 9 Cranch 195–99. Appeal from U.S. Circuit Court, Md. Appellate Case No. 675. Argued 3 Mar. 1815.
6 March	Ship Societe, 9 Cranch 210–12. Appeal from U.S. Circuit Court, Ga. Appellate Case No. 689. Argued 3 Mar. 1815.
10 March	Otis v. Watkins, 9 Cranch 356–58. Error to Supreme Judicial Court of Mass. Appellate Case No. 586. Submitted on written arguments.
10 March	Gettings v. Burch's Administratix, 9 Cranch 373–74. Error to U.S. Circuit Court, D.C. Appellate Case No. 649. Argued 21 Feb. 1815.
11 March	The Nereide, 9 Cranch 412–31. Appeal from U.S. Circuit Court, N.Y. Appellate Case No. 707. Argued 6–9 Mar. 1815.

1816

10 February	Henry v. Ball, 1 Wheat. 3–6. Error to U.S. Circuit Court, D.C. Appellate Case No. 692. Argued 8 Feb. 1816.
12 February	Davis v. Wood, 1 Wheat. 8–9. Error to U.S. Circuit Court, D.C. Appellate Case No. 691. Argued 8 Feb. 1816.
14 February	The Mary and Susan (The Privateer Tickler v. Fourteen Casks and Four Baskets of Merchandize), 1 Wheat. 35–45. Appeal from U.S. Circuit Court, N.Y. Appellate Case No. 702. Argued 10 Feb. 1816.
16 February	The Samuel, MS opinion, 1 Wheat. 13–19. Appeal from U.S. Circuit Court, R.I. Appellate Case No. 661. Argued 6 Feb. 1816.
23 February	Anderson v. Longden, 1 Wheat. 91. Error to U.S. Circuit Court, D.C., Alexandria. Appellate Case No. 714. Argued 23 Feb. 1816.
26 February	Thompson v. Gray, 1 Wheat. 81–84. Error to U.S. Circuit Court, D.C., Alexandria. Appellate Case No. 713. Argued 22 Feb. 1816.
28 February	Corporation of New Orleans v. Winter, 1 Wheat. 94–95. Error to U.S. District Court, La. Appellate Case No. 720. Argued 24 Feb. 1816.
4 March	The Astrea, 1 Wheat. 127–28. Appeal from U.S. Circuit Court, Ga. Appellate Case No. 728. No date found for argument.
5 March	Matson v. Hord, 1 Wheat. 131–41. Appeal from U.S. Circuit Court, Ky. Appellate Case No. 644. Argued 21–22 Feb. 1816.
6 March	Taylor v. Walton, 1 Wheat. 141–51. Appeal from U.S. Circuit Court, Ky. Appellate Case No. 723. Argued 27 Feb. 1816.

[6 March ?]   The George, MS opinion, 1 Wheat. 409–14. Appeal from U.S. Circuit Court, Mass. Appellate Case No. 729. Argued 4, 6 Mar. 1816.

7 March   Patton's Lessee v. Easton, 1 Wheat. 477–82. Certificate of division from U.S. Circuit Court, W. Tenn. Appellate Case No. 629. Argued 11, 14 Feb. 1815.

8 March   The Nereid, 1 Wheat. 178. Certificate of division from U.S. Circuit Court, N.Y. Appellate Case No. 798. Argued 8 Mar. 1816.

15 March   Harnden v. Fisher, MS opinion, 1 Wheat. 301–4. Error to U.S. Circuit Court, N.Y. Appellate Case No. 763. No date found for argument.

18 March   Walden v. Gratz's Heirs, MS opinion, 1 Wheat. 295–98. Error to U.S. Circuit Court, Ky. Appellate Case No. 743. Argued 8 Mar. 1816.

21 March   Brig Eliza v. Chazel, MS opinion, unreported. Appeal from U.S. Circuit Court, Ga. Appellate Case No. 748. Argued 15 Mar. 1816.

21 March   United States v. Stackelburg and Cargo, MS opinion, unreported. Appeal from U.S. Circuit Court, Ga. Appellate Case No. 744. Argued 14–15 Mar. 1816.

22 March   The Commercen, MS opinion, 1 Wheat. 395–406. Appeal from U.S. Circuit Court, Mass. Appellate Case No. 749. Argued 16 Mar. 1816.

22 March   The Hiram, MS opinion, 1 Wheat. 444–47. Appeal from U.S. Circuit Court, Mass. Appellate Case No. 752. Argued 18 Mar. 1816.

22 March   Ammidon v. Smith, 1 Wheat. 457–62. Certificate of division from U.S. Circuit Court, R.I. Appellate Case No. 701. Submitted on written arguments.

1817

8 February   Greenleaf v. Cook, 2 Wheat. 16–18. Error to U.S. Circuit Court, D.C. Appellate Case No. 674. Argued 5 Feb. 1817.

10 February   The Carl Gustaf, MS opinion, unreported. Appeal from U.S. Circuit Court, Ga. Appellate Case No. 756. Argued 19–20 Mar. 1816.

10 February   McIver v. Ragan, 2 Wheat. 28–31. Error to U.S. Circuit Court, W. Tenn. Appellate Case No. 698. Argued 5–6 Feb. 1817.

12 February   Slocum v. Mayberry, 2 Wheat. 9–13. Error to Supreme Court, R.I. Appellate Case No. 492. No date found for argument.

19 February   Beverly v. Brooke, 2 Wheat. 101–9. Error to U.S. Circuit Court, D.C., Alexandria. Appellate Case No. 759. Argued 11 Feb. 1817.

21 February   Coolidge v. Payson, 2 Wheat. 66–75. Error to U.S. Circuit Court, Mass. Appellate Case No. 754. Argued 10 Feb. 1817.

24 February   McCoul v. Lekamp, 2 Wheat. 112–17. Error to U.S. Circuit Court, Va. Appellate Case No. 766. Argued 12 Feb. 1817.

4 March   Rutherford v. Greene's Heirs, 2 Wheat. 196–206. Error to U.S. Circuit Court, W. Tenn. Appellate Case No. 767. Argued 24–25 Feb. 1817.

5 March   Fairfax v. Catlett and Wife; Catlett and Wife v. Fairfax, MS
             opinion, not reported. Appeal from U.S. Circuit Court, D.C.,
             Alexandria. Appellate Case Nos. 667, 718. Argued 8 Feb. 1817.

5 March   The London Packet, 2 Wheat. 372–73. Appeal from U.S. Circuit
             Court, Mass. Appellate Case No. 807. Argued 4–5 March 1817.

6 March   Johnson v. Pannel's Heirs, 2 Wheat. 207–21. Appeal from U.S.
             Circuit Court, Ky. Appellate Case No. 781. Argued 25 Feb. 1817.

11 March   The Argo, 2 Wheat. 288–89. Appeal from U.S. Circuit Court,
             Mass. Appellate Case No. 801. Argued 10 Mar. 1817.

11 March   Morgan's Heirs v. Morgan, 2 Wheat. 297–302. Appeal from U.S.
             Circuit Court, Ky. Appellate Case No. 810. Argued 8 Mar. 1817.

14 March   Chirac v. Chirac, 2 Wheat. 269–78. Error to U.S. Circuit Court,
             Md. Appellate Case No. 800. Argued 3 Mar. 1817.

15 March   Laidlaw v. Organ, 2 Wheat. 195. Error to U.S. District Court, La.
             Appellate Case No. 780. Argued 20 Feb. 1817.

15 March   The Anna Maria (Butts v. Stites), 2 Wheat. 331–35. Appeal from
             U.S. Circuit Court, Md. Appellate Case No. 816. Argued 11 Mar.
             1817.

15 March   Lenox v. Roberts, 2 Wheat. 376–77. Appeal from U.S. Circuit
             Court, D.C., Alexandria. Appellate Case No. 783. Argued 13
             Mar. 1817.

15 March   Hopkins v. Lee, not reported. Appeal from U.S. Circuit Court,
             D.C., Alexandria. Appellate Case No. 782. Argued 13 Mar. 1817.

1818

5 February   Jackson v. Clarke, 3 Wheat. 12. Error to U.S. Circuit Court, N.Y.
             Appellate Case No. 823. Argued 5 Feb. 1818.

6 February   The Friendschaft, 3 Wheat. 45–52. Appeal from U.S. Circuit
             Court, N.C. Appellate Case No. 831. No date found for
             argument.

10 February McIver v. Kyger, 3 Wheat. 53–57. Appeal from U.S. Circuit
             Court, D.C., Alexandria. Appellate Case No. 758. Argued 4 Feb.
             1818.

11 February The Samuel, 3 Wheat. 77. Appeal from U.S. Circuit Court, R.I.
             Appellate Case No. 661. Not argued (see entry under 16 Feb.
             1816).

11 February The San Pedro, 3 Wheat. 78. Error to Superior Court, Miss.
             Terr. Appellate Case No. 776. Not argued.

18 February Hughes v. Union Insurance Company, 3 Wheat. 163–67. Error
             to U.S. Circuit Court, Md. Appellate Case No. 828. Argued 12
             Feb. 1818.

18 February Swan v. Union Insurance Company, 3 Wheat. 170. Error to U.S.
             Circuit Court, Md. Appellate Case No. 829. Argued 12 Feb. 1818.

19 February Olivera v. Union Insurance Company, 3 Wheat. 188–96. Error to
             U.S. Circuit Court, Md. Appellate Case No. 791. No date found
             for argument.

19 February Shepherd v. Hampton, 3 Wheat. 204. Error to U.S. District
             Court, La. Appellate Case No. 883. Argued 16 Feb. 1818.

19 February   Patton v. Nicholson, 3 Wheat. 207. Error to U.S. Circuit Court, D.C., Alexandria. Appellate Case No. 886. Argued 19 Feb. 1818.

21 February   United States v. Bevans, 3 Wheat. 386–91. Certificate of division from U.S. Circuit Court, Mass. Appellate Case No. 866. Argued 14, 16 Feb. 1818.

24 February   United States v. 150 Crates of Earthenware, 3 Wheat. 233–34. Appeal from U.S. District Court, La. Appellate Case No. 887. Argued 19 Feb. 1818.

24 February   Hampton v. McConnel, 3 Wheat. 235. Error to U.S. Circuit Court, S.C. Appellate Case No. 875. Argued 14 Feb. 1818.

2 March   Houston v. Moore, 3 Wheat. 434–35. Error to Supreme Court of Pa. Appellate Case No. 881. Argued 28 Feb. 1818.

4 March   The Atalanta, 3 Wheat. 415–417. Appeal from U.S. Circuit Court, Ga. Appellate Case No. 891. Argued 23–24 Feb. 1818.

7 March   Evans v. Eaton, 3 Wheat. 503–18. Error to U.S. Circuit Court, Pa. Appellate Case No. 841. Argued 26–27 Feb. 1818.

14 March   United States v. Palmer, 3 Wheat. 626–35. Certificate of division from U.S. Circuit Court, Mass. Appellate Case No. 904. Argued 12 Mar. 1818.

1819

2 February   Dartmouth College v. Woodward, 4 Wheat. 624–54. Error to Superior Court of N.H. Appellate Case No. 892. Argued 10–12 Mar. 1818.

3 February   Philadelphia Baptist Association v. Hart's Executors, 4 Wheat. 27–51. Certificate of division from U.S. Circuit Court, Va. Appellate Case No. 869. Argued 25 Feb., 4 Mar. 1818.

5 February   The Divina Pastora, 4 Wheat. 63–65. Appeal from U.S. Circuit Court, Mass. Appellate Case No. 895. Argued 4 Feb. 1819.

8 February   Williams v. Peyton, 4 Wheat. 77–83. Error to U.S. Circuit Court, Ky. Appellate Case No. 838. Argued 2 Feb. 1819.

8 February   The Experiment, 4 Wheat. 84. Appeal from U.S. Circuit Court, Mass. Appellate Case No. 804. Argued 8 Feb. 1819.

15 February   The Sybil, 4 Wheat. 98–99. Appeal from U.S. Circuit Court, S.C. Appellate Case Nos. 915, 931. Not argued.

17 February   United States v. Howland, 4 Wheat. 114–18. Appeal from U.S. Circuit Court, Mass. Appellate Case No. 604. Argued 4 Feb. 1819.

17 February   Sturgis v. Crowninshield, 4 Wheat. 191–208. Certificate of division from U.S. Circuit Court, Mass. Appellate Case No. 896. Argued 8–9 Feb. 1819.

20 February   McMillan v. McNeill, 4 Wheat. 212–13. Error to U.S. District Court, La. Appellate Case No. 928. Argued 18 Feb. 1819.

24 February   Brown v. Gilman, 4 Wheat. 277–92. Appeal from U.S. Circuit Court, Mass. Appellate Case No. 914. Argued 13, 15–16 Feb. 1819.

6 March   McCulloch v. Maryland, 4 Wheat. 400–437. Error to Court of Appeals, Md. Appellate Case No. 938. Argued 22–27 Feb., 1–3 Mar. 1819.

9 March   Miller v. Nicholls, 4 Wheat. 315. Error to Supreme Court of Pa. Appellate Case No. 357. Argued 8 Mar. 1819.

11 March   McIver v. Walker, 4 Wheat. 451–52. Error to U.S. Circuit Court, E. Tenn. Appellate Case No. 893. Argued 13 Mar. 1818, 4 Mar. 1819.

12 March   McArthur v. Browder, 4 Wheat. 491–96. Appeal from U.S. Circuit Court, Ohio. Appellate Case No. 922. Argued 10 Mar. 1819.

Appendix II
Calendar of Miscellaneous Papers
and Letters Not Found

Beginning with Volume VI, the editors adopted a policy of presenting calendar summaries in a separate appendix. Any inconvenience resulting from this separation is more than offset, they believe, by keeping the main body of the volume reserved for documents selected for printing in full. In this volume calendar entries have been prepared for letters and certificates on behalf of Revolutionary War veterans seeking pensions; pro forma correspondence with Secretary of State John Quincy Adams, in which the secretary transmits copies of printed public documents and requests acknowledgment of receipt; and other routine documents such as a fire insurance declaration and powers of attorney for selling shares of stock in the Bank of the United States. Entries have also been prepared for letters not found whose contents are at least partly known from extracts or summaries in the catalogs of auction houses and autograph dealers. Most of these letters, if extant, would be printed in full.

All calendar entries begin with the dateline in italics, followed by information (in parentheses) describing the document and its location. The contents of the document are then stated in summary style; however, extracts from letters not found are quoted in full. Where necessary, footnotes have been subjoined to calendar entries.

To John Lowell

[1814], Richmond (summary of ALS, *American Book-Prices Current in 1937–1938* [New York, 1938], 507). Discusses Lowell's *Review of a Treatise on Expatriation.*[1]

1. See JM to Pickering, 11 Apr. 1814 and nn.

To Joseph G. Cogswell

23 April 1815, Richmond (summary of ALS, American Art Association-Anderson Galleries, Inc., Catalog [New York, 1929], item #102; also listed in *American Book-Prices Current in 1930* [New York, 1931], 672). Asks Cogswell to send erring son home from Harvard College.[1]

1. See JM to [Cogswell?], 9 Apr. 1815 and nn.

To Joseph G. Cogswell

29 May 1815, Richmond (printed extract of ALS, Robert F. Batchelder, Catalog No. 17 [Ambler, Penn., 1977], item #243). JM thanks Cogswell for taking care of his "very culpable son."[1] Says he could not get a bank draft from Boston but is sending one from New York, which he hopes will suffice. "Be so obliging as to present my respectful compliments to the President and say that I received his letter at the same time with yours.[2] I am much obliged [b]y the measures he took for the correction of John, and am truly chagrined that a son of mine should have proved so unworthy of his attentions, and should have thrown away the advantages he might have derived from the instruction which he might have received. My son will never forget his obligations to you, and I intreat you to believe that they will ever be retained in grateful recollection by your obliged and obedt. servt. J. Marshall."

1. See JM to [Cogswell?], 9 Apr. 1815 and nn.
2. Letters not found. John Thornton Kirkland (1770–1840) was president of Harvard from 1810 to 1828.

Fire Insurance Declaration

17 October 1815, Richmond (DS [printed form], Records of the Mutual Assurance Society of Virginia, Vi). JM declares for fire insurance on four buildings situated on his square of four lots in the city of Richmond: dwelling house ($6,750), office ($850), laundry ($150), and kitchen ($100).[1]

1. This is a printed form (No. 1651), with blanks filled in by special agent Lewis M. Rivalain and signed by JM (also signed by the agent and by two freeholders affirming the appraisal). Beneath the form is a plat showing the locations and dimensions of the insured buildings. These are the same buildings shown on JM's 1796 declaration, except that the 1815 declaration no longer shows a stable in the northwest corner of the square. The 1815 declaration shows an addition to the dwelling house and an enlarged office with brick walls (*PJM*, III, 16–18).

To [Benjamin W. Crowninshield?]

16 February 1816, [Washington] (printed extract of ALS, Carnegie Book Shop, *Autographs*, Catalogue No. 315 [New York, 1970], 19). Recommends Richard Barton [Smith] as "an applicant for the warrant of midshipman. . . . I have the utmost confidence in his personal merit & in his being educated . . . as to fit him for the service."

To [Josiah Meigs?]

15 June 1816, Richmond (ALS, RG 49, DNA). Encloses copy of will of the late Col. William Heth.[1]

1. This letter is part of a file of documents relating to Heth's military bounty lands. JM was one of Heth's executors. The partially torn cover indicates the letter was addressed to the Land Office in Washington. Josiah Meigs was then commissioner of the Land Office.

From John Quincy Adams

23 October 1817, Washington (letterbook copy, RG 59, DNA). In circular to federal judges and other officials, Secretary of State transmits copy of laws enacted by Fourteenth Congress.

To John Quincy Adams

28 October 1817, Richmond (ALS, RG 59, DNA). Acknowledges receipt of documents sent by secretary of state on 23 October.

From John Quincy Adams

20 November 1817, Washington (letterbook copy, RG 59, DNA). In circular to federal judges and other officials, secretary of state forwards copy of reports of Supreme Court cases decided at the February 1817 term.

To John Quincy Adams

20 [25?] November 1817, Richmond (ALS, RG 59, DNA). Acknowledges receipt of Supreme Court reports sent by secretary of state on 20 November.

To Unknown

21 February 1818, Washington (typescript of ALS, supplied by Charles Sessler, Inc., Philadelphia, 1967). In reply to letter of 20 February,[1] JM states that U.S. law "respecting foreign judgments is I believe perfectly and generally understood. It would however be improper for me to make any certificate on the subject. If Mr. Holken[2] wishes to bring the subject officially before the minister of France, his best plan will probably be to take the opinion of the Attorney General of the United States & submit that opinion to his consideration."[3]

1. Letter not found.
2. Possibly John Holker, formerly consul general of France.
3. No opinion on this subject by Att. Gen. Wirt has been found.

Certificate of Revolutionary War Service

1 May 1818, Richmond (ALS, RG 15, DNA). Certifies that Clement Hasty enlisted in Capt. William Blackwell's company in the 11th Virginia Regiment in 1776 and served out his three-year enlistment. In accompanying note JM tells Hasty he recollects "perfectly your enlistment" and hopes his certificate "may be of use."[1]

1. Hasty (ca. 1756–1821), of Culpeper County, had applied for a pension under the act of 18 Mar. 1818, which provided for pensions to all officers and private soldiers of the Continental line who served nine months or longer and who from "reduced circumstances" were "in need of assistance." He eventually received a pension of eight dollars a month, the amount established for private soldiers who could prove need (pension file of Clement Hasty, RG 15, DNA; *U.S. Statutes at Large*, III, 410–11). See also *PJM*, I, 6 and n. 5, 8, 10, 13, 16, 25, 28.

From John B. Colvin

3 October 1818, Washington (letterbook copy, RG 59, DNA). In absence of secretary of state, clerk of State Department sends a set of Wait's edition of public documents.[1]

1. *State Papers and Publick Documents of the United States, from the Accession of George Washington to the Presidency, Exhibiting a Complete View of Our Foreign Relations since That Time* (10 vols.; 2d ed.; Boston, 1817; S #42211), published by T. B. Wait and Sons.

To John Quincy Adams

5 October 1818, Richmond (ALS, RG 59, DNA). Acknowledges receipt of Wait's edition of public documents forwarded on 3 October.

To James Monroe

20 November 1818, Richmond (summary of ALS, Robert K. Black, Catalog No. 86 [Upper Montclair, N.J., n.d.], 23). Supports appointment of Corbin Braxton to federal office. Recommends him because of his character and notes Braxton's recent misfortune in being shipwrecked with his slaves off the coast of Florida while en route to settle in that new territory.[1]

1. Corbin Braxton (d. 1822) was the third son of Carter Braxton, a signer of the Declaration of Independence. Monroe's endorsement on the letter noted that someone else had already received the appointment (Frederick Horner, *The History of the Blair, Banister, and Braxton Families before and after the Revolution* [Philadelphia, 1898], 165, 167; John Sanderson, *Biography of the Signers to the Declaration of Independence*, V [2d ed.; Philadelphia, 1828], 89).

Certificate for Dr. George Watson

11 December 1818, Richmond (copy, PU). Asked by a friend of Dr. Watson "to state the estimation in which he is held in Richd," JM states "that as a man of science a physician, and a gentleman" Watson "has long and I think deservedly stood high in the public Opinion."[1]

1. This certificate is included in a pamphlet of letters and statements by prominent Virginians writing on behalf of Watson (1784–1853), who was then applying for the

chair of anatomy at the University of Pennsylvania. A native of Louisa County, Watson attended the College of William and Mary and studied medicine at Edinburgh and Paris from 1805 to 1808. He pursued further medical education at the University of Pennsylvania, receiving his M.D. in 1809. Watson then commenced a long and distinguished career in Richmond. The appointment to the anatomy chair went to Philip Syng Physick, the surgeon who operated on JM in 1831 (*Richmond Portraits in an Exhibition of Makers of Richmond, 1737–1860* [Richmond, Va., 1949], 202; Joseph Carson, *A History of the Medical Department of the University of Pennsylvania* . . . [Philadelphia, 1869], 152).

Power of Attorney

21 January 1819, Richmond (printed, *Niles' Weekly Register* [Baltimore, Md.], LIII [1837], 51). JM gives blank power of attorney to transfer five shares of stock in the Bank of the United States.[1]

1. In 1837 William Smith, formerly a senator from South Carolina and then a Jacksonian candidate for the Alabama state legislature, charged in a speech that JM had acted improperly in deciding McCulloch v. Maryland because of his ownership of stock in the bank. This charge provoked a response from JM's defenders, including Benjamin Watkins Leigh, who provided documentation on JM's ownership and transfer of bank stock for publication in the Richmond *Whig* (later reprinted in *Niles' Weekly Register*). According to Leigh's information, JM purchased seventeen shares of stock in 1817 and disposed of them before the decision in McCulloch. The five shares designated to be transferred by the above power of attorney were sold at par ($100 a share) to James H. Lynch on 21 Jan. 1819. Thomas P. Cope, who filled in his name on the blank, acted as attorney to make the transfer. Lynch certified that he advised JM "not to sell; but he assigned as his reason for selling, that he did not choose to remain a stockholder in that institution, as questions would come before the Supreme Court . . . in which the bank might be concerned." For the disposal of the remaining twelve shares, see Power of Attorney, 5 Feb. 1819 and n. 1 (App. II, Cal.).

Power of Attorney

5 February 1819, Washington (printed, *Niles' Weekly Register* [Baltimore, Md.], LIII [1837], 51). JM appoints Robert Adams as attorney to transfer twelve shares of Bank of the United States stock in JM's name and thirteen additional shares in his name as executor of William Marshall. These twenty-five shares were to be assigned to Thomas Marshall of Fauquier as trustee for the widow and heirs of William Marshall.[1]

1. See Power of Attorney, 21 Jan. 1819 (App. II, Cal.). According to the transfer clerk's certificate, dated 24 Aug. 1837, these shares were transferred to Thomas Marshall on 8 Feb. 1819.

To Unknown

11 February 1819, [Washington] (summary of ALS, *American Book-Prices Current* [New York, 1929], 741). Replies to solicitation of office seeker.

To John C. Calhoun

18 February 1819, [Washington] (ALS, RG 107, DNA). JM informs secretary of war that Samuel Elliott, Joseph Parker, John Laws, and Spencer Edwards served for three years in his company during the Revolutionary War. Encloses affidavit concerning Parker's poverty.[1]

1. These veterans had applied for pensions under the act of 18 Mar. 1818 (pension files of Spencer Edwards, Samuel Elliott, John Laws, and Joseph Parker, RG 15, DNA; Certificate of War Service, 1 May 1818 and n. 1 [App. II, Cal.]).

From John C. Calhoun

20 February 1819, Washington (letterbook copy, RG 107, DNA). In reply to JM's letter of 18 Feb., secretary of war transmits report from principal clerk of Pension Office and a pension certificate for John Laws.[1]

1. See JM to Calhoun, 18 Feb. 1819 and n. 1 (App. II, Cal.). The enclosed clerk's report noted that a certificate for Spencer Edwards had been issued on 9 Jan. and that those for Samuel Elliott and Joseph Parker had not yet been acted upon (James L. Edwards to Calhoun, 19 Feb. 1819, RG 15, DNA).

To John C. Calhoun

8 May 1819, Richmond (ALS, RG 15, DNA). Encloses affidavits in support of Joseph Garner's application for a pension.[1]

1. Garner (ca. 1754–1840) applied for a pension under the act of 18 Mar. 1818. Originally from Fauquier County, Garner had enlisted in JM's company in 1775. He moved to Georgia in 1802 and then to Alabama in 1820 (*PJM*, I, 5, 8, 9, 16; IV, 30–31; pension file of Joseph Garner, RG 15, DNA).

From John Quincy Adams

5 August 1819, Washington (letterbook copy, RG 59, DNA). Secretary of state forwards copies of documents ordered to be printed during first session of Fifteenth Congress. Documents of second session have not yet come to hand.

To John Quincy Adams

18 November 1819, Richmond (ALS, RG 59, DNA). Acknowledges receipt of the journals and documents of the second session of the Fifteenth Congress.

From John Quincy Adams

25 November 1819, Washington (letterbook copy, RG 59, DNA). Secretary of state forwards more documents printed by order of the Fifteenth Congress.

Appendix III
The Brig Caroline v. United States
Opinion
U.S. Supreme Court, 16 March 1813

Marshall's opinion in the brig *Caroline* was published in Brockenbrough's edition of Marshall's circuit court cases. According to Brockenbrough, the case was an appeal from "the sentence of the district court of the United States, at Norfolk," which was heard and decided at the November 1819 term of the United States Circuit Court. In fact, Marshall prepared this opinion for a case decided at the 1813 term of the Supreme Court, which had been appealed from the United States Circuit Court for South Carolina. The opinion was not published in Cranch's report, however, which contains only the Court's summary judgment. The manuscript eventually found its way into the collection of circuit court opinions that Marshall turned over to Brockenbrough to prepare for publication.

Brockenbrough's brief headnote is based on the opinion itself, not on any additional documentation of the case. He simply assumed—erroneously—that the case came from the district court at Norfolk; and he evidently assigned a November 1819 date because the manuscript was placed among other circuit court opinions of that term. Misled by Brockenbrough's original error, the editors searched in vain for this case among the records and papers of the circuit and district courts for Virginia and North Carolina. The discovery that the opinion actually belonged to a Supreme Court case of 1813 occurred too late to include it in Volume VII of this edition. In these circumstances, the editors decided to publish the opinion (formerly believed to be an 1819 document) as an appendix to the present volume.

The *Caroline* was seized by customs agents in the port of Charleston in May 1810 for violating acts of Congress concerning the slave trade. A decree of the district court condemning the vessel was affirmed by the circuit court in May 1811. William Broadfoot, claimant of the forfeited brig, took an appeal to the Supreme Court, where it was argued on 24 February 1813. The Court rendered its decision on 16 March (7 Cranch 496–500; U.S. Sup. Ct. Dockets, App. Cas. No. 513; Brig Caroline v. U.S., App. Cas. No. 513).

The brig Caroline
     v   ⎱
The United States   ⎰

¶1   The Caroline was seized as being forfeited to the United States for being concerned in the slave trade in violation of the acts of 1794 & 1807 or of one of them.[1]

¶2   The peculiar odium attached to the trafic in which this vessel is alleged to have engaged ought not to affect the legal questions which belong to the case.

¶3   The information charges that the Caroline ["]after the 22d. day of March 1794 was built fitted equipt loaded or other wise prepared within a port or place of the United States or caused to sail from a port or place of the said United States by a citizen &c for the purpose of carrying on trade or trafic in slaves to a foreign country &c."

There are other counts in the information; but as the observations made on this apply to them also, it is deemed unnecessary to recite them.   ¶4

The charge contained in this information is understood to be that the Caroline was either built, fitted, equipt, loaded or other wise prepared within a port or place of the United States, or that she was caused to sail from a port or place of the United States. It is not alleged that all these acts were performed but that some one of them, it is uncertain which, was performed. This information will be strictly & literally true if the Caroline was either built, fitted equipt loaded or other wise prepared within a port or place of the United States; or was caused to sail from a port or place of the United States.   ¶5

In such a case, it is deemed essential to the validity of the judgement that it should be such as the law will authorize the court to render on proof of any one of the acts charged in the information. If any one of two or more acts be innocent, & the information charges that one or the other of them has been committed, it would violate the clearest principles of law to pronounce judgement against the accused. If the law should inflict forfeiture on a vessel which should sail out of port on a certain day & an information should charge that a vessel did sail on that day or did not sail on it, all would concur in declaring that no sentence of forfeiture could be pronounced against such a vessel. So if several acts be prohibited under several penalties, & on one of them the penalty of forfeiture be inflicted, the information must charge in explicit terms that the particular crime to which the law has annexed forfeiture as a penalty has been committed, or the court cannot adjudge the thing to be forfeited. If for example it be forbidden by statute to build or fit a vessel for the slave trade, & to building or fitting be annexed a penalty of $2000, but to fitting be super added a forfeiture of the vessel, the information must charge a "*fitting*" of the vessel or the court cannot adjudge her to be forfeited.   ¶6

These positions seem to me to be incontestible. If this be correct it only remains to enquire whether the statute inflicts forfeiture on each of the offences charged in the information.   ¶7

The act declares that no person shall "build, fit, equip, load, or otherwise prepare any ship or vessel within any port or place of the United States, nor shall cause any ship or vessel to sail from any port or place within the same for the purpose of carrying on any trade or traffic in slaves to any foreign country."   ¶8

It is perfectly clear that each of these acts is prohibited; but it is equally clear that, if the law had proceeded no further, the vessel would not have been forfeitable for either of them. To the legislature it belongs to define punishment as well as crime, & courts would certainly step very far beyond their province were they to annex forfeiture to offences to which the legislature had not annexed that penalty. In order to determine whether all or any of the offences enumerated in the part of the act which has been recited, be cause of forfeiture, it will be necessary to examine that part of the law which prescribes the punishment.   ¶9

The law proceeds to say "And if any ship or vessel shall be so fitted out as aforesaid or shall be caused to sail as aforesaid, every such ship or vessel, her tackle, furniture, apparel, & other appurtenances shall be forfeited to the United States."   ¶10

¶11   The penalty of forfeiture is here annexed only to the act of "fitting out as aforesaid," that is for traffic in slaves; or to the act of sailing for the purpose of engaging in that traffic.

¶12   It is unusual for a legislative act when it has enumerated certain offences, to vary the language by changing the enumeration when penalties are to be annexed to those offences if the intention be to punish them all in the same manner. When a form of expression is used applicable to the enumeration of several distinct offences, & a penalty is afterwards inflicted on one or more of them, leaving others out of the recital, the mind is drawn to the conclusion that, in the opinion of the legislature at least, the offences are distinct, & the punishment is to be different. In legislative acts we are not accustomed to such a parsimony of words as to expect, where several offences are enumerated, that the legislature, if it means to punish them all in the same manner, will drop several of them in that part of the sentence which recites the offences to be punished, meerly to avoid that expenditure of words which would be incurred by repeating the enumeration. If then the offences were not materially variant it would seem to be a fair construction of such an act to presume that the legislature supposed some distinction to exist between them.

¶13   But in this case the offences are totally different from each other. To build a vessel & to fit out a vessel are two distinct acts as clearly separable from each other as any acts whatever. The terms are applied to distinct & different operations. To build a vessel is to construct her, to fit her out is to prepare her for sea after she has been constructed. They are no more the same act than to build a house & to furnish a house are the same.

¶14   I cannot admit that the legislature ought to be considered as having omitted the word "built" in that part of the act which enumerates the offences which are cause of forfeiture, from an idea that the word "fitted out" could apply in this place to a vessel "built" but not "fitted out." In addition to the well established meaning of the words, the clause inflicting forfeiture does itself show that in using the term "fitted out" the legislature had in contemplation a vessel equipt for her voyage. The words are "such ship or other vessel her tackle furniture apparel & other appurtenances shall be forfeited to the United States." This is obviously the state of a vessel actually fitted out, but a ship may be built without "tackle, furniture, apparel, & other appurtenances."

¶15   The 2d. Sec. inflicts a penalty of $2000 on any person who shall build, fit out, equip, load or otherwise prepare or send away any ship or vessel, knowing or intending that the same shall be employed in the trade or business prohibited by the act.

¶16   On an information against the builder of a ship not concerned in fitting her out, would it be a defence to say that the legislature used the word "building" in the same sense with the word "*fitting out*"; and as he had not "fitted out" so he had not "*built*" in the sense in which that term is used in the law? I cannot be mistaken when I say that no gentleman of the bar would hazard such a defence. And yet I cannot perceive the difference between saying that under the 2d Sec. no ship can be considered as built unless she be fitted out, & saying that under the 3d. Sec. the words built & fitted out have the same meaning.

¶17   The plain sense of the law appears to me to be this. In the first section various offences are enumerated to two of which, "fitting out & sailing," forfeiture is annexed. In the 2d. Sec. the penalty of $2000 is inflicted on any person

who knowingly commits any one of the offences. As this information charges
that one of several offences has been committed, & they are not in law each of
them cause of forfeiture, I should, so far as I can trust my own judgement, be of
opinion that a sentence of forfeiture ought not to have been pronounced.[2]

AD, Marshall Judicial Opinions, PPAmP; printed, John W. Brockenbrough, *Reports of
Cases Decided by the Honourable John Marshall* . . . , I (Philadelphia, 1837), 384–88. For JM's
deletions and interlineations, see Textual Notes below.

1. *U.S. Statutes at Large*, I, 347–49; II, 426–30.

2. The Court remanded the case to the circuit court, which was directed to allow the
libel to be amended. This decision also applied to the case of the ship *Emily*, which had
been condemned along with the *Caroline* for violating the slave trade laws. On retrial
sentences of forfeiture were again pronounced against both vessels. In 1824 the Supreme Court affirmed these decrees (7 Cranch 500; 9 Wheat. 381).

Textual Notes

¶ 3 l. 4	trafic ~~or traffic~~ in
¶ 4 l. 1	the ~~indictment~~ information;
¶ 5 ll. 1–2	the ~~informati~~ ↑Caroline↓ was
¶ 6 l. 10	& ↑on↓ one
ll. 13–14	If ↑for example↓ it
l. 14	or ~~equip~~ ↑fit↓ a
l. 15	or ~~or equipping~~ ↑fitting↓ be
¶ 7 l. 1	If ↑this be correct it↓ only
l. 3	the ~~libel~~ information.
¶ 9 l. 7	of ~~n~~ [*erasure*] forfeiture,
¶10 l. 3	tackle, ↑furniture,↓ apparel,
¶12 l. 1	for ~~the legislature~~ ↑a legislative act↓ when
l. 2	language ↑by changing the enumeration↓ when
ll. 3–4	offences ↑if the intention be to punish them all in the same manner.↓ When
l. 6	others [*erasure*] out
l. 11	in ↑that↓ part
l. 12	punished, ~~in order~~ ↑meerly↓ to
l. 13	the ~~words~~ ↑offences↓ were
l. 14	of ~~the~~ such an act to ~~suppose~~ presume
¶14 l. 1	legislature ~~wa~~ ought
ll. 2–3	offences ~~only cited~~ ↑which are cause of forfeiture,↓ from
l. 4	In ~~additi~~ ↑addition↓ to
¶15 l. 2	or ~~otherwise~~ send

INDEX

In addition to persons and subjects, this index includes the titles of all cases mentioned in the documents and in the accompanying annotation. Identifications occur at or near the first mention of a person. If a person has been identified in an earlier volume, the volume number and page reference follow the name in parentheses. The editors prepared the index with the aid of NLCINDEX, a program developed by Charles T. Cullen of the Newberry Library in Chicago. NLCINDEX is an adaptation for microcomputer of CINDEX, a mainframe indexing program designed by David R. Chesnutt of the University of South Carolina.